Frontline Feminism
1975-1995

*Essays from Sojourner's
First 20 Years*

Edited by Karen Kahn

Foreword by Robin Morgan

aunt lute books
SAN FRANCISCO

First Edition
10 9 8 7 6 5 4 3 2 1

Aunt Lute Books
P.O. Box 410687
San Francisco, CA 94141

Cover Photos: Marilyn Humphries , except lower right photo by Ellen Shub
Cover and Text Design: Pamela Wilson Design Studio
Typesetting: Pamela Wilson Design Studio
Senior Editor: Joan Pinkvoss
Associate Book Editor: Vita Iskandar
Managing Editor: Christine Lymbertos

Production:	Cristina Azócar	JeeYeun Lee
	Kerstin Carson	Dolissa Medina
	Heather Lee	Kathleen Wilkinson
Production Support:	Denise Conca	Tricia Lambie
	Jonna K. Eagle	Melissa Levin
	Jamie Lee Evans	Norma Torres

Printed in the U.S.A. on acid-free paper.

Library of Congress Cataloging-in-Publication Data

Frontline feminism, 1975-1995 : essays from Sojourner's first 20 years / edited by Karen Kahn : foreword by Robin Morgan. — 1st ed.
  p.   cm.
  Includes index.
  ISBN 1-879960-43-5. — ISBN 1-879960-42-7 (pbk.)
  1. Feminism—United States—History—20th century.   2. Feminism—New England—History—20th century.   3. Women—United States—History—20th century. 4. Women—Women—New England—History—20th century.   5. Sojourner (Cambridge, Mass.)—History.
HQ1402.F76   1995
305.42'0973'0904—dc20
                                                                    95-33433
                                                                    CIP

Acknowledgments

Many people have made this book possible. Most especially I am grateful to the *Sojourner* board and staff for allowing me six months leave from my position as editor of the newspaper to work on this project. I especially thank Amy Pett for serving as editor in my stead, and Linda Wong and Catherine Corliss who shared the major burden of my absence. During the six months I worked full time on this project, I lived in Honolulu, Hawaii. Thank you to all the women who welcomed me into their community and made my stay not only productive but enormously fun. I am especially grateful to Margaret Nielsen, who made it all possible, by providing me with a home and office (along with two furry companions, Sushi and Muffin, to keep me company while I worked); to Susan Miller for computer assistance, without which I could have never completed this manuscript; and to Rochelle Lee Gregson for office supplies and much more. For encouragement, advice, and comments along the way, I'd like to thank Carolann Barrett, Laura Briggs, Robin Carton, Jean Gould, Amy Hoffman, Kate Hogan, Demita Frazier, Kathi Maio, and Sandy Martin, Laura McCloskey, Nora Mitchell, Emily Skoler, and Meredith Smith. I thank *Sojourner* interns Judith Goldberger, Sarah McGrath, Rachael Saller Bender, Amy Yee, and Wendy Wu for fact checking and helping with the permissions. Thank you to Gary Kahn and Karen Rudolph for pushing me to seriously consider doing this anthology, and to my parents for providing financial support. Finally, thank you to all the women who have contributed to *Sojourner* over the years, especially those who agreed to have their work reprinted in this anthology; to my editor, Joan Pinkvoss, for insightful comments and patience as I struggled to finish the manuscript after I returned to *Sojourner;* to the production staff at Aunt Lute Books for their incredible attention to details; and to Patricia Gozemba, for reading everything and being there always.

Dedication

To all the women who have created *Sojourner* over the years: staff, volunteers, board and committee members, production workers, advertisers, donors, subscribers, and, most importantly, the contributors, whose stories, photographs, and drawings are the heart of the feminist press.

Editorial Note

This is a collection of newspaper articles that spans twenty years. Needless to say, during that time, there were many changes in *Sojourner*'s style conventions and in the general usage of certain terms. In order to make the book easier to read, it was necessary to make some stylistic choices. Most of these follow *Sojourner*'s present conventions. For example, "Black," when referring to people of African descent, is capitalized, though it has not always been so throughout *Sojourner*'s history. Similarly, I have made changes in the notation of numbers, abbreviations, times, etc., to provide consistency throughout the volume. I have not, however, changed "Black" to "African American" or "America" to "United States," style conventions that the newspaper adopted in more recent years. Readers will also note the use of "Third World" in the '70s and early '80s to refer to women of color in the United States as well as throughout the world. Since this was common usage at the time, I have let it stand, although I have consistently capitalized "Third World."

A note on the use of "we." It is difficult to write a book about the feminist movement in the third person, when you have been a part of that movement for many years. I have tried to be as careful as possible about the use of "we" and to use this universal pronoun only in places where I mean to refer to all women, all feminists, or our whole society. The context should make these differences clear. I have not used "we" where I refer to specific groups of women that represent my own identity: white, middle class, lesbian, or Jewish.

Finally, as noted, a number of the articles in this volume have been edited for length and clarity. The original articles are available in numerous libraries and archives throughout the country and should be referred to for historical accuracy.

Table of Contents

Chapter 3: The Politics of the Family

Chapter 4: Reproductive Freedom

Chapter 5: Women's Health

Chapter 6: Sex and Sexuality

Chapter 7: Violence Against Women

Chapter 8: Building an Inclusive Movement

Foreword

by Robin Morgan

"With the moral chaos that surrounds us on every side, the corruption in the state, the dissensions in the church, the jealousies in the home, what thinking mind does not feel that we need something new and revolutionary in every department of life?" So wrote the women founding a new feminist newspaper, adding, in defense of its name: *"The name speaks its purpose. It is to revolutionize. It is radicalism practical, not theoretical. It is to affect changes through abolitions, reconstructions, and restorations. It is to realize ancient visions, answer long-uttered prayers, and fulfill old prophecies."*

The sentiments are as timely as tomorrow, but the date was January 1868. The women were Elizabeth Cady Stanton and Susan B. Anthony. The newspaper was *The Revolution.*

It was impossible then, and it still is, to calculate the significance—in fact, the centrality—of the feminist media to the women's movement. During this contemporary wave alone (erroneously called the second wave when it's actually closer to the ten thousandth), the patriarchal media have pronounced the movement dying or already dead, every year, with tedious reliability, since 1969 (in 1968, they were busy proclaiming that the incipient movement wouldn't get born to begin with). Relentlessly faced with such premature death certificates, where would we be without the alternative—a media of our own? Paraphrasing Susan B. Anthony, Donna Allen noted, when founding the Women's Institute for Freedom of the Press, "Freedom of the press belongs to those who own the press."

In "mainstream" (for which read: patriarchal) journalism, it's a given that newspapers are the most ephemeral form of print communication, that yesterday's papers are, well, good only for wrapping fish. And print media (including books) in a feminist context carry a particular irony, since two-thirds of the world's illiterates are female. It's no wonder, then, that the poorest women in the so-called developing countries of the South cite "education" as their first longed-for priority, neck-and-neck with reproductive freedom—before nutrition, better housing, or economic relief. Perhaps it's because even in the industrialized world women had to win the right to education that we value our books and periodicals so. We certainly treasure them: attics, basements, cellars, and apartment closets often hide stores of hoarded feminist magazines and newspapers—the more delightful then, to have a twenty-year "sampler" of *Sojourner*'s best, between book covers, for keeps. After all, feminist newspapers constitute a veritable "herstory" of the women's movement, wave after wave, and now country after country as well; would we know of the existence of a thriving Arab women's movement in the

1920s, were it not for the legacy of at least two dozen different feminist magazines and journals published in Beirut during that period? Feminist media—newspapers, magazines, journals, quarterlies, and the like—have not only reflected the political growth of the movement, but defined and shaped it as well, and had the same effect on individual women's lives.

For instance, I think of myself as a book writer and an organizer. Yet only in sitting down to write this foreword for the long-awaited *Sojourner* anthology have I realized how inextricably my own life has been entwined with the feminist media. First and foremost, as a devoted reader and subscriber. But also: from writing token pieces on "women's liberation" in the "New Left" newspaper *Rat* in the late '60s, to being in the group of women who seized that paper in 1970 for a "women's issue" (we never did return it to the boys), to decades of doing interviews with, writing articles for, and publishing poems in many different feminist periodicals, to my years at *Ms.* magazine—as contributing editor, later editor-in-chief (of the revived, ad-free *Ms.*), and now consulting editor—I could chart my life along the lines of feminist periodicals as easily as along the lines of my own books, or groups I've been in, or any other milestones. And of all the grants made by the Sisterhood Is Powerful Fund (the first feminist foundation, set up with royalties from that anthology), the seed monies that helped found many contemporary feminist periodicals somehow make me proudest.

But as or more important than the impact on any one of us, the influence of feminist media on the movement as a whole continues to be crucial. *Sojourner: The Women's Forum* is an excellent case in point, for a number of reasons. It is now one of the grand old media institutions of this feminist wave, founded in 1975 (already managing to stay in print eighteen years longer than Stanton and Anthony's short-lived *The Revolution)*. Furthermore, it has consistently maintained a remarkable level of excellence for two decades, and has positioned itself inclusively on issues, constituencies, analyses, and even geographical regions.

Flourishing high above its original roots as a Boston-area women's newspaper, *Sojourner* has branched out to cover national and international feminist news. It publishes fiction and poetry worthy of a literary magazine. Its reviews—of books, films, music, performance art, visual art—are fair, witty, unsentimental, and plain *useful;* they're actually a lifeline for women living in more remote areas where, for instance, a local feminist bookstore browse isn't an option: such reviews at least give a clue as to what to *order.*

Then, of course, there are The Issues. You know, the ones the boys call "women's issues," which simply means everything (since women are the majority of the human species, how can all issues *not* be women's issues?). Violence against women, economics, peace, environment, electoral politics, pornography, women's studies, redefinitions of sexuality, of spirituality, of family, of power itself. . . . The book you hold in your hands is testament to *Sojourner*'s reach—and grasp, too.

Whether struggling with divisions of race, age, class, sexual preference/orientation, ability, ethnicity, nationality, culture, or any other barriers between women, the theoretical debates and tactical analyses, the discussions, the dialogue between writers and readers persists bravely, vulnerably, intelligently. No constituency is ignored for long, whether rural women, or women institutionalized in prisons or hospitals, or young girls, or rebellious nuns, or militant old women. There is honest anger in these pages, and lovely wicked humor, and a passion—in all senses of the word—for women. (A pleasant bonus is the invaluable perspective lent by hindsight, which teaches how certain schisms that seemed to loom so large at one point eventually fade, outlasted by the commitment of the long-distance-runner activists.)

And what of the next twenty years, putting us well into the new millennium? I believe, as technology shrinks the planet and women further expand the movement, that global feminist networking, issue-overlap, information exchange, and unifying strategies and actions will more and more become central to our political lives—not at the expense of local or grassroots activism, but because of, in linkage with, and in support of it. We can certainly celebrate the energy explosion of feminist print media all over the world: *Mulherio* (Brazil), *Kvinder* (Denmark), *Noon* (Egypt), *Nouvelles Questions Feministes* (France), *Emma* (Germany), *Manushi* (India), *The Crane Bag* (Ireland), *Noga* (Israel), *Donna* (Italy), *Agora* (Japan), *Al-Raida* (Lebanon), *Fem* or *Mujer* (Mexico), *Sister* (Namibia), *Asmita* (Nepal), *Broadsheet* (Aotearoa/New Zealand), *La Tortuga* (Peru), *Voice of Women* (South Africa), *Poder y Libertad* (Spain), *Woman's Voice* (Sri Lanka), and *Women's Exclusive* (Zambia). That's only a general *sampling*, nor does it include specialty periodicals (health journals, literary magazines, professional quarterlies, newsletters, etc.). Furthermore, new ones are born every day—and such "feminist newspapers of the air" as FIRE (Feminist International Radio Endeavor) use radio to reach pre-literate women thirsty for freedom and for news of other women.

In that context, the inspiration and challenge to *Sojourner* is great, especially if it's true, as I believe it is, that feminism is literally the politics of the 21st century: a worldview, an inclusive, connective, profound politics uniquely capable at this moment in history of saving sentient life on this small, endangered, fragile blue planet we call home.

That's a big "beat" for *Soj* to cover. But she's managed it so far—and so well, too. So she will. And in the process, she'll offer us "radicalism practical," and "realize ancient visions, answer long-uttered prayers, and fulfill old prophecies."

Here. *Read all about it.*

Robin Morgan

Introduction

Sojourner: The Women's Forum

When *Sojourner* was founded in 1975 as "the voice of the MIT women's community," few could have guessed that it would eventually become one of the most successful women's newspapers in the United States. After all, how could the Massachusetts Institute of Technology, a bastion of male privilege, provide fertile ground for such an endeavor? Yet it did, precisely because a women's newspaper was so necessary. Isolated on a campus where men outnumbered women by six to one, women faculty, staff and students needed a way in which to communicate with each other and explore their experiences. An MIT librarian wrote in answer to the question, why a women's paper? "[I need a] place where I, as a woman, can voice my feelings about the Institute and comment on general problems which affect me."

Chancellor Paul Gray's initial grant of $1,700, however, was only enough to fund two issues of *Sojourner*. Soon the founding mothers were on their own, raising funds through subscriptions, advertising, single-copy sales, and donations (just as the paper does today), and they realized that *Sojourner*'s survival would require expanding beyond the MIT community. After its first year of publication, *Sojourner* became Boston's "Feminist Journal of News, Opinion, and the Arts."

Sojourner's editorial mission differed from many of the other feminist journals launched during the '70s in that it did not support any particular feminist theoretical or political agenda. The editors took the paper's mission as a "forum" seriously, explaining to readers at the end of the first year of publication:

> *Our strength comes from serving the feminist community, and offering a place where feminists (women and men) can explore ideas and events in an attempt to shape their own experience and our collective experience toward changing our lives and society. We do not believe that there is a "correct line" of action or thought, and we will not exclude opinions because we do not agree with them (unless they are racist, sexist, or homophobic).*

Although "and men" crept into this early statement of purpose, *Sojourner* has rarely published articles by or about men. For twenty years, *Sojourner* has been a voice for women—first at MIT, then in Boston and New England, and eventually all across the country.

In its early years, *Sojourner*'s editorial process involved community meetings, in which anyone could participate in deciding what would be published in the current month's issue. This process appeared "democratic" on the surface, but, according to writer Kathi Maio, community involvement was more "token" than real. Women who wrote for the paper regularly or were involved in other aspects of its management and production were considered "staff," and their opinions carried more weight. In the end, if there was disagreement, the editor had final say.

What made *Sojourner* different, however, was its approach to editorial content. Most of the material in the paper was unsolicited. This allowed for diverse styles, opinions, and topics, but created a somewhat random feel in terms of what events or issues might be addressed. Early issues covered everything from "The Roots of American Feminism," the ERA, and alternative health care, to the abduction of millionaire heiress Patti Hearst, rape, and prostitutes' unions. The growing women's culture scene received at least as much attention as political issues: not only did *Sojourner* publish original poetry, fiction, illustrations and photography, but it regularly reviewed women's music, books, theater, and art, and interviewed writers and artists such as Adrienne Rich, Olga Broumas, Judy Chicago, Alix Dobkin, Kay Gardner, and Holly Near.

Sojourner has retained its early editorial mission throughout its twenty-year history, although the staffing structure and content of the paper have changed. By the '80s, it became clear that if *Sojourner* wanted to represent the diversity of women's experiences, it could not rely entirely on unsolicited material. A more concerted effort was made to solicit writing on a regular basis from women of color in particular, but also from other women who have often felt marginalized by mainstream feminism: working-class and poor women, lesbians and bisexuals, disabled women. More recently, *Sojourner* has looked to expand the age range of contributors, seeking out both old and young women to write for the paper. As a result, *Sojourner* has become a far richer conversation between women. And "conversation" is what *Sojourner* has always been about.

What has made *Sojourner* unique—and what makes this anthology so exceptional—is that the paper has never relied on a steady pool of "staff writers." There have been no columnists or editorial writers. Consequently, articles have been written by literally thousands of women from around the world, many of them grassroots feminist activists who have shared their passion about the particular issues that move them. Others have written to share personal stories—of recovery from addiction and childhood abuse, of coming out and falling in love, of raising children and constructing new families. *Sojourner* has been a place for work that, as one contributor recently wrote, "may be too raw for mainstream publications" (Laura Bernell, September 1995). But most importantly, *Sojourner* has been, and continues to be, a place where women not only read of each other's experiences, ideas, and feelings, but respond—with a click of recognition or with outrage, with a new vision or with a counterargument, but always with a sincere commitment to change.

Frontline Feminism

In editing *Frontline Feminism*, I have tried to recreate the dialogue that I have found so central to *Sojourner*'s mission throughout my eight-year tenure as the paper's editor. From early on, I believed that this anthology would prove most useful as a kind of "intellectual history" of second-wave feminism, in which readers could follow the process by which women have come to understand the social, political, and economic context that shapes their experiences. Consequently, rather than searching for the "100 Best" articles, I began by identifying political issues that had received the most coverage and seemed most significant in the development of the feminist movement. Because of lack of space, some of the issues I originally hoped to cover—for example, the women's peace movement and the international feminist movement—had to be eliminated. I also eliminated *Sojourner*'s arts coverage; film, book, music, theater, and visual arts reviews, because of their historic specificity, are, for the most part, difficult to anthologize. Thus, this book is by no means representative of *Sojourner*'s entire breadth as a publication. But even with limiting the scope of the anthology, I was able to achieve my initial goal: each chapter provides varied perspectives on a single political issue (or related complex of issues) and, thereby, contributes to our understanding of how women have constructed the theory and practice of one of the most significant social movements of our time.

I begin the book with a chapter that explores the history of "identity politics." Chapter One sets the stage for what follows by exploring the development of the multiple feminist movements that emerged during the '80s around race, class, ethnicity, age, sexual identity, and physical ability. Contributors speak to the differences among feminists and the problematic universalization of white, middle-class women's experiences. In the chapters that follow, these differences are raised in the context of how feminists have addressed specific issues—economic injustice, the politics of the family, reproductive freedom, health, sex and sexuality, and violence against women. Chapter Eight returns to the questions raised in Chapter One, by exploring how feminists have built alliances across differences and how we might seek to broaden these alliances in the future. Having come full circle, Chapter Eight suggests that without an agenda that speaks to *all* women, from the most disenfranchised to the most privileged, feminists will not be able to hold back the right-wing assault of the '90s.

The Legacy of the Second Wave

Since *Sojourner*'s earliest days, the conservative pundits have been predicting the demise of the feminist movement. But as this anthology makes eminently clear, women have been doggedly pursuing their rights for the past two decades. Though the media has often characterized feminism as "white and middle-class," such a characterization makes invisible the many movements that have emerged among women of color in the United States, among poor and working-class women, and among Third World women throughout the world. For the last two decades, many feminists have been engaged in a dynamic conversation about women's lives and their experience of oppression across difference. They have also been actively involved in making change: creating feminist institutions, overturning laws that institutionalized women's second-class status in the home and the workplace; challenging cultural assumptions about gender, family, sexuality, education, religion, and so on. This anthology should put to rest the cavalier dismissal of second-wave feminists as "victim" feminists, who in the '90s have come to be depicted as whiners wallowing in unfounded fears of violence and discrimination.

Second-wave feminism, like all social movements, has been a complex and dynamic interaction among women and men, grassroots organizations and powerful social, political, and economic institutions, activists and theorists, reformers and revolutionaries, conservatives and radicals. There has never been a single voice, a single vision; just millions of women changing their lives and the world around them. By bringing together over 100 of these voices in a single volume, I hope this book serves as a testament to the courage, persistence, and determination of a generation of feminist activists who have worked unceasingly over the last two decades to expand the possibilities of all women's lives.

CHAPTER ONE

Claiming Our Identities

Between 1967 and 1970, women in the United States took to the streets. They disrupted the Miss America Pageant (though no bras were burned), hexed Wall Street businesses, took over welfare offices, boycotted consumer products, held mass demonstrations to legalize abortion, held strikes and sued employers, took over left-wing underground newspapers and the offices of the *Ladies Home Journal*. Feminism's second wave had arrived.

Emerging out of the social and political ferment of the '60s, this new social movement never had a clearly defined leadership or a single agenda. Almost immediately, a liberal wing coalesced around the founding of the National Organization for Women (NOW), with its platform for "equal rights." Women active in the civil rights and antiwar movements—and angered by the sexism of the male leadership—formed the more radical and amorphous "women's liberation movement." These radical feminists hoped for more than equality—the liberation of women, they argued, would require a social revolution, in which gender itself would become irrelevant.

Organized into small, ever-changing political groups, radical feminists initiated the practice of "consciousness raising," in which they developed political theory by sharing the commonalities of their experience. Women met regularly in small discussion groups to talk about and analyze relationships—marriage, sex, pregnancy, children, family—as well as their experiences in school, the workplace, and in negotiating the health care system. They discovered that many of the experiences they thought were personal—mistreatment by male partners, lack of success in pursuing careers, objectification, lack of respect for their intelligence—were the shared experiences of women living in a male-dominated society. Consciousness raising (CR) caught on among liberal feminists as well (NOW eventually sponsored CR groups throughout the country), and soon it seemed that women everywhere were discovering "the personal is political" and demanding change: reproductive rights, affordable child care, economic rights, and respectful relationships based on equal partnerships not servitude. Sisterhood was, indeed, powerful.

The sisterhood, however, soon dissolved in a plethora of differences. The white, heterosexual, middle-class women who came to dominate the movement named sexism as the primary source of women's oppression, effectively silencing women who experienced a complex array of oppressions in their lives. In their enthusiasm to build a theory and a movement that challenged male domination, these women failed to recognize that, for many women, "feminism" was too narrowly defined. The movement did not address their concerns as women of color, as working-class or poor women, as women with a wide range of sexual identities.

Though initial explorations of identity may have been limited, as we will see in this chapter, the process of exploring identity remains at the very heart of feminist theory and practice. What is important, as Pam Mitchell points out in "The Poor and Working-Class Support Group" (1984), is that the process has changed. "The difference," she writes, "is that as painstakingly as early feminists used CR to seek out the similarities in the experiences that each had previously thought her own unique problem, a decade or so later we were busily digging our way out of the very prison of 'sameness' that this early feminist process created." As the articles reprinted here show, explorations of identity eventually broadened the scope of the feminist movement by challenging oppressive behaviors within the movement, encouraging the celebration of cultural differences, and expanding the feminist agenda beyond its white, middle-class origins. Today, when we speak of "the feminist movement," we are really talking about a loose coalition of movements, many of which have developed around specific identities such as race, class, sexual orientation, age, size, or physical ability.

By the mid '70s, when *Sojourner* began publishing, the women's movement had gone through a number of difficult and harsh transitions in which lesbians and heterosexuals had found themselves sharply divided on issues of theory and practice and the last remaining connections to the movements of the New Left had been severed. As Alice Echols shows in her book, *Daring To Be Bad: Radical Feminism in America, 1967-1989* (University of Minnesota, 1989), a new movement was emerging, which placed greater emphasis on "lifestyles," creating community, and building permanent institutions that would bring the revolutionary future into the present. For the most part, these communities and their new cultural institutions—women's music, women's bookstores and presses, land-based women's communes, women's credit unions and other businesses—were dominated by lesbian feminists, though any woman who considered herself woman-identified was welcome.

In this context, explorations of identity became particularly significant. The new institutions were seen as developing out of consciousness of female/lesbian identity. As Susan Rennie and Kirsten Grimstad wrote in their *New Woman's Survival Sourcebook* (Knopf, 1975):

Women-identified explorations are occurring today...in all of what we call "women's culture"—which is often more precisely lesbian culture made available to all women. This is perhaps the most profound and ultimately far-reaching expression of our politics—the incredibly difficult and moving discovery of a woman's world view that will inform the conception and reality of women's power to change their lives and their culture.

This woman's world view was defined in direct opposition to the hierarchical, competitive, aggressive, and violent male world view. Though not everyone agreed on the origins of male aggression—nature vs. nurture—most agreed that it was important for women to create a life-affirming culture that valued the earth, relationships, cooperation, and caregiving. During *Sojourner*'s first decade, much of the paper was devoted to the celebration of this new women's culture. Interviews with its major stars—Adrienne Rich, Mary Daly, Kay Gardner, Alix Dobkin, Teresa Trull, Holly Near—and reviews of women's music festivals, books, plays, and art shows were at least as significant as articles that covered political issues such as the ERA, reproductive rights, women's health, and violence against women.

Much of this new culture was being created by white, middle-class women. For those who fit in the rewards were enormous—for the first time, women could celebrate their identities as women and lesbians in the comfort of exclusively female communities—in women's centers, bookstores, restaurants, coffeehouses, and bars. For those who lived in more isolated communities, annual music festivals brought them into contact with lesbians who had thrown open the doors of their closets and were celebrating life with a new sense of joy and freedom. But for many women, these feminist communities did not turn out to be the utopias they had hoped for. Working-class and Jewish women and women of color, though equally committed to feminism, lesbianism, and the women's movement, often felt invisible and marginalized. Not only did the feminist agenda exclude, for the most part, issues such as race and class exploitation (for example, middle-class feminists pursued the legalization of abortion without giving much attention to sterilization abuse, which primarily affected poor women of color), but differences in cultural style silenced those who did not fit in.

Black women, particularly Black lesbian feminists, were the first to challenge the narrowness of the feminist agenda (as represented by both mainstream and radical feminist groups) and the exclusionary nature of the "women's community." In response to the racism of the women's movement and the sexism of the Black liberation movement, in 1975, Black feminists in Boston founded the Combahee River Collective. Using the feminist concept of exploring identity in order to develop their own politic, the collective wrote in their 1977 statement:

The focusing upon our own oppression is embodied in the concept of identity politics. We believe that the most profound and potentially most radical politics come directly out of our own identity, as opposed to working to end somebody else's oppression. In the case of Black women this is a particularly repugnant, dangerous, threatening, and therefore revolutionary concept because it is obvious from looking at all the political movements that have preceded us that anyone is more worthy of liberation than ourselves....

We believe that sexual politics under patriarchy is as pervasive in Black women's lives as are the politics of class and race. We also often find it difficult to separate race from class from sex oppression because in our lives they are most often experienced simultaneously.

Particularly concerned with struggles where race, class, and gender intersected, in 1979, Combahee responded to the murder of twelve Black women in Boston by writing and distributing a pamphlet about the connections between sexual and racial violence and economic exploitation (see Barbara Smith, "Black Feminism: A Movement of Our Own," 1984).

The pamphlet, written in English and Spanish, also included practical advice on how women could protect themselves. By refusing to accept the racist and sexist assumption that the murders were insignificant because the victims were "prostitutes and runaways," the Combahee pamphlet reinforced what many women in the Black community understood intuitively: it could have been any one of them. Moreover, by combining a race and gender analysis, Combahee was critical in building a coalition between Black community groups and white feminist groups to fight racist and sexist violence across the city.

Members of Combahee explored Black feminist and lesbian identity by sponsoring cultural events as well. In October 1978, the collective members joined with other women in the Boston community to sponsor "The Varied Voices of Black Women," in which West Coast musicians Mary Watkins, Gwen Avery, and Linda Tillery and poet Pat Parker demonstrated that white lesbians were not the only ones creating a new women's culture. Though the concert was first and foremost a celebration of Black lesbian feminist identity and culture, it was also an attempt to broaden the white feminist community's understanding of feminist and lesbian identity. That some white women, including *Sojourner*'s reviewer, found these gifted performers threatening indicated that there was much work to be done to build an inclusive, multicultural women's movement and community. Many readers, across racial differences, perceived this December 1979 review in *Sojourner* (not included here), which referred to "hostility" between the Black performers and white audience members, as racist. The controversy prompted *Sojourner*'s editors to pay more attention to issues being raised by women of color in the community, particularly the marginalization of their voices. The February 1979 issue of the paper focused specifically on "Third World" women (primarily African American), while racism was the theme of the May 1979 issue.

Increasingly, in the late '70s and early '80s, *Sojourner* ran first-person articles, interviews, and reviews addressing a broad spectrum of identities. Similarly, during this period, Persephone, one of the new feminist publishing companies, was publishing groundbreaking books such as *The Coming Out Stories* (lesbian identity), *This Bridge Called My Back* (women of color), and *Nice Jewish Girls* (Jewish lesbians). Women were gaining voice, claiming their identities, and expanding the boundaries of feminist communities by challenging racism, anti-Semitism, and classism. In 1983, *Sojourner* published two guest-edited issues, one produced by African-American women and one by Jewish women. Then, in 1984 the first issue on class appeared. Each of these special issues sought to use identity as a framework for challenging oppression. For example, Cheryl Clarke wrote in "New Notes on Lesbianism" (January 1983),

I name myself "lesbian" because this culture oppresses, silences, and destroys lesbians, even lesbians who don't call themselves "lesbians." I name myself "lesbian" because I want to be visible to other Black lesbians.... I name myself "lesbian" because being woman-identified has kept me sane. I call myself "Black" too, because Black is my perspective, my aesthetic, my politics, my vision, my sanity.

And in the November 1984 issue, Pam Mitchell wrote of poor and working-class women:

Like everyone else in this country we had breathed in certain assumptions and prejudices about class all our lives. In deciding to meet and discuss our backgrounds, we were allowing ourselves to face the self-hating, self-denying voices in our own heads as well as possible defensive or dismissive responses from other people. First of all we had to establish that we indeed existed, and then that we were worth fighting for.

By the mid '80s, women were asserting a complex range of identities and exploring the ways in which they had been silenced in the past. Of particular importance have been challenges to white male definitions of femininity which oppress all women, but are particularly detrimental to those who can never conform: old women, disabled women, fat women, masculine women, women of color. In claiming their identities, these women have pointed out that women in this society are rewarded for being young, thin, light-skinned, and fragile-looking. Those who can't or won't conform to gender stereotypes, and thereby challenge the society's definition of women, face economic discrimination, inadequate health care, violence, and social isolation.

Just as women of color, poor and working-class women, and lesbians have built their own movements to address issues that have been marginalized by white, heterosexual, middle-class feminists, so have disabled, fat, and old women. Disabled women have fought to make feminist culture accessible (through Braille, audiotape and large-print media; sign interpretation;

and wheelchair accessible events); fat women have confronted the hatred that most women feel for their imperfect bodies and the ubiquitous dieting that is as true for feminists as nonfeminists; and old women have challenged the ageism of young women who assume that old women, though they might be interesting as "community historians" (assuming they are willing to tell their stories), would have no interest in participating in feminist political and cultural events.

Challenging invisibility is one means of challenging the powerful forces of sexism, racism, class oppression, homophobia, ageism, and ableism that support the patriarchal, capitalist social and economic order. For example, when lesbians and gays come out, they challenge sex role stereotypes, the heterosexual norm, the nuclear family, and religious doctrine, all of which support patriarchal power. When working-class women assert their identities, they challenge economic exploitation by disrupting the myth that all "Americans" are middle class, whether they are CEOs or maids, professionals or factory workers. As the Combahee River Collective asserted, when we examine the roots of our own oppression and struggle for our liberation, we learn a great deal about the forces arrayed against us.

But identity politics has its limits as well. Although exploring our identities can lead to coalitions as we begin to see the interlocking nature of oppression, our vision may also be circumscribed by our inability to see past the boundaries of our own lives. For example, feminists who have been hurt by pornography have been unable to build alliances with sex workers who are trying to legalize (and legitimize) their profession (see Chapter 6: "Sex and Sexuality"). Another example is lesbians and gay men who, in campaigning for the "equal right" to serve in the U.S. military, miss the opportunity to create alliances with those who oppose the military's use of violence to oppress Third World peoples around the world (see in Chapter 8: Neta Crawford, "Out of the Closet and into a Straight Medal Jacket?," 1993). As we will see in the following chapters, building an inclusive movement requires an analysis that goes beyond our individual experiences of oppression to one that examines issues from the full range of our experiences. Otherwise we create a theory and a practice that presumes the universality of our own, limited experience, making it more difficult for feminism to effectively challenge the political, economic, and social structures that circumscribe *all* women's lives.

JANUARY 1983

New Notes on Lesbianism
by Cheryl Clarke

"Black lesbians" sounds formidable and intimidating. Did not bell hooks in *Ain't I a Woman* (South End Press, 1981) avoid the issue of Black lesbianism in the context of her feminist arguments for reasons she has never been able to explain that we (lesbians) know? "Black lesbians"—it is stark and startling. Did not Alice Walker (*Black Scholar,* Fall 1981), an avowed nonlesbian, state that she would prefer, among others, the term "womanist" to the name "lesbian"? "Black lesbians"—sounds like a Thelonious Monk tune. Lately, even I have been plying myself with such questions regarding my lesbianism: Why do I call myself a lesbian? Why do I elevate who I sleep with to politics? Why do I not pursue a more revolutionary politic—a polymorphous perverse vision of the world and of living? "Come out of the shoe box of lesbianism." "Do not be so cushioned in the narrow politics of sexual preference." "Are *labels* really necessary?" have been reverberating inside me regularly lately.

Black women like pretty names. Remember the names of Black girls in our lives growing up? Blossom. Queen Esther. Countess Peace. Floresta. Carleasa. "Black lesbians" is certainly different sounding. What Black person or Black lesbian in Harlem, on Chicago's South Side, Atlanta, Newark, Brooklyn, L.A. can relate to Sappho or the Isle of Lesbos, where white women were said to have migrated to cavort and become amazons? I wonder if they held Black lesbians slaves? Lesbos, as Alice Walker suggests in her *Black Scholar* review of *Gifts of Power: The Writings of Rebecca Jackson (1795-1871)* (University of Massachusetts Press, 1981), was not the origin of lesbians. Lesbians like Black folk came into existence in what is now known as the Kongo, where language began (thus, Black lesbians' facility for talk, storytelling, and advice-giving). So, perhaps, for Black women to call ourselves lesbians is anachronistic as Black women have obviously been lesbians longer than all women, according to Walker. Is "womanist" any more viable though? It is not the name that the prevailing culture despises but rather the act...of lesbianism, womanism; the interdependence of women and women, the fucking, the eating, the smells, the juices, the vaginas that our enemies despise. If Black women called ourselves something more neutral like "Black azaleas," would other Black women be more willing to identify with the politics of woman-bonding? If we were to call ourselves "Black azaleas" instead of "Black lesbians" would Black women be more willing to identify their woman-bonding as political? Would the Black community be any more willing to accept our definition, our naming? "Black azaleas"—sounds like a less foreboding Monk tune. "Black Azaleas."

In *Black American Literature Forum* (Vol. 14, No. 4, Winter 1980), Black feminist critic Deborah McDowell takes issue with "Towards a Black Feminism Criticism," written by Black lesbian feminist Barbara Smith and published in *Conditions Two* (1977), for its lack of "precision and detail." McDowell demands that Smith and others like Smith who write from a—Gasp!!!—lesbian perspective, pin our aesthetic to the page or folk will get confused. Not only may Toni Morrison's *Sula* (Knopf, 1973; Plume, 1987) as Smith suggests, be interpreted as a—Gasp!!!—lesbian novel, we might also be able, based upon Smith's criteria, to interpret Jean Toomer's *Cane* (Liveright, 1975) from a lesbian perspective: i.e., some writers who are not lesbians might be interpreted as advancing a lesbian aesthetic or ideology inadvertently.

The term "lesbian" has been denigrated, degraded, and made synonymous with disease. And feminists (lesbians) have rescued and reclaimed it as Black folk have rescued and reclaimed "black." And "lesbian" *can* mean "nigga" as June Jordan tells us in *Civil Wars* (Beacon Press, 1981), especially if it's Black lesbians doing it, especially if "nigga" means field hand, crazy nigger, outsider rebel, trickster, Ananci, or guerrilla. But if "nigga" means "unconscious, continuing self-hatred," as Jordan proffers in her 1976 *Ms.* article, "A Declaration of Independence I Would Just As Soon Not Have," reprinted in *Civil Wars*, "lesbian" is not the equivalent of it. It is hard to believe that Jordan has not edited out or recanted that whole passage in which she denigrates lesbians; even for 1976 the attitude was reactionary! Maybe June Jordan should have used "bulldagger" in the analogy if she wanted to evoke the negative of lesbian—at least the terms "nigga" and "bulldagger" are equivalent. And if she still really believes that "lecherous, exploitative, shallow, acting-out and pathological behavior" is synonymous with lesbian, then maybe June Jordan ought to find out more about lesbians. Get some balance, sister.

Who one sleeps with is important. It just is. Sexuality is not neutral, personal, or a private matter. Just because we can keep it private, personal, closeted, repressed, the world still revolves around who sleeps with whom and the power implicit in that. Whoever one is. Whom one sleeps with never does not matter. Folk constantly think about who sleeps with whom and where. If I, an avowed lesbian and feminist, were to say that I still sleep with men, what do you think would be the response from my lesbian-feminist sisters? If I come out as a lesbian in the various Black groups I find myself among, am I not buked? If I label myself "bisexual," then who would trust me? So, who one sleeps with is a key issue, because the act speaks to how far one might go in perpetuating or tearing down the empire. As a lesbian, a feminist, and a "nigga," I am about the radical restructuring of all systems—whomever I sleep with.

Economically, lesbians thwart capitalism—and the blacker the lesbian the more she should attempt to thwart capitalism and the more she does. Lesbians or women who are "lovers" do not wed themselves to the institution of exclusive heterosexuality which expresses itself unabashedly and unashamedly at every turn in our daily existence as women. Of course, lesbians are victimized economically like all women in capitalism, but there are additional threats to the economic and emotional survival of women who are lesbians—whether we are "out" or not. We can lose jobs, our children, our lovers, our freedom, our lives because we are lesbians in a homophobic culture. Thus, many Black women who love women are loathe to identify themselves as lesbians. Some of us feel we don't need another "handicap," "strike against us...we already Black." Being a Black lesbian is not easy, and the more non-middle-class, nonbourgeois elite the lesbian, the harder it is. There are fewer mechanisms in everyday life and in the institutions that run our lives for dealing with homophobia than there are to deal with racism or sexism. People recognize racism and sexism as legitimate oppressions. Many folk still feel the best medicine for homosexuality is to string the "queer" up on the nearest tree.

I name myself "lesbian" because this culture oppresses, silences, and destroys lesbians, even lesbians who don't call themselves "lesbians." I name myself "lesbian" because I want to be visible to other Black lesbians. I name myself "lesbian" because I do not subscribe to predatory/institutionalized heterosexuality. I name myself "lesbian" because I want to be with women (and they don't all have to call themselves "lesbians"). I name myself "lesbian" because it is part of my vision. I name myself "lesbian" because being woman-identified has kept me sane. I call myself "Black," too, because Black is my perspective, my aesthetic, my politics, my vision, my sanity.

A woman does not have to be sleeping with a woman or women to cultivate a lesbian perspective. McDowell, hooks, and Jordan, for example, could cultivate a lesbian perspective. Such cultivation might be therapeutic for their antilesbian attitudes. Any self-determined woman can call herself a lesbian if she is about affirming herself and other women.

The issue of lesbianism, as politics, as a way of being in the world, as just plain life needs talking about, not silence, not subterfuge, not coyness. Every time I meet a Black woman, who lives somewhere in the hinterlands of South Jersey, who has been making her way with a woman, in isolation, in the closet, cut off from community, and who thinks she's the only *"one,"* it becomes ever clearer how much self-determined Black women, Black lesbians, Black feminists, Black lesbian feminists need to do some naming and claiming regarding our tradition of woman-bonding, e.g., *lesbianism.*

This article has been edited for length and clarity.

POSTSCRIPT 1995

At this writing, I remain firmly convinced that our "enemies" despise "women and women, the fucking, the eating, the smells, the juices, the vaginas," although today, our enemies are different. Some of the Black feminists of whom I was "sharply critical" (Kahn, letter, June 1995) in 1983 have sharply revised their thinking on Black lesbian feminism. I have revised my thinking, too—both on Black lesbian feminism and about Black feminists who do not claim a lesbian politic.

I count Alice Walker, Deborah McDowell, and June Jordan among my teachers, allies, and friends. Walker's *The Color Purple* (Simon & Schuster, 1982) was profoundly informed by Black lesbian feminism. McDowell's astounding article, "That Nameless…Shameful Impulse," on the lesbian subtext of Nella Larsen's 1929 novel *Passing,* opened a whole new area of inquiry in African-American literary studies, from which I have benefited.

Jordan has taken many affirmative stands on love between women in her writing since the 1976 *Ms.* article and the 1981 publication of *Civil Wars:* e.g., her poem "From Sea to Shining Sea," (*Living Room,* Thunder's Mouth, 1985), her insightful essay, "A New Politics of Sexuality," (*Technical Difficulties,* Vintage, 1994), and her exquisite *Haruko/Love Poems* (Serpent's Tale, 1994), a whole series of which are devoted to love between women.

The positions of bell hooks (a.k.a. Gloria Watkins) baffles me more today than in 1983, despite her formal shift in "Reflections on Homophobia and Black Communities" (*Outlook,* 1988). In this essay, hooks admits to homophobia among Black people, albeit no worse than in any other community, without consciously implicating herself. She seems more nonplussed about Black lesbians who show up at parties or meetings with their white lovers than about homophobia and heterosexism in Black "communities." Her "reflections" are, as usual, provocative. In a June 1995 interview in *The Chronicle of Higher Education,* hooks still manages *not* to implicate herself, as she fantasizes about someone else's desire: "(T)here are probably many more young women thinking, wouldn't it be great to have sex with bell hooks, than young men." See also, "In Our Glory: Photography and Black Life," in *Art on My Mind* (New Press, 1995) for an update of her preoccupation with Black women and white women in lesbian relationships. Yet, I do not foreclose the possibility that bell hooks' thinking and writing on Black lesbian feminism will get beyond voyeurism. I look forward to the day.

NOVEMBER 1984

The Poor & Working-Class Support Group

by Pam Mitchell

"Poor and Working-Class Women's Support Group," our banner proclaimed at its first public appearance, at a march in Boston in the spring of 1981. And across the bottom, though you wouldn't know it from photographs taken at the time, giant letters made of lavender-colored felt asserted, "Invisible No More." Ironically, its blue tint rendered the line itself invisible: like a ghost with no reflection in a mirror, the photographic process left the illusion of empty space where in reality these bold words stood.

It was a disappearing act highly symbolic for the 50 to 100 women from poor or working-class backgrounds who found their way to the group's monthly meetings at some point during its two-year history. Perhaps the sign was acting something out for us. As much as we wanted to assert our presence in a women's movement too often blithely labeled "middle-class" even as we sat in its midst unacknowledged, as much as we wanted to stamp in indelible ink our identities, our values, our particular pains and passions onto the movement to which so many of us had given so much of ourselves despite persistent feelings of not belonging, many of us felt a certain ambivalence toward this particular "coming-out process"—a desire to jump off the banner ourselves and run back into hiding. After so many years of feeling weird or crazy or "less than" or somehow wrong, it seemed like we all needed heavy doses of acknowledgment, affirmation, and support from each other in order to feel strong and sure enough to take a public stand. The poor and working-class support group provided many of us with just that kind of support and self-awareness. By the time our banner showed its face again—at the Boston Gay/Lesbian Pride March a few weeks later— the shy letters had been replaced with more photogenic and insistent ones. "Invisible No More," the pictures taken at that event declare firmly; the imprint of the group itself, and the startling self-discoveries and revelations, the intimate friendships, and the stirrings of pride and ambition that it allowed, are etched as firmly in the lives of many of its members.

Like everyone else in this country we had breathed in certain assumptions and prejudices about class all our lives. In deciding to meet and discuss our backgrounds, we were
allowing ourselves to face the self-hating, self-denying voices in our own heads as well as
possible defensive or dismissive responses from other people. First of all, we had to establish that we indeed existed, and then that we were worth fighting for. The nay-saying voices
(both internal and external) generally carp on variants of a few predictable—and somewhat
contradictory themes: 1) There is no working class (and certainly no poor people, except
for a few lazy bums) in this country; 2) Certainly you can't claim to belong to it (even though
it doesn't exist, the working class has certain attributes and if you lack any of them—which
nearly everyone does—you can't claim membership); 3) Who would *want* to belong to it
anyway—it consists of, say, a bunch of reactionary, beer-guzzling rednecks and passive stupid breeders (specific content of the negative stereotype may vary from region to region);
and 4) Why don't you stop complaining and put your energy into people who *really* have
it bad? (This last one has been used within the women's movement on occasion to pit white
working-class and poor women against working-class and poor women of color, to the lasting benefit of no one. Working-class white women have been told through the words and
deeds of other white women, and sometimes by our own self-denying voices, that demanding space and resources—through our inclusion in affirmative action efforts, for example,
or through our demands for workshops at conferences that relate specifically to our issues—means taking from women of color.)

If that particular setup—the pitting of "less-privileged" whites against "even-less-privi-
leged" people of color—has a familiar ring to it, it should; it is, after all, a favorite national
pastime, and one that is a key factor in the perpetuation of racism, though, because of class-
blindness, it is one that has often been overlooked (or worse, reenacted) in feminist efforts to
fight racism. In reality, any working-class or poor person of any color or ethnicity who grows
up in a multiracial community has watched the pecking order in action, as whites are set up to
keep people of color under them instead of allying with them to eliminate the inequality that
hits them all to varying degrees. Often the people of color are neighbors or coworkers or classmates of the white people, or are trying to be. Evidence of such firsthand knowledge of how
racism and classism can reinforce each other has been sadly lacking in the women's movement.

According to Sheila Kelly, one of the women who first set the poor and working-class
women's support group into motion, it was discussions about race among working-class
white women that planted the seed for the group. Kelly reports that throughout 1980 many
small groups of white feminists were meeting in the Boston area to discuss and combat racism. But, she says, these groups assumed that experiences of all white women were the same.
The predominance (and the dominance) of white women from middle-class or upper-middle-class backgrounds in these discussions led them to believe that whites and people of color
occupy separate worlds, with all white people growing up as they did (comfortable, guilty,
and in very white environments).

Kelly and other white, working-class women she knew began comparing notes about
experiences and attitudes around racism, and something clicked. When word came that the
New England Women's Studies Association was planning a conference on racism for February 1981, Kelly and friends felt certain that the issue of class would be overlooked by the
mostly middle-class organizers and participants that an academic conference would be likely

to attract. They called the organizers, requesting that one of the small groups scheduled for the beginning of the conference be specifically for white women from working-class backgrounds. (This group would be limited to whites only because the organizers had already planned for women of color to meet separately during this part of the conference.) The conference organizers reportedly refused to build this request into their structure, but allowed a working-class caucus to convene informally. Kelly reports that the women who showed up were "starved" for more contact with each other and traded phone numbers. Out of this the poor and working-class group was born.

When I started attending the group a few months later, it was already well organized. Each month the participants—ranging in number from about fifteen to forty and always including some new women—would number off into small groups to discuss a previously-arranged topic. Sometimes the topic focused on how growing up poor or working-class affected our circumstances as adults: our financial insecurity with no family backup or connections, for example, or our job histories and attitudes toward work and money, or our conflicted attitudes toward our families' lifestyles and choices and their attitudes toward ours, or our experiences with middle-class and often "downwardly mobile" friends, roommates, lovers. Other times we focused on our childhoods: on our pride and shame about our backgrounds, including details about our pasts and our families that we had felt the need to gloss over or avoid in middle-class company; on our childhood experiences with people of different races and ethnicities and with racism; on the values we grew up with about religion, sex, emotionalism, violence.

"It was the first time in my life I felt like I didn't have to fight for space in a group," one woman told me recently. There was a tolerance and a mutual respect and a sense of exploration at our meetings as we stumbled on common themes and threads and noted differences. I am a little too young to have experienced the first rush of the consciousness-raising (CR) groups of early feminism, but the discoveries, the clicks, the surprised exclamations of "You mean it's that way for you, too?!!" must have been similar. The difference is that as painstakingly as early feminists used CR to seek out the similarities in the experiences that each had previously thought her own unique problem, a decade or so later we were busily digging our way out of the very prison of "sameness" that this early feminist process thus created.

As we compared stories, I began to realize that it was something of a miracle that we had found each other, considering the denial of class in the society at large and our own confusion about how we fit into the larger picture. This picture was made even more bewildering by the fact that, if we felt alienated from much of the women's movement because of its middle-class assumptions and style, most of us were to some extent alienated from the lifestyles we grew up with, as well.

We found that our confusion about our class identities had started early in our lives. During one meeting, when the discussion topic concerned the identity we each grew up with, every participant in my small group reported that her parents had communicated that their family was some version of "middle class." ("Lower middle class" was a particularly popular label.) "Of course we're middle class," one woman's father had told her. "Some people are better off than us, and some people are worse off, and we're somewhere in the middle."

Our parents' lack of eagerness to claim working-class status was understandable. By the time most of the women who participated in the support group were born—in the '50s and '60s—any possibility of socialism in the United States had been (temporarily) smashed: anyone with anything to lose had learned to keep her or his distance from "commie" ideas of the working class as a source of power and pride. Meanwhile, with the economy expanding, a growing demand for white-collar workers, and unions still powerful enough to deliver economically to blue-collar workers, with some luck and some individual enterprise, most people could get at least a little ahead (temporarily, anyway). Given these conditions, it made a certain amount of sense for less-privileged people to deny the very existence of class distinctions as part of a strategy of blending with the middle class. Perhaps the working class would wither away; if not, one could at least hope to leave it behind. (Even my parents, who were long-time Communists and champions of the working class, saw my father's high-stress, low-paying clerical work as the big "step up" from the mining and small farming his father had done, though every night as a child I fell asleep to the familiar sound of their fights over lack of money.) But these decisions on the part of our parents left many of us growing up with little sense of who we were and led to seeking self-definition by constantly comparing ourselves to people supposedly "above" or "below" us.

A lot of the women raised working-class reported being taught to feel competitive with (and fearful of) those who knew real poverty. "There was always food on the table" was a phrase I heard often from the working-class women, a distinction that put that sector of our group closer to the "middle" than other women in the group who grew up poor. "At least we were never on welfare" was another common line from many of the working-class women, though when someone asked how many women's families had ever received any form of public assistance, a lot of hands went up. For most of us, poverty was at best just a layoff or an accident or a death away.

Though the group was explicitly for poor *and* working-class women, sometimes the feelings of competitiveness and "superiority" the working-class women had been raised with, and the fact that the poor women in the group were outnumbered and often felt invisible, threatened to recreate a hierarchy of our own making. In our discussions of taking pride in our backgrounds and in our families' accomplishments, my small group spoke about finding ways of feeling good that were not at someone else's expense and that didn't imply a link between wealth and worth. We did not always succeed at that even within our group, and when the group decided to disband (in 1983), tensions between working-class and poor women were left somewhat unresolved. According to participant Marcia Duvall, who would have preferred closing the group's membership in its waning months, the fluidity and lack of continuity of the drop-in structure made bringing to the surface underlying conflicts, such as the one between poor and working-class women, feel unsafe and futile. She believes that for the same reasons, other sore spots within the group, such as ethnic differences and fat oppression, were never adequately addressed.

Even in the era of growing affluence that most of us grew up in, any child could see that even if she was in fact "somewhere in the middle," some people were "higher up" in that "middle" than others, some families had access to music and dance lessons, vacations overseas, and "nice" houses like the ones we saw on TV, while others didn't. As we got older, we also learned that some people's parents did interesting and prestigious work that they had some control over, while our own—if they had work at all—were often forced to grovel for their bosses and endure unsafe conditions and interminable boredom.

If the women who were drawn to the support group had had a hard time figuring out what class it was that we grew up in and "belonged to," this was in part because there have been significant ways in which we *didn't* "belong." If it's true that there is no "typical" member of the U.S. working class, that no one fits into some well-defined mold, it is nonetheless also true that when compared with the majority of our parents and siblings, the women showing up at the support group had things in common with each other that made us a particularly atypical bunch. Our membership was limited to women who were in the particular circle that would hear about our meetings through word of mouth and would feel comfortable once we got there. Most of us were in our twenties or thirties. Few of us were mothers with obligations that might prevent us from spending our Sunday afternoons with each other. Though the group was expressly open to both straight and lesbian women, the overwhelming majority of those showing up were lesbians. While many Jewish women passed through the group and a few stayed, women from Christian backgrounds seemed most often to feel at home and to keep coming back. (As someone from a mixed Jewish and Christian background, I felt in this group that though a part of me finally could become visible, could belong, my Jewish identity was still in hiding, feeling threatened and unacknowledged.)

And though this was obviously not representative of the poor and working classes in the Boston area, nearly all of us were white. This de facto segregation existed partly because the group arose in a context (at the New England Women's Studies conference) that was deliberately all-white, as an externally imposed strategy for combating racism (a strategy about which there were differing opinions within our group) and partly because word of its existence circulated in mostly white circles. Once established the group's white face probably perpetuated itself. Though an occasional woman of color passed through, it seemed that most, understandably, preferred to meet in groups in which they were not so thoroughly outnumbered.

Different both from the families we came from and from "typical" (or at least stereotypical) feminists, we were a homogeneous bunch in significant ways. Many (though not all) of us went to college—often the first in our families to do so, sometimes against our families' wishes, and most of us with the help of financial aid packages that were suddenly being given out like candy as we were coming of age (and which have as suddenly dried up since then, locking out our younger working-class and poor counterparts). Of course, the packages did have strings attached—the mere mention of student loans in the support group caused a collective shiver. But we (and the parents of some of us) were under the illusion that once our college degrees magically eased us into the middle class, the loans could easily be paid. Since so many of us attended college in the hippie days of the late '60s to mid '70s, we hadn't had to worry about our lack of expensive wardrobes or our "lack of taste" in clothes (read: different taste) because, as one woman in the group wryly put it, "we came into style in the '60s."

But by the early '80s we were no longer "in style." When I found the support group, I was glad to discover that I was not the only one at the time watching in bewilderment as many middle- and upper-middle-class former classmates and friends once so disdainful of ambition and wealth started "drifting" into expensive professional schools and cashing in on family connections. Women who didn't come from privilege could wonder together what it was that made us different, and though we might have liked to attribute the differences to greater purity, our virtuous commitment to antimaterialism was beginning to wear thin in the face of high inflation and unemployment rates.

Of course, I had noticed before that when times get tough, differences in access to wealth can become dramatically apparent. I got one of my first lessons in class when I transferred from a community college to a middle-class university in 1971. When I arrived, everyone was hitchhiking because it was hip and "ecological" not to own a car, but shortly thereafter, as parents learned of the hitchhiking rape-and-murder spree then hitting campus, a thousand cars bloomed overnight and I was one of the few people left standing. (Not that my mother wasn't worried about me: "You will take the bus, won't you?" she urged me on the phone.)

But the leap from the acceptance of parental cars (and stereos and vacations and skis and hair dryers and down parkas...) to the inheritance of middle-class status and income makes the realities of class more obvious to me. It's aggravating to figure out that a lifestyle of making-do that could be a lifetime sentence for many of us was a passing fad for others and that attainment of the career or the house that would require of some of us nearly limitless resolve and a great deal of luck comes to others as the path of least resistance. But without the awareness that class barriers exist, and without close contact with people "on the same side" of those barriers, it would be much easier to fall into self-blame and harder to come up with realistic strategies for getting what we want, whether what we want includes a "middle-class" career, a class-less revolution, or "only" an acceptance and pride in what we are and where we come from. I thank the women who attended the support group for being there to help me make sense of the '80s.

Some women who attended the support group regularly until it broke up in 1983 have told me that their most intimate friendships grew out of that group and that they now tend to stay away from organizations and activities dominated by middle-class women. I don't know whether our presence has been missed in environments in which we always felt unseen anyway. But it seems clear that, at least to each other, the women of the poor and working-class women's support group are indeed "invisible no more."

NOVEMBER 1994

The Cost of the Gold Stars:
An Interview with Dorothy Allison

by Patti Capel Swartz

Patti Swartz spoke with Dorothy Allison in March 1994, just prior to the publication of her book of essays, Skin *(Firebrand, 1994). Much of their conversation was about class. In the excerpt that appears here, Swartz and Allison talk about their experience growing up in work-ing-poor families.*

Patti Swartz: *Tell me about your new book,* Skin.
Dorothy Allison: It's a book of essays. The hardest thing I ever did in my life. I just don't have a comfortable relationship with reality. I much prefer writing fiction, where I can take a piece of reality and step outside and sharpen it. Sticking to the literal truth proved to be really enor-mously difficult. It took me way longer than I intended. The book is in part a way to rescue a lot of writing I've done on the subject of class.

In your essay, "A Question of Class," you talk about being splintered.
Oh, hell, yes, shattered. Some days I feel like I'm a glass lamp that people put back to-gether with scotch tape: mostly I put myself back together. And under heat, it tends to get real fragile. And life is heat.

In my head, I have a kind of picture of you as a child, very much like Bone [the pro-tagonist of Allison's novel, Bastard Out of Carolina *(Dutton, 1992)].*
In many ways.

Reaching for the comfort of the mother's body before you were five, standing by her hip.... The reaching that children do that we sometimes deny. I'm not sure if that's what you mean by what you just said.
It's a piece of it. But...one of the hard things that happens is that if you are reaching for your mother, if you love your mother and value her and the other women around her, and everything around you tells you that there is something wrong with her and the women around her, if everything that you run into outside the reach of her hip communicates to you that your survival depends on getting away from her, and her people, her family, your family, that's where some of the damage comes from. Pretty much that's what happens to kids who grow up in working-class, working-poor families. It's part of the process of growing up, any-way. We tell all kids that there's something wrong with identifying with and wanting their mama. But we tell that to working-class kids in a way that is particularly cruel because we devalue their mothers.

And we devalue the child at the same time.
Especially girls. Because you see yourself in your mother and when you're told con-stantly that what you see there is a "bad" or "wrong" thing, you don't know who to become. You don't know what to work for. It works on all kinds of levels. (Sighs.) There are so many social sins that it's possible to commit, and when all of those social sins are necessary for your survival, you're caught in a trap that ensures no escape. When I was a child, in the '50s, women, "good" women, were not supposed to work outside the home. *Nobody* in my family could afford not to have the women work outside the home.

That's one of the class issues that I think is pretty vital. Because women working out-side the home have been ignored.

Oh, and the kind of work they do. I mean, if you do work outside the home, you're supposed to look like those women on television. (Laughs.) Nobody in your family looks like those women on that television. God, I can remember watching—what was that wretched TV show—"Julia," and thinking, "Lord, if every Black child in the country is looking at her and thinking that their mama has to look like Julia, then we are in worse trouble than I thought."

Do you remember "Hazel"? Hazel was just about the only person I saw on TV who looked like anybody I knew, anybody in my family. She was this broad-hipped, broad-faced woman. She was the maid. And I knew, that's us. (Laughs.) [There are] multiple messages. The primary message is that you are not important, your people are bad. It's no surprise to me that I had very few cousins who didn't go to jail. It's no surprise to me that I had very few women cousins who didn't start having babies as teenagers. People give you back what you expect from them. And what this society has expected from them is pretty vicious.

That's true. Plus there's a lot of effort to keep things the same.

One of the ways they do that, that is infinitely problematic, is they tend to pick one, especially in families as large and poor as mine. That's one of the scary things that I realized at a really young age because I got picked at a really young age. By that I mean that they decide that one out of every large group will get recognized and pulled out and rescued. I wasn't exactly rescued...

Glasses from the Lion's Club...

Yeah. I wouldn't be able to see now—I have very bad vision—if the Lion's Club hadn't paid for my glasses.

Scholarship...

Being invited to join the advanced classes in school.... That's a marvelous thing, scholarships are a marvelous thing. I don't know what I would be if I hadn't started getting those awards and those little savings bonds for going to school when I was in junior high. And those little gold stars. But every goddamned gold star they give you tells you that you are different, you are special. But because you are different and special, you are proof that nobody else in your family is worth anything. Because if you can earn a gold star and your little sister can't, she might as well die. The undertone to everything that they give you is a message that says that you are infinitely separate, and you have to learn to hate all those people around you who can't do the things that you are being praised for being able to do. It makes you split at the core, because you can't hate the people that you are born loving and not borrow damage from it. I'm just, at 45, beginning to be close to my sisters. And that separation that split us off, part of it was my earning those gold stars. I was in junior high, and I've always known it. Everything that I ever did that won an award was another source of pain and shame at the same time that it could have been a source of pride. And it was, in some ways.

I got a few gold stars.

Well, they leave scars. And I don't know any way around it. I don't know.... Christ, I do it when my nieces do something and win some kind of attention. I send them things; I do everything I can to stroke and encourage them, because I don't know what else to do, but I try to do it in a way that doesn't separate them out from their families, that doesn't require that they have to have contempt for their families at the same time. That's what I hold this society responsible for. I want to know why, with all of that praise, there had to be so much contempt for everything.

I have always wondered why I had to be a chameleon—to try to be a part of whatever group so that I didn't stand out, so that nobody would know; I spent an awful lot of time trying to be a chameleon instead of trying to put my life back together. It took me a long time to realize that all of those people, they were in me and they would never, never go away, and it was okay to love them. I guess that's why I like your work so much. The love comes through. The anger and the love and the search.

Takes a long time, though. What I would like to see is a way that we could stop losing decades. 'Cause to me it seems to be a pretty constant pattern. I mean, I hunt out working-class kids, 40-, 50-, 60-year-old working-class kids—this is not a term that applies to age—and when I find them, I almost always find that they've lost a decade—sometimes two or three. When they didn't go home, when they were being a chameleon, when they were erasing who they were and creating this false person that they could be in public and hating themselves at home. I suspect—because mostly I find people who manage to make some connection and begin to get back who they were—I suspect that the ones who don't, die.

I had to come pretty close to that before I could start trying to find the person that I really was.

I worked awfully hard at it. I still think it's a miracle I'm not dead. I mean, aside from my childhood, it's a miracle I didn't find a way to kill myself when I was 24. 'Cause, Lord, I was looking. There was no answer. There was no way to be in the world and be who I really was and not be caught in the cauldron of hatred and shame. It was impossible. I can't drink. I'm physically incapable of drinking. It's something that's common, at least, with the women in my family. I don't have the pancreas for it. I tried really hard to develop a capacity for drink. I tried really hard to find a way either to numb myself or die. There was no way to accept the trap I was in. And I ran away from all those gold stars for a while, because I couldn't accept that either. Because every time they give you any recognition, you can see the hatred. It's that "dancing dog" thing. You know that term? I first heard that term from Jewelle Gomez and Cheryl Clarke, and as soon as I heard it, I thought, "That's it!" It's not that you can dance, but it's that a dog can dance.

And so that is remarkable!

Yes. (Laughs.) Aren't you extraordinary! My goodness, you can read! My Lord! And you're from *that* family! I don't think anyone else in that family has read for fourteen generations! You want to kill people who talk to you like that, shame your family like crazy. It's not praise.

No, it's not.

The thing that I find is extraordinary is that with all that damage, that when you go home again—and I mean that in the large sense—when you make that connection, what's waiting for you is this enormous well of energy and strength. They never wanted to let you go. Your people never wanted to let you go. Hmmm (shaking her head and reflecting). God knows, they certainly seem to be entirely proud of me.

DECEMBER 1984

Black Feminism: A Movement of Our Own

by Barbara Smith

The following talk by Barbara Smith was delivered as part of the series "Naming/Claiming/ Changing: Sojourneys with Black Women," organized by Boston's Women's Theological Center. Before Smith's speech, Brandeis sociology professor Karen Fields spoke on "Remembering One's Kin," reading excerpts from Lemon Swamp and Other Places: A Carolina Memoir *(Free Press, 1985), a moving and fascinating first-person account of her grandmother's life in eastern South Carolina.*

I liked Karen's talk a lot, one reason being that it was about a topic I love: Black women and Black women's culture. Inherent in many of the things Karen was describing to you are the reasons that we need Black feminism, "a movement of our own." For instance, she talked about how the men in her family did not want the women in her family to go out and work for white women. This was not merely about going out to work but about having to go out and work for white people, and I was wondering if women who are not women of color understood the profundity of that remark. Women of color are still taking care of white women's babies, and when I see a woman of color walking toward me with a baby carriage in front of her, I always pray, "Let it be her child, instead of a child she was hired to take care of." It is all work, honorable work, but when you're taking care of someone else's child, often your own child is at home by herself, not necessarily being looked after. This is a real sign of what Black women's experience is about: many of us never experienced domesticity, never got to stay home and be bored and oppressed in that way. We were too busy going out working for wages and being racially, sexually, and economically oppressed at the same time.

Karen also talked about the importance of honoring the places from which we came and the women and men who brought us here. As Karen expressed, most of the thinking of conscious Black women today comes from the people who raised us. Those are the roots of Black feminism, and I want to talk about why we need Black feminism, what kinds of organizing we have done, what we are doing now, and what I see us doing in the future.

Our politics, our commitments, our energy are passed on from the people in our families and in our past. I think this is different in some cases for people of color than for people who are not. If you are white and have class privilege, then if you want to do right, you have to rebel. But as a person of color, as a lesbian, that's not necessary for me; I don't have to rebel against the people who raised me in order to do right. Often we have a kind of connection to the people in our families, our people of origin, that is perhaps not as hard to come by as the connection that some women are fighting very hard to establish and keep with their families, because we don't have to rebel in order to be the people we are and do the work we need to do.

It is important to note that the historical impetus and inspiration for the contemporary Black women's movement—which began as early as the '60s, with Black women critical of sexism in the civil rights movement and Black power organizations—came out of the whole history of our people in this country and in Africa. The names of Harriet Tubman and Sojourner Truth are constantly invoked as our Black feminist foremothers but thousands upon thousands, if not millions, of Black women in the nineteenth and twentieth centuries explicitly devoted their lives to the examination and eradication of the oppression of Afro-American women. In the introduction to *Home Girls* (Kitchen Table: Women of Color Press, 1983), I wrote: "I am convinced that Black feminism is on every level organic to Black experience." All of us, as Black feminists, have been called names—"traitors to the race"—and have been told that we're dividing the race, etc., because "Black issues are racial issues solely." But, as I said, I believe Black feminism is organic to the Black experience.

This point cannot be made too strongly because there has been such a tendency in the Black community to dismiss feminism, even when it is practiced by Blacks and led by Black women, as only applicable to the white race—even though sexual oppression, of course, cuts across all races and cultures with disastrous and violent results. One reason that this disavowal has been possible is that there has been such a dearth of accurate information about what grassroots, radical women's groups, including groups of women of color, have done. If the only thing I knew about feminism was what I read in *Ms.* magazine, I would think it was irrelevant and a waste of my time, too. But as a Black feminist and a lesbian, I have access to information about—and I experience—the crucial work that progressive feminists are doing. As I wrote in *Home Girls:*

> *I have often wished I could spread the word that a movement committed to fighting racial, sexual, economic, and heterosexist oppression, not to mention one which opposes imperialism, anti-Semitism, the oppressions visited upon the physically disabled, the old, and the young, at the same time that it challenges militarism and imminent nuclear destruction, is the very opposite of narrow. I always felt that Black women's ability to function with dignity, independence, and imagination in the face of total adversity—that is, in the face of White America—points to an innate feminist potential. To me, the phrase "act like you have some sense," probably spoken by at least one Black woman to every Black child who ever lived, says volumes about keeping your feet on the ground and your ass covered. Black women as a group have never been fools; we couldn't afford to be.*

We come from a tradition of struggle, and so it is only natural that women in our particular groups would be take-care-of-business kinds of people. (I think this extends to all women of color, not just Afro-American women.) We have always faced sexual oppression, always faced racial oppression, always faced economic oppression. Certain conditions came into existence in the late '60s so that a women's movement—a resurgence of a women's movement—grew in this country. And with it came the blossoming of the feminism of women of color. But Black feminism is not a new concept.

Why do we need Black feminism? I will read to you from the opening paragraph of the Combahee River Collective statement, which summarizes the basic oppressions we are trying to fight (and which is reprinted in *Home Girls*). Much Black feminist history happened in Boston. The Combahee River Collective was a Black women's organization that began here in 1974. We wrote in 1977:

> *We are a collective of Black feminists who have been meeting together since 1974. During that time we have been involved in the process of defining and clarifying our politics while at the same time doing political work in our own group and in coalition with other progressive organizations and movements. The most general statement of our politics would be that we are actively committed to struggling against racial, sexual, heterosexual, and class oppression. We see as our particular task the development of an integrated analysis and practice based upon the fact that the major systems of oppression are interlocking. The synthesis of these oppressions creates the condition of our lives. As Black women we see Black feminism as a logical political movement to combat the manifold and simultaneous oppressions that all women of color face.*

So there you have it—the fact that as women of color we face all the business that they put out there. We found that if we were going to combat it, we were going to have to develop a kind of politics that would meet all those "isms." It was difficult—still is difficult—for many people to cope with the idea that sexual politics affects the lives of women of color. The fact that Third World men could possibly be oppressors as well as oppressed is a very difficult admission, and there have been many open debates and confrontations about it. But we are beginning to understand that you can be an oppressor and oppressed simultaneously, and that it's nothing new. The question is, "What are you going to do about that fact?" Feminists of color have also been threatening to our communities because we expect people to change. Once you figure out that all these things are occurring and ruining people's chances for better lives and freedom, then you have to change—but nobody likes to do that, and it's been difficult for people of color to understand, particularly when the women's movement has been portrayed as white. That's one of the reasons for making explicit Black feminist or Third World feminist statements. Sometimes people ask me, "Why do you have to say you're a feminist?" or "Why do you have to say you're a lesbian?" I try to explain that if I don't say it, then nobody *knows* why I have the particular commitment that I do. They won't know why I view political reality the way I do. I was lots of things before I was a feminist. I was an activist. I certainly was Black before I was a feminist. Feminism is something I claim because I claim it in the name of Black women.

One of the reasons I can do that is that most of the organizing I have done around sexual politics has been with other women of color, particularly other Black women; I never had the experience, say, of being in NOW [National Organization for Women] for five years and then having to dispense with the whole thing. In 1973, the National Black Feminist Organization had its first regional conference in New York, and my sister Beverly and I went to it. I think we both agree that in many ways it changed our lives to be in a room with so many Black women who, in 1973, were saying that they were feminists; in 1984, there are still many women who won't say it. It was an incredible experience, and a lot of our work since then has been with other Third World women. We worked on very broad-based and far-reaching issues, particularly in the Combahee River Collective, and I would like to be more explicit about some of the things I feel most embodied what we meant and what I mean by Black feminism.

I'm thinking in particular of 1979, when twelve Black women were murdered in Boston in less than six months. If you lived in Boston at the time, I'm sure you remember the murders. If not, you probably never even knew they happened; they got no media coverage because, after all, they were only Black women. I speak all over the country, and when I'm talking about feminism and organizing, I often talk about the murders because for me that was a pivotal time, in some ways the culmination of everything I had done, learned, tried to do until then. And I have found in going across the country that Black women are being murdered in droves and waves and epidemics all over: in Columbus, Ohio, at least three Black women have been murdered in the last few months. They always try to say that the murders are not connected, but when it always happens to a Black person who also always happens to be female and probably lives in a poorer section of the city, how can they not be connected? They are logically connected.

When the Boston murders happened, one of the most important things that occurred was the building of coalitions unprecedented in Boston's political history. As I observed Mel King's [mayoral] campaign of 1983 from New York, where I live now, I thought, "This is not the beginning of a coalition, not the beginning of the rainbow concept. We did much of that in 1979, when our section of the city was terrorized by these murders." All kinds of groups came together, people who ordinarily did not talk to each other then. It was incredible during this period of extreme crisis to be trying to bring together elements who had never worked together before.

When the murders were first talked about, in January or February, they were discussed solely as racial crimes. By April, six Black women had been murdered, and there was a march in the South End to the sites where some of them had been found, followed by a rally. The speakers talked about race, but no one said a damn thing about the fact that sexual violence is the name of the game, and that it's global. It doesn't matter what the context is: if you're a woman, you're bound to suffer from it. I'm sure you know how many regimes all over this globe are practicing fascism, and whenever you read about cases of torture, disappearance, or political imprisonment, and the victim is a woman, you know that part of that torture is sexual violence. And where do the military and right-wing forces get that idea—could it be because rape is a national pastime?

I left that demonstration really upset, because I knew that it was six Black women who'd been killed and that I and all my friends were potentially the next victims—there was more happening than just racial politics or class politics. So the Combahee River Collective wrote a pamphlet about how sexual violence connects to racial violence and economic exploitation and listing things to do to protect yourself. It was the first published, tangible thing that came out about the murders that people could use. It was the first thing that did not dismiss the murders or imply that these women deserved to die because "they might have been prostitutes or runaways."

We printed 2,000 of the pamphlets at first, and they were gone almost immediately. (Even some of you who were involved in that work may not know that at least 30,000 were distributed by the time we were finished: we kept going back to the printer.) The pamphlet was originally printed in both English and Spanish because we assumed, as Black feminists, that our concern was not just with Afro-American, English-speaking people, or with people who could read English. We wanted every woman to feel some kind of solidarity and some kind of protection. And there were many other activities around the murders besides the pamphlet; it was a coalition. I saw people sitting together in rooms who I didn't think would ever have anything to do with each other, although I'm not saying that there weren't whispers and looks behind people's backs—for example, a lot of the people who showed up for the work were, of course, lesbians, white lesbians. There was an interesting mix, much like the Mel King campaign.

This organizing embodied the kind of work that I feel is most important. It was a coalition effort that got at a bottom-line issue—murder—and dealt with a feminist issue, sexual violence. I always feel the need to honor it, particularly when I'm standing on the very soil on which it happened. Those of us who lived through it should always respect ourselves for the work we did, for showing power and resistance instead of lying down and taking it.

What kinds of things are we doing now as Black feminists? Given that we're affected by every kind of oppression, every kind of "ism" that affects Third World women and Third World people, you can imagine the range of our work. One of the things that has happened in recent years is the building of Third World women's institutions, like Kitchen Table: Women of Color Press, the Third World Women's Archives in New York City, the Black Women's Health Project in Atlanta, the Black women's self-help groups in Washington, D.C.—I could list about three pages of activities. Institution-building is absolutely crucial, because we don't ever know what we think until we ask ourselves, don't know what we need until we ask ourselves. We have to sit down and communicate, just like Karen did with her grandmother. I'm sure her identity was much more solidified after talking to this other Black woman connected to her by blood. That's why we need autonomous institutions and why we're building them.

But we are not separatists. That's a common misconception about feminism in general and about Third World feminism, too—that because we say we're Black and female, we must be separatists. We know, like anyone with common sense, that our fate is tied up with all the people of our race—men, women, and children. It's important for me to always try to express that, because I am a lesbian and have been stereotyped as such. Because I was Black before I was a feminist, Black before I knew I was a lesbian, I do not see cutting off the people who fought those battles. We are all locked together, and many Third World men understand exactly what I mean. I have great respect for our families, for our people. Black feminism is not about separatism; it's about autonomy.

What about the future? One of the things that I have been most enlivened by is the fact that it is no longer strictly a Black feminist movement that I am a part of, but a Third World feminist movement. And not only am I talking about my sisters here in the United States— American Indian, Latina, Asian American, Arab American—I am also talking about women all over the globe. I was fortunate enough to go to London twice this year for two book fairs, international events. We were talking about women's politics, not just publishing, and although we had never met one another, we basically agreed that we needed to talk about sexual, racial, class, anti-imperialistic, antimilitaristic politics. I think Third World feminism has enriched not just the women it applies to, but also political practice in general. For instance, the first time I heard the phrase "rainbow coalition" was when I went to the second National Third World Lesbian and Gay Conference in Chicago in 1980, which was called "A Unified Rainbow of Strength." We were talking about rainbows then; it was not just media hype. And we influenced the politics of other movements, like the Jesse Jackson [presidential] campaign, because we believed in coalitions before other people did.

I feel our work is cut out for us, as always. We are in a huge amount of trouble created by mad people at the top, and we're constantly trying to rectify the situation. I see the process of rectification as what Black feminism is all about: making a place on this globe that is fit for human life. If we do that, then we will have done a whole lot, particularly if that means that the new society we create respects people like you and me.

MARCH 1985

A New Spelling of Our Name
by Audre Lorde

The following is an edited version of a speech given by Audre Lorde as part of the Boston Women's Theological Center's series, "Naming/Claiming/Changing: Sojourneys with Black Women."

I'm very happy to be here to look around and see your faces. The last time I read in the Boston area, about two years ago, I promised myself that I would not read here again. I felt so unprotected in the women's community; I felt the racism and the gulfs so real and so unbridgeable. But we change. I look out now and see so many different faces, faces of women of color, and it makes a difference. I believe in our differences and in our use of them. I'm very pleased to be here tonight.

In my talk tonight, I'm going to read poetry because that is the strongest and most powerful way I know of changing my name and sharing the renaming with you. There is an ancient West African custom of naming and renaming as a ritual of renewal; as we gain new powers, we acquire a new spelling of our name. We rename ourselves as a recognition of new resources within us. I stand before you now—Black, lesbian, mother, feminist, poet, warrior—knowing that each name I give myself can set up a difference or a negative resonance with some one of you, and yet knowing also that each piece of myself is a source of power for me.

And that power is not abstract. I know that if I do not use the muscle of my being in the service of whatever vision I can maintain of our future, then I am a liar or a fraud. The names we shun are only new and unaccepted spellings of our hearts' desires turned around, new ways of staying afraid and impotent. We have been raised to fear, and as soon as we begin to rename ourselves—use all of who we are for change in our lives and in the world around us—we stand outside the borders of what has been, and that is very difficult.

But there is no other way. Nobody is going to do it for us—nobody, in other words, is going to come along and take the theory and give it flesh. No one else is going to live out the things that you and I believe. But we are not alone, as Bernice Reagon says and as I remind myself very, very often. "Each of us is here because somebody did something before we came," and we can learn by feeling that. We can learn from each other, and we can share what it is we have to learn.

The process of renaming, of respelling our names, is part of learning to live a self-conscious existence, gaining a deepening consciousness of self through everything we do. I know for myself—and I hope that each of you recognizes—the necessity for that self-consciousness. There's a certain kind of phraseology that always burns me up: when people say that other human beings "happen to be." I know what it costs for me to live, and I encourage and remind you to recognize what it costs you to live. Yes, it hurts, but it's part of empowerment. None of us "happens to be" anything; we either act or are acted upon. The title of this next poem comes from two of the phrases I hear most often: "To the Poet Who Happens To Be Black and the Black Poet Who Happens To Be a Woman." I like the title.

To the Poet Who Happens To Be Black and the Black Poet Who Happens To Be a Woman

I.
I cannot recall the words of my first poem
but I remember a promise
I made my pen
never to leave it
lying
in somebody else's blood.

II.
I was born in the gut of Blackness
from between my mother's particular thighs
her waters broke upon blue-flowered kitchen linoleum
and turned to slush in the Harlem cold
10 p.m. on a full moon's night
my head crested round as a clock
"You were so dark," my mother said
"I thought you were a boy."

III.
The first time I touched my sister   alive
I was sure   the earth took note
but we were not new
false skin peeled off like gloves of fire
yoked flame   I was

stripped to the tips of my fingers
her song   written into my palms   nostrils   belly
welcome home
in a language   I was pleased to relearn.

IV.
No cold spirit strolled through my bones
on the corner of Amsterdam Avenue
no dog ever mistook me for a bench
nor a tree   nor a bone
no lover envisioned my plump brown arms
as wings nor misnamed me condor
but I can recall without counting
eyes that canceled me out
like an unpleasant appointment
postage due
stamped in orange   red   purple
any color
except Black   and choice
and woman
alive.

V.
I cannot recall the words of my first poem
but I remember that promise
I made my pen
never to leave it
lying
in somebody else's blood.

I have just returned from a trip to Cuba, which was a very affirming journey, very hopeful, as well as very frustrating. I found Cuba a vital, encouraging society, and yet as a Black lesbian feminist I also found certain contradictions. They have not yet solved all of their problems of racism, of sexism, of homophobia. But I saw these forces within Cuban society as contradictions—meaning, in other words, that there was another basic truth. And this felt affirming and possible, for change, because in this country that we share, we do not speak of contradictions—we merely live them out. And often we live them out in rage and silence, so that they are forever untouched and unused.

For instance, how many of you know the name of Eleanor Bumpurs? Eleanor Bumpurs was a depressed, 66-year-old Black woman who lived in public housing in New York City. She was evicted for one month's nonpayment of rent. Because she was emotionally disturbed, the marshals who came to evict her brought with them six policemen and two shotguns. And when Eleanor Bumpurs did not open her door, they blew out the lock, entered her apartment, and fired two shotgun blasts at her, one of which tore off her right hand, the second of which blew out her chest. Eleanor Bumpurs was a 66-year-old depressed Black woman who was evicted from public housing with two shotgun blasts for nonpayment of one month's rent. Eleanor Bumpurs's story is not a contradiction. The killing of Black people in cities of this country is an accepted practice, becoming more so. Yet each one of us sitting in this room must come to name ourselves Eleanor Bumpurs.

And each one of us sitting in this room must come to name ourselves Renee Green. Do any of you know who she was? Renee Green was a 29-year-old Black woman who was evicted from her apartment with her two-month-old child and went to live with her sister and her two children. But they were evicted from that public housing because Renee had been dropped from the welfare rolls, unable to keep up with various forms. At that point she killed one of her sister's children and was about to kill her own, when a SWAT team broke in and blew her head off. Renee Green was 29 years old, and she is one spelling of all our names.

And so I would ask each one of you, what is the name of the woman who sleeps over the grating of the building down the street from the place where you are working? I read that one quarter of the homeless people in Boston are women; I read that their median age is 34 and decreasing. So that muddled old woman in the supermarket is not really so old. What is her name? Is it one of yours? We waste so much of our power as women when we accept only the names that are given to us by others, even though those are the names by which we first recognized each other, by which we first came together.

Now, for whatever reason you have come here and whatever you hope to get, I ask each of you to sit for a minute, reach deep inside of you, and feel what it means to you personally to be a citizen of the most powerful country in the world. For those of us who are Black, it is not enough to say, "I'm Black—I do not have a part of that power." For those of us who are women, it is not enough to say, "I am a woman—I stand outside that power." Each one of us is responsible. That responsibility and that power are relative, but they are real. And if I do not identify that power within myself, if you do not identify it within yourselves—own it, learn to use it for the future—it will be used against us, against you and me and our children and the world. It is as simple as that. What does it mean to be a citizen of the most powerful country in the world, to be a citizen of that country that stands on the wrong side of every single liberation struggle on this earth? Feel, feel the responsibility of that, not just in your hands that touch each other, but walking out of here, and at 3:30 on Sunday afternoon, so that it is a part of your consciousness all the time, personally.

Take the Philippines, where American money props up the Marcos dictatorship in direct opposition to the Philippine people; where girls as young as nine years old prostitute themselves with Philippine government licenses to servicemen in U.S. airbases so that their families can eat; where Mila Aguilar, 32-year-old Philippine woman, mother, journalist, activist, poet, is now imprisoned for speaking truth to her people—and she is only one of many. She is a poet who used her power, recognizing that she might have to pay dearly, and she has.*

I ask you now to feel what it means to be a citizen of a country from which $500 million a year flow to racist South Africa, where 14 percent of the people—white—own 90 percent of the land and where 86 percent of the people—Black—own 10 percent of the land. Seven million Black South Africans have been dispersed over the last nine years, driven into wastelands called locations, called reserves, called bantustans, called death by starvation and thirst. Water is trucked in once a week; women sit by the roadside and hold dust-mouthed children who cannot even cry. A white American journalist asked a white South African journalist about this, and the white South African responded, "You have solved the problem of your indigenous people—we are solving ours." Six Black South African children die every half hour from malnutrition; that means that while we are sitting here, 24 Black South African children will die from starvation. Yet white South Africa has the highest standard of living of any state in the world, and that includes the United States. Every other Black child in South Africa dies before the age of five or, to put it another way, 50 percent of Black South African children born are dead before their fifth nameday.

Five hundred million American dollars flow into white South Africa annually. How many of those dollars are yours? How many of those dollars do you control? Where does your credit union invest? Where do you bank? What is the position on divestment of your savings bank? Do you own stock? Does your company do business in South Africa? This is about renaming, using whatever power we have, relative as it is. A group of us are in the process of organizing SISA, Sisterhood in Support of South Africa, and we ask your support as we begin making more and more contacts. Remember the name: it means "mercy" in Xhosa. The women of South Africa—are their names not our names also?

Each of us has a responsibility to identify whatever power we can touch and to use it, and so I ask you in the name of my South African sisters to educate yourselves about what is happening in South Africa. Do not expect to find this material in the daily newspapers, or on the evening news; subscribe to the African National Congress news briefings, or ask your library to subscribe. Do any of you know who Winnie Mandela is? Winnie Mandela is a South African freedom fighter whose husband, also a freedom fighter, has been in prison for twenty years. She has raised her children in exile, in prison, and under ban. Being "banned" means that she is moved out of any society in which she can function; she is not allowed to meet with people, to attend funerals, or to speak publicly. Banning orders are renewed every five years, and the last time Winnie Mandela's ban was renewed, there was not a word about it in the *New York Times,* or in any newspaper in New York—and there was so little news that night on television that a feature was run concerning the rules of the road. That's why you don't know what is happening in South Africa, and why you cannot expect the media voices of the structure to which I hope you are opposed to educate you.**

The next poem is dedicated to a group of South African women I met in Germany, whose names are also ours, and the title of it is "Sisters in Arms":

Sisters in Arms

The edge of our bed was a wide grid
where your fifteen-year-old daughter was hanging
gut-sprung on police wheels
a cablegram nailed to the wood
next to a map of the Western Reserve.

I could not return with you to bury the body
reconstruct your nightly cardboards
against the seeping Transvaal cold
I could not plant the other limpet mine
against a wall at the railroad station
nor carry either of your souls back from the river
in a calabash upon my head
so I bought you a ticket to Durban
on my american express
and we lay together
in the first light   of a new season.

Clearing roughage from my autumn garden
cow sorrel, overgrown rocket gone to seed
I reach for the taste of today
The New York Times finally mentions your country
a half-page story
of the first white south african killed in the "unrest"
not of Black children massacred at Sebokeng
six-year-olds imprisoned for threatening the state
not of Thabo Sibeko, first grader, in his own blood
on his grandmother's parlour floor
Joyce, nine, trying to crawl to him
shitting through her navel
not of a three-week-old infant, nameless,
lost under the burnt beds at Tembisa
my hand comes down like a brown vise over the marigolds
reckless through despair
we were two Black women touching our flame
and we left our dead behind us
I hovered   you rose   the last   ritual of healing
"It is spring," you whispered
"I sold the ticket for guns and sulfur
I leave for home tomorrow."

And wherever I touch you
I lick cold from my fingers
taste rage
like salt from the lips of a woman
who had killed too often to forget
and carried each death in her eyes
your mouth a parting orchid
"someday you will come to my country
and we will fight side by side?"

*Keys jingle in my passageway threatening
whatever is coming belongs here
I reach for your sweetness
but silence explodes like a pregnant belly
into my face
a vomit of nevers.*

*Yaa Asantewaa turns away from the cloth
her daughters-in-law are dyeing
the baby drools milk from her breast
she hands him half-asleep to his sister
dresses again for war
knowing the men will follow.
In the intricate Kumasi twilights
quick   sad   vital
she maps the   next day's battles
dreams of Winneba   sometimes
visions the deep wry song of beach pebbles
running after the sea.*

So I stand here—Black and lesbian, feminist, poet, mother, warrior—feeling my power, attempting to use it, doing my work, part of which always is to ask each one of you how you are doing yours, because I am a new spelling of each of your names, as you are of mine. I come from a long line of Black women who cherished their lovers, nourished their children, and spoke the truth as they saw it, and for that we have always been called many names, depending on whether the speaker loved us or hated us. And rest assured, as you do your work, you will be called many names also. It is not easy to own our power, sometimes in the face of enormous opposition. It is not easy to learn how to use it. But we can, just like we can work when we are afraid. We can use our power even when it does not sit easily. And remember: none of us will be alive 300 years from now. The time is now. If you wait until you are not afraid, you'll be sending little messages on the ouija board, cryptic complaints from the other side.

In 1986, the Philippine people ousted the Marcos dictatorship. Philippine society, however, continues to suffer from extreme economic inequities.

**On April 29, 1994, the people of South Africa, voting in their first democratic, multiracial election, elected Black South African freedom fighter Nelson Mandela to head a new, multiracial government. The U.S. antiapartheid movement was crucial to bringing about the changes that made such an election possible. Today, Black South Africans still suffer from severe poverty, as the new government attempts to reshape the entire social, economic, and political landscape.*

DECEMBER 1986

Dina: Deep, Joyful Ways of Being Jewish

by Carole Ann Fer and Gloria Melnitsky

In early October [1986], several contributors to The Tribe of Dina: A Jewish Women's Anthology *(Sinister Wisdom, Issues 29/30; Beacon Press, 1989) came together in Cambridge, Massachusetts, to share readings from* Dina *and celebrate the Jewish New Year 5747. The event had a homey feeling; the readers shared the stage with a living-room lamp and flowers, and the evening ended with the appearance of homemade pastry delights and the passing of honey and apples, to be shared in accordance with tradition. The sense of warmth continued the next day as we interviewed the editors of* Dina, *Melanie Kaye/Kantrowitz and Irena Klepfisz, about the anthology and the context from which it grew. We began by asking how* Dina *was conceived.*

Irena: The initial impulse to do a Jewish women's anthology grew almost immediately from *Nice Jewish Girls,* which Melanie and I had both contributed to. That book [originally published by Persephone Press in 1982] generated great enthusiasm and energy among Jewish women; we hoped it would also generate a lot of creative writing, which we could then put together in another Jewish women's anthology. That impulse was realized with *Dina,* but other issues that emerged over the three and a half years shaped the book into what it is now.

Gloria: What are some of those other issues?

Irena: Melanie and I were both doing a lot of workshops on Jewish identity and the issue of assimilation. We wanted to move away from a focus on anti-Semitism, which we found very depleting, and toward the other issues women raised in these workshops—"How to return to Jewishness?" "What do I do?" Of course, we didn't have formulated answers, but the question of "reclaiming" became another impetus for the anthology.

Melanie: Another important thing happened—well, it was worse than important: in June of 1982, Israel invaded Lebanon. The invasion reverberated through the Jewish community and through the lesbian and feminist community, and we wanted to incorporate what we learned from that. We had a need to know more about what was going on in the Middle East and we wanted to connect with the feminist, lesbian, peace, and civil rights movements in Israel. We also wanted to deal with the anti-Semitism that had been stirred up in the Left, but in a way that wasn't simply reactive; we wanted to find a positive way to deal with the issue of Palestinian self-determination in the Middle East.

Carole Ann: American Jews focus on Israel, identify with it a lot, particularly because so many Jews in this country are of Ashkenazi background, and that cultural tradition was destroyed, along with most of the Sephardic culture in Europe. Of course, Israeli and American reactions to Israel are important aspects of your book that we'll get to. But for those Jews who don't want to focus on Israel for their cultural connection, there is a wealth of other possibilities.

Irena: There are many ways of being secular and Jewish, but these options aren't very visible in the U.S., because the focus is on the synagogue or Israel. Even in feminism the focus has been on reforming the synagogue and on women rabbis. Yet in workshops women often say, "I'm not religious. I'm not spiritual." And they might not be interested in Israel, or they might be anti-Zionist. But they want to reclaim something.

The issue of who is the "real Jew" always comes up in groups. Everybody seems to think there is someone else in the room who is more real or legitimate. Melanie and I will come into a group of women and suddenly we're the real Jews because we wrote a book or something. Then I'll go to YIVO [the institute for Yiddish research] in New York and I'll feel like I'm a total ignoramus and they're the real Jews.

Melanie: The synagogues are what's visible in the U.S., although something like 10 percent of American Jews are members. I think when people want to reidentify with the culture, they go to what is visible, and here, that's religion.

As I was growing up, I felt embarrassed about my lack of "Jewish" education, about not knowing Hebrew. I associated these with people with more money, who got to have a culture and take pride in it. I was too busy trying to learn not to sound Brooklyn, because Brooklyn meant lower class, meant getting stuck with the lives of my parents and the people around me.

Irena: Yiddish culture doesn't reside with the middle class. Upward mobility was often a way of getting away from the culture, discarding it. You read in Anzia Yezierska's stories about class splits within a family, the children moving away from the mother and the culture.

Gloria: Negative feelings about Jewishness often get focused on the women, especially on mothers. That's who needs to be disowned or escaped from.

Carole Ann: Tied to this is the myth that there are no longer any working-class Jews, which makes us invisible.

Melanie: I think that, statistically, Jews are better off economically than we were 40 years ago, and that fact is used against us. First it makes working-class Jews invisible. Jewish women are doing about the same economically as other women in this country—which is not that great. Then, Jews have done about as well and about as poorly as other immigrant groups who came here at the same time, when the economy was opening up: there are approximately the same numbers of Jewish poor as Italian and Polish poor. There does continue to be a large group of Black poor, who have watched the immigrant groups cut ahead of them economically and in terms of acceptance in this country. This is clearly a function of the persistence of racism and of the disruption of Black culture due to slavery. But there's a way that even middle-class Jews have not been able to assimilate, because they stand out in a way that middle-class Italians or Germans don't.

It's hard to maintain any sense of class in this country. Class issues are so confused, especially around race and class. Even people in unions think that if you're normal, you're middle class. Jews are in a good position to do some of the sorting-out about class. Why? Because we need to: class issues are used against us. We need to untangle anti-Semitism from serious class issues. I think poor people *should* be angry at rich people, but it's not fair for poor people to be angry at Jews as Jews. That doesn't serve anybody. August Bebel said, "Anti-Semitism is the fool's socialism."

Gloria: As we talk, I find myself making mental checklists: "Who else grew up orthodox, from what countries, what generation?" It feels like I'm checking off little boxes, marking which issues I can relate to each of you on, rather than letting myself feel the experiences we have in common. I know it's because the reality of our individual and family histories is complicated—complicated for profound and tragic reasons.

Carole Ann: For years, wearing a Jewish star on a chain represented, for me, my parents being forced to wear the yellow star. Could you talk about what it means to choose not to pass and to wear a star in this country?

Melanie: I wear a Jewish star [necklace] in this country, but when I went to Israel, I stopped wearing it because I felt that it said something untrue about me—that I was religious or right wing or that I didn't want to be seen as an Arab. I wear it here for different reasons. I'm 41 now, and I started wearing a star when I was about 35. I had never worn one growing up in Flatbush, in Brooklyn, where it felt normal to be Jewish and wearing a star meant to me that you were religious. But years later, when I was living in New Mexico and feeling alternately invisible or disliked as a Jew, a woman drove through from Georgia with a decal of a Jewish star on the window of her van. My first reaction was fright—her car seemed marked for all kinds of hatred. But at the same time, I found her because of that; I knew she was a Jew. I started wearing a star and learned a lot. Sometimes it helps me to find other Jews and sometimes it's a way of saying, "This is who I am."

Irena: I've learned that Jewish symbols change under different circumstances and at different times in Jewish history. I went to my first-ever synagogue service in 1982; it didn't mean the same thing that it would have meant to my parents in 1925. I come from people who were virulently antireligious, Bundists and other socialists. Putting on a Jewish star is violating my whole Jewish tradition and heritage, but Jewishness changes. I'm not a member of the Bund in the middle of Warsaw in the 1930s. When I started to wear a star, after the invasion of Lebanon in 1982, I felt it was the opposite of the *gela lata,* the yellow star. I wanted to be identified as a Jew, although even in New York City it terrified me. It felt important.

Gloria: There are many, many decisions we make every day about how we pass for non-Jewish or don't pass. I guess wearing a star eliminates some of those decisions.

Melanie: I'm a teacher, and every semester I used to have to figure out how to come out to my students as a lesbian and not have them get totally focused on it. Then I had a book of poetry published, and on the back it says, "Melanie Kaye, lesbian." Now I don't have to say it every time. The star is similar: it isn't always my responsibility to say that I'm Jewish.

I made another important decision about passing. My father had changed our family name from Kantrowitz to Kaye. After he died in 1982, I decided to take the name back, partly to reverse the process of assimilation. I also didn't want to disown the history that made him change it, though, and that's why I have the name "Kaye/Kantrowitz." I'm forever spelling it and explaining it, and I can understand a small part of why he changed it. It's different to choose the name consciously now, and not to have to operate during World War II like my father did, dealing with people blaming the war on Jews. My fantasy is that all the Jews with the name Kaye will take back their names.

Gloria: Along with the (relative) freedom that we have in this country at this time to assimilate or not to assimilate, there also comes a struggle to keep our cultures together and an ambivalence about that struggle.

Melanie: Assimilation is a double-edged sword. People came to assimilation out of fear and need, but one of the reasons people are now talking about how to reverse the process is that it hasn't given people or their descendants what they were looking for.

Irena: Assimilation wasn't just a response to fear and need. Some people felt that shedding cultural, religious, and national differences was a good thing. It was a conscious act.

Melanie: That taps into a basic issue. Part of the way assimilation has happened in this country is that American Jews have been cut off from the Jews in other countries. For most American Jews, whose families came from Europe, there is a lost thread that has to be groped for. The thread is like a rope across a chasm, and that chasm is the Holocaust. There's no place to go back to; the ground was destroyed. So it takes a lot of work to remake the connections.

Irena: Culture is so difficult. It's hard to maintain any culture in the U.S., and not just for Jews. You don't even have a thriving Yiddish culture in New York City. To keep a language, you have to stay in groups and speak it. I do translations from Yiddish, and I don't know if they're more part of the problem or part of the solution. I want the works to be accessible, yet that doesn't encourage people to get to know Yiddish. Yiddish has been dying for a long time now, like the Jewish people.

There is academic interest in Yiddish now. Some people say that means Yiddish is really in trouble: if the academics are interested, there must be a corpse on the table!

Carole Ann: One of the most exciting things about *Dina* for me, Irena, was your poetry that combined Yiddish and English. I loved seeing that in print.

Irena: How do you do something Jewish in a non-Jewish language like English? There are pieces in English in *Dina* that have that oral Yiddish quality—the Trina Hope piece and Grace Paley's and Vera Williams's. Put them together and they share something. They're in English...

Irena and Melanie: But with a Jewish accent.

Melanie: It's a parenthetical style. You have to get a lot of information into each sentence, because reality is complex. I don't know if I'll ever have the time and energy to learn Yiddish. I learned ancient Greek and Latin in graduate school. People don't speak those languages, but the cultures they represent, the stories and myths, came into our culture. I think something like that may happen with Yiddish, which is why I think Irena's translations are so important.

Irena: Jewish women are robbed in this area—robbed of Yiddish, robbed because of the Holocaust, and robbed because, who pays attention to women, anyway? Women who wrote in Yiddish can give us an important connection to our pasts, tell us how women lived. I've been looking at some short stories written by Yenta Sardofsky in 1925 about women in *di bavegung,* the movement. There's a gold mine of information that the men weren't writing about.

Melanie: I feel pleased that *Dina* talks about the tradition of radical Jewish women, active in feminism, in building unions, in class struggle. When Clara Lemlich, the sixteen-year-old woman who started the ladies' garment workers' strike in 1906, said she was tired of listening to speeches, she said it in Yiddish; I don't know how old I was when I realized that. Half of Emma Goldman's lectures were in Yiddish. Those of us who see ourselves as progressive Jewish feminists have a proud history going back to those women and beyond, back to Europe.

One thing that hampers American Jews in building Jewish identity is that Americans are so American-centered; part of understanding who Jews are as a people means recognizing the different experiences of Jews in different countries, Jews from different places. The terms that people have used in discussing Jewish experience usually don't fit. For example, people try to say that the category "Ashkenazim" is white and "Sephardim" is Third World, but that doesn't make sense if you trace what "Sephardim" means. It refers to people who came from Spain and then lived in Arabic countries with an Arabic culture. Some then ended up in Germany or in Holland. This doesn't mean that "Sephardim" isn't an important and distinct category but, like all Jewish experience, it has to be conceptualized in its own terms. The history of the Jews is very convoluted, and the categories aren't very neat. That's frustrating for non-Jews to deal with. It's frustrating for Jews, too.

Carole Ann: Your book strives for an international perspective on Jewish women.

Melanie: This came out of our work on building Jewish identity. There were two different cultural directions to go in: to reclaim the familiar, the things we have lost, and to connect with Jewish traditions that are not our own, expanding our picture of what it is to be Jewish. For example, the Sephardic songs in Ladino collected by Judith Wachs are the same stories I've heard all my life, but in another language. There are gaps in *Dina,* places we feel we didn't do enough. With Russian Jews—

Carole Ann: and Ethiopian Jews.

Irena: The rich diversity is always there, even though we are not always in touch with it. If you think of *Nice Jewish Girls, Dina,* and then a continuity, a *truly* international book is the next stage. We had planned to do that this time, but because of limited resources, we didn't do as much as we wanted to.

Carole Ann: You did get the opportunity to network and connect with some Israeli women, and that was a focus of *Dina.*

Irena: When we put together the section called *"Kol Haisha*—Israeli Women Speak," we had in mind making a bridge, giving information from a base that would seem acceptable to American Jews who are afraid to deal with the issue of Israel. In talking about Israel, there is always that thin line: is the speaker being anti-Semitic? With *Dina,* we wanted to have information that could be heard, with no fear that the book was produced by self-hating Jews.

Melanie: We determined to make connections with progressive people in Israel. We got a grant, and we went to Israel and interviewed two dozen women at the end of 1985 and in early '86. We had contacts with some feminists and lesbians, and people were enormously receptive. Despite the tensions many Israeli women feel about American feminists wanting to take over Israeli feminism and not really wanting to understand Israeli feminists' issues, we felt extremely welcome.

Carole Ann: Were you able to bring back much new information about progressive movements for peace within Israel?

Melanie: In Israel, the Left is a much more important movement, numbers-wise, than its U.S. counterpart. There's a lot of activity and discussion and immediate need in the areas of peace, civil rights, the economy. We went to the Peace Now demonstration just before the Israeli withdrawal from Lebanon was announced, and we were struck by how well-behaved the crowd was. The Israelis don't have any tradition of civil disobedience. Any kind of opposition to the government is a very recent phenomenon there, and that makes a difference in the Left. There are some anti-Zionist groups in Israel, but the Left's definition of itself has been Zionist, which is very different from what you'll find in leftist groups in the U.S. An Israeli opposition movement is gathering now, as people define themselves as needing to challenge a government doing the wrong thing. There are large numbers of Israelis who challenge what their government is doing, and it's very important for American progressive Jews to connect with the progressive people in Israel to strengthen that movement.

Irena: I realized when I got back from Israel how very little information we get here. For example, when Peace Now had its first public meeting between the Israelis and Palestinians on the West Bank, it was a nine-line article in the *New York Times,* whereas, in Israel, it was a major event. American Jews have to make a concerted effort to become informed about Israelis who are doing this kind of work, because the mainstream papers aren't going to tell you what is really going on.

Melanie: That particular event happened the day after the U.S. bombed Libya. That bombing was a very polarizing thing in terms of Arab/Israeli relations, making it much more difficult to imagine any kind of peaceful settlement, and that's what made the headlines. Then there was a teeny article on page nine [about the public meeting on the West Bank]. Progressive people, primarily progressive Jews, are going to have to bring that kind of thing to people's attention, to make them realize there's a chink in the wall in the Middle East.

Gloria: Political work is a positive expression of Judaism for many women.

Melanie: One of our hopes is that *The Tribe of Dina* inspires joyful, positive, deep ways of being Jewish. The reading last night marking the Rosh Hashanah holiday really moved me. I haven't always celebrated the Jewish holidays; my work life is not structured around them the way lives are sometimes structured around Christian holidays. It takes a lot of work to find meaningful ways to celebrate. But then the music, the creative literature are so nourishing; they make me happy to be part of this culture.

Carole Ann: That's reflected in the book, with your inclusion of art, photographs, and sculpture, as well. And *Dina*'s ending is empowering.

Irena: We end the book with a section called *"In Gerangl/*In Struggle," which is basically made up of suggestions and exercises for consciousness raising around Jewish identity and anti-Semitism. One exercise is to identify the prejudices you were raised with about other Jews—what the sources of those prejudices were, how they were passed on.

Melanie: The book includes ideas about how women can work politically on Jewish issues—ways of forming coalitions within the Jewish community and working with Jews you may not always agree with, as well as ways of working as visible Jews in coalitions with non-Jews. We hope we have made a contribution to a greater understanding of the Jewish people and our connections to one another.

FEBRUARY 1987

SOME CLARIFICATIONS FROM MELANIE AND IRENA

DEAR *SOJOURNER:*

Thanks very much for your interview with us in the December issue. As anyone who has seen her spoken words in print knows, talking and writing are two different things, and we have found in our words—spoken by us, transcribed and edited by Carole Ann Fer and Gloria Melnitsky—some statements that are either wrong, unclear, out of context, or distorted from what we intended. We are taking this opportunity to set these distortions straight.

To say that Jewish women are faring about the same economically as other women is true, but the word "other"— read, "average"— obscures difference. White women earn more than women of color, especially Black women, Chicanas and Latinas, Native American women, and recent immigrants from Central America and Southeast Asia.

To say that middle-class Jews have not been able to assimilate to the extent that middle-class Germans or Italians have is half true, half false: true about Germans and many other ethnic groups; utterly false about Italians, who, as long as they are visibly, identifiably Italian, are never permitted by mainstream culture to forget it.

To say that large numbers of Black people continue to be very poor (as opposed to many immigrant groups) "due to slavery" mystifies a crucial fact. Afro-Americans did not choose to come here, not even to escape terrible oppression and poverty. The difference between chosen and forced entry, between immigration on one hand and capture and enslavement on the other, is referred to, but not with sufficient clarity.

To say, "When I started to wear a star, after the invasion of Lebanon in 1982...I wanted to be identified as a Jew" seems to indicate pride in the invasion instead of what was intended, a response to the upsurge of anti-Semitism and the desire to be visibly Jewish *and* opposed to the invasion, to retain and intensify Jewish pride during a difficult time.

To say, "Yiddish has been dying for a long time now, like the Jewish people" sounds like a serious, mournful statement, instead of the ironic full-of-laughter remark that it was. People *say* Yiddish is dying, that the Jewish people are dying, but in reality, interest in Yiddish actually increases and the Jewish people go right on surviving.

Sephardim refers to Jews who originated in Spain and Portugal, some of whom then lived in Arab countries with Arabic culture, some of whom ended up in Germany, Holland, South and North America, and elsewhere.

True, it is difficult to get information in the United States about the peace movement in Israel and especially about joint Israeli-Palestinian peace attempts, but it is not impossible. *New Outlook, Israleft,* and, of course, the *Jerusalem Post* are all useful and available.

We appreciate the opportunity to offer these corrections.

Mit khaverteshaft (in sisterly comradeship),
Melanie Kaye/Kantrowitz and Irena Klepfisz

AUGUST 1988

Where I Come From
God Is a Grandmother

by Paula Gunn Allen

Paula Gunn Allen presented the following lecture at a conference entitled "Reading and Writing the Female Body" at Grinnell College in Grinnell, Iowa.

I am not sure what the phrase "issues of gender identity" means exactly, so I am not clear about how it has affected my writing. If it means do I write from my experience, which necessarily embraces my womanness, do I make aesthetic choices on the basis of my gender, do I consciously write from and to a sense of women as my community of reference, or do gender-based politics and insights impact on my thought, style, structural choices, and subject matter, the answer is that issues of gender identity, like my gender identity itself, have affected my writing in a number of fundamental ways, as do the issues of class identity, racial identity, political identity, geographic and regional identity, and cultural identity.

But while these seemingly thin-air abstractions inform my work, they are embedded securely in the rock of practicality and physicality, and it is, finally, from my practical, physical experience that my writing and the spiritual, political, and cultural comprehensions it details arise. I think the bases of my writing are the land (New Mexico) and the people of my formative years. The land: a vast, intense, spirit woman, whose craggy fastnesses, deep dry waterways, miles and miles of forest and wilderness, reaches upon reaches of mesas, 40,000 deep skies where thunderheads of frightening force and awesome majesty sail ponderously, give me my primary understanding of womanness, of gender in its female sensibility. The people: how they talk, what they say, what they think, how they understand human experience within the powerful intricacies of the creaturely and supernatural enwebbing that is called "the planet, our lives, the tribes" provide me with a multiplicitous dimensionality within which I experience my gender's significance.

With a woman's voice and out of a woman's body, I shape the songs of my land, tribes—and my tribe is less Laguna than Cubereno, mostly Francis of the Cubero branch. It is largely rural, deeply spiritual, intensely political, not so much because I am "naturally" those things in and of myself, but because the people who nurtured me and had the most profound impacts on me were and are those things. Where I come from, where I aim my work toward, multilinguisticality, multiculturality, multispirituality, and multigenderality are the normal order of things. The place I come from is like San Francisco: there the women are tough and the men are pretty. And so, because I come from Cubero and because I come from a cultural, racial, and genetic whirlpool, my idea of what constitutes gender differs greatly from the American middle-class norm that has largely contextualized the entire subject.

I was born into a world that was surrounded by huge stone mesas and a woman mountain whose name in Laguna is "Woman Veiled in Clouds," in Acoma is "Woman Who Comes from the West." Cubero is a tiny village of adobe houses respectfully hunkered down at her feet. Nearby is the sacred small mountain we call "Flower Mountain," a towering vulva raised up under volcanic thrusts of grand passion. I have climbed her lava cliffs tired and sweating, and found myself, after several difficult hours of trekking, seated amidst the rainbow, engulfed in multicolored flowers that covered her soft-sloping mons and looked down, secure on the softness of grass and gentle slope, far above my village and the others nearby.

My village was Mexican, Chicano, a land-grant town. The rest of the villages were Laguna, Pueblo, Indian. They were named Seama, Paraje, Laguna, Casa Blanca, New Laguna, where the Santa Fe trains used to stop to take on water and fuel, to unload people, mail, and merchandise.

Where I come from, everyone spoke two or three languages. My father spoke four well and knew enough of three more to get along. They were Arabic, Spanish, English, Laguna, Acoma, Zuni, and Navajo. By rearing I knew that monolinguality was abnormal, though by preference based on my own personality (who does not like to leave anyone out) I am largely so deformed, so deviant that I speak only English for the most part.

Similarly, in my world, where adults of significance to me were as likely to speak German, Spanish, Kere, or Arabic as English as their home language, they were as likely to eat *cus a mitwe* as beans and chili, *atole* (blue cornmeal mush) as Cream of Wheat, celebrate Feast Day as Easter, have early childhood memories of the KKK burning crosses on their lawns as those of wandering the sandstone mesas and riding horses as a way of getting to work. In all of this, my experience was in the feminine mode, but what that means in my world differs considerably from what it means in some others, particularly in the world where discussions of "sex, gender, and identity" take place.

I was raised in a place and a way that bears only superficial resemblance to mainstream America's way of childrearing, by people who were as confused about what anything in America means as I am. Some of them, of course, thought they knew all about it; others were depressingly fearful that they knew too little about it, and that they and their children would suffer because of the lack. But whether sure or unsure, in truth, none of them had more than the dimmest notion of how white Americans see the world, or what in the world they mean by any word, thought, or deed. We could follow the forms pretty accurately, but what the content was mostly eluded us.

I knew that boys were different from girls, that they grew up and might become fathers and grandfathers, that they did things like keep store or run for senator, that men had deep voices and attended Lion's Club meetings at which they roared in voices that woke little girls, but I didn't realize that gender identity would mean or could mean that some people have worth because of what my mother refers to as their "pendant," while others who are differently endowed had less or no worth. I didn't know that the people around me, Indians—excuse me, I mean Native Americans; Mexicans—I mean Spanish-Americans or Chicanos (whichever generation is listening); Arabs—excuse again—I mean Lebanese-Americans; or Jews had less worth even *with* pendants. As for Black people, the only ones I knew moved away from Cubero before I was old enough to remember playing family games—adults included—of Kick the Can and Hide and Seek with them, so surely I didn't know they were of no worth along with the rest of us.

See, my mother and sometimes her uncle, an Indian, fixed the plumbing and appliances when they broke. She moved furniture when she wanted it moved, including the upright piano. I never saw my father with a monkey wrench, a screwdriver, or a pair of pliers—nor did I think the less of him for that. On the other hand, my mother had been to the university while my father was a high school drop-out. She spoke French as well as Spanish and could read both of them, and she listened to operas and read literary masterpieces. He preferred Seboyeta Chicano *musica,* swing, blues and scat, and read the newspapers, westerns, and *Bambi* (to me). I thought that women were the ones who got educated and men were the ones who tended the business. Both rode horseback, both climbed mesas, both drove cars, both did whatever they could do. My mother cooked and kept house, but since she was the educated one (and we all valued education) keeping house wasn't a second-class occupation in my mind.

When, at age six, my parents sent me to convent school to board there under the tutelage of the Sisters of Charity, I was required to wear dresses all the time, even after school. My mother argued quietly for jeans for me because I was always tearing my dresses, getting them dirty. I didn't know that might mean I was unfeminine: I thought it meant I was a normal child. My mother wore pants, my grandmother wore pants; I didn't know that pants are male and dresses are what low-statused individuals wear. We female-types wore dresses on high-status occasions, like Mass, Christmas, going to the city, going out to dinner. I thought dresses were what ladies dressed up in, as suits were what men dressed up in. Pants were what people wore to work or play in.

When I was in my late twenties or so, reading Betty Friedan and other (white) feminist theorists, I realized that one big reason my siblings and I had so much trouble understanding the Anglo world we lived in was because we had our ideas of gender role backwards. Our father acted like women are said to act, and our mother acted like men are said to act. He worried, nagged, expressed fearfulness over our adventurousness, our appearance, our manners. He fretted and fussed, cried, wrung his hands, was emotively expressive. She was calm, rational, self-contained, inclined to view emotionality as a male weakness or a Lebanese trait that should be discouraged.

The older I get the more I notice the great difference between my notions of what constitutes femininity and masculinity and the white world's notions about it. Every time I read a sentence that goes "women (do, say, think, feel)" or "men (do, say, think, feel)" I always ask, however silently, *which* women? *which* men? For, frankly, none of the men and women I grew up with did any of the described behaviors, or they did some but not the others, or did entirely undescribed ones. And that list of people I grew up with includes Anglos, but they were rural—ranch folk, New Mexicans, not much better acquainted with middle-class American mores than we were. In white, middle-class America, for example, at least in its feminist branch, women are relationship-oriented, nurturing, socially aware, nonviolent, kind, gentle, tender, giving, self-sacrificing, caring, emotionally centered, and emotionally expressive. Men are violent, abusive, cold, logical, rational, uncaring, individualistic, competitive, selfish, uncaring, and emotionally unexpressive. Where I come from these traits are more likely to mark different ethnicities than genders: the Indian people are inclined toward unexpressiveness of emotion (as that term is understood in the world of white intelligentsia); both genders can and do engage in violent attacks on one another. Indian, Lebanese, and Chicano men are very concerned with their children and families, individualism is an Anglo trait (male and female), as is competitiveness, though interpersonal rivalry is practiced by both genders among the Lebanese and Chicano populations, while group competitiveness in the sense of jealousy and social ostracism is definitely a Laguna institution.

In any case, for all of us, Anglo norms, including its gender norms, are obscure. None of us come by them naturally, so to speak. My mother's mother learned how to be Anglo at Albuquerque Indian School; her husband, my mother's stepfather, learned how to be Anglo rather late in life. He was raised in southern Germany where he grew up an impoverished German Jew; my father and his sisters learned Anglo ways in convent school (the girls) or at St. Mary's (the boys), only after they had spent their early childhood, up to over seven years of age, in Seboyeta where they were raised by a mixture of Lebneni, their parents and grandparents being from Lebanon, or Seboyetanos.

I remember the first time I came across the concept of "gender." When I was eight or nine I was reading *My Friend Flicka* and *Thunderhead*. This boy had gotten a filly, Flicka. I asked someone what a filly was, and was told it was a young female horse, like "yearling" was a cow that wasn't grown yet. Oh. Later, the term "gelding" came up, and I didn't know what a gelding was. I puzzled over it for some time before asking what it meant, and was told it referred to a horse that wasn't a stallion. That was clear as mud. I gave up and tried a dictionary, where I stumbled up against that odd word, "gender." I knew the word from grammar class: a noun has three genders—masculine, feminine, and neuter.

What, please, is a neuter? I thought the question, but have never asked it aloud until now, when my attempts to write this have forced me to address issues in my own consciousness that have been waiting around for attention for some time.

As a child I think I viewed the nuns and priests as neuter. That is, they weren't masculine or feminine as far as I could see. I was shocked to discover some nuns' underwear flapping on the clothesline one bright morning at convent school. I think I believed that nuns were like my dollies. Unlike me, they didn't have anything that would mark them male or female, which made them neuter.

In English, males, that is, boys and men, are said to be masculine, and women and girls are said to be feminine. Neuter is castrated. It started out to be masculine, then got cut off. I knew *that* eventually because I was at a branding at my girlfriend's ranch one summer around the same time I read the novels and saw the undies on the line and was offered some "Rocky Mountain Oysters." As usual I didn't know what they were talking about and finally asked. They told me, laughing. I declined the offer. I remember the horror that settled in my stomach and my groin as I contemplated the information I was given. They did *what* to those cattle? I think I asked why they did that, and was told something about wildness and fat and markets, but maybe that was later.

The issue of gender has played a central role in my consciousness (and therefore, in my writing) because it has been a thorny issue (you should excuse the expression) for a very long time. I suspect that at deep levels I was somehow afraid that I could fall into that horrible category, neuter. Maybe the right pronoun for me was not "she" but "it." After all, my own beloved horse Bole was a gelding, and short-legged to boot. And I did have trouble doing girl things like not tearing my dresses and remembering to cross my legs at the ankle. I was learning what gender in America means.

In the '60s, when I became personally rather than only theoretically aware of the issue in its political sense, I spent many months trying to get a sense of what feminine (female) meant to me. I resurrected my life's experiences, contrasted them with what feminist friends described as theirs. There was little match, and I wondered what it meant. I was in graduate school before I could comprehend that professors would bestow my grades on the basis of my gender. I was not surprised at their behavior when I finally "got" it, but at my inability to recognize that the political is always personal long before; that the abstract is always experientially true. My friends and my reading had told me about it, and I had been a practicing feminist for some time—in theory, at any rate, in terms of "women" as an abstract group (that's how we're supposed to think about everything in the white man's world), but that the theory had practical affects on Paula had eluded me. I wondered why.

I found out about the connection when I had a professor who assigned grades on the basis of gender and profession. He allotted A's to those he thought would become scholars and critics, lesser grades—no matter the merit of the work—to those who, in his estimation, would not. At least, that's what rumor said. Rumor also had it (this from a co-student, male) that this professor never gave A's to poets and writers, to those of us who were in the MFA program, because we wouldn't be critics. Another rumor (this from a flaming feminist friend, female) that the professor never gave A's to women because they would leave the profession to have babies. As I was guilty of both errors, and as I was into this guy for ten graduate hours, and as I had my heart set on a four-point average, I was not only incensed but profoundly depressed. I imagine that the only reason rumor didn't accuse the professor of allotting less-than A's to people of color was because I didn't know any other graduate students in English of that persuasion, or they'd have had a rumor too!

Predictably enough, I got a B for five hours of course work in the seminar in the first quarter, and I was very distressed. I had had another English professor read my paper on William Carlos Williams before I turned it in, and she thought it was A work. The next quarter I worked even harder, but received a B again. It was a long time before I could set foot on a university campus without becoming ill.

This experience, my first conscious (and very traumatic) experience with gender-typing, while devastating, strongly affected the ensuing course of my professional life. Looking back I realize that the experience made me a critic and scholar whose work is mostly concerned with women: our aesthetics, our cultural forms in various cultural settings, our history, our multitudinous ways of being in the world—modern or tribal, American or non-Western—our philosophies, our variegated experiences over hundreds and, more recently, thousands of years. Here it is, twenty years later and I'm still reacting to rumors about Prof. W. and my interpretation of that devastating B.

Years after leaving Oregon where I took the ten hours with the "chauvinist" professor (as I styled him in my kinder moments), I decided to reread the papers I had turned in to him. Imagine my chagrin when upon reading the papers, I realized that, in my opinion, they didn't deserve a B at the graduate level. I wouldn't have given them a C! I read his comments on them and had to revise my opinion of Prof. W. and of Paula Brown, which had been my name those many years before. I also had to reassess my position on the issues of gender identity and its impact on my work.

To do so, I again thought for a long time—months—about what gender meant. How does one go about deciding what is female, what is male? I had taken a number of those funny tests that determine your gender identity—a couple in psychology classes, a couple in magazines—and I had always come out with an even number of masculine and feminine characteristics. Did that mean I was neither? Both? The tests were screwy? I was neuter? Maybe, I thought, it meant I was a lesbian, which by this time I was, or "androgynous," whatever that means. Or maybe it meant something I couldn't imagine because the universe of discourse from which such tests are developed and to which they speak didn't offer other ways to think about gender identity.

But I am a half-breed American Indian/Lebanese-American woman, born in Cubero into a family that doesn't necessarily participate in the above-mentioned universe of discourse. I am also a political, politicized person who knows, as all who did '60s rebellion and/or civil rights work and thought know, that "psychological" tests are culture-biased and that the whole notion of "gender" is culturally prescribed: that is, what it means to be feminine or masculine is culturally defined. In fact, the idea that there are two genders and no more is itself a culturally prescribed notion, one that many tribal people did not and do not hold even now. It may be that my "masculine-feminine equipoise" as judged on whitemen's tests is a consequence of some cultural suppositions about what each of these mean rather than a description of anything "universal" as white intellectuals are pleased to describe their world view, a possibility I explore one way or another in much of my work.

In Indian country a woman is seen as strong and powerful. She is associated with "hard" things, like rocks, mountains, and clay, and with growing things like corn, beans, and squash. She is Mother of the Deer (all of the animal people); Grandmother of the sun; source of life, certain forms of rain and lightning; Mother of the Kachinas and the gods, bringer of architecture, social institutions, religion, and political authority. Male qualities include many that are transient or transitory such as feathers, smoke, clouds, and the sun, certain forms of rain and lightning. It is true that men engage themselves traditionally in certain occupations while women engage in others, but the point is that woman-ness is not of less value than man-ness. Indeed, it is preponderant; it is the source of human male and human female, the giver and bestower of life, ritual, afterlife, social power, and all that is sacred.

Passivity (as whites define it) is not a trait ascribed to women, but among a number of tribal people is considered to be a characteristic of a mature individual. One noticeable feature of novels by and about Native Americans is that the male protagonists are always passive—more passive than the female characters, though neither is likely to do aggression or self-assertion as whites define those behaviors. However, the women in those novels, as the women in Native American communities, are notable for their decisiveness, clarity, independence, and self-direction.

My point is not that Indians do it better than whites (though they might, who knows?), but that "gender" is a cultural precept and is culturally prescribed. What constitutes gender role, what "men" ascribe to "women" differs culture to culture. It is not true that all men see women as powerless, ready victims, passive receptacles of male authority, naturally and necessarily under the domination of men, though a number of theorists of feminist or academic bias imagine that such is the case. I submit that the assumption is itself racist, classist, and presumptuous.

Given that masculine and feminine mean different things to different peoples in different settings and over different times, it seems reasonable to assume that "feminine" signifies what a female person does or thinks, and "masculine" signifies what a male thinks or does. An action, thought, or feeling cannot determine the identity of a person; rather the gender of the agent of an action determines the action's gender. Gender, in this view, is not an aspect of human identity because it's an adjective or adverb, not a substance or a content. It shapes, as a glass shapes a beverage, but intelligence requires we not confuse the glass with the drink!

Given these multitudinous understandings of what feminine means in a tribal universe of discourse as opposed to what it means in an Anglo Euro-American university universe of discourse, the issues raised in my mind and work by the question of gender identity differ greatly from those more often considered before audiences such as this. For me the questions are more about why and how white people get to the arguments they are having, what those arguments mean, how they compare to other possible arguments, and what those others might mean and be. And for me, finally, the issue is personally political—that is, politically significant to my personhood. In the white universe, discussion went from an agreement that men are powerful and smart, to a belief that they are stupid and malevolent—which, linguistically, is not a far leap.

In modernist, "progressive" or liberal America, we began by saying that men and women are the same (a strikingly peculiar notion to my way of thinking), then moved to arguing about which was superior, which inferior along somewhat different, somewhat the same lines. Certainly many on both sides of the Anglo-European gender barrier have suffered from cultural absolutes about either, and those of us who, like my horse, Bole, do not fit either category have suffered at least as much. Certainly the issues raised by the whole idea of gender impact heavily on identity, and therefore on writing and creativity. Neuter creativity seems to me to be a contradiction in terms—on the order of bureaucratic mentality, another oxymoron.

One's acculturation, however mindless it seems to be, cannot help but seriously affect one's expression in life—and writing can never be more than life expression, or another of the things humans do on their way to death. But for me the question of gender is inextricably linked to the question of land. If earth is our Mother, a female Supernatural Being, if rock and angle and plant and star are Her, are female, then what does that say to the other culture's side of the story? "Powerless" is not a realistic way to define a Being who rains us into drowning, who tsunamis us, volcanoes us, mudslides and avalanches us, earthquakes, hurricanes, and droughts us, who famines us, burns us to a crisp in her radiant embrace, who drags on our muscles and skins, who takes us to her and holds us relentlessly in her arms.

Where I come from Woman is rock and towering peak, wild animal and domestic pet, grandmother and mother, sister and aunt, soft penetrating rain and sheets of fire in the sky. She is Originality, Creativity, Thinking Herself. Where I come from God is a woman, her name is Thinking Woman, and she is everything that is, including whatever is male. I take my cue on how to be Womanly from her, though admittedly, She's an impossible act to follow. My work focuses on how She is, and who She is, though I think that had that conversation about gender, sex, and identity not come up in academic and, eventually, in popular circles, my work would have taken quite another turn, found quite another focus. Perhaps I would not have written at all, but made pottery or raised sheep or gone to the beach and never worked. Or maybe, just maybe, She wouldn't have thought me here at all.

JUNE 1992

Constructing the Lesbian Self
by Karen Kahn

One day, in the mid '80s, one of my roommates came home with a small, lavender button that proclaimed a new lesbian identity: "butchy femme." We loved that button and gave it an honorary home near the bulletin board that hung over our phone. Though I would never have proclaimed myself a femme, not even a butchy femme (maybe a femmy butch?), whenever that button caught my eye, I smiled. There was something about the very act of having put those words together that signaled a playfulness about constructing our identities that had long been lacking in our lesbian-feminist communities. I smiled not because I thought being butch or femme was amusing, but because butch and femme, constructions of identity that had been exiled in the androgynous '70s, still resonated with meaning in my lesbian world. Though I may not yet have been aware of the richness of butch-femme lesbian herstory, intuitively, I recognized butches and femmes as women who had struggled to love each other in a homophobic world before my time. I was fascinated by these lesbian images, and though I had many assumptions about the rigidity of "roles" in the pre-Stonewall decades, the "butchy femme" button suggested, at once, the reclaiming of these foremothers and a new flexibility in the construction of lesbian identities.

Joan Nestle, cofounder of the Lesbian Herstory Archives in New York City and author of *A Restricted Country* (Firebrand, 1987), has been a leader in giving us back our herstory and restoring respect for the lives of pre-Stonewall butches and femmes. In *A Restricted Country,* through personal memoir, fiction, and analysis, she told us her story of growing up femme in the '50s and brought to life the working-class butch-femme world that formed her community.

Now she has a new book, *The Persistent Desire: A Femme-Butch Reader* (Alyson Publications, 1992), an anthology of writings by some 70 butch and femme lesbians. The diversity of experience, the complexity of identities, the richness of the social fabric—and the persistence of desire—described here are likely to put the final nail in the coffin of the myth that butch-femme couples were pale imitations of their heterosexual role models. As Nestle herself suggests, in the introduction to *The Persistent Desire:*

> *At the crux of the modern discussion about butch-femme identity is the question of its autonomy: does the longevity of butch-femme self-expression reflect the pernicious strength of heterosexual gender polarization—or is it, as I would argue, a lesbian-specific way of*

deconstructing gender that radically reclaims women's erotic energy? Are femmes and butches dupes of heterosexuality, or are they gender pioneers with a knack for alchemy?

The authenticity of the voices in this volume answers that question: these are women, who in Nestle's words, "believe in the originality of their choices."

I spoke with Nestle about her new book in late March, when she was in Boston for OutWrite '92, the annual gay and lesbian writers' conference. This is a book close to her heart, and throughout our conversation, I could feel her passion—not just for the subject but for each woman who, by contributing to this anthology, risked sharing the intimate details of her life. "Every woman who contributed to this book performed an act of courage," Nestle said proudly. This book, she wanted me to understand, belongs to all the contributors, not just to her.

Writing about our lives is always a courageous act, but Nestle was referring to a particular vulnerability for these writers whose "way of loving" has been disparaged not only by straight society but by their lesbian sisters as well. Nestle called the book *The Persistent Desire* "as a way of keeping faith to the old, a way of saying that we have been scorned, rebuked, ridiculed, ostracized, but [this way of loving] does not go away.... It seems to me that when women, [especially butch women], choose to risk their lives the way they did, and do, that it gives desire a very profound meaning."

The anthology is divided into two parts, probably best described as pre- and post-lesbian-feminism. Although chronologically there may be some overlap, the important distinction is the context in which the writer identified as butch or femme—whether she did so outside or within a lesbian-feminist community. In the first section of the book (about two-thirds of the whole), we hear how femmes and butches lived their lives prior to the second wave of feminism and about the great pain and alienation the rejection of these identities by lesbian feminists caused, especially for femmes. In the second section, we hear from lesbians, many of whom have come out in the last decade, who are claiming butch-femme identities in a feminist context. These voices, Nestle suggested, "make a new statement. If butch-femme was this oppressive rigidity that no one would choose...[then] there is something really interesting going on when women now [are choosing it]. That to me is very exciting. I don't have to argue that old point anymore about 'we were forced to do it.'"

True to her avocation as a community historian and archivist, Nestle begins the anthology in the mid-nineteenth century, with a short letter by William Cullen Bryant about a butch-femme couple. This piece is followed by a few early twentieth-century representations of butch-femme lesbians, including a short story by Radclyffe Hall. But the majority of the pieces in the first section portray femme-butch life in the '40s, '50s, and '60s. Many of the contributors are working-class women, from varied racial and ethnic backgrounds, who found their homes in the lesbian bar scene of the time, but there are also a number of international voices—women from South America, Australia, the Philippines. Their stories add another layer to our understanding of the lesbian lives presented here. As Nestle explained in the interview, "It was very important to me that there would be international voices, and I would have liked more.... By including [them], I wasn't trying to say butch-femme is an essential identity; I was saying that it is a way of loving and of self-identity that exists in different cultures in a recognizable form but is very specific [to that culture]. For instance, Marivic

[Desquitado], from the Philippines, does not call herself a 'butch'; she calls herself a 'tomboy,' and that means something different."

Identity is key here. "Butch-femme is not the only way for women to love or the only way to be," Nestle insisted. "In fact, I say just the opposite. It's an identity, which means you really can't fake it very satisfactorily. You can't do it out of a liberal desire to do something you think is radical. It has to come from the place where desire comes from, and, therefore, you can't preach someone into being butch or femme.... I write and express for those for whom it's a lived, gut feeling, and for those who are interested."

Lesbian feminists, at the height of the political '70s, rejected butch-femme as "role-playing." On the surface, butch-femme couples did appear to be playing at man and wife, imitating the hierarchical, sexist heterosexual model of relating. Butches seemed to have more freedom, to be the active sexual partners, and to rely on their "femme wives" to take care of them, while femmes appeared to do just that: staying home, caring for the kids if there were any, and being "passive recipients" when it came to sex.

But as the many contributors to this volume make clear, and as Nestle underscored in her comments to me, the complexities of real lives were lost in these stereotypes. Yes, Nestle said, "these identities were strong and very rigid-appearing in public places, because adherence to those self-presentations said you were not an enemy but a member of the community.... I think it is really hard to recreate for women who weren't there what the public stance of butch and femme meant in terms of claiming a safe territory." She went on to tell me a story from her own life, about how she escaped entrapment during an afternoon at the Sea Colony, a lesbian bar she frequented in New York City. "I stopped in during the afternoon, and there were three people in the bar: Maria, the bartender; myself; and this woman sitting at the bar having a drink. The minute I saw her I knew she was a policewoman, because she mixed up the butch-femme codes.... It was that rigidity that protected us."

However, that rigidity did not necessarily deny self-expression. "For myself, the friends that I knew, and for many women in this book, butch-femme was a very malleable personal life. We did things in public for many different reasons, but we were not simplistic human beings. So when butch and femme women were at home in their bed, there were many different exchanges that went on."

The Persistent Desire, in many ways, is a rebuttal to the argument that butch-femme "roles" are necessarily self-limiting. Nestle expresses the anthology's fundamental premise most eloquently when she writes in her introduction, referring to contributor Deanna Alida, who died in an accident last year, "I will always think of Deanna when I say we are not speaking of roles but of identities. Her butch self was not a masquerade or a gender cliché, but her final and fullest expression of herself."

But what is *butch?* Gayle Rubin, in her essay "Of Catamites and Kings: Reflections on Butch, Gender, and Boundaries," defines *butch* as "a category of lesbian gender that is constituted through the deployment and manipulation of masculine gender codes and symbols." There are as many ways to be butch, she tells us, as there are ways to be male maybe more, since the fact of being female adds another layer of complexity to the discussion and manipulation of gender identity. If you make your way through all 500-plus pages of *The Persistent Desire,* you will know that she is right. Gender identity is complex and, often, even paradoxical. Each generation has reshaped butch identity, and even within single communities, butches express a wide range of individuality (and the same, of course, is true for femmes). In this anthology, we meet stone butches who derive sexual satisfaction purely from pleasuring their femme partners, passing women who make their livings in factories that hire only men, butches who feel inadequate because they will never be men, and butches who glory in the complexities of being female and masculine. All, however, express some level of discomfort with the traditionally defined category of femaleness, a category that never fit their experience of self.

Contributor Jeanne Cordova grew up feeling more like a boy than a girl:

I thought I hated being a woman, that I was really a man trapped in a woman's body, a transsexual. At the wizened age of twenty-one, I'd nearly fulfilled my ambition. In the eyes of my girlfriend and friends I'd almost become a man. But in this new role I remained foreign to myself.

Gay liberation and feminism led Cordova to a new conclusion:

If men and women weren't divided and gender were accepted as fluid, I wouldn't be perceived as deviating from a nonexistent norm. And neither would the other one or two billion queers like me. I wasn't transsexual. I was simply individual, gender and psyche, a recombinant dyke.

Today, Cordova takes great pride in her butchness:

Being a butch—like being a woman, a lesbian, having a soul—is not something I can dismiss. I believe butches are born, not made. Since this is my birthright, I choose to glory in it. When I comb my hair back and strut out my front door, being butch is my hallelujah.

But gender confusion can also cause deep and lasting pain. Cherríe Moraga describes that pain in a 1981 conversation with Amber Hollibaugh:

To be butch, to me, is not to be a woman. The classic extreme-butch stereotype is the woman who sexually refuses another woman to touch her. It goes something like this: She doesn't want to feel her femaleness because she thinks of you as the "real" woman and if she makes love to you, she doesn't have to feel her own body as the object of desire. She can be a kind of "bodiless lover." So when you turn over and want to make love to her and make her feel physically like a woman, then what she is up against is queer. You are a woman making love to her. She feels queerer than anything in that.

This is a pain, often based in shame, brought on by a society whose hatred for women is only surpassed by its hatred for masculine women. In two stunningly passionate, fictional memoir-like pieces, Leslie Feinberg describes the hatred that butches faced in the '50s, the violence that often marred their lives, and the internal anguish it caused. Her survival, she says, rested in the arms of her femme lovers, who offered the love that healed:

And I'm wondering: did it hurt you, the times I couldn't let you touch me? I hope it didn't. You never showed it if it did. You knew it wasn't you I was keeping myself safe from. You treated my stone self as a wound that needed loving healing. Thank you. No one's ever done that since.

"Stone butch" is a category of lesbian gender identity that comes up more often in the first section of *The Persistent Desire*. Today's generation of butches define themselves differently, yet there is continuity. At a 1990 forum on butch-femme identities, Sue Hyde defined her butch self this way:

I am butch because I express desire for a woman in terms of how I can make her feel. I need—and it's with no small amount of need—to be my lover's best lover. I need to know from her that the failure I experienced at adolescence, that moment of horror when I realized I could never be a man and in this culture I would never quite be a woman either, can be transformed and transcended through her profound pleasure and my pleasure at hers.

The emotional content of Hyde's statement was echoed by Deanna Alida at the same forum. "Being a butch," Alida stated, "is living with a strong defense and with a deep, deep vulnerability."

But the vulnerability of butches is balanced by the strength that it takes to announce their lesbian presence in the world. Femme partners of butches recognize that strength, that characteristic dyke rebelliousness, and love them for it. During our conversation, Nestle described her feelings as a femme who loved and continues to love butches. "What is so astounding to me about both this history and its present lived reality is that there is an incredible vulnerability that coexists with a tenacity of courage and desire. They never cancel each other out, but they create a special poignancy that I think enters into the loving and enters into the bonding of these two people. What I mean by that is, as a femme woman, part of my loving of my butch partner is the sense that I have to protect her; I have to protect her against a world that sees [butches] as these freaks, particularly when they are recognizable."

So much for the stereotype of the butch protecting the weaker, more vulnerable femme. In fact, the femme voices in this volume are powerful, passionate, and often angry. Not surprisingly, the once silent partners of old-time butches become more vocal in the latter section of the anthology, following the historical changes wrought by feminism. "Feminism changed the world for us, for femmes, in a very profound way," Nestle told me. She subtitled the book *A Femme-Butch Reader* to signal the change: "As a femme woman," she explained, "I feel it is now time to reverse the order.... It was a symbolic statement that I think that the femme woman has been the least understood, the least visible. As a femme feminist, it was very important to me to put my sisters first at this moment of history."

The pain, the joy, and the paradoxes involved in constructing femme identities emerge from a reading of this anthology as quite different from the experiences of butches. Femme contributors describe struggling with the same self-hatred that straight women in this society must fight. For example, Paula Austin writes in "Femme-inism":

Femme often carries the stigma of the word feminine, and being feminine has traditionally meant powerlessness, passivity, everything that being a woman has traditionally meant. When I first came out, I wanted to be butch. I wanted to outwardly defy patriarchy in general, and men in particular.

Self-expression that relishes the feminine in a society that hates women and devalues all human characteristics associated with females is bound to be mired in internal contradictions. Thus femmes look to their lovers—often butches—for reassurance that they can in fact be loved for the womanness that they want so badly to love in themselves. Pat Califia expresses a sentiment shared by many of the femme contributors to *The Persistent Desire* in "The Femme Poem":

Because with you it's finally safe
To be a woman.
The feminine qualities
That win me the world's contempt
Put a light in your eyes,
Make you feel like you're finally
Getting a little of what you deserve.
That's why I keep coming back …

Similarly, from Amber Hollibaugh:
I can't not be a femme, just as I can't not be a lesbian, because with butches I really do
know what it is to be a woman.

Not that one can only be a femme with a butch or vice versa. As Gayle Rubin writes:
There are butch tops and butch bottoms, femme tops and femme bottoms. There are
butch-femme couples, femme-femme partners, and butch-butch pairs.

When I asked Nestle if her femme identity is inextricably linked to being with a butch woman, she replied, "One thing I had to come to terms with is that I would be a femme even if I was alone in the world." Her femme identity is "everything I do. It's a philosophy of life. It is a social stance—to be a femme woman, in those social senses, means...to be generous, to be nurturing...to be exploratory...to be lustful in all things, not just sex, to like to join in difference."

But it is also an erotic stance. Both butches and femmes are announcing their desire through their self-presentations—it is a language that is understood, and manipulated, in a kind of erotic conversation that cannot be reduced to the stereotypical image of the sexual encounter between an active butch and passive femme. Notably, in this volume, femmes express the deepest sexual passion—their desire is right there on the surface where you can almost touch it and feel the heat. For example, in "Her Thighs," Dorothy Allison's femme narrator describes slowly seducing her repressed butch lover:

Bobby shifted and cleared her throat and watched me while I kept my mouth open
slightly and stared intently at the exact spot where I wanted to put my tongue. My eyes were
full of moisture. I imagined touching the denim above her labia with my lips. I saw it so clearly,
her taste and texture were full in my mouth. I got wet and wetter. Bobby kept shifting on the
couch. I felt my cheeks dampen and heard myself making soft moaning noises—like a child in
great hunger. That strong, dark musk odor rose between us, the smell that comes up from my
cunt when I am swollen and wet from my clit to my asshole.

This kind of wanting, of uncensored sexual desire, is most often associated with being a "slut" in this society. To have this kind of desire for women is certainly something we are taught to be ashamed of. In many ways feminism, by insisting that women's sexual desires were not evil, helped femmes overcome that shame—but at the same time it heightened all the contradictions of femme identity.

In the feminist '70s, Nestle points out in "The Femme Question,"

Femmes became the victims of a double dismissal: in the past they did not appear culturally different enough from heterosexual women to be seen as breaking gender taboos, and today they do not appear feminist enough, even in their historical context, to merit attention or respect for being ground-breaking women.

Butches often slipped easily into the androgynous '70s, shedding suits and ties for flannel shirts and jeans. Their rejection of the "feminine" fit the politics of the time. Fitting in was more difficult for their femme counterparts, who were seen as decidedly unfeminist in high heels, makeup, and other accoutrements of females in patriarchal society. Some tried to shed their femme identities, but they were left feeling lost, their sexuality impoverished, their fury often turned inward as they tried to hide their true selves from the movement that had so much to offer them as women. Some, like Amber Hollibaugh, felt suicidal:

The only time I ever tried to kill myself was when I tried to figure out how I could live with my politics and the fact that I was femme. That didn't come from just a political community that I felt would judge me...I said to me, I can't be a part of my own political agenda if the way I want women to make love to me is as a butch to a femme. It meant that I thought I had to choose between my political vision and my sexual desire. I'd already faced that to be a lesbian. I'd already walked that razor blade. So to choose against the women I wanted to be with to have the political ideals that I absolutely founded my life on seemed to be an intolerable contradiction.

Femme rage simmering below the surface spilled out and became vocal in the early '80s, especially following the now infamous Barnard Conference, Towards a Politics of Sexuality. This conference, picketed by Women Against Pornography, sparked the "sex wars," which still divide our communities: heated and angry debates over not only butch/femme, but s/m, pornography, sex toys, even penetration. Although, as Nestle stated, "the sexual judgments have gentled" in recent years, Lyndall MacCowan's letter to Nestle from April 1991 makes clear that the anger has not fully dissipated:

And what I'm angry at is feminism, specifically lesbian feminism, despite its being a movement whose benefits I can name and touch, and whose philosophy has shaped my entire adult life and the history of my generation. I am angry because its message has been plain these past two decades: as a lesbian who is femme, I'm not considered worthy of liberation.

When I asked Nestle if she shared this anger, she told me that writing *A Restricted Country* and now having given "a much wider range of women who love this way" a chance to tell their stories through the anthology, have made a difference. "[I no longer feel] the sort of primal anger I had, being again made a freak by a movement I helped build—in some senses, I've gotten what I asked for, which was a place in history."

In restoring this history, and in reopening the discussion of lesbian gender identity, Nestle has done a great service for our lesbian communities. In the '70s, we rushed to embrace the concept that gender was not destiny. But as Nestle sees it, "The discussions around gender were political discussions. I don't think we ever got to discuss the gender we [lesbians] were. We discussed it in terms of economics (women as workers who should get paid), but we never got around to talking about what the gender of being female meant to us as lesbians. We never got to the complexity of a gender discussion—the women who didn't feel like women....What this book raises is that we can look at how we experience womanness and maleness, and whatever those things mean. When lesbian is in front of it, it's a whole new thing."

Nestle admitted that even she wanted to reduce those complexities when she first began writing about butch-femme. "In *A Restricted Country,* I was cleaning up the act a lot. I said butches never wanted to be men and that wasn't true. There were butches who wanted to be men. So I had to face my own shames and ask myself, 'Why did I have to do that act of self-protection? Why couldn't I just have said that there were women who had gender complexities that we don't have a language for?' It made me face a lot of truths."

The truth is that our communities have been painfully divided by sexual rhetoric for at least a decade, and we cannot afford to keep hurting one another. As lesbians, whether we construct our identities as butch or femme, lipstick lesbian, androgynous professional, or Queer Nation punk, we face an increasingly repressive society in which hate crimes against lesbians and gay men continue to increase at astonishing rates. It is time to listen to the voices of those whose "gender complexities" we don't understand, to embrace difference rather than setting ourselves up as the gender police (as happened at last year's Michigan Womyn's Music Festival when male-to-female transsexuals were excluded). "I think the big danger is to confuse sexual rhetoric, which we always need because we are an oppressed people because of our sexuality, with the complexity of our personal sexual lives," Nestle emphasized toward the end of the interview. We still know very little about the relationships between biology, sexuality, and gender. Listening to the voices of our lesbian sisters—from the past as well as the present—without passing judgment—is the first step in "getting down to it and seeing how we are queer." *The Persistent Desire* is a tremendous resource for doing just that.

MAY 1994

Presenting the Blue Goddess: Toward a Bicultural Asian-American Feminist Agenda

by Sonia Shah

We all laughed sheepishly about how we used to dismiss the South Asian women in our lives as doormats irrelevant to our cultural location. For most of us in that fledgling South Asian-American women's group in Boston, either white feminists or Black feminists had inspired us to try to find our feminist heritage. Yet neither movement had really prepared us for actually finding anything. The way feminism was defined by either group did not, could not, define our South Asian feminist heritages, which for most of us consisted of stuff like feisty immigrant mothers, ball-breaking grandmothers, Kali-worship (Kali is the blue goddess who sprung whole from another woman and who symbolizes "shakti"—Hindi for woman-power), social activist aunts, and freedom-fighting/Gandhian great-aunts. In many ways, white feminism, with its "personal is political" maxim and its emphasis on building sister-hood and consciousness raising, had brought us together. Black feminism, on the other hand, had taught us that we could expect more—that a feminism incorporating a race analysis was possible. Yet, while both movements spurred us to organize, neither included our culturally specific agendas—about battering of immigrant women, the ghettoization of the South Asian community, cultural discrimination, bicultural history and identity, and other issues specific to our lives.

Today, our numbers are exploding in our immigrant communities and the communi-ties of their progeny, and subsequently, in our activist communities. Our writers, poets, artists, and filmmakers are coming of age. Our activism, against anti-Asian violence, battery, and racism, is becoming more and more inspired and entrenched. Yet our movement for Asian-American feminism faces crucial internal challenges. Long-time Asian-American femi-nist activists such as Helen Zia, a contributing editor to *Ms.* magazine, wonder, "What makes us different from white feminists or Black feminists? What can we bring to the table?" And they complain that "these questions haven't really been developed yet."

Our needs, our liberation, and our pan-Asian feminist agenda have been obscured by a Black/white dichotomy that permeates both activist movements and the mainstream. This racialist essentialism has divided us, stripping us of the tools we need to articulate an Asian-American feminism. Our movement, in all of its different forms, has been forced to smash itself into definitions, assumptions, and activist protocols that simply don't work for us. So, while we have been able to get a lot of good work done, and will continue to do so, we haven't been able to show each other, tell each other, or teach each other, about what Asian-American feminism really means.

The movements of the '60s, out of which the first wave of Asian women's organizing sprung, collided with the mainstream in defining racism in Black and white terms; racism is still defined as discrimination based on skin color. These earlier activists also, to some extent, elevated discrimination based on skin color to the top layer of oppression. According to these assumptions, an assault on an Indian because she "dresses weird" is not racist; the harassment of a Chinese shopkeeper because she has a "funny accent" is not racist. Neither are as dis-turbing, unacceptable, or even downright "evil" as, for example, an attack on a Black person because of her skin color. Racism is seen as a problem between people of different skin colors, between Black people and white people, and one must be in either the Black or the white camp to even speak about it. Those of us who are neither Black nor white are expected to forget ourselves. Whites try to convince us we are really *more like them;* depending upon our degree of sensitivity toward racist injustice, we try to persuade Blacks that we are similar to them. This narrow definition has distorted mainstream perceptions of anti-Asian racism and has distorted even our perception of ourselves—we either don't see ourselves as victims of racism or we see ourselves as victims of racism based on skin color.

For example, many Asian-American women have described Asian women's experi-ence of racism as a result of stereotypes about "exotica" and "china dolls," two stereotypes based on the fact that we look different from white people. Of course, we do encounter racism that emanates from these stereotypes. But there are many more layers of oppression just as unacceptable and pernicious as this discrimination based on skin color. By focusing solely on "racial" differences, however, we fail to see them for what they are, and we fail to name the reality of our experiences.

For our experiences of oppression are in *many* ways qualitatively different from those of Black and white people. For me, the experience of "otherness," the formative discrimination in my life, has been a result of culturally different (not necessarily racially different) people thinking they were culturally central: thinking that *my* house smelled funny, that *my* mother talked weird, that *my* habits were strange. They were normal; I wasn't.

The Black/white paradigms of both feminist and civil rights struggles create false divisions and false choices for Asian-American women. Not long ago, a group of South Asian women organizing against battery held a conference on South Asian women. Recent emigrees, the conference organizers tended to hail from greater class privilege than the parents of second-generation South Asian Americans. This difference led second-generation South Asian American activists, born and bred in the United States, to boycott the conference, charging that the organizers, because of their class privilege and because of their relative newness to the Asian-American community, sidelined issues of U.S.-based racism and discrimination.

This is a false division, especially dangerous in such a relatively small activist community. When first faced with U.S. racism and its Black/white constructs, immigrants with class privilege, even activist ones, are apt to dismiss racism as "not their problem." (As it has been defined by the mainstream, strictly speaking, it isn't.) Efforts by second-generation (and beyond) activists, to convince our sisters at other locations on the culture/class continuum that what we suffer is similar to what the Black community suffers are fraught with difficulty precisely because we have been confined to the Black/white paradigm. We need to use an accurate portrayal of our own experiences of racism, defined on *our* terms, to create alliances with our sisters across generation, class, and culture gaps. As long as we don't, false dichotomies will continue to divide us.

As Asian-American women, Asian women in America, American women of Asian descent, or however we choose to think of ourselves, we all grapple with conflicting signals and oppressions in our lives because we are all situated, to differing degrees, in both Asian and American cultural milieus. We suffer not only cultural discrimination (as men do as well) but our own form of cultural schizophrenia, as we receive mixed and often contradictory signals about priorities, values, duty, and meaning from our families and greater communities. We encounter sexist Asian tradition; racist and sexist white culture; antiracist nonfeminist women heroes; racist feminist heroes; strong proud Asian women who told us not to make waves; strong proud non-Asian women who told us *to* make waves, and on and on.

We all reconcile these tensions and oppressions in different ways: by acting out a model minority myth, for some; by suffering silently, for others; by being activist, for still others. These conflicts, born of cultural duality, along with the experience of cultural discrimination, are what unite us as Asian-American women across our differences. But this commonality has been obscured; there is no room for cultural duality in a world where one is automatically relegated to one racial camp or the other based on biological fact. But as we grapple with conflicting signals and oppressions in our lives, we can reimagine and reinvent ourselves and our priorities. The cultural schizophrenia, the feeling of not belonging to either or any culture, is not necessarily a burden; it is also an opportunity for us to recreate ourselves. We do it every time we encounter a conflict anyway; why not politicize this process of cultural reconciliation, and tag it for feminism and liberation?

We need to reclaim our cultural duality as our commonality and, also, as our greatest strength: for the good of our movement and to save ourselves. When the poor immigrant Asian woman who follows an abusive husband to the United States, who doesn't speak English and is cut off from the women who supported her in her home country, is beaten nearly to death by her one contact to the outside world, she needs a bicultural feminism. Not one that helps her go back to Asia, nor one that suggests she become a typical liberated "American" woman. She needs an activism that recognizes the cultural discrimination she will encounter in this society, while still empowering her to liberate herself in this country (with money, legal services, shelter, and support). She needs a bicultural feminism that will recognize and politicize the cultural reconciliation she must undergo to liberate herself: for example, by reimagining her duty as an Asian wife as a duty to herself.

When my little sister, who is just beginning to see herself as a sexual person, thinks she is a "slut" for wearing tight jeans, she needs this bicultural feminism. Not a mainstream white feminism, which might suggest she throw away her tight jeans because she is objectifying herself, nor one that simply suggests she revert to the dress of her "homeland" and wear a revealing sari—but one that would affirm that she doesn't have to abandon Indian values of filial respect or whatever it is that makes her fear appearing "slutty." It is possible that my parents, first-generation Indian immigrants, reject the trappings of American sexuality, such as tight jeans, as culturally alien. My sister's subsequent interpretation, however, that Indians are antisexual stems from her assumption—promulgated by mainstream society—that there is but one culture, not many. If you don't appreciate the trappings of sexuality, you don't appreciate sexuality. The fact that tight jeans are a particular, cultural expression of sexuality is obscured. An Asian-American feminism that emphasized cultural duality and reconciliation would subvert such narrow-mindedness. There are many cultures, many sexualities. My sister needs to name the cultural conflicts she is involved in for what they are and to reconcile her visions of sexuality and empowerment within the cultural confines of white patriarchy and Indian patriarchy. A bicultural feminism would ensure that she does this in a feminist, liberatory way.

As bicultural feminists with multiple identities, we are empowered to enter the broader discussion and struggles around us with something more substantial than identity politics and a slightly different take on the Black/white dichotomy. The concept and practice of the extended family, for example, might lead us to apply our critical reinventions to the struggle for accessible child care, where we can shift the turgid debate away from paid care to building cooperative care centers and encouraging work-sharing. Understanding social and linguistic difference within Asian-American families, we can apply our insights to the current debates about gay parents raising potentially straight children, or to white families raising children of color, by advocating for the fitness of the child's cultural community rather than for the fitness of the parent. Remembering our histories as Asian women, we can apply our sense of outrage over issues such as the Japanese internment during World War II, "brain drain" immigration to the United States that has robbed the Third World of its professional class, and past and present treatment of refugees to the struggle for just immigration policies. We can reinterpret Asian paradigms of filial and familial duty as social responsibility. We can use antimaterialism as a basis for building an ecological society.

I remember, in that South Asian American women's group, we were all looking forward to Mira Nair's film, *Mississippi Masala*. We took Nair as a kind of model—a seemingly progressive Indian woman filmmaker who had gained the financial backing necessary for reaching wide sectors of the South Asian community. *Masala* was the first film we knew of that would portray an Indian-American woman in her cultural milieu as the protagonist.

I don't know what Nair's intentions were, but her Indian-American protagonist was little more than a standard Western-defined beauty, her biculturalism little more than occasional bare feet and a chureedar thrown over her shoulder. Although a refugee from Uganda living in Mississippi with Indian parents, she was phenomenally unconcerned with issues of race, history, culture, and gender. Given the dearth of accessible activist commentary on biculturalism and feminism beyond the Black/white divide, even a sympathetic "opinion maker" like Nair can hurt our movement, by portraying us as little more than exotic, browner versions of white women who by virtue of a little color can bridge the gap between Black and white (not through activism, of course, just romantic love). If Asian-American women's movements can effectively unite within bicultural feminist agendas, we can snatch that power away from those willing to trivialize us, and Masala and our less sympathetic foes beware.

Editor's note: A longer version of this article appears in The State of Asian America: Activism and Resistance, *edited by Karin Aguilar-San Juan (South End Press, 1994).*

OCTOBER 1994

Prisons
by Margaret Robison

I was sitting in my hospital bed in Mercy Hospital in Springfield, Massachusetts, writing in my journal, when my pen ran out of ink. I laid the pen down on the table that extended across my stomach, then turned my head to my left and looked at the extra pen on the window sill beside my bed. I needed that pen. Straining, I reached my right arm as far as I could, stretching my fingers toward the pen. I tried again. But I couldn't reach far enough across the left side of my body, paralyzed and lead-heavy from my stroke. I rang the bell for a nurse or an aide, then lay back and waited. As I waited, I felt the familiar panic building in my chest once more. Again, the deepening realization that I was imprisoned in my own body.

Not that I'd never felt imprisoned in my body before. As a teenager I thought of my body as something I wanted to escape. It wanted to eat pecan pie and ice cream, fried chicken and french fries when I wanted to be movie-star-thin like the other girls. It had insistent sexual feelings when, according to Mother, Daddy, and the Baptist Church, I wasn't supposed to have such feelings until after I married. If then. My nose sometimes ran with mucus. My arm pits sweated. And once a month I bled between my legs, blood sometimes leaking onto my underpants, and once staining a skirt so that I had to wear my raincoat all day in school.

But now I knew what it felt like to be imprisoned in not only a body that sweated, ran with mucus, and still occasionally bled, but a body in which one whole side had forgotten how to move at all. I couldn't escape from a burning building to save my life. I couldn't even reach my pen. It might as well have been in the next room or at home on my writing table. Panic beat in my throat.

Stacked on my table were the new poems Tracie M. had sent me from the prison where she was an inmate. I knew that she felt I'd abandoned her by leaving my position as creative writing teacher at the prison. Now I didn't have the energy to read her poems.

Though I wasn't able to give Tracie the critical feedback that she wanted, Tracie herself was on my mind a great deal as I lay in the hospital for months, unable to move from bed to wheelchair without assistance. I thought a lot about prisons then. Before my stroke I had led a theater/writing workshop together with actress Sheryl Stoodley in the prison in Lancaster, Massachusetts. There I met Tracie as well as a number of other memorable women.

They were often on my mind during the months I spent in Mercy. I thought of Lisa and her rich, full voice as she sang "Amazing Grace" to me after my mother's death. I thought of the pain in Lynn's eyes as she looked down at her hands and arms deeply scarred from years of drug addiction. I remembered how Christina's father held the phone receiver to the ocean so that she could hear the waves. In my mind, I heard the voices of the women: *I was looking for something, I don't know what it was. My mama beat me with a wet electric cord. My Daddy was always gone, my Daddy always gone. Sometimes I'd rather be dead. Sometimes I hate myself so bad. You think you got it bad? Let me tell you—How do you tell a child that you murdered her father?* And the taped voice of Zeneida, who could neither read nor write, played itself in my mind. In the first published prison journal, I'd quoted her:

I don't want to be in prison.... I hate the rooms. I hate the bathrooms.... Every time I think about the mountains, they are so beautiful.... Today I sat outside. I looked at the trees. I looked at the sky. I looked at this little bird. He was free. I wanted to be that bird so bad.

Now Zeneida was dead of AIDS at 38. I still grieved over the loss of Zeneida, though I was grieving for myself as well. "I'm reaching for my life," she'd said. So was I.

Now I lay, paralyzed, unable even to reach across my own body for a pen.

Sometimes I imagined being back at Lancaster, in Putnam cottage where Sheryl and I spent so many intense evenings in a large room on the third floor, talking, listening, writing, acting with the women. I imagined what it would feel like to walk up those stairs, lifting my paralyzed left arm and putting my hand on the banister; to be able to walk down the hall to the rooms of the women; to be able to walk on the grounds.

To be able to walk at all. Anywhere.

Given the opportunity, I asked myself, would I trade lives with a woman in prison, serving her sentence for her as she lived in my body for me?

It felt like an eternity that I waited for an aide to get my pen for me.

Now I was always waiting for something—waiting for someone to transfer me from bed to wheelchair, waiting for someone to bring the bedpan in the middle of the night, waiting for someone to lift me off the toilet and pull my pants up as I leaned against the bathroom wall, waiting for my bath, waiting for visitors, waiting for meals. Lines I'd written for the prison play that we collaborated on kept running through my mind:

Wait for the mail.
Wait for meals.
Wait for a visitor.
Wait for release.
Wait for a phone call.
Wait for meds.
Wait for the doctor.
Waiting to live.

Waiting to live. Would I change lives with a woman in prison?

In Mercy, time passed quickly as long as I was in therapy. Therapy not only demanded my total physical focus but my mental focus as well. I struggled with finding a way to communicate to my left leg that I wanted it to raise itself from the exercise mat in the gym. I struggled to keep from falling when I tried to take a few steps outside the parallel bars. Or—in speech therapy—struggled to say the word *paralyzed* or *immensity* or *remorse*. It was when I was alone, with nothing separating me from my own feelings, that time slowed to an agony of waiting.

Waiting not so unlike the waiting I had done in the state mental hospital the summer I left my husband the first time. Then I could find no safe place in my mind to go, no place where there wasn't pain or rage or a howling despair hiding in every fold of consciousness. There for 21 days I wrote the journal through which I claimed myself as a writer. Time was my obsession then. The clock on the wall of the locked ward with its calm, predictable face became my focus. That and the clock in the dining hall and the ten-minute difference between them. Over 20 years ago and I still remember those clocks. As I remember the walk to and from the dining hall, past the place on the stairs where a handful of shattered glass from a window pane lay shining dully in a pile of dust and dead wasps.

Being in the prison in Lancaster immediately took me back to my experience at the State Hospital—the all-pervasive undercurrent of mistrust ("they're poisoning us," another patient whispered as we stood in the medication line, "they're poisoning us"); the sense of confinement that seemed to include not only external physical confinement but limitations on the psyche as well. Something to do with power and the lack of power. A condescending, controlling attitude as tangible and as deadly as the thick cigarette smoke filling the visitors room that first night as I sat listening to the story of how an abused woman came to murder her husband. Listening, I sucked in my breath and held it as my entire body registered the thought that I could have been that woman.

Would I trade lives with a woman in prison?

How did I answer that question when I was in Mercy? Did I answer it? Now I no longer remember, although, given my fear, my seizures of panic during those early days after my stroke, I can imagine me thinking that I would feel unbounded relief for such a trade. To be free of my paralyzed body—to be able to walk again, to move my arm and hand, to speak clearly and with ease. Yes! I can imagine myself saying. Yes!

But perhaps, pushed to give an answer, even then I would have opted for keeping my own body. Though I suspect that this is true, of course, I'll never know for sure. When I answer the question now, my answer comes from a position of being a great deal more mobile than I was when I could not reach across my body to pick up my pen. The fingers on my left hand are still unable to do more than curl like a claw at the end of my arm. And I walk painfully slowly, using a leg brace and cane, slinging my paralyzed leg stiffly. But I might make it out of a burning building now, if the stairs had a good, sturdy hand rail; if I was fortunate enough to have my leg brace on and my cane in my hand when the fire broke out; if the fire was slow moving; if there wasn't a crowd of people pressing against me to throw me off balance.

Whatever my answer might have been to the question I asked myself in Mercy, my answer now is "no," I would not change lives with a woman in prison. Not because the lives of all women in prison are more difficult than mine. They aren't. My reason for keeping this body (given such a choice) has nothing to do with either opting for an easier way out, or accumulating martyr points for enduring life in a crippled body. My reason for keeping my body is precisely that—it is mine. And it's home. Home to my feelings. Home to my thoughts.

I don't know why I had the stroke. I don't know why I didn't have a heart attack instead or lung cancer or the lupus one doctor thought I had. Or no physical catastrophe at all. I did know that I could not go on living the way I was. I no longer had the energy to travel from school to school as poet-in-residence; I no longer had energy to invest so much of myself in a group of children and teachers only to have to say goodbye to them and begin again someplace else; I no longer had energy to try to hold the worlds of public school and prison together in my mind and heart. I had lived through too many profoundly important experiences without having adequate time to deal with my own emotional responses. I was completely burned out. I knew my life had to change. But did change have to come through such drastic means? Was the stroke an accident of nature, or the result of whatever caused both my grandmothers to die of strokes? Did I myself do something—either consciously or unconsciously—to cause the stroke? Was my life better as a result of it?

Lying on my hospital bed that day, I felt panic. Certainly then I couldn't imagine a hopeful future. But I felt gratitude when an aide finally came and handed me my pen. As I wrote in my journal then, I felt the relief that only comes when I find a way to hold my feelings in words.

Over the months I spent in Mercy, as I became more accustomed to living in a paralyzed body, my panic attacks became less severe though my anxiety level continued to be high. How was I going to be able to go home alone when getting from the bed to the wheelchair by myself was a major undertaking? Who would help me bathe and dress? How would I be able to sleep alone with no nurse to come in the night if I needed her? Often I fell asleep with my earphones on and a monotonous voice repeating, "You are in control, you are in control," while my whole existence was threatened, my whole life falling apart.

In August I went home to the apartment I'd left in May. I did not go home to the life I'd left. I could no longer drive from town to town to lead poetry workshops for children. I could not talk clearly enough to teach the women's workshops that I'd advertised just before my stroke. Nor did I have the physical energy or coordination. The writing workshop I'd been scheduled to lead at the university in the summer had been taught by someone else. And the prison project was long since over.

My life was now focused on therapy, both physical and speech, which meant three trips to Cooley Dickinson Hospital each week and many hours of therapy at home. I also had to learn to live with the almost constant presence of people I'd never met before, but who were now helping me, not only with therapy at home, but personal things like bathing and dressing. I was becoming used to a world that months before was totally foreign to me.

Even being in prison is not all negative. For all the complaining the women did, there was a good bit of talk about positive results that came out of the experience of imprisonment. "Prison makes me strong," Zeneida said, and I believe that was just as true as her intense longing to be out of prison. One woman wrote anonymously about the results of her addiction to cocaine: "I was part of the living dead.... I turned myself in.... I know now that jail saved my life."

Perhaps it did. Though I would say that turning herself in was probably the first step toward saving her life. I don't understand how a life can be saved unless that person wants to save it. And I believe Zeneida was made stronger by prison because she wanted to grow stronger. As I wanted to grow stronger. Whatever caused my stroke in the first place, the important thing was what I chose to do with it.

In the prison play, I quoted these words by Tracie:

But then I got six to ten for armed robbery. That's a good chunk to be locked up. But it's not the worst punishment, and I know that probably sounds weird....I don't know if there's a god or not. I don't know if there's a plan. But it just seems like my time. That it's my time to figure things out. I have to find out about me.

Now it's my time. I've spent much of it in a wheelchair parked at my writing table overlooking the Deerfield River flowing just outside my window. I've thought a lot about my life. And I've worked at healing. Not only from my stroke, but from all the wounds in the life that brought me to it—a painfully difficult childhood and adolescence; a 23-year marriage that I finally terminated on grounds of "cruel and abusive treatment"; a sexual assault by a therapist I'd trusted; long hours of teaching that—even as they enriched my life—exhausted me both physically and emotionally; and the end of a love affair that left me grief-stricken.

Is my life better than it was before my stroke?

No. It's not better to have to wear a leg brace and use a cane for what slow walking I do. It's not better to have seizures that terrify me or to live with a level of exhaustion I'd not even imagined. It's not better to speak each word with difficulty and effort. It's not better to experience such staggering loss and to feel the grief and anger that come with such loss. It's not better to be unable to lean down and pick my grandson up in my arms.

And yes. It's better to know the new friends I've made because of the stroke, people who have contributed enormously to my life. It's better to be searching for forms to hold my many experiences of working with children. And to think and write more about women in prison. It's better to have time to sit at my writing table and watch mist rise from the water in early morning, the mountain darken against the sky in evening. It's better to have time to record my dreams and learn to listen to their messages. It's better to be sitting here writing and to be gaining more insight into myself through the writing. Not that I've not worked all my life on gaining insight just as I've worked on healing from as far back as I can remember. I have. Only, the stroke gave me a new lens through which to examine my life, and I've used it.

This morning I spent several hours reading through the journal entries and poems that Tracie sent me when I was in Mercy—pages and pages of writing about being beaten, being raped when she was seven, being forced into prostitution when she was twelve. She wrote about her mother's alcoholism and her own, wrote about poverty.

Tracie is out of prison now. I hope she is continuing to use writing to find her way. As I sit here at my writing table, pausing from time to time to look out at the river, and beyond it—to the mountain—I think of Tracie. I think of Catherine, Christina, Elaine; I think of Diamond, Jo Ann, and Lisa; I think of Lynn, Phyllis, Maggie and Ruth; I think of Zeneida. Thinking about them keeps me company.

I, too, am trying to write my way out of prison. A prison of silence as tangible as the closet I was locked in when I was a young girl—a small, hot closet thick with the stench of my own vomit. A prison of emotion frozen inside me since early childhood because I was taught that I had no right to my feelings. A prison of memories still hidden behind fear, and only hinted at through dreams, paintings, and poems. A prison of experiences unclaimed, thoughts unexpressed.

My body is not the major prison in my life. Certainly, its disabilities limit my range of possibility, even as the limitations themselves have their own gifts to offer—time to watch the white goose that floats so gracefully near the river's far shore even as I write; time to remember the moving stories children have shared with me about their lives; time to release the emotions that have filled my heart in response to those stories.

My body is a friend doing its best to give me messages that—though sometimes difficult to hear—I need to hear and accept in order to grow more whole. And the more I say, see, and feel of my life, the more I bring into consciousness the memories stored in bone and muscle, tissue and organ, the more healed I become.

Today, May 1, 1994, is the fifth anniversary of my stroke. Even after these five years of recovery—recovery and acceptance of what I've not recovered and may never recover; even with the terror I've experienced, the sorrow, despair, anxiety, anger, I continue to call the stroke "a terrible gift of healing." Not that I believe the stroke came to me like an angel with blessings on its breath. I don't. For whatever reason, the stroke happened. A blood clot traveled to my brain and stopped the flow of oxygen, destroying pathways of communication, leaving messengers from my arm and leg unable to find their way home to my devastated brain. Speech as I'd known it died that day. My sense of balance, my sense of my own body's relationship to the earth itself was obliterated.

I will probably never know for sure my own role in causing the stroke, or how much choice I might have had in the matter. However, almost from the beginning, it was clear to me that I had a choice as to how I would live with the stroke. I could look at it as tragic and debilitating, or as a gift, however terrible and terrifying that gift might be. In accepting the gift, bit by bit I'm coming home to myself.

Response to previous article:

JUNE 1995

NOT IMPRISONED, JUST A FACT OF LIFE
by Mary Frances Platt

I am not a disabled woman who is imprisoned in her body or who has overcome or strives to overcome her disability or the limitations that result as a fact of that disability. I am a radical crip who struggles to stay alive in an ableist culture that: attempts to genetically "screen out" my kind prebirth; would rather institutionalize me than provide me with the resources to hire in-home consumer-directed assistance; and prefers "cutting the cord" to developing and funding adaptive equipment and effective nonnarcotic pain medication that would assist me in living my life.

Ableism is what makes my life intolerable, not the fact that I use oxygen, a wheelchair, and daily personal assistance. Dealing with bureaucratic bullshit in order to survive; fighting daily for my basic rights under the Americans with Disabilities Act; finding responsible personal assistants; and enduring ridiculous pain levels because of my lack of money to pay for acupuncture, chiropractic, massage, and homeopathy, and my unwillingness to be drugged into oblivion—these are what "diminish" my life, not being a wheelchair and oxygen user.

Disability is a fact of life, a fact of life that nondisabled feminists do not want to acknowledge. It is especially a fact of life for those of us from poor and working-class backgrounds and from cultures of color. In October 1994, with the publication of "Prisons" by Margaret Robison, *Sojourner* showed that it too would rather print the words of disabled women that most reflect the nondisabled view of disability than the radical crip, antiableist view of living disabled. Margaret's personal experience of becoming disabled and living with disabilities is just that: her personal experience. The feminist press consistently publishes writings on the personal experiences of women with disabilities that encourage readers to look at how one can overcome disabilities, or learn to live within limitations—or, if we're lucky, as in the case of Margaret's piece, disabled women becoming comfortable in and owning their bodies. I own my fat, disabled, oxygenated body. I will not rehabilitate to an acceptable, inspired, level of walking. I will always need nightly, if not daily, oxygen due to a polluted planet. It is not my fault that I am disabled. I cannot image it away or pass as nondisabled to make you more comfortable about the fact that disability is more and more a fact of life as the earth gets more and more polluted, used, and abused by white humans.

Meanwhile, feminists continue to hold events, run businesses, and live in wheelchair-inaccessible spaces. Feminists continue to put out our words in average-size print and not in braille, large print, *and* audio tape. Feminist festival organizers refuse to hire antiableist women who promote integrative access, and the only nondisabled feminists involved in the disability rights and antiableism movements are the friends, lovers, and families of people with disabilities. The majority of feminists feel fine about genetic genocide of people with disabilities through prenatal "screening," abortion of disabled fetuses solely on the grounds of disability, and removal of nutritional and life support to those whose lives are "not worth living." How many times have feminists said, "I don't care if it's a boy or a girl, I just hope it's all right." "All right," of course, being the equivalent of not disabled.

In the past year, the feminist press has expounded on the joys of a daughter pulling the plug on mother, how important nursing homes are for disabled and old people, and, now, how having a disability is similar to being imprisoned at MCI [Massachusetts Correctional Institution]-Framingham. Prison is a horrible punishment used as a tool by dominant cultures to keep nondominant cultures oppressed. Disability is not a punishment. It's just an everyday fact of life. These are dangerous ableist, ageist, racist, and classist analyses that need to be challenged within the feminist press.

Why is it that the words of radical crips connected to disabled, antiableist, and antioppression cultures are not being published? Most women I know who are connected to the antiableism movement have an integrated model of looking at how oppression works within dominant cultures to oppress, exclude, and discriminate against nondominant cultures. Why is it that those of us with those models, words, and viewpoints are not getting published, hired, or allowed access to feminist culture? Because it is simpler and more comfortable to allow in only those disabled women who may be coming from a medical model, as opposed to a cultural model, of disability. It is less threatening and more familiar to have some of your ableist stereotypes validated, and not to be challenged to look at how you participate in ableism in your own life by focusing on images of pity or adoration for overcoming disability. It is less scary not to be presented with your own worst fantasies of becoming disabled or with the knowledge that, at any second, you too could join this oppressed group.

It's time to stop participating in ableism, time for feminists to consider the interruption of plug pulling, genetic screening, and forced institutionalization of old people and people with disabilities. We are not tragic, pitiful, or disgusting. We are alive, kicking and screaming, fighting for our lives, and quite tired of those lives being trivialized, medicalized, infantilized, and romanticized. As radical crips, we are a faction of people with disabilities, and it's time that the feminist press, and not only the feminist disabled press, reflect *our* visions, realities, life experiences, and struggles, too. Stop choosing to showcase those most like your nondisabled selves, and start publishing the words of radical dyke, bi, and hetero crips who are part of the antiableist movement. Stop holding wheelchair-inaccessible, perfume-laden, spoken-English-only events that bar all but the nondisabled, nonallergic, hearing population. Stop bashing radical crips cuz we scare the shit out of you with our strong words, angry demonstrations, and bizarre theories of integration.

My radical crip friends are dying faster than I can keep up with. I know too many who have taken their lives for lack of what's needed to keep living a disabled life. Feminists must stop contributing to this growing backlash against the rights of disabled people to live out our disabled lives in the ways that we choose. Start participating in our struggles and making space on stage, in print, in your homes, schools, and businesses that welcomes, invites, and includes us. Stop making excuses about why not or how come. Just do it. You need us drooling, plugged-in, wheeling radicals to show you just how to survive on a polluted planet where a trip to the 7-11 could result in a trip for a wheelchair fitting. You need us obnoxious, infamous, won't-go-away, mouthy crips to learn more about interdependence and survival. Becoming antiableist is not an act of choice for people with disabilities, or an act of charity for the nondisabled. It's an act of survival for all of us.

© 1995 Marilyn Humphries

© 1995 Ellen Shub

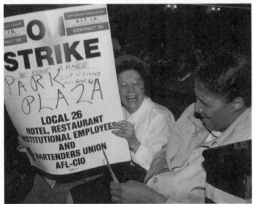

© 1988 Linda Haas

CHAPTER TWO

Economic Injustice

When feminism's second wave began, one issue stood out among all the others: economic discrimination. Married women who didn't work were economically dependent on men, and women who did seek paid employment, either out of necessity or the desire to pursue a career, faced a highly segregated work force, persistently lower wages than men, and few opportunities for advancement. A 1963 report by President Kennedy's Commission on the Status of Women documenting widespread discrimination against women catapulted women into action. Their first victories: the 1963 Equal Pay Act, requiring employers to pay men and women performing the same job duties the same salaries, and Title VII of the 1964 Civil Rights Act. With this act Congress barred all forms of employment discrimination based on race and sex and established the Equal Employment Opportunity Commission (EEOC) to investigate complaints and enforce penalties.

The Equal Pay and Civil Rights Acts have by no means ended economic discrimination against women. In fact, though women have made significant economic strides since the '60s, in 1994, women still earned only 71 cents to every man's dollar. For Black and Latina women the situation was even worse, with Black women earning 65 cents to every man's dollar and Latina women earning 54 cents. During the '80s, Reagan's economic policies increasingly impoverished women. By the mid '90s, one-half of all single-mother families in the United States lived below the poverty line.

In this chapter, we look at the way in which women's economic status has shaped women's lives and the strategies women have used since the '60s to overcome their dependence on men and men's salaries. Although as the statistics suggest, by and large, women are still poor, much has changed for women in the work force. Affirmative action (passed by executive order in 1967) has given women access to a wider range of careers, including the once-exclusively white male skilled trades; unionization and pay equity campaigns have improved women's wages in traditionally female occupations such as nursing, teaching, and clerical work; and antidiscrimination laws have forced employers to hire women without regard to age, marital status, or motherhood. Nonetheless, many women, particularly single mothers with small children, remain outside the work force where they must rely on an inadequate, degrading, humiliating, and increasingly punitive welfare system.

In the mid to late '60s, three different groups of women began to confront the economics of women's lives. The middle-class, liberal women who founded the National Organization for Women concerned themselves with issues such as job discrimination and pay equity; radical feminists began to unravel the relationship between the nuclear family, women's economic dependence on men, and capitalism; and poor women demonstrated, as part of the National Welfare Rights Organization, and organized for changes in the welfare system.

In *Sojourner*'s earliest years, the theoretical concerns of radical feminists, along with the practical concerns of working women, shaped the coverage of economic issues. Women were creating new economic theory, drawing on Marxism and the work of turn-of-the-century feminist Charlotte Perkins Gilman. Gilman wrote a book entitled *Women and Economics* in 1898, in which she explored the history of man's economic domination of woman. Analyzing the "sexuo-economic" relation, which she considered problematic, Gilman wrote: "Woman's economic profit comes through the power of the sex attraction. When we confront this fact boldly and plainly in the open market of vice, we are sick with horror. When we see the same economic relation made permanent, established by law, sanctioned and sanctified by religion, covered with flowers and incense and all accumulated sentiment, we think it innocent, lovely, and right.... But the biological effect remains the same. In both cases the female gets her food from the male by virtue of her sex-relationship to him." As a solution, Gilman suggested that "wives, as earners through domestic service, are entitled to the wages of cooks, housemaids, nursemaids, seamstresses, or housekeepers."

Gilman's work inspired a movement, in the late '60s and early '70s, for "wages for housework" (see Molly Lovelock, "Wages for Housework: The Idea's Everywhere," 1978). Feminist activists involved in various issues from day care to welfare to assisting displaced homemakers (divorced women who have difficulty entering the work force because they lack "job-related" experience) supported the concept, particularly because it could unite women across class boundaries. Whether married to a wealthy man or living as a single mother on welfare, almost all women support the economy through unpaid labor. Not only do men benefit directly through increased leisure time; the entire capitalist system thrives because the caregiving work of wives, mothers, sisters, and girlfriends leaves men free to devote themselves to their places of employment. As Randy Albelda points out in her 1994 article, "The Misogyny of Welfare Reform," any job that pays enough to support a family assumes that there is a wife at home doing limitless unpaid labor, from laundry, shopping, cooking, and cleaning to child care. If women were paid for this labor, their independent income not only would provide protection in cases where their marriages dissolve but would allow them the freedom to raise children on their own. Women would not be penalized for being single mothers.

Wages for housework is a radical concept that continues to have some support in the '90s, particularly among welfare rights advocates. As Pat Gowens points out in "Impoverished Women Pose Solutions" (1993), middle-class feminists have largely abandoned the campaign, putting their efforts into ending workplace discrimination instead. Although these goals are important, feminists have generally ignored the question of who will do the caregiving work. Not all mothers want to work in the paid labor force, especially working-class and poor mothers who have access only to low-wage, service industry jobs. Should these women be punished for staying home to raise their children?

Having failed to address the question of unpaid labor in the home, many working women have found themselves run ragged by the double burden of a full-time job and caring for a family. As Elaine Bell Kaplan notes in "I Don't Do No Windows" (1985), men have not taken up the slack. To lighten the burden of household responsibilities, if they can afford it, middle-class women hire domestic workers: working-class and poor women, very often women of color, who work for low wages in the only jobs available to them.

These employer/employee relationships are fraught with conflict, because, as Kaplan points out, middle-class women have not, for the most part, looked critically at their own role in exploiting a vulnerable female population. When middle-class women employ domestic workers at low wages (without even making required social security payments), refuse to offer their employees benefits such as vacation pay or sick time, and treat them as if they are ignorant, irresponsible, or invisible, these employers undermine the possibility of cross-class and cross-race alliances.

Since the '60s, as more women have entered the labor force (some out of the desire to escape the "domesticity" of the '50s, most out of economic necessity), challenges to gender discrimination in the workplace have become common. As noted above, the 1964 Civil Rights Act called for the creation of the EEOC; by 1969, the EEOC had received 50,000 complaints of gender discrimination. Women filed class action suits as they discovered that they were paid less than men for the same jobs. In 1977, the women of NBC settled for $1.7 million. Similar suits led to major settlements at the *Washington Post,* the *New York Times,* and at publishing houses such as Houghton Mifflin. Women also worked through unions, particularly in the public sector, challenging employers wherever they found that they did not receive "equal pay for equal work." Even so, statistics in the mid '70s revealed that women still earned only 59 cents on the male dollar.

Looking at the statistics, women realized that the wage gap was not simply the result of women being paid less than men for the same work. The real problem was job segregation: across the board, women's jobs paid less than men's jobs. And job segregation, in the '70s, was extreme: 99.2 percent of secretaries were women as were 98.5 percent of dental assistants and 96.7 percent of nurses. Yet less than 10 percent of "skilled workers" and less than 5 percent of top managers were women. Even in fields with more women, such as medicine, women were clustered in lower-paying jobs. A new concept was introduced: comparable worth.

Throughout the '80s, efforts to increase women's wages have focused on comparable worth (see Johanna Brenner, "A Socialist-Feminist Perspective on Pay Equity," 1986). Using this concept, employers reevaluate pay scales according to the skills, responsibilities, and working conditions each job entails. Such reevaluations have been fairly successful when undertaken within the context of a single employer creating a single job evaluation system. However, when an evaluation is done across disparate job categories—for example, the jobs of all public employees—the criteria used may be sex- or class-biased. For example, men's dirt such as grease may be considered a negative working condition, while women's dirt such as bodily fluids is not. Or hazards such as working on scaffolding are measured, but not hazards such as VDT terminals. Equally problematic is the high value given to years of education over skills that may be learned through experience—for example, caretaking (a traditionally female skill) or tree trimming (a traditionally male skill). In each of these cases, the criteria reinforce existing gender and class hierarchies. Thus, in order to create a deeper level of social change, feminists need to reexamine the criteria used in comparable worth studies. As Johanna Brenner points out, when "value to the public" is the primary criteria for determining compensation, pay differentials decrease dramatically.

One of the primary ways in which women have fought for pay equity and other job-related benefits has been through unions. While we often think of unions as organizations of white male construction workers, in the late '70s and early '80s, union campaigns in female-dominated workplaces became more common. As early *Sojourner* articles reflect, clerical workers were among the first to begin such campaigns. Between 1973 and 1974, numerous associations of office workers formed around the country, including Boston's 9 to 5. These groups, which eventually merged and affiliated with the Service Employees International Union, assisted clerical workers in numerous union campaigns, winning major victories at Columbia and Yale universities by the mid '80s and at Harvard University a few years later. Through unions, nurses significantly increased salaries as well as respect for their profession; in recent years, flight attendants, cannery workers, hotel workers (usually men and women of color) have all won significant union victories (see Harneen Chernow and Susan Moir, "Feminism and Labor: Building Alliances," 1990). These victories have been significant, not only because they have provided women workers with the clout to demand higher pay, but because the unions have looked to improve working conditions in other ways as well. For example, the Boston University clerical workers union fought for child care provisions in their contract, Boston hotel workers included language to improve access to affordable housing, and female flight attendants have used their unions to end age, weight, and marriage restrictions that often meant that flight attendants lost their jobs by the time they turned 30. As of the early '90s, the Coalition for Labor Union Women (CLUW), founded in 1974, had over 15,000 members; unions have become a significant player in working women's lives.

Unions have played a role in improving the economic lives of women not only in the United States, but internationally as well. Throughout the world, women tend to be clustered in low-wage sectors of the economy: for example, the garment industry and high-tech assembly plants. In the '80s, under pressure from the World Bank and the International Monetary Fund (IMF) to repay their enormous foreign debts, numerous Third World countries established "free trade zones," or "maquiladoras." In these economic zones, multinational corporations employ cheap Third World labor—usually women—to produce goods that are shipped to the United States duty-free. Maquiladoras generally operate without environmental and labor regulations; the supposedly "submissive" workers are paid a few dollars a day, much less than even nonunionized U.S. workers.

But maquila workers have been organizing around the world for higher wages and better working conditions. The process of politicization that Rebecca Ratcliff describes among Mexican women in "Women United across Borders" (1987) is happening in countries such as Guatemala and the Philippines as well. As in the United States, women in other countries who become active in union struggles begin to challenge male domination in all aspects of their lives, becoming leaders in societies in which they have long played subordinate roles.

Though women have been able to use unions to improve working conditions in some traditionally female occupations, they have not had as great success in prying open the doors to the high-paying unionized trades. Entering the trades was another strategy that U.S. women pursued in the '70s to increase women's economic power—union construction jobs usually paid at least $10 an hour more than the usual service and clerical jobs available to women. Early issues of *Sojourner* include numerous articles about women leaving their office jobs, rolling up their shirt sleeves, and becoming carpenters, masons, and electricians (see Carly Lund, "Women Build Careers in Construction," 1982). Though during the '70s it was difficult to break your way into an apprenticeship program, many women thought the barriers would fall after 1978, when the federal government established quotas for federally funded construction sites: 6.9 percent women on work sites and 20 to 25 percent women in apprenticeship programs. Even with these affirmative action guidelines, however, women have made little headway in the trades. In the early '90s, women were still struggling at 2 percent of the construction labor force, the same percentage they had reached in 1983. As Susan Eisenberg notes in her 1989 article, "Tradeswomen: An Endangered Species?," more than ten years after their initial entry into the trades, women still faced the same isolation and harassment that they did during the early years. Such conditions—which lead not only to loneliness, but danger—drive women to leave their jobs "voluntarily," making it all the more difficult to increase their numbers. As Eisenberg argues, without the support of the women's movement, the situation is unlikely to improve. This is particularly true in the face of a right-wing Congress and Supreme Court intent on dismantling the affirmative action laws that have been used to challenge the exclusively white male domains of construction and other unionized jobs such as firefighting and truckdriving.

Though affirmative action, pay equity, and nondiscrimination laws have improved working conditions for middle-class and some working-class women, the majority of women workers in the '90s continue to be concentrated in low-wage jobs, particularly the rapidly expanding service sector of the economy. As Rebecca Johnson explains in "Do We Kill Ourselves on Purpose?" (1994), Reagan-era economic policies had a particularly disastrous impact on poor and working-class women. Though 19 million jobs were created during the '80s, these were almost entirely minimum-wage jobs, with no benefits. A full-time, minimum-wage job pays $9,360, less than the federal poverty level for a family of two. These are the jobs available to most women, because as Johnson points out, by the end of the Reagan era, the service-sector made up three-quarters of the U.S. economy.

Reagan-era economics affected poor and working-class women in other ways as well. As Kip Tiernan and Fran Froehlich point out in "Homelessness: Crisis or Chronic Condition" (1989), during the '80s, homelessness skyrocketed. Massachusetts had two homeless shelters in 1982; seven years later, in 1989, the state funded 120 shelters. During that same period, 8 million people living in the United States had fallen below poverty level, while the national budget for affordable housing had decreased by 70 percent. Reagan built only 25,000 housing units, as compared to the 300,000 built during the Carter administration. Tiernan and Froehlich estimate that in Massachusetts, 75 percent of the homeless are families and 80 percent of these are living on welfare payments made through Aid to

Families with Dependent Children (AFDC). The homeless, in other words, are primarily poor women and children.

The attack on poor women and children, which began with Reaganomics, continues in the '90s under the guise of "ending welfare as we know it." Welfare was first established during the Depression to help women without husbands stay home and take care of their children. During the late '60s and early '70s, a national welfare rights movement, led primarily by African-American women, successfully lobbied and demonstrated for increases in benefits and an end to some of the most humiliating practices of welfare departments, such as midnight raids in search of men living illegally with women receiving benefits. Unfortunately, internal conflicts led to the dissolution of the National Welfare Rights Organization in the mid '70s, leaving an organizational gap just as the right wing was beginning to flex its muscles. Local organizations survived but did not have the power to resist the dismantling of social services that has marked the '80s and '90s. Today, women who receive public support are blamed for just about every problem we face as a society: poverty, drugs, violence, homelessness, the failure of children in school, and so on. As Randy Albelda argues, however, forcing welfare mothers to take minimum-wage jobs ("workfare") does nothing to relieve poverty among women and children. Nor does it help children who are left alone without the supervision of an adult in neighborhoods that, because of poverty and the despair it brings, have become increasingly violent and dangerous. It does, however, decrease government expenditures, so that the rich can continue to benefit from lower taxes.

Throughout the late '80s and '90s, *Sojourner* charted the increasing impoverishment of women through articles on the shifting nature of the economy, homelessness, and welfare. Responses to these articles have made it evident that tensions have increased between poor mothers who rely on state support for their families' survival and "working" mothers (see Tori Joseph, "Poor Women Need To Take More Responsibility," 1994). Though in the '90s, organizations such as NOW have joined hands with welfare rights organizations to demand a minimum family income, a higher minimum wage, affirmative action, and affordable day care and health care, feminists have not been immune to the increasingly conservative public rhetoric that blames mothers who receive welfare for the failures of public policy. Women, however, cannot afford to divide ranks. The current attacks on poor women are part of the larger right-wing agenda to force women to realize that they cannot survive without the support of a male "bread-winner." Now, more than ever, feminists need to build alliances between middle-class and poor women by developing an economic agenda that meets the needs of all women.

MARCH 1978

Wages for Housework: The Idea's Everywhere

by Molly Lovelock

The labor which the wife performs in the household is given as part of her functional duty, not as employment. The wife of the poor man, who works hard in a small house, doing all the work for the family, or the wife of the rich man, who wisely and gracefully manages a large house and administers its functions, each is entitled to fair pay for services rendered. To take this ground and hold it honestly, wives, as earners through domestic service, are entitled to the wages of cooks, housemaids, nursemaids, seamstresses, or housekeepers.
—Charlotte Perkins Gilman, *Women and Economics*, 1898

Wages for housework is not a new idea. Virginia Woolf suggests it in *The Three Guineas* (1938). Women of the Paris Commune proposed it during the French Revolution. A "housework analysis" was crucial for early theorists of the modern women's movement. As a broad perspective, "wages for housework" has influenced almost every feminist issue, from abortion to displaced homemakers to workplace organizing.

Wages for housework demands us to look at women's work and at women's lack of money. The facts are familiar to many of us: a 1970 survey by Chase Manhattan Bank showed that wives of Wall Street employees work 99.6 hours a week in the home, performing services that would cost $257.53 on the open market. (Poorer women presumably spend even more time on housework, with fewer babysitters and appliances, more mending and budget food preparation.) Without money of our own, women are often trapped. Unpaid work is "worthless"—as experience in finding a paid job, in "economic terms" (no one includes it in the GNP) and for self-value in a money-oriented society. Economic dependence has kept many women in intolerable marriages.

Within the general wages for housework perspective are many approaches and groups seeking economic security for houseworkers: the Martha Movement, welfare rights organizers, social security activists, displaced homemakers.

One approach calls itself "Wages for Housework," a source of confusion since they are only one of a number of people and groups proposing wages. Also referred to as "Power of Women Collectives," they have branches in this country and abroad. Selma James, one of the leading spokespeople for this group, coauthored *The Power of Women and the Subversion of the Community* (Falling Wall Press, 1973, 1975), with Italian Mariarosa Dalla Costa.

Dalla Costa provides some of the underlying framework for the ideology of the "Wages for Housework" group. From a Marxist-feminist perspective, she stresses the housewife's indispensable role in capitalism: "[T]he figure of the boss is concealed behind that of the husband. He appears to be the sole recipient of domestic service, and this gives an ambiguous and slavelike character to housework. The husband and children, through their loving involvement, their loving blackmail, become the first foremen, the immediate controllers of this labor." The housewife provides labor (ironing work clothes, packing lunches), emotional bandages (calming her husband after a hard day), and future labor power (raising children). All these directly benefit big business and bosses; therefore, capitalism should pay women a wage.

Other feminists, though, see this approach as too narrow. Big business, bosses, and the structure of paid labor are, for them, one aspect of patriarchy. Housework does benefit capitalism but also provides real services and leisure time for husbands.

Betsy Warrior and Lisa Leghorn in the *Houseworker's Handbook* (Women's Center, 1974), provide some of the key arguments for this perspective. As members of Cell 16, one of the original feminist groups in the late '60s, they proposed a number of ideas associated with the current wave of feminism. Betsy Warrior's 1969 article "Reasons for Houseworkers to Unite" first urged compensation for housework.

The *Houseworker's Handbook* doesn't compromise: it states right out that unpaid work is usually considered slavery. "When slavery applies to the female it's invisible, a 'natural' role, a 'biological' condition that's taken for granted: wife, domestic." Leghorn and Warrior don't believe that housewives and mothers are too lofty and sacred to be paid. "If receiving a wage for your work is mercenary and wrongheaded (as certainly many men will hotly proclaim in the instance of housework) then let these men undertake a serious campaign against wages being paid for any and all work not just women's work." They know the benefits housework provides men, particularly leisure time. "Time is a birthright we're all given. But women give up much of this birthright to men. In every field, men have profited from this in direct proportion to what women have lost." And they stress that unpaid work degrades women more generally—for instance, in determining suitable jobs and salaries for women in the paid labor force. With the article "Battered Wives" and her later "Working on Wife Abuse," Betsy Warrior focused attention throughout the country on battered women. She emphasized that wife-beating is the "occupational hazard" of the housewife without independent income.

The poor woman in the quote from Charlotte Perkins Gilman works just as hard as the rich. The *Houseworker's Handbook* points out: "Your wages shouldn't depend on your husband's wages, as your work is independent of his. If he left you or died, you would still have almost the same amount of work to do. Your income should not be dependent either on the kind of man you are with (rich man, poor man, drunkard, gambler, etc.) or your ability to get a man. This is inconsistent and unfair and forces women into relationships for reasons other than personal compatibility."

A "wage" as a percentage of the husband's salary doesn't really provide independence either, for the wife still relies on him to pay her. Most wages for housework advocates stress that the government could pay women. For instance, the family allowance in England pays all mothers, based on the number of children. In richer families, this "income" is returned to the government in taxes. Meanwhile, however, the woman directly controls some money.

Lisa Leghorn and Kathy Parker in "Towards a Feminist Perspective of Women in the Economy" (unpublished manuscript) use the *perspective* of wages for housework to reveal women's universal lack of economic power. Women in China get no workpoints for household chores. In Sweden, despite laws and social reform for women's equality, housewives still have the major responsibility for work in the home; child care spaces are limited. Parker and Leghorn stress that, although unpaid labor oppresses women everywhere, strategies (of which payment for housework is one) must reflect the specific economy and culture.

Almost all feminist organizing, in fact, recognizes the burden of unpaid housework. Day care advocates know childrearing is a *job,* deserving payment and support. Welfare rights organizers stress that women should earn a living wage. Activists against world hunger point out the role of women in subsistence agriculture, unsupported by governments or development programs. Wives of wealthy men are at refuges for battered women, with no resources for escape. For workplace organizers, unpaid housework contributes to women's low job status, and by creating a "second shift" in the home, makes union work difficult for many women.

Some feminists see wages for housework as a poor strategy, one that could be used to keep women in the home. Others feel that housework is real work and women should be paid for it. Whatever we think about strategies of wages for housework, though, the overall perspective has influenced us all.

AUGUST 1985

"I Don't Do No Windows"
by Elaine Bell Kaplan

Despite the fact that Black domestic workers have been pioneers among U.S. working women, they have received little feminist attention. Their work experience, however, provides important insights into the interactions among racism, classism, and sexism—and between Black and white women.

This essay is based on interviews I conducted with white, middle-class women (and their husbands) who employ domestics, women who work as domestics, and the daughters of both. Interviewing the white women first, I found that to many of them, the domestics, or "housekeepers," were just faceless and nameless lower-class women. I then interviewed the women who worked as domestics, asking open-ended questions about what it means "to work for a white, middle-class woman in her home." Gradually, certain patterns emerged that reminded me of all the women I knew who work as domestics, including my mother, who is still working at 72.

My interviews convinced me that domestic work involves more than the usual friction between employers and employees of different classes. It struck me that the women involved break the normative pattern of work by employing or working for other women—and that they have much in common with each other. After all, both housewife and domestic are expected to service and maintain men and children, and both are dependent on the wages of a man. In fact, the housewives' husbands indicated that they see their wives and maids as "interchangeable." When asked, "Who does the housework in your home?" one husband said to me, "When the maid doesn't come or doesn't finish her work, I tell her to just leave it—my wife will finish it."

My interviews indicated that in this situation many housewives seek to maintain class and race privileges vis-à-vis their domestics—and thus collude with the patriarchal and capitalist system that oppresses both groups of women. My research drew out several "housewife power strategies" that support the going social order and structure of privilege. Yet, for both groups, paid and family work blend together, creating an unending day of caring for and waiting on others. When the maid cannot work, the housewife must.

The Haves and the Have-Nots

The history of Black women as domestic workers is rooted in the slave legacy. Slave women were engaged in the "double day" long before it became common among free families. In fact, as Julie Matthaei has noted, since the earliest days of slavery, Black women have "combined personal service and skilled production" *(An Economic History of America,* Scholar Books, 1982). After emancipation, domestic work was one of the few occupations open to Black women in the South; in the North, white immigrants dominated domestic work until immigration was stopped during World War II.

Although it was after the war that large numbers of Black women began working as domestics in the North, as early as 1935, Black journalists happened upon a scene in New York City they called the "Bronx Slave Market." Dozens of Black women gathered early every morning to parade in front of wealthy housewives who came to "buy their strength and energy for an hour, two hours, or even a day at the rate of fifteen, twenty, or, if luck would be with them, thirty cents an hour." Under the watchful eye of the housewife, the women would be permitted to scrub floors on bended knees, hang precariously from the windowsills of mansions, luxurious apartments, and modest middle-class homes, and strain and sweat over steaming tubs of heavy blankets, spreads, and furniture covers. They were rewarded for their day's work with a single dollar bill, if that: "More often, the clock is set back an hour or more. Too often she is sent away without pay at all."

Today, 172,000 Black women give personal service as domestics in private households, at pay that is still very low. (My mother and most of the maids I interviewed earn between $3,000 and $6,000 per year, about $5 an hour). And, like the women of the Bronx Slave Market, they do not receive health care, sick days, or paid vacations, unless, as one woman said to me, "Mrs. Coleman is going away or it's a big one like Thanksgiving or Christmas." In addition, they are expected—like slave women—to serve the personal needs of their employers "in a civilized manner, respecting the social ways of their owners," in Matthaei's words.

Today's employers of domestic workers have the privilege of hiring these women to do, as one said, "cleaning and other things I don't want to do." In fact, some of the housewives I interviewed have always counted on these women to service them: "We always had what we used to call maids.... I don't want to give you the impression that we were that wealthy ... my mother would just contract these women.... For a long time we had women who lived in the house, who helped take care of the house and helped take care of the kids." Housewives hire domestic workers so that they can pursue career and leisure activities: "I have an awful lot of help. The housekeeper does the things I don't want to do. If you want to have children and have a career, I can't think of any other way to do it."

All of the housewives I interviewed said that the housekeeper helps them because their husbands will not. One woman recalled growing up in a household where housekeepers did everything for her; she was "shocked" to find, when she married, that she was expected to clean the house: "My dear, I never made a bed in my life until I got married.... I was almost incompetent in a lot of ways: never cooked, never washed, never picked up my clothes because they were gone when I got up. So marriage was, physically speaking, a harsh blow. When I woke up...the same things were there that were there the night before." She complimented her housekeeper: "[She] is excellent. She does everything—the cleaning, the meal planning, the marketing—and knows what's going on in the house. She keeps this place very clean, which is a big thing because I am very fussy."

These women's statements touch the very heart of my argument. The housewife, or a woman she supervises, is expected to cook and clean, but her husband is not. The domestic worker enables the middle-class woman to avoid a confrontation with her spouse about sharing household duties; she serves as "middle woman" between he who has power and she who needs it. But her presence emphasizes the fact that women—all women—are responsible for cleaning the house, at the same time that it releases the housewife to become a lady of leisure or a career woman.

The domestic worker, whose labor represents the convergence of racism, classism, and sexism, reminds us that women's increasing entry into the labor market does not necessarily mean liberation. For the most part, these women extensively or totally support their families on their wages. Most of the maids I knew or interviewed had to raise four or five children; my mother's salary went a long way in helping maintain seven children on my parents' low income.

Of course, modern technology has changed housework to some extent. My mother does not have to scrub floors on her knees like the women of the Bronx Slave Market, and domestic workers like Ella Mae Robinson clean rugs with vacuum cleaners and put dishes into a dishwasher while clothes tumble dry. Now, Ella Mae says, "I get a good deal of work done in one day" (in fact, she cleans two houses daily). She describes a typical day: "I work as quickly as I can. I dust all the rooms, vacuum, mop the kitchen, clean the bathrooms and cabinets, put dishes in the dishwasher, and do some ironing. Many times I have to take the clothes to the cleaners, feed the cat, wash the woodwork, and pick up the clothes off the floor and off the chairs. Most women like me and this Christmas I got a blouse."

But the new appliances have caused Ella Mae to speed up, and in working for two employers, she is subjected to two totally different sets of whims and moods. And, typically, Ella Mae does the dirtiest, most dangerous, and most physically demanding work in the house, lifting furniture, cleaning away large amounts of trash, and using harsh chemical cleaners. The wife, if she helps at all, establishes her race and class difference by ordering the maid to handle items like oven cleaner, wax remover, and painting materials while she rearranges closets and shelves.

The women I interviewed did not in any way feel that they have the right to decide what to do or when and how to do it. The housewives give them a list of chores and, in addition, tell them which cloth should clean the silverware and how many different types of polishes they must use in the bathroom and on sinks and kitchen floors. In this way, the madam is able to show the maid who is in charge and, at the same time, deny her work experience. Over the years, Ella Mae has tried to "tell 'em, 'Don't give me no list. I know what to do.' But they keep right on doin' it. It makes me feel like I don't know how to work. I have to keep askin' her for the next thing to do. It slows me down and then I have to work real hard to get done by the end of the day."

The casual nature of the maid's work sets her up to do whatever the housewife wants; she may have to act as a secretary or babysit children without any additional compensation. My mother decided not to take jobs where children were involved. "They make you stay with the kids while they go to the movies and you can't say anything about it. And they tell you they gonna come back at eight, and they come back at ten, and you have to go home to your own kids. They don't care.... And money don't vary no matter how much extra I work." The fact of no extra pay for extra work was a recurring theme in my interviews.

In general, the housewife sets the wages and conditions of work according to her own preferences, knowing the maid's dependence on her job, which is often her family's only source of income. Domestics have little opportunity to influence hiring and firing practices or to establish minimum working conditions. The communication that would be necessary to make changes in their work conditions and relationships never occurs; neither the domestic nor the housewife verbalizes tensions. The reason for the maids' silence is clear. It is not that they are deferential: they are trapped by racism, sexism, and the class system. What is left unsaid between the domestic worker and her employer enhances what I call the "housewife power strategies."

Space as a Power Strategy

Each weekday morning, Ella Mae Robinson takes the bus across town to her employer's home. Once the Black woman leaves the Black community, she encounters cultural differences which suggest that she can no longer be completely at home. She must make some kind of change in the way she acts. She must compromise. Trudier Harris has found that of all the elements that govern the Black domestic's interaction with the white world, "space, with its implications both physical and cultural," is perhaps the foremost:

The black woman is presumably at home in her own environment; but when she enters the white woman's kitchen, she moves into a culture which is at least apart from her own, if not alien or openly hostile. Black town and white town have metaphorical connotations as well as physical dimensions.... [W]hen she immerses herself in the white culture, she loses the psychological security derived from familiar surroundings and must make adjustments accordingly. (From Mammies to Militants: Domestic Service in Industrializing America, University of Illinois Press, 1981)

Ella Mae Robinson realizes that once she opens the door to her employer's middle-class home, she has to conform to a script written out by her mother's mother and her mistress's mother and grandmother. She also knows that the madam believes that however "motherly" her maid, she is not "like one of the family." (Most of the women I interviewed wondered how any employer "gets away with saying we are part of the family," as one put it.) So both women take their places on the one terrain where they share powerlessness: the family home. The cleaning lady readies her pots and pans in the kitchen, while the housewife sits at her desk in the den writing down her list of instructions, ready to confront this woman with whom she shares so much—yet who is so different.

Paid domestic work in other people's homes involves exposure to the particular frustrations and resentments generated by extreme asymmetry in power and wealth. In the private home of the housewife, the maid is not a person. For example, the housewife can strategize to separate herself from the domestic. Harris writes about employers who establish the kitchen—or, as she calls it, a "Niggers room" associated with cleaning supplies, food, and dirt—as the space in which the domestic must stay most of the day when she is not cleaning the other rooms. The Black woman cleans the living room, dining room, bedroom, or bathroom, then retires to "her room." There she sits when she has time for sitting, and there she waits for requests that she go to other parts of the house. One white woman I interviewed wondered why, when she was at a relative's home for dinner, her cousin's maid did not join them in the living room. "I thought she couldn't possibly be working in the kitchen all the five or six hours I was there."

The housewife, however, has the right to enter the domestic's designated turf whenever she feels the need—for instance, to strike up a conversation. Since the domestic is not considered a person, she is sometimes required to listen to the housewife's discussion of her personal business. Yet, as one woman put it, "You're not supposed to have an ear or to understand. Or they'll discuss racial issues, talking about how 'they' are trying to move into the neighborhood. You're not supposed to hear that, either." Louise Jackson, a twenty-year veteran of domestic service, confronts this problem all the time. Her strategy, she says, is to "keep my views to myself."

When I asked my mother to explain what domestic work is all about, she hesitated. In all those years of rising early in the morning to catch the bus and coming home late in the evening after serving food at numerous cocktail parties, she had never been asked about her job. "How do you get along with them?" I finally asked. "Do they talk to you about their family and do you talk about your family to them?" My mother answered, "I have to listen to them, but I don't talk. It's none of their business. When they ask me how I'm doing, I say, 'just fine.' That's all I say. They want to know my business so that they can tell their friends."

My mother's experience is not that different from other domestic workers'—all of whom saw their work as alienating. For example, when I described my mother's feelings about her work to several domestics, they nodded their heads in agreement. One maid said, "Yes, I can believe it. Most likely she spends her whole day responding to her employer with head nods or one-liners like, 'Yes, I understand,' or, 'No, I don't,' or, 'How nice.' If it's a personal issue, she says, 'It's too bad.' She makes all the appropriate responses—like a robot who is not expected to have feelings or ideas."

Actually, I saw my mother's response as a strategy of her own in which she had the power to keep her personal life away from the housewife. Domestics have other strategies, as well, like passing around stories about their experience. In fact, Alice Childress wrote a novel about her experience as a domestic, and authors like Toni Morrison and Alice Walker have peppered their work with characters who are domestics. Other women, less educated or less inclined to write their stories, will use other strategies. For instance, although they generally work alone, some domestics—usually those women who work in apartment buildings—will go out of their way to meet other domestics in the laundry room or in the elevator. According to my mother and other domestics I interviewed, they pass the time advising each other on bad and good employers and how to handle them. A few domestics will praise the housewife who, one woman said, "really treats me well—we respect each other." The domestic may also demand that the housewife call her "Mrs. James," while she calls the housewife "Grace." Although this is not a common occurrence, several employers I interviewed mentioned that they were expected to address their maids this way.

Appearance as a Power Strategy

Another strategy that the housewife uses to separate herself from the maid is to affect an appearance different from the domestic's. While the housewife chooses whatever she wants to wear, she keeps the domestic worker dressed as a charwoman, especially when she is working backstage—in the kitchen. But once the domestic worker is at front stage—say, at parties—she is expected to represent her employer's class status (although not her sex, hence the uniform). Trudier Harris notes:

> Just as cleaning and cooking are expected, so too is a certain physical appearance. The maid is expected, for example,....to wear a uniform, which aside from its practical functions symbolically negates individuality. When the black woman takes off the clothes in which she has ridden the train or bus to her job and puts on that uniform she becomes the maid, not somebody's mother or sister or wife. Her primary function is to serve the needs of the family which has thus defined her. (Ibid., 1981)

While many maids do not wear uniforms today, they are still expected to wear "some depersonalized dress." When maids are not on stage, the uniform is designed to eliminate all sense of them "as women, as sexual beings," Harris points out.

According to the maids I interviewed, clothing is a real source of conflict. Usually they wear old housedresses that add years to their age: I recall going to meet my mother once at work and being surprised when she came to the door wearing an old, faded housedress. This was not the same woman I had seen leaving the house earlier. Ella Mae Robinson talked about the way her employer reminds her of the dress code: "Honey, you could hear Mrs. C gettin' all excited and makin' a big deal over my clothes. I hate to have to answer her questions about why I'm 'looking extra pretty today.' She makes sure I get them clothes off before she moves one step."

The dress code is a device to enhance the separation of the wife from the domestic. I suggest that this strategy helps alleviate the housewife's feelings of powerlessness: after all, the domestic worker and her employer are really "interchangeable." The construction of appearance, like the division of space (and the gift-giving strategy I will discuss), works to make the maid experience her inequality. At a deeper level, these strategies also serve to emphasize the madam's claim to femininity; definitions of femininity are class-bound, and the attributes of helplessness and delicacy are applicable only to a comparatively small number of females of the dominant class, "the mass of women beneath them being compelled to undertake many forms of strenuous and unladylike activity," in Jacklyn Cock's words *(Maids and Madams,* Raven Press, 1980).

The Gift-Giving Strategy

Loyalty, awareness of another's power, and the notion of reward are all elements of gift giving. Marcel Mauss, in fact, has called it an alternative to war—an interpretation that can be applied to housewife gift giving. Domestic service, of course, reveals the vast and frustrating difference between maids' standards of living and their employers', a rare work situation. As Cock has pointed out, constant exposure to what other people have, and what she herself does not have, can be called the essential job experience of the domestic servant.

My mother's tiny apartment was overloaded with expensive sheets, blankets, dresses, and shoes that obviously cost more than the $50-per-month rent we paid. Such gifts create what Trudier Harris calls the "grossly absurd" incongruity of living in a tiny walk-up apartment, barely able to make rent or refrigerator payments, yet eating expensive meats and owning countless decorative bowls. These handouts—or "service pans," as they were called in slavery days—are considered job benefits by housewives, who may also use them to resolve guilt about their wealth: "I certainly feel that I have more than enough food and clothing here, and she must need some of these things. I don't mind sharing them. We are so fortunate, you know, and these things are still good. I think it cheers her up."

The gifts are also designed to discourage requests for increases in domestics' usually meager pay. One housewife, however, thought that her maid did not deserve gifts: "Every maid we have seems to have some kind of attitude. I just don't understand it. So we give them things to keep them pleasant. We understand their situation. But boy, oh boy, we give them a lot." After all, this woman's thoughts probably run, the Black woman who works for her should be grateful for the privilege. To request more money is to be ungrateful and uppity; it means stepping out of place, an injustice recognized by cleaning women like Ella Mae Robinson. She realizes that the hand-me-down dresses and leftover food she receives as "gifts" cannot possibly compensate for the physical deterioration of the body—for the bad backs and feet and varicose veins—that inevitably results from a maid's hard work. (My mother literally shuffles after 40 years of working on her feet.)

Here I want to stress that, on some level, the housewife suspects the maid of envying her status and wealth. And given the class and race position of the two women, it is safe to say that the housewife is quite satisfied with the status quo and wants nothing more than to maintain it. The "have-not," the maid, is apt to be less satisfied. As George Foster writes, there is "growing fear in the middle and upper classes of the consequences of the envy of the lower classes, of minority ethnic groups," because, he notes, an inferior can take from a superior only through an aggressive act. Thus, the superior who suspects that her servant is envious "fears the evil eye." She worries about being seen eating an expensive dinner or wearing expensive clothes; she fears "outright attack." Gifts like Ella Mae's blouse should therefore be seen as the housewife's superficial attempt to soothe the domestic's feelings, to alleviate her possible hostility and envy. At the same time, however, the housewife uses the blouse to reinforce her class privileges, since Ella Mae cannot reciprocate.

The Invisible Family

Like slave families, the families of domestic workers lose out because the employer's needs take priority. I recall my mother's late-night phone calls requesting that someone pick her up at the bus stop, and some women I interviewed expressed resentment at having to serve at cocktail parties that extended well into the evening. The housewife has the ability—the right, she assumes—to maintain that her family's needs and desires come first. Of all the strategies she employs, this is certainly the most exploitative, and its impact is cross-generational.

For example, in Ella Mae Robinson's family, and my own, the eldest daughter (generally not the son) is assigned the care and feeding of her sisters and brothers until the mother returns. This kind of arrangement sets the daughter up in direct competition with her mother over who defines what has to be done when. Many daughters of domestics talked about the conflict that results. One said, "I could boss my sisters and brothers around during the day, but when my mother got home, she never would say that I did a good job. She would immediately find something I did wrong. By the time I was fifteen years old, I was sick of taking care of kids. And I never could play with the other kids."

Her story touched a chord in me. As the oldest daughter, I watched over my sisters and brothers and managed to boss them around a great deal. I remember cooking dinners for them when Mrs. Brown decided that she needed my mother to serve at her parties, and I recall, at twelve, scolding my brothers and sisters like a good mother when they did not follow my orders. My extremely fussy attitude led to several major arguments with my mother over who should establish rules for the children. My mother disagreed sometimes and gave in others.

At the time, it was not clear to me or to my mother why we had to grapple with these problems. But my role as a surrogate mother matched that of girls in nineteenth-century Britain, who were expected to contribute indirectly to the economic maintenance of their households by acting as "little mothers" to the younger children. Jacklyn Cock observes of this pattern:

[T]he mother's two economic roles as wage-earner and as housewife frequently conflicted, and when the demands of outside work had to be put first, her female children automatically took over the household duties, which involved not only the housework and cooking but also the tending and care of the younger members, as well as nursing the sick members of the family. Thus, to allow the mother to go to work, the elder female children frequently had to relinquish the opportunity of going to school and stay home , (Ibid., 1980).

Another point that came up in my interviews is the stigmatization of Black domestic workers by their own families. Many of the domestics' daughters recalled that when they were children, long before they had any sense of why their mothers had to do domestic work, they were ashamed to tell anyone about their mothers' jobs. One woman said that her mother worked as a secretary, and I shudder to think I used to tell people my mother was a housewife—I was so embarrassed.

Yet, in my interviews, the housewives' daughters often stereotyped the domestic as a matriarch or tower of strength—tender, kind, tough, and supportive (in some cases, more supportive of them than their own mothers). Although they generally did not know much about their maids' families, one daughter said that she felt her mother did not want her to know about the domestic's family: "If I asked our housekeeper any questions about her family, my mother would frown." Most of the daughters claimed to "love the maid like a second mother," as one put it. And they believed that the maids loved them—so much that they would happily render free psychological counseling to both daughter and mother. Some women said that they could talk to the maid when they could not talk to anyone else.

We All Know Who the Boss Is

It is well known that white men used Black slave women as sexual partners, and accounts of domestic workers having to "give it up" to their employers' husbands are common. But the women I interviewed did not talk about sexual relationships with their employers' husbands; it may not be a problem for them, or they may not be willing to talk about it. They did mention sexual harassment, however. For example, when my mother was younger she was harassed quite often in full view of party guests and the madam. The husband, everyone suggested, was "joking around" or "too drunk" to be held responsible for his actions. And, according to my mother, the madam "pretended not to notice." (Actually, I suspect Mrs. Brown took one look at this cleaning woman in her matronly dress and decided that she could not count—as a woman. Then again, perhaps the housewife cannot afford to notice that the cleaning woman is a woman, too.)

The employer's husband may also figure in the maid's strategies to keep the housewife in her place. In fact, Ella Mae Robinson credited herself with knowing "who the real boss is." She took it upon herself to tell me that domestics know that the housewife's husband, not the madam, has the ultimate power—and that they will use that knowledge to their advantage. One domestic worker said, "Whenever Mrs. Jones tells me to wash the windows, I wait until Mr. Jones is home. I tell him that I didn't want to bother Mrs. Jones, but I can't wash no windows. He understands and takes care of it."

A housewife I interviewed told me: "I was uncomfortable about having maids, because I got out of the university with this very socialist/Marxist idea we were not supposed to hire maids. But we needed one, so I hired a Black woman to live in. I didn't want her to dress in dirty clothes—I gave her my clothes so that she would look nice in the house. But my husband opposed my dishing out food for this lady—he said that she had to take food out of the pot herself. She started to take advantage of me—I suppose she saw that he was in control, and she totally disregarded me. I couldn't get her to do anything. I told my husband, 'I think part of the problem is that she sees you obviously controlling me, that I have no power.' I said to him, 'Please don't relate to the maid. Let me do it.' But he wouldn't keep out of it."

As long as women feel powerless, they will continue to abuse other, more vulnerable women. They will have to see the way in which they reinforce their oppression by acting in concert with male domination. They will have to understand that both of them are—maids. I reported earlier one man's response to my question, "Who does the housework for your family?" Now I want to add another man's typical reply to that question: "Oh, the cleaning? The housekeeper or my wife does a great deal, because I just don't notice the dirt."

Conclusion

The "housewife power strategies" I've described push the domestic into a corner and may entrap her daughter, and she has to evolve strategies of her own. These two sets of strategies create a push-pull dynamic that has deep impact, yet is so subtle that the women may not grasp what is really going on in their struggle with each other.

This tension between domestics and housewives would certainly be lessened by a domestics' union. But organizing and unionizing will not completely change how domestics are treated by women with more privileges, privileges that lead to assumed "rights" and to collusion with the real oppressors. And Angela Davis's suggestion that business firms hire out domestics, thus eliminating the personal aspects of the housewife-maid relationship, might mean lower wages for them. In addition, such business arrangements take out of the hands of domestic workers what little control they have: they cannot decide when or where to work. But if the domestic worker does not gain more control over the oppressive work relationship I have described in this essay, I predict that the same kind of interaction will occur between clerical workers, who are increasingly young Black women, and office managers, the majority of whom are middle-class white women.

I think this essay suggests some answers to a question I am often asked: "Why are Black women staying away from the feminist movement?" Some people assume that Black women's issues are different from those of the movement, and to some degree this is true. But we need to look more closely at why Black women who must work all day for white women may not want to join them in supporting feminist causes, even when they really believe in women's rights. This point is painfully clear in an incident that Audre Lorde recounted in her essay, "The Uses of Anger: Women Responding to Racism" (*Sister Outsider,* Crossing Press, 1984): "I wheel my two-year-old daughter in a shopping cart through a supermarket in Eastchester in 1967, and a little white girl riding past in her mother's cart calls out excitedly, 'Oh look, Mommy, a baby maid!'" The mother did not correct her child, Lorde notes. What we need, I propose, is further exploration of the interaction between Black and white women in order to understand why we have never had a "sisterhood." I suggest this essay as only a beginning, a chance to open the other eye, so to speak, to how women treat women.

Author's note: I want to thank for their valuable comments on this essay the Berkeley Women of Color Collective, Lewis Kaplan, Maresi Nerad, Anne Stolz, and Lucy DePertuis. I'm also grateful to Arlie Russell Hochschild, whose project on dual-work families was the source of the housewife interviews.

This essay also appeared in Competition: A Feminist Taboo, *edited by Helen Longino and Valerie Miner (Feminist Press, 1987).*

APRIL 1986

A Socialist-Feminist Perspective on Pay Equity
by Johanna Brenner

Comparable worth adds an important new dimension to women's struggle for economic equality. It raises issues not raised by either "equal pay for equal work" or affirmative action demands. Most important, comparable worth focuses attention on the systematic devaluation of women's work and the connection of that devaluation to more general denigration of women and womanly activities (the overvaluation of male skills and the lack of recognition given to skills, such as nurturance and sensitivity, associated with femininity). By attacking directly the question of how skill is defined, comparable worth allows a revaluation of many "nonelite" jobs—jobs that require relatively low levels of formal education—and, therefore, of jobs done by the vast majority of women who have a high school or community college education. By focusing on skill, effort, responsibility, and complexity of jobs, and by comparing jobs right across the board, comparable worth can be applied to the work of all women, helping to raise the pay of women in clerical, pink-, and blue-collar jobs.

So what's wrong with "comparable worth"? Nothing, so long as we are careful about how we argue for it and organize around it. Thus far, arguments for comparable worth have accepted the basic hierarchical organization of power and prestige in capitalist society and the vast differences in the opportunity for self-expression, rewarding work, and life chances between a small elite and the majority. If we hope to build a movement that includes working-class women and women of color and asserts a vision of society in which people live in equality and mutual respect, then we need to pay special attention to challenging those structures that perpetuate inequality and the ideas that justify hierarchy.

Most campaigns for comparable worth aim only to distribute people meritocratically into a hierarchy of jobs, to decide where women's jobs should be on the ladder—should a secretary get paid more or less than a truck driver? A favorite theme of comparable worth campaigns is to compare nurses to skilled male blue-collar workers: in the Denver campaign, a common example involved nurses and tree trimmers, and a recent pamphlet by the Democratic National Committee Women's Task Force compared nurses and sign painters. The message is that nurses are smarter because they are more educated—what an outrage it is that smart nurses are paid less than dumb tree trimmers! There is often an unwarranted assumption that educated people are smarter or more motivated or more *something* than less-educated people. One "proof" of the need for comparable worth often used by feminists is that a woman with a college education makes as much on average as a male high school dropout; the "inequality" here is that "smart" women get paid less than uneducated men. But this kind of elitism can easily be turned around on women and divide us. If nurses are smarter than truck drivers, then aren't nurses also smarter than secretaries? Than waitresses?

Comparable worth studies do take into account more than education in evaluating jobs and may help raise the pay of women with rather "low" levels of formal education who do jobs demanding responsibility and requiring skills: we all know how crucial the clerical staff is to any organization. One of the major breakthroughs of comparable worth is that it helps make the contributions of women's work visible. Nonetheless, I would also argue that if we uncritically accept the terms within which most job evaluation studies are done, we will tend to divide women by class and race, allowing comparable worth remedies for women's low pay actually to increase the gap between women managers and professionals and other women workers, as well as between white women workers and working women of color.

Traditional job evaluation systems rate supervision of other workers and handling finances high as measures of "responsibility." This tends to reinforce the higher pay of managerial positions compared to other women's jobs that also involve responsibility—for instance, child care work. Working conditions and "effort" are generally weighted much lower than responsibility or skill. There is reason to expect that comparable worth adjustments will favor clerical workers compared to women in service and manual work.

While Black and Latina women have gained clerical jobs over the last decade, Third World women are still much more concentrated in service and operative jobs (38 percent of Black women and Latina women, compared to 24 percent of white women).

One remedy is to challenge the schemes themselves—the factors used, how they are weighted, and so on. But, while certainly necessary, this strategy alone remains insufficient. It shifts even more control over bargaining to technical experts in union offices and/or government commissions. The less control workers have over the implementation of comparable worth, the more easily employers will use it in politically divisive ways. For example, the state of Washington will implement a comparable worth program over ten years during which the wages of auto mechanics will be frozen or granted small increases, while the salaries of nurses (found to be underpaid relative to the mechanics) will rise until they reach parity. In a successful strike by women clerical workers at Yale, on the other hand, the union used the idea of comparable worth to argue for their right to higher pay without tying their salaries to a job evaluation scheme or to the wages of other workers.

Comparable worth campaigns are necessarily limited because they are aimed at sorting and selecting among jobs. Yet, if a job were judged in terms of its value to the process of production or to the public, then all jobs would be much more equal. For example, the secretary, the orderly, and the lab tech are just as necessary as the nurse and the doctor to deliver care to the patient. Workers whose jobs do not take a long time to learn (e.g., sanitation workers) certainly do worthwhile work. In addition, it seems to me we ought to contest the idea that people's income should be determined by where they fit in a corporate hierarchy. Pay is necessary for our survival and ought to be determined by our needs. Simply because men have laid claim to higher pay than women in the name of their "breadwinner" role is no reason for women to abandon the demand for pay to meet our needs, regardless of the kind of work we do.

As long as pay differentials exist, comparable men's and women's jobs should be paid equally. But feminists need to go further than this. We do not agree that a woman secretary should make half the pay of a woman manager because male managers make twice as much as male stockroom clerks. A movement that intends to speak for all women can hardly afford to accept such inequalities in opportunity and position between us. When comparable worth studies open pay scales up to negotiation, feminists ought to be arguing for reduced pay differentials between *all* workers as a key part of the changes.

Finally, feminists need to think about more than the pay attached to most women's jobs. We have to address the quality of the jobs women have. If we're looking at the work people do, then let's ask whether those jobs are productive, safe, and interesting, as well as how much they pay. Sometimes we are so busy trying for parity with men that we ignore the limitations of what most men have. Traditional male jobs pay more, but many are boring, dirty, and dangerous. Women's rights that we should be raising in comparable worth campaigns include not only pay equity and the right to traditional male jobs but also the right to meaningful, safe work. We need to pay attention to the routinization and de-skilling facing many women clerical workers and the threat that mechanization will eliminate their jobs—a threat that may increase as comparable worth gains lead to clerical wage raises. Finally, we need to ask whether the jobs women are doing—and the "comparable" jobs done by men— allow us to use our talents and skills and to develop new ones. These are issues that can be addressed now, and not only in some visionary future. A society as wealthy and productive as the United States can provide all of us with rewarding work.

Excerpted from the original.

AUGUST 1982

Women Build Careers in Construction
by Carly Lund

One hundred and fifty years ago, Thomas Carlyle said, "A fair day's wages for a fair day's work...is the everlasting right of man." Today a lot of women are looking toward the kind of fair wages available in the hitherto exclusively male domain of construction. Unskilled union laborers make $12.20 per hour, while skilled journeymen command double and even triple that amount. Also provided are liberal employee benefits, including dental work, optical care, pensions, and life insurance, as well as free schooling and on-the-job training.

As recently as five years ago, women in construction were conspicuous by their absence. The semantics of the industry clearly revealed its bias with such union designations as the "International Brotherhood of Electrical Workers (IBEW)" effectively warning females away. In April 1978, however, the federal government helped ensure access by establishing nationwide goals and timetables for the hiring of women on federally contracted and sub-contracted projects. At present, the federal goal is 6.9 percent for women, but city and state governments may set higher quotas for individual jobs.

Contractors and labor unions responded, albeit sluggishly and unwillingly, to the regulations set up by the Office of Contract Compliance Programs (OCCP), and training programs like the now defunct Women in Construction (WIC) Project and special CETA [Comprehensive Employment and Training Administration] courses successfully helped the first women to pioneer their way onto construction sites and into the security of union jobs.

How effective has the OCCP proven to be in continuing to ensure women access to a share in these jobs? And what is it like for the women—and men—who must work out new relationships in the changing world of gender-integrated construction?

Interviews with contractors, labor union officials, and construction workers provided me with some not-so-simple answers to these key questions.

At Boston's Copley Place construction project, I spoke with Janet Palladino. Two years ago, she was a short-order cook making minimum wage. She was attracted to construction mainly by the high salaries. But the physical aspect appealed to her, too. She said, "My body keeps in shape. I feel very healthy. And my pocket feels healthy." Her friend, Lynne Saya, agreed and added, "I'll take a challenge any day."

Both these young women are members of the Laborers' International Union, and they work hard for their pay, "just as hard as the men," said Lynne. Janet told me, "Yesterday we were jackhammering concrete. The vibration kills you. My hands go numb and they ache and ache." She added, "But it's not as tough as last winter. We were working on the 40th floor and it was freezing. The only way up was ladders. There I was bringing back coffee for twenty guys trying to get up the ladder." They exchanged wry grins and Lynne interjected, "On my job, the guys get the coffee."

The issue of who gets the coffee fades into insignificance beside the much more volatile one of sexual harassment. Most women agree it's a problem, but many understandably wished to remain anonymous when discussing it. A woman at the Copley site told me, "The men are nice and they're kind, but there's a sex joke here, a sex joke there, a pinch, someone's going to grab me." Another said, "That's men's nature. It gets tiresome but you have to expect it." Some felt the problem was minimal, that "it depends on your attitude." Another agreed, "The men enjoy seeing a girl on the job and that's okay. There's a lot of gorgeous guys out there, too..."

Perhaps the real measure of the depth of feeling on the subject was demonstrated at a recent meeting of the Network of Women in Trade and Technical Jobs (NWTTJ). The topic was sexual harassment. Jill Feblowitz told me, "It was unbelievable. Twice the usual number of women showed up. The meetings are supposed to last until 9 p.m. This one didn't end till after 11 p.m. The discussions were very heated."

In March of this year, Feblowitz became a licensed journeywoman electrician in the IBEW. She was the first woman in Local 103 and one of only fifteen in Massachusetts who are certified. Four years ago, she was drifting from one low-paying job to another, working as a waitress, office clerk, or salesperson. As a union apprentice she was provided with free schooling and well-paid on-the-job training. She graduated second in a class of 54— 49 of whom were men. Now she is making $16.58 per hour and says, "I have a lot of confidence in myself, not just in my work but in other areas of my life." She sees much that is positive for women but is aware of the problems, too. A big concern is how hard women must struggle to gain acceptance and respect. As Martha Holley expressed it, "At first, they don't think you're capable. They don't take you seriously."

One woman who has refuted both counts is Barbara "Bootsie" Grace. Six months ago, CECO Corporation made her the first woman "foreman" in the Massachusetts Laborers' Union. She told me, "I really didn't think you would see a female move up like that. I was very lucky. I had everybody behind me." As a single parent supporting two young children, Grace saw the high wages as a way of making ends meet. Her job as foreman "petrified" her at first, but she gained confidence as she realized, "I know what I'm doing. And I get along very well with my crew. I had a couple of guys who didn't take me seriously and I had to get tough with them. Your crew can make you or break you. This job is my meal ticket."

One of the most persistent myths among men in construction is the idea that women don't need to work. The prevailing opinion I heard was that "women belong at home cooking spaghetti for their husbands and children." The fact that many women don't have husbands and must first earn the money to buy the spaghetti was ignored. The real issue here is that these men fear they might lose their jobs to a woman. A common statement was, "I think it's wrong that a woman might get the job just to fill a quota and some guy who has to support his family is out of work."

Coupled with this concern was a sense that women on the job are a threat to the men's masculinity. Most men insisted that "women just aren't strong enough" for some jobs. One said bitterly, "I don't want women on the job. It used to be that the old-timers did the easy jobs like sweeping up. Now the women do them. What are the old-timers going to do?" Here again, the myth obscures reality. The fact is that with the advent of technology, construction has become automated to the extent that brute strength alone is less often necessary. Interestingly, most men agreed that women do work hard. One of the most hostile I spoke with admitted, of the lone woman on his crew, "She will try. I'll give her that. She'll pick up something heavy, and she will struggle till she drops."

Despite stereotypical attitudes and prejudices against women in general, the majority seemed sincerely disposed to make the best of the situation. One man who has been a crane operator for 27 years summed up what most felt: "I don't mind women on the job. You learn to accept it and live with it. Lots of them are very nice. And they work really hard, harder than a lot of the young guys. But I don't want to lose my job to someone less qualified just to fill a quota."

Change is painful, but I got the feeling from both men and women that "at the same time it's exciting...to be in a social-change-type situation and see people change to respond to it."

The OCCP has taken the first steps in making workplace changes to protect the rights of women who are currently working or who seek to work in the industry. But there is much more to be done if the program is to achieve maximum effectiveness. At present, regulations and guidelines apply only to contractors, who then are expected to request the cooperation of the unions to help them meet quotas for the hiring of women. Union officials told me that before government mandates, virtually no women were taken into unions.

Louis Mandarini, Sr., business agent of Boston Local 22 of the International Laborers' Union, stated bluntly, "If contractors didn't have to hire women, they wouldn't hire them." Officials at Perini Corporation, a worldwide construction company, complained that unions often fail to supply a sufficient number of qualified women to fill quotas.

Whatever the reasons, quotas are not being filled at the Copley Place site where the Massachusetts Turnpike Authority has authorized a goal of 10 percent female work-hours. According to Agnes McCann, compliance officer for the site, the actual female work-hours average about 7 percent. She explained that the unions reported a lack of qualified women available. Union officials like Mr. Mandarini make no secret of the fact that they believe "women don't belong in construction." It seems clear that without monitoring and compliance programs for unions, existing OCCP mandates remain weak and subject to abuse.

A beginning has been made, however, and women like Beth Coffey are finding a whole new world to explore. She thinks women should be aware that they don't need special skills and aptitudes to get into the field. "My qualifications for apprenticeship in the Plumbers' Union were a degree in Home Economics and a job in a health food store weighing out raisins and sesame seeds," she laughed. She finds the men in her union friendly and helpful. "There is room for optimism," another woman told me. The union newsletters used to begin, "Dear Sir and Brother." Now they start out, "Dear Brothers and Sisters."

This article has been edited for clarity.

AUGUST 1989

Tradeswomen:
An Endangered Species?
by Susan Eisenberg

At the Second National Tradeswomen Conference held in Chicago this past Memorial Day weekend, there was a lot of anger and frustration over our isolation and invisibility—a good bit of it directed toward the women's movement. Like those children parents think are grown and off on their own, doing just fine, female carpenters, electricians, ironworkers, and plumbers are back on the doorstep, needing to call on the family for support.

What causes alarm among tradeswomen are simple statistics. Women, in 1983, made up only 2 percent of the construction industry work force. In 1988, statistics again showed women at only 2 percent of the construction work force. When tradeswomen imagine where they might expect their numbers to be in ten years, the answer obviously has to be: locked in at 2 percent—unless dramatic changes are made. Rather than being pioneers of the industry, breaking the barriers of "men's work," we seem to be on the endangered species list. This should be a cause of grave concern to feminists.

A cap of 2 percent, which has become the industry's response to affirmative action, accomplishes two things. First, it ensures that women workers will be isolated, and that, eventually, those with other options will likely leave "voluntarily." Two percent women translates to one other woman on a job of one hundred workers. And no guarantee that you'll like her. It means that having a woman on a jobsite at all is still rare enough so that the cultural dynamics of the work need not adapt to include women workers. Each time a woman walks onto a jobsite she still risks being seen as an unwelcome invader of a "just-guys" scene. As a transition phase, I think all women who entered male-monopolized job fields expected and accepted this. After ten years, it's a bit much to ask.

Second, it marginalizes women so severely that their involuntary removal, at any given time, could be easily accomplished. Tradeswomen themselves are the primary advocates, re-cruiters, lobbyists, publicists, monitors, and organizers for female affirmative action goals in construction. It has become too many hats for too few heads.

What a 2 percent cap most certainly does not do is provide an economic alternative to sig-nificant numbers of women. Remember, affirmative action and comparable worth were twin goals of the '70s multi-issue women's movement, for achieving economic empowerment for women. Yet, at present, out of 420 job categories listed by the Department of Labor, 70 percent of working women are in only 20 of these categories—not surprisingly, among the lowest-paying.

Women who now earn over $20 an hour in construction, with good health benefits, pension plans, and annuities, owe their jobs to the organized women's movement of the '70s (and to the civil rights movement that paved the way). Before the 1978 guidelines mandating quotas for women on federally funded construction sites, women in union construction were extremely rare. And if tradeswomen pass into oblivion in the next decade, we will be another

I-thought-that-battle-was-won which fell through the cracks of the fragmented women's movement of the present.

Remember that splash of articles ten years ago, when the nontraditional woman worker was hot? Just about every magazine or newspaper had its article and accompanying photo—almost always of a woman doing something scary or holding a tool that was very large. The woman would say how the guys weren't too bad, she enjoyed working with her hands, and the pay sure was great. Some coworker would say how, gee, she handled the work better than he'd expected. We say you're okay and you say we're okay, and we can stay. Understood. Very polite.

Both the daring images and the politeness have outworn their usefulness. Photos that once energized me now catch in my throat: the female ironworker walking a beam...the linewoman making a splice high up on a pole...exotic images meant to thrill and excite. But how many people in their right mind would want to walk across a beam at the top of a skyscraper?! or tie in 480 volts live hanging from a safety belt?! If you wanted to convince someone to learn to drive would you hand them the wheel at rush hour on Route 128 or start out in an empty parking lot on a Sunday afternoon? A lot of these photos were posed. Can't you find a bigger wrench? a female plumber would be asked by a reporter. Seen in isolation, they belie the step-by-step training that builds self-confidence and demystifies trades skills.

Not that tradeswomen don't get off on this image-hype ourselves. I'd be lying if I didn't confess that I enjoy the gasps when I point out the container crane in Charlestown where I worked 100 feet up in the air, 100 feet out on a boom, on a ladder, in the rain on a 4-foot-wide platform with a railing on only one side. The other side: a 100-foot drop, either into water or onto concrete (depending on which side of the boom you were on). And I gasp myself, because I can't imagine ever doing it again! (Since that day I've learned to answer "yes!" when someone asks me if I'm afraid of heights.)

Competent women. Whose work is routine. Women who are routinely competent. Like we think of skilled men. These are the images we need to cultivate and display. Remember the images used by the government, during World War II, when the intention was to attract women to these jobs? Images that make the work seem ordinary, rather than freakish. Which is why I loved the performance at the Tradeswomen Conference developed and directed by Marty Pottenger, a carpenter and performance artist from New York City. In eleven minutes, and to music, an ensemble of tradeswomen framed a miniature house, complete with roof, plumbing, and—as the finale—a light! Boston plumbers Maura Russell and Cathy Greenspan and Local 103, International Brotherhood of Electrical Workers [IBEW], apprentice electrician Vicky Chapman were among the wildly applauded cast.

And then there's the other side, characterized for me by "Sesame Street," which I watch several times a week with my children. Here's a program that very consciously deals with equity issues, but clearly falls short. I cringe every time I see Maria working in the fix-it shop. She's been running the place for years now (she may have entered there on an affirmative action slot herself), and she still doesn't seem like the person you'd choose to repair your broken toaster. She lacks the assurance that should come with her years of experience. Outside the fix-it shop, she lacks the mechanical sense that's so telling in tradeswomen, and, at great cost, denied to most women. One "Sesame" segment, which has haunted me since I saw it, is about firefighters. A four-year-old African-American girl is wishing to be a firefighter.

The camera shows her gazing at firefighters putting out a fire, in their big coats, dragging hoses, climbing ladders. One clearly imagines the writer/producer deciding to have an African-American female be the child to gaze longingly, as though this image would portray the idea that people of all races and sexes could grow up to be firefighters. What I saw was quite the opposite. There were no African-American (or any other) female firefighters among the group the girl was watching. What she could see was that this important and exciting activity was not for people like her. Has so little changed?

Which brings up the issue of politeness. When there are so few women out there, the situation begs for an explanation. Either 1) women are not able to do the work, 2) women do not want to do the work, or 3) women are discouraged from doing the work.

Since World War II's Rosie the Riveters were certainly billed as quite capable, and since we know from history that they had to be fired and forced from their jobs, let's jump right off to door number three (and make a note to consider if our behavior is always consistent with these beliefs. A lot of tradeswomen suspect that more women distrust our ability than would admit it). We need to address the complexity of how women are discouraged—not only by the concrete, measurable, or litigative violations, and not only by the obvious bad guys, but by subtler forms and earliest sources of discouragement and by all of our complicity.

We *all* need to be affirmative action monitors, asking where the women are and, when we have the power, requiring their presence. By March 1980, there were to have been 6.9 percent women on federally funded jobs. Ten years later, one would be hard-pressed to find a jobsite in the nation where these minimal goals have been achieved. We need to coordinate recruitment efforts when union apprenticeship slots open, so that women who are unemployed, underemployed, facing layoffs can have access to this training. We need to challenge the sex-segregation in vocational schools whose facilities predominantly serve male students. We need to demand answers and change. As the Reagan Supreme Court dismantles many of the affirmative action gains we have come to depend on, we will need to develop bold legislative initiatives.

The groups of women (and, sadly, very few men) who struggle around issues of pay equity, around issues of affirmative action, around issues of poverty, tend to be disconnected from one another. The absence of a multi-issue women's movement is painful. In these grim times, as we all struggle to keep ourselves afloat, and to keep particular programs or issues alive, we'll need constant reminders to keep a wide-ranged economic agenda and create ways to overlap our work.

FEBRUARY 1990

Feminism and Labor: Building Alliances

by Harneen Chernow and Susan Moir

Too often the struggles of working-class women in unions have remained invisible to the feminist community. The feminist press has largely avoided reporting news about union organizing, contract battles, strikes, and other labor activities, which involve increasing numbers of working women. By remaining ignorant about unions and labor, the middle-class feminist community is missing an opportunity to build alliances with working-class women. In the past few years, women in unions have had many important victories. For example:

• The women of the mineworkers' families organized themselves as the *Daughters of Mother Jones,* a powerful strike-support organization, which has been essential to the success of the nine-month-long United Mine Workers' strike.

• Flight attendants, who are predominantly female, have taken on new leadership in the airline unions as shown through difficult and lengthy strikes at TWA and Eastern Airlines.

• Over 3,500 clerical and technical workers (overwhelmingly women) at Harvard University, building on earlier victories at Columbia and Yale universities, won union recognition and settled their first contract as members of the Harvard Union of Clerical and Technical Workers/American Federation of State, County and Municipal Employees (HUCTW/AFSCME).

• District 65, United Auto Workers (UAW), representing 850 clerical and technical workers at Boston University, won groundbreaking child care language in their 1988 contract. Then, the Boston School Bus Drivers Union, United Steelworkers of America (USWA), Local 8751, used the Boston University workers' model to win company funding for a child care planning committee.

• Over 600 tradeswomen from around the world met in Chicago at the Second National Tradeswomen Conference to discuss issues confronting tradeswomen and plan strategies for greater access to the trades for women.

• Increasing numbers of women union members in the Communication Workers of America (CWA) and International Brotherhood of Electrical Workers (IBEW) emerged as leaders in the recent NYNEX [telephone company] strike, demanding paid health insurance, pay equity, and an end to the electronic monitoring of VDT users.

• In Watsonville, California, 1,100 mostly female Chicana cannery workers went on strike for eighteen months, during which time not a single union member crossed the picket line. The strike ended in a historic victory for Latina trade unionists and cannery workers everywhere.

Throughout the country, women are looking more and more to organized labor as a vehicle for change. As increasing numbers of women become single heads of households, more women are demanding the same wages and benefits that are paid to unionized men (also known, in part, as pay equity or comparable worth). And while in theory these victories are as significant to the women's movement as they are to the labor movement, the feminist community has often failed to embrace these struggles as our own.

There is, of course, good reason for many of us feminists to cringe when we hear the word "union." A commonly held stereotype of organized labor has been of closed-minded white men, sitting in back rooms, making deals. Mainstream media has supported this image by presenting unions as corrupt, unresponsive to their membership, led by bureaucrats, and in bed with management. With this public perception, it is no wonder that our feminist comrades often question our union involvement. Why would women become active in the world of unions and labor?

The collective organization of workers in unions is the sole means of empowerment at work. As working people and as women, we know that when rights are given based on someone's good will, they can easily be revoked in disagreement or anger. Once a union contract is negotiated, however, issues such as raises, benefits, and fairness are no longer dependent on someone else's good will. They become the legal and guaranteed rights of all union members. This means that working women have a concrete way to deal with sexual harassment, wage inequities, unsafe working conditions, racial discrimination, and other work-related problems; that women have the right to demand fairness and have the support of their union when demanding these rights.

For example, a District 65/UAW member at Boston University who files and settles a sexual harassment grievance but chooses not to return to her job has the right to transfer to a vacant equivalent position within the university. The employee is guaranteed this right whether or not she wins the sexual harassment grievance.

On a more national scale, the Service Employee's International Union (SEIU), AFSCME, and other service-sector unions have been at the forefront of the struggle for parental leave legislation and, in addition, have won maternity leave benefits for their members at the bargaining table. These same unions have filed most of the lawsuits demanding comparable worth and are involved in an ongoing struggle to increase the economic and social value of what has been defined as "women's work."

It is true, of course, that unions have always been dominated by white men. While the early twentieth century saw an initial rise of women union members located in the newly formed garment industry, and the late '30s and '40s saw another increase in the number of women union members as women entered the wartime industrial sector, union leadership remained predominantly male. Even today, as the growth of the largely female public- and service-sector unions has coincided with a greater awareness of women's inequality, most of the top labor leadership is still male.

It is also true that the majority of unions have moved away from their democratic roots. It is for these reasons, along with the loss of jobs in the industrial sector and the increased power of big business during the Reagan era, that unions have been on the decline in the United States. The problem lies not in the concept of unions as a viable workplace organization, but in the composition of the present-day leadership and their agenda for change.

The leadership in unions has begun to change, however, and is changing from the bottom up. In the public, service, health care, and retail sectors of labor, many women serve as elected union officials, are representatives to union/management committees, are stewards (union representatives) at their worksites, and are paid union staff. In many cases, these women have built powerful coalitions in order to be elected to positions traditionally held by men.

These coalitions have been the building blocks of the progressive labor movement. This movement is made up of working women and men, people of color, and lesbians and gays who have a commitment to union democracy and a vision of unionism that includes equal representation for all working people. The goal of progressive labor is to make our unions what they were created to be.

The growing power of union women and other progressive allies in the labor movement reached a new plateau in the fall of 1988.

Question 2, Something New

When the blue-and-white bumper sticker "Question 2, Bad For You" started appearing in Massachusetts in the fall of '88, it was a mystery to many feminists and other progressives who are not connected with the labor movement. The ensuing high-profile fight between the labor unions and the antiunion Associated Building Contractors made most people aware that Question 2 was an attack on the prevailing wage law in the construction industry. (This law requires state-funded construction to be paid at the prevailing wage in the area, meaning at union rates.) There was another story, however, that went largely unnoticed and unreported.

Even though the most obvious beneficiaries of the prevailing wage law are white men working in the skilled building trades, the fight against Question 2 united the labor movement in an unprecedented way. The progressive labor movement, led by women and people of color based in public- and service-sector unions, individual progressive activists in the building trades, and community-based organizations who work with labor unions, understood that if the highest hourly wage dropped so would the lowest. And those low-wage workers are overwhelmingly women and people of color. For all women who work for a wage—union *and* nonunion—Question 2 was, indeed, "bad for you."

Equally important to bringing about the unity that defeated Question 2 was the understanding in the Massachusetts labor movement that the powerful construction unions could not win this fight alone. As the percentage of union-built construction has declined, so has the power of the unionized building trades. Concurrently, those sectors which form the base of the progressive labor movement, women and people of color largely concentrated in service-sector jobs, have witnessed an expansion in their membership.

These two dynamics—the widespread understanding that Question 2 was an attack on the entire working class in Massachusetts and the growing power of the progressive sectors of labor—resulted in women and the communities of color providing the critical education and organizing that defeated Question 2. The fact that the building trade unions would have lost without progressive labor has been widely acknowledged and has begun to change the operating assumptions of even the most conservative of the "old boys" in the building trades and state labor federation. The defeat of Question 2 was in every way a women's victory.

Feminism Plus Unionism

The alliance that brought us to victory in the battle over Question 2 is both novel and fragile, and yet it can provide insight and inspiration as we look to the future. Credit for the growth and influence of women in the labor movement goes to twenty years of modern feminism. This is the variable missing from earlier eras, when women's participation in the work force increased but their power did not. The name and ideology of feminism belongs to women labor leaders and activists as much as it does to anyone. We need to claim it and use it since we too stand for the end of oppression of all women.

As feminists active in labor we are committed to expanding the role of women in unions and to using unions as a vehicle to change the role of women in society. Women currently make 70 cents to every dollar made by men and are still clustered in low-paying, dead-end service-sector jobs. By organizing more women into unions, we can struggle more effectively for women's economic empowerment and demand those benefits (such as child care, pay equity, health and safety, parental leave, job security) that are vital to working women and important to us all.

To those feminists whose view of the labor movement might be limited by outdated stereotypes, we are your allies. As long as the role of unions in women's lives goes unrecognized by the women's movement, working-class women and organizations will continue to be excluded from the movement.

As feminists, there is much we can to do to begin building an alliance with women in labor. For example, the next time we walk by a picket line, as many of us did during the NYNEX strike, remember that those strikers are our sisters, and their struggle is our struggle. (Passersby are welcome to join picket lines.)

The next time we hear of a boycott involving a labor dispute, such as the ones against Eastern/Continental and California table grapes, honor the boycott. Think of the working people who are putting their livelihood on the line: the female flight attendants who are fighting for decent pay and rights and respect for airline workers and the Latina farmworkers who are miscarrying and giving birth to deformed babies from picking grapes sprayed with pesticides. And before we rush to endorse Evelyn Murphy for Massachusetts governor based solely on her politics around choice, let's also research her position on labor and the stance she has taken in the past toward the rights of working women.

Although the alliance between the feminist and labor communities will not emerge without struggle, we look to the '90s as a time when these parallel movements will continue moving toward a common understanding and the sharing of common work. Organized labor represents 17 to 19 percent of the work force. Although this figure represents a decline from earlier times, labor still has more members then any other social/political organization in this country. Unions are a powerful force, and as they continue to take on broader community issues such as affirmative action, housing, and reproductive rights, the alliance between labor and women's organizations should grow and flourish. With the increasing assaults on the rights of women and working people, feminists and unionists need to work together and to take advantage of the knowledge, culture, and skills that each movement has to offer. The result could be unstoppable change in the struggle for women's liberation.

Authors' note: The authors wish to thank their many union sisters and brothers who have offered ideas, comments, and criticisms. The conclusions expressed are our own.

FEBRUARY 1987

Women United Across Borders
by Rebecca Ratcliff

In all of us a seed was planted. We weren't going to be exploited anymore, by our bosses or our men.—Rosaria, a Mexican garment worker

On October 16, 1986, in the crumbling remains of the 1985 Mexican earthquake, hundreds of garment workers and their supporters gathered to celebrate the one-year anniversary of the September 19th Garment Workers Union, the first independent, all-women's union in Mexican history. The following week, from October 22 to 25, the union hosted the International Exchange and Solidarity Conference. Meeting in the union's makeshift headquarters of tents and aluminum buildings, women from feminist organizations, labor unions (including the United Farm Workers and the Watsonville Cannery Strikers), and development agencies from Canada and the United States discussed strategies and shared resources and information with their Mexican hosts.

The *costureras* (garment workers) had a lot to teach; a year of impressive organizing against formidable obstacles had catapulted them to the forefront of the Mexican women's and labor movements. In the process of establishing and expanding their union— 4,000 members strong now, with 12 factory contracts and 15 more pending —they had been forced to challenge the traditional Mexican system of labor unions and male dominance in their own communities, as well as their own government's complicity in ever-expanding efforts of multinationals to exploit cheap female labor around the world. Their victories and their fervor make their story an inspiration to feminists everywhere.

That story begins with an earthquake that struck Mexico City on September 19, 1985. The city's garment district was devastated; close to 1,600 women were killed as the buildings that housed the garment shops collapsed. As the garment workers formed brigades to rescue their buried coworkers, their bosses aided by the Mexican military, brought in trucks to pull out their machinery. "I stood outside the factory where my daughter worked," recounted Maria Lopez, a mother of one of the buried garment workers. "We could hear the women moaning inside, but the army roped off the area and kept us from going in. When the owners arrived, I thought surely they would help us. But they just pulled out their equipment and left our loved ones to die."

From this tragedy, political consciousness arose. Mexico's strong labor movement and relatively progressive labor laws have distinguished it to some extent from other Third World countries such as the Philippines or South Korea, where union organizing has been illegal and dangerous. Yet for twenty years, garment workers who protested unsafe working conditions and illegally low pay were ignored by the government and by the state-supported unions. Controlled by the corrupt Congress of Workers (CT) and directed by the state party, the Institutional Revolutionary Party (PRI), most Mexican unions have helped maintain the political and economic status quo while effectively locking workers out of union decision making. "Before the earthquake we would only find out that we had a union when the CT official came around to collect our dues and tell us what our negotiated salary was," said one new member of the September 19th Union.

"It took the earthquake to shake me out of my stupor," said Evangelina Corona, the secretary general of the new union. "My life has been turned upside down. I've had to redefine what it means to be a worker as well as a woman." With 40,000 garment workers unemployed, and many being denied the severance pay they were legally entitled to, the newly politicized women realized that to protect their interests they needed an independent union controlled by women workers. On October 17, 1985, they delivered a petition to the women's representative of the CT, Hilda Anderson, demanding recognition of a union and a meeting with Mexican President de la Madrid. Ms. Anderson's suggestion that the garment workers be incorporated into an already-existing union within the CT was greeted with boos from the petitioners. This demonstration was the first most of the women had ever participated in. The second came two days later, when they marched on the Presidential Palace to demand registration as an independent union. With the help of sympathetic media attention and support from the community, progressive lawyers, and trade unionists, the costureras won the official recognition they sought.

With the strength of the new union behind them, the garment workers began their next campaign. Using pressure tactics such as camping out in front of their bosses' houses and reconstructed factories, they began negotiations for severance pay. Thus far, 80 percent of the union's members have won their compensation.

They also set out to establish a truly democratic organization while unionizing more workplaces. An eighteen-member National Executive Committee was created to set the course of the union with the guidance of feminist and leftist women's support groups, and it was decided that ultimate decision-making power would reside with assembly meetings made up of delegates from each factory. Since many union members were illiterate and politically inexperienced at the beginning of the struggle, a union-run school was set up, offering courses in literacy, labor laws, the union's bylaws, the history of the working class, and women's liberation.

As the union established itself, its members faced increasing harassment and government repression. For example, during the annual workers' march in Mexico City on May Day, an event supported by the Mexican government, the army and the special antiriot forces blocked the garment workers from taking part in the procession of state-controlled unions. And speaking of the violence committed by bosses and CT scabs, one garment worker described an attempt to vote in a September 19th contract in the *Comercializadora* plant: "Since I was the first to vote, and they knew I was supportive of the September 19th union, they hit me. They said if garment workers voted for the union they would kill [the workers'] families."

The factories and the government have good reason to feel threatened by the independence and militance of the September 19th women. Garment workers, the great majority of whom are women, are the lowest-paid industrial workers in Mexico, receiving an average of $3.50 per day. A compliant female work force has been the cornerstone of the U.S. and Mexican governments' Maquiladora program, a system that sets up transnational "assembly lines" whereby U.S. companies ship parts to Mexico to be assembled (often in illegal sweatshops or in workers' homes) and finished products are then shipped back to the United States duty-free. The garment industry has been a mainstay of the Maquiladora system, which parallels programs in other Third World countries; these programs, developed in the '70s and early '80s, allow U.S. companies to pay lower wages, avoid labor regulations, and take advantage of patriarchal structures that promise a submissive labor force.

In the face of such powerful and determined opposition, a unique multiclass women's alliance has emerged to support the decidedly nonsubmissive Mexican garment workers. Women's support groups made up of hundreds of students, community organizers, and political activists arose in the aftermath of the earthquake to offer economic aid and political guidance as well as a feminist perspective. (Though their numbers dwindled down to dozens after the initial postquake period, members of these groups have continued to provide the costureras with essential services and inspiration.)

Support groups helped the union set up a dispensary to provide striking and unemployed garment workers with food and other essential items. As one unemployed garment worker remarked, "I have five kids and I am the only one to provide for them, so I must depend on the dispensary to feed them."

The support groups have also helped garment workers cope with the resistance many have met from their families as they step outside of traditional female roles. "My husband and in-laws did not want me to leave the house at night to take part in meetings and demonstrations," said one union member who is still struggling to get her severance pay. "They say my place is in the house."

In the separate space that one union member referred to as "a world of women," many garment workers have been transformed as they've discovered their potential as women. "They say that women are more sensitive and weak," said member Alicia Garcia. "That's not true. We can't continue to be submissive. Now I'm not just a mother. Now I have a more important role in society working together with other women."

Educational material developed by the garment workers and their support groups states: "As women we have to fulfill the needs of others and last ourselves. When we start working in a factory we again encounter the same subordinate relationship that we had in the family, which makes it difficult to establish a worker-boss relationship in which we stand up for our interests as women." Their analysis consistently connects the patriarchy they face in their homes with the broader economic and political forces they are struggling against in the workplace.

The battles of the garment workers occur at a time when the welfare of all Mexicans is at a critical point. With a 40 percent unemployment rate and inflation at 100 percent, the Mexican economy is dependent on loans from foreign (primarily U.S.) banks and the International Monetary Fund (IMF). In order to qualify for loans the Mexican government must acquiesce to strict IMF austerity programs that limit spending on social services and to economic policies that facilitate foreign investment. The IMF is also promoting the expansion of the Maquiladora program to provide Mexico with funds to repay its debts, which amount to roughly a third of the country's budget.

On October 23, garment workers joined with other unionists, peasants, urban poor people, and students in a national march in Mexico City to protest debt repayment at the people's expense. At the march they handed out a leaflet explaining their position. "To the people of Mexico, we the costureras of the 19th of September Union march this day to show our opposition to the payment of the debt because we are the workers and the people of Mexico who will no longer pay with our lives."

While U.S. companies may profit from the drastic restructuring of Mexico's economy in order to pay its debts, North Americans lose jobs as Mexicans are forced to work for inadequate pay. As policymakers and businessmen continue to pit U.S. workers against Mexican workers, the women of the September 19th Union have called for unity across borders. They challenge North American women to do their part in addressing labor issues and in changing the nature of the cloth that binds women together both within and between countries. It was in this spirit that the recent Conference for Solidarity and Interchange was organized.

"We feel the need for struggles such as ours to be connected internationally," said a paper distributed to conference participants. "We need to exchange ideas, information, and experiences with other activist women—to discover the global tendencies of the garment industry, to learn methods of struggle that working women are employing in different countries, and to develop tactics of local and global resistance."

Speaking to the women of North America as well as those from Mexico, a representative of one of the garment workers' support groups urged: "We feminists should extend our demands.... Feminism to us is not just a demand to have the freedom to determine our motherhood and control our bodies, but also to defend the rights of women as workers and to fight for better working conditions on all fronts."

OCTOBER 1986

Women Are the Housing Wars' Wounded

by Joni Seager

The horror stories about housing in Boston never seem to end—and most of them are true. The survivors of the September apartment scrimmage are now consoling themselves, perhaps, with the security of another year's lease, or with roommates who seem okay even if they aren't the people you'd choose to live with the rest of your life. There's also a more bitter consolation for most of us—that no matter how bad it is for us, there always seems to be someone who's worse off.

Most of the people who are worse off are women. We all know who they are: the elderly Black woman in the South End who is being displaced from her $95-a-month one-room "bedsitter"; the single mother in Somerville with three children whose rent just doubled as a new landlord took over the building; the young pregnant woman who has taken the last beating from her drunken boyfriend and has fled into the night and into a void; the 58-year-old suburban woman whose husband has walked out, leaving her with an empty house, no job, and a hefty mortgage. As winter draws nearer, the homeless aren't far from sight, and despite most media coverage that portrays "the homeless" mostly as *men* huddled in groups on street corners, in Boston (and in most other major cities) well over half of the homeless are women and their dependent families.

Statistics on the feminization of poverty, on the homeless, on household composition and household incomes underscore the impression that, increasingly, the people who are scraping the very bottom of the housing barrel are women. Housing *is* a women's issue, and it's a feminist issue. Not just because it's mostly women who are losers in the housing wars, but also because a feminist analysis of housing turns out to be among the most cogent in explaining what has gone wrong with housing in this country, and why.

Most of the voices we hear on "the housing issue" are the tones of dull male economists, and the "analysis" they present is generally boring and certainly disconnected from the everyday realities of the people who are actually living with a housing system that simply does not work. What is most remarkable about conventional housing "analysis" is the extent to which it is gender-blind and gender-dumb: despite the indisputable evidence that "the housing crisis" is a crisis especially for women, in "serious" economic analysis women are never mentioned. This, then, is an attempt to reclaim "the housing issue" for women by starting with a clear image of women as the walking wounded in the housing wars and offering an analysis that puts women and gender relations at its center.

It is easy to explain what we mean by "the housing crisis." The crisis has two components: first, there is not enough of the right kind of housing to meet the needs of the population that must be housed, and second, the housing available is too expensive. Why, though, is there a housing crisis? Why the mismatch between housing stock and housing needs? Why the cost? And why is the crisis more profound for women? The answers are interlinked.

Most housing analysis assumes that capitalism is the central structuring force in housing—and that the class and power relations of capitalism explain the nature of housing and the ups and downs of the housing market. This is certainly, but only partly, true. A feminist analysis shoves patriarchy and patriarchal gender relations onto center stage in the housing debates.

Two-thirds of the American housing stock consists of single-family, detached houses. It is this preponderance of single-family, low-density, American-dream housing that is the key element in the mismatch of housing availability and housing needs. The housing crisis stems directly from this form of housing, in combination with an economic system in which housing is treated as a commodity, available only to those who can meet the price. So, to answer the question of why a housing crisis and why a crisis especially for women, we have to ask why we have the type of housing we do, and why housing is a high-priced commodity.

The single-family American-dream housing stock and the "commodification" of housing are neither universal nor inevitable. The structure of housing in urban America —both its physical form and its economic relations—was self-consciously and deliberately created and shaped by social policies and ideologies. Our housing system was created (and much of today's housing built) in the late 1800s and early 1900s. (There are several good social histories of housing that make this point, including most of the books of Dolores Hayden; I can't repeat the historical analysis here, but need to work from this as a basic given.) We can get at the roots of our current housing crisis if we can determine why housing in America was shaped the way it was. Who was served by this (now dysfunctional) structure of housing?

The answer that critical or radical housing analysts give to this question is that low-density, single-family, American-dream housing suited the needs of capitalism, and it certainly is true that single-family housing generates huge demand for materials, supplies, and consumer goods (whereas multiple-family dwellings conserve and combine material demands). And it is also true that turn-of-the-century industrialists tried to quiet labor unrest by encouraging workers to buy into the American dream and by saddling them with large mortgage commitments. Single-family, low-density housing and the commodification of housing did suit the short-term needs of capitalism. But feminists argue that, perhaps more important, this type of housing served the needs of patriarchy.

The low-density (and suburban) housing ideal that we live with today (and struggle with) developed from an ideology of the separation of the public and private, productive and nonproductive, male and female worlds. "Home" and "family" were supposed to be private, protected places as far removed as possible (emotionally and spatially) from harsh industrial realities: men forayed out into the productive sphere to earn the wherewithal to support a nonproductive wife and family. Separating out the worlds of women and men may or may not have served the needs of capitalism: it certainly served the needs of patriarchy by keeping women at a remove from the labor market and dependent on men. The nature of housing enforced the exclusion of women from the productive sphere, and it was very explicitly designed to do so.

At the same time, making housing a high-priced commodity meant that access to housing depended on one's position in the labor market. Conversely, this meant that housing was beyond the reach of those who were most marginalized in the productive sphere—this was why housing could be used as a status symbol. But the group of people who were most marginalized (and very specifically *intended* to be marginalized) in the productive sphere were women. In turn-of-the-century urban America, as the foundations for our housing stock and housing policies were being laid, women had access to housing mostly through men.

Women are still the most marginalized group in the productive sphere, and still their access to housing is primarily through men. Women who try to live on women's wages and perhaps support a family without the help of another adult wage-earner cannot afford the kind of housing that is available. But they aren't intended to—housing is still constructed as though the housewife-at-home nuclear family were the norm.

Statistics on the feminization of poverty illustrate the financial chasm between housing and women. In the United States, 74 percent of all the poor are women and their children. If a woman works at a minimum-wage job (and more women than men work at the bottom of the occupational ladder), she'll earn $6,968 per year. If she has two children, this wage will place her below the poverty level. If she's on AFDC, she and her two children will get $65 per month, including food stamps.

Clearly, housing is not just a problem for women who are officially "poor." To understand why women are at such a disadvantage in the housing market, we have to understand the economic structural inequality of *all* women: women earn the least, work in low-esteem and low-pay jobs, are marginalized in part-time work, are least unionized, and have the fewest work benefits of any group of workers. And, of course, these disadvantages are compounded for Black women, Hispanic women, and recent immigrants.

Let's stop for a moment and review what a feminist perspective reveals about the housing problem.

• The most preferred and most available type of housing is that which maximizes women's dependence on men-as-breadwinners and which maximizes women's exclusion from the productive sphere by physically isolating them in environments of least opportunity. (Suburbs are a huge monument to patriarchy.)

• It is women who are given the major emotional and logistical responsibility for the family but are given the fewest resources to meet those needs; they are discriminated against in the labor force and consistently economically marginalized. The feminization of poverty is the inevitable result of decades of discrimination against women in the labor force, now accelerated by misogynist policies of the Reagan administration.

• When housing is a high-priced commodity, women are the least equipped to buy it, especially women who are trying to house themselves without the dual (and higher) income of men.

• With rapid changes in the structure of families, and most especially the rise of single-parent, women-headed households, the mismatch between available housing and women's needs is acute: single-family, low-density houses in far suburbs are too expensive for most women and, in any event, are not especially appropriate for their housing needs.

On top of this huge wall of patriarchy, there are the logistical problems that women who try to house themselves and their families face. Landlords won't rent to "single mothers"; landlords won't rent to women trying to live collectively; landlords won't rent to families with children; financial institutions discriminate against women; there is no day care; there are few alternatives to the private, American-dream housing market.

Rather than question the structural assumptions about how and why housing is shaped (with an eye to reshaping it), planners and policymakers have been spinning their wheels for years trying to find various band-aid solutions. "Public housing" is the most u-biquitous "solution." Public housing was originally intended as a vehicle for lower-income families to achieve self-esteem and an entree into the American dream. It has become warehousing for people who just can't keep up—and most of those people are women.

Women dominate the public housing population, and most of the 11,000 people now on Boston Housing Authority (BHA) waiting lists are women and their dependent families. The BHA hasn't built any new family housing since 1954; the Reagan administration cut housing assistance funds by 60 percent between 1981 and 1985. Public housing replicates the patriarchal model: just as the middle-class housing ideal kept women dependent on male breadwinners and isolated in a far suburb, public housing keeps women isolated in inaccessible, often dangerous, forgotten, and blighted urban neighborhoods, far from services, jobs, or public transportation, dependent on a bureaucracy for monthly payments. We are warehousing poor women, and once again, the "where" and "why" of housing become significant in assessing women's housing options. The safety net of public housing—such as it ever was—is wearing thin, and it is mostly women who are falling through.

The surest sign of the crisis in housing is the swelling population of homeless. The numbers are staggering: an estimated 9,000 homeless in Boston, 60,000 in New York City, 25,000 in Chicago, 10,000 in San Francisco. Behind most of these statistics are women and children who have been forced out of whatever housing niche they once occupied: most of the homeless in most cities are women and their dependent children. At latest count, there were an estimated 1,200 homeless families in Boston looking for shelter—and shelter space for 345.

People *become* homeless, people not much different from you and me. The ways in which women become homeless are specific to women—and specific to women's overall status in society. Domestic violence accounts for an estimated 40 percent of all family home-lessness. Elderly women more often than not (and much more often than men) have no pension—because they didn't hold a job during their married younger years or because the job they did have was part-time, nonunionized, and/or without benefits. Elderly women are among the poorest of the poor and are especially vulnerable to being made homeless. Women with fixed incomes or low incomes who have children to raise find their options limited, es-pecially since there is no system of day care. A rent increase can put them on the streets.

Any housing solutions that do not address the structural inequalities between men and women in this society are band-aids. This doesn't mean that the struggle is so large as to be unapproachable. Certainly, we must fight for rent control, for a renewed commitment to public housing, for innovative crisis shelters such as transitional housing. But it also means that we must broaden our agenda in housing battles. Day care is a housing issue; di-vorce is a housing issue; transportation is a housing issue; economic justice in the workplace is a housing issue. Housing activists and feminist activists have overlapping agendas but have not to date done much coalition work. The housing crisis is embedded in a set of so-cial and economic relations that place women as adjuncts and subsidaries of men and the nuclear family. It is clear that that's no place for women.

JUNE 1989

Homelessness: Crisis or Chronic Condition

by Kip Tiernan and Fran Froehlich

Understanding The Problem

Violence *against* women in Massachusetts continues relentlessly, whether it is of an intimate variety or administered legally *by* federal or state government in the form of homelessness—one more brutal assault on poor women and now their children. In Massachusetts, and other states, taxpayers are picking up the tab for it.

In all, the Commonwealth will expend $158.4 million on individual and family homelessness services in FY 88, with approximately $35.6 million in federal reimburse-ment projected in return. This is a 1,500 percent increase since 1983. (Massachusetts House Ways and Means Committee Report, May 1988).

One might well ask, did any of this go toward permanent housing? The answer is probably "not much."

Women and children are the fastest-growing group of homeless citizens of the Com-monwealth. In fact, of the counted 10,000 homeless people, 75 percent are families and of those, 80 percent rely on Aid to Families with Dependent Children (AFDC) as their principal means of support. So we're talking about poor women and their children. We now have about 2,000 children—homeless—living in motels and welfare hotels in this state alone.

The buzz word in the '70s was "shelter." It was replaced in the '80s by the word "transitional." All of it has to do with a growing underclass, of mostly women and children, whose needs were not met when the crisis began many years ago, and whose needs have now exploded across the charts to include housing, food, medical and legal services, transportation, day care, job training, rape crisis counseling, mental health care, drug counseling, elderly services and, most recently, services related to AIDS.

Several years ago, we began doing some research on the harsh increase of homelessness in Massachusetts: the skyrocketing rents, the federal and state cutbacks on all basic human services, the emergence of the service industry, the increase in the number of shelters rather than adequate housing and jobs. We came up with the notion that one of the fastest growth industries in the Commonwealth was the shelter industry.

The crisis has reached shameful proportions because the root causes have been ignored. And now poor people, like their big corporate brothers Chrysler and the Savings and Loan industry, need a bailout—not a handout. Instead, what they are getting is woefully inadequate to meet even the most basic human needs.

One might well ask, who benefits from this? The landlords for one, the real estate industry—the same industry that has been left unchecked, unmonitored, uncensured for the past 30 years. Boston now has the highest rental costs in the country, with the poor and working poor having no chance at all of ever buying their homes. The ultra-poor cannot afford to live anywhere anymore, especially in their own neighborhoods. So shelters have become the catchall.

According to a report last year by the U.S. House of Representatives, 67 percent of all homeless people in the United States are homeless because there is no affordable housing for them. How did that happen? For one, the Housing and Urban Development Agency (HUD) hasn't even requested funds for housing for a long time. In fact, from 1981 to 1987, HUD pulled out $32 billion or close to 70 percent of the entire housing budget allotment for those years. In addition, the high cost of the military has greatly inhibited the construction or replacement of public and low-cost housing. What we have allowed in the name of national security, we would call crimes against humanity in any other country of the world. Since 1982, 8 million more Americans have fallen below the poverty level.

This is a very difficult story to write, as one [Kip Tiernan] who opened up the first drop-in and emergency shelter for women in the country—Rosie's Place—fifteen years ago, in 1974, when we were told there weren't any homeless women in Boston. In fifteen years, you would think the problem might have been solved or at least seriously looked at. But conditions for poor women have worsened over the years, and these women have been especially hard hit by the housing "crisis." (It was a crisis fifteen years ago—now it is a chronic, accepted fact of life).

Women are more likely to be poor anyway. In fact, almost half of all female householders were poor in 1987, compared with one-eighth of all families with children. They are even less likely to be homeowners and, despite their lower incomes, they are getting short-changed on housing subsidies. Most federal subsidies go to married couples or male householders. Families headed by women are paying the highest average proportions of their incomes for rent. Single female parents under 25 are now paying close to 80 percent of their incomes for rent. In fact, most of us are now paying between 40 and 50 percent of our incomes for rent.

In 1968, Congress established a goal of 600,000 additional units of low-income housing. That goal has never been met. Under Gerald Ford, we got 200,000; under Jimmy Carter, we got 300,000; and under Ronald Reagan, we got 25,000. George Bush doesn't think we even have a housing problem. ("There might be some homeless people out there," he grudgingly admitted during the presidential campaign.)

During the Reagan years, there were severe cutbacks in housing, food stamps AFDC, Head Start, medical and legal services, drug programs, the Women, Infants, and Children (WIC) supplemental nutrition program. Poor women lost 70 percent of all monies budgeted for services. In addition, the minimum wage has not increased since 1981, although the cost of living continues to increase. America's answer to all of this seems to have been "hide-them-don't-house-them." And so in desperation we all came up with what we thought were temporary but compassionate alternatives—shelters.

In 1982, Massachusetts had 2 state-funded shelters. Today, seven years later, we have well over 120—with lots of nonstate-funded shelters here and there as well. Next year we say we need 20 more family shelters, several individual shelters, and at least 20 mental health group homes.

The reality of our lack of affordable housing has been denied for years. So have the statistical counts of homeless people in shelters. When Rosie's Place first opened, there were, nationally, about 250,000 homeless people—a statistic denied by the Nixon administration. Three years ago, we on the shelter scene were saying there were perhaps two to three million homeless people—a statistic denied by the Reagan administration. Reagan suggested people slept on grates because they wanted to. His attorney general Ed Meese said people went to soup kitchens because they were too cheap to go to restaurants. (But then, this was the administration that told us ketchup was a vegetable.) Philip Clay of MIT suggests if we do not do anything substantive about affordable housing, by the year 2003 there will be 19 million homeless people in our streets. Homelessness is increasing nationally at the rate of 30 percent a year.

And the politics of space is not limited to Massachusetts or even the United States. Homelessness, largely a product of far-right political ideology, which lacks all ethics and has no real concern for poor and working-class people, is globally pervasive. As far back as 1983, the *Wall Street Journal* reported a homeless phenomenon emerging in Europe. Needless to say, the homeless situation has worsened in Europe, but then there are also Brazil, South Africa, Japan, India, Pakistan, Sri Lanka—even Russia—and all the refugee populations on the African and Central and South American continents. These refugees are mostly women and their children. It is men, who have a lust for global domination, who orchestrate the problem. The victims are always the most vulnerable, the least able to challenge the systems that create the brutality, and they are the first to fall.

Women, poverty, and homelessness obviously all go hand in hand. Sorting out female populations at Rosie's Place alone leads one to believe that we have not yet seen the catastrophic results still to come. It, however, does become depressingly apparent that shelters are no answer, nor was Rosie's Place ever, by any stretch of the imagination, meant to be a solution. Which leads one to the next reflection—if shelters aren't an answer, is homelessness the question? We believe homelessness is the most visible result of bad social and economic policy...one to which many of us have accommodated ourselves in the name of altruism. But alleviating the suffering is only part of the answer—eliminating the causes is the other, and here the road gets very bumpy indeed.

Getting To The Roots

We are not saying close the shelters. We desperately need them; but we are suggesting that by not dealing with the root cause of homelessness, namely poverty, we are girding ourselves into the warehousing and structured isolation of a permanent, chronic American underclass. How does such a thing happen? We believe it is because the priorities of the ruling class are being met at the expense of the underclass, whose basic human needs simply are not being met.

We decided that there were at least five major social arenas that affect the lives of poor people: class assistance, economics, housing, sheltering, and culture. Class assistance includes AFDC, legal and medical services, day care, and employment training, all of which, as noted above, suffered severe budget cuts under the Reagan administration. Economics refers to changes in mean income, minimum wages, the rise of the service industry, real estate, banking, plant closings, hostile takeovers, Proposition 2 (a citizen's referendum in Massachusetts that significantly reduced taxes and had a serious impact on public services). Sheltering includes city/state/federally funded shelters, non-state-funded shelters, soup kitchens, deinstitutionalization, motels/hotels, health care for homeless people, homeless children's educational needs, and philanthropy. Under housing we are looking at changes in the availability of affordable housing, and under culture, the ideology that continues to accommodate homelessness by calling it a "crisis" and, thus, finding a logical solution in "temporary" shelters. We want to briefly address several of these factors, before moving on to solutions.

Housing: As neighborhoods become gentrified, rents go up, making it virtually impossible for poor and working-class people to stay in their own neighborhoods. In Boston, over the last ten years, as in other areas of the country, those who could afford condos bought them. In 1977, there were 2,000 condos in Boston; in 1980, 6,000; in 1985, 21,000; and in 1987, 30,000. Correspondingly, in Boston, we lost 50,000 to 60,000 rental units, all the residential hotels, and most of the single room occupancies. That accounts for some of the homelessness, we suppose.

At the same time, during the condo years, the number of families needing rental housing doubled. Between the years 1982 and 1984, 80 percent of apartments under $300 a month simply disappeared. In 1985, the average rent in Boston was $661 a month—you would need an income of about $30,000 a year to afford that. Well, AFDC mothers don't have anything near that—in fact, Massachusetts AFDC single parents are still living close to 30 percent below the poverty level, so there is a vast discrepancy in what they have and what it costs to live in Massachusetts.

In the meantime, we are losing more housing stock. There's the expiring-use housing stock—federally funded developments whose mortgages will all be paid up within the next five to ten years. And once these mortgages are paid, the developers can do what they want and chances are all subsidized tenants will be taking another long walk to nowhere.

Although "condoizing" has slowed in the Boston area, and moved westward, the real estate industry continues to push for more profits with referendums such as Proposition 1-2-3, which will appear on the Cambridge, Massachusetts, ballot in November. This referendum is being touted by the industry as a way of ending homelessness by giving tenants the opportunity to buy their own apartments. The ordinance itself reads, "Any tenant who has occupied a controlled rental unit for a period of at least two years shall be entitled to purchase and occupy his or her unit as a condominium unit owner, if tenant and landlord so agree." Under this binding referendum, condo conversion of rent-controlled apartments would result in the immediate loss of affordable housing. And 70 percent of the real estate in Cambridge is apartment rental. For landlords, realtors, and developers, it is a veritable goldmine. It means to the lowly tenant the permanent loss of affordable housing. It means the beginning of the end of rent control. While it is being bandied about as a method of preventing homelessness, it is one more cruel and abusive method of getting rid of poor people once and for all.

Economics: The middle class, the class by which America has always defined itself, is fast disappearing, according to Barbara Ehrenreich, 1987 fellow at the Washington-based Institute for Policy Studies. Statistically, the middle class is that part of the population that earns near the median income—say the 20 percent that earns just above the median income plus the 20 percent whose earnings fall just below it. But in more subtle terms, it is the class by which we identify "The American Way of Life"—homeownership, college degrees, financially comfortable future expectations, the ability to afford such amenities as two cars or a summer place. But today those who identify as America's middle class aren't doing as well as they might. A baby boomer's father might have spent 14 percent of the family income on housing costs. Today's homeowner must set aside at least 44 percent of the family income on housing costs alone.

Public policy of the '60s and early '70s favored a downward distribution of wealth. But Ronald Reagan came to town; and life for America has changed, it seems, forever, with the drift towards a two-tier society, which began shortly before Reagan's presidency. Lenore Weitzman, author of *The Divorce Revolution* (Free Press, 1985) writes that an ex-wife's disposable income is likely to fall 73 percent in the year following divorce, while her ex's rises by 42 percent. Today, single moms account for half the U.S. households in poverty. According to the census bureau, the current income gap between the richest and the poorest in the United States is wider than at any other time since the bureau first began keeping such statistics in 1947!

According to some economists, there are deeper structural reasons for a disappearing economy. Moving from a manufacturing to a service economy at the rate of the loss of 11.5 million jobs since 1979 has not helped. Just since 1986 Massachusetts-based companies have laid off 17,000 workers, as a result of corporate takeovers. The insatiable appetite real estate developers have, scarfing away at housing; the low-paying service jobs; the disappearing middle class; the state and federal debt have all played into the price some of us are paying so that others can have everything they desire.

Sheltering: The shelter industry is big business in Massachusetts, make no mistake about it. When state-funded shelters began, in 1982, costs were running about $4 to $6 million. It has increased every year to the present cost of $158.6 million spent on state programs to shelter people, for housing advocates in welfare offices, for 707 vouchers to try to prevent homelessness, for food programs, for more shelters, for educational monies for homeless children, for training more people how to be respectful of homeless people. We are spending more and more money, not to solve the problem but to service the problem itself. Something is wrong with this picture!

We have finally managed to institutionalize poverty itself. We are one perilous step closer to case-managing poor people or to designing a new form of social control. Sure they need services—like the rest of us. But what poor people really need is the money to manage their own lives.

Culture: "Situations of cultural acceptance breed accommodating complacency" (Walter Brueggmann, *The Prophetic Imagination,* Augsburg Fortress, 1978). There has been a cultural acceptance of shelters in this country, in lieu of solving the problem of poverty. Certainly gentrification, artificial altruism, cultural Christianity, liberalism, and all the other "incremental -isms" that keep people poor are part of the total gestalt of homelessness. How we perceive it is how, or if, we address it. If homelessness continues to be looked at—after all these years—as an emergency and a crisis rather than a political and economic death sentence for a particular class of people, a chronically accepted fate for millions of women and their children, what hope can we have?

As urban ministers, as community organizers, and as the creators of several basic human needs alternatives in Boston, we feel there is a lot of hope out there and that there is still a lot to hope for. We have the capacity to end poverty and homelessness in this country. What we lack is the political will to do it. Homelessness and its ancillary agonies—economic deprivation, hunger, lack of adequate medical, educational, legal, and political access—have all inspired systems to deal with the growing overwhelming problems, but we have not managed to turn the problem around or to solve it or even to prevent more from happening. The cultural acceptance of all of this, and the elaborate devices to deal with it, manage it, identify it, create new myths about it, control it, and spend millions to alleviate it, has not stopped more people from becoming homeless.

The Road Toward Solutions

Peter Townsend, a British sociologist, said, many years ago, "Poverty is not just the result of inequities or inequalities but rather a particular consequence of action by the privileged to preserve and enhance their wealth and deny it to others: a kind of shoring up of the status quo to help perpetuate a brutal two-class system, in which the poor have no chance of survival at all." He said this about England but it might well be said of the United States.

More and more women and children are falling, faster and faster, through whatever safety nets are still in place. Public policy is certainly at fault. But the priorities are established by federal and state administrations. We might begin the challenge by examining why we continue to treat homelessness as if it were a vast social service problem instead of an economic and political judgment on a whole class of people. The terms of the debate must be changed. We certainly need to develop another set of ethics. We require a loud critical voice because real criticism can only begin in the capacity to grieve, the most visceral announcement that things are not right. We must bring hurt into public expression, and shelters and soup kitchens are not where to begin. They have become the burnt offerings of the twentieth century.

There is a vast distinction between charity and justice, and homelessness and poverty are justice issues. As urban ministers, we are well aware that justice, according to the Bible anyway, means the sorting out of what belongs to whom and the returning of it to them. The outrageous cost of real estate and rents is not so much a profitable business as it is a rip-off, and those who can't afford to be ripped off any more end up in shelters, where we have ended up creating an ethic around needs rather than creating a need for a new ethic. Michael Harrington, in *The New American Poverty* (Viking Penguin Books, 1985), refers to it as "the cruel innocence." He says, "We are truly innocent of the impact and the reality that it is the structures of the systems which make many of us very comfortable that are creating these crises and these problems." Ethics, said someone on a "Bill Moyers Show" recently, is a minority movement in this country and it is not for wimps. According to *Webster's,* ethics "is the science of moral duty: broadly the science of ideal human character based on the practice of moral principles." But we in this country have defined ethics to mean almost anything we want. We have developed a market-value ethic around property and an "incremental ethic" around the needs of poor people.

Whatever happened to solidarity—anywhere, not just within the women's community? Has our world become so terribly complex that we are forced to deal with only one agony at a time? The April 9 pro-choice demonstration in Washington, D.C., was a terrific opportunity to broaden the base of women's politics. We kept hoping that the leadership would stretch the agenda beyond reproductive rights to include the economic deprivation of an entire generation of women whose lives and their children's lives are endangered on all fronts.

Have we allowed the fundamentalists to define the women's agenda in such narrow terms? To narrow our capacity to deal with more than one abuse at a time? Basically a privatized religious movement, Christian fundamentalism centers around the individual rather than the community—it excludes all that is considered by them to be "different," and that certainly takes in a multitude! Real community, on the other hand, is a cooperative style of addressing everyone's needs. In Washington, we lost an opportunity to further radicalize the privileged. Many of the privileged women who were there could go home and continue to enjoy their privileges, whether it was an affordable, safe abortion or an affordable apartment.

The possible dismantling of *Roe v. Wade* is one more terrifying piece of the unraveling of the thread of hope we had in the tapestry of women's rights. Women—all women—must again voice the rage we used to have around all issues—issues that poor women should not have to face alone, unsupported. We must address poverty—the economic humiliation of women due to inadequate federal and state support, the dizzying high cost of living, the cycle of poverty that keeps poor women and their children poor—if we claim to care. We must believe we can change things. And it will take all of our combined and collective and communal strengths and courage and faith to sort out the truth. We live in what is mistakenly called an informational society. It is very hard to distinguish the truth, but only when we can look at the results of what is called "truth" can we see who benefited.

The times require a shared vision—an ethic, a political and spiritual ideology that begins to sort out what belongs to whom and returns it to them. Only in working together for the common good—the common wealth—will we find it together. We believe in this common language and ethic, this common bright red thread that dominates the tapestry of our very existence. We believe we can find that world we looked for a long time ago, but only if we are willing to look at the real reality of our lives insofar as that reality affects the lives of so many more around us.

APRIL 1994

Do We Kill Ourselves On Purpose? Thinking About Structural Adjustment

by Rebecca Johnson (with thanks to Abbey Lincoln)

> Do we kill ourselves on purpose?
> Is destruction all our own?
> Are we dying for a reason?
> Is our leaving on our own?
> Are the people suicidal?
> Did we come this far to die?
> Of ourselves are we to perish,
> for this useless, worthless lie?

At the height of the East Coast real estate boom of the late '80s, the *Boston Globe* ran an article about life for poor women with children on Cape Cod. The story featured a woman who lived in a tent during the tourist season because no property owner would rent a unit to her at a reasonable rate. She could find housing in the winter, during the off-season, but from the beginning of May till after school started in September, she and her children lived in a tent, moving from one campsite to another.

> are we dying for a reason?
> is our leaving on our own?

The last time I was in New York City, friends took me to Harlem. The streets of the main shopping district were lined with women and men selling goods off blankets and small tables, out of boxes and the backs of cars. These folks are just the most public manifestation of a largely invisible informal economy. This economy consists of illegal activities such as selling drugs and stolen goods as well as trading and selling legal goods and services outside of the venues recognized by the Internal Revenue Service. By its nature—informal, unregulated, frequently exploitative—this economy both injures and benefits those cut off from the larger, intentionally inaccessible, prosperity surrounding Harlem and its residents.

> *Are the people suicidal?*
> *Did we come this far to die?*

A resurgent component of the informal economy is the sweatshop. In the apparel industry, immigrant women in Boston, Philadelphia, New York City, and many cities in California are paid "$1.20 to $3.00 for a garment that takes up to one hour to sew. Eventually the contractor will be paid $10 to $20 for the item, which may have a price tag of $50 to $75 when it leaves the retailer" (Elizabeth McLean Petras, "The Shirt on Your Back: Immigrant Workers and the Reorganization of the Garment Industry" in *Social Justice*, Vol. 19, No. 1, 1992). Working conditions are dangerous in these shops, and in order to keep up with the piece rate system, women frequently must enlist their children in the production of garments at home and in the shop.

> *Are the people suicidal?*
> *Did we come this far to die?*
> *Of ourselves are we to perish,*
> *for this useless, worthless lie?*

No, the people are not suicidal, but we are uninformed. During the '92 presidential campaign, we listened to rhetoric from rich white men whose chief desire was to "make America great again." Bill Clinton employed rhetoric about welfare reform aimed at the sympathies of workers who felt themselves separate from and somehow oppressed by the women and their families in the previous examples. Neither George Bush nor Bill Clinton talked about how, in the previous ten years, the U.S. government created the poverty we see daily on our streets, the suffering in our homes, and the tension in our communities. The citizens of many Third World countries could tell us how these things happened. They would tell us about "structural adjustment."

Structural Adjustment Policies

What was called Reaganomics or trickle-down economics in the United States was just another manifestation of economic policies common in the Third World. Known as structural adjustment policies (SAPs), these economic policies have increased the poverty of numerous countries that have been forced to endure the austerity and debt-reduction measures such policies entail. Most of us don't realize that the increased suffering and decline in living standards for the majority of U.S. women has resulted from government policies very similar to those imposed by the World Bank and the International Monetary Fund (IMF) on these "developing" countries. We need to ask three questions: What is structural adjustment? What does it feel like for poor women in the Third World? And, how and why did the Reagan/Bush administrations impose these policies on the United States? But first we need to understand the international structures created to carry out these policies—the IMF and the World Bank.

After World War II, the United States was the ascendant economic and political power. The IMF and the World Bank, along with the General Agreement on Tariffs and Trades (GATT), were created after the war as the mechanisms through which the United States could impose large-scale economic policies on the world. Through the promotion of free trade, capitalist-style competition, and the concentration of capital in the hands of relatively few corporations, these organizations address their primary concern—creating a more favorable business climate and increased profits for transnational corporations operating all over the world.

In the '80s, the World Bank and the IMF implemented SAPs in over 70 countries. The results were devastating. Money was devalued, social services were discontinued, any structures a government might have used to protect its citizens from the effects of capitalism were dismantled. Presented as remedies for such conditions as "severe inflation, stagnating or deteriorating industrial and agricultural output, prolonged trade deficits, and the inability to attract development funds," SAPs helped spawn the economic "miracles" of oppressive regimes such as those in Peru and the Philippines, where poverty is endemic (*Reaganomics and Women: Structural Adjustment U.S. Style—1980 to 1992*, Alternative Women in Development, 1992). Women in these countries, as well as many others, experience dislocation from rural areas and subsistence farming as they are forced to move to overcrowded urban centers, where little access to health care and increased exposure to violence often lead to premature death.

How Structural Adjustment Works

The World Bank and IMF become involved with a country when its foreign debt has reached unmanageable proportions, when it needs help with "free market" economic development, or when it is experiencing some short-term stability problems. The IMF creates debt management and austerity programs. The World Bank deals with longer-term issues of economic development, primarily by providing money for development programs. GATT—the final layer of this complex international management of the world's economy—rounds out the measures imposed on these countries as it works to reduce barriers to the free movement of trade. The North American Free Trade Agreement—NAFTA—is one aspect of GATT and of structural adjustment. The general idea is to assist "developing" countries to manage their extremely high-interest debt and to create an economic atmosphere conducive to development.

Countries burdened with SAPs exist very close to our borders. Jamaica has struggled with IMF-imposed austerity measures for over 25 years. In the early '60s, Jamaica was experiencing difficulty repaying its foreign bank loans, and inflation was running at over 400 percent. The IMF designed a program in two parts: first came stabilization, then structural change. Stabilization demands austerity measures. In Jamaica, stabilization resulted in the currency losing over half of its value. Unions and other employee associations were suppressed as wages and salaries were reduced. The government was forced to spend less on health care, social programs, and education. At the same time, trade policies were "liberalized"—that is, made more compatible with the international economy. These policies heavily favored the United States and Great Britain. The government-controlled bauxite industry (bauxite is the raw material for aluminum) was privatized. Land reform was ended in the interest of space for the production of commodity crops such as sugar.

After the IMF deems a country's economy stabilized, it institutes projects and policies that result in structural changes. In Jamaica this has meant that the government has permanently lost control of the bauxite industry and can no longer try to create a favorable trading environment for Jamaican products. For example, much of the raw sugar grown in Jamaica is processed into rum and exported, forcing Jamaican citizens to pay high prices for imported refined sugar.

Banking is no longer totally government-controlled either. The value of the Jamaican dollar is tied to international money markets and constantly decreasing in value—in 1988 the exchange rate was nine Jamaican dollars to one U.S. dollar. Last year it was twenty-five Jamaican dollars to one U.S. dollar.

In the '60s, Jamaica was moving toward a more socialist form of government. It received support from Cuba in the form of technical assistance and support for its health care and education systems. At one time, most rural health clinics were staffed by Cuban doctors. Cuban technical assistance supported the educational system's programs for universal literacy. As a result of structural adjustment, the size of the central government has been drastically reduced and progressive tendencies toward land reform, universal health care, and education have been squelched. Clinic staffs are now down to one doctor visiting two or three times a week, and almost no nighttime emergency care is available. Jamaica's educational system has become one of the most elitist in the Caribbean; poor children have almost no access to higher education.

These policies create the most hardship for women. Poor women are largely responsible for the welfare of their families. As access to land has been reduced, and village-based fishing has declined (fishing is now dominated by industrial fisheries), tourism has been given free reign. Once a state-run industry, tourism has been privatized and the industry now controls the best land, access to running water, and many jobs. Women looking for work are forced to travel great distances to tourist and other urban centers; either they must leave their children back in the rural areas with relatives or take them to overcrowded urban shantytowns. As food production is reduced and the prices of fresh fruits and vegetables steadily increase, these women have more and more difficulty caring for their families.

As an SAP takes effect, the economy in a country like Jamaica becomes open to the exploitative labor needs of transnational corporations. Rather than maintaining indigenous agriculture and sustainable production, the government provides the raw materials and workers to manufacture export-oriented products and commodities. Essentially, the government is forced to trade the welfare of its citizens and its autonomy for foreign bank loans and development grants.

Structural Adjustment in the United States

Women in the United States don't experience the level of poverty of women living in shanties in the Philippines, Jamaica, and Nigeria. But conditions for poor women have worsened in the past twelve years in large part due to government economic policies similar to those experienced by women in the Third World.

In *Reaganomics and Women: Structural Adjustment U.S. Style—1980 to 1992*, the women of Alternative Women in Development (Alt-WID) provide us with a detailed description of the results of the Reagan years. According to Alt-WID, Reaganomics was a response to severe inflation, stagnating industrial and commercial output, prolonged trade deficit and a perceived budget deficit, and general government inefficiency. Reagan's stated goal was to reduce radically the government's role in the economy.

During the Reagan years the dollar lost some of its value and spending for social programs was sharply reduced. Through antilabor activities and policies, workers lost the ability to keep relatively high wages. The Reagan/Bush administrations altered the tax system to benefit capitalist enterprises and the rich. Many public agencies were sold and many services were privatized. Regulation of financial institutions was significantly reduced.

What did these structural adjustment policies accomplish? Certainly, the U.S. economy grew. This growth was "fueled by military spending, high consumption patterns financed largely by debt of individuals, corporations, and the federal, state and local governments" (Alt-WID, 1992). There was certainly prosperity for the minority, but the majority of U.S. citizens felt a relative decline in income and an increase in economic hardship. Women bore a disproportionate share of this hardship—in 1988, according to Alt-WID, "1 in 7 women was poor, 1 in 6 was living without health coverage, and 1 in 3 of all female-headed families lived below the poverty level." (Poverty level in 1993 for a family of three in Massachusetts was $12,000 per year.) African-American, Latina, and Native American women fared much worse.

The creation of 19 million jobs in the '80s did little to increase the prosperity of poor and working-class women, regardless of their race. Almost three-quarters of jobs n the United States are service-sector jobs. These jobs fit the pattern of the type of work that rises up during a time of structural adjustment: jobs with low wages and few or no benefits. The majority of women in this country, and their families, are working poor, and they hold these low-wage, no-benefit service-sector jobs. With these jobs, they struggle to raise their children and keep their households together.

Welfare Reform as Structural Adjustment

But the impression given by national politicians is that our country is full of welfare cheats living extravagantly off the labor of a hard-pressed middle class. These women—and the implication is that they are mostly women of color—must be forced to work. Hence the cry for reform of public welfare systems. Structural changes in social service and entitlement programs are an integral part of making a national economy more conducive to capitalist corporate activity. It reduces a citizen's expectations of her government and increases the number of people at the mercy of exploitative, low-paying jobs.

Recently, a trend toward using free-market strategies to "free women from dependence on public welfare" has gained prevalence in many states. This free-market approach falls under a set of programs called Self Employment Programs (SEPs). SEPs are considered a progressive reform. They exist in Illinois, Maine, Minnesota, California, and approximately twenty other states. They emphasize entrepreneurship, independence, and market-driven venture development. Poor women are encouraged to enroll in programs that help them to enhance their entrepreneurial skills. These programs emphasize personal development, with special attention to personal appearance and comportment, and prepare women to start their own businesses. Women with little access to those factors that make for successful small businesses—access to capital in the form of family or personal money; convenient, affordable child care; and secure living situations—are encouraged to create microenterprises, small businesses such as catering, door-to-door cosmetic sales, house cleaning, and the like that can be operated from their homes. I have heard women in such programs talk with pride about their increased skills, while fretting over their long days of entrepreneurial activity and unpaid homework (frequently sixteen to eighteen hours), inadequate or nonexistent child care, reduced access to health care, and little or no access to capital. They feel isolated and forced into a competitive lifestyle with none of the family or social supports that accompany capitalist attainment. And, like most small businesses, these fail at least as frequently as the 90 percent of other businesses created in a three-year period. For these women, failure can mean loss of housing security, humiliation, and an even more precarious financial situation than the one they had on welfare.

Creating Just Alternatives

There is a better way. Most of us, if asked to describe the conditions needed to thrive, can readily list economic, social, and spiritual resources that make each day possible: things like a supportive community, access to enjoyable and safe work, access to income, time for oneself or worship or nature. Some of us grew up in cultures responding to social oppression in creative and life-affirming ways. African-American history is full of examples of communities organizing to create economic stability while organizing for the economic rights denied by the larger society. More fundamentally, Native American culture has a deep and rich understanding of how a people can provide for the needs of all. Much of that information was suppressed or driven underground by the first imperialist assault of European conquerors on this continent, but the knowledge still exists. Both Native American and African-American cultures, in their historical attachment to the land, their willingness to protect members from the assault of a violent culture, and their deep commitment to righting the economic wrongs perpetrated on their people have much to teach us about the structure of economies that benefit people. Indeed, there are people, organizations, and movements in this country seeking to create security and economic justice through the creation of worker- and consumer-owned cooperatives, alternative strategies for access to land and housing, and new government policies focusing on creating progressive tax structures, social welfare reform, and participatory community economic development (for example, the American Friends Service Committee's Women and Global Corporations Project, in Philadelphia, Pennsylvania; California Network for a New Economy, in San José, California; and Grassroots Economic Organizing, in New Haven, Connecticut).

We see homelessness on our streets every day, struggle to afford our own health care, are alarmed at the increased violence in women's lives, and perhaps, live personally closer to the edge than in any time that we can remember. We may wonder who is causing this situation, feel resentful toward all those people benefiting from public assistance when we are struggling, let anger overwhelm our ability to think critically and ask the question "but why?" Why are more women poor? Why are the only solutions suggested the ones that benefit transnational and domestic corporate interests? Why are we pitted against workers in Mexico, the Philippines, South Korea, the Caribbean, who, after all, have the same needs for access to income and economic security? And when the answers to these questions make you angry enough, you will decide that, no, the people are not suicidal and, no, we are not meant to perish. Then act. Listen to progressive discussions of NAFTA, welfare reform, and poverty. Contact groups like Alt-WID, your local community land trust, or progressive welfare reform organization, and join women all over the world organizing for the right to live with dignity, in safety, free of the exploitation of policies created by our government to benefit the military, transnational corporations, oppressive regimes, and irresponsible bankers. Remember, together we can defeat this useless, worthless lie.

Author's note: Much of this article grew out of discussions with women at a conference in April 1993 sponsored by the Nationwide Women Program of the American Friends Service Committee. The "Roundtable on Women and the Global Economy" was a four-day discussion involving women from Honduras, Mexico, South Korea, Germany, the Netherlands, the Philippines, Canada, and the United States. Thank you to Luisa Maria Rivera for her concise and insightful description of structural adjustment.

JUNE 1994

The Misogyny of Welfare Reform: Corporate America's Cycle of Dependency
by Randy Albelda

"Reforming welfare as we know it" is a great idea if it means getting poor women and their children out of poverty. Unfortunately, what is being touted as welfare reform is *not* about alleviating poverty. Rather it is a thinly guised economic assault on poor women, who are being punished for lacking access to male income. Attacking welfare is also a ruse: public debate is being redirected away from the real problems that ail many families—especially single-mother families—in the United States. Those problems include lack of child care, poor wages, and jobs that assume someone else will do all the necessary unpaid work at home and in our communities.

Talking about welfare reform scores big points politically. The key to all of the current reforms is to replace the Aid to Families with Dependent Children (AFDC) benefits with mothers' (and deadbeat dads') wages. And if poor mothers don't work, there's lots of punishment in store for them. The ultimate punishment is ending welfare as we know it by simply cutting people off the welfare rolls. The linchpin of President Clinton's current welfare proposal is the two-year limit. Any woman who has received AFDC for any 24 months (they do not have to be consecutive) is no longer eligible for AFDC—regardless of the age of her children.

Another popular punitive welfare "reform" is workfare, which requires the adult recipient of AFDC to perform unpaid services in return for AFDC benefits for her and her child(ren). If she does not perform the free work, she and her family are "sanctioned," meaning they lose their cash benefits. Workfare is supposedly designed as preparation for entering the workforce, but there is no evidence that workfare significantly improves skills or wages after a mother goes off AFDC. Further, anecdotal evidence suggests that many workfare placements do not allow women to care adequately for their children in the event of emergencies or even routine illness.

Another popular punitive proposal is the "family cap." This proposal denies AFDC mothers any additional AFDC benefits upon the birth of another child. Legislators in New Jersey have already approved this measure, and several states are considering it. No empirical evidence substantiates the claim that women have more children just to get an additional meager amount of money (in Massachusetts— a relatively high-benefit state—an additional child gets you $60 a month). In fact, all the evidence points to just the opposite: the average number of children in AFDC families is exactly the same as in other families with children, and the average number of children in AFDC families in low-benefit states is greater than in high-benefit states. The proposal makes as much sense as arguing that the federal income tax deduction for dependents encourages people to have more children (at $2,350 a child for families in the 33 percent tax bracket, this deduction is worth $65 a month).

Few other national issues are driven more by myth than welfare. And, more importantly, few other economic issues are more important to women. Why is this the case?

First, welfare is one of the few national policies almost entirely directed at women and their children. Second, the likelihood of having to rely on welfare at some point in one's life is much too high for any woman— at any given time, one out of every six women is a single mother. But most important, welfare policy is the best indication of what our economic system and policymakers think about women's work—which is not much!

Consider two facts: 1) two-thirds of all people who receive AFDC benefits are children, and 2) one-half of all single-mother families in this country have incomes that are below the poverty line. These two facts are not unrelated. While most are familiar with the term "feminization of poverty," in many ways, the phrase is not accurate. What is really going on is what economist Nancy Folbre has termed the "pauperization of motherhood." Most women, while making considerably less than men in the labor market, for the first time in U.S. history, can support themselves. However, most women cannot support themselves and children on their own—hence, the unbelievably high rates of poverty among single-mother families.

Policymakers have always associated poverty with lack of work either because the economy could not generate enough jobs or because people were unskilled and/or unmotivated. Since the '80s, welfare policies have promoted paid labor (and with it education and training programs) as a means for AFDC recipients to get out of poverty. After all, most women today do paid work, want to work, and in many families, there is little choice in the matter. In the '90s, however, fewer and fewer state welfare proposals want to fund the education and training components necessary for women to find work that could, in fact, support their families; now policymakers primarily promote paid labor with punishments for not working.

The notion that one can eliminate poverty by going to work is a distinctly male policy model. It is time to think about female poverty differently. Single mothers work plenty—both at paid and unpaid jobs. Despite what politicians and the public think, the causes of poverty among single-mother families have less to do with paid employment and more to do with two facts of all mothers' lives: most women earn low wages when they work, and most women must spend time raising their children. Replacing wages with AFDC reduces welfare rolls—it does not reduce child and female poverty.

"Putting mothers to work" is not the most important issue in the welfare debate. Single mothers with children over the age of six work more hours, on average, than do mothers in two-adult families. One-third of married mothers work full-time jobs—about the same percentage as single mothers. The issue is not work. The problem, of course, is time and money. A full-time minimum wage job pays $9,360, which is less than the poverty line for a family of two in 1993. One half of *all* women over 18 and under 65 years of age who worked in 1991 earned less than $13,000.

Ironically, the expectation that all able-bodied adults must work and want to work—one of the women's movement's greatest achievements—has fueled the flames of substituting wages for AFDC benefits. The notion that women's economic independence is predicated on their ability to enter the labor force, on the one hand, has become accepted by society, and, on the other, has helped to fuel the feminist backlash. Though the right wing doesn't get very far by arguing that women should stay at home and raise their children, it has made tremendous in-roads in blaming feminists for "wanting it all"—children and jobs.

The feminist movement has not demanded enough for women who work. For while economic independence comes with the ability to enter the labor force, it begs the question of who is going to take care of the children. The time has come for those concerned with women's economic equality to take a hard look at how society has managed to expect all individuals to do paid work while not ever discussing socializing the costs of raising children.

The key to understanding the misogyny behind welfare is that our market-based system rewards only paid work (and increasingly, we are a society that is rewarding that work less and less, as evidenced by men's falling wages). Despite all the hoopla around family values, economically speaking, we are a society that absolutely does not value the work done in families.

Families typically must rely on wages and salaries to support themselves. Few own enough property to live off interest, dividends, and rent. In order for any family member—male or female— even to get to work every day requires a significant amount of unpaid labor in the home. And if there are children in the home—the work is immense. Despite the fact that unpaid labor is a crucial component to *any* worker's ability to get to work, we have an economic system in which the jobs that pay enough to support a family (i.e., "breadwinners' jobs") are ones that assume a wife at home doing limitless unpaid labor (or they assume there is no caregiving done in the home at all). Good jobs are "jobs with wives."

The reason why half of all single-mother families in this country are poor is not that single mothers are lazy, have no initiative, or are unlucky. The primary reason single-mother families are poor is that there is one female adult responsible for supporting a family. These women *must* do unpaid work, which naturally limits their time to do paid work, and when they do paid work, they are paid significantly less than men.

Welfare reform that argues that work is the answer ignores the realities of women's lives and deeply devalues the work all women already do. Raising children takes time. It is also costly. This is true for all families. It is physically impossible both to take care of children (yes, school-age children need time, too) and have a full-time job without some help—paid or unpaid. Two-adult families where both parents work do an incredible juggling act that is virtually impossible with only one parent.

Single mothers, especially those with school-age children, already do paid work (over 70 percent of single mothers with children over the age of six have paying jobs). Further, the incredibly high rates of voluntary participation of AFDC mothers in employment and training programs is testimony to the deep desire to get a good job. But work is not enough. Mothers need jobs that pay them enough to buy child care and feed their families. Mothers need jobs that allow them to take care of sick children who can't attend day care or school. Mothers need jobs in which they have health care benefits. The issue is not desire or effort.

What single parents (in fact, most parents) lack is not work effort but time and money. Two-parent families have the benefit of two incomes to pay for child care or the option of having one work while the other takes care of the children. Single mothers cannot both work for pay and take care of their children without the appropriate supports—namely, high incomes or very cheap child care and after-school programs.

Politicians and corporate leaders are no fools. They know the facts. To cure what "ails" single mothers is not the point of the welfare reform that is being proposed. Much more to the point would be child care reform, wage reform, and job reform—and not just for single mothers. If women are to work, affordable, quality child care must be available. If women are expected to support their families, they will need to be paid at wages that make this possible. One way to ensure decent wages is through comparable worth legislation—legislation requiring comparable pay for jobs with comparable skills—which would boost women's wages in traditionally female jobs. Finally, if both men and women are going to support their families, we need a jobs program. Very few people have "wives" these days. What we need are jobs without wives for men and women— jobs that require no more than 30 hours a week and pay a living wage so that we can all take care of our families and our communities.

But to pursue policies that would benefit all women—not just single mothers—would mean that women with children could choose to live without the support of a man. An important component of welfare "reform" is precisely to make this option remarkably unattractive. Behind welfare reform lurks a struggle over the "right" types of families. In short, this is a struggle about women's choices at the most fundamental level.

Women choose to raise children without male support for varied reasons: some do it rather than remain in abusive situations; others have been left by men; others simply have decided they want children whether or not there is a male support; others have children as a means of shoring up self-worth in a society that values them little. Despite the reason, it is precisely the choice to bring up children without a man—actually without a male income—that is at the heart of this issue.

What also lurks behind welfare reform is an attack on the most politically and economically disenfranchised group in the United States—poor women and their children. The attack diverts attention from the real economic and political problems of our society: an economic structure that competes with, rather than accommodates, the necessary work of taking care of ourselves, our families, and our communities.

Families, U.S. businesses, and the government have become "dependent" on women's unpaid labor. The cycle of dependency we need to be addressing nationally is not single mothers' sustained need for government income supplements to support their families. That dependency is nothing new: mothers have always been dependent on income supplements; typically, they just came from a man she was related to (her husband, father, brother). What is new is our economic system's simultaneous dependency on cheap female workers *and* their unpaid work at home.

Families are hooked on unpaid labor because they can survive in no other way. Someone has to do it. The future labor force cannot be sustained unless they are taken care of as children. Currently, businesses are reaping the benefits of women's (and increasingly men's) lower wages and their unpaid work, but individual families are paying the price. As the two-working-parent family becomes the rule rather than the exception, who do we think is taking care of the kids? How long can businesses assume that every worker has a wife?

The dependency on unpaid labor also serves those in political power well: the attacks on single mothers allow the federal and state governments to reduce their welfare rolls and at the same time avoid discussions about the taxes that would have to be raised or budget cuts implemented if we dared to socialize the cost of raising children.

We must break the cycle of dependency on women's unpaid and cheap labor. Let's truly end welfare as we know it and have some real welfare reform. It is vital that women see welfare reform as a key component of any women's economic agenda. Until we begin to talk seriously about socializing the cost of raising all children, paying women what they are worth in the labor market, and instituting a 30-hour week, all women—but especially low-income women—are economic losers.

SEPTEMBER 1994

POOR WOMEN NEED TO TAKE MORE RESPONSIBILITY

DEAR *SOJOURNER:*
"The Misogyny of Welfare Reform" wants us to believe that poverty results from unpaid labor in the home, low-paying jobs, the cost of child rearing, and the unresponsiveness of government to the special needs of mothers. This is idealistic feminist rhetoric, which fails to take into account three very important factors.

The first is the role of personal responsibility. We have lost sight of the fact that we make decisions that have consequences for which we must accept responsibility. A woman who drops out of school at sixteen, leaving herself unprepared to enter the job market except at the low-paying end of the spectrum, must then cope with the results of her decision. The fact that God gave women the biological ability to have children does not give us the right to procreate whenever we choose. Parenthood is a serious responsibility. We have a responsibility to ourselves, our unborn child, and society to be able to provide for that child. If we cannot or are unable to purchase services such as child care, we must reconsider becoming a parent until we are able to do so. Delayed gratification is not a crime.

The second factor is the role of government in our lives. The United States is a land of opportunities, not guarantees. There is an unfortunate and pervasive sense of entitlement in this country that transcends all social and economic levels. If we want something that is unattainable on our own, we want the government to provide a "program" or other mechanism by which we can have it—*now!* The government is not designed to be a surrogate parent or caretaker for its citizens. Nor is it meant to rescue us from ourselves and the decisions we make. To make the government or anyone else responsible for the decisions we make creates an atmosphere where failure to bring our wishes to fruition makes us feel unjustifiably victimized. This is an unhealthy, unproductive, and self-defeating message for women to internalize.

The third factor is the role of the women's movement in the poverty of women. It has produced both positive and negative results. We have gained freedom while becoming isolated and alienated from those sources of support that our foremothers relied on: i.e., the extended family, informal child care, the community, and the church. We have attained control over our bodies and removed the stigma of having children outside of marriage while all but absolving men of responsibility for supporting their offspring. Now, Albelda is suggesting we want independence, provided that we are able to rely on governmental assistance when it is convenient. And we want equality, provided that it takes into account our special childbearing skills with special privileges. Is welfare reform truly misogynistic or are we asking for the world to be handed to us on a gold platter?

Poverty is a fact of life. It was present when this country was founded and, realistically speaking, it will be a part of this society when the world comes to an end. We will never eliminate it, but we can lessen the numbers of people affected by it. Doing so means recognizing and behaving in a manner that acknowledges and respects the reciprocal relationship between the individual and the government.

Individuals need to make responsible decisions that minimize their risk of vulnerability to financial disaster. The government needs to stop funding programs on the "cause of the month plan" and to begin concentrating on providing adequate safety net programs we all need in case of unforeseen and unpredictable crises.

It is time for society to hold people accountable for those decisions that they alone have control over. And it is time to stop blaming the government for not taking responsibility for things over which it has little, if any, control.

Tori Joseph
West Dennis, MA

MARCH 1993

IMPOVERISHED WOMEN POSE SOLUTIONS

DEAR *SOJOURNER:*

It's good to see you reporting about women and poverty. I'd like to update you on some of the goals/solutions to the poverty of women that impoverished women ourselves are proposing. Too often our voices are not heard by those expounding on the problem, even within the feminist movement.

One of the primary reasons for the poverty of women worldwide is that we perform the caregiving and caretaking work, which in most cases is *unpaid labor.* We provide the child care, training, supervision, and nurturing for most children; do most of the housework in most homes; and care for most of the elderly or disabled people who need care. Since we usually do, and have historically done, this caregiving work for free, this work is also one of the lowest paid jobs in the world when we *do* get paid for it.

Although we all know that women perform this crucial work for free, few modern-day "problem solvers," whether politicians, business people, or feminists, will acknowledge that our poverty is simply a result of the *unpaid* nature of nurturing work. Instead, they argue that the solution is to push us into those types of work that pay living wages and to eliminate sexual and racial discrimination in the workforce.

Of course, all decent people want to eliminate discrimination. And we all want women to be allowed to work in any and every job that we choose. However that will never solve the problem of the poverty of women, nor will it solve the problem of our communities' needs for loving, competent, skilled caregivers and caretakers! If we all quit caring for the children, the old, the sick, the earth, how will we survive? And no, mothers cannot simply add on a full-time *paid* job while continuing to provide full-time care. That is called the double workday, and it is violently oppressive and counterproductive.

It is obvious that the solution to the poverty of women is to include our work in the labor force so that it is paid and so that caregiving is recognized as equally important as the work of doctors, lawyers, business people, and therapists. The question of how we will pay the caregivers is a challenge that needs to be addressed by all progressive people.

Women in Ottawa, Canada, are organizing around the slogan "Mothers Are Women," while trying to persuade the feminist movement to include the issues of mothers and other caregivers in their agenda. They publish a magazine called *Homebase,* which allows mothers who provide child care and homemaking in their homes to unite and validate one another. Some of their ideas for paying caregivers include an idea from Mother Earth's Centre in Toronto, Canada. They recommend that homebased caregivers receive an income of not less than that of the average income of fully employed wage-earners in the community (about $25,000 a year). The income would be paid by the government, preferably local government. They also support fully subsidized out-of-home child care. They state that any healthy community recognizes that adults who are full-time caregivers, and the children in their care, are at the heart of every viable human community.

Another activity of the Canadian Mothers Are Women (MAW) movement involved lobbying the Canadian Justice Department to include the work of at-home childcare and domestic workers in the census and national accounts. MAW has also actively lobbied within the National Action Committee on the Status of Women (a national governmental women's group) to reflect the reality of and state the objectives of mothers and women at home in the struggle for their equality.

Closer to home is the "Wages for Housework" group, with offices in Philadelphia, Los Angeles, San Francisco, London, and Trinidad. This group works with both local governments as well as the United Nations to open the debate on paying women for the work we do. They have produced journals, literature, T-shirts, buttons, towels, postcards, and greeting cards to promote the message of the importance of *paying* women for caregiving and caretaking work.

The Welfare Warriors, a group of single moms working out of Milwaukee, Wisconsin, produce a bilingual mothers' publication, *Welfare Mothers Voice,* and staff a MOMS helpline to make the voices of impoverished mothers heard in their own communities as well as in the world of government, business, and feminism. The Welfare Warriors advocate a guaranteed income for all caregivers, comparable to the Social Security stipend received by mothers who care for children of a dead or disabled dad. (The requirements that the father be deceased and that he have been attached to the labor force would have to be eliminated.) They recommend that the government provide this income as long as the children are dependent (to age eighteen). The Welfare Warriors argue that the current system, which punishes and stigmatizes children and mothers in homes where the fathers have abandoned or abused them or cannot earn enough to support them, implies that the only deserving caregivers are those who manage to be left by dead or disabled dads. (Is that a message to kill the deadbeat dads?) The Welfare Warriors argue that all children deserve the support of the community, and all caregivers need to be paid.

We urge feminists to keep these issues alive, to debate, discuss, and deliberate how our communities can begin to value, pay, and promote the work that women do and that the community needs for its survival. Women at home on the farm, the city block, and in the suburbs have always been the caretakers of the community as well as the home. We cannot afford to eliminate this work. *Someone has to do it.* We are losing our sense of community and the sanity of our communities in this focus on the workplace versus the home. We need workers in both places. And we need to pay *all* of our workers.

Pat Gowens
Milwaukee, WI

© 1994 Marilyn Humphries

© 1986 Linda Haas

CHAPTER THREE

The Politics of the Family

Over the last three decades, the nuclear family has been at the very heart of the battle between progressive and conservative forces in the United States. Feminist challenges to the nuclear family—an institution seen as fundamentally oppressive to women—have run head-on into a growing religious Right, fearful that the collapse of the "mother-father-2.5 children" unit is responsible for all the social ills of late twentieth century society, from poverty and violence to teenage pregnancy and AIDS. Right-wing politicians such as Jesse Helms, Bob Dole, and Newt Gingrich have used that fear to promote a conservative social and economic agenda that has two goals: to reassert white, heterosexual male privilege, and to dismantle the welfare state. At the heart of their strategy has been the construction of a "profamily" ideology that attacks abortion, welfare, and gay rights, all of which symbolize the freedom of women to live without men. In this chapter, we look at debates within the feminist movement around constructing families and raising children, particularly within the context of the profamily ideology that has gained cultural and political hegemony over the last two decades.

For white, middle-class feminists of the '60s and '70s, the male-dominated, child-centered nuclear family was the single most important site of female oppression. In 1963, Betty Friedan's *The Feminine Mystique* (W. W. Norton) highlighted the oppressive nature of the ideology of domesticity, which had flung women out of the work force and into suburban homes, following World War II. Though Friedan's critique did not challenge the patriarchal structure of the family, her criticisms resonated with thousands of middle-class, college-educated women who had "chosen" full-time homemaking in lieu of careers and found themselves bored and isolated. These were not the happy wives/mothers of "The Donna Reed Show," "Father Knows Best," and "Leave It to Beaver," women content in their roles as full-time caretakers and second-class citizens. Angry that they had been hoodwinked into believing that domesticity could provide an emotionally and intellectually fulfilling life, they joined the women's movement in search of expanding opportunities and began to challenge sex discrimination in education, business, and the law.

Radical feminists were even more critical of the family. In 1970, Shulamith Firestone published *The Dialectic of Sex: The Case for Feminist Revolution* (Morrow), in which she argued that the family, and women's oppression, originated in women's need for food and protection during pregnancy and while nursing her young. Freeing women from the biological constraints of reproduction and making childrearing a responsibility of society as whole, Firestone argued, would go a long way in dismantling the oppressive family structure. Radical feminists demanded "free 24-hour day care," as the first step toward socializing child care responsibilities (see Molly Lovelock, "Bringing Up Baby: The Day Care Question," 1981).

The family was problematic in other ways as well. As the primary site of gender socialization, the family was where girls and boys learned the rules of femininity and masculinity respectively. While girls were taught to gain fulfillment from taking care of others, boys learned to wield the power of masculinity. Mothers were idolized but exploited, expected to serve everyone's needs but their own. Trapped by the conflicting needs of self, spouse, and children, mothers were never as perfect as their children expected and carried all the blame for their children's problems from childhood to adulthood. In fact, mother-blaming was a venerable tradition reinforced by the popularization of Freudian psychology during the '40s and '50s.

Moreover, feminists declared, families kept women economically dependent on men. Not only were women expected to stay home and focus their entire lives on caretaking (if their families could afford it), but women who did work were paid less than their male counterparts because they "didn't need to support a family." This economic dependence left women vulnerable to violence—battering and incest, feminists discovered, were a "normal" part of family life—and to poverty in cases of abandonment or divorce.

Some radical feminists felt so strongly about the reactionary nature of the family that they limited the number of married women allowed into their political groups. How could women, legally—or even emotionally—attached to men, free themselves from patriarchal control? they asked. These feminists looked for alternative ways of constructing their lives. Many chose to live in lesbian feminist collectives (see Gloria Z. Greenfield, "Thoughts on Lesbian Living Collectives," 1978), but others chose to live alone or in more diverse collectives that included men and/or children. In 1979, Karen Lindsey wrote "Familiar Friends Are a Natural Resource," expanding the notion of family to what has come to be called "chosen family": those on whom we depend emotionally (and sometimes for economic help as well) but to whom we may have no blood relation and with whom we may not even share a home. Lindsey challenged the image of the isolated, lonely, spinster by arguing that women living alone were not necessarily living without "family." The families they created for themselves, however, were free of the oppressive, heterosexist, and patriarchal structure of the traditional nuclear family.

For many women in the '70s, experimentation with alternative lifestyles was fundamentally connected to their politics. Lesbian feminists, in particular, felt they were putting "the personal is political" into practice as they established rural and urban communities, in which they shared resources, ate vegetarian food, and tried to create a women's culture based on principles of cooperation and nonviolence. But what about married feminists?

According to Molly Lovelock ("Married Feminists: Fish Out of Water?" 1978), married feminists often felt like "fish out of water," unwelcome in a movement that seemed to hold so much promise yet often seemed hostile toward women attached to men. Moreover, balancing family with meetings, demonstrations, and women-only events could be difficult, making it harder for married women to become involved in the movement at the same level as lesbians who were building their lives around movement activities. Yet marriage often made women feminists. Once married, women confronted some of the culture's most sexist practices: expectations that women would change their names, give up career aspirations, make homemaking and children the center of their existence, and defer to their husbands when it came to making significant family decisions. Married feminists were very much on the frontlines in the sense that they struggled every day to create egalitarian relationships within the most sexist of institutions.

The tension between married and unmarried feminists took a different form in the '80s, as evidenced by Susan Shapiro's article "Motherhood: Choices That Divide Us" (1988), written exactly one decade after Lovelock's piece. By the late '80s, the context in which feminists examined the choices of marriage and motherhood had changed radically. The pronatalist and profamily ideology of the Right, which brought us the defeat of the ERA, the antiabortion movement, campaigns to reverse human rights legislation guaranteeing the civil rights of gays and lesbians, had clearly made inroads on the Left as well (see Ellen Herman, "Still Married After All These Years?," 1990). Popular culture once again celebrated domesticity, while villainizing the single career woman. New reproductive technologies pressured women to pursue childbearing at any cost.

Moreover, by the '80s, women of color were raising questions about the feminist critique of the family, suggesting that families were not only sites of patriarchal oppression; i.e. in communities of color, they argued, families were often sites of resistance. The family maintained cultural traditions, taught children to be proud of their heritage, and provided support to resist the racism and ethnocentrism of the larger society.

In this context, experiments with alternative lifestyles gave way to a resurgence of traditional marriages and a baby boom that even crossed over into lesbian-feminist communities. By the '90s, with lesbians and gays demanding the right to marry (in 1994, the Hawaii state superior court ruled that "heterosexual only" marriage was a form of sex discrimination, setting off a larger movement throughout the country), Firestone's 1970 call to dismantle the family seemed only a whisper from a distant past. Feminists who remained committed to alternatives—to living alone or in groups, to not having children or to raising children in a collective environment—were now the ones who felt alienated (see J. Kay, "Childlessness," 1992).

The question of "choosing children" had become a divisive issue within lesbian-feminist communities by the mid '80s (see Ellen Herman, "The Romance of Lesbian Motherhood," 1988). Those who had committed themselves to the lesbian community for the very reason that it represented "unconventional" womanhood—women living without the constraints of children and family—felt abandoned by sisters who seemed to be bowing to the "profamily" pressure of the '80s by creating their own version of the nuclear family—two moms and a baby. Long-time lesbian mothers, many of whom had had children before coming out and had always felt unsupported and slightly alien within the primarily childless lesbian-feminist communities of the '70s, felt angry that children were now "in." But for many, the choice to have children represented a kind of "lesbian coming of age": lesbians had overcome the internalized homophobia that led them to believe that they were unfit mothers. Choosing children could be seen as an act of resistance against a limited, heterosexist definition of family, particularly in the face of antigay legislation such as that passed in 1985 in Massachusetts, which denied lesbians and gay men the right to raise foster children.

The decision to become a mother is, as Ellen Herman points out, the most personal of decisions, yet it cannot be removed from the political context in which women live their lives. For lesbians, the choices become more complex as they face decisions about how to have and raise the children they desire. Both artificial insemination and adoption are options most often reserved for heterosexual married couples. Though both routes have become popular among middle-class lesbians (both are expensive, making them inaccessible to many women), it is not always easy to find a sperm bank or an adoption agency that accepts lesbian clients. Both methods have their drawbacks, the first leaving the child without a known father, the second raising complex issues of race and class, as adopted children are most often from poor, Third World countries. For lesbians who choose known donors, the role of the father in the child's life must be determined as well, an issue that is made all the more complicated by legal and social policies that tend to support father's rights over those of a nonbiological mother.

Choosing children is, of course, a privileged "choice." Most women find their families shaped by economic, social, and political forces beyond their control. As Mi Ok Bruining and Roxanna Pastor argue in their 1989 articles on international adoption ("Made in Korea" and "The Honduran Baby Market"), the privilege of white, middle-class women to adopt is predicated on the lack of choices available to women in the Third World. In the case of Korea, the patriarchal state and social order forces "unwed mothers" to give up their children, while in Honduras and other Central American countries, women sometimes sell their children out of sheer economic desperation. Noting that, when it comes to adoption, one mother's gain is another's loss, Judith Beckett wonders in "Birthmarks: A Birthmother's View of Adoption" (1989), why we so easily accept this transfer of children from the poor to the wealthy. "Who benefits," she asks, "when children are taken from single, poor, Hispanic, and teenage women in this country—indeed from any woman—and placed in traditional (patriar-chal) 'families'?"

Indeed, who benefits from the various social and economic policies that affect family life? Though in the United States there is a great deal of talk among politicians, religious leaders, and talk show hosts about sup-porting families, the reality is that the U. S. government does less for fami-lies than any other Western, industrialized country. The myth of the nuclear family—a working father, mother at home raising the children—has a greater impact on public policy than the realities of family life. Today, in the United States, less than 20 percent of families conform to this ideal picture. Even in two-parent families, most women work out of financial necessity. Yet women still earn significantly lower wages than men; day care is still expensive and inaccessible; and workplaces are still organized with the assumption that men will pursue careers while their wives will carry the major share of family responsibilities. Even the 1993 Family and Medical Leave Act, Congress's great effort to support families by guaran-teeing the right of parents to take time from work to care for sick children, provides only *unpaid* leave, an unaffordable option for most working par-ents. Public policy refuses to support working mothers, because the politi-cal and economic elite of this country want to reinforce the illusion that women are supported by men, thereby maintaining a marginalized, low-paid work force that can be lured in and out of the workplace as needed.

Of course, as public policy experts are well aware, the reality is that, in the United States, 47 percent of Black families, 23 percent of Latino families, and 14 percent of white families are "female-headed house-holds." Though feminists are often blamed for this "breakdown of the American family," this demographic shift is primarily the result of eco-nomic policies that have led to the deindustrialization of the U.S. economy. Without high wage industrial labor jobs, men can no longer afford to sup-port families; in this context, the traditional nuclear family is obsolete. But because social welfare policy does not provide the means for women to both care for their children and support them economically, 50 percent of female-headed households live at or below the poverty line. As Kate Huard writes in "Casualties of the Patriarchal War" (1989), "parenting is not val-ued in our capitalist society in such a way that life can be supported eco-nomically.... One of the major reasons 'people' (read: women) are on welfare in the first place is because they are the unsupported primary care-takers of dependent children." Yet, as Huard notes, welfare payments and other social supports are so stingy and punitive that it is almost impossible for women and children to escape the destructive forces of poverty. Real families struggle every day for survival because the state, convinced that it can drive women back to men (even without providing adequate jobs), refuses to provide the social and economic support necessary to raise healthy, well-educated, and socially responsible children. Conservative efforts to "downsize government" may rest on a "profamily" ideology, but the goal—to support capitalist expansion by cutting taxes for corporations and wealthy individuals while reducing support for poor women and children—is about as antifamily as one could imagine. (For more on single mothers and welfare reform, see Chapter 2: Economic Injustice.)

Though economic changes may have had the greatest impact on family life over the last three decades, we cannot ignore the influence of the feminist and gay liberation movements. In analyzing how the nuclear family oppressed women and children, feminists created a wider vision of possibility. Women are exploring new options—living alone or with other women—pressing for more egalitarian marriages, raising children on their own, and divorcing without shame. The lesbian and gay movement has legitimized alternative families, claiming that gay families, with or without children, deserve the same social respect and economic support (tax credits, health care, etc.) as other families. But new visions require a new social context. Without a movement that continues to press for social and economic policies that allow women to live autonomously, without the economic support of men—including legal and accessible abortion services, affirmative action and pay equity in the workplace, affordable day care and health care, antidiscrimination laws that include lesbians and gay men, and state support for women raising young children—few women will be able to *choose* to live outside the confines of traditional family structures.

FEBRUARY 1978

Married Feminists: Fish Out of Water?

by Molly Lovelock

A Married Woman: She has a clerical job with an insurance company. Two of her children are in school; she has makeshift arrangements for the third because day care is too expensive. Her doctor has recommended a hysterectomy. Her husband helps out sometimes with the dishes, but she can't push him too far: his paycheck keeps the family going. Both she and her husband spend as much time as they can with their children—they want a good future for them. She's not a feminist. She hasn't the time or the interest to go to a women's center or demonstrate for abortion rights. But it's for her that the women's movement exists.

A Radical Feminist: She works housecleaning, typing, and doing other odd jobs. She's involved in several women's organizations and often goes to meetings four nights a week. Other evenings she goes dancing at a women's bar, has dinner with friends, or works on an article she's writing. Before the women's movement, she was active in the Left and in tenant organizing. She's not married. She hasn't the time or the interest for husband and children. The women's movement exists because of her efforts.

There are few married, active feminists in the Cambridge-Boston area. I know because I am one and had to actively seek out other married feminists for this article. "A fish out of water," one woman described us. What role do we play in the women's movement? How does feminism affect our married lifestyle?

Married feminists are actually in all types of women's activities. There are few, certainly, in lesbian-separatist groups although we're not totally absent even there. More married feminists are involved in day care and in the health movement. We're not just in NOW [National Organization for Women] (which recently elected its first full-time homemaker as national president). In fact, Boston NOW has relatively few married members; recent task force emphasis has been on lesbian rights and "women in transition" (women recently widowed or divorced).

Married women have some obvious disadvantages within the women's movement. One problem is time. When are we home? When are we at meetings? To various degrees, we have a life outside the women's movement, aside from our feminist friends. Married feminists have to make more choices if attending a feminist event—a lesbian can bring her lover to the Holly Near concert or to a potluck supper and discussion group, but a married feminist either attends feminist events alone or goes someplace else with her husband.

"Women's space" can create problems for married feminists. No one I talked to longed to include her husband in feminist gatherings. However, telling another woman that an event is closed to her male friend may be especially awkward for a married feminist, who may want to say that you can be a feminist and still be with a man. It is painful if husbands or sons are hurt by antimale rhetoric from within the movement. Sometimes this is inevitable and beneficial; other times it's not.

Rare, but especially damaging, according to most of the women I talked to, is being totally ostracized or condemned as a married woman. One feminist reported a whole variety of criticism when she recently got married. Another told of a coworker in a feminist organization who reacted: "What! Not you—*married?*" Other married feminists consciously choose groups or activities that minimize personal scrutiny or lifestyle criticism. One woman talked about more subtle discrimination, such as scheduling policymaking meetings during the dinner hour. (This is particularly difficult for women with children.)

Married women, though, have certain advantages as feminists. One is some protection against "burn-out." For a woman without other commitments, the pressure to work day and night on the movement may be overwhelming (especially in Cambridge). To have a husband or children say, "You promised to go to the beach with us Saturday!" may be justification for time off, which we otherwise might feel guilty about taking.

Several women I talked to were radicalized as feminists by marriage. One woman described the anger she felt not being able to keep her own name, being isolated in a new location, being treated differently by friends and coworkers. This experience "tipped her over the top" from being aware of women's issues to being a radical. Another woman had the experience of seeing herself in *The Feminine Mystique* (W.W. Norton, 1963) and admits that the book totally changed her life.

Being married may enable us to make contact with women some feminists rarely meet. Sixty percent of U.S. women are married. We are not necessarily converting the wives of our husbands' coworkers or the mothers of our children's friends, but we may be in touch with their concerns. Feminist issues such as day care, abortion rights, birth control, or sterilization abuse can affect our lives directly.

One woman felt marriage put her more in touch with her own anger against men. It's impossible, if married, to isolate ourselves in a cozy, women-only world. Someone is always there to remind us that we're "*Mrs.* John Jones," that the work we do is irrelevant, that we should care about dishwashing liquid.

On the other hand, marriage can bring some *tangible* benefits, sometimes known as "heterosexual privilege." Marriage may make us look "safe" to potential employers. We are less subject to male advances. Spouse benefits like health insurance are valuable. A long-term commitment and a working husband may allow a woman to choose feminist activities instead of a full-time job. No one I talked to wanted to be "supported" by a husband—obviously an uncomfortable position for a feminist. But on the other hand, the full-time control of an employer—or of the welfare department—makes certain political and other work difficult.

As married feminists, we are a "presence" in the movement. Among feminists, we're there, doing work and caring about issues like anyone else. Maybe we mitigate the tendency to equate lifestyles with politics. Since some women in the movement *do* equate the two, it was reassuring to see that the women I talked to didn't want any "political credit or blame" for being married.

Finally, on the outside we're a presence, too. People see us married, sometimes with children, yet still involved in radical activities. Perhaps this makes it easier for some women to take that first step toward feminism.

Being married, then, has both negative and positive connections with our feminism, although generally the women I talked with felt their marriage helped their work as feminists.

What about the reverse? What effect does feminism have on our marriages?

Some of us find feminism makes large demands on our time. We'd like to see our husbands (or children) more, although we want to maintain our independent priorities and feminist activities. Routines of setting aside a certain evening to be home, or crossing days off the calendar are never totally satisfactory. This conflict is heightened since our husbands don't always have a "cause" analogous to our feminism, nor do men in general put as much time and effort into their same-sex friendships.

Feminism, though, has expanded the concept of marriage so that more lifestyles are possible for married women. One feminist can spend most evenings at home with her husband. Another can live across the street from hers. Husband and wife can split child care and paying jobs in various ways, although, like most women, the feminists I spoke to who had children assumed the major burden. Even if everything is split equally internally, society has different expectations for wives than for husbands, and these expectations are impossible to avoid.

No one spoke of her "liberated marriage" (as Caryl Rivers did in a *New York Times* article). Perhaps, ultimately, we're feminists because that's never possible (any more than being a "liberated woman").

Feminism does mean that our marriages, in order to continue at all, are more egalitarian. Sometimes this equality was always a natural part of the relationship; other times it was hard and painful to develop. One woman admitted that she and her husband stayed together only because they didn't want to go through a divorce—their only alternative was to change the marriage and themselves. Another woman pointed out that feminism made her realize how much was required of a "nonsexist" husband. Equal sharing of housework is so symbolic that it can obscure other problems. In many cases, these problems were more acute for women who were married for a while before they became feminists.

Marriage as a lifestyle has feminist implications. One woman said feminism, for her, had to do with the *quality* of her relationships. Marriage has to do with commitments, generally an unpopular idea, but ultimately a very feminist one. Several of the women I spoke to said they found it especially rewarding to raise children within the framework of that commitment.

Marriage can be "asexual." Knowing someone very well creates the potential to relate as *people*. Relating to a person who happens to be a man was brought out by several of the women I talked to, including one woman whose previous long-term relationships had all been with women.

Would we get married again? Most of us said we would (but only to the husband we already have). Marriage has been more patriarchal, more damaging to women than almost any known institution. Married feminists, whatever their lifestyles, are still a part of this institution but are in a particularly good position to be critical of it. We are trying to live our lives differently than other women have been able to in the past. We have no models except our own lives. For the women's movement to grow, it must admit women of many lifestyles, including married feminists.

FEBRUARY 1978

Thoughts on Lesbian Living Collectives
by Gloria Z. Greenfield

Discovering a writing technique to present my experiences in collective lesbian living has been most difficult. After many unsuccessful attempts with sentence structure, I decided to allow my thoughts to flow into the typewriter and out onto the paper. The following is a collage of thoughts from a participant in a four-year-old collective lesbian lifestyle.

collective living for lesbians is an everchanging process/the older the collective becomes the more it changes because the individual lesbians—the atoms—change with experiences and maturity/that is, our needs change/

the beginning of the collective—or the hand-fasting ceremony—the agreement, the moving in, the arranging of the household—is perhaps the easiest stage of the collective process because that is when we are most ignorant of the questions that need to be asked to decide if this particular situation is possible/

one of the reasons we do not know the questions to ask is because of the absence of recorded role models/even if collective lesbian living has occurred successfully we surely don't have many primary sources to rely on/therefore, lesbians involved in collective living are involved in an artistic process/we are all artists in that we intentionally use materials such as experience, imagination, and vision to transform a patriarchal reality into a gynergetic reality/we have been very creative/

i find it necessary to make a distinction between those lesbian collectives who see their situation as temporary and those lesbian collectives who have made a life commitment to each other/how can anything be a life commitment you may ask but let me remind you that we more easily accept a life commitment from couples—especially heterosexual couples—and not because they are healthier but merely because society expects that heterosexual couples be loyal and dedicated to each other while lesbian relationships are seen as temporary/lesbian collectives need to create our own social expectations and the most important expectations being that we are dedicated to our quest and loyal to our commitment/

during the summer of 1976 charlotte bunch participated in a lesbian panel discussion in new york city where she mentioned her experience with collective living in the furies—an early lesbian collective in washington, d.c./becoming divorced with feelings of hostility, she did not speak with much hope/rather, she implied that collective living was nearly impossible/after all, they tried and couldn't succeed/

i remember her words piercing my soul because i did not need to hear her negative conclusion/i needed to hear some lesbian say, yes, i am involved in a lesbian collective and we saw these problems approach, or we got involved in these particular problems and this is how we decided to get beyond it and this is how we learned from it, because our commitment was to succeed in developing a lifestyle that was healthy, supportive, and lasting/so charlotte's words were lurking threats to me/i was afraid that when problems occurred her words would take form in my mind and block imagination that is necessary for solution/

there are many issues involved in a lesbian living collective/for instance, clothes: should we each recognize the closets in our bedrooms or should we create one collective closet/should we purchase clothes that will fit all of us/my collective began with individual closets, asking each other if we could wear each other's clothes at particular times/when we moved into the country, we created one closet/after all, there's not a great variety of clothing that is needed in an isolated farm country situation/and besides that, we didn't have the money to buy new clothes/it wasn't very long before we forgot that we ever had our own clothes, and that we each had a particular style of dressing/ when we eventually moved back to the boston area, we ignored the closets in our bedrooms and put all of our clothes into one closet/as time went by, and we settled back into urban living—which is our preference—we slowly became aware that we preferred wearing clothes that suited our individual tastes, and that fit us/our financial situation was also changing—we all found jobs that allowed us the luxury of buying clothes occasionally/yet, we were each intimidated by the structure we had established of a collective closet/

to make the issue more complicated, we were sharing all our money/when we moved to the country, there was never an excess of money/every penny went toward paying for heat and potatoes/therefore, there was never an opportunity to use the collective money for items such as personal clothing or going to the movies/after we returned to the city and the finances changed, it seemed difficult to break out of the pattern established/it was difficult to say, yes, i am going to use some of our money to buy myself a shirt that makes me feel like an individual because it's my style and my size/within a couple of months we changed our financial structure/an assessment was made of the monies needed to meet collective expenses, and we maintained a joint account to meet the expenses/in addition, we each began personal accounts/the assessment of our collective expenses and responsibility to meeting that assessment also allowed us to assess what our personal needs were/if i wanted to go cross-country for the summer, i could do so without feeling irresponsible to the collective/my financial responsibility was clearly defined and working to save extra money for the trip became a personal decision/

i feel that the most important issue that we are dealing with right now is change: how do we maintain a supportive environment while an individual collective member is experiencing changes in her self image/how do we avoid being threatened by the inevitable effect it will have upon the collective/how do we avoid being caught up in structures that are no longer relevant to our present situation/

when our structure is not flexible enough, it is very easy for the collective to be more sapping than supportive/more energy is needed to adhere to a structure rather than to invest that energy into positive change/the result might be a feeling of suffocation and entrapment/the instinct will be to escape/i think that the most important experience that i can share is that the collective lesbian lifestyle is a constant evolutionary process, and that the moment it resigns itself to pattern, it begins to decay/

SEPTEMBER 1979

Familiar Friends Are a Natural Resource

by Karen Lindsey

Shortly before last Easter, I was chatting with my friend Kathy and another friend of hers, who was planning to spend the holiday with his family. What was Kathy doing? he asked.

Kathy grinned, looked at me, and said, "Oh, I'm spending Easter with my family, too." The "family" was me—we'd planned to get some work done and then take a long Scrabble break together.

Kathy and I have lived in the same building for over a year, and though we're close friends and spend a lot of time together, this was the first time either of us had verbalized what we both knew our relationship to be. We were, and are, family.

Each of us has perfectly good parents and siblings, with whom we enjoy perfectly good relationships. But adults need families outside of those they grew up with. Conventionally, of course, this need has been met by spouses and children; unconventionally, by roommates and commune-mates. But the assumption about the person living alone is that she has no family other than the one she grew up with.

This assumption is rooted in the narrow definition of family that the straight world has always accepted, but also in the contempt and disbelief that both the straight and countercultures have always felt for the person who chooses to live alone. It's either unnatural or it's bourgeois individualism—or it's a way of treading water till the right man (or the right commune) comes along to rescue you. If you really treat it as a lifestyle, you're antisocial, unwilling to make commitments, or at least self-deceived.

I *like* living alone. So does Kathy. We've both lived in a variety of roommate situations, good and bad. We've both made clear, comfortable choices about how we want to live. I need solitude; I need to know for at least part of every day that there's no one else around, and I need to have some control over what time of day that is.

I also like companionship, support, and warmth, given and received. I like to be cheered in my triumphs, babied when I'm sick. I like family. So does Kathy. So does my friend Mark, who also lives in the building and is part of my family (though not of Kathy's—they hardly know each other). We didn't move into the building together, or at the same time. But a major factor in both Kathy's and Mark's choice of the building was the fact that I lived in it.

For people who live alone, the effort put into relationships—into creating family (which is a form of close friendship, though not all close friends are family)—is precious and conscious. Every moment spent with people is deliberately chosen—family is an ongoing choice, never simply a given state of coexistence.

It helps, of course, when your family lives in the same building, but it's not necessary. One of the happiest couples I know—the sort of warm, committed, monogamous couple that makes you believe in the possibility of heterosexual happiness after all—have been together for nearly ten years. They live in apartments on the same block and spend much of their free time together. They're considering moving into larger quarters, in two separate apartments.

Their relationship has affected my fantasy life, I'm sure. I still dream, from time to time, of Mr. Right—you know, the perfectly nonsexist guy who'll take one look at my shiny teeth and realize he can't live without me. For a long time, in my daydreams, Mr. Right and I lived in a cozy little apartment together, like the one I lived in with Mr. Not-So-Right in another lifetime. Once I started living alone and realizing how much I needed space, I built an extra room onto my dream house: Mr. Right and I now had separate studies. Then, in the midst of a brief relationship, I realized that I really like sleeping alone—that glorious feeling of being able to toss and turn without crashing into another body was very seductive. I added a separate bedroom to the dream house. When I realized how much I enjoyed eating dinner alone without interrupting the mental flow of whatever I was working on, I decided there was no point in sharing the john either. There's a place in my mind where Mr. Right and I now live, in perfect Hollywood harmony and in adjacent apartments.

But Mr. Right isn't quite as important as he used to be. The great love would be nice, but it wouldn't fill all my needs for love and companionship—and it wouldn't have to. I have loving friends, and I have family-friends. With Kathy especially, there's that wonderful linkage of closeness and casualness that betokens real intimacy. We see each other, at least briefly, nearly every day, no matter how busy we are. Sometimes I bring work up to her apartment and we work separately and companionably. Sometimes, for two or three weeks, our time together is confined to hurried half-hour visits. But we're always there for each other, and we always touch base.

Of course, there's not the security traditional families ostensibly offer: we've made no promises, no long-range plans to stay together. But I know that, if either of us considered moving, the other would be a major factor in the decision.

I'd like to mention here my third family—actually, in chronology, my second. Feminist columnist Ellen Cantarow has written about the low priority put on on-the-job relationships in our culture. But these can be among the warmest and closest of family relationships. Before I moved to Boston in 1971, I'd worked for ten years as a proofreader at *Newsweek*, first part-time, then full. During the week I worked with three other readers, all much older than I was, all more conservative in lifestyle and politics. Except for Dale, we all lived alone. There were long stretches of time without work, during which we read, wrote letters, and talked. We talked about Dale's wife and son, about Ed's elderly parents and his young niece, about Jane's and my cats. We analyzed TV shows we'd seen the night before. The conversations themselves were never intimate, but a sweet, domestic intimacy grew among us. We savored each other's little triumphs, fretted (though never intrusively) over each other's sadnesses. Dale and I played inane practical jokes on each other, while Jane and Ed ritually rebuked us.

Leaving there was the hardest part of leaving New York. Two years ago, when the *Mary Tyler Moore Show* aired its final episode in which the newsroom personnel were all fired and went their separate ways, I sobbed for an hour, reliving my own departure from Ed and Dale and Jane. But I'm luckier than the fictional Mary Richards: my office family is still there. I go back to New York three or four times a year, and when I do, I head for *Newsweek* as soon as possible. We share our news, and I sit with them while they work. Sometimes we chat, sometimes not. It's fine when we don't— the affection, the companionship, the warm familiarity are enough. These family visits mean as much to me as visits to my parents or brothers do.

Living alone doesn't necessarily mean living without family—it simply means not cohabitating with anyone. There are all kinds of families. I've been very lucky in mine.

OCTOBER 1981

Bringing Up Baby:
The Day Care Question

by Molly Lovelock

"Free 24-hour day care!" Day care was part of every feminist and radical platform ten years ago. Now we hear about it mostly when there are cutbacks in state funding, or as another "dilemma" of middle-class parenthood, like choosing a pediatrician. Where really is day care now in our organizing strategies?

Day care centers themselves can be political communities but seem to be increasingly less so. My son is in a cooperative day care center, formed a decade ago by activists who pressured Harvard University into providing free space. At one recent meeting, the issue of diversity of children vs. co-op participation came up. One parent couldn't understand the reason for the discussion. Why did it matter? What did diversity or the theory of co-ops have to do with her baby or her own day-to-day problems?

Stepping back, though, even choosing to use a day care center may be a radical move. However, this isn't what I'm hearing these days. There's been little growth of new centers in this area since the activism of a decade ago. Feminists, like those who wrote *Ourselves and Our Children* (Random House, 1978), talk about guilt in sending their children to day care centers. A report like the 1974 Corporations and Child Care by the Women's Research Action Project, which outlines the vast differences between profit-making day care like the Living and Learning Centers and parent- and teacher-controlled centers, would probably never be written today. The Child Care Resource Center says most of the good day care literature, films, and tapes date from the early '70s.

The choice of child care has become privatized. Parents, mostly mothers, frantically put their names on ever-growing waiting lists, interview babysitters, and call everyone for referrals. No one organizes. We hustle to grab those hours without our children in tow.

Family day care—individuals working at home—seems popular. It is cheaper than many alternatives and can certainly provide warm, caring attention for children. But these workers are isolated and often overburdened, and may well be women with more conservative values. Interestingly, even feminists don't seem to talk much about questions of children's sex roles or race issues with the motherly person they've found. We're so grateful to have *found* someone.

State funding is being cut from day care programs. Proposals are being made now to provide babysitting through "workfare." Under these suggestions, welfare mothers would become slave laborers. I also cannot imagine a worse way to get quality day care. I remember how little I cared about my charges as a teenager, with babysitting the only paid job I could get.

Some of the only real activism around day care now comes (as it always has) from welfare mothers, single mothers, Black mothers, and day care workers. Those of us with more privilege, and maybe a little more time or money, are busy with other things. Ten or fifteen years ago, when we really weren't allowed in jobs, when we were expected to be full-time Mommies, *then* we saw the reason for day care. Then it was political for us, and we organized, demanded, and gathered together in political communities called day care centers.

For some of us, day care activism may not be from direct self-interest. But the indirect potential is enormous, and we've been sitting out for too long. First, I believe day care centers to be absolutely crucial. Assuming they are controlled by parents and workers, and not by corporations and government, they can be important for the development of children's attitudes toward violence, racism, or sexism. Working in a day care center, even with the low wages, seems to me altogether preferable to working at home. One has colleagues, can get support, and is recognized.

A center supplies stability. When a teacher leaves, things still continue. Parents meet other parents and children, which makes their job easier.

All this seems radical. It shifts responsibility for children from mothers to a community. Day care creates alliances across race and class, but only if we look beyond individual situations.

Day care activism has been low. We're either mothers with almost no resources, mothers who have worked out individual solutions or nonmothers. But right now we need organizing that's going to work. And day care does work—we've already proved that.

It's time for pulling out some successful strategies. Militant tactics seem to have the best potential to make effective use of our scarce resources and mobilize us. We should once again take over buildings, strike. These things are direct and logical for day care, while less appropriate for the ERA. We need space. We need time. We can't work as mothers or as paid workers without day care.

More militant actions may be safer when done "for children." Significantly, such direct tactics can also be very effective (and less risky) when carried out by those of us with more money, better jobs, better credentials. Suppose every woman earning over $15,000 took her child to work instead of just using our hard-found individual solutions. Suppose we all demanded day care together. Now suppose all *men* earning over $15,000 did the same.

We need to shake ourselves. Day care centers could be more political, parents could be more political about their child care "dilemma," and feminists everywhere need to see day care in a broader perspective. It means the future of generations. It means women's very survival now. It's the very best bet, I think, for real militancy that could have enormous returns.

AUGUST 1985

Outside the Sisterhood:
Ageism in Women's Studies

by Barbara Macdonald

Barbara Macdonald delivered the following speech at the 1985 National Women's Studies Association (NWSA) conference held in Seattle at the University of Washington.

I have not come here out of NWSA's spontaneous concern about ageism. I am here after a four-year fight, after other older women along with me wrote to the NWSA planning committee and demanded that ageism be addressed at a plenary session. We insisted that NWSA confront the question of how it is possible that the last 30 years of women's lives have been ignored in women's studies. This morning I have twenty minutes to speak about that topic.

From the beginning of this wave of the women's movement, from the beginning of women's studies, the message has gone out to those of us over 60 that your "sisterhood" does not include us, that those of you who are younger see us as men see us—that is, as women who used to be women but aren't anymore. You do not see us in our present lives, you do not identify with our issues,...you patronize us, you stereotype us. Mainly you ignore us.

But it is worse than that. For you yourselves—activists and academicians—do not hesitate to exploit us. We take in the fact that you come to us for "oral histories"—for your own agendas, to learn *your* feminist or lesbian or working-class or ethnic histories—with not the slightest interest in our present struggles as old women. You come to fill in some much-needed data for a thesis, or to justify a grant for some "service" for old women that imitates the mainstream and which you plan to direct, or you come to get material for a biography of our friends and lovers. But you come not as equals, not with any knowledge of who we are, what our issues may be. You come to old women who have been serving young women for a lifetime and ask to be served one more time, and then you cover up your embarrassment as you depart by saying that you felt as though we were your grandmother or your mother or your aunt. And no one in the sisterhood criticizes you for such acts.

But let me say it to you clearly: we are not your mothers, your grandmothers, or your aunts. And we will never build a true women's movement until we can organize together as equals, woman to woman, without the burden of these family roles.

Mother. Grandmother. Aunt. It should come as no surprise to us that ageism has its roots in patriarchal family. But here I encounter a problem. In the four years it took to get NWSA to address ageism, feminism has moved away from a position in which we recognized that family is a building-block of patriarchy, the place where sexist hierarchical roles are learned and the socialization of girls takes place, the unit by which women are colonized, manipulated, controlled, and punished for infraction. From that basic tenet of feminist theory, both mainstream and radical feminists have moved back to reaffirming family. Mainstream feminists are buying the notion that as long as a woman has a "career," family is a safe and wholesome place to be. Radical feminists have affirmed family as the source of our cultures—as a way of understanding our strengths and our oppression as Black, Jewish, Hispanic, Asian American, Native American, working-class women. This return to family is reflected in our writings, where less and less is father seen as oppressor, but more as another family member, oppressed by white male imperialism. (*And, believe me, he is.*)

It will be for future feminist historians to explain how it was that in our return to family we never questioned its contradictions of our earlier feminist theory. Not that we can't contradict our own feminist beliefs—they aren't written in concrete. It's just that we never acknowledged the contradictions.

Nor can history fail to note that our return to family coincides with a reactionary administration's push back to family values, any more than it can ignore that our lesbian baby boom coincides with Reagan's baby boom to save the Gross National Product.

But if we are to understand ageism, we have no choice but to bring family again under the lens of a feminist politic. In the past, we examined the father as oppressor, we examined his oppression of the mother and the daughters; in great detail we examined the mother as oppressor of the daughters. But what has never come under the feminist lens is the daughter's oppression of the mother—that woman who by definition is older than we are.

The source of your ageism, the reason why you see older women as there to serve you, is the family. It was in patriarchal family that you learned that mother is there to serve you, her child, that serving you is her purpose in life. This is not woman's definition of motherhood. This is man's definition of motherhood, a male myth enforced in family and which you still believe—to your peril and mine. It infantilizes you and it erases me.

This myth of motherhood is not a white American phenomenon, although nowhere, I believe, is it as bad as in white imperialist culture. Barbara Christian, in her book *Black Feminist Criticism* (Pergamon, 1985), points out how this myth is uncovered in Alice Walker's fiction about Afro-American life and by Buchi Emecheta's writing about Ibuza life. The myth is summed up by an Ibuza saying: "The joy of being a mother is the joy of giving all to your children." It is internalized by the young mother, but then internalized and perpetuated by her daughters, so that even when—as in Emecheta's *The Joys of Motherhood* (Braziller, 1979)—the mother has come to some insight, her daughter continues to see her as existing only for self-sacrifice.

The old woman is at the other end of that motherhood myth. She has no personhood, no desires or value of her own. She must not fight for her own issues—if she fights at all, it must be for "future generations." Her greatest joy is seen as giving all to her grandchildren. And to the extent that she no longer directly serves a man—can no longer produce his children, is no longer sexually desirable to him—she is erased more completely as grandmother than she was as mother.

It is for these reasons—because of everything you learned in family—that you, as feminists, can continue to see the older woman as a nonperson. It is for these reasons that you believe our lives as old women are not important and that we exist only to serve you.

We have all been so infantilized in family that we have never made ourselves, as daughters, accountable as oppressors of the mothers—and we should know only too well that the failure to acknowledge the oppressor in ourselves results in confused thinking and a contradictory image of those we oppress. Thus, you who are younger see us as either submissive and childlike or as possessing some unidentified vague wisdom. As having more "soul" than you or as being overemotional and slightly helpless or as a pillar of strength. As "cute" and funny or as boring. As sickly-sweet or dominating and difficult. You pity us, or you ignore us—until you are made aware of your ageism, and then you want to honor us. I don't know which is worse. None of these images has anything to do with who we are—they are the projections of the oppressor.

I want to close by giving three very recent examples of ageism in some of our best writing as feminists. These are writers whose work I admire. But the ageism in their writing will be passed on through women's studies to other young women if it is left on the shelves unexamined, and I am not willing any longer to leave it there. *These writers are no more ageist than the entire women's community.* They have not personally failed me—they, like all the rest of us, have been failed by the women's movement.

In Ruth Geller's novel *Triangles* (Crossing Press, 1984), we use our living grandmother as a character, and we make her the comic relief. We show her photograph on the back cover, with a blurb making her the subject of laughter—and most of the laughter is that she is not in on the joke. And yet the sisterhood publishes this book, reviews it, and is silent.

In *Between Women*, edited by Sarah Ruddick, Louise DeSalvo, and Carol Ascher, we bring together a fine collection of essays on the relationship of female biographers to the famous women whose lives they have chosen to write about. But, believing in the myth of motherhood, many of these biographers, not satisfied with status by association with these strong famous women of the past and present (such as Virginia Woolf and Simone de Beauvoir), proceed to turn their subjects—most of whom chose not to have children—into their mothers. This is no equal association between women. This is ageism, and as though these women had not given enough, the biographers (women in their fifties) in page after page ask to be mothered, nurtured, and have their lives blessed by their subjects. And still the sisterhood reviews this book, finds nothing offensive about it, and is silent.

In her essay "Half of a Map," Sandy Boucher, one of our best feminist authors, writes of old women who have been helpful to her: "I would be *them* one day, and if I could be...as generous of myself as they were, then I could be proud to be old." Apart from the intolerable patronizing, only a male myth of motherhood makes this feminist think my pride in being old consists in my generosity to younger women. And still the sisterhood is silent.

I have to say of women's studies that when you make the lives of women over 60 invisible, when you see us as your mothers and fail to examine your oppressive attitudes, you are letting the parameters of women's studies be defined by men—by the man in your own heads. But there is more than that. In the consciousness raising of the late '60s and '70s, in the contributions to feminist theory that grew out of those years, in the development of women's studies that followed, we planned curriculum with an entire piece omitted—that of age and the oppression of ageism. We cannot now patch up those structures in twenty minutes to cover the gaps of our ignorance. We have no choice but to go back once again, as we have had to do before, cover old ground in new ways, and rebuild this time with a wholeness that includes all women and all the years of our lives.

Excerpted from the original.

OCTOBER 1985

AN OPEN LETTER TO BARBARA MACDONALD

DEAR BARBARA:

I have for some time read, admired, respected, and learned from your writing, and so when I read your comments about *Triangles* in the August *Sojourner*, I was deeply distressed. You write: "In the novel *Triangles*, by Ruth Geller, we use our living grandmother as a character, and we make her the comic relief. We show her photograph on the back cover, with a blurb making her the subject of laughter—and most of the laughter is that she is not in on the joke. And yet the sisterhood publishes this book, reviews it, and is silent."

There are several reasons why your comments disturb me. When I decided to write *Triangles*, I did not come to my grandmother—to Sophie Geller, the woman—to exploit or revere her or to "use" her as comic relief. What I was *trying* to do when I wrote the character of Rose was to show an old woman who is still fiercely individualistic, who has struggled to live her life as she wants in spite of all the pressures and demands that society and the family have put on her for the past 80-plus years, and in spite of how others misunderstand and misinterpret her actions. The reason I began *Triangles* by picturing Rose sitting on the stoop was because I wanted to avoid doing precisely what you criticize the women's movement for—seeing her through the eyes of, or as an adjunct to, a young woman. I wanted to show her in her own life, as her own person, as well as I could given my own limitations.

I tried also to portray Sunny, the main character, as a young woman who has ageist attitudes—who, for example, while desperately struggling in her own relationship with a woman, smiles condescendingly at her grandmother's struggles with *her* friend. I did not portray Rose as weak or helpless or a pillar of strength, "cute" and funny or dominating and difficult. I tried simply, to see her as she is. Perhaps I succeeded; perhaps I failed. Some day I will reread the book and make my own evaluation, and for now, I don't know. But please do not make me—or my book—into something we are not. Do not "use" me—or my relationship to or portrayal of my grandmother—to make political statements about the women's movement, however urgent and necessary those statements may be. And please, do not judge my book by its cover.

When I decided to dedicate the book to Sophie, I knew immediately that I would not write a simple dedication from me to her, but try to make the dedication *hers*. And when the incident occurred that became the blurb, I knew that the dedication would be her statement to me about the book itself. Perhaps my intent was too esoteric or my meaning too subtle, but in any case that, in fact, was my intent—not to "use" Sophie as comic relief. If the joke was on anyone, it was on me. I had worked for years on this book, been consumed by it, and yet when you came right down to it, which was more valuable? To my grandmother, having good eyesight is more valuable than writing a book. And though her comment made me initially laugh, her perspective stayed with me and put those five years in which I was driven, focused on a single task, into a different light.

Best wishes,
Ruth Geller

Excerpted from the original.

MARCH 1988

The Romance of Lesbian Motherhood
by Ellen Herman

Even while the sex and gender culture is growing more conservative, some affected communities are growing more radical, and activism is on the rise. Last October, in what was the largest civil rights demonstration in U.S. history, 750,000 gay men and lesbians came together in Washington, D.C., to express outrage at the government's shameful response to the AIDS crisis and the until-you-die stigma attached to being "queer." Suggesting that gay people are unfit to be parents has been one of homophobia's mainstays; insisting that gay people do not deserve to keep their children is a cruel but dependable form of punishment.

In addition to the homophobia that has surfaced everywhere in response to AIDS, recent statistics about hate crimes directed against gay people have gone through the roof, to be added to the mountains of paper already documenting violence against women, Blacks, Jews, and other marginalized groups. These are frightening reminders, indeed, that social outlaws remain lightning rods for hostility and violence. But indicators that public homophobia is increasing do not seem to be stopping many lesbians from turning the whys and hows of motherhood upside-down. Lesbians are bringing children into their lives self-consciously after they come out, with the result that the relevant question is changing from whether we will be allowed to keep custody of our children to what kind of parents we have the strength and vision to become.

Accepted estimates are that 10 percent of adult women are lesbians, and that 20 to 30 percent of lesbians are mothers. That means there are somewhere between three and four million lesbian mothers in the United States alone. These numbers are not new. They speak the truth that lesbians have always had children in their lives as a result of heterosexual marriage, adoption, and foster parenting. Lesbians have been mothers as all women have been mothers, because of love and pain and choice and lack of choice.

Sisters are "doing it for themselves," and this trend suggests an exciting possibility: that the self-respect of women and gay people is at an all time high and that theories about transforming the experience and institution of motherhood are being put into daily practice. There is, however, another, less positive possibility to consider: that lesbians are being affected by a heavy dose of "pronatalism," the ideology that woman's anatomy is woman's destiny, that being a mother, particularly a "birth-mother," is the quintessential, compulsory female experience.

What has been termed the "lesbian baby boom" is occurring at a time when back-to-motherhood propaganda is on the rise. Heart-rending stories about childless couples who take dramatic steps to become parents are reported as national or even international news as well as human interest items. In one recent example, a 48-year-old South African woman, Pat Anthony, gave birth to triplets for her 25-year-old daughter, Karen, who had lost her uterus three years before, after a life-threatening but ultimately successful delivery. Following the birth of their son, Karen and her husband, Alcino, reportedly became tormented by the knowledge that Karen could not bear more children, and the entire extended family was caught up in their pain. Finally, Pat offered to act as an "incubator." After being given hormone treatments and slim chances of success by doctors, Karen's eggs were harvested, fertilized with Alcino's sperm, and then implanted in Pat's uterus. Even though the Vatican pronounced all forms of artificial procreation to be "morally illicit" in March 1987, when Pat Anthony was in her third month of pregnancy, most reports of the triplets' birth in October celebrated the event as a selfless act of maternal love as well as a medical miracle. Pat Anthony had this to say: "I never thought I was doing anything really different, just what anyone would do for a daughter deprived of having children."

The popular and consumer cultures are pushing the joys of children and families, too. Television shows like "Thirtysomething," a series devoted almost exclusively to the home life of two yuppies and their new child, celebrates domesticity directly. Previously considered to be simply boring or even the kiss of death to television ratings, parenting is now being elevated to high drama. Those who pay attention to advertising are also familiar with images that make embarking on motherhood seem more like a shopping spree in a reproductive supermarket than a decision affecting the most profound possibilities of life. Marketing reproduction as a lifestyle choice with a hefty price tag distorts what parenting is about. Children do cost time and money, but luxuries like designer diaper bags and necessities like child care are equally inaccessible to most parents. Designer motherhood just offers women more reasons to feel that the job they are doing is not good enough.

Lesbians are not immune from any of these cultural pressures. Lesbian moms may be a crack in the "pronatal" facade, but it is not clear how deep that crack is, and the damage we hope to do to patriarchal ideas and arrangements is far from automatic. "Choosing children" is not necessarily a step towards social change. The radical potential of lesbian motherhood is embodied in our unique political consciousness as women who live at the crossroads of sexual and gender oppression. Will we continue the work we have begun—building our movement, our understanding of power, and our community of celebration and resistance?

There are, of course, numerous other questions that are obligatory features of becoming a mother and simultaneously living as a lesbian (or simply living independently from men), and we seem to be quite obsessed with them all. How do you get pregnant? What do you tell the social worker from the adoption agency, your family of origin, and your employer? What form will your "family" take? Will there be a nonbiological comother or other parent(s)? When do you come out to a child? If the biological father is known, how will he, or men in general be involved in the child's life? If you've never met the father, what do you tell the other parents in the playground when they ask whether your child looks like you or his father? *Can you sleep naked after you have a baby?*

Local women recently had a chance to address these and other questions about the current lesbian baby boom when more than 800 women from the Boston area, other parts of New England, the East Coast and Canada gathered at UMass/Boston for a conference, titled "Children in Our Lives." Panels explored "Race and Class" and "Political Strategies," among other topics. More than 30 workshops offered something for almost everybody, from "Raising Adolescents and Teens" to "Lesbian Divorce" to "Sex and the Lesbian Mother." Informal caucuses were held, films and videos were shown, and, in addition to child care, several creative sessions were held just for kids, including "How/ Whether to Tell Your Friends" and "Are You My Other Mother?"

Nine women worked for a symbolic nine months to produce this event. Their work falls in the proud tradition of other local lesbian mothers who have organized against homophobia and for civil rights and dignity. Some of their predecessors are: Tykes and Dykes in the early '70s, the Lesbian and Gay Parents Project in the late '70s, and the Lesbians Choosing Children Network, formed just a few years ago. According to conference organizers:

In struggling through the planning for today's conference, we have tried to address some of the difficult questions that arise in the lesbian community over children and our various relationships with them. In working together, we ourselves have had to struggle with some of the race and class issues that we hope the conference will take up.... There is no single experience of lesbian mothering and this conference makes no attempt to synthesize one. Similarly, we understand that lesbians' relationships with children can take many forms and that motherhood is not the only way that we have children in our lives.

Most conference participants I spoke with said they had been looking eagerly forward to the conference and felt enthusiasm about the day's events. Still, there was a lingering feeling of uncertainty about what this movement of lesbians toward children and motherhood actually means. It is a credit to the organizers' vision that difficult political and philosophical questions could be asked (even if they could not be answered) as freely as the practical ones that seem to occupy so many of us.

A tone of openness was set in the morning, at the first panel, entitled "Considering Motherhood." Diane Raymond (philosopher, activist, and mother) offered a number of insightful observations and questioned the notion that lesbians who choose children are necessarily making a progressive political statement. She also touched on the controversial point of whether or not any of us have a "right" to have children and suggested that dependence on a "rights" framework perpetuates the concept of children (and, by implication, women) as private property, little more than things to be owned and controlled. She encouraged lesbians to take a hard look at whether we are reproducing new variations on old sexist themes. For example, do we act on the belief that there is such a creature as a "real" mother and that biology is central to defining her?

Holly Bishop (a therapist and mother) described her work on the Lesbian Mother Study, an ambitious-sounding attempt to document the motivations and expectations of lesbian mothers-to-be. Participants in the study will be followed for the next 20 years. Like Raymond, she criticized cultural pressures on all women (lesbians included) to become mothers, but also pointed out that thousands of chosen children are living proof that our individual and community self-respect has come a long way. She expressed optimism that lesbian moms and their kids would pose serious challenges to homophobia and sexism. Two other panelists offered personal anecdotes about the experience of becoming mothers and told stories of the daily battle to integrate a life and identity—loving as a lesbian and as a mother—considered a contradiction in terms by the mainstream.

The panel on "Race and Class" tackled the notion of "choice" and exploded it. Andrea Rogers (long-time feminist activist and mother) spoke with emotion and bitterness about her experience as a white, working-class feminist. "I don't think I knew what class oppression was until I got into the women's movement." She also had some very angry words for "women out chasing the almighty sperm." "What are they going to teach their children about race and class? Where the hell are they? Nothing has changed."

Susan Moir, another long-time white working-class feminist activist (who describes herself as a "recovering lesbian mother") echoed Rogers's angry frustration:

I'm here as an artifact to say the same thing I said many years ago. The women's movement has been dominated by the values and strategies of white, middle-class women and that continues to be so. It's good that people are having kids, but there is a lot of bitterness about the idea of choosing children when most of us were knocked up and had no choice. For women to "choose girls" is an extreme exercise of privilege and makes working-class women and women of color the grunts who raise boys and deal with sexism. Outside of this space, I am your sister in the struggle against the enemy. In this space, we need to talk about class conflict.

Roberta Wilmore, a Black mother, told movingly of her own childhood memories, her parents' belief in education, and her struggle to raise a child and remain true to herself. She also spoke of her loneliness and painful alienation from the lesbian community. "In the lesbian community, as everywhere else, there is public opinion, and when you go against it, you get a lot of criticism. I have not found the strength in the lesbian community to raise my son the way I want to."

Julia Perez, writer and mother, took up this thread and concluded the panel by calling the idea of "politically correct lesbian motherhood" nothing more than a dangerous excuse to raise children in isolation and keep them from contact with "the other."

In the afternoon, Angela Bowen (writer, activist, mother, grandmother) delivered an inspiring keynote speech to an appreciative audience. Her excitement and sense of humor were infectious, her ideas serious and thought-provoking. "We, of all people, don't need to romanticize motherhood. It is a forever fact that never ceases to be. Deep down, we will never be totally free again." Saying that feminist consciousness required it, she asked the logical, yet surprisingly unspoken question: Why become mothers? Then she built on one of the day's themes, that equating motherhood exclusively with "choices" (whether the donor should be known or unknown; whether to come out to every other parent in the playground; how to include male role models in a child's life) risks directing us away from what could be lesbians' most significant contributions:

> *What will you teach your children? What relationship does choosing children have to all the personal and political work you did before? Or do you have more important concerns now that your child's welfare is at stake? Will you try to raise children who can be your friends and allies later in life? Or will they be little yuppies mixed and matched so that they do not feel the discomfort of being different? Will you be busy hiding for the sake of your choice children? These are the choices to be made here.*

Bowen concluded her talk by offering a personal thought that doubtlessly stirred many feelings: shock, discomfort, and relief, too. "If I had to do it all over again, I wouldn't do it myself."

Jan Clausen has written: "We don't move by rules; we move toward that love." I believe, in theory, that motherhood should be the most personal of decisions, never in need of defense or justification, never chosen or not chosen for reasons of political principle. In practice, I think that motherhood is many things: a way women satisfy curiosity, ego, the need to control something in life, and the desire to extend ourselves and what we believe beyond our own lifetimes. A strong feminist movement is the only thing I feel ready to trust to help this and future generations of women challenge the "pronatal" prescription that nurturing children and others must occur at the cost of our own freedom. We must insist that reproductive choices not be individual sacrifices. Only then will motherhood be an equal opportunity to participate in a future of social change.

This article has been edited for length.

AUGUST 1988

Motherhood: Choices that Divide Us
by Susan Shapiro

There is no doubt that our society is prejudiced against women who don't have children. This bias is reflected in our media, our language, and in the daily assumptions we are bombarded with by even the most well-intentioned people. When the women's movement of the late '60s and early '70s responded by affording us the support and freedom to choose lifestyles other than marriage and motherhood, some feminists took an extreme stand: having babies was bad, staying home with them was worse, and giving birth to sons was abominable. While it is rare these days to hear such feelings expressed directly, the vestiges of antimotherhood sentiment remain with us, a pervasive undercurrent that can no longer be dismissed as the radical fringe. The result of all the intolerance both within the movement and the dominant culture is an unacknowledged division between those of us who have children and those who don't.

Ironically, though our feminist counterculture, as well as society at large, is allegedly based on a belief in freedom and choice, the wide range of lifestyle options open to women today is threatening to both spheres. While society fears alternatives that don't support a patriarchal system (lesbianism, spinsterhood, childlessness), many feminists are threatened by choices that appear to perpetuate it (marriage, motherhood within the nuclear family). Certainly there are times when motherhood isn't a question of choice. A large number of women, particularly those who are poor and/or uneducated, become mothers without ever having made the choice to do so. And some women are infertile or otherwise physically unable to give birth. While these are significant problems with widespread ramifications, in this article, I specifically address the implications of choice and refer primarily to women for whom giving birth, adopting, or not having children has been a conscious decision.

As I read and listen to people speak about some of the complex issues surrounding motherhood—reproductive technology, adoption, choosing not to have children—I am struck by the ways in which feminists are criticizing and hurting each other. As a mother, I am particularly sensitive to comments that attack or devalue motherhood, but I know many women feel equally judged and reproached for not being mothers. It seems lines are being drawn as if there were clear sides and correct answers when we have barely begun to articulate the real questions.

Two recent articles illustrate some of the tension, criticism, and resentment that are creating a rift among feminists. In "Womb Worship" (*Ms.*, February 1988), Paula Weideger maintains that the old hierarchy has returned, "the one in which mothers perch at the top and non-moms huddle down below." She criticizes feminist supporters of Mary Beth Whitehead (biological mother of "Baby M") for "retreating to notions of the sanctity of the womb," and mothers in general for their attitudes of superiority and "arrogance about the wonderfulness of mothering." Nonmothers, she says, have been called selfish and narcissistic, and she questions whether they are more shallow or self-indulgent than women who have babies so they can buy designer outfits for three.

In "The Romance of Lesbian Motherhood" *(Sojourner,* March 1988), Ellen Herman worries that lesbians are being affected by a "heavy dose of pronatalism" and criticizes "back-to-motherhood propaganda" such as the news story of a woman bearing triplets for her daughter and television shows like "Thirtysomething," which "celebrates domesticity directly." Like Weideger she makes reference to "designer motherhood." And after voicing concern about "public expressions of contempt for selfish women who choose not to reproduce," she goes on to say what motherhood is to her: "a way women satisfy curiosity, ego, the need to control something in life, and the desire to extend ourselves and what we believe beyond our own lifetimes."

It seems to me that Herman, in an article that clearly attempts to be fair-minded, inadvertently lists only the most selfish of reasons for having children. Both articles ultimately illustrate that all of us, whatever our choices, are being accused of selfishness. And the fact is, we *are* all "selfish," those of us fortunate enough to make choices that work in our own lives. Didn't we learn way back in Feminism 101 that a degree of selfishness was good for us? It's ironic that within the women's movement, with its focus on loving and valuing ourselves, with its "prochoice" politics, we may be criticized as selfish or egocentric when it comes to our decisions about having or not having children.

Two of the factors that influence current feminist thinking about motherhood originate in our larger culture: a strong pro-nuclear-family trend and the emergence of reproductive technology. Nowhere is the back-to-traditional family value more evident than in the media. Movies such as *Moonstruck, Hope and Glory,* and *Fatal Attraction* zoom in on family photographs, symbolizing the endurance of nuclear family despite all odds. A number of new television programs also focus on traditional families with babies and young children. "Day by Day," a prime-time sitcom in which both parents have left high-powered careers to work in their at-home day care center, is a modern-day "Father Knows Best." The antihero is, of course, a materialistic, work-obsessed, child-hating career woman. (On the other hand, "Heart Beat," a series which focused on women's health care and just happened to feature a lesbian as one of the regulars, lasted less than two months. "Molly Dodd," a program about an independent career woman, has also been canceled.)

The problem here is not that the nuclear family is being represented, but that it is overrepresented. (Perhaps even more fundamentally, it is misrepresented. Not all nuclear families are the ageist, sexist, homophobic institutions that the media portrays.) While a traditional patriarchal structure in which men have all the money and power is certainly oppressive, the Nuclear Family per se (man-woman-child/ren) is not the big bad wolf outside the door of Alternative Lifestyles. The problem with film and television is the narrow focus, the distortion of the larger picture, the lies of omission. But as feminists respond to this cultural trend with understandable anger, the distinction between symptom (an overrepresentation of traditional lifestyles and values and the near-invisibility of other lifestyles and values) and underlying problem (an intolerance of alternatives) sometimes blurs. Resentment and defensiveness build between mothers and nonmothers, women with traditional and alternative lifestyles, and we inadvertently reinforce a narrowness of vision instead of expanding our possibilities.

In addition to this media phenomenon, as the result of current reproductive technology we are also facing complex ethical dilemmas concerning motherhood. Surrogacy raises questions about baby-selling, potential exploitation of poor and Third World women (especially with the advent of *in vitro* fertilization), legislation of morality, control over women's bodies, fathers' rights, and much more. I initially responded to the "Baby M" case on a purely emotional basis: there is no higher law than the bond between a mother and child. No financial arrangement or document, particularly one originating within a class-biased, male-dominated legal system, should be so binding as to prohibit a mother from keeping her child. But the more I thought about it, the less sure I was that such a simple answer was possible.

It's easy for me to empathize with the birthmother. The image of a baby being physically wrested from her is a powerful and upsetting one. But what would this "higher law" say about adoptive parents? Certainly adoptive mothers are among the most nurturing and loving parents I know. At what point does a woman adopting a child become a mother? Is being told there is a child for her to adopt the emotional equivalent of a woman's learning she is pregnant? When does bonding occur? Is this strictly emotional bonding any less profound or legitimate than such a connection with a physical counterpart?

With whom could we possibly entrust judgments in situations like the "Baby M" case if they are to be determined on an individual basis? (It is terrifying to realize how readily the courts and media can paint a justifiably stressed and frightened woman as an incompetent hysteric.) And though I find my sympathies lie more with both mothers than with the father, I can't entirely dismiss paternal emotions and fathers' rights.

In the face of all these murky questions and media distortions, we become easily threatened and defensive, clinging to our own preferences and rejecting that which is different. Our language begins to include terminology like "pronatalism," which starts out referring to the ideology that all women want or should want children, but like any of the "isms," becomes a convenient accusation, in this case whenever we don't like something that portrays parenting as important.

As we realized how profoundly our language influences attitudes and values, feminists began to implement much-needed revision. "Fireman" became "firefighter," "girl" was no longer an acceptable way to describe an adult female, etc. When the label "childless" was recognized as having a negative value, some feminists went to the opposite extreme and replaced it with "child-free." But the suffix "-free" implies liberation from something one should be rid of ("pest-," "disease-," "rust-"). (I don't imagine infertile women who would *like* to have children or mothers whose children have died think of themselves as "child-free.")

The suffix "-less" often indicates a lack of something that should be present ("penniless," "friendless"), but since it literally means "without" it can also have positive connotations ("fearless," "painless"). Perhaps "childless," like "spinster," is a word that needs to be reclaimed as positive when referring to a choice—not as a definition of who someone is but as a simple description of a particular aspect of some women's lives.

Another expression that warrants examination is "the sanctity of motherhood." This reference, often heard in discussions of cases such as "Baby M," is generally used with sarcasm. By implication, it dismisses the possibility that motherhood may, indeed, have an element of the sacred. It is important to differentiate between "holy" and "holier than thou." When I heard feminist theologian Elizabeth Dodson Gray speak on the sacredness in women's lives, I was deeply struck by her suggestion that birth itself was a sacred process, certainly as holy as the patriarchal rituals surrounding it. For me, giving birth—becoming a mother—was as close to a sacred experience as I've had. I was filled with a profundity, an awe, a reverence for some life force outside and within myself. Yet until now, my feeling has been a well-kept secret—partly because it was so personal but also because it sounded foolish, overemotional, or worse, condescending. What does acknowledging the sanctity of motherhood say about nonmothers?

I think the basic question underlying much of the debate surrounding motherhood issues is, *why do women choose to have children?* and its corollary, *what does this say about women who choose not to do so?*

If motherhood is an instinct, does this mean women who don't choose it are abnormal? If raising children is a selfless gesture, are nonmothers by definition narcissistic? If choosing to become a mother is neither instinctual nor selfless, is it an egocentric and therefore bad choice? Obviously, motherhood can't be reduced to simple terms. Whether a woman is ambivalent or very clear in her decision, there are many components that may be influencing her feelings: economics, age, lifestyle, family history, current relationship status, cultural and family pressure, biology, personality, and more. Even these factors are not clearcut, but filled with ironies and contradictions. One woman may want children to recreate the loving family structure in which she grew up, while another wants them to create the family bonds she never had as the daughter of abusive or absent parents. On the other hand, a woman may not want children so as not to replicate her painful experience of a nuclear family—or because her friends and relatives already meet her familial needs.

One of my friends does not want children, in part because the primary relationship she has chosen is demanding and requires a lot of work. She doesn't think it would be fair to them or to the child to bring a third person into the relationship. Another friend gave a similar reason for wanting a child. Her primary relationship was too demanding, too intense. She feels that having a baby strengthened their bond, allowing them to share in something wonderful but deflecting some of the one-to-one intensity that had begun to be a problem.

"Nonmother" can also be problematic as a label that describes someone in terms of not being a member of a dominant group. The solution is not to replace one value-loaded expression with another but to examine the contexts in which we use these expressions. People are not generally labeled "catless" or "cat-free," because our worth as women or as human beings is not deemed contingent upon whether or not we own pets. But in an article about cats, one might use the expression "non-cat-owner" or "catless" without any negative implications just as in this article I refer to "nonmothers" as women who have made the legitimate *choice to* be without children. "Non," like "less," can be neutral or defined by context ("nonconformist").

There are probably as many combinations of reasons for wanting children as there are people who want them. Some of us feel an "instinct" to nurture (which for a number of women can be realized by supporting and caring for children and/or adults who are not our biological offspring). Others mention an "instinct" or wish to carry on bloodlines, give life, perpetuate the species, or create a sense of immortality. And some women may have what appear to be overtly selfish motives such as holding on to a man or having someone to take care of them in their old age. (These "selfish" reasons are based on fears created by a society that does not provide adequate emotional or economic support for women, especially old women.) There are many cultural/social incentives for procreating which encompass self-image, relationships, and a society that views childless women as less than fully developed, childless couples as incomplete. But I think the primary reason for wanting children is that along with myriad fears and inconveniences, there can be many joys connected to motherhood: a deep mutual love and commitment; the opportunity to play, teach, and learn in an ongoing way; infinite funny and poignant moments. In addition, motherhood (including pregnancy) is a major life experience many of us don't want to take the chance of missing.

The choice to remain childless is equally complex and can be more difficult in that there is little support for it in our larger culture. Reasons for choosing this option include insufficient social and/or financial support, work (political and otherwise) that does not leave enough time and energy for raising children, and concerns about overpopulation and nuclear holocaust. But I think women often choose not to be mothers for the same reasons we choose not to be gardeners or doctors or electricians. While many of us find motherhood enriches our lives, others know they would find it boring, draining, and frustrating. They may not be attracted to the idea of pregnancy and have little or no interest in raising a child. Although motherhood is clearly an enormous political issue, it may be useful to view it not only in a political context but also as a vocation—one to which some of us are drawn and others are not.

Our current perspective on motherhood is far too narrow to accommodate the wide spectrum of individual needs and legitimate preferences that women have. One need not go far to encounter prejudice against any position on the "motherhood scale." At-home-by-choice mothers, "working" mothers, impoverished mothers, adoptive mothers, infertile women, women who choose childlessness, as well as those of us who don't fall directly into any one of these categories, are all victims of someone's judgments and assumptions based solely on our motherhood status.

I find myself with a lot of questions and not too many answers. But I do know that as feminists we have a problem that's not going to go away until we face it. The tension that exists between women whose motherhood choices differ is often subtle, unacknowledged. Certainly childbearing does not always factor into relationships between mothers and nonmothers. But given the hard decisions that will be called for as the result of reproductive technology and the public stands many of us will take, we must carefully examine our feelings and attitudes about motherhood with an understanding of the complexities involved.

Some women do indeed act smug and superior in terms of their motherhood; and some are disparaging and insensitive toward those of us with children. ("Children are something to be stepped on," said one feminist in a group in which I was the only mother.) But these attitudes all ultimately stem from feelings of being threatened or unaccepted or powerless. In the feminist community we must acknowledge and work through prejudice against motherhood within the nuclear family, just as we must demand that the mainstream support and empower women with alternative lifestyles. In searching for ways to give greater visibility to nontraditional choices, we must support alternative media and feminist filmmakers. Perhaps we need to invent new language. We need more honest dialogue, within the pages of women's periodicals and among ourselves in groups, workshops, and individually. And certainly those of us with children must, by word and example, teach them the values that can someday empower all of us to make our own best choices.

OCTOBER 1992

Childlessness

by J. Kay

Like many stories, this story keeps changing. Like many decisions, the deciding comes first, the reasons come later. *Childlessness*. It's a strange word. "Ness"—a state of being. "Less"—

without. But our language, at least has no other, less negative, word—a state of being, with?—that describes quite the same thing.

In 1979, when my friend Janet told me she had decided to get a tubal ligation, I wondered. I hadn't realized before that you could decide to get a tubal ligation. I guess that I had assumed—if indeed, I had ever thought about it before—that someone else made that decision for you. For medical reasons. For control. For punishment. I had heard about women in prison and in mental institutions. I had recently worked on a political event for Puerto Rican independence. I had learned about unsuspecting women in Puerto Rico who had been subjected to forced sterilization.

When Janet told me about what she was going to do, we were both 31. We both had been affected by the confusion and idealism of the late '60s, early '70s. We often had had conversations about population growth, the egotism inherent in families, and the necessity of incorporating social responsibility into our personal lives. Although I don't think too many personal decisions are made on the basis of startling statistics or altruism, who knows exactly the convoluted and intricate ways social realities impress themselves upon our minds and actions? Janet was married. She had had two abortions. One legal, after *Roe v. Wade,* and one before, not. She and her husband wanted to adopt a child, rather than have one of their own.

Okay, I thought. Probably whoever was in charge of tubal ligations would think it made sense for her. Besides, she had her husband to back her up. Had her husband to grant permission, in case that man in charge (I imagined a man) demanded another man's permission.

I didn't. I wasn't. I hadn't. And I might just as well have been 21 rather than 31. I mean, my life stretched before me like that. As though I would live forever. I loved taking my time, observing. I loved learning and political activity and working at idealistic jobs, just enough to support myself—no more. Maybe it would not be true to say I wanted my life to continue exactly as it was. But if I wanted it to change at all, I wanted it to change slowly, as it would—with no socially predetermined plan.

I have never felt driven to marry and have children. Even at 31, marriage seemed, at best, like something a long way down the road. Thoughts of having a family seldom entered my daydreams. Not even as a teenager. In my daydreams, I was usually living alone in a stark but pleasant room, surrounded by art books, a radio playing classical music. In my daydreams, I was sitting at a huge wooden desk writing. In my daydreams, my mate was an unobtrusive lover who would visit late in the evenings.

"I'm thinking of getting a tubal ligation," I told my boyfriend, Jake. He was driving his orange '70 Volkswagen bug, and I was sitting next to him, close enough to chart the response on his profile. His face changed. The thought was visibly upsetting to him. I'm quite sure not because he was thinking of any stake he might have in the decision. He didn't want to marry. He didn't want children. "That seems drastic," he said. Or maybe he said "unnatural" or "unwomanly." I don't think he said "unwomanly," but somehow that thought came through.

"I'm tired of taking the pill. I feel like I'm poisoning my own body with it. Besides I just want to decide about something, to decide once and for all." Those were the reasons I would have given then. I can't remember if I actually gave them at that time. More likely, I quickly changed the subject. Or he did. I never told him—even though we stayed together for a number of years afterwards and then broke up and then got together again. I never told him. I never told my best friend at work. I never told lots of people. I had to tell one person, though, because the outpatient clinic required that someone pick me up afterwards. I told my friend Alice because years before I had helped her when she needed an abortion.

But I'm getting ahead of myself. I couldn't get the tubal ligation immediately after the seed had been planted to do so. I didn't have health insurance, and I didn't have the money to pay for the operation. Within a few months, however, I took a full-time job with the state of Illinois. I deliberately chose an HMO that included free tubal ligations as part of its benefits.

It all seems pretty willful, doesn't it? Though I've never regretted the decision, I did go through a long period some years afterwards wondering about myself. What was driving me? What had made me so determined? I still am not sure of the answers to those questions. But determined I surely was. Even the HMO doctor did not deter me—though he very well might have. His face, like Jake's, changed when I brought up the idea.

The prejudice that the HMO doctor exhibited toward tubal ligation fits into a long, ignoble tradition of the medical profession. The prejudice has manifested itself in diverse ways depending upon whether or not the woman in question was a woman of color or white, whether or not she was poor or middle class. Coercive practices tied to eugenics and race purification abounded in the first half of the century and are still extant in some parts of the world. Not that long ago, doctors performed the "Mississippi appendectomy" on Black women in the South by tying their fallopian tubes without their knowledge. As eager as doctors have been to sterilize some women, they have been just as reluctant to sterilize others. Until 1970, doctors usually refused requests for voluntary sterilization from unmarried women or from women whom they did not feel had enough children. Sterilization committees at hospitals even devised an age-parity formula. The woman's age times the number of her children had to equal 120 in order for a sterilization request to be honored.

My HMO doctor bombarded me with questions, many of which were not medical in nature. I answered patiently. No, I had never been pregnant. Yes, I was sure I didn't want to have a baby. No, I didn't have a husband. And so forth. He stood above me, a tall, robust man whose very physical presence could have been intimidating. Strangely, though, I stayed calm.

After the interrogation came the horror stories. Something about how I might begin bleeding profusely years after I had the tubal ligation. I'm not kidding; he said that. I knew, then, he was simply lying for whatever reason of his own. I had done enough reading to know there was little risk involved in the procedure. Though his reaction angered me, anger was not the overriding emotion. I felt detached, and if his irrationality had not been inconveniencing me so much, I might even have been amused that I had the power to threaten him so. The meeting ended with him saying the only way he would perform the operation was if I would see a psychologist first.

After thinking about it for a few days, I wrote a letter to the HMO to complain. Within four days, I received a phone call and an interview with the head of the HMO. She couldn't have been more apologetic or sympathetic. She did not question my motives but simply assumed I had made a decision that was right for me. Within a few weeks, she had an appointment at an outpatient clinic with another—a non-HMO—doctor set up for me. I felt very grateful.

"Freedom is not in fragments. A nonfragmented mind, a mind that is whole is in freedom," says the twentieth-century spiritual teacher Krishnamurti. *"Freedom of choice denies freedom; choice exists only where there is confusion. Clarity of perception, insight, is the freedom from the pain of choice."*

I think about this quotation often. I think about it in relation to childlessness. I think about it in relation to women's liberation. I think about it when I think of my own determination to have a tubal ligation. As I have already intimated to you, I do not fully understand that determination. But I do feel that having a tubal ligation was one of a few times in my life that I was acting with clarity and freedom. When I agonize over a problem and then make up my mind, I do not feel that same clarity and freedom. When I try to crowd all possibilities into my life I do not feel clarity and freedom.

And isn't that what we are often pressured (or pressure ourselves) to do? I mean, crowd all possibilities into a life. What is motivating so many women, aged 35 to 45 (and younger women, as well), who become obsessed with the need to have a baby "before it's too late"? More and more lesbians are "deciding" to have babies. More and more single heterosexual women are "deciding." One must ask why, at this time, so many women feel pressure to decide in this way. What social and political pressures are affecting that choice? Or can we even call it *choice* when so often women truly feel obsessed about childbearing (to the extent that the act of becoming pregnant can become a major economic project, almost a way of life) and conversely so seldom feel truly free or happy not to bear a child at all?

This story, I have said, like many stories, keeps changing. The deciding comes first, the reasons come later. The reasons elude; the reasons, like the story, change. At age 43, I suddenly, for the first time in my life, become intensely interested in science. I read ferociously. I read about chimpanzees and chaos and information and quantum mechanics and relativity and the human brain. I read science in the same way as I have read literature, biography, psychology, history, and theology for many, many years before I realized that science had something important to say to me, too. I read subjectively. I read to find out my place in the universe. I read to find out who I am and why I act the way I do.

When I read about chimpanzees and evolution, I learn that the intelligence of a species has a lot to do with life span, especially the years lived after reproductive activity. Jane Goodall tells us that some female chimpanzees may live past childbearing years, but female humans are by far the most successful females of any species at living long lives after the childbearing years. Freed from the constraints of childbirth and childrearing, older females help develop the intelligence of the whole species by passing on accumulated knowledge and wisdom. That's how the theory goes. I speculate and wonder. In an overpopulated world, do the childless serve a similar evolutionary function?

Reading about science can only make us wonder about, not know, the mysteries of life—those mysteries that we ourselves unwittingly participate in. That's how I feel about childlessness—that it is something of a mystery, surely just as mysterious and miraculous as bringing a child into the world.

I have told you that I have never regretted having had a tubal ligation. And that is true. But that is not to say my life ended up happily ever after. When I am feeling alone or insecure, I look for understanding especially among other women who consider themselves liberated from constraints of gender conditioning. I don't expect to find understanding everywhere, but I feel taken aback when I don't find it where I assume I will.

Once when I went for a routine examination at a women's clinic, I saw a practitioner's face change in the same way Jake's and my HMO doctor's faces had changed. I had just told her in response to a question that I once had had a tubal ligation. She just couldn't understand if I had never had a child, how I could have freely chosen to do such a thing. I hadn't expected to find such incredulity at a woman-centered clinic.

Once a good friend surprised me in a similar way. We were discussing her decision to have a child at the age of 41. Because she had been unable to become pregnant, she was going to try *in vitro* fertilization. "You know," she said, "even though you have had a tubal ligation, you could have a child that way, too." The underlying assumption clearly was that I must by now regret my decision, that anyone my age without a child must really want to have one.

Life goes on. The stories change. The reasons change. We learn. We speculate. We live with who we are, like it or not. Sometimes we find understanding, often we don't.

But today is a beautiful day in May. So, really, who cares about any of it? In my neighborhood, pink and white blossoms perfume the air. Tulips, jonquils, lilacs, and bridal wreath mark the boundaries between modest bungalows with vibrancy and good will. In the park across from my apartment, young men amuse themselves by bouncing balls and insulting one another's mothers.

I write in that stark room I always daydreamed about. I have the wooden desk and lots of books. The rent is cheap. The walk to the corner store is not long and is rather pleasant along the length of Kosciuszko Park, past a playground where agile urban children hang from their knees and walk on their hands, past benches where lovers hold hands and unkempt men and women drink alcohol from glass bottles barely disguised in brown paper bags, past the tennis courts where partners shout in Polish and Spanish, past the basketball court where Blacks and Latinos and whites compete for the nets, and today past a glorious cherry tree whose limbs are bent with the weight of rowdy nine-year-olds.

On my way back, I meet five-year-old Shawn, who lives in my building, and his friend Brenda. Shawn's skinny arms are hugging two huge branches of cherry blossoms. Leftovers, evidently, from the vanished nine-year-olds. Brenda carries a modest bouquet. "Look how they have hurt the tree," I say to Shawn and point to the jagged end of a rudely torn branch.

"They are for my mother," Shawn says, his face shining with unmitigated joy.

"You could have given her a small bouquet like Brenda's," I protest. But Shawn isn't listening. The day is too beautiful for lectures, no matter how well intentioned or deserved.

"Do you have any gum?" he asks smelling the peppermint on my breath.

"He really likes gum," Brenda adds. I take a pack from my pocket and offer a stick to Brenda and then one to Shawn.

"Thank you," Brenda says. "Thank you," Shawn echoes, though he usually forgets that nicety. I am about to walk on my way when Brenda says, "Happy Mother's Day."

Yes, that's right. Today is Mother's Day. Though I sent a card and gift to my mother a few days ago, it has completely slipped my mind. For a moment, I feel disconcerted by Brenda's good wishes, so I laugh and shrug my shoulders. "Thank you," I say. "Happy Mother's Day to you guys, too." Now they are the ones caught off guard by the greeting. So all three of us laugh. Then I wave goodbye; they wave cherry blossoms, and I walk back to my apartment alone.

This essay also appeared in Childless by Choice, *edited by Irene Reti (HerBooks, 1992).*

MAY 1989

Made in Korea
by Mi Ok Bruining

I was asked to write about my perspective on Korean adoptions in the United States. As an adult Korean adoptee who was adopted by a white family in the United States, I want to address five areas of concern which both U.S. and Korean societies will have to address if we are to understand and transform the 40-year-old phenomenon called adoption. These include cultural and economic factors used to justify Korean adoptions, and the social, political, and racist attitudes that pervade the process.

When Korean and U.S. adoption officials are asked why so many children are being adopted from (South) Korea and sent abroad to developed nations, the reasons are most often based on cultural and economic factors. The highest percentage of children are adopted from Korea (an estimated minimum of 75,000 children have been adopted worldwide in the last three decades through the existing international adoption industry). Spokespersons who represent the most established and enduring adoption agency, Holt International Children's Services, Inc., and other agencies propound that Korea is an underdeveloped, Third World, economically struggling nation and that strong, ancient cultural standards sanction the adoption of Korean children by other nations. However, as with most controversial but seemingly harmless situations, social, political, and racist attitudes pervade these arguments. The answer lies in what is *not* discussed not in what is explained.

I adamantly dispute these standard reasons for the export of Korean children, because for as long as Korean children have been sponsored and adopted by U.S. families, the United States has been politically and militarily involved with Korea. This fact is not merely an historical coincidence but a direct reflection of the political and economic exploitation of "Third World" nations, including Korea by the United States throughout history.

The ramifications of U.S. involvement with Korea are seen in the export of Korean-made products: clothes, electronics, and most recently, automobiles. Korea is no longer an underdeveloped, struggling nation. It is a developing, technologically powerful country with economic ambitions similar to those of other developing nations.

The reasons that Korea continues to send her children away to the United States and other lands drastically differ from the reasons for which I was adopted more than twenty years ago. I was born in 1960, a time when Korea was severely crippled by the aftershocks of the Korean War. The land was ravaged; people were starving in the fields and begging on the streets. Families were torn apart, children separated from their parents, either by disease or abandonment. I was one of thousands of children who were abandoned and left to be brought to the increasing number of orphanages hastily being built to accommodate the inundation of orphaned children. The city of Seoul was a mass of rubble and the United States responded to the needs of the children by establishing organizations to allow U.S. families to sponsor and/or adopt orphaned children. Those children who were not adopted right away were sponsored by families or individuals who supported the child with letters, money, clothes, and so on.

I was one of those sponsored children, having been abandoned at three months old, processed through one of the several police stations in Seoul, and dropped off at Il San, the largest orphanage at the time, which was established by an Oregon farmer and his wife. My photo was sent to a family in New Jersey who decided to sponsor a Korean child because they had read of the plight of children in Korea in a local newspaper. They read about Harry and Bertha Holt, who built the Il San orphanage, and the Holt Orphan's Fund, and responded by sending me money, clothes, letters, and toys. Later, when they realized that I wasn't about to be adopted right away (not all children were adopted immediately), this family decided to adopt me. The adoption process took nine months, and I arrived in the United States in 1966. I was five years old, almost unadoptable because of my age: I was getting too old to be "cute" anymore.

The circumstances of children in Korea today are very different, but their needs and issues are no less vital and immediate. The pervading and unavoidable issues today do not include poverty and disease but societal constraints and oppression. In 1960, when I was born, it was expected that I would be abandoned if my birthmother could not provide for me. Korea was ravaged by war: there was no social welfare system, no housing to shelter homeless families, no halfway houses for pregnant, unmarried women. Human rights were minimal (with little progress today).

Today, just as twenty years ago, women who give birth to children out of wedlock are forced to relinquish their babies. The pressure is greatest for unmarried women in the lowest income bracket; however, regardless of class and income status, the pressure is immense for all unmarried women who become pregnant. These are the Korean children who are being adopted all over the world.

When I returned to Korea in 1984, I visited the adoption agency I had been adopted through and toured the orphanage I had lived in for the first five years of my life. For the first time, I experienced Korean culture and the social implications of adoption in Korea. I began to wonder why the domestic adoption program in Korea was so small and powerless. I asked about birth control and the foster care program in Korea. I inquired about the clinical practices of the social workers who counseled unwed, pregnant women. I asked about the availability of abortion in Korea. The answers to all these questions disturbed me. Very little tangible information was voluntarily offered, and what information I received was obscured by righteous excuses, which these agencies believe justify their work, actions, and attitudes.

I was outraged but not surprised that sex education is not taught in the home or schools. Korea is not extraordinary in its belief that adolescents and teenagers are not sexually active. If high-school-aged girls and boys are not having sex, where are all the babies coming from? The answer is that denial is global. I learned that birth control is offered to the mother after she has relinquished her child, but not surprisingly, nothing is demanded of the father for his responsibility in producing an unwanted child. I don't know if abortion is illegal, but it is vehemently discouraged and not accessible to most women. Besides the economic unavailability, there are strong beliefs that a woman is committing an immoral, life-killing act. For all of Korea's westernized attitudes, the society is still very oppressive in its treatment of women.

We must not ignore the fact that the adoption program in Korea is funded and administered by the Korean government, which is governed by men. The Korean government establishes and regulates the policies and programs for the adoption industry. The executive director (a man) of the largest adoption agency in Korea was appointed by the Korean government.

Many people, especially in the United States, see only the benefits of these children being adopted. In concept, the idea is a noble one. The "orphaned" child is given a loving family and provided with a home and all the material comforts each child deserves, and the family is provided with a child to love and care for. And, well, the birthmother, she wasn't "able" to care for her child, right? The answer is correct in the Korean case only because the pregnant, unmarried woman is approached by a representative of an adoption agency and is "counseled" to relinquish her unborn child. The adoption agency provides housing and prenatal care, pays all the medical expenses, and guarantees a reentry back into society as a contributing citizen. In essence, there is no social or economic future in Korea for an unmarried, pregnant woman who refuses to relinquish her child.

Both the United States and Korea have marketed the adoption industry so well that there is a "trendy" demand for Korean infants and young children. The availability of these children has only recently been noticeably reduced by the huge number of U.S. families applying. There are currently ten U.S. families applying for each healthy child in Korea. The application process and wait for Korean children is more complicated and longer now, especially for Korean female infants. It seems that most pre-adoptive families prefer female babies because girls are considered "cuter," more intelligent, have fewer behavior problems, and they can be dressed up. These assumptions are based on and perpetuate stereotypes of Asian girls and women, who are seen as docile, accommodating, obedient, quiet, soft-spoken, nonconfronting, and exotic.

There are many more issues I have not addressed, like the inadequate domestic foster care program and domestic adoption program in Korea and the United States' "righteous," imperialistic attitude that U.S. families can better provide for these children, many of whom are not orphans, but are relinquished by unwilling women, coerced by a corrupt government. But my most immediate concern is the fate of the children considered unadoptable, those left behind to face unpromising futures as societal outcasts. These are the sibling groups, the older children, the ones who are disabled and mentally retarded. Korea has hidden these children away just as the United States has hidden its infant mortality rate; poverty; homeless, elderly, and institutionalized disabled populations; and child abuse and incest statistics. One of the few attempts Korea has made in providing for these "unadoptable" children is by making it quicker and easier for U.S. families to adopt them.

As a feminist, I see many dimensions to the issue of Korean adoptions and all foreign adoptions in which we exploit and export living, breathing products known as children. I escorted Korean children to the United States on three occasions with mixed feelings and a bad taste in my mouth. I felt neither pride nor disgust, but a gnawing feeling inside that this— foreign adoption—is not the answer, but only a tiny, insignificant band-aid on a huge, open, gaping wound, covered by an enormous, hideous amount of denial. I cannot begin to address the racist attitudes toward adopting Korean children or other foreign-born children without attacking the "Asian model minority" myths and stereotypes that pervade U.S. society. We, as Asian Americans, are either the "enemy," seen by the generations before my own as the ones the United States fought against in World War II and the Vietnam War, or we are the super-intelligent computer and math whizzes. There is very little in between where we are considered individuals, unique as human beings.

My own awareness and consciousness has been raised through great pain, isolation, and alienation. I have been rejected by the local Korean community because I have white parents, and I have been rejected by the white society because I am Korean. I am unique as an Asian-American woman, a woman of color, and a Korean-American woman. I experience a dual heritage on a daily basis, as do all children who are adopted from Korea to the United States. Though it may be easier for Korean children today because there are more of them, the issues are just as immediate and undeniable. I appeal to the adoption agencies, to the Korean government, to adoptive parents, to other adoptees, and to the postadoption services professionals to look again at the reasons for Korean adoptions, because they do not always justify this 40-year-old phenomenon. The price of denial, imperialism, racism, and oppression of Korean women will be paid by the children who are adopted, but most especially, and importantly, by those who are left behind.

Until the United States and Korea address the five elemental issues (social, political, economic, cultural, and racial) discussed in this article, adoptions must continue to provide homes for children who need them. It will take years of social change, drastic changes in the goals of both the United States and Korean adoption industries and governments, and new policies across these very powerful institutions to enable new possibilities for the lives of relinquished Korean children, and the women who give these children up. I have this obscene image in my mind of Korean babies and "adoptable" children being put on an 11,000 mile-long conveyor belt stretching from the maternity wards in Korea to all of the major airports in the United States. I am hoping that in my lifetime, if the conveyor belt must exist, that it will transport children considered "unadoptable" along with the basic human rights, freedom of choice, and dignity that all children and birthmothers deserve.

This article has been edited for clarity.

MAY 1989

The Honduran Baby Market
by Roxanna Pastor

Throughout history, first world nations have used the labor force in the Third World for economic gain. In Honduras, the women who work in the free-trade zone manufacture products from baseballs to bras. While they are paid better than if they worked for a Honduran enterprise, they are paid far less than what a woman in this country would earn for exactly the same job.

In the past eight years, the Reagan administration invested $8 billion in Central American countries. Unfortunately, the money served to militarize the region and stabilize the existing economies rather than to create jobs. As a result, up to 15 percent of all Central Americans have been displaced from their homes, more than 160,000 have died, and two of every five Central Americans cannot afford their basic food needs.

The acute economic crisis brought on by the state of war has directly affected the lives of women. Unable to find jobs, let alone training opportunities, they have been forced to seek other means of survival. In Honduras, some have moved near the areas where the United States soldiers are stationed. There they can sell their bodies at a much higher rate than in other parts of the country. Unfortunately, one of the consequences has been the increased spread of sexually transmitted diseases. This is particularly worrisome in a country where, in the rural areas (most of the country), there is one doctor for every 15,000 people and one nurse for every 50,000 people.

Women who do not have enough to eat have also found themselves having more children. Living in a day-to-day manner leaves little opportunity or money to go to the clinic and seek contraceptives, which are scarce and expensive. Just as they have little access to health clinics, they have less access to the government-controlled adoption agencies. (Adoption is not as common as in the United States and, until the late '60s, adoption was illegal by the mere fact that there was no adoption law.)

Some of these women are relieved when someone wants to adopt a newborn who they know they will not be able to feed. Often they give up their children in exchange for a promise of a good life for the baby or for $25 or $50. The women who give up their children usually are approached by adoption "merchants" at the public hospital after giving birth on the sidewalks or in hallways due to the lack of beds.

These newborns are then taken to homes known as "fattening houses," where up to fifteen children are kept at a time. One woman is paid a miserable salary to care for all the children who are waiting to be adopted by U.S. couples and who, in the meantime, are gaining weight. "Fattening houses" and this type of illegal adoption transaction have been discovered in Honduras and Guatemala. Depending on who is involved in the business, they are prosecuted or not, but the practice has not been stopped. In Mexico, the government has taken a more active role to recover children who have been kidnapped or sold to U.S. couples.

The main problem the baby "merchants" face is that the baby of a malnourished woman who has not received any prenatal care is not necessarily a healthy child. As the demand for babies has increased (as Third World adoptions have become more popular), the merchants have resorted to other strategies. In Honduras, they have paid teenage girls to get pregnant; the merchants then follow the young women throughout their pregnancy to make sure they eat well and receive some kind of prenatal care. Once a baby is born, and if the baby is healthy, the mother is paid $50 for the product. This practice is not very different from what we call "surrogate motherhood" (in the United States); however, it is substantially cheaper.

I have chosen the words "merchants" and "product" rather than adoption workers and babies because the way these adoptions take place is an illegal business, not a transaction between a woman who cannot care for a baby and one who wants a child. The needs of the women involved are only important to the degree that they affect the business. A woman in the United States who is considering adopting a baby from the Third World must take into account these situations, and not solely her wish to obtain a newborn baby.

As a child care worker, I am acutely aware of the hundreds of children both in Honduras and in this country who would benefit from a family who could care for them. I also know, however, that the type of adoptions described above are just one more way of exploiting women. I feel very strongly that women in the United States who have chosen to adopt a child from a Third World country have the responsibility to investigate the situation. It is the first step they can take to show respect for their future child.

AUGUST 1989

Birthmarks: A Birthmother's View of Adoption

by Judith E. Beckett

The article from the *Valley News* has been sitting on my desk since last October when it first appeared. Each time I walk by it and glimpse the headline I'm horrified. The words scream out at me: "Babies Stolen for Adoption." I don't know what to do about those words, that pain.

The South-North News Service article by Lucy Hood begins: "Guatemala City—Nadia Popol was nursing her infant son at home one Sunday morning in Guatemala City's slum when two men with knives burst through the door and took her child away.... One of the intruders restrained Popol's aunt and two sisters while the other struck Popol on the head and grabbed the baby from her arms."

I shudder reading it. As international adoptions have become common in this country I've anguished over the terrible social, political, and economic circumstances that must contribute to the (non)choice my sisters in the Third World make in surrendering their children for adoption. Do they understand, I wonder, that the foreigners into whose arms they are entrusting their babies are partially responsible for their present desperation? Do they know it's not coincidence that the focus of international adoption activity has shifted from Korea in the late '50s and early '60s to Vietnam in the '70s and then to Central and South America in the '80s as political and social turmoil (and U.S. involvement) have also shifted there? And why has it never occurred to me before that babies might actually be *stolen* for adoption?

Finally, in Nadia Popol's screams I hear the echo of my own. Are they so different?

I am screaming and screaming. There are other women in the labor room screaming, too. I know one of them. We are both from the home for unwed mothers. The nurses yell at us: "Push! Don't you want to have this baby?" I hold on to my baby for as long as I can, but finally they take me to the delivery room where I see in the mirror that she's about to be born. Soon she's screaming, too. Her head is born, her body still inside me, but she's screaming.

I decide to take care of her for the five days that we're together in the hospital. It seems to me the first days of my daughter's life may be important to her. I want them to be filled with love, and I want her to know during these first few days that she is wanted and cared for—I'm not going to let them take that away from us.

When the nurses bring her to me to be fed, I talk to her incessantly. The other mothers in the room wonder at how I can talk to her so much, but I want her to remember my voice, to remember her mother. I stare at her face, trying to memorize it. It must be enough to last me forever.

When the May [1989] issue of *Sojourner* appears in my mailbox, I'm jubilant. The headline reads: "Whose Children? The Politics of International Adoption." Inside are articles written by two adoptees: Mi Ok Bruining is a Korean woman adopted by a white family in the United States during the '60s; Roxanna Pastor is a Honduran woman adopted in her own country before there were any adoption laws. A third article is written by Carol Aubin, a woman who has adopted two South American children. I'm excited to see feminists taking on the issue of adoption as their own!

A voice is missing, however. I note grimly that none of the women who gave birth to any of the four adoptees mentioned above are represented: all the forces of sexism, racism, and classism at work in this world conspire to make sure that doesn't happen.

I learn instead from others in this issue of *Sojourner* that the women surrendered their children in the hope of obtaining a better life for them, because they were unmarried and needed to deny their motherhood, or because they were so poor that the child most certainly would have died anyway. All of these reasons are related to issues of race, sex, and class. These "reasons" intellectualize the mother's pain and serve to keep us a step removed from her suffering.

Not to be able to care for one's own children is a great shame. That is, it's shameful, but I'm not the first in my family to feel shamed in this way. My maternal grandmother, Johanna, was married to an alcoholic when she gave birth to my Uncle George in 1910. When she finally left her husband's alcoholism and cruelty and went to work in a matchbox factory to support herself, she had to put her son into foster care. He remained there until she married her second husband, my grandfather, around the time of World War I. It's a secret in our family that my grandmother had two husbands and placed her child in foster care. Her secret, her poverty, and her suffering were related to her class and her powerlessness as a woman.

On my father's side of the family, my grandparents were servants who came here from England. My grandmother was a cook, my grandfather a butler. They found positions working on an estate in Connecticut, but were not allowed to keep their children with them. They placed my father and my Aunt Muriel in foster care where they both remained until they were grown.

Adoption and foster care are institutions similarly related to issues of racism, sexism, and classism. This relationship is fundamental and unchanging over time, worldwide and in this country. The situation in the United States when my daughter was born parallels that which Mi Ok Bruining describes in Korea today: "The pervading and unavoidable issues today do not include poverty and disease but societal constraints and oppression.... Today...women who give birth to children out of wedlock are forced to relinquish their babies. The pressure is greatest for unmarried women in the lowest income bracket; however, regardless of class and income status, the pressure is immense for all unmarried women who become pregnant."

Today in the United States, things have not changed much from what they were when my daughter was born, except that, for the time being, some women have the option of abortion.

Still, 23 percent of U.S. children are born "illegitimately" each year. The word "illegitimate" is defined by *Webster's Ninth New Collegiate Dictionary* as "not recognized as lawful offspring; not sanctioned by law." And it is the patriarchy that decides which offspring are "sanctioned" and which are not. A further definition of illegitimate, "departing from the regular, erratic," reminds me of the *Sojourner* article about the Grandmothers of the Plaza de Mayo (Rita Arditti and M. Briton Lykes, January 1989): "The dictatorship's strategy was to try to change the identity and the future of the children by changing their affiliation. Evidence for this comes from the military's own words: 'Personally, I did not eliminate any child. What I did was to give some of them to beneficent organizations so that they would find new parents for them. Subversives educate their children into subversion. That has to be stopped.'"

Feminists need to ask who benefits when children are taken from single, poor, Hispanic, and teenage women in this country—indeed from any woman—and placed in traditional (patriarchal) "families."

At the home for unwed mothers, I have a box of baby clothes that my sister saved for me from her first child. I take the little things out, wash them, fold them, and put them back again very neatly. Even though my parents won't bring my baby home, I tell myself that I'll keep my baby. I'll find a place to live, get a job, and find someone to care for her and keep her safe while I'm working.

My social worker tells me that my baby's birth certificate will be stamped ILLE-GITIMATE. She asks me how I think my child will feel when she goes to school and the teacher asks everyone what their fathers do for a living. What will my child answer? She asks me who I think will marry me when I already have one child born out of wedlock.

And then my social worker tells me that if I "give my baby up" she'll be adopted by a "good" family. That she'll have "all the advantages" that I can't give her. That she'll have two parents who want her very much. She says my child will be part of a "family."

I agree to adoption. On the fifth day, I walk away, leaving her in the hospital. This is the hardest thing I have done in my life. Three months later, I'll go to a lawyer and sign the papers that will separate us forever. I'll swear on the Bible that I'll never try to find out where she is.

In Argentina, the Grandmothers of Plaza de Mayo are searching for their grandchildren. The grandmothers estimate that some 500 children were born in concentration camps run by the military throughout the country during the brutal repression between 1976 and 1983. Hundreds of kidnapped pregnant women gave birth in these camps before being tortured and murdered. Their children were then placed for adoption, in some cases given to those very individuals who had tortured and killed their parents. Some of these children have been found outside of Argentina, having entered the international adoption market.

A decade later, the grandmothers are aided in their search by modern technology. Blood tests which identify genetic markers prove that the child in question comes from a certain family with 99.95 percent accuracy. Arditti and Lykes write: "At the center...is the issue of restitution of the children to their legitimate families.... They have been denied the knowledge of their history and origin, and objectified as property. Without the knowledge of the truth of their origins, the children remain disconnected from their history, living a life of lies."

To search is an act of civil disobedience, as Joyce Pavoa said at the American Adoption Conference in Nashua, New Hampshire, last October, but I can't forget my daughter as I had been assured I would. While she's growing up, I don't marry or have other babies. I search for her only in the faces of other women's children. Internalizing the adoption professionals' judgment that I'm inadequate as a woman, I'm depressed, self-destructive, and filled with self-hatred; I'm often physically ill. Her birthday is the hardest time for me.

In the '70s, I become a feminist. Things begin to feel a little better as I learn to love my body, my femaleness, even my genitals. An astrologer tells me I'm like a flower just beginning to open. By the time my daughter is eighteen, I am able to call the adop-

tion agency where my daughter was placed and have my name, address, and medical information appended to her file so that she has access to it should she decide to search. This is all I'm allowed to do.

Then I read Mary Daly and Merlin Stone. I discover the Goddess and understand that the relationship between mother and child is the primary relationship in life. I wonder why family is defined as father, mother, and child—denying this fundamental bond—and why fathers determine which children are "legitimate" and which are not. (This is no different than it was a thousand years ago when fathers decided which child would be allowed to survive—usually the males—and which would be exposed to die on the hill!)

I begin to create rituals to bring my daughter closer to me. I celebrate her birthdays and, after seeing Ronda Slater's play,...a name you never got, in October 1987, I stop worrying about the oath I took and hire a searcher to look for her. The death of six-year-old Lisa Steinberg a month later (Joel Steinberg, the criminal lawyer hired by Lisa's birthmother to arrange an independent adoption for her, had kept the child and abused and finally killed her with a blow to her head) fuels my sense of urgency. For the first time, it occurs to me that the family who adopted my daughter may not be "good."

Within four months, I find my daughter in the same city and within several blocks of the apartment where I live.

I believe the pressure put on young women to relinquish their babies for adoption is now greater than ever, and that the desire for adoptable babies is a driving force, both consciously and unconsciously, within the movement to make abortion illegal. In fact, this now seems to be official U.S. policy. President Bush states in *Newsweek* on May 1: "We must change from abortion to adoption."

There are 2.4 million infertile couples in this country today. Technologies such as IVF (*in vitro* fertilization) and GIFT (gamete intrafallopian transfer) have helped only 5,000 couples so far to conceive and bear children, while between 50,000 and 140,000 children become available and are placed for adoption annually. (These figures are hard to pin down because so many adoptions are arranged privately.) Many city and county adoptions are free, but private adoptions cost $5,000 to $10,000 and may be as high as $30,000. International adoptions run between $6,000 and $10,000.

On the other hand, 1.6 million abortions are performed each year in this country. According to the same article in *Newsweek,* women with incomes less than $11,000 per year are three times more likely to have an abortion than those with incomes over $25,000. Hispanic women, unmarried women, Roman Catholic women, and eighteen- and nineteen-year-olds are also most likely candidates. These are the women who will be asked to carry their babies to term and surrender them for adoption if *Roe v. Wade* is reversed. Feminists looking at who births the babies and who gets the babies cannot ignore the class issues involved.

In fact, the Supreme Court's recent decision in *Webster v. Reproductive Health Services* already allows for states to severely limit access to abortions. In developing feminist theory, we need to remember that to save unborn lives we must love and help mothers. And that children are not consumer goods. Be aware, furthermore, that in the competition for a limited supply of infants, the patriarchy has set up woman against woman. Finally, understand that it is not the right of any woman to have and raise a child to adulthood. It is a privilege, and that privilege is very much related to the issues of racism, classism, and sexism, which feminists must be committed to eradicating.

It's a beautiful spring evening in May, but as I walk toward the restaurant where I have agreed to meet my daughter after our 24-year separation, I'm trembling inside, I'm breathing too fast, and my knees feel weak. I begin to think I might faint. I have to stop to talk to myself.

"Listen," I tell myself sternly, "this is not the hardest thing you've ever done in your life."

I turn in to the flower shop a block from the restaurant to buy her some flowers, "Carnations and daisies," I tell the man behind the counter. "Baby's breath?" he wants to know. I smile. "Yes, baby's breath," I agree. And I know then that everything will be all right.

My daughter Phebe and I were reunited one year ago this month. This Mother's Day I received a card from her on which she had written: "I love you so much and count my blessings every day—thank you for finding me." Her relationship with her adoptive parents is also excellent, and they love her dearly.

SEPTEMBER 1990

Still Married After All These Years?
by Ellen Herman

Imagine an outdoor gathering of several hundred properly attired young women, located somewhere in the New England countryside. They are sitting in neat rows, shielded by a tent from the sun's punishing heat, listening in rapt attention to an address by a stately, older member of their sex. The speaker, who carefully notes that women are capable of a variety of independent accomplishments, concludes her remarks with a ringing defense of domesticity's virtues. Marriage and motherhood, she assures them, will brighten their lives and benefit their society. Wild applause follows.

An anecdote from the prefeminist dark ages? Hardly. This took place recently, when Barbara Bush spoke at Wellesley College's commencement exercises. If one of feminism's first accomplishments was to challenge domesticity as an imperative defining the permissible limits of women's potential, domesticity has, in the last twenty years, been redefined again. This time, it has been transformed from a stifling to a stylish way of life, entirely compatible with the brave new world of equality. The claim that women's status has improved dramatically in private because it has improved dramatically in public is pervasive. It does not matter that this claim bears a very dubious relationship to the actual conditions of most women's work and family lives. It does not matter that recent surveys of family life illustrate that what has changed is the readiness of men and women to use words like "equal" and "mutual" to describe their domestic relationships, even while tangible measures of "equality"—like the number of hours spent changing diapers or the number of dollars in men's and women's paychecks—are still light years away from that balanced ideal.

The Motherhood Report, for example, published in 1987 and based on such a national survey, clearly documented that the vast majority of mothers were "discontented" with their male partners because of their refusal to provide emotional and practical support for childrearing. In other words, trendy images of involved dads were entirely mythological, yet the authors concluded that "feeling overburdened [as a mother] is a state of mind."

For more than twenty years, the relationship between women's status in the family and women's status in general has been at the center of feminist analysis, debate, and activism. Can the position of women in the family explain why gender has such unequal consequences for men and women? Do biological differences between men and women, or the social organization of those differences within the family, account for the gap between "human beings" and "women"? Since the second wave of feminism first appeared, women's traditional roles in the family—as mothers and wives supporting men who are much more than fathers and husbands—have compelled the attention of feminists and antifeminists alike.

Dismantling the Nuclear Family

In the late '60s, the radical young women who reclaimed the derisive term "feminist" and made it central to their own developing political identities pinpointed the family—specifically, the Western, patriarchal, bourgeois, child-oriented nuclear family—as the most important source of women's oppression. They criticized the legal contract by which women were categorically assigned to economic dependence and lifetimes of domestic labor in exchange for promises of male support; the gender socialization process, conducted within the family, which trained girls and boys to expect separate and unequal experiences in life; the sexual double standard for repressing women's sexuality (or at least channeling it in exclusively procreative directions), while constructing a different set of rules and regulations to regulate the supposedly untameable chaos of male desire; and the ideology of romantic love for being a pretty masquerade covering the ugly consequences of all the other inequalities that families contained: routine domestic violence and sexual assault. Feminist radicals, in sum, criticized the family for being rigid and obligatory and women's functions within it for being obstacles between them and full human status.

Such criticisms demanded concrete and immediate changes. Marriage as an institution came under fire. Of what use was this institution to women, feminists asked, if its continued viability required economic subordination, disproportionate childrearing responsibilities, and a profusion of other gendered restrictions in women's lives? The Feminists, a New York group, developed numerical quotas in 1969 that limited the membership of legally married women and women living with men, a controversial action that clearly illustrated the growing conviction among radical feminists that both formal and informal marriages were major obstacles in the path of women's humanity.

A few years later, when compulsory heterosexuality was called into question, an important element of lesbianism's appeal was that it defied the sexual prescriptions of family life. If anything, the erotic pleasures of coming out were secondary benefits.

Feminists concerned with exposing the cozy relationship between patriarchal families and capitalist economies went further. Without wifely and motherly services, the economy would instantly crumble. Demanding "wages for housework" was therefore more ambitious than demanding that women's domestic labor be dignified with decent wages. It contributed to an understanding that women's liberation and capitalism were contradictory, that "profit" was conceivable only when more than half the population went unpaid for a vast amount of work.

Beyond challenging marriage and the domestic division of labor as oppressive to women, the feminist critique of the family suggested that reproductive control was a prerequisite to anything resembling equality. Efforts to repeal states' criminal abortion laws before *Roe v. Wade,* and to create organizations like JANE in Chicago, which provided safe and affordable underground abortions before 1973, expressed feminists' commitment to bodily self-determination, to a society in which all children were wanted, and—most importantly—to a culture where assessments of women's worth would not be categorically based on gender, and especially not on reproductive decisions.

In *The Dialectic of Sex* (Morrow, 1970), Shulamith Firestone took these insights into the sexual politics of family life further than many other early feminists were willing to go. The fact that the family was organized around a reproductive unit, she theorized, was the nub of the problem; that only women reproduced the next generation for the benefit of the species as a whole was the cause of their degraded state. Firestone concluded that reproduction itself would have to be altered, artificially if necessary, to guarantee that genital differences between males and females would not matter socially. Equally shocking was her blunt statement, *"pregnancy is barbaric,"* and her dismissal of natural childbirth as countercultural brainwashing.

Whether or not they agreed with *The Dialectic of Sex,* feminists in the late '60s and early '70s wanted to see the trajectories of their own lives transformed. They were not motivated by abstractions. These young women, many of whom had not yet made their own reproductive decisions, wanted the freedom to design their present and future families in myriad ways, without penalty: to love women or men, to have sex with one person at a time or several, to live with or without children, to participate in parenting without necessarily participating in reproduction, to experiment with different household forms. Only when they could invent families of all kinds—without fear of ridicule or self-loathing—could women hope to attain genuine individuality, rather than categorization as captive members of a sex/gender class. For their boldness, and for their transgression of a major tenet of family life—that women's pursuit of personal happiness must be subordinated to a common family good—they were called selfish bitches.

The name-calling has persisted because women continue to become feminists out of a desire to change their own lives. For two decades now, storms of anxiety and organized backlash have offered clear evidence that the feminist critique of the family was subversive after all, that it succeeded, at least partially, in exposing the many weaknesses of that sacred institution and carving out a path toward viable alternatives.

The Profamily Agenda

Accusations came first and most forcefully from the new Right, that well-funded and sophisticated network of organizations that gained national momentum during the '70s in its effort to roll back the gains of feminism (and other social movements of the '60s) and make America a man again. Profamily groups like Phyllis Schlafly's Stop ERA (also called the Eagle Forum), Anita Bryant's Save Our Children, Inc., and Jerry Falwell's Moral Majority protested the wave of "permissiveness" they believed was responsible for skyrocketing divorce rates, visible and shameless homosexual communities, objectionable textbooks, uncontrollable teenagers, and other alarming examples of moral decay.

At the heart of the backlash (at least among women) was the belief that traditional family roles accorded special privileges to women and that feminist activism and consciousness threatened to liberate *men* by stupidly repudiating the preferential treatment that women had managed to extract from them, especially economic support and property inheritance during marriage and alimony and child custody after divorce. The nuclear family was, according to this view, an arrangement among hostile members; new Right activists were utterly unconvinced by the feminist vision of a voluntary family. Men, they believed, would bestow neither paychecks nor plumbing services on women and children, except under great duress. Without compulsion, the family would simply disintegrate, leaving its weakest members face-to-face with a heartless world.

To the extent that feminism successfully tapped widespread longing for noncoercive relationships, the new Right was correct in holding feminism responsible for endangering the survival of prescriptive family forms. Women (and some men) began experimenting with collective forms of childrearing, nonmonogamous relationships, friends as family, and coming out. But the backlash came quickly, before feminists had developed enduring alternatives and proved, in practice, that men, women, and children might actually want to share their lives for reasons other than sheer necessity or obligation. A vision of a better family was one thing. Giving up the family one had without any assurance of what would take its place, was something else altogether.

The new Right encouraged women and men to aggressively defend the very meager protections that currently existing families offered against the ups and downs of the market or, in the cases where they offered none, to have faith that such protections could be willed into existence. This fact was not lost on the Left. Especially after Reagan's election in 1980—a shining moment for the new Right—and the defeat of the ERA in the spring of 1982, interest in family issues grew on the Left as well. Advocates of a Leftist "profamily" strategy included Michael Lerner (currently the editor of *Tikkun*, a progressive Jewish magazine), who started an organization called Friends of Families in hopes of "recapturing the family issue."

Leftists like Lerner wanted to see the ERA passed and abortion rights maintained, but above all, they saw "profamily" policies as a way to make some political headway against the hallmarks of Reaganomics: increased unemployment, capital flight, de-skilling, union-busting, and severe cutbacks in basic social services. According to the profamily Left, it was Reagan's trickle-down program—not domestic violence and sexual abuse, unequal intimacy between men and women, or repression of all sexual expression other than compulsory heterosexuality that had families teetering on the edge of survival. Profamily leftists shared the new Right's romantic conception of the family as a harassed haven in a dog-eat-dog world, a place where love could survive and flourish, if only it were given a fair chance.

If the profamily Right and Left were both willing to deny or ignore the numerous dangers to women and children that feminists had so unceremoniously pointed out were built into family structure, some feminists in the '80s were too. Forced onto the defensive and still reeling from the defeat of the ERA, liberal feminists like Betty Friedan decided that reactionary "antifamily" feminism was to blame and that it was time for the women's movement to enter a "second stage," in which women and men would march forward together as equal partners, transcending gender's tiresome polarizations and the very definition of feminism itself.

Making the family a happy place would be the goal of this new stage. Those too stubborn to consider men as good or equal partners until they learned how to do laundry and be supportive listeners were merely harping on annoying old problems or, worse, denying their most profound wishes to have and love children.

Many cultural feminists ended up in more or less the same place as liberals like Friedan—spurning the essentials of the initial feminist critique and reaffirming women's traditional roles—but for entirely different reasons. Campaigns against rape, pornography, and other sexual abuses in the '70s and '80s were particularly important in convincing many feminists of what new Right women had been saying for years: that the inherent violence of male sexuality presented huge dangers to women and that some vehicle had to be found to control it in the interest of protecting women, civilization, even the planet. Where the new Right believed the family could do the job, cultural feminists offered a number of options, ranging from separatism to state action. Cultural feminists celebrated what their predecessors had criticized: a "women's culture," somehow connected to the terms of biological reproduction and, therefore, "nature" and "life."

By the early '80s, many socialist feminists, who remained convinced of the family's centrality to capitalism and women's oppression, had begun to notice that the nuclear family was vanishing, but without much assistance from feminists. The profound questions that women of color asked of a women's movement that presumed to speak for all women, but which hardly included all women or even had a clue about the diversity of women's concerns, did a great deal to inform white, middle-class feminists about the kinds of families many women and children lived in—divorced ones, poor ones, female-headed ones. Feminists had aimed their first arrows at the nuclear family, which made everyone who fell short of that white, middle-class ideal seem either invisible or irrelevant, and racism and class bias conspired to perpetuate this narrow focus.

But long-term demographic trends toward nonnuclear, non-male-headed families—in all racial and ethnic groups—became harder and harder to ignore as time passed. (In 1955, 9 percent of white families and 21 percent of families of color were headed by women. By 1975, the percentages were 13 and 44 respectively, and these families were much more likely to be poor than nuclear families.) Reagan's budget cutbacks and "de-industrialization" (the loss of full-time, unionized, well-paid industrial jobs in favor of part-time, nonunion, poorly paid service-sector jobs) tossed more women and children into poverty and gave even more credibility to voices previously marginalized within the women's movement, whether for reasons of race, poverty, or educational disadvantage.

Unlike partisans of the new Right, the profamily Left, or liberals, most feminists who explored the feminization of poverty did not claim that domestic violence was the price of male unemployment or ignore it altogether in order to romanticize the picture of family-as-refuge. Nor did they suggest that women's growing economic independence was the culprit. They simply pointed out that the family's traditional source of revenue—men—was increasingly inadequate to support the population decently (even where men still counted as members of the family), and that neither women's increased labor force participation nor the government had begun to make up the difference.

While these feminists concluded that women and children were losing ground for reasons of structural inequalities within the family and economy, the new Right blamed impoverishment on feminism itself. Feminists added full employment, guaranteed annual incomes, and a full range of social services to their agendas in an attempt to assert that families were both diverse and deserving of social support. In the meantime, organizers on the Right spread fears that the best kind of nuclear family had been damaged beyond repair. By irresponsibly loosening men's economic obligations, they complained, the women's movement had left swarms of helpless women and children to fend for themselves.

By the early '80s, headlines heralding "post-feminism" suggested that if feminism wasn't actually dead, its glory days were certainly long since past. Young women took eagerly to the pages of national newspapers and magazines to call feminists "throwbacks" and "the anomalies of a radical decade." Women, they said, had finally managed to get beyond feminism and could avoid the bitterness, isolation, and all around pain of their older sisters or mothers.

Also by the early '80s, many lesbians who had come out within supportive feminist communities during the '70s shifted their attention from demanding that lesbianism itself be recognized as legitimate to gaining support for lesbians whose families included children. The "lesbian baby boom," in which lesbians have children after coming out, reflects both straightforward demographic facts (the first generation of post-Stonewall lesbians reaching their childbearing years) and complicated realities of political progress and backlash.

On the side of progress, "choosing children" would have been utterly inconceivable without the gay movement, which has done so much to make lesbians think of themselves as both loving and loveable, hence raising serious doubts about the perception of lesbian mothers as automatically unfit and their children as necessarily damaged. On the side of backlash, the trend toward "choosing children" is occurring, not coincidentally, at a time when the message that childlessness means loneliness is louder than it has been since the '50s. Why shouldn't lesbians be as vulnerable to such pressures as heterosexual women, perhaps even more so, if having children can be offered as evidence that lesbians are capable of approximating a semblance of "normality"? Many lesbians have settled into stable couples and conventional-looking domestic arrangements in preparation for parenting, an entirely understandable development since they face the same pressures as all mothers do and have better than usual reasons to fear poverty and lack of support.

But what does this do to lesbians (or heterosexual women) who don't choose children, either because they are uninterested in parenting or because they would prefer a different kind of parenting than is possible as a single mother or as part of a couple? The profamily backlash is the major reason why these questions are rarely asked, even among lesbians; it explains why the desire for children is accepted without question but its absence is treated as a matter of nervous curiosity. The result is that women without children are left further outside the definition of legitimate family than ever before, a direct affront to responsible adulthood.

Reacting to Reaction

Feminists have had to react to all the reactions of the past twenty years while also surviving themselves in the extremely conservative climate that has existed in this country for over a decade now. Some, for example, who were quick to criticize Michael Lerner's Family Bill of Rights for ignoring most of what feminists had been saying about the destructive inner workings of the family might well feel grateful today to see elements of its program enacted: accessible and humane social services, community-controlled child care, federally supported construction of affordable housing.

With bare-bones family leave legislation recently vetoed by the president, the Women, Infants, and Children (WIC) nutrition program cut with barely a complaint to be heard, and state legislatures all around the country competing to produce the most draconian abortion laws ever written, reforms like Lerner's begin to look practically utopian. It is not original to suggest that prolonged attack will exact a toll from any movement even when it also elicits renewed activism, as in the case of reproductive rights since last year's *Webster* decision. Even with the upcoming nomination hearing of David Souter likely to unleash the most energetic outpouring of angry activism among women that this country has seen in some time, it seems important to acknowledge that *Roe v. Wade* is very unlikely to survive. Although the landmark case has not been formally rolled back yet, it probably will be soon. The downward slide will not begin on the day that *Roe* is rubbed out of federal law; women have been paying dearly, for a decade at least, for the judicial trend toward restricting abortion rights.

Is the current frenzy to protect *Roe* at all costs (and I count myself as frenzied as anyone) obscuring a future in which women's freedom will include far more than abortion rights? Determination to salvage every scrap of reproductive choice we can is entirely appropriate, but forgetting that it is a salvage operation means forgetting both our deepest criticisms of the family and our most imaginative goals. Women are still the objects of routine sexual violence and objectification. We do not control our sexual or our reproductive destinies. Our work remains, by definition, less important than that of men. How can we possibly hope to control our lives while the irrationalities of racism, poverty, and other forms of systematic oppression have the power to make us sick (literally) and desperate? Defending *Roe* by ignoring that women and children are poor, hungry, and illiterate is no defense at all, nor will even the most stringent guarantees of abortion rights magically eliminate poverty and hunger. To save *Roe,* or to make plans for safe abortion services in a post-*Roe* environment are among the most crucial tasks feminists face today. Neither, however, will achieve a feminist family, that is a family that produces equality and individuality in all its members.

The women's movement is not to blame for failing to transform in twenty-odd years an institution that has lasted for thousands. But we are to blame if we have lost track of transformation as an ultimate goal. If we cannot imagine (or worse, no longer believe in) a culture where the difference between mothers and nonmothers will be meaningless—because parenting will not require martyrdom and women's humanity will not rise or fall depending on reproductive choices—then we have succumbed to the profamily onslaught. If we find it impossible to state publicly that "the family" should have as many different forms and meanings as there are ways of envisioning affectional and sexual bonds among humans, then we have allowed sexist anxieties to contaminate our vision of a truly human potential. If we refuse to believe that our personal choices have been affected by our social context—by insisting that the families we live in merely reflect where we happen to be located on a developmental ladder called "growing up" and our reproductive decisions revolve only around the ticking of a biological clock—then, on top of everything else, we are also kidding ourselves.

If we do not know that building families capable and worthy of love involves tremendous risks, then we have forgotten that freedom is not safe and sound, but that women want and must have it anyway.

MARCH 1995

Poor Mother Under Siege
by Kathi Maio

Friends, let me warn you right now that it's going to take me a while to get into the *film* in this film review. The movie brought up so many issues, that I feel a (more than usual) need to put it into the social context of current events. But I'll tell you up front that the film in question is a small, British picture that isn't easy to watch, but which all Americans should see. (How's that for a come on?)

Okay, I won't hold out. It's called *Ladybird, Ladybird*, and it was made by one of the few great, progressive feature filmmakers making movies in the English language. The director's name is Ken Loach. And, although most of his movies are not available in this country, his three most recent films—*Riff-Raff* (1992), *Raining Stones* (1993), and his latest, *Ladybird, Ladybird*—have all received limited theatrical release in this country. (Meaning: see *Ladybird* now, while you have the chance, for the opportunity may not come again!)

But, please, indulge me while I digress a bit. For one of the reasons Ken Loach is so important is that he has dedicated himself to doing something Hollywood never does (and that few independent American filmmakers—outside of, perhaps, John Sayles—even attempt), and that is to create a body of work that honestly tells the stories of poor and working-class people.

Never has it been more important that popular culture give a voice to the invisible "masses." Because never in my lifetime has American society exhibited such vicious contempt for the poor.

These are scary times. And the signs are everywhere. Yet none of the reactionary social indicators—not even the reproductive health clinic murders—has frightened and disgusted me as much as the ever-increasing attacks on "welfare mothers." For this hatemongering against poor women isn't something you can even kid yourself is coming from a few crackpots or political extremists. Listen to the sound bites issuing from the mouths of even supposedly liberal politicians, and you realize that "unwed teen mothers" and "welfare mothers" have become the most socially acceptable scapegoats for *all* of our social ills.

It's not surprising that Newt Gingrich should spout off about how our "welfare state"—oh yeah, that land of milk and honey built out of a whopping 4 percent of the federal budget—is encouraging twelve-year-old girls to have children and their teenage male playmates to impregnate them. What else can you expect from a guy like that?

I just expect more from the general populace of the United States. And they're not only disappointing me, they're terrifying me.

The scariest thing isn't that some guy in a December *Newsweek* should write (in an essay about how society needs to use "shame" as a "benign tool" against women who bear young out of wedlock) that "the fact remains: every threat to the fabric of this country—from poverty to crime to homelessness—is connected to out-of-wedlock teen pregnancy." The part that really gives me the willies is how many of us in this country read or hear this kind of statement and nod our heads in agreement.

Hello? How did we come to get things this mixed up? Poverty is the cause, not the effect. Why is it that all the politicians and national journalists are pointing their fingers at the poor instead of at corporate America with their billions in tax breaks or at the country's wealthiest—who, according to the conservative figures of the Census Bureau, as a fifth of the overall population, received 48.2 percent of *all* household income in 1993?

The fact that it's poor *women* who are taking most of the hits makes it all the more absurd. As if some fifteen-year-old female who has only known poverty, very possibly abuse, and almost certainly unsafe neighborhoods, and bankrupt, ineffective schools, could somehow be the villain of the piece.

This current frenzy of accusations against single mothers on AFDC (Aid for Families with Dependent Children) dovetails all too snugly into an even larger trend to demonize and disempower motherhood, especially single mothers, throughout society. There are the cases you regularly hear about on the news. And I don't just mean the media monster stories like Susan Smith.

There was the Virginia mother who lost custody of her child for a being a lesbian. There was the Oregon mother who lost custody of her child because she held a job (as a grade school teacher, of all things), while her ex-husband's new wife was a full-time homemaker. There was the Texas mother who was charged with felonies that could put her in prison for life because she permitted her two daughters to go on a (court-mandated) parental visit with their father, who later killed himself and the two children in a drunk driving accident.

And there was young Jennifer Ireland, who was doing everything society says it expects of a single mother. She was caring for her daughter, Maranda, while trying to force the child's father to financially support his child. And she was attending college (on scholarship) full-time to make a better life. But because she left her daughter in a *licensed child care center* for 35 hours a week, a judge took the child away and awarded custody to the father.

Everywhere, mothers are under attack. In courtrooms and on the floor of Congress we are being condemned. And it's anguishing (and angering) to behold.

It seems crazy to have to defend motherhood in a country that, according to lore, finds its glory in mom and apple deep dish. But it seems that we've come to that. And yet, there are bad mothers. (Just as there are far too many bad, neglectful, abusive dads—although politicians and reporters seem much less interested in *them*.) And few of us would side with a mother just because she gave birth to a child. If a youngster were truly at risk, we'd all like to think that we would think first of the rights and well-being of the even more powerless child.

Of course, if you ask that judge in Michigan he would say that's exactly what he was doing when he yanked little Maranda away from her mom. To me, the Jennifer Ireland case is a no-contest example of justice denied. But some cases would be hard for even a close personal friend of the family to decide—much less a social worker or judge who knows little of the day-to-day life of a mother and her children.

And that is the kind of case that Ken Loach unflinchingly portrays in his new film, *Ladybird, Ladybird*. Written by first-time feature scripter Rona Munro, the film is "based on a true story." And it's the kind of story that needs to be told on both sides of the Atlantic.

The film opens at a karaoke pub in London. A woman named Maggie (Crissy Rock) is singing the Bette Midler song, "The Rose," with great feeling, and an occasional flat note. A man in the bar, a Paraguayan refugee named Jorge (Vladimir Vega), is struck by the emotional power of her singing and approaches her.

Maggie can't pronounce Jorge. (She gives up quickly, and calls him George.) And, at first, she can't give voice to the pain Jorge has sensed within her. Then, her story spills out. She is the mother of four children, by four different dads. All of them recently "taken into care" by authorities.

Raised in a family where her father brutalized her mother (and sexually abused her, we later learn), Maggie has also been abused by lovers. In an effort to get away from the latest, a batterer named Simon (Ray Winstone), she had fled with the children to a women's shelter. One evening, on a night out on a singing gig with a bar band, she is called "home." A fire had broken out in the shelter, where she had left her children locked in their room. (For their own protection, she tells police.) Her eldest son was badly burned in the fire, and social services had deemed them all "at risk," and had placed them in foster care.

Maggie's children *are* "at risk." From Maggie's lack of good judgment, but also, the film shows, from a lack of social supports. When forced to later choose between losing her children forever, or entering a detentional "family center" that will, social workers tell her, help her "rehabilitate and cope" (but which Maggie can plainly see is an institution full of its own style of violence), she goes, instead, back home to her batterer.

It is another mistake in a life of no-win options. And Maggie loses her four kids for it.

Still, there is new hope for a time. Jorge is a good man, who wants to make a new life with Maggie. And although, as an undocumented worker, he can only get below-subsistence wages working for the unscrupulous owner of a fast-food stand, Jorge and Maggie set up housekeeping in a council flat, and await the birth of their first child.

But the state is watching. It sees that Jorge is a foreigner, and (judging by Maggie's history with men) assumes that he is abusive. So, when Maggie has her baby and is uncooperative with the snooping caseworkers who come to call, her new daughter is ripped away from her, never to be seen again.

Maggie is filled with despair and a consuming rage that she cannot mask in any way. No matter how hard she tries, Maggie can't seem to play the game. Because she is certain that it is a game she has no chance in winning. The system has all the power. Maggie has none. Not even the power to control her emotions—the only thing left her. She lashes out at the bureaucrats who can decide the fate of her children.

The social workers, lawyers, and magistrates judge Maggie to be "beyond help." And so, they offer her nothing but denunciation. And since the Maggie they see is (understandably) a snarling, obscenity-spitting fury, they feel more than justified in separating her from her fifth child. And, when she defiantly has another child with Jorge, authorities wrest her sixth child away from her while she is still in the hospital.

This is Maggie's story. But as much as Loach and Munro try to keep Maggie's perspective, they are careful not to paint their protagonist as a saint. Nor do they portray the film's social workers as fiends. These are careful, possibly even caring, bureaucrats who are trying, in accordance with government guidelines they've been given, to do right by children. But how can they fairly decide whether Maggie is a fit mother or not, knowing the little they do about who she is and how she lives?

They cannot. And that is the point of the film.

Ladybird, Ladybird encourages us to think about how we define concepts like "good mother" and "bad mother." I suspect that many bureaucrats, here and in Jolly Old, define a good mother as a woman who is a middle class or better, well-educated, unabused (as well as unabusing) full-time homemaker who never works outside the home because her husband brings the good life home to her and the tykes. Well, a lot of women would fill most or all of that profile, if they only could.

But if your life is far from ideal, does that mean that you have no right to be a mother? And even assuming that the state should take children away from women they judge to be "bad," who do we trust to make those shattering decisions?

We can't put off thinking about these issues any longer. Ken Loach knows that. That's why he gave us *Ladybird, Ladybird.*

At one point in the film, Jorge tells Maggie about how he had to leave his country, on threat of death, for speaking out about human rights. "Suffering," he tells her, "has a job to do for the government." We believe it about South American dictatorships, but we hate to think that it could be true here.

And yet, all of Newt's proselytizing about orphanages brought to my mind the haunting image of Maggie living in an apartment with a wall of pictures of the babies she lost forever. And that reminded me of the mothers of the Plaza de Mayo, who marched through the streets of Buenos Aires clutching pictures of their disappeared children.

If we're not careful, there may soon be a generation of disappeared children in this land of mom and apple pie.

This article has been edited for length.

NOVEMBER 1989

CASUALTIES OF THE PATRIARCHAL WAR

DEAR SOJOURNER:

I have read about all the pros and cons of parenting, prolife vs. prochoice, single vs. coparenting, gay vs. straight, but it all becomes pointless when parenting is not valued in our capitalist society in such a way that life can be supported economically. I have been a single parent for seventeen years. I spent thirteen of those years on welfare. One of the major reasons "people" (read: women) are on welfare in the first place is because they are the unsupported primary caretakers of dependent children.

Working single mothers and others suffer the guilt and shame of watching their children grow up to be angry, depressed, hostile juveniles for whom no services exist at all until they get into trouble. These mothers have to work. They cannot make enough money to pay someone to care for their child and to pay the high cost of living. Women who are facing divorce are the most heartbreaking, and so many of them are. We are creating a new poor, a cheap labor pool of devastated young mothers who are watching their children self-destruct. Having children is not a matter of being "politically correct." They are not revolutionary "toys." They are very direct casualties of the Patriarchal War, and until something is done to stop this destruction, it would only be politically correct to choose not to have children at all. That is, if one can avoid being raped. It does not even make sense to go on welfare, when a welfare check does not even pay the cost of housing.

If giving birth is not a women's issue, I don't know what is. I would like to see us fighting, not for the right to abort, but for the right to give birth, if that is what we choose. We have a society that creates the necessity for abortion, and as long as we ignore the real issues that create that necessity, prochoice is not about choice at all.

Kate Huard
Worcester, MA

CHAPTER FOUR

Reproductive Freedom

Since the earliest days of women coming to feminist consciousness, reproductive freedom has been at the center of their agenda. This is because reproductive freedom is about women controlling their own bodies—determining whether, when, how, and with whom they will have children—a fundamental requirement of true liberation. Although abortion rights have become the focal point of this struggle, the agenda for reproductive freedom encompasses a wide range of reproductive rights, including safe and effective birth control; an end to exploitative practices such as forced sterilization, unnecessary hysterectomies, and cesarean sections; and adequate economic and social supports for pregnancy and childbirth. In the '80s, feminists also turned their attention to the new reproductive technologies, asking important questions about whether these technologies serve women's interests. This chapter addresses each of these topics from a variety of perspectives, tracing the development of the feminist reproductive rights agenda since *Roe v. Wade,* the 1973 Supreme Court decision legalizing abortion.

Sojourner began publishing in 1975, just two years after the *Roe v. Wade* decision. Immediately following the Supreme Court decision, abortion rights came under attack from the right wing. By 1977, Congress had passed the Hyde amendment, eliminating federal funding for poor women's abortions. As Jezra Kaye makes clear in her 1977 article, "Abortion: A Question of Control," the battle then moved to the state level. In Massachusetts, activists prevented the passage of the Doyle/Flynn amendment, which would have cut off state Medicaid funding, but other states were more successful. By 1995, only thirteen states still provided public funding for abortions.

In the late '70s, the mainstream women's movement, absorbed in the struggle for the ERA, ignored these first attacks on abortion access. Race and class bias prevented most middle-class feminists from realizing the attack on poor women's access to abortion was only the first volley in the battle to limit the impact of *Roe v. Wade*. Though *Sojourner* covered the passage of the Hyde amendment, the Supreme Court decision to uphold the amendment, and the Massachusetts fight over the Doyle/Flynn amendment, the struggle over abortion rights did not figure prominently during the early years of publication. Notably, no articles appeared by women who would be directly affected by the loss of public funding or teenage women whose access to abortion was being seriously curtailed by parental consent laws.

With the election of Ronald Reagan in 1980, however, it became clear that *Roe v. Wade* was not the end, but the beginning, of the fight for reproductive freedom. The New Right placed abortion at the center of its campaign to roll back the gains of the feminist movement. They began with the Human Life Amendment (HLA), an attempt to pass an amendment to the U.S. Constitution declaring that human life begins at conception. As Judith Barrington points out in her October 1981 article, the implications were stark: "the HLA will not only make abortion a crime equal to murder or manslaughter, it will also make the use of the pill, the IUD, or any form of birth control that operates on a fertilized egg, also murder." Barrington's argument, that reproductive freedom is essential to the sexual liberation of all women—lesbian, straight, single, or married, and thus highly threatening to our male supremacist society—represented the views of the radical wing of the reproductive rights movement. This wing was, to a large extent, silenced by the "prochoice" movement of the '80s, which veered sharply away from making any link between abortion and women's sexual freedom.

Though the HLA never passed, the '80s saw the emergence of a powerful grassroots organizing effort to stop women from having abortions. In 1985, *Sojourner* reported bombings at the Pensacola, Florida, Ladies Center clinic and at a Washington, D.C., clinic, and arson attacks on two clinics in Washington state. These attacks escalated in the late '80s, as did the popular "nonviolent" clinic blockades organized by the prolife group Operation Rescue. In response to this all-out effort to overturn *Roe v. Wade*, the leaders of mainstream reproductive rights organizations such as Planned Parenthood and the National Abortion Rights Action League (NARAL) dropped the language of women's liberation and began to couch demands for reproductive freedom in terms of "choice" and "privacy." As Marlene Fried argues in her 1987 article, this decision to fight for "choice" rather than "justice" made it clear that mainstream activists were willing to compromise the rights of their poor sisters in order to appeal to those who, in fact, had choices. This limited the breadth of the visible movement and prevented the reproductive rights movement from gaining allies among poor women and women of color concerned with a broader range of reproductive rights issues, including public funding, sterilization abuse, teenage pregnancy, prenatal care, and infant mortality.

Although *Sojourner* addressed the issue of forced sterilization as early as 1976 (see Judith Herman, "Sterilization Abuse"), it was the Supreme Court's 1989 decision in *Webster v. Reproductive Health Services* that finally allowed the voices of reproductive rights activists who had long advocated for an expansion of the agenda to be heard. In the *Webster* decision, the Supreme Court not only affirmed the rights of states to deny public funding for abortions, but also asserted that states could demand that public hospitals not perform abortions. The Court also allowed the preamble to the Missouri law, which states that "life begins at conception," to stand. Though the Court did not overturn *Roe v. Wade*, with this ruling the justices made it clear that they intended to limit the rights not only of poor women but of all women seeking abortions. Many feminists recognized the immediate need to reevaluate the strategies of the prochoice movement.

The shift in the debate is evident in the profusion of articles addressing reproductive freedom that appeared in *Sojourner* from 1989 through 1995. These included articles addressing reproductive freedom for disabled women, the high rate of infant mortality in African-American communities, the criminal prosecution of pregnant women for "providing drugs to a minor" (meaning the fetus), and the coercive use of new hormonal birth control methods such as Depo-Provera and Norplant (see articles by Karen Schneiderman, 1989, Evelyn C. White, 1991, Charon Asetoyer, 1993, and Asoka Bandarage, 1994). Although some of these issues had been addressed in earlier years, the voices of women of color significantly transformed the discussion. Access to abortion was placed in a larger context in which women once again claimed not only the right to "choice," but the right to information and resources necessary for *all* women to control their own bodies.

Although abortion was certainly at the center of the struggle for reproductive freedom throughout the '80s and early '90s, a new topic also emerged in the pages of *Sojourner*—the new reproductive technologies. As early as 1981, Ruth Hubbard wrote a piece, entitled "Implications of Pregnancy Intervention," in which she raised questions about the increased use of amniocentesis and ultrasound, even in cases where a woman could expect a perfectly normal pregnancy. Hubbard predicted a trend which would become more ominous throughout the next decade: that medical intervention would wrest control of pregnancy away from women themselves, just as it had in earlier centuries when doctors had managed to squeeze midwives out of their role as the primary caretakers of pregnant women (see Evelyn C. White, "Lay Midwifery: The Traditional Childbearing Group," 1991).

Today, as Hubbard feared, amniocentesis and other forms of genetic testing have become routine aspects of prenatal care. In addition, many women subject themselves to much more complex procedures in order to become pregnant in the first place. Feminists disagree about whether these practices, including *in vitro* fertilization, various forms of embryo transfer, and surrogacy provide women with greater options or are, in fact, so experimental as to be exploitative (see articles by Rita Arditti, 1985, Ruth Hubbard et al., 1987, and Dion Farquhar, 1995). In either case, these new technologies have markedly changed the pregnant woman's relationship to her body. Where the fetus was once a part of her, inseparable until the time of birth, it is now seen as a separate entity, visible on an ultrasound screen, transferable from one body to another, able to be nourished by its genetic mother or by any other woman. The technology has fed the right-wing antiabortion ideology that a woman is simply the vessel in which the fetus grows, leading to the absurd situation in which the fetus is now seen to have rights that may come into conflict with the rights of the mother. As Ruth Hubbard, Nachama Wilker, and Marsha Saxton point out in their 1987 article, "Of Fetuses and Women," a Santa Clara Juvenile Court in California had recently proposed legislation that would "make the fetus a dependent of the juvenile court system in situations where the mother's behavior is judged to be harmful.... If a pregnant woman is not willing to follow court orders,...she should be placed in a medically controlled environment."

Although such legislation has not yet passed constitutional muster, feminists are carefully watching two other trends that weigh the value of the fetus against the rights of the mother: women forced to undergo court-ordered cesarean sections and fetal protection policies. In the first instance, women are denied the right to refuse surgery on their own bodies; in the second, they are subject to job discrimination. In all of these cases, we see the rights of pregnant women (and sometimes "potentially" pregnant women) becoming increasingly restricted as the society places greater and greater value on the life of the fetus.

Though the new reproductive technologies have fed antiabortion ideology by making the fetus a visible entity separate from the mother, these technologies have supported another practice as well—selective abortion. As several authors point out in this chapter, the eugenic potential of these technologies is frightening. Antiabortion activists have used the medical establishment's bias toward encouraging women to abort disabled fetuses as a means of recruiting disability activists to their cause (see Karen Schneiderman, "Disabled Women Need Choice, Too," 1989). On the other side, prochoice activists, ignorant of disability issues, sometimes use disability as a reason to support the right to choose. This focus on the fetus, however, avoids important social questions. In a society in which disability is shunned, and individual families are forced to bear all the costs of raising a disabled child, we have placed women in an untenable situation. As disability activists have argued, rather than putting so much effort and social capital into weeding out imperfect children, maybe as a society we should be supporting the needs of disabled people and their families.

Reproductive freedom is a cornerstone in the struggle for women's liberation. If at first feminists thought that legal access to birth control and abortion would transform their lives, they have since learned that the issues are more complex. Legal access, without economic and social support, is not enough. *Roe v. Wade* does not guarantee poor women access to abortion; hormonal birth control methods may be hazardous to women's health; reproductive technologies may be liberating but they also have the potential to once again reduce women's control over their own bodies. In the articles that follow, though the authors speak from different points of view, they share a single vision: a society in which women are guaranteed—through law as well as social and economic power—the right to determine if, when, and how they will have children.

SEPTEMBER 1977

Abortion: A Question of Control
by Jezra Kaye

I.   It's nine a.m. A line of people snakes up the stairwell at the State House. The guards have not organized this very well. People are flowing into all the corridors.

We are going to the hearing on the Doyle/Flynn Medicaid abortion bill.

Already, I'm exhausted. Everyone is tired, and nothing has happened yet. It's only nine o'clock.

"Prochoice" people (people who support a woman's right to choose abortion, for whatever reasons) are wearing buttons that say "CHOICE." "Right-to-Lifers," or "prolifers," have brought their kids. The kids are white. They are wearing professionally made T-shirts that say "CHOOSE LIFE."

For reasons beyond my control and for the purposes of this campaign, I and the majority of Americans who, according to all reports, favor the right to choose abortion, have been branded "antilife," or, if you will, "money-hungry abortionists."

It is said that the Catholic Church has a budget of $30,000 for their legislative campaign in Massachusetts alone. In part, that money covers advertisements in local papers, printing of T-shirts, payment for workers who canvass door to door to get people out to hearings like this one.... $30,000 is not much money for an effort like that, but it *is* 30 times more than the prochoice groups have.

II.   Waiting in line at the ladies' room, I start talking with Dorothea Manuela. She has come to the hearing to testify. "Yeh," she says, "I had an abortion. It was one of those Lysol jobs. I was eighteen. I have three children now. I was lucky. I'm lucky to be alive. After the abortion, I was hemorrhaging so bad I went to the hospital. The doctor said, 'Tell us who gave you this abortion and we'll treat you.' Of course, I refused. So he wrote on my slip that I had refused treatment, and he sent me home."

III.   On August 4, 1977, the federal government cut off Medicaid funding for abortions. The move was carried out by Health, Education and Welfare (HEW) Secretary Joseph Califano. It affects 300,000 women every year.

Since 1973, when the Supreme Court declared abortion to be legal in the United States, there has been a 40 percent decrease in the rate of "maternal" deaths (even the medical classification of who dies indicates that a pregnant woman is already, in official eyes, a mother). This is because women who were not physically capable of giving birth did not have to do so. But, more significantly, it is because women stopped, by and large, killing themselves with back-alley and self-induced abortions. Seventy-five percent of the women who died from illegal abortions in 1969 were Black. As of August 4, the situation that killed these women is in force again.

IV.   In the hearing room, Representative Marie Howe (R-Somerville) is testifying. She trembles as she stands before the chairman. "Your honor," she says, with a rising note of hysteria in her voice, "I sit in this room and my heart almost stopped beating when I saw...I saw a man walk into this room...he walked in and he got a standing ovation...he gets a standing ovation, and *do you know what he did?* He strangled *a little Black baby boy to death with his bare hands! He..."*

She is gavelled down. In January 1975, Dr. Kenneth Edelin, a Black physician, was brought to trial after performing an abortion. The charge was murder. The trial dragged on for six weeks. Now he sits in the hearing room and the supportive energy of half the people there flows out to him as Marie Howe screams. "Hmmmm," a Black friend who is with me mutters. "Don't tell *me* she's so all fired up about the lives of cute little Black babies." But she is, in her own way. These people have made a curious separation between the value of the life of a fetus and the value of the life of an adult. Ken Edelin is sitting very still. I am shaking inside.

There are men and women in this room who think they are fighting for the lives of innocent children. They are inflamed with holy purpose. They rant and gesture and quote God. There are also women and men in this room who know that we are fighting for our *own* lives. We are as vehement as our opponents. But they have the power—the money and influence—and we know it. In general, we speak quietly and respectfully, and we quote statistics.

Although there are women and men who testify for and against this bill, at the core, this is an action that has been perpetrated on women by men. Over and over, at the testimony for the Doyle/Flynn bill, I hear the bill's supporters claim that this issue is a *moral* issue. I do not agree with them. I (and many other women who have united together to defeat this attempt and the ones that will follow to deny us our abortion rights) believe that this issue is one of *control.* Who will control women's bodies? Will it be the state, with its programs of sterilization, its laws against "prostitution," its assumption of guilt toward women who are raped? Will it be the Church, with its male hierarchies, its doctrine of original sin (a woman's sin)?

Or will it be us?

V.   The Catholic Church, one of the major funders of the "Right-to-Life" movement, has not always been antiabortion. In fact, abortions were permitted in the Church until 1869. Except for a brief period between 1588 and 1591, when Pope Sixtus V forbade all abortions, the Church held that a fetus was not "vivified" until 40 days after conception—in other words, it was not considered to be a living thing, and abortion was held to be "not irregular." In 1869 Pope Pius IX forbade all abortions, changing the Church's position on vivification. However, as Catholics for a Free Choice and other religious groups involved in the prochoice struggle are quick to point out, the Church's present position has never been an official encyclical or an official Church doctrine.

Why has this conflict emerged so startlingly in Massachusetts and in America in general in 1977? The answer is, of course, that the conflict never died. Rather, prochoice forces relaxed their guard after a 1973 Supreme Court judgment that seemed to secure the right of abortion once and for all. However, the 1973 decision rests on ambiguous legal grounds, and can be, as we are now seeing, circumvented by a variety of tactics. The Supreme Court decision justified abortion on the grounds of *the right to privacy.* The right of privacy is an implied right, deriving from the Bill of Rights. Thus, the 1973 judgment does not rest on a tangible part of our national law. Nowhere does the law state that there is any such thing as a right for individuals to control their bodies.

"Prolifers" have asserted again and again that they will not rest until they have called a Constitutional Convention that would make abortion illegal in America by banning it with a constitutional amendment. It is necessary for 35 state legislatures to petition the government in order to call such a Constitutional Convention. This year, Massachusetts became the ninth state to do so.

VI.   No form of contraception is 100 percent effective. Even if you now use contraception you *can* get pregnant. And the number of unwanted pregnancies is staggering. Every year, 30,000 women *under fifteen* become pregnant. (I think it is safe to assume that the majority of these are unwanted pregnancies.) Of women between the ages of fifteen and nineteen, 600,000 more have what they describe as unwanted pregnancies. Even among married couples who claimed to be practicing contraception on a regular basis, the rate of contraceptive failures (either human or mechanical) is over 200,000 a year. Every year, in America, close to one million women seek abortions. It is a traumatic and difficult choice that will mark most of these women, even when made under "the best" of conditions.

What alternatives to abortion exist? This year, in Massachusetts, the legislature voted against a bill that would have insured the legality of providing teenagers with contraceptives. On the other hand, the Department of Health, Education and Welfare estimates that it has been paying for between 100,000 and 200,000 sterilizations a year. These sterilizations were performed on poor women.

We all know that 200,000 poor and Third World women did not walk into HEW offices and say, "I want to be sterilized." Even those who *did* agree to the operation most likely did not do so with full knowledge of its consequences or of the other alternatives that may have been available to them. We have no way of knowing how many of these sterilizations were done with the informed consent of the women involved. In fact, HEW did not even keep accurate records of how many sterilizations were performed, period.

But in Puerto Rico, where the Bureau of Public Health might aptly be nicknamed the Bureau of Sterilization, records were kept—and they are frightening. *Forty percent* of Puerto Rican women of childbearing age have been sterilized to date.

VII.   Despite "prolife" propaganda to the contrary, no one is "proabortion." No one is happy about abortion, or thinks that it is a great solution to the personal and social problems created by unwanted pregnancies. The label of "prochoice" was carefully chosen and represents an awareness of the conflict that women experience in choosing abortion. It signifies a belief that such a choice must be made on the basis of deeply personal and intuitive principles.

Just as different supporters of the "prochoice" position hold different views about the issue of fetal viability, which "prolifers" so simplify in their slogans, so do proponents of a woman's right to choose differ on the meaning we assign to this battle we have entered together.

Some view abortion as primarily a medical issue. They feel that abortion must be available as a backup procedure in the case of contraceptive failure, and they see the present attacks on abortion rights as creating primarily a practical problem.

Others, like myself, do not feel that that view goes far enough. We believe that this struggle is basically a political one. Thus, the issue is not only whether some well-to-do women will have abortions while other, poorer, women will not. The issue is not whether women should be "granted" the privilege of having abortions by a contemptuous male power structure intent on punishing women and minorities for every social failure down to and including the mechanical failure of contraceptive devices designed and manufactured by men. The issue is one of *control*.

One million women every year have held that abortion, no matter how painful a choice, is a necessary means of pursuing our mental, physical and social welfare. Will we have to beg for these medical services? Will we have to die for them?

This article has been edited for length.

OCTOBER 1981

Aborting Women's Choice
by Judith Barrington

More and more feminists are coming to understand that what we are seeing now is a very real backlash against our movement's advances over the past ten years. It is not coincidental that a massive attack on abortion rights is being mounted at this time. In the nineteenth century, when abortion was first seriously prosecuted in this country, governmental interference again coincided with a period in history when the women's movement appeared to be seriously threatening the stability of patriarchal society.

What we need to understand is just how central the whole issue of reproductive freedom is to the wider issue of women gaining autonomy in society and control over our lives—the freedom of women to live outside the model of dependence on men, if we choose to do so. Because reproductive freedom fundamentally threatens our sexist society, abortion is an issue that needs to be understood and supported by *all women*, as well as by men who support the ideals of feminism. I particularly stress, in this context, that abortion rights are important to lesbians, celibate women, sterile women, women outside of childbearing years, and also to women who would not personally choose to have an abortion, as well as to those women who might either choose or need to have an abortion at some time in our lives. It is politically vital that all people who believe in autonomy for women fight against the current attack on abortion rights.

In order to understand why abortion is so crucial to all women, we have to look at the issue in the context of the entire spectrum of reproductive rights for women. In order to lead our lives freely and independently, we must have control over if, when, and under what circumstances we will bear children. The availability of abortion is just one of several rights that women need in order to experience this kind of control of our lives and our childbearing capacity. Equally important are the availability of birth control and proper sex education, research into safer methods of birth control, the end of unnecessary hysterectomies and other medical abuses, and an end to racist government policies that prevent women from having children we want. Governmental control is equally as destructive when it operates through selective sterilization of poor and Third World women as when it encourages or forces the birth of white, middle-class babies. It is all part of a policy that assumes government to have the right to control our fertility by forcing some women to bear more children and others to bear less. And reproductive freedom involves the right of every woman to decide for herself when she wishes to bear a child, including the possibility of single women and lesbians to make that choice under whatever circumstances they choose.

The federal government is currently involved in promoting a whole series of changes that are designed to get women back "where they belong"— that is, back being dependent on men, as wives and mothers. It is a clearly thought-out approach that attacks women on a number of different fronts, from the economic cutbacks that aim to make it financially impossible for women to survive independently— and particularly as single mothers—through legislation that will make it illegal (and, by implication, morally and ethically wrong) to control our reproduction by using certain forms of birth control or abortion.

The proposed Human Life Amendment will not only make abortion a crime equal to murder or manslaughter, it will also make the use of the pill, the IUD, or any form of birth control that operates on a fertilized egg, also murder. Again, this legislation has an effect on all women, even beyond the horrors that will descend upon those women who resort to illegal abortions, those women who die of self-induced abortions, or those women who may be legally attacked while trying to perform an abortion (since the law allows a person to intervene, attack, and possibly kill someone who is about to commit a "murder"). We may all find ourselves under surveillance in the government's effort to prevent abortion "murders." Women who miscarry may have extreme difficulty in getting medical assistance: in Nazi Germany, when abortion and birth control were banned, women who miscarried had somehow to "prove" that their miscarriages were indeed spontaneous, before they could be treated.

If you are still in doubt as to how this proposed legislation could affect you (as a lesbian or a celibate, for example), what about the consequences of rape or incest, to which all of us are vulnerable? This legislation would put the survival of the fertilized egg above all considerations of the pregnant woman, no matter what the reason for her pregnancy. It would become, in effect, the legal duty of every woman who becomes pregnant, for whatever reason, to protect the fertilized egg, even if that meant lying flat on her back to prevent miscarriage, taking drugs that might be dangerous to her for the sake of the fetus, or otherwise circumscribing her activities in the interests of remaining pregnant.

Probably the most fundamental reason why abortion is an issue that is crucial to all women is the complex connection between reproductive rights and female sexuality. Some people think that the opponents of abortion simply want women to find some other, "better" way of controlling our reproduction: better birth control, for example, would remove the necessity for abortion in many cases. This is not, in fact, the case.

Organizations such as Planned Parenthood confirm that the same people who oppose abortion also strongly oppose sex education in the schools and the availability of birth control to teenagers without parental consent. These same people, again, are strongly (often violently) opposed to gay rights, and in fact, oppose such things such as the Equal Rights Amendment (ERA) on spurious grounds that relate, quite unnecessarily, to sexuality, such as the argument that the ERA will lead to homosexual marriage. All these positions have one thing in common: a fear of, and opposition to (and often obsession with), any form of sexuality for *women* that is not directly concerned with childbearing.

Women who enjoy an autonomous sexuality are profoundly threatening to our male supremacist society: after all, women who can *choose* when and how to be sexual can also make other choices—and some of those choices may make us less available to men and, ultimately, threaten male control over our lives. Women who are single, women who live with men outside marriage, lesbians, women who live with other people whatever their ages and relationships, as well as all women who take charge of our sexuality outside or inside the heterosexual institution of marriage—all of us threaten the concept of female sexuality being first and foremost an instrument of reproduction that is controlled by men.

If we are to continue our expansion of our potential and strive toward fuller, more creative and fulfilling lives, we must protect our right to express our sexuality in whatever way we choose. We cannot be creative or vital women if our sexuality, which is such an intrinsic part of us, is to be controlled by men, whether individually or by governmental interference. The current opposition to abortion rights is part of an attempt to put female sexuality back "where it belongs": inside marriage, producing children. We cannot let this happen.

Excerpted from original.

THE HUMAN LIFE AMENDMENT

SECTION 1.   With respect to the right to life, the word "person" as used in this article and in the Fifth and Fourteenth Articles of Amendment to the Constitution of the United States applies to all human beings irrespective of age, health, function or condition of dependency, including their unborn offspring at every stage of their biological development.

SECTION 2.   No unborn person shall be deprived of life by any person; provided however, that nothing in this article shall prohibit a law permitting only those medical procedures required to prevent the death of the mother.

SECTION 3.   The Congress and the several states have power to enforce this article by appropriate legislation.

This version of the Human Life Amendment appeared in an article in the February 1981 issue of Sojourner.

MARCH 1987

The Right to Choose: Sanitizing Feminism

by Marlene Gerber Fried

Nationwide, the antiabortion movement has a strategy: working toward criminalizing abortion altogether by limiting access to abortion now. This past fall, four states—Massachusetts, Rhode Island, Arkansas, and Oregon—had referenda on their ballots that would have done just that. In Massachusetts, Question #1, a proposed amendment to the state constitution, would have made it constitutional for the state to regulate or prohibit abortion and to deny public funding for abortion. These serious challenges were defeated in each state. However, the campaigns raised important questions for our movement.

Access to safe, legal abortion is a necessary condition for women's freedom. But real choice for women requires much more. The new Right understands this; its attack on abortion is part of its overall attack on women's freedom. Therefore, we must combat efforts to erode reproductive rights by broadening the political base of the abortion rights movement and widening its agenda. We need to evaluate our strategies with these goals in mind.

In this article, I want to look at some of the ways the prochoice movement has reacted to the challenges from the Right. I will focus on the campaign to defeat Question #1 in Massachusetts, the Campaign for Choice, because it is a good example of general tendencies within the movement: defensiveness; isolation of abortion from other aspects of reproductive freedom; framing of the issue in terms of civil liberties rather than women's liberation and sexual freedom; framing of strategy and politics around the concerns of white, middle-class people. All of these barriers to the wider goals can and must be overcome if we are to build a movement that can defend and expand reproductive rights for all women.

The abortion rights movement essentially folded after abortion became legal with Roe v. Wade in 1973. While more radical segments of the movement mobilized after the passage of the Hyde amendment in 1977, not until the threat of a federal constitutional amendment that would ban all abortions was posed in 1981 did a visible mainstream abortion rights movement reemerge. But when it did, it formed as a reaction to the backlash, not as a proactive voice for feminism. The new abortion rights movement rarely dared to talk about abortion or women's rights, preferring instead to focus on the intolerance and extremism of the other side. In order to stem the antiabortion tide, the prochoice movement has attempted to sanitize its own demands. Insisting on abortion rights as a necessary condition of all women's sexual freedom is seen as too threatening, too risky, too selfish. Instead, the movement has turned to the more innocuous and ambiguous language of "choice" and personal freedom. Once, the women's movement fought to bring women's reproductive lives out of the private sphere and into public debate, arguing that our personal choices were political.

How is it that the women's movement is now arguing that abortion should be in the private, not public, domain?

This is not true for the entire abortion rights movement. Some activists have argued for a radical reproductive rights approach that would link abortion to other aspects of reproductive freedom, an approach that would look squarely at the fact that the reproductive rights of poor women and women of color are attacked first. However, those with this perspective have had to struggle simply to put abortion and women's lives back into the debate. There seems to be no place at all in the ideology of "choice" for public discussion of women's needs for autonomy and sexual freedom and for the societal changes that would make these possible.

Strategically, the prochoice movement, trying to hold onto past gains, has not pursued new ones, either by solidifying its own membership or speaking out to the public. *Roe v. Wade* has not been the first step of a feminist agenda for reproductive control; it has become the only step. It has been defended by appeals to the right to privacy, to the importance of keeping the government out of our personal lives, and to religious tolerance.

In Massachusetts, both antiabortion erosions and prochoice responses have roughly followed this pattern. Massachusetts was one of the first states to attempt to cut off state funding of abortions with the Doyle/Flynn bill in 1979; the first state to require parental consent for minors seeking abortions; and one of the first states to prohibit state employee health insurance from covering abortions.

Since the Hyde amendment, a succession of groups defining themselves as reproductive rights groups has focused on access to abortion rather than simply on the legal right to abortion. The Reproductive Rights National Network (R2N2) is the most recent of these. But the mainstream groups, more visible, have taken a different tack. Planned Parenthood, Mass. Choice (the National Abortion Rights Action League affiliate), the Religious Coalition for Abortion Rights, the Civil Liberties Union of Massachusetts, the League of Women Voters, and the National Organization for Women have framed the abortion issue in civil libertarian terms. Therefore, when these groups formed the Coalition for Choice (later the Campaign for Choice), which essentially ran the campaign to defeat Question #1, the campaign took the civil libertarian approach.

The defeat of Question #1 in Massachusetts and of similar referenda in the other three states was extremely significant. While abortion rights were not expanded, holding the line is a victory when those rights have steadily been eroded. If these defeats force the opposition to drop this particular strategy, these campaigns will have had much wider implications.

At the same time, we must examine the fact that, after the prochoice movement spent a half-million dollars and mobilized thousands of activists, the antiabortion referendum was defeated with only 58 percent of the vote in a state that is supposedly almost 80 percent prochoice. We had hoped for a larger victory and need to think about the implications of this vote.

From the beginning we were on the defensive. The antiabortion movement initiated the referendum, and backed by overwhelming support from the state legislature, antiabortion activists controlled the amendment's wording and the timing of its passage through the legislature. Therefore, for almost four years—from 1982 when the first version of the legislation that ultimately became Question #1 was passed—the strategy of the abortion rights movement in Massachusetts was substantially shaped by this impending referendum. Groups were reluctant to take up other campaigns, afraid of diverting attention and re-sources away from the battle that would need to be fought if the proposed legislation were to go on the ballot. Four years is a frustratingly long time to be on hold and simultaneously to maintain a sense of urgency within the activist community—especially given that a great deal of energy went into diffusing the threat: lobbying the legislature to prevent the issue from coming before the voters.

More significantly, the politics of this campaign were defensive—shaped reactively rather than proactively. The Campaign for Choice decided to frame the issue in terms of choice, privacy, and freedom from government intrusion. Its early ads against Question #1 urged, "Keep Free-dom Legal in Massachusetts." One really had to read the fine print to understand that abortion was the issue. Campaign literature focused exclusively on these messages:

Vote no in November to keep this personal private decision about childbearing free from legislative intrusion. The decision to have an abortion is extremely difficult and deeply personal; this amendment will take that decision out of women's hands and place it in the hands of state legislators. Vote no on Question #1, protect your right to privacy; Massachu-setts can't wait to come into your bedroom. I want to help defeat this assault on the freedom to make a private choice on abortion.

We must remember that a positive feminist stance was the breeding ground for the le-galization movement in the early '70s. We have to respond to the attacks on abortion, and even though we do not control the timing or place of the attacks, we can control the terms of our response. The prochoice movement's defensive stance implies that we will settle for less.

The decision to fight for choice rather than justice is itself a decision to appeal to those who do have choices. This strategy contributes to keeping the visible movement primarily white and middle class. While individual Third World activists and women's groups did sup-port the campaign, their levels of participation and involvement were low. This is not new for the abortion rights movement, despite the fact that the abortion rights of poor women, of whom a disproportionate number are women of color, have been assaulted first. For in-stance, had Question #1 passed, the most immediate consequence would have been an end to state-allocated Medicaid funds for abortions. Thus this campaign seemed to offer a chance to make alliances with activists and groups fighting for the rights of poor women—yet the campaign did not do so.

The women's movement in this country has a history of trading away the rights of women of color and working-class women in favor of gains for more privileged women. Be-cause of this history, we must consciously and aggressively make clear that we are not about to do this in the present. Minimal steps, at least, must be taken for a multiracial and class-con-scious movement for abortion rights to become a reality. For poor women, the legal right to abortion is empty without access. To be inclusive, the women's movement must take a strong stand not just for abstract choice but for practical access to abortion.

When it came to Medicaid, the Campaign for Choice was too shaky, seemingly afraid of the issue. In 1984, the antiabortion forces won an initiative that stopped Medi-caid funding in Colorado. Polling data seemed to indicate that the loss came because of the unpopularity of Medicaid—for abortion in particular and for social welfare funding in general. Some leaders of the Massachusetts Campaign for Choice appeared willing to use this data to support the argument that a Medicaid abortion is cheaper than paying for the birth and upbringing of unwanted children, if that had looked like a winning strategy. While this argument was never officially used by the Campaign for Choice, some member groups did use it in speeches and in writing. This strategy, however, trades away the rights of poor women to protect the rights of more privileged women, women who do have economic choices. It reinforces the view that reproductive choice—the decision to have children as well as the decision not to—is a privilege and not a right. Framed this way, the struggle for choice is at best of concern only to some women and at worst won at the expense of the rights of poorer women.

Posing abortion as a private matter, as all literature from the campaign did, is also problematic. Ever since *Roe v. Wade* made privacy the basis for the legal right to abortion, the prochoice movement has seized on "privacy" as its buzz word, ignoring the fact that private behavior requires social supports if we are *all* to enjoy privacy rights. Making privacy the central pillar on which legal abortion stands undermines Medicaid abortion. Our opposition in the Question #1 campaign was quick to seize on this and to argue that state funding of abortions should be opposed precisely because abortion is a private matter, arguing that the prochoice movement cannot have it both ways.

Placing abortion in the private sphere is problematic in more general ways as well. The appeal to privacy masks the political nature of female sexuality and social relationships and undermines the hard-fought struggles of the women's movement to show that the personal is political. Women do need the power and autonomy to make decisions about our reproduction. Access to legal, safe abortion is a step toward achieving that power. It is a political necessity, not a private solution to a private problem. Substituting the right to be left alone for empowerment will give us neither personal nor political freedom.

The final political aspect of the campaign that I want to examine is its single-issue nature. The decision to run a single-issue campaign has long-range implications. The stated mission of the Coalition for Choice was, "The purpose of this organization shall be to educate the public and block legislative approval of a proposed antiabortion amendment to the state constitution and other attempts to restrict abortion rights" (Coalition for Choice, revised agreement, September 26, 1984). In practice, the coalition restricted itself to working on the initiative, although some coalition members did defend abortion rights in other ways. This way of posing the issue led the coalition to alienate part of its most natural constituency—those whose other nonabortion reproductive rights were being challenged. Perhaps the clearest example of this was the relationship between the Coalition for Choice and those organizing against the state's foster care policy. In May 1985, Massachusetts became the first state to effectively prohibit gay men and lesbians from becoming foster parents. Lesbian activists have long been in the forefront of struggles to defend abortion rights; many of those active in organizing the Foster Equality campaign were also active against Question #1. Despite the fact that the individual groups that composed the coalition steering committee all opposed the foster care policy, the coalition refused even minimal steps to allow the opposition a public voice in the Question #1 campaign and gave the governor, who promulgated and promoted the foster care policy, prominence in the campaign. The message: lesbian and gay rights were to be sacrificed in the pursuit of abortion rights.

Ironically, this general strategy of isolating abortion rights from related rights makes the prochoice movement itself more vulnerable. In the Reagan years, all progressive movements have been challenged. Many movements have decided to go it on their own, believing that linking their issues to others will weaken the chances of winning anything. Abortion has been one of the main casualties of this mentality. Because abortion has been in the forefront of the larger new Right agenda, other movements have sought to steer clear of abortion politics. Meanwhile, the new Right has made links between issues and organizations that have greatly strengthened their ability to challenge reproductive freedom in its broadest sense on many fronts at once.

While the 58 percent to 42 percent defeat of Question #1 was a significant victory, activists need to think beyond simply winning or losing a particular battle. Did this campaign contribute to the long-range effort to build a movement capable of fighting for the rights of all women? I believe that only by doing so can we hold on to and expand the rights we have won.

As a member of R2N2-Boston, I worked on defeating Question #1 for over three years. I represented R2N2 on the steering committee of the Campaign for Choice. R2N2 developed its own literature and developed independent activities in conjunction with other groups who shared our perspective. My experience in this campaign has left me with more questions than answers about the future of reproductive rights organizing. While I have been critical in this article of the mainstream movement, I am aware that the more radical tendency has also not been successful in achieving these wider goals. We need to examine our own politics and strategies as we try to answer these questions: What is the role of small reproductive rights groups like R2N2 in campaigns that are essentially shaped by the mainstream prochoice movement? How do we articulate a broad and positive feminist agenda while at the same time defending against the specific challenges to abortion rights now? How can a reproductive rights movement emerge from or build upon a civil libertarian consciousness? Can campaigns like this one help create a feminist movement that is genuinely speaking and fighting for the concerns of all women?

The politics and strategy of the Campaign for Choice reflect the national prochoice movement's general tendency to shy away from the more controversial aspects of abortion rights. Such a response has only emboldened our opposition. The antiabortion movement has a clear agenda both for the long run and in the present. The new Right uses each campaign to build support for its goal of criminalizing abortion and uses the antiabortion campaigns to build support for its "profamily" agenda. It has been aggressive politically and ideologically and has managed to gain the moral and psychological initiative over the past several years. The abortion rights movement needs to look at this carefully. Our defense of abortion rights is based on very strong feminist grounds. Obscuring these has made us more vulnerable to ourselves and to our opposition.

However, I am sensitive to the fact that perhaps in the '80s choice and privacy are compelling messages. The Campaign for Choice selected these on the basis of its interpretation of polling data. While skeptical of the polls, I was surprised when audiences responded fervently to appeals to keep the government out of our private lives. People linked their prochoice stance to a perceived similarity between the abortion amendment and Massachusetts' mandatory seat belt law, which was also being challenged on the November ballot. Both seemed to symbolize the threat of government interference in private decision making. It was difficult to gain a hearing for efforts to discuss the amendment in the context of women's rights to control our own bodies, sexual freedom, and social justice. Privacy and choice have become the lens through which abortion rights are filtered.

These questions are not unique to the abortion rights movement. With the exclusion of gay sexuality from constitutional protections of privacy, the gay and lesbian movement is also falling into the privacy trap as it opposes sodomy laws. As in the abortion debate, activists against bans on sodomy have argued primarily against government intrusions into personal lives. Privacy is replacing sexual freedom as the goal of the lesbian and gay movement.

I do not think that feminists engaged in reproductive rights organizing should moderate our demands. We must rethink the relationship between our objectives in a particular campaign and our long-range goals. The heat of a specific campaign makes it difficult to see beyond the goal of winning. With the immediate threat having passed, we can begin to assess our movement. I hope that this article will be helpful in promoting the discussions we need in order to move ahead.

This article has been edited for clarity.

JUNE 1989

An Open Letter to My Mother
by Catherine Houser

DEAR MOM,

You chuckled when I told you I was going to participate in the march on Washington to keep abortion safe and legal. Do you remember? It was a nervous laugh, an audible exhale of pain and fear. "Just don't get arrested," you said emphatically; then, barely, as if some ancient power outside yourself was moving to stop them, came the words, "If I was there, I'd go with you, Cathy." Your words, the sound of your voice, labored and sad, reached in and, as it does when parents use your name in a sentence, tap danced down my spine. I knew you were telling the truth, Mom, however difficult it may have been to say that, to give silence words.

I'm on a bus with 50 other women. The youngest, a nine-year-old, is asleep in the seat behind me; the eldest, a grandmother, is up front, turned around in her seat, talking to a small attentive group about the chemicals on the apples. The woman in front of me is reading *Food and Wine* magazine; the one across the aisle, Thomas Hardy's *The Mayor of Casterbridge*; and in back of her, the pages of Salman Rushdie's *The Satanic Verses* slap a fresh breeze my way every minute or so. Tomorrow morning as we begin the march on Washington we will be a half-million souls of one mind fighting to keep the right to our own bodies. There's a place for you here, Mom.

You must know, Mom, that I'm doing this as much for you as I am for me. Do you know? Do you know that I know? The news of your abortion came to me in the middle of the night when I was fourteen. Remember, in 1971, when Steve was a senior in high school, and he'd gotten that girl pregnant? You were talking to him about it late one Saturday night while I, having been stirred from sleep, lay in my bed, listening. Then, through the darkness came the truth of your own abortion. Here's what I remember...1961, alone, across the border into Mexico, a butcher, the money, then home the same day to Dad and the five of us. In an adolescent second I wondered who it might have been, then I began the lifelong process of grieving for you, Mom. The pain you must have felt coming to the decision that five children were more than enough and that six would be much too much. I wonder, did you know then, in 1961, on any conscious level, that Dad was an alcoholic? Did you have the words? It would be years before they would call what Dad was doing to the boys and me and Diane child abuse. Still years more before I would remember and, in giving memory voice, heal. But you, nearly twenty years ago in that little living room in the middle of the Arizona desert talking to your seventeen-year-old son, lacked the language. I remember hearing you tell Steve, you "just knew" the abortion was the right thing to do. Your knowledge was visceral, your decision private, and, except for that one night in 1971 as you tried to inform your son and his girlfriend of their options, so has your truth about that illegal abortion been visceral and private. But, Mom, you know, silence can be deadly.

I will break the silence today, Mom. I understand it was a silence born of necessity—a silence born of illegal acts and unspeakable agonies. But it is a silence that has, in my lifetime, become obsolete. Don't you see that if you, and millions of women like you, continue this code of silence about your illegal abortions, we as your daughters and your granddaughters are likely to suffer the same fate. So I am here today to bear witness for my friends who have had necessary, safe, legal abortions; for my high school friend to whom I loaned $300 for an abortion the first year it was legal; and for you, Mom—mostly I am here for you. I am not you. I do not know what went on in that place you went to in Mexico in 1961; I cannot tell your story. But I am of you, and I have my own visceral truths born of that shared female space. Simone de Beauvoir wrote that "it is at her first abortion that woman begins to 'know.'" My "knowing" began that night I lay listening to the hushed waves of your voice held quiet by the walls of those tight rooms. You spoke in the cadence of truth; through senses I had not yet discovered, I heard. I will march today, Mom. For you, for me, for all of our daughters, I will tell what I know.

DECEMBER 1989

Disabled Women Need Choice, Too
by Karen Schneiderman

Amidst the demonstrations, lobbying efforts, clinic defense, confrontations, conferences, and all-night conversations over cups of cold coffee, we see the dismantling of a fundamental right, one that supersedes the power of the Supreme Court and cuts to the core of what it means to make decisions about our bodies: our right to choose abortion. No leaders can make that decision for us. As the states fall like leaves, some in neat piles, others in total disarray, those of us in the prochoice movement raise our voices in anger and song. I report to you as a disabled woman, a potential target of the antichoice movement, which capitalizes on my vulnerability and my tentative social status in trying to seduce me to join its ranks.

Disabled women have never held lofty positions in the prochoice movement. How could we, when families, institutions, schools, churches, and the medical establishment have determined we are barely sexual beings? Issues of choice—childbearing and abortion—have been given little consideration and the right to make such decisions has been stripped from us. How could we enter a woman's movement, have any political opinion that mattered, when we spoke without a context? Those who biologically exist as female, but are told to deny or suppress our sexuality, have too little data to speak boldly about our own rights.

The antichoice movement has chosen us as one of its targets, a clever tactic, particularly when it singles out those women with genetic disabilities. This movement questions how we could be so selfish as to support aborting a fetus when we, as disabled "babies," were not aborted by our own mothers. If they had done so, the argument goes, we would not be here to make a decision. This overidentification with the fetus causes many women to choose to have an unwanted child out of guilt. Of course, the fact that the mothers who came before us did not have the information to determine whether or not to give birth to a disabled fetus is not discussed. We who conceive and then choose abortion are being selfish, denying that fetus the same rights we had to live, as fetuses, the antiabortionists claim.

Thus, the woman who feels she cannot or does not want to have a child is put in the position of explaining why her value as a disabled adult is greater than that of her fetus. Although her argument may seem similar to those of an able-bodied woman, when one recognizes that, historically, disabled women have been almost exclusively robbed of all of their sexual choices, the discussion takes on a more serious dimension. Should we heed the warning that in the pursuit of the perfect child we are eliminating a culture, the words ringing with overtones of holocausts all over the world? As the geneticists research to find disease and disability within the womb, while counseling disabled women against childbearing, should we then fight for the right to have a disabled child whether we want to or not, simply to defy the medical establishment?

If my mother had had the knowledge that her daughter was initially a genetically disabled fetus (spina bifida), would she have had an abortion, had it been legal?

Would she have found other means to abort, had it not been legal? Probably. However, that aborted fetus would *not* have been her now 35-year-old daughter, oppressed by her disability, her gender, and a system that does not support parents or nurture children; neither would she be a woman who is getting along, keeping up the struggle, even enjoying moments of her life. It would have been a complex genetic structure gone awry, with the potential to be born a baby who could not walk and who would have continued medical problems. Does this mean she should have aborted? Not necessarily. If a woman and, hopefully, a partner are ready to accept their child's years of hospitalization, watching their child survive surgery upon surgery with no promises, then no government should intervene in that decision. Yet the antichoice movement would make such births legally imperative, ignoring those for whom the work would be impossible.

Stated plainly, being disabled, as separate from our other labels (for the moment), is no joy. Disability culture is an artificial construct; people huddle together to fight outside prejudices, but beyond that they may have little else in common. In this respect, disability culture is very unlike the shared indigenous cultures of ethnic or racial groups. Even in the extreme scenario of a world where all disabled fetuses were aborted (and that would be highly unlikely in a society that *allowed* for choice), no races, nationalities, or genders, proud of their distinctions despite the criticism of the world, would be eliminated. The family unit would not be destroyed. Moreover, the so-called disability culture could not be completely eradicated, since not all disabled people become so during gestation. Accident, illness, and, finally, age produce disability in almost all of us before we die.

Instead of trying to save unborn disabled fetuses, should we not concentrate on creating the healthiest, most respectful and all-encompassing universe for those disabled individuals who are already here, and who are entitled to education, work, recreation, and even, for some, the possibility of a cure? Our society rehabilitates disabled people without giving them a place to go once they leave the hospitals or institutions. Laws already in place do little to assuage the physical and psychological pain of being unhealthy. True, some disabled people are generally healthy, but none of us can afford to ignore the fact that health care is a major issue in our lives. It is not an issue of valuing disabled fetuses less; it is a question of how willing we are to support those of us who are disabled and already here. To those who see the aborting of disabled fetuses as genocide, we must respond that we seek not a perfect race, but rather to give people the right to give birth to children who are wanted and who will be cared for appropriately. This is not a question of the right of the mother against the right of the fetus.

The antichoice movement attempts to evoke guilt, self-doubt, and a phony sense of pride in the disabled community through the aspects of ourselves that are often most insecure: our sexuality and ability to parent. True, it is healthy to integrate our disability into the description of who we are as women: to see it in its rightful place and with careful respect for our successes. As I choose to identify myself in that way, I also define myself as a woman, a daughter, a worker, a friend, and any other number of categories. Let us not accept the able-bodied guilt espoused by the antichoice movement and take it as our inheritance, at the expense of what we know from our own experience. We should not further separate ourselves from other women and impose upon ourselves the additional burden of having children we do not want. We should fight for a prochoice agenda, and that goal must include all women, regardless of the propaganda that imposes sanctity on the disabled fetus. We, as disabled women, know better.

DECEMBER 1994

Abortion Terrorists: Guerrillas in the Midst

by Loretta Ross

America's latest domestic terrorist threat is a volatile mixture of antiabortion extremists and the racist Right. To an alarming extent, the antiabortion movement—once known for its prayer vigils and nonviolent clinic blockades—is gathering white supremacist recruits and using their tools: vandalism, arson, bombs, and murder. The murders of Drs. David Gunn and John Britton and clinic escort James Barrett at reproductive health clinics in Pensacola, Florida, are a dangerous escalation of the battle over women's rights. A cloud of fear hovers over every clinic in the nation.

This wave of antiabortion violence surprised many who thought that Bill Clinton's election would mean the end of the battle. The opposite happened. The legal attempts by antiabortionists to put an end *to all* abortions have failed. They have chipped away at abortion access with clinic blockades, waiting periods, parental consent, the Hyde amendment. But they have not stopped women from overcoming even these complicated hurdles to make their own decisions and take care of themselves.

Whenever the anti's get desperate, they get mean. The last wave of bombings and arson was in the late '80s, when Ronald Reagan failed to pass the Human Life Amendment, which would have constitutionally prohibited all abortions. Between 1977 and 1983, there were a total of eight bombings and eighteen arsons reported to the National Abortion Federation (NAF). For a briefer period, 1984 to 1986, there were a reported 24 bombings and 21 arson attacks as disappointment in Reagan grew.

Former Operation Rescue director Keith Tucci has called Clinton the "bloodiest president in our history [who has] wiped out twenty years of legislative work on behalf of the pre-born." Today, antiabortion leaders despair because funds have dried up. Some blockaders are going home, turned off by the ugly aggressiveness of tactics such as pouring foul-smelling chemicals inside of clinics. Fewer people are willing to be arrested. A hardened core of rank-and-file zealots with lengthy arrest records is all that is left.

Confrontational direct action groups had adopted the image of the bloody fetus as the symbol of their "in-your-face" type of activism. But dwindling troops mandated even more extreme measures. From 1986 to 1992, there were fewer than 10 death threats and harassing calls to clinic staff per year. A year after Clinton's election, this number jumped to 61. Stalking doctors became a favorite hostile and threatening tactic. No stalking incidents were reported to NAF until 1993, when 140 such reports were registered. The wave of terror turned fatal in March 1993 when Michael Griffin killed Dr. David Gunn in Pensacola, Florida.

A new breed of antiabortion activists has emerged. As clinic blockades have failed as an effective strategy, a growing group of extremists has made saving the unborn a job (or at least a mission). Some of these protesters have multiple arrest records in many different states. Others are loners living on the ledge of society seeking an opportunity to jump. When they jump, they try to take someone with them.

Some leaders of the antiabortion movement have attempted to portray Griffin and Paul Hill, the Presbyterian minister who was convicted for the July 1994 murders of Britton and Barrett, as "lone psychos," but the murders show that they are just part of a growing number of antiabortion terrorists willing to use lethal violence.

What is most disturbing is the way these antiabortion fanatics link their acts to their "Christian" beliefs. In his book, *Should We Defend Born and Unborn Children with Force?*, Paul Hill describes his vision of a zealous underground that murders people for "disobeying God's laws" on abortion, homosexuality, and other "crimes." His vision comes from the Biblical tale of Phineas, a priest who killed two sinners with a single spear thrust and became

a symbol of righteous zeal. The same story guides the Phineas Priesthood, a white supremacist group that murders people for interracial mixing.

This is only part of a disturbing pattern linking antiabortion fanatics and the racist
right. The leaders of the antiabortion movement, many of whom claim they do not support
the stalking and murdering of doctors, don't seem to realize that their rhetoric has attracted
people more committed to violence than to saving unborn babies. The neo-Nazi youth
movement is visibly entering the fray. Skinheads in Oregon, Texas, and Florida have demonstrated at clinics. They were not repudiated by their "mainstream" counterparts.

The similarities of white supremacists and antiabortion extremists are striking: both
rely on spiritual prophecies to shape the beliefs of their followers and to exhort them to violence. They are also equally obsessed with all aspects of sex and sexuality, homosexuality,
abortion, pornography, feminism, and single mothers.

If nothing else, the murders of Gunn, Britton, and Barrett lay to rest the notion that
the antiabortion movement is about saving the lives of babies. In reality, it has always been
about controlling the behavior of women. Unable to convince women not to get abortions, the
movement has resorted to low-intensity warfare: killing the doctors and burning the clinics.

Instead of trying to control women, antiabortionists need some critical discipline
within their own ranks. But disciplined nonviolence is difficult to maintain with leaders such
as Randall Terry broadcasting thinly veiled threats against doctors. Speaking on a Cleveland
radio broadcast on August 8, 1993, Terry said the following about a Colorado physician who
performs abortions: "I hope someday he is tried for crimes against humanity, and I hope he
is executed."

Terry has apparently abandoned peaceful methods to stop abortion. He is now affiliated with the U.S. Taxpayers Party, a Christian Patriot group that grew out of the tax
protest movement of the '70s. Christian Patriots believe, among other things, that the
Federal Reserve should be eliminated, that all federal tax and welfare programs should
be ended. They advocate the use of citizen-organized militias to combat alleged con-
spiracies by foreign governments to militarily invade America. The notorious Posse
Comitatus, whose members have been involved in shootouts with federal marshals, typi-
fies the Christian Patriot movement. Significantly, the U.S. Taxpayers Party also supports
armed "citizens' militias" to enforce its specialized interpretation of the Bible and the
U.S. Constitution.

A month after his speech in Cleveland, Terry went one step further: "I want you to just
let a wave of intolerance wash over you. I want you to let a wave of hatred wash over you.
Yes, hate is good."

Racist organizations couldn't have said it better. Tom Metzger, leader of White
Aryan Resistance (WAR), himself convicted of encouraging followers to commit murder, supports Paul Hill: "You've got to admit this guy has some style at least; he's not
begging for mercy but smiling at his keepers.... If the guy who did the shooting in some
way protected Aryan women and children, then WAR condones the killing." Other racists chimed in, including former Invisible Empire Knights KKK leader John
Baumgardner in Florida: "The recent killing of the clinic doctor was a political assassi-
nation." He finds "some merit in the deed" but is dissatisfied with unsupportive
attitudes of some in the antiabortion movement.

As murderers and racists have sought to dominate the antiabortion movement, their deeds have overshadowed even the best propaganda efforts of antiabortion spokespersons, eclipsing more moderate voices. Sensitive to this potential public image disaster, some antiabortion leaders are trying to distance themselves from visible ties to violence and white supremacists. In Florida, John Burt, a former Klan member and now a leader of the extremist antiabortion group Rescue America, denounced murder as a tactic. Burt, however, was Griffin's supporter and worked with Hill to identify Dr. Britton last summer. Is it simply coincidence that the same guy was connected to all three deaths? Rescue America also acknowledges that racist groups support its cause but dismisses charges of racism.

Is this the truth or is it a public relations smokescreen to avoid criminal charges?

For women who need abortions, it hardly matters. Incidents of abortion clinic violence are escalating at frightening rates. In 1992, there were 8 reported death threats at clinics. A year later, there were 65. In September 1993, a man was arrested at a Dayton, Ohio, clinic with a .22 rifle and 30 rounds of ammunition. The week after the July 29 murders, a clinic in Falls Church, Virginia, suffered a likely arson, while in Philadelphia, a man in possession of at least five Molotov cocktails was arrested outside a clinic. In Vancouver, Canada, Dr. Garson Romalis was shot by a sniper outside his house on November 8, 1994.

The Justice Department's decision to post federal marshals at clinics most susceptible to attack is a belated and much-needed measure. But armed guards are not enough. What about the doctors and patients who are stalked by these fanatics? Abortion services already are not available in 83 percent of counties in the United States, forcing women to endure great hardships in exercising their legal rights. There is only one provider in Mississippi. It won't take long to eliminate access altogether.

It is time for the prochoice movement to go on the offensive against these terrorists. Aggressive prosecution of violators of the Freedom of Access to Clinic Entrances Act will winnow down even further the available pool of protesters. Activists must monitor and photograph each antiabortion protester at the clinics, so that dossiers can be developed to assist law enforcement in prosecuting those who break the law. Research, monitoring, and organizing assistance is available from groups like the Center for Democratic Renewal, in Atlanta, Georgia, or the Fund for a Feminist Majority, in Arlington, Virginia. Tensions between providers and advocates must be addressed. Often, when trouble breaks out at a clinic, directors don't welcome the support offered by community activists. They are afraid to draw more attention to their clinic. However, the people who commit crimes against clinics and staff operate best under a cloak of secrecy. Exposure damages their cause and makes a mockery of their professed belief in the sanctity of life.

Prochoice activists must understand that every significant freedom movement in the United States has been marked by tremendous sacrifices. Fighting this kind of terrorism takes vigilance and courage. Exposing the links between antiabortion fanatics and the racist Right is a first step. The evidence is right in front of our eyes. Antiabortionists often plant crosses at the alleged "graves of the unborn" to profess their devotion to their cause. How long will it take before they start setting those crosses on fire?

OCTOBER 1976

Sterilization Abuse

by Judith Herman

Forced Sterilization In The United States

In 1973, two Black sisters in Alabama, aged twelve and fourteen, were sterilized in a federally funded family planning program. Their mother had been persuaded to give her consent by making an X on a form that she could not read. She did not know that the operation was permanent.

In the same year, a white mother in South Carolina revealed that the area's only practicing obstetrician routinely refused to deliver a third child to women on welfare unless they consented to sterilization. As his nurse explained it, "This is not a civil rights thing or a racial thing, it's just welfare." In a six month period this doctor had performed 28 sterilizations, mostly on Black women.

In Armstrong County, Pennsylvania, Norma Jean Serena, a Native American woman, is suing hospital and welfare officials for involuntary sterilization. Her tubes were tied immediately after the birth of her third child, while she was medicated and exhausted from the delivery. She was not aware that she had been sterilized until the following day, when she was persuaded to sign a consent form. Her medical chart states that the operation was performed for "socioeconomic" reasons.

In Los Angeles, ten Chicana women have filed a class action suit against hospital and state health officials charging that they were either coerced or deceived into being sterilized. Some were presented with consent forms while in labor. Others never signed forms at all and only learned later that they had been sterilized.

Sterilization: U.S. Policy

Sterilization as a means of controlling population in Third World countries has been a part of our government's policy for years. In Puerto Rico, the laboratory for U.S. population experiments and testing ground for the pill, over one-third of all women of childbearing age have already been sterilized.

In the last five years, this policy has come home to the mainland. Since 1970, female sterilizations in the United States have increased almost threefold. Between 600,000 and 1,000,000 procedures are now performed on women each year. Poor women and women of color are heavily overrepresented: 20 percent of married Black women have been sterilized, compared to about 7 percent of married white women. Of Native American women, 14 percent have been sterilized.

The increase in female sterilization has come about not in response to women's demands (as in the case of abortion), but as the result of governmental policy and pressure from hospitals and doctors. In 1971, Nixon appointed John D. Rockefeller III to be chairman of a commission on "Population and the American Future." Rockefeller has been eminent among the promoters of the idea that the "population explosion" is responsible for poverty in the world. A natural enough idea for a Rockefeller. The commission advised that "slowing the rate of population growth would ease the problems facing the American government in the years ahead. Demand for government services [read welfare] will be less than it would be otherwise, and resources available for the support of education, health, and other services would be greater. "

Funds for Sterilization, Not Social Services

Though Nixon rejected the commission's report because it recommended legalized abortion as one method of limiting births, many of the commission's recommendations have been put into effect. Between 1969 and 1974, federal allocations for family planning increased from $11 million to $250 million, while funds for Head Start, child care, and community health were repeatedly cut. By 1974, the Department of Health, Education, and Welfare (HEW) had modified its guidelines to require states to provide family planning services to welfare recipients. And most recently, HEW has announced that states will be paid 90 percent of the cost of sterilizations for poor women, but only 50 percent of the cost of abortion. This gives hospitals and clinics an incentive to promote an irreversible birth control method and to discourage the method that gives the individual woman the greatest amount of flexibility and personal control.

At the same time that government policy has swung around to promoting population control within this country, medical policy has also shifted in favor of liberalized guidelines for sterilization. In part, this may be because the medical profession has accepted the Rockefeller line on overpopulation. In a recent survey, 94 percent of gynecologists polled in four major cities said that they favored *compulsory* sterilization for welfare mothers with three or more "illegitimate" children. As Dr. Curtis Wood, president of the Association for Voluntary Sterilization, puts it: "People pollute, and too many people crowded too close together cause many of our social and economic problems.... As physicians, we have obligations to our individual patients, but we also have obligations to the society.... The welfare mess, as it has been called, cries out for solutions, one of which is fertility control."

Practice for Surgeons

Even more than ideology, doctors' interest in surgical training has led to the promotion of sterilization, especially in major teaching hospitals. Women who want birth control are talked into sterilization, without any discussion of the risks involved (sterilization is at least as dangerous as the pill or the IUD) or the available alternatives.

Women who definitely want sterilization are often persuaded to have a hysterectomy, rather than the far less complicated tubal ligation, simply because a hysterectomy is a more interesting and challenging operation for the surgeon-in-training. As a medical student at Boston City Hospital reported: "The name of the game is surgery—bring the patient in, cut her open and practice, and move her out. While she is there she is an object, treated coldly, patronizingly. Backs are turned on patients, questions are unanswered, operation permit forms are not explained. It is jokingly said that the only needed prerequisite for a hysterectomy is not to speak English. It isn't much of a joke."

Minimal Federal Guidelines

As a result of the case of the Relf sisters in Alabama, HEW was ordered to set up guidelines for sterilizations supported by federal funds. The guidelines were minimal, but they did include a requirement that the patient be told that sterilization is permanent and that she be assured that she would not lose any benefits such as welfare, if she refused. A 72-hour waiting period was also required between the time the woman signed the form and the performance of the operation. This was included to allow the woman to change her mind if she had signed under duress. Almost a year after the court order, the American Civil Liberties Union (ACLU) reported that most of the hospitals they surveyed did not bother to comply with even these minimal guidelines.

Feminists Slow to Respond

Feminist reaction and organizing around this issue has, until recently, been slow. In part, this may be because white, middle-class women have not felt the pressure. If anything, breeding is still encouraged among more privileged women. A young, white, married woman who lives in Lexington, Massachusetts, tells her obstetrician that she plans to have only one child. "But my dear," he exclaims, "you are just the sort of person who should have four or five!" This happened recently to a friend of mine. It probably happens all the time to women who get their care from private obstetricians rather than from public clinics.

Another reason that feminists have been slow to understand the threat of sterilization abuse is that the population control establishment, which is promoting sterilization, has been our ally in the abortion fight. As a result, it has been hard for us to be clear about the fact that their purposes are very different from ours.

When the feds increase funding for family planning twentyfold, they are interested in limiting births, especially among poor women. They have decided for the time being that there are too many of us. *They are not interested in our right to control our bodies.* It is important for us to be aware of this, especially when we cooperate with them around specific issues.

Women Organize to Fight

In the last year, women have begun to fight forced sterilization in an organized way. In New York, the Committee to End Sterilization Abuse (CESA) has developed model guidelines for sterilization that include a 30-day waiting period and a rigorous definition of informed consent.

After a long struggle within the bureaucracy of New York's Health and Hospitals Corporation, a citizen's group has succeeded in getting their guidelines adopted as hospital policy. In the process, they provoked opposition from a large segment of organized medicine and the population control establishment, including Planned Parenthood, the Association for Voluntary Sterilization, the American College of Obstetricians and Gynecologists, and HEW. Enforcement of the new guidelines will depend on constant vigilance and pressure from consumer groups.

In California, the ten women who are suing the state have succeeded in getting a court order that halts the use of federal funds for sterilizing women under age 21. The judge also ordered the state to rewrite its Spanish language consent form so that ordinary people can understand it. These may seem like token victories, but at least they are a beginning.

This article has been edited for length.

SEPTEMBER 1994

A New and Improved Population Control Policy?

by Asoka Bandarage

The United Nations International Conference on Population and Development begins in Cairo, Egypt, on September 5. At that conference, representatives of international governments from the Northern and Southern hemispheres; population control agencies such as Agency for International Development (USAID), the International Planned Parenthood Federation (IPPF), and the United Nations Population Fund (UNFPA); and nongovernmental organizations (NGOs) will meet to set the agenda for international population control strategies into the twenty-first century. As feminists, we must look critically at population control strategies and how they affect the lives of women, particularly poor women of color living in the Third World.

Malthus: The Father of Population Control

Malthusianism is one of the most pervasive, if not the dominant, responses to the current global political and economic crisis. It derives its name from the doctrine articulated, in 1798, by English clergyman-turned-economist Thomas Malthus. Malthusianism sees the numerical increase of the human population as the root cause of natural resource depletion, poverty, and social unrest—and population control as the primary solution.

As global problems worsen and policymakers are pressured to find quick solutions, Malthusianism is resurging in many overt and covert forms. Many leading scientific bodies, environmental organizations, and United Nations agencies have been issuing warnings and declarations to the effect that if population growth in the Third World, which accounts for 95 percent of current global population growth, is not controlled quickly, the planet itself is doomed to extinction.

A joint statement issued by the U.S. National Academy of Sciences and the Royal Society of London in 1992 claims that if current rates of population growth continue, "science and technology may not be able to prevent either irreversible degradation of the environment or continued poverty for much of the world." More than 70 leading population and environment agencies also signed a "Priority Statement" in 1991 arguing that "there is no issue of greater concern to the world's future than the rise in human population" and that "the United States and all nations of the world must make issues of human population growth a priority in this decade."

At the International Forum on Population held in Amsterdam in 1989, policymakers set targets for global fertility reduction for the first time in many years, arguing that it is an essential development strategy for the '90s. Also, the World Bank has been increasingly demanding that Third World countries accept stringent population control programs as a condition for receiving World Bank loans. Many Third World governments have adopted strong family planning programs, pursuing fertility reduction through extensive use of economic incentives and numerical targets—predetermined numbers of "acceptors" of specific contraceptive methods. In the United States, too, the calls for an official population control policy have been growing in recent years, along with plans to introduce economic incentives and new, long-acting contraceptives.

Reversing the policies of the Reagan-Bush administrations against funding for abortion, the Clinton administration is vigorously reasserting U.S. leadership in international family planning. USAID is working closely with corporations, multilateral organizations, the media, and universities, as well as with other industrialized nations, particularly Japan, to forge a consensus on the urgency for global population stabilization. In advance of this month's [September 1994] world population conference in Cairo, the U.S. public was subjected to a vast lobbying and media campaign designed to increase the "emotional edge" to the population question and to increase funds for more effective methods of population control for the Third World as well as U.S. urban areas.

Since the time of Malthus, population control ideology and policymaking have evolved in many directions, ranging from open support for eugenics and coercion to reproductive choice as a basic human right of women. Demographers Bernard Berelson and Stanley Lieberson, for instance, in the 1970s called for a "stepladder approach" to population ethics arguing that population control programs should begin with less severe methods and ascend to harsher methods as situations warrant them. At the time they put forward their theory, they hoped that a "disaster ethic" requiring measures such as "randomizing medical care" would not arise since the "disease" of overpopulation would be cured in the years ahead.

Today, however, many environmentalists in the North have accepted the "disaster ethic" as inevitable and are advocating coercion as a necessary evil in the race to stabilize global population. Maurice King, professor of public health at Leeds University, for example, has called for a removal of oral rehydration and other human-life-sustaining methods from public health programs in the Third World as a means to control population growth and ensure environmental "sustainability." If the environmental movement and policy planning move increasingly in a Malthusian direction, we are likely to see more and more triage policies that sacrifice human rights of poor people in the name of environmental sustainability.

However, most official population policies drawn up in preparation for the Cairo conference claim "opposition to coercion" and attempt to present population control within a more humane framework, calling for women's reproductive choice, health, and human rights. They emphasize family planning as a precondition for gender equality and women's empowerment and advocate expansion of reproductive health interventions beyond fertility control to include maternal and child health, prevention of sexually transmitted diseases (STDs), HIV/AIDS, and so on.

The "New" Reproductive Rights Agenda

The new emphasis on women's reproductive rights is an improvement on the earlier U.S. and international population policies, which paid scant attention to women's needs. Indeed, when compared with right-wing fundamentalist opposition to abortion and women's reproductive freedom, this neo-Malthusian family planning position seems liberal and consonant with feminist struggles for reproductive choice and human rights for women.

The assumption, however, that the goals of population control and women's rights are inherently compatible is mistaken and, in fact, dangerous to the interests of poor women who are the targets of population control. The distinction between population control and birth control must be emphasized here: population control involves external domination over people's reproductive lives whereas birth control involves individual autonomy and empowerment.

Social change movements need to build coalitions and alliances to find effective, long-term solutions to the complex problems facing the world. Yet it is important to bear in mind that *ruling* interests tend to confuse and co-opt social movements by manipulating progressive terminologies, offering funds, and using other tactics. There are many historical precedents to the co-optation of liberal feminist birth control struggles by population control interests, especially in the United States.

During the early decades of this century, the birth control pioneer Margaret Sanger, who started out campaigning for working-class and women's rights, capitulated to the eugenicist efforts to control the numbers of the poor, the working class, minorities, and new immigrants. This change happened when Sanger came under the financial and political influence of the population control movement with its openly eugenicist ideology. Later, in the '70s, liberal feminist organizations such as the National Organization for Women (NOW) and the National Abortion Rights Action League (NARAL), leaders in the abortion rights campaign in the United States, refused to join the struggle for stricter federal regulations of sterilization. They did so because sterilization abuse was not a major concern of white, middle-class women and because they did not want to lose the support of the population control organizations that were opposed to those reforms. But, in taking such a stance, the liberal feminist organizations distanced themselves from the interests of poor women in the United States, particularly Black, Latina, and Native American women who have suffered greatly from forced sterilization. Liberal feminist organizations have continued to take a narrow view on reproductive rights, equating "choice" with abortion. They see the so-called prolife movement as their enemy and the population control movement, despite its relative silence on abortion during the Reagan-Bush era, as largely their ally.

Many international women's reproductive rights organizations are now working together with population control organizations and relying on the latter's monetary and political support. Yet, since its beginning after World War II, population control has been a male-dominated, Eurocentric, numerically oriented enterprise, its financial and technological power emanating from Washington, D.C., and New York City to the far corners of the Third World. This is an alliance of which we should be cautious, especially when we see many of these women's organizations define their work within the analytical framework of population stabilization.

As population control organizations adopt and adapt the language of women's rights, population control subsumes women's health concerns. As fertility control is presented increasingly as the means for women's empowerment, feminist criticisms of coercion and experimentation within family planning programs get softened; the resurgence of eugenics associated with the growth of new reproductive technologies gets overlooked; and the social structural roots of women's subordination and the global crisis tend to be forgotten.

The leading actors in global population control are the pharmaceutical companies selling contraceptives; the medical and scientific community developing new technology; the demographers producing the numbers; the bureaucrats at USAID, the World Bank, UNFPA, WHO, and IPPF designing programs; the public relations experts marketing family planning; and the lobbyists raising funds. Their reproductive rights agenda does not seek to decentralize the techno-bureaucratic command structure of population control or challenge its inherent authoritarianism.

Nor does the "new" reproductive rights agenda seek to change the population control movement's modes of operation. For example, it does not call for the abolition of numerical targets and economic incentives, although the abuses associated with them have been widely documented. Targets and economic incentives are still routinely used in many family planning programs, especially those in Asia. Targets in themselves may not be wrong, but the pressure put on family planning workers to meet targets often results in violations of reproductive and human rights as well as corruption and fraud.

Studies from India and Bangladesh show that midwives anxious to meet their sterilization targets and increase their earnings often fail to offer nonterminal birth control methods to their clients and neglect their work in childbirthing. Doctors moved by their dedication to the cause of population control and pressure to meet their own targets and increase their earnings perform tubectomies with undue haste in the unhygenic environments of mass sterilization camps or they refuse to take out IUDs and the hormonal implant Norplant when women complain of serious side effects. In addition to health care workers, in many Asian countries, schoolteachers, shopkeepers, village officials, military officials, and others with social authority have been integrated into population programs through targets and incentives. In Thailand, for example, in many cases, the provision of basic social services like roads, transportation, and latrines have been tied to the acceptance of contraception.

Economic incentives offered to poor people to accept sterilization, IUD insertions, or hormonal contraceptives make genuine reproductive choice a fiction. How can the acceptance of sterilization or contraceptives in order to collect money to buy food constitute reproductive freedom? This question has applicability in the United States, too, where many state legislatures have put forward bills attempting to tie welfare payments to fertility control, particularly the use of Norplant. Judges in the United States have also used Norplant in a punitive way, by forcing some poor women to "choose" between acceptance of Norplant and incarceration.

While family planning is increasingly promoted in the name of women's reproductive choice, rarely do family planning programs offer poor women a choice in the selection of birth control methods. This is why female sterilization continues to be the leading method of fertility control in the world. Where nonterminal methods are made available, long-acting, hormonal methods are promoted over less invasive technologies. Despite the new rhetoric asserting the importance of women's health and empowerment and need for greater male participation in fertility control, the use of quick-fix, provider-controlled, female contraceptive methods is currently being expanded. For example, in Africa, there is a big push to increase the use of methods such as the injectible hormone Depo-Provera and the hormonal implant Norplant despite poor health care facilities and the rapid spread of STDs and HIV.

While leading population control organizations such as USAID's Office of Population speak publicly of integrating family planning within a broader health care framework, in private correspondences officials argue that family planning should not be "held hostage" to strict health requirements and that "medical barriers" to contraceptive provision such as Pap tests and breast exams should be reduced. In other words, the position that maximum access to contraceptives should override safety and ethical concerns continues unabated. Women are seldom told of all the side effects and contraindications. Furthermore, poor women, whether they be in the South or the North, rarely have access to routine, quality health care essential for relatively safe use of high-tech methods such as Norplant and Depo-Provera.

Starting with the pill, modern methods of birth control have been experimented with mostly on the bodies of poor women of color, quite often without informed consent. The dumping of the Dalkon Shield IUD in the Third World after it was taken off the market in the United States due to damage to women's health; the testing of Depo-Provera among tribal women in Thailand and Black women in Atlanta, Georgia; and widespread use of Norplant in Indonesia and other countries are just a few examples. The latest "miracle" methods, such as the antipregnancy vaccine being experimented with in India and elsewhere, and the nonsurgical female sterilization pellet, Quinacrin, being tested in Vietnam, could have serious side effects on the health of women as well as their offspring.

Yet the alliance of population, reproductive rights, and environmental groups does not question whether contraceptive methods that alter hormonal and immune systems will affect the ecology of women's bodies and the sustainability of human reproduction. There does not seem to be a place for these concerns in the global consensus on population that has been forged "on the road to Cairo."

Still, a number of feminist groups in the South as well as a few international feminist networks based in the North continue to emphasize the use of safer, low-tech, barrier methods with access to legal abortion as a backup method. They point out that women's health and their ability to have control over their bodies must come before the goals of population control. They also emphasize the advantages of barrier methods for the prevention of STDs, including HIV, in the Third World. But as the population control hysteria grows, feminist voices emphasizing safe methods and democratic process over the goal of population stabilization are marginalized. Their challenge to the dominant forces of technical-scientific "progress" and bureaucratic authority is shunted aside as "extremist" and "radical."

The introduction of coercive and experimental fertility control methods in the context of deepening poverty and patriarchy can make family planning a force for women's victimization rather than liberation. Perhaps the most extreme example is the spreading use of sex-selection tests such as amniocentesis in China and India, as well as other countries. Population control pressure coupled with deep-rooted preference for male children and the wide availability of modern sex-determination technology have resulted in a situation where increasing numbers of female fetuses are being aborted. The sex ratios of many Asian countries are increasingly biased against women. Yet no calls are being made against sex-selection in the new reproductive rights agenda prepared for the Cairo conference.

Nor are participants in the Cairo conference addressing the irony of demanding severe control of fertility in the South while pronatalist policies and new reproductive technologies for fertility enhancement such as *in vitro* fertilization (IVF) are being promoted in the North. Just as the pressure on poor women of color not to bear children increases, the pressure on middle-class women, especially white women, to bear children increases.

The alarmist calls for fertility control also tend to overlook the fact that, in all regions of the world, birth rates are declining. Population is increasing not because of extremely high fertility as much as the exponential nature of growth and the high proportion of people already of childbearing age. Given this reality, couples can be made to limit childbearing only with extreme coercion as exemplified in the case of China's one-child family policy and its drastic consequences for women's reproductive and human rights.

However, the small-family norm and even childlessness can become voluntarily acceptable to many people with fundamental social transformations, particularly economic empowerment and social and psychological freedom for women. Although neo-Malthusians recognize the correlations between women's poverty, education, and fertility, they make hardly any provisions for women's education and economic survival in their population programs and financial disbursements. The new reproductive rights agenda asserted by population control organizations, the United Nations, and USAID position papers for the Cairo conference do not address these concerns seriously or honestly. They fail to challenge economic policies coming from the North, such as the IMF/World Bank Structural Adjustment Programs, which are worsening poverty, especially women's poverty, and as a result contributing to their need for large families. By upholding corporate, "free trade" economic policies, the so-called new reproductive rights agenda fails to provide the economic and social security essential for reproductive freedom of women.

A Global Class Consensus

The liberal reproductive rights, population control, and environmental groups constitute a global class alliance and consensus representing dominant economic and political interests. It seeks solutions to the global crisis within the confines of the twin forces of modern technology and capital—technocapitalism—and the Malthusian framework.

Most environmentalists now agree that population is not the only factor that has impact upon the environment. They also identify affluence and technology as having decisive impact upon the environment. Yet when it comes to providing solutions, Malthusian environmentalists inevitably advocate population control over consumption control or the development of environmentally appropriate technologies. Thus, in *The Population Explosion* (Touchstone, 1991), Paul and Anne Ehrlich argue that "because of time lags involved, first priority must be given to achieving *population control*" (emphasis in original). The joint statement by the U.S. National Academy of Sciences and the Royal Society of London mentioned earlier, also recognizes that conservation of resources and energy in the "developed world" are needed for environmental protection. But it too claims that "unlike many other steps that could be taken to reduce the rate of environmental changes, reductions in rates of population growth can be accomplished through voluntary measures." Such arguments place the costs of environmental sustainability on the poor while denying that population control in the Third World has been and continues to involve coercion.

Despite their public criticisms of overconsumption of resources by the North, Third World governments and elites are pursuing the same model of technocapitalist growth and consumption as the North. Working in collusion with their Northern counterparts, they too are vigorously promoting population control in place of fundamental social transformations such as redistribution of wealth and resources and the adoption of appropriate technologies of production and reproduction.

The Malthusian analysis is narrow and superficial and its solutions elitist and ultimately ineffective. Since the time of Malthus himself, socialist, Marxist, Third World, and feminist analysts and ecologists have been presenting alternative perspectives that place population and human reproduction within the context of economic production and gender, race, and class dynamics. Progressive movements including feminist and environmental movements today must not be confused and sidetracked by the benevolent terminology of Malthusianism, including its more liberal reproductive rights variant. Instead, we must look at the actual policies, their implementation and effects on poor women and their families and continue challenging the population control establishment. More importantly, we must strengthen political-economic analyses that go to the historical roots of the contemporary population explosion and global crisis and seek democratic and sustainable solutions to these problems.

JANUARY 1988

DALKON SHIELD MAKERS ORDERED TO PAY DAMAGES

A federal judge has ordered A.H. Robins to set aside $2.48 billion to settle claims from thousands of women injured by its defective intrauterine device (IUD), the Dalkon Shield. A.H. Robins had offered $700 million, and lawyers for the Dalkon Shield Victims Association asked for $7 billion. More than 220,000 women filed claims. Lawyers for the association say that many will receive only token sums because their injuries were minor or because they lack evidence connecting injuries to the IUD.

Claimants suffered from infertility, spontaneous abortions, injuries from pelvic infections, and some births to babies with brain damage. Critics say that the Dalkon Shield's design resulted in bacteria being drawn into the normally germ-free womb. A.H. Robins denied liability, saying the shield was not more dangerous than other IUDs and blamed the health problems on sexually transmitted diseases. The company refused to take them off the market until 1974.

A.H. Robins sold 3.3 million Dalkon Shields in the United States and abroad between 1971 and 1974, when they were officially withdrawn from the market. In 1984, it was discovered that Dalkon Shields were being dumped into Third World markets and sold to United Nations' family planning programs.

MARCH 1993

A Nation in Distress

by Charon Asetoyer

And indeed, if it be the design of Providence to extirpate these Savages in order to make room for cultivators of the earth, it seems not improbable that Rum may be the appointed means. It has already annihilated all the tribes who formerly inhabited the sea coast.
—from the diary of Ben Franklin (1700s)

Let us put our minds together and see what kind of life we can make for our children.
—Sitting Bull (1800s)

It becomes clear who was the savage and who was the civilized man.

Historical Overview

In 1973, two doctors from Seattle, Washington, David Smith and Kenneth Jones, identified an irreversible birth defect that occurs when alcohol is consumed during pregnancy. They called it fetal alcohol syndrome (FAS) and noted its effects: mental retardation, deformed facial features, and stiff joints in the hands, arms, hips, and legs.

This naming of FAS by "modern man," however, was not our first knowledge of the correlation between alcohol and the birth of unhealthy children. As early as 428 to 347 B.C., in the Laws of Plato, we find warnings about alcohol consumption during pregnancy: "Any man or woman who is intending to create children should be barred from drinking alcohol." Plato believed that all citizens of the state should be prohibited from drinking alcohol during the daytime and that children should not be made in bodies saturated with drunkenness. He went on to say, "What is growing in the mother should be compact, well attached, and calm."

In 322 B.C., Aristotle was quoted as saying, "Foolish, drunken, harebrained women most often bring forth children like themselves, morose and languid." In ancient Sparta and Carthage, the laws prohibited bridal couples from drinking on their wedding night for fear of producing defective children. Even in the Bible (Book of Judges 13:7), an angel warns the wife of Manoah, "Behold, thou shalt conceive and bear a son, and now drink no wine or strong drink."

If the great philosophers were aware of the relationship between alcohol and birth defects, why has it taken so long for modern medicine to reach the same conclusion?

Ben Franklin's diary serves as a reminder that the colonial governments of what are now referred to as the United States, Africa, and Australia all used alcohol in one form or another to manipulate and control the local inhabitants of the continents they invaded. Alcohol was often used as a form of money with which to barter with local inhabitants for land, food, and animal hides. Colonial governments knew that indigenous people had no experience with alcohol and, therefore, were vulnerable to its effects. As Franklin makes clear, annihilation of indigenous people through alcohol became the unofficial policy of the colonial (U.S.) government.

Throughout U.S. history, the government has continued to use alcohol to control, manipulate, and murder Native Americans. Alcohol has been legal, illegal, and legal again at the whim of various presidents. The most recent change in the laws pertaining to alcohol use among Native Americans was in 1953, when the Eisenhower administration once again legalized the sale of alcohol to Native Americans. Knowing this history, we should not be surprised that alcoholism remains a major health problem among Native Americans, nor that alcoholism results in the birth of significant numbers of children with FAS.

The Women and Children in Alcohol Program

Of all women who drink alcohol during pregnancy, 40 percent will give birth to children suffering from either FAS or a lesser condition known as fetal alcohol effects (FAE). FAE occurs four to six times more often than FAS, and though a less serious birth defect, we must not underestimate it. The effects are: below average intelligence; learning disabilities; visual, speech, and hearing problems; hyperactive behavior; and a short attention span. FAE may also be accompanied by some of the same physical disabilities as FAS. FAE children usually are not detected until they enter school, where they are often seen as children with discipline problems. On Native American reservations, it is estimated that anywhere from one in nine to one in four children are born with FAS or FAE.

To address the problems of alcohol consumption among Native American women and its impact on their children, the Native American Community Board (NACB), a nonprofit project based on the Yankton Sioux Reservation in Lake Andes, South Dakota, developed the Women and Children in Alcohol program. NACB was founded in 1985 to improve the quality of life for indigenous people and to ensure the survival of our culture through increasing awareness of health issues pertinent to our communities and encouraging community involvement in economic development efforts.

Women and Children in Alcohol was the first program of the NACB, and this focus resulted in NACB opening the first Native American Women's Health Education Resource Center in 1988. Located on the Yankton Sioux Reservation, the center addresses many of the unmet needs of women and children identified during the initial program, including: child development; nutrition; adult learning; women's health issues, especially reproduction, AIDS and other sexually transmitted diseases, and cancer prevention; and environmental issues. It is not enough to go out into the community and spread the word about FAS/FAE. Information is important; however, there is more to it than that.

Blaming the Women

Early on, we discovered that when people learned of FAS/FAE, they were quick to blame mothers and their children. No one wanted to examine the larger picture, to ask questions about why women drink when pregnant. What about men's involvement in this, the peer pressure to drink in a community where alcohol use has become the accepted norm? What about the idle time in communities where the unemployment rate is often as high as 85 percent and the high school dropout rate is over 60 percent? What about the high rates of domestic violence and sexual assault in our communities and the lack of community agencies to address these issues? It is easy to say that a mother's drinking causes an FAS/FAE child to be born, but it is far from the whole truth.

Women who are chemically dependent don't plan to get pregnant and give birth to unhealthy children. They are often the products of abusive childhoods or of homes where their parents drank. They were introduced to alcohol at an early age—I've known children on reservations addicted by the time they were ten or eleven years old. As adults, these women have many health problems of their own: liver damage, diabetes, and other conditions related to alcohol abuse. But these are not uncaring mothers. Chemically dependent mothers love their children as much as other mothers—no matter how unlikely this may seem to outsiders. They must also live with the guilt that society imposes upon them for having given birth to imperfect children. Every day they are reminded that had they not consumed alcohol during pregnancy, their children would probably have been normal and healthy.

Chemically dependent women who seek treatment find one barrier after another blocking their paths. Only a small number of alcohol and drug treatment centers take pregnant women. In our four-state area, there is only one such center designed for Native American women. The Kateri program, in St. Paul, Minnesota, will take women through their sixth month of pregnancy (due to complications with Title 19, women cannot receive medical coverage if they stay beyond this point). This program, however, is in the process of being closed down because of problems with state and county funding.

Even if a woman is able to find a treatment center, in most cases, she will be unable to have her children there with her. If she is lucky enough to have supportive and available family members, she can leave her children with them; otherwise, she must turn them over to foster care, where she may fear that they will be abused and neglected. Most Native American women will not turn their children over to foster care unless ordered to do so by the courts.

Of course, someone must pay for women to enter treatment centers. Often, for poor women, the only means of gaining access to treatment is through a court order. But more often than not, when a woman is prosecuted for crimes related to chemical dependency, the courts find it easier and cheaper to terminate parental rights or to sentence a woman to jail than to provide treatment.

In recent years, it has become more and more common for prosecutors to charge women with child abuse or with giving a controlled substance to a minor in cases where a woman has continued to drink or take drugs during pregnancy. Judges want to punish women for engaging in what they consider self-indulgent behavior. They see these mothers as abusive rather than ill. The court may not even consider the fact that the woman being prosecuted may have tried to gain access to unavailable services.

Women of color are reported to authorities eight times more often than white women for giving birth to babies who are drunk or who have controlled substances in their blood. These women are often brought to the attention of authorities by social workers or doctors who deliver their children. But what have these service providers done to help these women deal with their addictions? In our communities, it is a sad fact that social service and child-protection workers are often aware of alcohol problems among children and adults but are unwilling to intervene because those in need of assistance are part of their own extended family or the family of a tribal council member. Because of the politics involved, a social worker may lose his or her job for trying to assist a child in need of services.

Several years ago, a doctor at the Indian Health Services Hospital on our reservation diagnosed a child with FAS. It turned out to be the tribal chairman's child. The doctor was transferred out of our hospital. It is easier for the problems of families and children to be ignored, for the entire system to become dysfunctional, and for all of the blame to fall on alcoholic mothers, who are given little or no support in the first place.

Sterilization Abuse

Since the courts are rarely interested in helping women to overcome their addictions, they have instead focused on how to prevent alcoholic and drug-addicted women from having children. Although judges have shied away from permanent surgical sterilization of women because of fear of violating women's civil rights, new contraceptive technologies have allowed judges to order women to be temporarily sterilized. This, too, is a violation of civil rights.

Norplant, a surgically implanted contraceptive that prevents pregnancy for up to five years, has become the sterilization method of choice among judges. Norplant must be implanted, and removed, by a physician; thus, the woman who is subjected to Norplant has no control over her fertility. She is sterilized. The same is true with the contraceptive Depo-Provera (an injected contraceptive that lasts for approximately three months), which was used to sterilize mentally ill Native American women in the '80s. Not only were these Indian women injected with Depo-Provera without their approval, but they were given the contraceptive before the FDA had even approved it for use in this country.

The first case in which a judge, as part of a plea bargain, ordered a woman to use Norplant, was in California in 1991. The woman, Darlene Johnson, was African American. The judge had little, if any, understanding of the potential harm that Norplant might do to this woman. He did not know that Johnson had health conditions that could become life-threatening if she were to be given Norplant. Should court officials who have no medical background be prescribing powerful medications? Will the courts assume legal responsibility if they endanger a woman's life in prescribing a potentially harmful drug?

Poor women, many of them women of color, have been targeted for sterilization not only through the courts but through bills in a number of states that require the use of Norplant as a condition for receiving welfare. Clearly, society takes the attitude that you reduce the risk of FAS/FAE babies by sterilizing women at high risk for giving birth to these babies. Reducing the risk of alcoholism and drug addiction among women of color and providing treatment for those in need is not a priority. This means that FAS/FAE and chemically dependent children often end up as orphans, dependent on the state for medical treatment as well as other social services.

Addicted mothers end up absent from home because they are still "using" and are out in the streets, in jail, or are dead after many years of substance abuse. Others must care for the children who may end up in foster homes or state facilities for the remainder of their lives. I have a close family member who has FAE. He lost his mother when he was seven years old due to an alcohol-related car accident. By the time he was fourteen, he had been in ten foster homes. Some were so bad that he experienced sexual abuse, drug abuse, and neglect. He is now 25 and has many problems with chemical dependency as well as with the law.

Society must take some responsibility for allowing a system to continue to function in this manner. It seems that it is easier to allow a system to be ill than to assist it in trying to get healthy. Both tribal and state courts have overstepped their authority in recommending or sentencing women to use Norplant or Depo-Provera. The bottom line is that this is sterilization, whether short-term or permanent, and such a policy carries with it strong connotations of racism and genocide when women of color are the intended targets. We cannot forget that in the mid '70s, the surgical sterilization of Native American women was common practice, with estimates running as high as 25 percent of all childbearing age women having been permanently sterilized against their will.

Conclusion

It is easier to blame women for being alcohol- or drug-addicted than to admit that society has failed to provide services that will help these women to work toward a healthy lifestyle. Though not entirely surprised by the response of the courts, I have been shocked by hearing health care professionals support sterilization policies. In a recent interview with an Indian Health Service doctor concerning Norplant and Native American women, he said that he "would support court ordering of Norplant for the prevention of FAS/FAE." Never during the entire interview did he mention or suggest that the system had failed in trying to assist women who are alcohol- or drug-addicted.

Fetal alcohol births are an indicator of a Nation in distress. What does this mean for the future of a Nation? For the existence of a culture? The quality of a Nation's leadership is derived from its people and the vulnerability of a Nation lies in its leadership. Health care professionals, social service workers, tribal leaders, lawyers, and judges—people in a position to create a positive response to this issue—have chosen not to do so. Thus, they must share the burden of guilt each time an FAS/FAE or chemically dependent baby is born.

OCTOBER 1994

WOMEN SUE NORPLANT DISTRIBUTOR
by Ellen Samuels

Three years after the hormonal contraceptive implant Norplant was introduced to the United States, more than 400 women have signed on to a class action lawsuit against Wyeth-Ayerst, the U.S. distributor of the implant. Citing scarring and excessive pain experienced during its removal, former users are seeking between $20,000 and $50,000 in damages each, as well as an injunction to halt untrained practitioners from purchasing and implanting Norplant.

The suit was filed in September 1993 by Jewel Klein, a Chicago district attorney, on behalf of an unidentified woman who had undergone three unsuccessful procedures to remove her implant. Klein reports that her office has been besieged by calls from women seeking to join the suit, many of whom report operations lasting two hours or more, and aftereffects such as serious bruising and nerve damage. One woman even lost nearly all use of her arm.

According to Wyeth-Ayerst, the implant, which has been used by almost a million U.S. women, can be easily removed in a procedure taking from fifteen to twenty minutes. It also says that it has established training centers where 28,000 doctors and nurses have learned about insertion and removal. But the company does not require doctors purchasing the implant to have received any specialized training.

According to Dr. Marc Deitch, vice president of medical affairs and medical director of Wyeth-Ayerst, the removal of the implant is also influenced by a number of variables, such as how the capsules were originally inserted, the procedure used for removal, and circumstances that are unique to each patient. Deitch, therefore, said, the company believes "that class action litigation is inappropriate."

Julia Scott of the National Black Women's Health Project (NBWHP) said, "We've always raised questions about whether the insertion and removal are as simple as they said it was." A special concern of the NBWHP is the possibility that keloid scarring, a form of scarring common among African Americans and people of Mediterranean descent, may further complicate removal.

"These are issues organizations of color have been raising from the beginning," agreed Luz Alvarez Martinez of the National Latina Health Organization, adding that Wyeth-Ayerst dismissed their concerns as "alarmist." Martinez said her organization has been ignored when calling for a registry of Norplant users, and "now the lawsuits are coming and we can't find all the women."

Martinez questioned why the problems with Norplant removal, which appear to stem primarily from faulty insertion, were not noted in the extensive international testing of the implant, which preceded its introduction in the United States. Ironically, a 1990 critical review of Norplant, published by the Amsterdam-based WEMOS/HAI Women and Pharmaceuticals Project, found that removal can be "difficult" and "extended," especially "when the implant is inserted too deep."

Prompted by the unpleasant, sometimes disabling, side effects of the implant, such as excessive bleeding, weight gain, hair loss, and headaches, approximately 50 percent of women seek removal by the third year, according to the National Women's Health Network, with about one-third of these in the first year of use.

Martinez and Scott both consider the latest Norplant developments to be consistent with the history of reproductive health abuses against poor women and women of color. Martinez has heard many horror stories of Norplant removal: one young California woman was told by her doctor that he would remove one of the six Norplant capsules for $75 and she could return when she had more money. Another woman removed her own implant, after being refused removal by the New Jersey clinic that did her insertion. The Native American Women's Health Education Resource Center in Lake Andes, South Dakota, is considering a lawsuit on behalf of a local woman who was told by her doctors that they would remove the implant only during a tubal ligation.

Referring to the issues now surfacing around Norplant as "an indictment of our entire health care system," Scott called for women to be given "safe choices" as well as "more choices" in the development of new contraceptive technologies.

MARCH 1991

Lay Midwifery: The Traditional Childbearing Group

an interview by Evelyn C. White

Shafia Mawushi Monroe dispenses with the formalities the minute you step into the office of the Traditional Childbearing Group (TCBG). Actually, a visit to TCBG bears no resemblance to a "standard" medical appointment. There's no sterility, stacks of confusing forms, or impersonal staff members. Instead, there's a comfy couch, a pot of tea, and a wall filled with photos of smiling babies.

Shafia and I had one of those long, loving, and laughter-filled conversations that Black women used to have over the back fence while they hung the laundry on the clothesline.

Times sure have changed for Black women. Our mothers may not have had executive suites or their own talk shows, but by and large, most of them had healthy babies. Their babies did not come into the world drug-scarred and trembling—three times more likely than white babies never to see their first birthday. While all may not have been perfect for Black women during the '50s and '60s, our mothers did not have to face a Reagan-wrought medical system that, at best, disregards and, at worst, totally disrespects Black women.

Shafia Monroe has made it her business to improve the pathway for Black children as they enter the world. We need to listen to this sister and support her as if our life depended on it.

Because it does.

Evelyn C. White: *Why don't you begin by telling me a little bit about how you became interested in midwifery. Was it something you always wanted to do as a child?*

Shafia Monroe: Actually, I didn't plan to be a midwife. I wanted to be a veterinarian until age fifteen. I always wanted to help animals, whether it was a dog having puppies or a pigeon with broken wings. If they needed help I was always drawn to them. This desire to help began when I was five years old. I think that was probably my calling, but I didn't realize I would be working with people who were in need. Even if you're pregnant and not sick, you still need help. It's another experience for you.

So at fifteen my mother passed away, and I moved in with an older woman and her family. She had three other children, and she was pregnant.

Was that here in Boston? Are you from Boston?

Actually, I'm from Alabama. But that was here in Boston. I lived with this woman in her house for about a year. I was very attracted to her pregnancy. I would rub her stomach and talk to her at night and shake the baby to feel it move. She said, "You know, you are really so good at this, you should really consider being an obstetrician." So I ran it by my father, about being an obstetrician, and he said, "You know you had a great aunt who was a well-known midwife in Alabama." I bought a book on midwifery. That was right around the time of the women's movement, too, coming back across the country, and the underground midwifery movement.

So at fifteen, I started reading more about it. Then at eighteen, I joined a group in Newton, [Massachusetts], called Homebirth Info Movement. I learned a little bit, but unfortunately, having to commute from Roxbury into Newton was a bit of a hassle at eighteen. I was the only person who was Black. They were nice, but there was a cultural difference, and I didn't feel comfortable with them. So I decided not to return, and, instead, I got a job at Boston City Hospital, 11 a.m. to 7 p.m., as a nurse's aide. I was lucky, I got on the newborn nursery floor. As soon as the baby was born back in the '70s, it went from the mother's body into a nursery. We're talking about second-old, minute-old babies.

Just taken away like that.

Yes. But there was an advantage to working in the nursery. During my year there I learned how to assess the health status of a newborn—how to assess their neuro-development, how to take their vital signs, how to remove extra fingers (sometimes they're born with six fingers), how to draw blood, and other skills needed for a well baby check.

The other thing, too, is that it was on the postpartum floor. For the breast-feeding, I got to take the babies to the mothers at night. And I think with any midwife, you learn best from the women themselves. I would ask them, "How was the birth experience? How was the pregnancy? How would you want it different? Why are you breast-feeding?" I learned a lot from one year talking in the middle of the night and listening to their stories.

Between 18 and 21, I enrolled at University of Massachusetts as a pre-med student, considering maybe getting into obstetrics. I was doing that, doing work at the hospital, and I was still running around trying to find midwives of color, which was really difficult. In 1972, you couldn't find many African-American midwives here.

In the North or Northeast?

The ones who I did find, who were from the South, they were old. Unfortunately, I think the system invalidated them. They didn't want to talk: "Oh, girl, that's an idea from a long time ago; you don't want to do that now, we got bottles, you don't have to do that now." And I was trying to tell them we did want to do that, that was positive.

But I did get some information from them. Midwives from Africa and the West Indies also taught me a lot. I met a midwife from Zaire who went to my university, studying to be a doctor. And I met a midwife from Pakistan, who helped me catch a baby. And then I met a midwife who was from Alabama, an older woman. We did a few births together. I learned more hands-on from her. She taught me how to do circumcision. Her grandfather did circumcision with a scissors. Nowadays you hospitalize babies. I'm personally not for circumcision. But if people are going to circumcise, I'd rather see them use the African approach where it means something—herbs are involved, there's a ritual; it's spiritual, not just something that's going to happen to this poor little boy. She taught another perspective on how to do it.

Then, at 21, I had my [first] baby, and I had a home birth. I couldn't find any midwives who would come into my area. There were no Black midwives. So I ended up using a white male doctor, which I wasn't happy about. But since I wanted a home birth no matter what, I dealt with him.

Two years later, I was pregnant again with my second child, a girl, and I went to this event and met a woman named Majeeda, who had just had a baby and had to use a white male doctor. We said we wished we could find a group and we said, "Let's get together and start a group!" And so we did. She invited some folks she knew, and I invited some folks I knew.

We called it the Traditional Childbearing Group, because this is the traditional way. Hospital births are nontraditional. Bottle-feeding is nontraditional. I tell people that this is the right name. We are truly traditional in the sense of the history of birth, and because we use information passed on by word of mouth. Look it up in the dictionary. For people of color, we are oral people. I teach midwifery, and how to be a parent, how to give birth, by talking. We give information by paper, but we do most of our stuff hands-on, touching and talking. This is what we've always done as Black women in this country—doing each other's hair, grabbing each other, hugging each other, slapping each other in jest or serious, whatever. So we choose that same approach within our framework, and it's very effective.

It's completely opposite in hospitals. Doctors don't talk to you. How can they in fifteen minutes? The nurse is the first twelve minutes. She does all the blood pressure, weight; you see the doctor a couple of minutes and you are out. You can't learn that way.

When I was pregnant with my five children, I went to clinics for all my prenatal care, though I was having a home birth. I did that as an investigator. So I knew firsthand what women had to go through. I sat there for many hours and walked into very impersonal care. I don't think I ever had a doctor who was Black or a midwife who was Black. They were always not of my community, not of my ethnicity, usually middle class, didn't understand my lingo. One thing I noticed was that they didn't touch you. They would say to you, "Oh, Shafia, how are you feeling?" I'd say, "I'm okay, but my back is killing me." They'd say, "Okay, let's get on the scale now." Not even acknowledge it.

Not even touch your back.

That's right. And with me, if your back hurts, "Well, take off that shirt, lay down and let's get the coconut oil out—or olive oil?" and we get into it. People call up and say, "My back hurts." I say, "Come on in." To me, that's what midwives do.

I used to go out to people. I did all my visits in people's homes. You learn more in someone else's environment. This [TCBG office] is not their home, even though it's warm. It's still not their house. I can't really see what their needs are here. We have pride. If we're poor, we don't say, "Well, I have no food in my house." If I make a home visit and they offer me tea, and I can see that their cupboard is low, I can see that they don't have any furniture or it's cold, they don't have heat. I can say, "Hey, sis"—I'll say it in a calm way, a sisterly way—"we can get you vouchers for some food, we can call ABCD and get you some heat."

A doctor will never know that. They don't know what people are going through on an everyday basis. And when they do know it, and they do make a home visit, it's very scrutinizing: "You don't have enough, we're going to get you services or we're going to file a 51A [a form filed with the state accusing a parent of neglecting or abusing a child] and take your baby out." We've never had to file a 51A in twelve years. I don't believe in that. Unless you're throwing kids out the window, literally. If there isn't a way to work it out, well then let's talk to your mother, let's talk to the baby's father; we have to be able to do something about this before we resort to having to bring in the outside, the authorities.

What is the difference between a lay midwife and a nurse-midwife? Do you need to be certified? What is your official status?

Well, the so-called lay midwife was first. We are the original midwife. It was a calling, or someone in the community appointed you because of your behavior or your personality. It was an honored position. But then in Europe—not in Africa and not in the South—but in Europe in the 1600s, they went through that whole witch-burning. I'm always clear with white America, that's not part of my history. We didn't get burned as witches in Africa; we were always honored, and we still are very respected today. But in Europe they did burn the midwives. They did push them out. It was a money thing. The doctors wanted to take over.

A nurse-midwife means you became a nurse first in a two- or four-year program, and then decided to continue on with midwifery studies, so you come out with the degree C.N.M. [certified nurse midwife]. For the traditional [lay] midwife, we are taught by other midwives: we use the apprenticeship program. Even though you have a calling, you still have to find another midwife who knows more than you, because we practice for many years. I try to practice what I call Afrocentric midwifery. That, and the Southern experience of mid-wifery—of Black midwives—is much different from the experience of middle-class white women who become nurse-midwives.

In this state, we have the Massachusetts Midwives Alliance, which is an organization of lay midwives statewide, a racially mixed organization. We have our own code of ethics, protocols, and an optional test to see if you're at a certain level. So if someone calls up and says, "I want Shafia Monroe as a midwife, what do you know about her?" they can run her name on the computer and say well, she took the test, she's certified, we know her, she is qualified. As opposed to Jane Doe, "She's not part of our organization. We can't give you anything about her. Use her at your own risk."

The disadvantage [of being a lay midwife] is we can't get third-party reimbursements. We can't get Medicaid to pay for us or Blue Cross/Blue Shield. I'm in a unique position be-cause I'm one of the most prominent midwives in this state who's Black. For twelve years, I've been out on the frontline fighting. Though we're not always liked by the physicians, they respect us. We work with some type of collaboration.

At this point, Boston and the country's getting desperate for solutions to the high cost of health care, and infant mortality is a problem for Black people across the country. We have to start being innovative, and they realize that.

Speaking of the high infant mortality rate, what's going on in Boston? Second in the nation?

I think third. Mississippi first, and maybe Chicago or Detroit.... But it's high enough. You know it's a twofold problem. I believe that as a people we should cure this problem. And I always tell women who come through here, if my father had a sixth-grade education and his mother had no education and she was able to birth healthy children that got through the first year of life, what's our excuse? We have to take some responsibility. You can control what you put in your mouth. I don't care if it's beans and rice and corn bread, it has got to be better than chips and Coca-Cola all day long. In a bad relationship? Get up and get out of it. Things you can control, let's start with that and then we can challenge the system.

At the same time, we don't want the system to get off the hook. Even if you're an educated, middle-class Black woman making over $30,000 a year, you're still at risk for infant mortality as opposed to a white woman of the same economic and educational background. It's the racism. I don't care how well you eat or how many herb teas you drink, you're going to have to fight racism on your job, in your neighborhood, and in your school system on a daily basis, and that's going to affect you. Why do you have higher blood pressure among Black women? Because we're angry. I talked to an herbal doctor who said, "You know, genetically, we're carrying anger in our genes because of slavery, and we have not been able to get it out yet."

That's what Toni Morrison talks about. The anger and the sadness from slavery, and I think that's part of the chronic depression among so many Black women and Black people in general. I think there's this residual sadness and anger in our DNA left over from that kind of stuff.

Yeah, we have to figure out among ourselves, how can we get rid of it? Any time you're oppressed it comes out through the lives of your children—premature births, etc. Infant mortality is not so much the baby dying, but how many babies who are born live are sick forever because they were born too soon or their mother carried them to full term but they were born too small? Any baby born under 5 lbs. 6 oz. is too small. The baby can't thrive inside, because the mother's not thriving.

A lot of women don't know that we have the highest death rate in the country. And I let them know we have the highest death rate because our babies get fewer health options; we have more parenting struggles, earlier exposure to drugs; and we have more diabetes, hypertension, strokes, obesity—

You name it.

The whole gamut. We've got it. I say we have got to start working on ourselves, loving ourselves: we have to be sisters.

What's the response like?

Very positive. I let them see things and tell them, "You're not being paranoid. What you're talking about is true. Yes, they are giving too many tests, and right, your visit was too short and the doctor was unfriendly, and you're right, he doesn't really care about you." These are teaching hospitals. They put teaching hospitals in Black areas, poor areas, and oppressed areas because we don't ask questions. We sign on the dotted line. We feel so grateful that they're even looking at us, with a fifteen-hour wait. I know all that stuff. I hug them. I tell them how good Africa is. I say find some of your people from the South. Ask your great-grandmother, how does she eat? Look at her teeth. Look at her skin. Look at our sisters and brothers in Africa.

In Africa their teeth are beautiful.

I tell them, because they were breast-fed and they eat vegetables. They can see that... "Oh, yes, my grandmother did say she didn't have a cavity." I say, "See, that was our history, but the white man took it off the books so we don't know. So we have to bring her back and ask them how."

Why are Black women so hesitant to breast-feed? I remember my mother breast-feeding my baby sister Phyllis, but I also remember her specifically sitting us all down and explaining to us what she was doing and not to be ashamed of it.

You're one of the more blessed ones. The system did a very good job. They took away midwifery, home birth, and breast-feeding. In the '50s, we were still breast-feeding and white America had stopped. They stopped in the '40s and went to bottles. So you're poor, you're Black, and here comes the white man who says, "Oh my god, not only are you poor and Black and ignorant, you're still breast-feeding! Ugh! You're outdated."

No progress. Still no progress.

Yes. I talked to a Black physician and said, "I'm a home birth midwife and I want you to help me with backup." And she went off, "Are you crazy, I'm against it. You know how long we fought to get in a hospital, and you're going try to take us back out." I said, "We don't have rights in a hospital yet." I understand that and I support that. We should have the right to birth where we want, that's all I'm saying. Why is it that only white, middle-class America has home births, midwives, and breast-feeding support, and we don't? And childbirth classes? You can't get childbirth classes in this area. Boston City Hospital offers them, and another place offers them all in Spanish. Otherwise you can go to two major white institutions—Beth Israel and Brigham and Women's. The class is probably taught by a white nurse.

What's the importance of having these services provided in the community by women from the community?

Most nurse-midwives, even if they come to the community, are not of color. They're white women, and they're serving Black people. Which is fine. Anyone can help anyone have a baby. Obviously, the doctors have been doing it for years. What's unique about having the community midwife is that when I see the mother at her home and help her, I'm going to see her again—we go to the same food store and I see them shopping or I go to a party or I'm at someone's house and we know the same people, so there's that continuity. But when you have to commute in and then go out, you don't see people—

Breaks the ties.

Right, breaks the ties. You only see them 9 a.m. to 5 p.m., usually in the clinic setting. You don't see them just walking down the street. The park that I go to, the same mother goes to with her kids, so I can see how she's bonding, how she feeds her kids, how she handles stress with children. Constantly educating.

Any midwife and any woman can teach people about empowerment of women, but I think for Black women, we need Black empowerment. We have a crisis right now. Our boys are killing each other and our babies are dying and we're having real hard times as a people. The '60s were the best years we ever had, when Black was beautiful—and with Black power. What happened? The white man killed him and arrested him because we were becoming too powerful, we started liking ourselves too much.

What is unique about the Traditional Childbearing Group is that we use an African perspective. You have to be political. I can take all the blood pressures I want, but it won't do anything if I don't teach folks, "Hey, genocide is alive and well in America." I don't care what they say, I believe that. The system does not want us, doesn't need us anymore.

Doesn't the struggle ever get you down?

I go home, and I get very depressed. My kids get after me, "Why are you like this?" They don't understand why I am so fanatical about this Black issue. I say, "Because I believe that until we define ourselves and fight for ourselves, we're not going anywhere." I always tell my son, "You have to look at the system brother. The white man wants you to go up and kill Black men because he doesn't want you to live either. That's why you can get a gun, but you cannot get a job. You can get crack, but you can't get an education." They always hear me say that. They say, "Ma ... " I say, "Look outside, what do you see? Can you go out? Can you ride your bike? Do you feel safe?"

Can't go outside, live, and do normal things like we did as kids.

Every time you go out, you hope you get back home in one piece. That's a reality. As a Black mother, having three Black boys, it's my reality. My sons go out, I always hug them, because I don't know if I'll ever see them again. That's not paranoia, that's reality. Every day is like another blessing if your children come back home. As a midwife, that's part of it. A midwife doesn't just catch babies. A midwife is an educator as well. I can say to a father some things that a male doctor could never say. "Now, I know you don't want to talk about this, but I know that you beat your wife. She didn't tell me. I saw her face. We have to talk about it. And I still like you and you love your woman, but you cannot handle this this way, brother. We've got trouble." And they'll open up because I've been in their house, I've drunk their water. I've used their toilet, and a lot of times before I got this office, they used to come to my house. That was my office. They came into my home, so we were equal. And they knew I didn't have any meat either. I'm poor like them, they know that. I have a commitment to their children, to their women, so they care about me. And I care about them. I can call them and ask for a favor and get it. I'm their midwife—I need a ride, a jump, I need a car, I need a babysitter.... So, that's nice. So that's the difference between traditional midwives who live in the community, as opposed to those who commute in and out.

Now I have to include gang violence in my parenting. Informally. I don't do things real formally. As we're talking, I just meet someone, "How many kids do you have?" "I have three kids, one's two, one's eight, and one's fifteen." I'll say, "Is that a boy or a girl? I have a four-teen-year-old. Is he in school now?" I just start talking, 'cause I know what they're going through. I make them aware. "Are you keeping track of him? You know where he's going? Is he having sex? Does he use condoms? Do you talk to him about sex? 'Cause if you ain't, who's going to talk to them? That's your child; forget being embarrassed, you don't tell him he's going to get AIDS, then you aren't going to have a son."

So that's all part of midwifery. It's not just checking the mother. It's the whole family, because the whole family affects this woman's life. If her son is out all night getting shot at or shooting somebody, she cannot grow a healthy baby. If her boyfriend is unemployed and strung out on crack or he has HIV or is getting laid up, that's going to affect her pregnancy. If her teen daughter is pregnant and not coming home at night, everything is going to affect her pregnancy.

Who pays for all this, especially if you can't get third-party payments?

Our first support came from the Boston Women's Fund. Since then, we have been getting great support from the Boston Foundation. We call them our Mother Group, our Mother Source. They make sure we stay intact. They've been giving us funding since 1987, $25,000 to $35,000. And we just got a state contract for the first time. This is very important for us, since we're the first group that's not associated with a clinic or a teaching hospital. They gave us a contract for $69,000. We can hire two people [to do outreach], knock on doors and stand at the bus stops and find pregnant women. And we do some fundraising. Once a year we give an event on African Women as Healers. It's for Black women only, to come together at night. We light candles, massage each other. We have a blast.

We have to rely on the grants because folks who come through, they can't afford it. The visit should cost $65 to $200. They get a complete history, blood work, Pap smear, gonorrhea culture, the massage with blood pressure, baby's heartbeat, the whole bit. We only charge $3, if they can pay, and of course, they can't pay. A lot of folks are on Medicaid but we can't accept Medicaid, so we don't charge them. If we say money, they just won't come. They'll go to the hospital for care, so we do it anyway. And we give childbirth classes and a lot of folks can't afford to do those either. So we do it for free. We like to believe the angel will come back. My thing now is I'm trying to get more women in the community to be midwives. I want my sisters to do it.

How many have you trained so far? How many apprentices?

Five have come through here in twelve years.

That's not a big number.

And only two are part-time active. I think the main thing is because of money. You can't make a lot of money. I couldn't make money, so what I had to do was develop the Traditional Childbearing Group so I could write grants, so we get paid for education. Midwifery is one component. But we need the state to legalize traditional midwives and let us get third-party reimbursements so we can help people who need to be helped.

So you have the doctors standing in your way right, 'cause they see you as a threat to their business.

Right. In the state of Massachusetts, to get any third-party reimbursements, you have to be licensed. And we don't have any way of being licensed in this state. There's no school for us to be licensed without becoming a nurse first. I don't want to be a nurse. In Africa, in Asia, and even Europe, midwives are not nurses. You either become a nurse or a midwife— they are two separate professions. Nurses are taught to work with sick people, and they're taught to be subordinate to male physicians as a rule. Midwives are independent, strong women who run a practice autonomously. They don't have to work for anyone, and they see pregnancy as a normal state.

Not a disease.

Right.

Now, concluding things. What do you want people to know? Why should Black women come here? People always say, "What happens if there's a problem with my baby? You don't have any machines. What are you going to do?" That sort of thing.

I'm glad you mentioned that. I want to say that with the Traditional Childbearing Group, and for myself, we don't try to force people to have their babies at home. What I see as the most powerful aspect of our program is that we teach Black empowerment, Black woman empowerment. No matter where you give birth—home or in a hospital—we want you to know that you're somebody, you have rights in the hospital, you have rights with your own birth midwife, you need to know how to interview her. You have to love yourself, you have to love your unborn baby and that your baby's being born Black. It already has something against it. You're all it's got and you have to get yourself empowered to keep this baby alive, so that he or she can make and be the great spirit that's meant to be, why it's coming here. You have to honor yourself and be proud, so that you can maintain your pregnancy and do it with dignity by taking care of yourself. You have to reach out to your pregnant sister and give her birth information and encourage her and rub her back and love and make her feel good about her new spirit coming into the world. Everything's against that child when it comes out. It's been born probably in a teaching hospital, by a white person probably, that really doesn't have any connection to it. So you're all it's got right now. So we have to go back to our history. Start with your mother and go to your grandmother, your great-grandmother, someone in your family who knows the power of your family line. Find out and try to live by it and do what you can do. You can read. You can eat right. You can breast-feed. And you can call us.

MAY 1985

Scrutinizing New Reproductive Technologies
by Rita Arditti

Sexuality is connected with all aspects of our lives, and when those connections change, the implications for our whole lives can be very great. I would like to raise some of the issues that will confront us more and more as the biological connection between sexuality and reproduction weakens through the development and use of new reproductive technologies. By "new reproductive technologies" I mean all forms of biomedical intervention that are offered as help when women consider having a child. Some of them—like artificial insemination, *in vitro* fertilization, embryo "flushing" and embryo freezing—are already with us. Others are still being researched: cloning, for instance, and ectogenesis, which is the complete development of the fetus outside the womb.

What these technologies are doing, put simply, is separating sexual contact from reproduction, making it possible for women to become mothers without engaging in sexual contact with males. This is an absolutely new development in the history of the species, and at first glance it could be seen as an unmixed blessing for women who do not wish to be dependent on men to have children. Artificial insemination (AI), for instance, is a relatively "low-technology" procedure, which women can perform without medical assistance, and, in fact, many children have been born in England and this country through AI. Groups of women have written guides for self-insemination and, using sperm from friends, have been able to bypass the medical establishment, which has in turn denounced them.

But despite the fact that AI is a very simple procedure, attempts are predictably underway to control it. In 1982, the British government established a commission, headed by Mary Warnock, to examine the issues raised by the new reproductive technologies. Its report, released in 1984, recommended that a special authority monitor those technologies, that they be made available only to infertile couples (heterosexual, of course), and that physicians have discretion to refuse anyone treatment. The implications of this are clear: heterosexual single women and lesbians do not qualify for these services, and it is questionable how much access minority, poor, disabled, and older women will have. The report has received wide acclaim both in Britain and abroad and will probably form the basis for English legislation; no such legislation now exists in the United States but many physicians in the field now operate in an ethical mode similar to that of the Warnock Commission.

The example of AI shows clearly the central question raised by the new technologies: who controls them? Who decides their development, use, and accessibility? The fact is that the medical profession controls contraception and childbirth and will control the artificial reproductive technologies as well. And it is medical control over reproduction that has given us the pill, the IUD, Depo-Provera, the DES tragedy, and proposed contraceptives that are even more frightening: subcutaneous implants that release hormones 24 hours a day in women's bodies [Norplant, introduced to U.S. markets in 1991]; plans for adding contraceptives to the food and water supplies of Third World countries; and sterilization, which is already rampant in the Third World and is offered insistently to minorities and poor women in this country. The medicalization of childbirth has also pushed the view of pregnancy and delivery as dangerous and pathological processes, with the result that the cesarean section rate has risen tremendously in the last twenty years and now stands at 25 percent of all births.

Even the medical establishment's handling of amniocentesis—the removal of amniotic fluid from a pregnant woman to examine the cells of the fetus—suggests an effort at "quality control" based upon a philosophy of human perfectibility through technology. Amniocentesis is a useful procedure for detecting genetic diseases, but we need to consider its social and political implications, especially because of the long and ugly history of eugenics, the attempted improvement of the human species through selective breeding.

Think, for instance, of the sperm bank—the Repository for Germinal Choice—established a few years ago by Nobel Prize winners so that women could have the "choice" of Nobel Prize babies. It is also possible to hear eugenic echoes in some of the prenatal screening programs, and they certainly raise the question of who will be allowed to be born. What kinds of defects will be considered so undesirable that women will subtly and not so subtly be pressured to abort an otherwise desired child?

Equally disturbing questions arise in connection with *in vitro* fertilization, which is beginning to be widely available in the United States. As of January 1985, 105 clinics and centers were offering *in vitro* fertilization to couples (again, I mean heterosexual couples, because this procedure is available only to women who are married or in a permanent relationship with a man). *In vitro* fertilization means fertilization "in glass," because the union between egg and sperm takes place in a flat dish called a "petri dish." The term "test-tube baby" is totally misleading, giving the impression that the baby is developed in the laboratory by physicians. Actually, after fertilization in the dish, the eight- or sixteen-cell embryo is implanted in the woman's womb or frozen and stored for later use.

Hundreds of babies have been born through this procedure, primarily in Western, industrialized countries. There is so far no evidence of abnormalities, but the issue is not settled yet: too few babies have been born and none has reached maturity. (The oldest child, Louise Brown, is only seven years old.) Yet there have already been claims by Dr. Wood, one of the leaders of *in vitro* fertilization in Australia, that the babies are not only healthy but actually "better" than "normal" babies. (Of course—he sees himself as the father.)

In vitro fertilization is increasingly presented as the technical solution to the problems of infertile women. But it remains to be seen how much of a blessing it really is and how much additional pressure it may put on women to keep trying to have children. The procedure is far from painless: it involves gruesome testing and long waiting periods, costs between $4,000 and $8,000 per attempted fertilization, and has a success rate of only 15 to 25 percent. Furthermore, although its specific effects on women's health are now unclear, it is so invasive as to be highly suspect. Described as "minor surgery," *in vitro* fertilization involves hormonal treatment to induce superovulation, general anesthesia, distention of the abdomen with an inert gas, two or three incisions in the abdominal wall, and insertion of a telescope and an aspiration device to collect the follicles. After fertilization of the egg, the woman receives another hormonal treatment so that her uterus will be better able to accept the embryo, and frequently the whole procedure ends with a cesarean section. The process can also rob a woman of control over her pregnancy: the egg taken out of her body can be fertilized with her partner's sperm or with somebody else's—and the resulting embryo can be checked for "quality" and then implanted back into her or into a surrogate mother, thus raising serious questions for society at large.

The portrayal of *in vitro* fertilization as a response to the desires and demands of infertile women is difficult to accept. If scientists are so sensitive to women's needs, why has no simple, safe, reversible contraceptive been developed? Contraception is an urgent priority for women all over the world, while *in vitro* fertilization reinforces a pronatalist ideology. It can also be seen as the medical response to the decline in U.S. births from four million a year in the mid '60s to just over three million annually in the mid '70s. Doctors, whose primary clientele is women, were faced with a decreasing number of patients requesting obstetrics, and infertility treatments and the new reproductive technologies came to the rescue.

Meanwhile, little information is known or being developed about the relationship between infertility and lifestyles, employment patterns, and standards of living. It seems likely that chemical poisoning of the air, water, home, and work environment is a heavy contributor to infertility; other possible causes, usually neglected, are stress (by no means insignificant for women), abdominal surgery, drugs and alcohol, smoking, weight, nutrition, endometriosis, cesarean sections, and sexually transmitted diseases. Most important, because it can be totally prevented, is infertility that is iatrogenic—induced by contraceptive technology like the pill and IUD, which have been shown to damage the female reproductive system both temporarily and permanently. (Interestingly, in the United States, it is the upper class that reports most of the infertility problems.)

Unfortunately, *in vitro* fertilization is not the only new reproductive technology that robs women of control over pregnancy by splitting it into discrete pieces. In a new U.S. procedure called embryo "flushing," a woman is fertilized through AI with the sperm of the partner of an infertile woman. The embryo is then flushed from her and transferred to the infertile woman—a process being patented by the company that developed it. The implications of this procedure for abortion are just tremendous. For example, Bernard Nathanson, a physician who once directed New York's Center for Reproductive and Sexual Health and has now joined the antichoice movement, has said, "The abortion of the future, then, will consist simply of early detection of the fetus, removal of it from the unwilling mother, and either transfer to a life support system or implantation into a willing and eager recipient." Much of our thinking about reproductive rights has been shaped by the assumption that pregnancy can occur only in women's bodies; when we talk about the right to choose, we talk about choosing what happens to our body. But what happens when what used to happen to our body is not happening in our body anymore, when fertilization and embryo development take place outside the body? In other words, who "owns" the fetus?

As we struggle with questions like these, there will clearly be many disagreements among women; infertile women, for example, may feel that their pain is not taken seriously enough. It may, in fact, be impossible to evolve a single "feminist position" on many of the new reproductive technologies. But we can work together to minimize coercion around them, to protect the health of women, and to expose the fallacy that they somehow lighten the burden of mothering. The impersonal reproductive technologies developed by males in a sexist society must not be a substitute for real changes in our society's oppressive construction of motherhood.

MARCH 1987

Wombs for Rent, Babies for Sale
by Rita Arditti

The current case of "Baby M" has finally put the issue of commercial surrogate motherhood squarely in the public eye. "Baby M" was conceived by Mary Beth Whitehead, a 29-year-old New Jersey homemaker, through artificial insemination with the sperm of William Stern, a 40-year-old biochemist. William Stern and his wife Elizabeth, a 41-year-old pediatrician, decided to delay raising a family until she completed her medical residency in 1981. In 1982, Elizabeth Stern decided not to become pregnant for fear that pregnancy and delivery would worsen her case of multiple sclerosis. The Sterns turned to surrogacy.

Mary Beth Whitehead signed a contract at the Infertility Center of New York, a private profit-making business whose founder and director is a well-known surrogacy advocate,

Noel Keane. According to the contract, Whitehead consented to give up the baby after the birth. William Stern's name would be on the birth certificate and Elizabeth Stern would file for adoption. Mary Beth Whitehead was to be paid $10,000 plus expenses and the Infertility Center would get $7,500. This kind of arrangement is not a novelty; more than 500 babies have been born this way as surrogate mother businesses have sprung up across the country in the last ten years. It is estimated that more than twenty businesses are operating currently.

But Mary Beth Whitehead changed her mind and decided she did not want to give up the baby. Although Whitehead was accepted in the surrogate mother program, in the psychological report that is done as part of the process of evaluating candidates, the psychologist reported that "she expects to have strong feelings about giving up the baby at the end" and "she may have more need to have another child than she is admitting."

While there have been other cases of "surrogate" mothers changing their minds, this is the first time that the contracting couple is contesting the decision. For the first time, our legal system—in this case, a New Jersey judge—will have to rule on the legality and enforceability of the surrogacy contract.

Only ten years since the surrogate business began, we have already come to this: six policemen entering a mother's home to take her child from her; the mother, still bleeding from the delivery, put in handcuffs and thrown into a police car while her neighbors watch; after the mother fled with the child, police from two states, the FBI, and private detectives hunting for the renegade mother and her child.

Things do not look particularly bright for Mary Beth Whitehead. The baby is now in temporary custody with the Sterns. Whitehead is allowed to visit the child four hours a week at a county home for wayward youths under the supervision of a sheriff's deputy. The judge has forbidden her to breast-feed her baby and has denied her request that her husband and two children visit the baby. The baby's court-appointed legal guardian has recommended that William Stern receive sole custody of the ten-month-old girl and that Mary Beth Whitehead be denied visiting rights for the immediate future.

Proponents of commercial surrogacy claim that women have always had babies for other women. One of their favorite citations is that of Sarah and Hagar in the Old Testament. Genesis 16 tells that Abraham had a child with his wife's handmaiden, Hagar, when Sarah could not become pregnant. What the proponents of the baby-selling business never mention is this: Hagar was a slave who had little control of her life, and when Sarah finally was pregnant and delivered Isaac, Hagar and her son Ishmael were cast out into the desert. Hagar was not producing a child for *Sarah,* but for *Abraham,* and a "second-rate" child at best.

Surrogacy raises profound questions regarding the rights of women as mothers, regarding what constitutes a family, regarding the social value we place on children, regarding how we relate to each other in a society that becomes more and more commercialized. We need to ask what is going on with the surrogate industry. What values exactly are being promoted behind the benevolent facade of "trying to help infertile couples"? Clearly not the woman whose body is being rented at an hourly wage of $1.57.

Clarifying the language is crucial to this discussion. The term "surrogate mother" is a misnomer, clearly reflecting the male perspective that pervades the issue. As Canadian feminist Somer Brodribb has pointed out, "The woman who carries and labours to give birth to a baby with her own ova and from her own womb is clearly a real mother. She is, however, a surrogate wife to the man whose legal wife is infertile." The 21-page surrogate parenting agreement drafted between the Whiteheads and William Stern clearly spells out that Mary Beth Whitehead is a "surrogate," while William Stern is the "natural father." But Mary Beth Whitehead is the natural mother, a fact that proponents of the surrogate industry want us to forget and disregard.

Surrogate wives provide men the opportunity to have babies who carry their own genes. This is not a minor detail in the surrogacy business. Couples have hired surrogates even when the now-infertile woman had children from a previous marriage because the present husband wanted a child "of his own." In *The Surrogate Mother* by Noel Keane and Dennis L. Breo (Everest House, 1981), the first client described is a man whose wife very much wanted to adopt, but he wanted to have his *own* baby. As he says in the book, "Maybe it's egotistical, but I want my own child. Adoption leaves me cold. I guess for some women, as long as they have a child it's fine. But for me, it's like if I see my child do something, I need to know that he's really mine. Like I say, maybe it's egotistical."

Having one's own child, a child with whom there is a genetic link, may indeed be one of the obsessions in our culture that we need to address. Why is it so important to have one's genetic offspring? What kind of values are we supporting if we give so much importance to genetic makeup? What is parenting all about? Is it about caring and loving children or is it a way to preserve one's own germinal line? How is this desire to have one's own children linked to patterns of patriarchal inheritance and descent? Why did William Stern feel, as he said, "compelled" to continue his family's bloodline? While the obsession with having one's own genetic child may operate for both women and men, in the case of surrogacy, it is the male who can act upon it. We need to think critically about these issues, particularly now when the developments in reproductive engineering make all kinds of combinations and permutations more and more possible.

Noel Keane is quite clear about what is going on when he says, "There is a simple reason why people prefer finding a surrogate mother to adopting: the child will bear the genetic imprint of the man." Keane claims that surrogate mothering is equivalent to artificial insemination, where a couple infertile because of male infertility can have a biological connection through the woman. This claim equalizes the ejaculation of sperm with the profound changes that take place in a woman's body during pregnancy and with the experience of delivery, and it ignores the biological connection between the woman's body and the child.

Proponents of commercial surrogacy say that the "right to privacy" guarantees procreative autonomy. But the right to privacy does not imply a right to obtain a child in any manner desired. If we invoke present social policy, we need to remember that the selling of babies is illegal in this country and that many states have laws prohibiting fees for adoption. Regarding the much vaunted "right to procreate," Angela Holder, head of the American Society of Law and Medicine, has pointedly said, "I do not think that the right to procreate includes the right to get somebody else to procreate. We don't usually have constitutional rights by proxy. Paying somebody to have a baby is baby-selling. "

Keane and other representatives of the surrogate industry claim that the fee paid to the mother is not for the baby. As one of the lawyers of his center has said, "We don't pay a woman for carrying the baby. We are paying for her time and loss of convenience." In the surrogate parenting agreement, they claim that the money is compensation for services and expenses, and in no way is to be construed as a fee for termination of parental rights or a payment in exchange for consent to surrender the child for adoption. But if that is the case, why is it that if the mother delivers a stillborn baby or the baby dies, she receives only $1,000?

In practice, commercial surrogacy can thrive because of class differences and exploitation of poor women. Contracts are drawn mainly between upper-middle-class couples and working-class or lower-middle-class women. The Sterns have a joint income of more than $90,000 per year. Mary Beth Whitehead is married to a sanitation worker with a salary of $28,000 per year. The Sterns are highly educated professionals, a biochemist and a pediatrician. Mary Beth Whitehead, sixth of eight children of a schoolteacher and a beautician, left high school before graduation, married at age sixteen and had two children before her nineteenth birthday. The Sterns have spent $60,000 or $70,000 so far on fees for lawyers, private detectives, and expert witnesses. Mary Beth Whitehead was hoping to use the $10,000 for the education of her two children. Surrogate companies see women in poor economic conditions as more likely to "behave." As Noel Keane puts it in his book, "Rich women, after all, are not likely to become surrogate mothers."

A woman's infertility has been identified as an upper-middle-class or upper-class woman's issue, to be taken seriously only if she is married and if she can afford the $20,000 or so that is needed for the expensive "solutions" to the problem. These "solutions," like surrogacy or *in vitro* fertilization, are not available to most Black women in this country whose infertility rate is one-and-one-half times higher than that of white women, but who are predominantly poor. In fact, the concern regarding Black women is just the opposite. The family planning agencies and a racist medical establishment fear overpopulation by people of color and large families headed by females. If there really were a concern for the infertility of all women, we would be seeing a very different type of public health policy, one that emphasized prevention of infertility and education about its numerous causes. Even so, surrogacy is a most peculiar answer to a woman's infertility. It clearly is not a treatment: the woman remains infertile.

Surrogacy reinforces the classic Western patriarchal view that the woman is the incubator of the man's sperm. She receives it from him and gives it back to him. She is the "maternal environment" for the development of his progeny, reduced to a container. Thus it is no surprise that surrogacy contracts set up an enormous surveillance system for controlling women's lives. The woman has to agree not to smoke, drink, or use any drugs during pregnancy. She is bound to obey all medical instructions of the physicians involved in the case. She has to agree to avoid any activity that might be against her doctor's advice. She has to comply with a strict prenatal schedule of medical visits and testing. If the woman does not fulfill all these conditions, she is liable for all expenses and also damages. In the case of "Baby Cotton" (the first British commercial surrogate), the mother was not allowed to have a home birth because of the added risks.

When attorney William Handel of the Surrogate Parent Foundation in North Carolina was asked why the firm demands that the surrogate keep his firm informed of her whereabouts at all times, he answered candidly, "Because she's carrying my client's child. It's nice to know where she is at all times. If she moves, we have to know. If she changes employers or insurance, we have to know. If anything traumatic happens in her family such as a death or a job loss—anything that could materially affect the contract in any way whatsoever—we have to know. If anything comes up, we deal with it. She breaches the contract if she does not tell us."

A new case is coming soon to the courts that will make the Mary Beth Whitehead case look simple by comparison. For us as feminists, this case, which opened February 18 in San Diego, will bring up the unprecedented exploitation of Third World women through the use of their bodies as breeders. According to the information furnished to me by her cousin and defender Angela Garcia, Alejandra Muñoz, a twenty-year-old Mexican woman, was brought illegally to the United States to be inseminated by the husband of her cousin, Natti Haro. The couple first asked Angela Garcia, who is Natti Haro's sister, to serve as a surrogate, but she refused. Muñoz was then asked by a member of her family to "help" her cousin by agreeing to an "ovum transfer." The insemination was performed at home. However, one month into the pregnancy, Muñoz was told that the embryo transfer could not be done and that she would have to carry the pregnancy to term.

Muñoz signed an agreement in which the Haros agreed to pay her $1,500, already well below the standard commercial fee of $10,000. After she signed, the couple added in handwriting, "I will give up my rights to the baby." The Haros now have custody of the baby and Muñoz sees the baby three times a week. But having never agreed to be a "surrogate mother," Muñoz wants to keep the child.

Muñoz has a second-grade education, does not speak English, and cannot read handwritten writing. She has not been able to get her medical records in the United States because the birth certificate was signed by Natti Haro and she used Natti Haro's name for medical insurance purposes.

Merlen Schneidewind, the Haros's lawyer, in trying to justify the couple's right to the child, said, "I don't want to sound cold, but we're looking at an uneducated, illegal alien here with no visible means of support," conveniently leaving out the fact that Alejandra became an "illegal alien" because the Haros brought her into this country to breed a child for them.

The potential for exploitation of Third World women, of which the Alejandra Muñoz case is already an example, becomes even stronger when we realize that the combination of techniques of *in vitro* fertilization and embryo transfer makes possible what is called "total surrogacy." Up to now, women used as surrogates furnished the ovum for the creation of the embryo. The new technologies allow for an egg fertilized in the laboratory to be implanted in the uterus of another woman. This woman's womb will actually act as the incubator for the embryo without having any genetic connection to it. Two babies have already been produced this way: one in Australia and one in the United States. Up to now, racism and the demand for a certain kind of looks have protected Third World women from being used as rented wombs, but with the new technologies, where the woman's body will not furnish the egg, many more types of women become possible surrogates. Couples would be able to hire poor Third World women to carry their child at spectacularly low wages. Some businessmen, like John Stehura from the Bionetics Foundation, speculate that one-tenth the current fee could be paid to such women, as in the Muñoz case. Quoted in Gena Corea's *The Mother Machine* (Harper and Row, 1985), asked what countries he had in mind, Stehura replied, "Central America would be fine." A woman from the Third World who fulfilled this function could even have a serious health problem, he added, "however if her diet is good and other aspects of her life are okay, she could become a viable mother for a genuine embryo transfer."

The media often portray the surrogate wife as happily handing over the child to the contracting couple. But as women start speaking up, we might hear from many other women like Mary Beth Whitehead. For instance, Elizabeth Kane (a pseudonym) who was this nation's first surrogate, has now started to campaign against the surrogacy concept. Initially, she says, "I brainwashed myself. I have not been able to bury my feelings about the loss of my son. I thought if I could share my healthy body, it would be a Christian thing to do. I was very naive. I considered it a medical problem. If people donate their kidneys, why not an ovary? I think surrogate motherhood is a rip-off. The only people who benefit are the attorneys and physicians doing the insemination." Kane flew to New Jersey to see Mary Beth Whitehead after reading her story in *People* magazine. Kane now defines surrogate mothering as "transferring pain from one woman to another," referring to the pain and anguish of the infertile woman and the pain and anguish of the mother. She now believes that commercial surrogacy should be banned in the United States.

The cases presently in court are significant because they will start setting precedents about the legality and enforceability of surrogate contracts. Realizing that the situation is getting out of hand, state legislatures are beginning to develop legislation. In New York, for instance, a report by the State Judiciary Committee has recommended that contracts for surrogacy be "legal and enforceable," opening up the way for legal recognition of commercial surrogacy. This is a dangerous precedent because, as George Annas, professor of health law at Boston University, has pointed out, "Surrogate motherhood has enough potential legal and personal problems surrounding it that it is unlikely to ever become popular unless laws are developed that encourage it by clarifying its legal status."

How is commercial surrogacy dealt with in other parts of the world? In England, the Warnock Report (the report of a committee set up to provide guidelines for human fertilization and embryology) has recommended that all surrogacy agreements be considered illegal contracts and, therefore, unenforceable by the courts and that legislation be enforced to ban commercial surrogacy. In Melbourne, the capital of the state of Victoria in Australia, legislation makes it an offense, punishable by up to two years in prison, to give or receive payment for acting as a surrogate mother. It is also illegal to publish any advertisement seeking a surrogate or offering to act as one. However, unpaid volunteers may legally act as surrogates.

The surrogacy cases in U.S. courts should be seen in the context of what is happening in U.S. custody cases. More and more men are being granted custody upon request, while mothers are losing custody for any kind of behavior that may make them look like "unfit mothers" in the eyes of a judge. As U.S. feminist Carol Brown has pointed out, the present trend may have the effect of restoring "father right," the father's paramount right to children. As she says, "If the father wants the children for the social pleasures of this new unit of consumption, he is increasingly able to get them. If he does not want them, and most do not, then he need not have them. The freedom is his."

As we move ever more rapidly into a society where everything has a price tag, it is after all not much of a surprise that a new kind of entrepreneur has emerged, one dealing with newborn babies. Commercializing childbirth means that the dynamics of the market will enter directly into one of the few realms of our lives that had, up to now, resisted that intrusion. The rules of the capitalist market, when applied to women's bodies and reproductive power, institutionalize women as breeders and devalue motherhood. It turns children into commodities, making them into objects that can be bought, sold, or returned if defective. The commercialization of women's procreative power promotes the exploitation of women and constitutes an attack on the dignity of all human beings. It should not be allowed to continue.

Author's note: I wrote this article after a stimulating brainstorming session with FINRRAGE (Feminist International Network to Resist Reproductive and Genetic Engineering) members Gena Corea, Sarah Franklin, Shelley Minden, and Janice Raymond. I thank them for their ideas and comments. I especially thank Gena Corea and Alison Ward for generously providing me the contacts to gather unpublished information for this article. The responsibility for the ideas expressed in this article, however, rests wholly with me.

Editor's note: On February 3, 1988, the New Jersey Supreme Court ruled that surrogate mother contracts involving payment were illegal. However, custody of Melissa Stern remained with her biological father, William Stern. Elizabeth Stern's status as adoptive mother was nullified and, several months later, visitation rights for Mary Beth Whitehead were reinstated.

APRIL 1987

Of Fetuses and Women
by Ruth Hubbard, Nachama Wilker, and Marsha Saxton

On February 22, 1987, the Vatican announced its doctrine on human reproduction in light of newly available technologies of artificial insemination, surrogate motherhood, *in vitro* fertilization, embryo transfer, prenatal diagnosis, and fetal therapy. Entitled "Instruction on Respect for Human Life in Its Origin and on the Dignity of Procreation: Replies to Certain Questions of the Day," the document contains no surprises and is in line with the Vatican's previous pronouncements.

In brief, the instruction forbids all forms of procreation that are not direct outcomes of the "conjugal act"—sex within marriage. This includes artificial insemination between married partners, *in vitro* fertilization in which married partners provide both eggs and sperm (the only kind now offered in the United States), as well as, of course, the use of these technologies by single parents or unmarried and nontraditional couples. It also forbids any experimentation on human embryos since it forbids their creation or manipulation outside a woman's body. When it comes to prenatal diagnosis and fetal therapy, the instruction is more discriminating: it permits procedures intended to benefit the particular fetus and only forbids those that needlessly endanger that fetus or that are carried out with the intent of terminating the pregnancy if the fetus is shown to have a disability or disease.

We are women's health and disability rights activists who have voiced reservations of our own about some of these technologies or their specific uses. This has led some people to misinterpret our position as sympathetic to that of the Catholic Church or the so-called right-to-life movement.

As feminists, we do not accept the underlying premise that the issues associated with these newly available technologies revolve around whether or not they interfere with the "natural" process of reproduction within marriage. And we also insist that a woman has the right to choose when and how to bear children, which must include the right to abortion, whatever her reasons. We oppose the instruction because it focuses entirely on the well-being of the embryo or fetus and disregards the needs of prospective parents. It supports a recent trend that views pregnant women as "fetal environments," where the fetus takes on the rights of personhood and can be seen as having rights that may be in opposition to those of the pregnant woman.

This idea is put forward not only by the Catholic Church. Some supporters of abortion rights argue that, once a woman decides to carry a fetus to term, she waives her right to an abortion and assumes the responsibility to provide a "safe environment for the child to be born of sound mind and body." For example, in a recent court case in San Diego, a woman was brought up on charges of fetal neglect for not following her doctor's orders. The case was thrown out of court. However, increasingly, courts and medical professionals are presuming to "speak for the unborn child [sic]." The supervisor of the Santa Clara Juvenile Court Unit in California has gone as far as drafting proposed legislation that would "make the fetus a dependent of the juvenile court system in situations where the mother's behavior is judged to be harmful.... If a pregnant woman is not willing to follow court orders...she should be placed in a medically controlled environment—possibly against her will—where she and her fetus could be supervised."

This concern for "unborn children" is also reflected in exclusionary employment practices now in effect at some major corporations, such as Digital and AT&T, where protection of a "potential fetus" and the recognition of reproductive hazards in the workplace have resulted in women of childbearing age being removed or transferred, even though they were not pregnant nor trying to become pregnant at the time. Such policies shift the responsibility for securing a safe and healthy work environment from employers onto women employees. Potential hazards are controlled by removing the women and not the hazards themselves, while little or no acknowledgment is made of the reproductive risks these hazards pose to men.

As feminists, our reservations about prenatal diagnosis and fetal therapy stem rather from concern for the rights of women and of people with disabilities. We can assume that most people would prefer to be healthy and to have healthy children. The question is how best to assure health for the greatest number. The health problems of most infants who are born ill or disabled are due to the fact that they are born either prematurely or too small and undeveloped, even though they are born at term. The main reasons for both are poverty, malnutrition, smoking, use of alcohol and other drugs, and inadequate or no prenatal care of the mother. Recently, the *Boston Globe* has reported on the adverse impact of poverty and poverty-related problems on the health of babies and pregnant women, with the greatest burden falling on women of color. Despite the fact that this information is common knowledge, a great deal more money is being spent on expensive programs to care for these very sick newborns or to diagnose health problems of fetuses than on developing economic and health supports that would make more women able to have healthy babies.

Increasing numbers of prenatal tests are being developed to diagnose relatively rare genetic and developmental diseases, giving women the opportunity to decide whether they want to terminate a pregnancy. This can, indeed, benefit women who have health insurance or can pay for the tests, if they are sure that they do not want to birth a baby with the particular problem that the test detects. Many of the disabilities that are being diagnosed such as neural tube defects (NTDs), sickle cell anemia, or Down's syndrome, vary from mild to severe: the tests cannot predict the degree of disability, only that it exists. However many tests exist, they cannot assure a healthy fetus. Women will continue to have children who need special services and social supports. Disability rights advocates have been pointing out that for most people with disabilities, the disability is less a problem than the resulting oppression: hostility, discrimination, and lack of services are what make it difficult to live with a disability. The increasing preoccupation with diagnosing rare "defects" reinforces discriminatory attitudes toward people with disabilities and individualizes problems that, in fact, are largely social. It also increases the sense of personal responsibility individual women are made to feel for having healthy children.

We are also concerned about the high level of technical intervention of some of these technologies, especially *in vitro* fertilization. To enter *in vitro* programs, women must consent to risky, exploratory operations with a very small chance of a successful outcome. *In vitro* fertilization also provides some of the technical know-how necessary for genetic and other manipulations of early embryos and fetuses. While we do not share the Vatican's belief in the sanctity of embryos, we worry about the potential use of embryos for genetic engineering because scientists do not know enough about how genes work. Any genetic alteration of an early embryo, if it survives, will enter its germ cells (sperm or eggs) and can therefore be passed on to its descendants. Scientists call this "germ-line gene therapy." Recently, the Recombinant DNA Advisory Committee (RAC) of the National Institutes of Health rejected a proposal offered by the Boston-based Committee for Responsible Genetics (CRG) that such research be forbidden until further notice. At present, the U.S. government does not fund embryo research because this would require approval by a special review board, which the Reagan administration has failed to appoint in deference to the radical Right. In contrast to "fetal rights" advocates, our concern is not so much with the morality of using human embryos for research purposes, but with the risks of manipulating embryos that will be implanted and allowed to develop.

Another objection we have with all these technologies is their expense, which by definition makes them accessible only to women and couples who can pay for them. This is especially important in the United States, which is the only industrialized nation besides South Africa without some form of national health insurance or national health service. So while poor women, and especially poor women of color, are still subject to medically unnecessary sterilizations, expensive technologies to counter infertility are being developed for those who can pay.

Since women are the ones who care for children, they must have access to the services they believe they need. Therefore, although we are skeptical that the development of increasing numbers of procedures for prenatal diagnosis and therapy benefits women, equity demands that the technologies that exist be available to all women, irrespective of their ability to pay. This means that women must get sufficient information about the tests, in a form they can understand within their own cultural context, so that they can make informed decisions about whether to use them.

Women must have the right to refuse prenatal tests and fetal therapy even if these become standard medical practice, because any attempt to test or treat a fetus requires that a procedure be done on the pregnant woman. Medical personnel and insurance carriers must not be able to discriminate against a woman or her future child because she has refused to have her fetus tested or treated in utero, and the courts must not have the power to force a woman to undergo such procedures.

Developing a feminist position on prenatal technologies is complex because, as always, we must take into account the diversity of women's needs, wishes, resources, and experiences, and also acknowledge the many contradictory pressures society puts on women to do what is "best" for our children.

JANUARY 1995

Reproductive Technologies Are Here to Stay

by Dion Farquhar

The question of whether reproductive technologies benefit or harm their users, providers, and society as a whole has become an important element of contemporary feminist debate. In 1993, there were 267 facilities offering assisted reproduction in the United States (not counting alternative donor insemination) that performed 43,975 cycles of treatment (Society for Reproductive Technology, 1993 Results). Reproductive technologies provide the medical capability to remove human eggs and sperm from one set of bodies, perform operations on them, and return them to the same female body, place them in another female body, or cryopreserve them. In addition to removing fertilization from the interior of women's bodies and transferring it to the laboratory, reproductive technologies also remove male ejaculation from its endpoint in the female body, reducing it to masturbation in clinic bathrooms.

All reproductive technologies separate reproduction from heterosexual sex and marriage. Potentially, that separation makes reproduction possible for those outside of the traditional heterosexual couple, offering new democratic family and parenting options. Not only are new individuals conceived as a result of technology, but so are new family, kinship, and parenting practices. Assistive reproductive technologies are expanding and challenging traditional views of just who may mother (or parent) a child today. Single heterosexual women, lesbians, single men, gay couples, and older women have fought for, and won, access to medical treatment. As more and more nontraditional would-be parents use the technologies, the ironclad identification of "mothering" with biology, heterosexuality, or even women, no longer holds.

Although there are obvious social benefits to removing reproduction from its biological constraints, many feminists take a passionately antitechnology position. I want to argue that because reproductive technologies are a growing part of the U.S. social, economic, and medical scene, the point is not to be for or against them, but to ask what contributions they might make to the realization of feminist goals. Our choices are not just between rejecting the technology entirely or debating it uncritically. Reproductive technology, like maternity, is neither entirely oppressive and exploitative nor all-empowering and fulfilling. A woman's relation to reproductive technologies will depend on many complex biographical and historical factors.

Antitechnology feminists such as Rita Arditti, Gena Corea, Andrea Dworkin, Janice Raymond, Robyn Rowland, Patricia Spallone, and others have produced a large body of literature opposing assistive reproductive technologies for their complicity with the Western liberal medical model of "disease," their essential sexual objectification of women's bodies and reproductive capacities, and for their unkindness to and abuse of women's bodies. Some of the points made by these antitechnology feminists are important and useful: e.g., their critique of our culture's compulsory natalism and the endemic sexism and racism of the Western medical model; their analysis of the problem of class (the high cost of using these technologies severely restricts access and encourages the exploitation of desperate donors); and their exposure of the fertility clinics' false claims and misleading statistics on success rates. The problem is that in demonizing the technology, these theorists preclude admitting any liberatory potential for these technologies, which sometimes do satisfy the desires of individuals to have children and may also expand our cultural understandings of family and kinship.

Ambivalence Toward Maternity

Underlying the demonization of technology that is evident in the opposition to assistive reproductive technologies is a radical ambivalence toward maternity. On the one hand, the antitechnology writing brims with an antinatalist stance that configures women's nurturance as unequivocally supportive of patriarchal domination. Women's desires for maternity are seen as the externally imposed burden of patriarchal ideology, a parasitic sapping of women's physical and emotional energies that deflects women's time and attention from more important aspects of public life—knowledge, power, money, and so on. Antinatalists find the whole project of helping women reproduce and become either genetic and/or gestational mothers problematic because it reinforces the already near-compulsory cultural bias toward maternity. The only shift, according to this antinatalist vision, is that rather than being controlled by individual men through marriage, women will be controlled by science and technology. Childbearing in this view is either rejected or suffered.

The same antitechnology literature, however, sometimes glorifies motherhood as the apogee of care and nurturance, the basis for an alternative ethics, and the source of women-centered knowledge. This pronatalist stance, though, is limited to "naturally" achieved maternity. Technological intervention is opposed on the grounds that it fragments unitary maternity, threatens to displace "natural" motherhood, and interferes in "natural" maternal processes. Pronatalist "natural" maternity is seen as unambiguously enriching to (all) women just as for the antinatalists, maternity is seen as a patriarchal rip-off of (all) women's unpaid and unappreciated reproductive and emotional labor.

This contradictory discourse forces antitechnology feminists to invoke "false consciousness" to explain (mostly) middle-class white women's escalating demand for high technology infertility services: "But sometimes women also collude because we have been brainwashed. The information and education we get is one-sided and male-centered and the hidden conviction creeps into our own minds that men and their technology must be better than our own body and our own experiences with it," writes Renate Duelli Klein ("What's 'New' about the 'New' Reproductive Technologies?" in *Man-Made Women: How New Reproductive Technologies Affect Women,* edited by Gena Corea et al. [Indiana University Press, 1987]). Reproductive technologies all "violate the integrity of a woman's body in ways that are dangerous, destructive, debilitating, demeaning; they are a form of medical violence against women," argues Janice Raymond in her latest book, *Women as Wombs* (Harper Collins, 1993). For anitechnologists, the female "experience" is universal; there are no exceptions, no individuals for whom they do not speak.

Whether pronatalist, antinatalist, or both, anitechnologists basically displace feminist ambivalence toward motherhood onto the technologies themselves. As feminist writer Michelle Stanworth, in her article "Birth Pangs" (*Conflicts in Feminism,* edited by Marianne Hirsch and Evelyn Fox Keller [Routledge, 1990]), has noted: "A focus on the degrading impact of conceptive technologies is attractive, perhaps, because it seems to make possible the impossible: to attack the coercive aspects of maternity, the way that motherhood makes victims of women—and to do so in the name of motherhood itself." In attacking technology, however, we hold infertile women to a higher standard of political purity, particularly since feminists have never successfully countered the pronatalist expectations of our society. Generally, we live in a culture in which "childlessness" is frowned upon and motherhood is still taken for granted.

The Technology Debate

A deep ambivalence about motherhood, however, is not the only reason that some feminists oppose reproductive technologies. Antitechnology feminists also write about the superficiality of the interventions. They assert that the high-tech medical treatment of infertility is a "quick fix" rather than a correction of underlying pathology. Prescribing *in vitro* fertilization (IVF) for the treatment of blocked, diseased, or absent fallopian tubes only bypasses them, providing a technological "fix" without ameliorating the underlying problem. Though this may be true, why should we necessarily feel that it is problematic to circumvent the malfunctioning part of the conception process, if this is the most direct route to bearing a child?

A related objection of antitechnology feminists to high-tech treatments is that they fail to address the underlying macro-epidemiological causes of infertility: environmental pollution, workplace toxicity, iatrogenic (physician induced) factors, untreated or undiagnosed pelvic inflammatory disease, among others. Ignoring such epidemiological evidence, they argue, greedy high-technology promoters focus only on treating the individual once she or he is found to be infertile.

Both of these antitechnology arguments point out critical gaps in the medical and popular representations of reproductive technologies; they are entirely valid as social analyses. These criticisms, however, like all the others, excoriate the technologies for their individual focus and failure to address the social causes of infertility without providing any possibilities for infertile people. The antitechnology position suggests that infertile women, whose wills are porous ciphers of the patriarchy, should "choose" to forego the use of such technologies. As Gena Corea and Jalna Hanmer have written in the prologue to *Made to Order: The Myth of Reproductive and Genetic Progress* (Pergamon Press, 1987), "the desire of some individual women to 'choose' this technology places women as a group at risk. With the new reproductive technologies, women are being used as living laboratories and are slowly but surely being divorced from control over procreation."

This position endorses a reproductive double standard for infertile people, approving, albeit idealizing, those who reproduce "naturally" and opposing the use of technology as pronatalist for those who experience physical or social obstacles. The imposition of a strict politically pure double standard on infertile people who wish to use such technologies is like blaming cancer patients for "choosing" individualist therapies like chemotherapy or radiation rather than campaigning for the reduction of pesticides or pollutants. Infertile people are no more or less responsible than the rest of the population for campaigning for a healthier environment or sterility prevention.

Conclusion

Like many aspects of life in the contemporary United States, reproductive technologies are a mixed blessing. There seems no point in simply opposing them, since they are here to stay. Moreover, why not endorse their contribution to ameliorating involuntary childlessness, while criticizing their problematic aspects? Reproductive technologies have the potential to change radically the nature of family and kinship. As feminists, we should seek to expand women's access to these technologies, to regulate the provision of services, and to build a social movement that addresses environmental causes of male and female sterility and infertility.

© 1994 Marilyn Humphries

© 1992 Marilyn Humphries

© 1992 Marilyn Humphries

CHAPTER FIVE

Women's Health

As we have seen in the previous chapter, the struggle for women's control over their bodies has been central to the feminist agenda. The struggle has taken place on many fronts: court battles have challenged laws limiting reproductive rights, street demonstrations have targeted beauty pageants and advertising that exploits women's bodies, and self-help groups have taught women basic facts about their own bodies. These self-help groups, which sprang up in the late '60s and early '70s, often as an outgrowth of consciousness-raising activities, formed the foundation of the women's health movement.

The early women's health movement was closely related to the movement for reproductive rights. As consciousness-raising groups turned their focus to sex and reproduction, women became acutely aware of how they had been denied knowledge of their own bodies, leaving control of all reproductive-related health needs—from birth control and abortion to pregnancy and childbirth—in the hands of the male medical establishment.

Historical research revealed that this had not always been the case. Women throughout the world had once been healers and midwives, and in many cultures, the tradition continued. However, in Europe, during the sixteenth and seventeenth centuries, many women healers were persecuted as "witches." Much of the art of healing through herbs and other natural remedies was lost as physicians took control of medicine. In the nineteenth century, U.S. medical doctors gained full control over their profession, by establishing training programs and licensing requirements that excluded women and people of color. Midwives found it more and more difficult to practice their art, as male doctors turned female reproductive functions into "illnesses" that only they could treat. Pregnancy and childbirth, once seen as a natural part of the female life cycle, became subject to medical interventions that often proved detrimental to women's health. Women began to ask questions: why were they unconscious when they gave birth? How could a drug as harmful as DES have been approved for preventing miscarriages? Why does the United States have such a high rate of cesarean sections and hysterectomies?

To regain control over their bodies, women realized they needed information. Self-help groups were one means of attaining that information. Modeled on consciousness-raising groups, they took the body as their subject. Women examined their own cervixes with mirrors and speculums, learning to recognize signs of health and illness. They also taught themselves to do menstrual extractions, a relatively simple procedure that could prevent pregnancy. They sought out information on alternative treatments for vaginal infections, menstrual cramps, and symptoms of menopause. In 1969, the Boston Women's Health Book Collective gathered much of this information together for the first time. With the publication of the self-help manual *Our Bodies, Ourselves*, the women's health movement had come into its own. By 1973, *Our Bodies, Ourselves* had sold 250,000 copies.

Early issues of *Sojourner* gave prominent coverage to the women's health movement, which by 1975 was having a profound impact on women's lives. Articles covered the opening of a women's health clinic in Cambridge, Massachusetts; encouraged women to consider using midwives rather than doctors for prenatal care and delivery; and reported on self-help forums sponsored by the Boston Women's Health Book Collective and other organizations. An August 1977 news story even reported a health-related civil disobedience action. Some 30 women attending a national conference for women involved in the feminist health movement conducted an inspection of the Tallahassee Memorial Hospital's maternity wing. According to *Sojourner*, "the inspection exposed unsafe and inhumane childbirth practices such as drugging of women in labor and misuse of fetal heart monitors leading to excessively high cesarean section rates." Four of those involved—including Carol Downer, a founder of the Feminist Women's Health Center in Los Angeles—were arrested and convicted on charges of criminal trespass.

Health activists like Downer understood the radical nature of the work that they had begun. During a 1972 police raid on the L.A. women's health center, Downer and Colleen Wilson had been arrested and charged with practicing medicine without a license—for administering yogurt for vaginal infections.

Though Downer won the "yogurt conspiracy" case, feminist health centers have barely managed to stay alive. Licensing regulations—designed to support the medical establishment—along with the virulent antiabortion movement (feminist clinics immediately began providing abortions following *Roe v. Wade*) have forced many clinics to close their doors, limiting women's access to health care to places like Planned Parenthood, for-profit abortion clinics, or traditional medical practices. Generally, these environments do not promote the self-help techniques popularized by the feminist clinics of the '70s.

Though few feminist health clinics have survived, the self-help movement had a profound impact on health care delivery, particularly for white, middle-class women. In learning more about their bodies, these women became more confident in approaching the medical system and demanding better care. Though women are still often ignored and mistreated by the medical establishment, more options are available. There are far more women doctors who run women-centered practices; midwifery services are once again available in most states; birthing rooms have replaced impersonal delivery rooms in many hospitals; and more information is available—*Our Bodies, Ourselves* is only one of several books now published by the Boston Women's Health Book Collective. Today, in any women's bookstore, you can find hundreds of books addressing women's physical and mental health needs.

As the health landscape changed for white, middle-class women, the urgency behind the self-help movement dissipated. This is evident in *Sojourner*'s lack of attention to self-help concepts throughout the '80s. Then, in 1989, Byllye Avery renewed the discussion with her article on the National Black Women's Health Project ("Black Women's Health: A Conspiracy of Silence"). Researching the subject of Black women's health, Avery discovered the women of her community suffered from extraordinarily poor health—and she decided to do something about it. Applying the self-help concept, she began to organize small groups of Black women to talk about their lives and learn about their bodies. Through the National Black Women's Health Project, similar groups have now been established in 42 states as well as in Nigeria, Cameroon, Brazil, and several Central American countries.

The self-help concept has spread to other communities, too; Asian-American and Latina health projects have sprung up as well as Boston's Women of Color Coalition for Health (see Linda Wong, "Women of Color Coalition for Health," 1993). These projects tend to focus on culturally specific educational workshops, self-help groups, and advocacy for women who find it difficult to access care through the Western medical system. These women may be immigrants who don't speak English, they may have very different cultural understandings of health and sickness, or they may simply be poor and of color and, therefore, mistreated by the Western medical establishment.

In addition to these kinds of self-help projects, focused primarily on communities of color, in the '90s, there has been an upsurge in self-help groups among college-age women who fear that abortion will once again become illegal (see Rachel Lanzerotti, "Women's Health in Women's Hands," 1992). More like the groups of the early '70s, members of these self-help groups see themselves as political radicals engaged in a form of civil disobedience. Like their predecessors, they focus on gynecological health and on performing menstrual extractions for group members.

Even more than the crisis around abortion access, however, it has been AIDS and breast cancer that have placed health care once again at the forefront of the feminist agenda. AIDS activists, who initially drew on civil rights, antiwar, and feminist traditions of protest and civil disobedience to create a new brand of "in-your-face" activism have inspired women health activists to return to the streets—and to broaden their agenda to include the health needs of poor women without access to insurance or service providers. Today, groups such as WHAM! (Women's Health Action and Mobilization) and the Boston Women's Community Cancer Project are changing the face of women's health care, by using direct action to focus attention on gender inequities in the allocation of research and treatment funds.

Although in the late '70s and early '80s, AIDS was seen as a "gay male" disease, by the mid '80s, many feminists, particularly lesbians, had become involved in AIDS advocacy, service, and activist organizations (see Cindy Patton, "Feminists Have Avoided the Issue of AIDS," 1985). Today, women are the fastest-growing infected population, and it is women who continue to press to see that the needs of HIV-infected women are being met (see Laura Briggs, "Women, AIDS, and Activism," 1995). Feminist AIDS activists have successfully demanded that the Centers for Disease Control change the definition of AIDS to include opportunistic infections that affect women. They have also lobbied to improve women's access to clinical drug trials and have created safe-sex information targeted toward particular populations, such as prostitutes IV drug users, lesbians or women of particular ethnic backgrounds.

One of the great legacies of AIDS activism, beyond its impact on the political and medical establishment's response to AIDS itself, has been the emergence of the women's breast cancer movement. Thus far, this movement has had a three-part agenda: to press the federal government to spend more money on breast cancer research, to change the research agenda from its focus on genetic causes to environmental toxins, and to raise public awareness about the dramatic increase in the numbers of women diagnosed with the disease in recent years. The movement has also drawn on the self-help concept of the '70s, establishing support groups, buddies, and underground treatment networks to help women who are living with the disease.

Sojourner's coverage of the breast cancer movement began in 1989, with the publication of Susan Shapiro's "Cancer as a Feminist Issue." Shapiro's article resulted in the formation of Boston's Women's Community Cancer Project, one of the first feminist groups in the country to begin to expose the politics of breast cancer research and treatment. As such groups began to organize in other parts of the country, the National Breast Cancer Coalition emerged, and breast cancer became part of the national health care agenda. "One in Nine," the slogan of the grassroots movement (a reference to figures that came out in the early '90s indicating that women had a one in nine lifetime chance of contracting the disease), has become part of our everyday discourse.

The emergence of this grassroots movement is reflected in a dramatic increase in the coverage of women and cancer, particularly breast cancer, in the pages of *Sojourner* throughout the '90s. During this period, *Sojourner* covered breast cancer more often than any other women's illness, with stories about environmental causes; the choices that must be made around cancer treatments, particularly mastectomy; how-to guides to breast self-exam; and personal reflections on illness and recovery (see Linda Quint Freeman, "The Breast Cancer I Have," 1993). These articles not only increased awareness around breast cancer issues but repoliticized women's understandings of our health care.

In addition to physical health, feminists have long been concerned with women's mental health and our treatment by the psychiatric profession. As early as 1972, Phyllis Chesler challenged the mental health system in her book *Women and Madness* (Doubleday). In 1975, Boston feminists founded the Elizabeth Stone House (see Molly Lovelock, "She Ain't Heavy, She's My Sister," 1982). The Stone House brought feminist principles to mental health care by using lay workers in a group setting to help women recover from the physical and emotional traumas that made them "crazy." Over the years, the work of researchers such as Jean Baker Miller (*Toward a New Psychology of Women,* Beacon Press, 1976), who have shown that women recover their mental health by building positive relationships, has been incorporated into the Stone House treatment plan.

Though highly successful (the Stone House recently celebrated its twentieth anniversary), feminist-oriented psychiatric care, particularly in institutional settings, is still not readily available. Judith Vincent's 1990 story of her treatment at a traditional psychiatric hospital ("Where I Bin") and Kate Millet's "Psychiatry's Crimes" (1991) make it evident that psychiatric institutions are still more often used to "keep women in their place" than to help them become independent and self-assertive human beings. The mental health liberation movement continues to fight the labeling, and subsequent discrimination, that mental patients face after hospitalization, as well as the abusive use of psychotropic drugs.

Since 1990, *Sojourner*'s annual health supplement has been one of its most popular issues. The topics covered in this chapter—the self-help movement, AIDS, cancer, and mental health—are only a few of those that *Sojourner* and the women's health movement have addressed over the years. Particularly important have been articles on alternative treatments for common female ailments such as PMS, endometriosis, substance abuse, and depression; the latest research on sexually transmitted diseases such as HPV; the debate over estrogen-replacement therapy for menopausal women; and the politics of the recovery movement (particularly with regard to "addictions" such as food, sex, and codependent relationships). There have also been discussions of diseases such as chronic fatigue syndrome, environmental illness, and lupus, all of which seem to affect women more often than men. During the early '90s, when health care topped the national agenda, *Sojourner*'s feminist writers tried to examine issues that were often marginalized in the discussion of national health care: for example, how does poverty impact health outcomes? What kind of care do women in prison receive? How will disabled women fare under the proposed national health plan? Will women be guaranteed full reproductive rights? What would be the advantages of a single-payer plan?

The national health care debate made abundantly clear what feminists had been saying for some time: health care is a political issue. As health care once again slips from national consciousness, it is up to feminists and other health activists to shape a national health care agenda that speaks to the needs of women, lesbians and gay men, people of color, and all people who are unable to access safe and affordable care.

NOVEMBER 1975

Women's Bodies: Self-Help
by Camille Motta

The women's movement has done a lot for us. It has taken some of us out of the kitchen, given us decent jobs and assured us of equal pay for those jobs. The movement has shown us that we are people, that we can function in the outside world and that, moreover, we don't necessarily need men to do it. In the process of gaining our personhood, women have pretty much experienced with each other and learned through each other. We have found ourselves through ourselves. In the sphere of our bodies and our health this is also the case. Self-help is women sharing their experiences, knowledge, and feelings. It is a positive act by which we learn of our own bodies and become comfortable enough with them so that we know and recognize when we are healthy and when we are not. Self-help is examining our own bodies. It is learning, by doing breast and cervical self-exams, what is normal and what is not. It is control over our own lives. Self-help is women relating to ourselves in order to demystify health care, the medical profession, and our own bodies.

Self-help is at the base of all the programs offered by the Women's Community Health Center in Cambridge. A collective of women who believe that they provide choices for women that the present health care system does not, the Women's Community Health Center was first conceived in the minds of several women in August 1973. At the first annual Women's Health Conference held in Boston in November 1973, a core group was formed dedicated to starting a women-owned and -controlled health center. Through frequent meetings the group solidified, and with highly successful fundraising programs, by April 1974 the Hampshire Street office was opened. Self-help groups began meeting. These are informal action-discussion groups geared toward understanding and sharing information about women's bodies and women's health care. Topics include breast and cervical self-exam, birth control, sexuality, and paramedical skills. These groups start each month and are held in four three-hour sessions.

In July 1974, the center began gynecological services and women doctors joined the staff: Florence Haseltine, Barbara Roberts, Suzanne Riggs. By September 1974, pregnancy screening and counseling services were underway, and a few months later, medical nights began to be held two to three times a week. In April 1975, special interest self-help groups were formed such as lesbian health care, menopause, and others. First-trimester abortions were first performed in May 1975, and the initial step in the procedure for clinic licensure, the certificate of need (a document stating that there is a need for this service), was approved by June 1975.

The Women's Community Health Center has thus evolved into a highly active and sorely needed women's health place. It is a center where women can learn about their bodies in a supportive, information-sharing atmosphere. All explanations are thorough, so that each woman can make educated decisions about her own health care. Charges are kept as low as possible. In addition to the above services, the center does phone referrals and counseling, maintains a reference library, which includes books, pamphlets, magazine articles, and news clippings of items of interest to women and issues fact sheets on such topics as vaginal infections and natural methods of birth control. Child care is provided upon request during services, and Spanish and Portuguese-speaking health workers are available.

This article has been edited for clarity and length.

JANUARY 1989

Black Women's Health: A Conspiracy of Silence
by Byllye Avery

The following is an edited version of a talk that Byllye Avery, director of the National Black Women's Health Project, gave in Cambridge, Massachusetts, in July 1988.

Getting Involved

I got involved in women's health around the issue of abortion. There were three of us at the University of Florida, in Gainesville, who just seemed to get picked out by women who needed abortions. They came to us. I didn't know anything about abortions. In my life that word couldn't even be mentioned without having somebody look at you crazy. Then someone's talking to me about how to get an abortion. It seemed unreal. But as more women came (and, at first, they were mostly white women), we found out this New York number we could give them, and they could catch a plane and go there for their abortions. But then a Black woman came and we gave her the number, and she looked at us in awe: "I can't get to New York..." We realized we needed a different plan of action, so in May 1974 we opened up the Gainesville Women's Health Center.

As we learned more about abortions and gynecological care, we immediately started to look at birth and to realize that we are women with a total reproductive cycle. We might have to make different decisions about our lives, but whatever the decision, we deserved the best services available. So, in 1978, we opened up Birthplace, an alternative birthing center. It was exhilarating work; I assisted in probably around 200 births. I understood life, and working in birth, I understood death, too. I certainly learned what's missing in prenatal care, and why so many of our babies die.

Birthplace

Through my work at Birthplace, I learned the importance of our being involved in our own health. We have to create environments that say "yes." Birthplace was a wonderful space. It was a big, old turn-of-the-century house that we decorated with antiques. We went to people's houses and, if we liked something, we begged for it—things off their walls, furniture, rugs. We fixed the place so that when women walked in, they would say, "Byllye, I was excited when I got up today because this was my day to come to Birthplace." That's how prenatal care needs to be given—so that people are excited when they come. It's about eight and a half or nine months that a person comes on a continuous basis. That is the time to start affecting her life so that she can start making meaningful lifestyle changes. So you see, health provides us with all sorts of opportunities for empowerment.

Through Birthplace, I came to understand how important our attitude around birthing is. Many women don't get the exquisite care they deserve. They go to these large facilities, and they don't understand the importance of prenatal care. They ask, "Why is it so important for me to get in here and go through all this hassle?" We have to work around that.

Through the work of Birthplace, we have created a prenatal caring program that provides each woman who comes for care with a support group. She enters the group when she arrives, leaves the group to go for her physical checkup, and then returns to the group when she is finished. She doesn't sit in a waiting room for two hours. Most of these women have nobody to talk to. No one listens to them; no one helps them plan. They're asking: "Who's going to get me to the hospital if I go into labor in the middle of the night, or the middle of the day, for that matter? Who's going to help me get out of this abusive relationship? Who's going to make sure I have the food I need to eat?" Infant mortality is not a medical problem, it's a social problem.

One of the things that Black women have started talking about regarding infant mortality is that many of us are like empty wells; we give a lot, but we don't get much back. We're asked to be strong. I have said, "If one more person says to me that Black women are strong I'm going to scream in their face." I am so tired of that stuff. What are you going to do—just lay down and die? We have to do what's necessary to survive. It's just a part of living. But most of us are empty wells that really never get replenished. Most of us are dead inside. We are walking around dead. That's why we end up in relationships that reinforce that particular thought. So you're talking about a baby being alive inside of a dead person; it just won't work.

We need to stop letting doctors get away with piling up all this money, buying all these little machines. They can keep the tiniest little piece of protoplasm alive, and then it goes home and it dies. You see what I'm saying? All this foolishness with putting all this money back into their pockets on that end of the care and not on the other end has to stop. When are we going to wake up?

Black Women's Health Project

I left the birthing center around 1980 or '81, mostly because we needed more midwives and I wasn't willing to go to nursing school. But an important thing had happened for me around 1979. I began looking at myself as a Black woman. Before that I had been looking at myself as a woman. When I left the birthing center, I went to work in a CETA [Comprehensive Education and Training Act] program at a community college, and it brought me face-to-face with my sisters and face-to-face with myself. Just by the nature of the program and the population that I worked with, I had, for the first time in my life, a chance to ask a nineteen-year-old why—please give me a reason why—you have four babies and you're only nineteen years old? And I was able to listen and bring these sisters together to talk about their lives. It was there that I started to understand the lives of Black women and to realize that we live in a conspiracy of silence. It was hearing these women's stories that led me to start conceptualizing the Black Women's Health Project.

First I wanted to do an hour-long presentation on Black women's health issues, so I started doing research. I got all the books, and I was shocked at what I saw. I was angry—angry that the people who wrote these books didn't put it into a format that made sense to us, angry that nobody was saying anything to Black women or to Black men. I was so angry I threw the book across the room and it stayed there for three or four days, because I knew I had just seen the tip of the iceberg, but I also knew enough to know that I couldn't go back. I had opened my eyes, and I had to go on and look.

Instead of an hour-long presentation, we had a conference. It didn't happen until 1988, but when it did, 2,000 women came. But I knew we couldn't just have a conference. From the health statistics I saw, I knew that there was a deeper problem. People needed to be able to work individually, and on a daily basis. So we got the idea of self-help groups. The first group we formed was in a rural area outside of Gainesville, with 21 women who were severely obese. I thought, "Oh this is a piece of cake. Obviously, these sisters don't have any information. I'll go in here and talk to them about losing weight, talk to them about high blood pressure, talk to them about diabetes—it'll be easy."

Little did I know that when I got there, they would be able to tell me everything that went into a 1200-calorie-a-day diet. They all had been to Weight Watchers at least five or six times; they all had blood-pressure reading machines in their homes as well as medications they were on. And when we sat down to talk, they said, "We know all that information, but what we also know is that living in the world that we are in, we feel like we are absolutely nothing." One woman said to me, "I work for General Electric making batteries, and, from the stuff they suit me up in, I know it's killing me." She said, "My home life is not working. My old man is an alcoholic. My kid's got babies. Things are not well with me. And the one thing I know I can do when I come home is cook me a pot of food and sit down in front of the TV and eat it. And you can't take that away from me until you're ready to give me something in its place."

So that made me start to think that there was something else to this health piece that had been really missing, that it's not just about giving information, people need something else. We just spent a lot of time talking. And while we were talking, we were planning the 1988 conference, so I took the information back to the planning committee. And Lillie Allen was there. And she brought the understanding that we are dying inside. That unless we are able to go inside of ourselves and touch and breathe fire, breathe life into ourselves, that, of course, we couldn't be healthy.

Lillie started working on a workshop called, "Black and Female: What Is the Reality?" This is a workshop that all of us are terrified of. And we are also terrified not to have it, because the conspiracy of silence is killing us.

Living with Violence

As we started to talk, I looked at those health statistics in a new way. Now, I'm not saying that we are not suffering from the things we die from—that's what the statistics give us. But what causes all this sickness? Like cardiovascular disease—it's the number one killer. What causes all that heart pain? When sisters take their shoes off and start talking about what's happening, the first thing we cry about is violence. The violence in our lives. And if you look in statistics books, they mention violence in one paragraph. They don't even give numbers, because they can't count it: it's too pervasive.

The number one issue for most of our sisters is violence—battering, sexual abuse. Same thing for their daughters, whether they are twelve or four. We have to look at how violence is used, how violence and sexism go hand in hand, and how it affects the sexual response of females. We have to stop that line, because that insult is the training ground for us.

When you talk to young people about being pregnant, you find out a lot of things. Number one is that most of these girls did not get pregnant by teenage boys; most of them got pregnant by their mother's boyfriends or their brothers or their daddies. We've been sitting on that. We can't just tell our daughters, "just say no." What do they do about all those feelings running around their bodies? And we need to talk to our brothers. We need to tell them, the incest makes us crazy. It's something that stays on our minds all the time. We need the men to know that. And they need to know that when they hurt us, they hurt themselves. 'Cause we are their mothers, their sisters, their wives; we are their allies on this planet. They can't just damage one part of it without damaging themselves. We need men to stop giving consent, by their silence, to rape, to sexual abuse, to violence. You need to talk to your boyfriends, your husbands, your sons, whatever males you have around you—talk to them about talking to other men. When they are sitting around womanizing, talking bad about women, make sure you have somebody stand up and be your ally and help stop this. For future generations, this thing has got to stop somewhere.

Mothers and Daughters

If violence is the number one thing women talk about, the next thing is being mothers too early and too long. We've developed a documentary called *On Becoming a Woman: Mothers and Daughters Talking Together.* It's eight of us mothers and daughters—sixteen ordinary people talking about extraordinary things.

The idea of the film came out of my own experience with my daughter. When Sonja turned eleven, I started bemoaning that there were no rituals left; there was nothing to let a girl know that once you get your period your life can totally change, nothing to celebrate that something wonderful is happening. So I got a cake that said, "Happy Birthday! Happy Menstruation!" It had white icing with red writing. I talked about the importance of becoming a woman, and, out of that, I developed a workshop for the public schools for mothers and daughters. I did the workshops in Gainesville, and, when we came to Atlanta, I started doing them there. The film took ten years from the first glimmer of an idea to completion.

The film is in three parts. In the first part, all the mothers talk about when we got our periods. Then the daughters who have their periods talk about getting theirs, and the ones who are still waiting talk about that. The second part of the film deals with contraception, birth control, anatomy, and physiology. This part of the film is animated, so it keeps the kids' attention. It's funny. It shows all the anxiety: passing around condoms, hating it, saying, "Oh no, we don't want to do this."

The third part of the film is the hardest. Here, Lillie works on communication with the mothers and daughters. We feel that the key to birth control and to controlling reproduction is the nature of the relationship between the parents and their young people. And what's happening is that everybody is willing to beat up on the young kids, asking, "Why did you get pregnant? Why did you do this?" No one is saying to the parents, "Do you need some help with learning how to talk to your young person? Do you want someone to sit with you? Do you want to see what it feels like?" We don't have anything. In this film, you see us struggling.

What Lillie does, which was hard for the parents, is that she creates a safe space where everybody can say anything they need to say. And if you think about that, as parents, we have that relationship with our kids: we can ask them anything. But when we talk about sex, it's special to be in a space where the kids may ask us, "Mama, what do you do when you start feeling funny all in your body?" What the kids want to know is, what about lust? What do we do about it? And that's the very information that we don't want to give up. That's "our business." But they want to hear it from us, because they trust us. And we have to struggle with how we do that: How do we share that information? How do we deal with our feelings?

Current Projects

The last thing I want to talk to you about are our current projects. We have 96 self-help groups in 22 states, 6 groups in Kenya, and a group in Barbados and 1 in Belize. In addition, we were just funded by the W. K. Kellogg Foundation to do some work in three housing projects in Atlanta. We received $1,032,000 for a three-year period to set up three community centers. The first is in the MacDaniel Glen Project.

At MacDaniel Glen, the community center space had been closed for four years. We convinced them that we could get this grant, and the housing authority spent

$55,000 fixing up the space. It's painted mauve and cream; there are new tiles on the floor, and we decorated it up to the ceiling. Our plan is to do health screening and referral for adolescents and women, and in addition to hook them up to whatever social services they need—help cut through the red tape. There will be a computerized learning and individualized tutorial program to help young women get their GEDs, along with a whole panel from the community who will be working on job readiness skills. And we'll be doing our self-help groups—talking about who we are, examining, looking at ourselves. You'll have to commit yourself to eight sessions.

In year two, we'll open up another facility, and in year three, a third one. The success of this program rides on our ability to work ourselves out of the job, because at the end of three years, we want it to be in the hands of the tenants. They'll direct the program, although the staff, director, social service people, and nurse may come from outside. Self-help developers and teen developers will be hired from inside the community. Fundraising will have to be done locally.

We hope this will be a model program that can be duplicated anywhere. And we're excited about it. Folks thought it was a big deal for a group of Black women to get a million dollars in Atlanta. We thought it was pretty good, too. Our time is coming.

This article has been edited for length.

This essay also appeared in The Black Women's Health Book: Speaking for Ourselves, *edited by Evelyn C. White (Seal Press, 1990.)*

MARCH 1992

Women's Health in Women's Hands

by Rachel Lanzerotti

Recognizing that women have been denied knowledge of our bodies, feminists have struggled on many fronts to put control of women's bodies into women's hands. Following on feminism's second wave in the late '60s, feminist health activists of the '70s promoted the concept of "self-help." They spawned a movement of women determined to learn about their bodies through self-education and self-examination and to use that knowledge to provide women access to safe abortions.

Abortion rights activists gathered in California in 1971 with speculum in hand to demonstrate vaginal and cervical self-examination in order to "confront...physical hang-ups in a physical way," to form another front of the women's liberation movement, and to address then-illegal abortion. The central organizing principle of this women's health movement was the "self-help group." A self-help group refers to women learning together about their physical and mental health by comparing and contrasting their experiences and knowledge. In many cases, they also learn by doing physical and/or gynecological self-examination. Today, these groups are reemerging.

Self-help inspires action: women helping themselves by taking control of the care and health of their bodies. The power of self-help for women's health lies in the possibilities of women coming together to question their most basic assumptions: definitions of "health" and "healthy," who provides health care, the meanings of access to health care, and what we have not yet learned but can learn about ourselves and each other.

What They Do

I interviewed four women from four different self-help groups on the East and West Coasts to find out more about how women are using self-help groups today. The women I spoke to—Ria, Loretta, Leah, and Alice—are between the ages of 21 and 30, are white, and have had some college education. All four became part of self-help groups because of other feminist/activist commitments that led to personal contact, through women's centers or other women's organizations, with women who were doing self-help. As their own groups of between four and seven women have developed, they have continued to learn from women outside their groups who serve as sources of information on numerous topics, such as how to do uterine size checks, where to get materials, and herbal remedies.

The self-help groups in which these women participate vary in the breadth of topics they address. Alice, a participant in an East Coast self-help group, described group activities that focus on physical and mental health. These include discussing sexuality and, more specifically, orgasm; talking about body image; "seeing and appreciating each others bodies" through massage sessions; and spending one meeting making flannel-cloth sanitary napkins. All of the women I spoke with mentioned sharing information —articles, books, and videotapes, as well as their own stories and knowledge—in their groups as essential. Self-help group participants decide together what they will do and learn about and how to use available personal and outside resources. The priorities, identities, and knowledge of participants, and the length of time they have worked together, usually determine what a group focuses on.

Ria, who has been with her East Coast group for three years, said that the connection to other women is what gives her self-help group vitality; the five women have become close through sharing different aspects of their lives. She said of their discussions about sexuality that the group is one of the few places where the question, "What is it like for you?" can be asked frankly. This question runs throughout self-help. By sharing factual information and by describing what has been important in their own experiences, women in self-help groups become close to other women, begin to demystify health care, and gain new perspectives on their own health. Discussions of "hidden" or "forbidden" topics, which can be difficult to speak about elsewhere, can take place in this setting.

Self-help groups almost always have a concrete focus on physical health and on women becoming familiar with their bodies. For some groups, this includes self-examination. The women I interviewed all practice basic gynecological self-examination within their groups. During gynecological self-exam, a member of the group inserts her own speculum— which in many feminist contexts has become symbolic of the goal of self-empowerment and self-knowledge—into her vagina to view her cervix using a mirror and flashlight. After looking at themselves, women may choose to examine each other. Leah, part of an East Coast group for just one month, described it as "just like looking in your mouth." Loretta, a college student on the West Coast, expressed the sense of wonder she felt when she saw her cervix for the first time in the self-help group she meets with. "Wow! so close and accessible, and so many women don't even know it's right there."

Self-examination may also include an external exam—checking for changes in the labia, clitoris, and vaginal opening—and bi-manual exams of each other—using two hands to feel the pelvic organs. Alice pointed out that her group closely follows "universal precautions" against HIV transmission: for example, everyone has her own speculum and they use latex gloves for examining each other manually. Groups also practice breast self-examination as another means of becoming more comfortable with their bodies. Observing and discussing changes in each individual over time—and differences among women in the group—allows the group to recognize the healthy states of each woman in the group. After doing self-exam together for long enough, they become familiar with their own and each other's health and can recognize potential health problems that manifest as unusual changes in their bodies.

When conditions are easily treatable by home remedies, the group may do so. All of the groups whose members I interviewed use or have some interest in using herbs in health care, for example. If they cannot alleviate the condition, the group at least is able to identify problems early. Assuming the participants have the financial and the social resources, then they may choose to see a health practitioner. As Alice explained, "We believe that we should acquire as much information as possible [about our health], but then there is nothing wrong with going with allopathic [conventional Western medical] treatment." In this way, women become more informed health care consumers in self-help groups and other health care settings. They recognize changes in their bodies, can ask more informed questions, and understand treatment options. In the '70s, the Boston Women's Health Book Collective, best known as authors of *Our Bodies, Ourselves,* publicized this basic self-help and feminist approach to women's health: encouraging women to get the necessary information to make decisions about our health and health care.

Menstrual Extraction

The most controversial practice of self-help groups is a procedure called menstrual extraction (ME). Developed by women involved in self-help in the '70s, ME is the removal of the contents of the uterus by slow suction and without dilation of the os (the cervical opening). It is done at the time of an expected menstrual period either to avoid a menstrual flow or as an early abortion method.

All of the women I talked to had participated in at least one ME. One of the main goals of the group during an ME is to give the woman receiving the ME control over the procedure at all times: she chooses a comfortable setting and who will be present (Ria even chose what music she wanted to hear for the most recent of her MEs), and she talks throughout the ME in order to set the pace and to describe how she feels. Usually the self-help group has been working together consistently and has learned to do ME in that context. However, two of the groups I learned about originally came together around the event of "emergency" MEs for women in the groups with unwanted pregnancies. Experienced members of other self-help groups, who had performed many MEs within their own groups, did these procedures.

Ria, whose group has done many MEs over the past three years, emphasized the importance of beginning self-help practice by becoming extremely familiar with all of the "basics" of self-examination, before ever doing ME. This was crucial to her as a safety measure and because she believes ME should be seen as part of self-help—a means of self-knowledge, not just as an abortion alternative.

All of the women I spoke with were cautious about confidentiality, particularly in speaking about ME. Their caution is not unfounded because of the links between self-help, ME, and abortion. Because ME can be used for early abortion as well as for removal of a month's menstrual flow, self-help groups (even those not doing ME regularly) could come under attack by antiabortion groups and under greater legal scrutiny for "practicing medicine without a license" should legal access to abortion become even more restricted.

Cynthia Pearson, program director at the National Women's Health Network (NWHN), describes self-help groups as having a "lightning rod effect" in the women's health and reproductive freedom movements. She asks, "If a legislature takes this right [abortion] away from us, is it right to take it into our own hands? [Self-help] could have a more profound impact of getting a larger number of people to look at the feminist analysis of health care." If they draw attention to themselves, some self-help groups could spark social and legal debate about reproductive freedom and, more generally, who should provide what kind of health care for women. Indeed, women, particularly women with few options, already find themselves caught in medical and legal conflicts over the "management" of their bodies.

Several of the group members mentioned conflicts in their groups over whether they are willing to perform MEs as a service to women outside the group who have unwanted pregnancies. They anticipate even more difficult decisions about the sharing of information that could put themselves and, in some cases, others at risk should abortion become even more restricted by the legal and political system. The debate centers on these legal concerns and on the safety of procedures performed on women who are not known to the group. Additionally, it addresses the central purpose of self-help as a whole approach to health and health care that is multifaceted and concerned with multiple issues, including but not limited to abortion.

The tension between conceptualizing self-help as an approach to health care and using self-help as a means to provide abortions ran throughout the interviews. Self-help is active "self-determination—taking control—empowering yourself," a creative process encouraging women to learn and to make decisions about their health care, I was told again and again. Alice spoke specifically about ME as "empowering: it felt like nobody had control over the description and knowledge of our bodies.... It was by no means carefree.... It was a powerful realization of our strength." However, Alice also addressed the reproductive freedom issues behind her personal involvement with a self-help group. She explained, "As a single mother—motherhood is so difficult, demanding, wonderful, and sacred; it has to be a choice. It has to remain a choice. I am more dedicated to both self-help and abortion rights after having [my son]." Her composite goals in doing self-help illustrate the complexity of political concerns behind self-help practices.

Self-help As An Organizing Tool

Self-help relies on a system of teaching and information exchange among women. Each woman I interviewed expressed an interest in eventually being able to pass on to other women the information she has learned through self-help. This is one means of using the group as an organizing tool, in addition to a learning and support group for individual members. Leah described the library of information that her group would like to compile, and in the short-term, she has a particular interest in telling other women about self-help through a postering campaign in her city. Ria also said, "We are interested in teaching what we know the way that we know it—to empower women, sisters friends.... I would like to see every woman learn about this once, and some will...stick to it." In keeping with this goal, Loretta described demonstrating self-exam for a fifteen-year-old friend, who is becoming sexually active, and for the girl's mother. Participants in Loretta's self-help group planned to do self-exam with their own mothers while they were home over the academic winter break. Passing on information in this way makes it accessible and less threatening. Judy Norsigian, director of the Boston Women's Health Book Collective, agrees that "once more aware, some individuals and [self-help] groups are motivated to become more active...[to] try out new strategies for community organizing or reaching different groups of women with a particular message."

Reaching different groups of women is difficult for these individual self-help groups, which are not associated with any broad-based organizations. Although self-help promotes access to information and supportive, humane, informed health care, for a variety of reasons it does not offer a form of health care that is widely accessible. In part, this is because of the inward focus of self-help groups. As Ria put it, "For me, [self-help] began as political, but it has become very personal." Also, concerns about confidentiality, stemming from the ambiguous status of ME, make it difficult for women to find one another other than through word-of-mouth.

Other issues also pose obstacles to women trying to use self-help as an organizing tool. Women's access to information is restricted in many ways. Some women interested in getting information about their bodies by doing self-examination simply cannot get speculums easily (medical supply stores consider speculums "medical devices," although tongue depressors and otoscopes, among other "invasive" instruments are not), so cervixes certainly are not as accessible as they might be. For many women, it is uncomfortable and awkward to talk about, let alone examine, our bodies in a group of women. This is just the surface of the many-layered ways in which we are denied access—in a tangible sense—to information about our own health. Both Pearson and Norsigian identified economic constraints as especially significant for many women in the United States. Some women will not have the time to spend in a self-help group or will not be able to get someone else to watch their children during meetings. For many reasons, other women may never hear about self-help at all.

But the concept of self-help is finding its way into new communities. In Connecticut, the group *Cosas de Mujeres* [Issues Affecting Women] offers "a bilingual, bicultural support group for poor and working Puerto Rican women with limited formal education.... The group is guided by the premise that empowerment for poor

Puertorriqueñas begins with a heightened understanding of and greater sense of power over their own bodies, especially in matters related to reproduction and sexuality." This group differs from the self-help groups I have described. The ten-week program starts out with a very structured agenda, facilitated by trained women from outside the group, and it does not involve gynecological self-examination.

The National Black Women's Health Project (NBWHP) maintains a network of self-help groups in the United States and internationally, providing a forum for Black women to empower themselves. The NBWHP grounds their Self-Help Developers' Manual in facts about the status of Black women's health in the United States, and they consider a variety of issues regarding the wellness of Black women. These materials have emerged from different communities and political contexts than the self-help materials that were the product of women's health activism in the early '70s.

If self-help groups can be flexible in meaning as well as in structure, self-help will affect many more women's lives. Women using the self-help tools of shared information, experiences, and analysis provide the first step in comprehending the multiple everyday and far-reaching issues—from using tampons to violence against women—that affect women's health and wellness in complex ways.

This article has been edited for length and clarity.

MARCH 1993

Women of Color Coalition for Health
by Linda Wong

Lack of access to culturally sensible and affordable health care is one of the silent killers of women of color today. Nearly 42 percent of AIDS cases among women and children in Massachusetts, for example, afflict Black residents, even though African Americans account for only 5 percent of the state's population. Similarly, only 40 percent of the city's residents reside in Roxbury, Mattapan, Dorchester, or South Boston, yet 67 percent of the city's sexual assaults occur in this minority-dominated area. Why are women of color, when compared to white women, disproportionally affected by poor mental and physical health? And what can be done to improve health care access?

The Women of Color Coalition for Health, a grassroots, health care education organization based in Roxbury, Massachusetts, is attempting to resolve these questions. Through workshops conducted by nine health educators, coalition members discuss health care issues with African-American, Chinese, Puerto Rican, and Vietnamese women. Similar workshops for Cambodian, Cape Verdian, Haitian, Native American, and West Indian Caribbean women will soon be organized.

Dorretta Dorrington, the assistant director of the project who is currently developing culturally and linguistically appropriate materials for the workshops, said that the barriers to good health and health care are enormous. The lack of money, health insurance, adequate child care, transportation, and linguistically appropriate information often prevent women from seeking medical help until it is too late. The jobs that women of color take because of the lack of economic resources also directly tie in with their illnesses. Domestic workers, for example, will "sooner or later" develop "rheumatism problems, arthritic problems, and dermatitis," Dorrington said.

The great lack of straightforward information on illnesses more prevalent among women of color than white women is also a problem. "Substance abuse," for example, "affects health in so many different ways that you don't have to go out and shoot [African-American] people anymore. You don't have to sterilize them anymore. Give them crack and you've done what you've needed to do," Dorrington said.

Another barrier blocking access to health care may be lack of familiarity with mainstream "American-style" medicine or prevention. More basically, women do not share the same ideas about their health, bodies, or disease. Women, therefore—particularly those from minority communities—are far less likely than women who identify with the country's English-based culture to seek care that does not match or respect their cultural beliefs.

There is "Western medicine versus Eastern medicine. Spiritual concepts around where diseases come from. You can tell people all you want to that HIV is a virus, and that viruses are transmitted," Dorrington said, "but there are other people who believe it's fate. It's sin. This is where the sensitivity comes in. How do you talk to people who may have that as their religious concept and not tell them, 'You're absolutely wrong?'"

One approach is to be nonjudgmental about people's beliefs, Dorrington said. For example, suggesting to people who have cancer and believe that they are to "live with it until they die" that other options to living with the disease exist, is a major step.

Reaching this step, however, requires work: hiring health educators, doing outreach to get women of color to attend health care workshops, and developing culturally sensitive and linguistically appropriate curricula. According to Spring Redd, director of the project, hiring educators who are sensitive to the needs of targeted communities requires a lot of "hitting the streets." "You can't just advertise in the *Boston Globe*," Redd said. "If you want people who are really connected to their own communities, and not just halfway connected, then you have to really advertise. You have to advertise [on culturally appropriate radio shows]. You have to go to [community] restaurants.... You have to pin up signs in doctors' offices. You have to pin up signs in supermarkets. You have to hand out job descriptions."

Once educators are hired, outreach to encourage women to attend the free workshops usually involves "piggybacking" onto existing social programs targeted to and located in specific communities of color. Kim Tuan Le, the Vietnamese health educator, for example, wrote letters to the Vietnamese American Civic Association, Metropolitan Indo-Chinese Children and Adolescent Services, Brighton High School, and the International Institute of Boston and received their permission to conduct health care workshops at their organizations.

Materials and curricula for the workshops are then developed to appeal to specific audiences. Juanita Lopez, the health educator for Boston-area Latinas, said that for women who can't read Spanish well, brochures have to be written very simply. For workshops geared to teaching young people about AIDS, a Spanish-language comic book depicting conversations about safe sex in "soap-opera-style" scenes may be more appropriate material than a simple brochure.

The crux of developing a successful "bridge" between health care resources and oppressed women of color, though, lies mainly with the ability of coalition members to understand and empathize with women in their communities. Spring Redd, an incest survivor and former battered woman who is currently living with breast cancer, implied that the coalition can be a place of "nurturing and support" for different women of color to safely talk about their mental and physical health. Similarly, Kim Tuan Le, a woman who fled Vietnam after the fall of Saigon and who later cared for Vietnamese women—including rape survivors—at a refugee camp hospital, says that the memories of her escape help her to act kindly toward the women who attend her workshops.

This article has been edited for clarity.

OCTOBER 1985

Feminists Have Avoided the Issue of AIDS

by Cindy Patton

In 1980, a new disease—Acquired Immune Deficiency Syndrome (AIDS), soon to be the most widely known disease of the twentieth century—was recognized among a small group of urban gay men. The early association of this disease with gay men skewed public perception, marking AIDS as a "gay disease" and negatively affecting research and public policy priorities. Although about 70 percent of those affected in the United States are gay or bisexual men, there are significant other risk groups. Among these groups are women.

Roughly 7 percent of the 13,000 U.S. cases (and a slightly lower percentage of the 350 Massachusetts cases) and about half of the non-U.S. cases are women. Women are at risk for AIDS in several ways, making it difficult to approach the special needs of women as a "community."

There has been little organized effort to define and organize around the needs of women with AIDS, in part because these women are hidden in the categories "intravenous (IV) drug user" and "other" or "noncharacteristic." West Coast women started a Women and AIDS Network, which for a time published educational material, but they were hampered by the lack of institutional support and the unwillingness of the feminist activist community to perceive AIDS as an important health and political issue. COYOTE, the San Francisco-based sex workers union, has been active in educating women in the sex industry and recently formulated policy statements on forced testing and safe sex. The most recent issue of *Our Bodies, Ourselves* contains a brief section on AIDS. Women have met in groups at nearly every AIDS conference to discuss the problems of women with AIDS, but much of our time has gone into supporting ourselves as we work in predominantly gay male organizations on a disease still discounted as a disease of perversion. Many of the U.S. women's papers have run an article on AIDS, often about the issues of women who have had problems with the medical or judicial systems. But despite the occasional articles hinting at the political and medical problems arising in the AIDS crisis, feminists have not mounted an organized effort to cope with the AIDS epidemic or its political aftermath. There are simple and complex reasons why feminists around the country have avoided the issue of AIDS, including burnout from other work, persistent homophobia, sex-negative attitudes, and fear of confronting such an unprecedented health problem.

Unfortunately, as most AIDS organizers have discovered, individuals and communities don't respond to the tragedy and urgency of AIDS-related illness and panic until someone they know gets AIDS. But because most of the women with AIDS are scattered throughout communities not structurally connected with the primarily white, middle-class feminist movement—recent Caribbean immigrants, prostitutes, IV drug users, urban poor, and isolated suburbanites—the majority of active feminists have not met a woman with AIDS.

AIDS is a terrifying disease, especially if you have watched someone waste away until death or listened to medical personnel state their refusal to care for patients or wondered whether you might have been exposed. The fear of AIDS circles closer to home until we do something to stop the panic and slow the spread of the disease—something personal *and* something programmatic.

Women who have not been exposed to the virus have a great deal of work to do in order to support women who have, and to support gay men. Gay men, whatever our political differences, *are* our allies. Feminists who continue to deny the similarity of women's and gay men's concerns at this historical moment should read the Eagle Forum pamphlet "ERA-AIDS" to get a sense of how the right wing lumps us together in a neat little package. The physical health and civil liberties of women and gay men are increasingly at stake under the Reagan regime, and AIDS is easy to manipulate into a divisive and punitive moral issue. The prejudice against anyone who tries to assert their independence from the traditional family model, the destruction of laws prohibiting discrimination, the erosion of the right to privacy for sexuality (under which the right wing includes abortion), the refusal of the government to produce accurate and nonjudgmental educational material about safe sex and safe IV needle use, and the ignorance of medical professionals outside urban areas about AIDS (and even in urban areas if the patient is female or not obviously a member of a risk group) are all problems that have a major impact on women. It is past time for feminist groups to include AIDS on their agenda. AIDS touches on all of the issues feminists have been concerned with for years: education about our bodies and the right and ability to make choices for which we are not penalized.

If women—and especially lesbians—as a community seem less affected by AIDS, it is primarily because we have not addressed the issue in a thoughtful way. Lesbians have AIDS; straight women have AIDS. If we have AIDS in lower numbers, we have experienced more than our share of the backlash. Lesbians are included in repressive legislation designed to limit the freedom of gay men, because, as one state legislator said, "They are perverted, too." Prostitutes have been caught in police sweeps on the pretext of public health. Historically in the United States, whenever prostitutes are subjected to stricter state repression, increased penalties for their amateur sisters are not far behind. Most mainstream feminists have averted their eyes from the rapid loss of sexual freedom—which includes freedom to know about and make choices about sexually transmitted disease. Feminists have tended to deny that we, our friends, or even unknown women are significantly at risk for AIDS, or that because of AIDS hysteria, women are at risk of having children taken away, losing welfare benefits, or being quarantined. Many feminists have lured themselves into thinking that because we—as a community—have so far been spared, to a degree, the onslaught experienced by gay men and IV drug users (ain't they women?), we are immune from AIDS. As a feminist and a gay activist, the denial I see in the women's community feels very much like the denial among gay men five years ago: "It can't happen here," "We aren't like those faggots in New York," "We aren't like...."

Those feminists who have been involved in AIDS organizing experience frustration and anger at our sisters' callous attitudes and refusal to believe the magnitude of the political and health problems caused by the AIDS epidemic. It *can* happen here, and it *is* happening here. It is essential that organized feminists advocate for accurate and nonjudgmental information about risk reduction that clearly explains low-risk sexual and drug use practices. Equally, as the political backlash of AIDS sweeps through our communities, often in advance of actual cases of AIDS, feminists must recognize and work with other communities in developing strategies to promote the right to privacy, quality health care, and policies that promote self-determination.

Two decades of second-wave feminism have taught women to extend our understanding of our own experience in order to find commonality with other women. Five years into the AIDS epidemic, feminists should make good on the promise of "global feminism." AIDS in the United States and internationally provides ample problem areas for connecting with feminist analysis and practice.

This article has been edited for length.

JUNE 1991

Women, AIDS, and Activism: Third Annual Women and AIDS Conference

by Laura Briggs

Women with AIDS die six to eight times faster after diagnosis than men. That bald fact speaks eloquently about the state of health care for women at risk for HIV infection: women's baseline health is often compromised. Women don't see health care providers because of lack of funds, because women often prioritize children's or other family members' care over their own, because when they are using alcohol and drugs they are afraid that their children will be taken away, or because they fear they will be drawn into the legal system because pregnancy has become a criminal condition. Without health care, women die.

When women with AIDS do see health care providers, they are misdiagnosed because they are not seen as a high-risk group or because common AIDS-related infections like pelvic inflammatory disease or chronic vaginal candidiasis are not officially considered to be AIDS. In the United States, 65 percent of HIV-positive women die without an AIDS diagnosis. If many gay men with AIDS have been left sitting in the waiting room, many women have not gotten through the door.

While the health care bureaucracy has failed to respond consistently to women's needs for AIDS-related health care, women in some African-American and Latino communities in the United States have been hit especially hard by the epidemic; AIDS is now the leading cause of death for Black women aged 15 to 34 in New York City, and nationally, AIDS is one of the five leading causes of death for women of childbearing age.

The third New England Women and AIDS Conference was held in Boston April 19 to April 20. More than 700 people—almost all of whom were women, about one-third of whom were people of color, and an easy majority of whom were lesbians—attended the conference. The event brought to the fore, in a way that few discussions of AIDS do, the life experiences of sex workers, drug users, and prisoners; issues of racism, pregnancy, sexual abuse, and violence; and the role of women as family caretakers. Many speakers testified that the problem of women and AIDS inevitably involves larger questions of how women's health care—as well as their economic, sexual, and social lives—is constrained in ways that make it difficult to prevent HIV infection or to establish adequate self-care when infected. As Jonathan Mann, former director of the World Health Organization's Global Programme on AIDS, put it, "A male-dominated society is a public health threat."

"HIV has simply magnified all the issues that we in the women's struggle have been working on all this time," added Dazon Dixon, founder and director of Sisterlove in Atlanta, an affiliate of the National Black Women's Health Project. Ironically, AIDS activism, often by men, has sometimes been more successful at winning health care and social service dollars than decades of advocacy by other groups. That has made for anomalous situations, where, for example, it may be easier for someone to access funds for drug treatment or prenatal care if she is HIV positive than if she is not. According to Janet Mitchell, chief of perinatology at the Harlem Hospital Center, "Health care for poor people is being systematically dismantled. The only way that poor women are going to get health care is if they have a disease that researchers are interested in."

Additionally, concern about AIDS has raised the visibility of populations usually viewed by government officials as outside the mainstream, including drug users, prostitutes, poor people generally, and pregnant women. "All this concern about women as 'vectors of the disease' has created a lot of "interest" in these usually invisible women," said Gloria Weissman of the National Institute on Drug Abuse. They are "justifiably suspicious of all the hands that are now reaching out to them," she added.

Prisoners, however, are regarded as a self-contained population and have not benefited even from the hand of self-interested and hysterical attention from the government that Weissman described. Rather, efforts at AIDS education, prevention, and self-empowerment undertaken by incarcerated women have, with few exceptions, been systematically quashed, according to Judy Greenspan of the American Civil Liberties Union (ACLU) Prisoner Project. Women in prison have much shorter survival times after an AIDS diagnosis than other women, because prisoners do not have access to anonymous HIV testing or to standard treatments, prophylaxes, or adequate nutrition.

Barriers to Care

While women have often been the focus of public-health efforts to prevent the spread of HIV infection, the dominant message has been for them to get men to change their behavior by wearing condoms. In the absence of women-controlled methods to prevent sexual transmission of the virus, said Weissman, such directives may be unhelpful at best. "In abusive relationships, getting partners to wear condoms may be more immediately dangerous than the risk of HIV infection."

According to Dixon, providing information about modes of transmission and safer sex are often inadequate to produce change in women's lives. "If we don't address the issues in women's lives in a way in which they feel safe and supported, we're not going to be able to do anything," she said. The question that women need to be asking themselves, Dixon said, is, "How do I get through the pain of whatever is holding me down and making me make unhealthy choices?"

Asian and Pacific Islander women and Native American women face particular jeopardy because of the extent of denial within those communities and neglect from federal and state officials as well as AIDS service organizations, according to Suki Terada Ports, founder and director of New York City's Family Health Project. AIDS organizations have made educational materials available in only a few, if any, of the 53 Asian and Pacific Islander languages spoken among U.S. immigrant communities. In addition, federal and state officials have refused to fund programs or research targeted to those communities because, officials claim, there are insufficient numbers of cases.

HIV infection and AIDS among Native American women have also been ignored, said Charon Asetoyer, not only because the numbers are low but also because they are wrong. When collecting statistics the Centers for Disease Control (CDC) counts only those Native Americans who live on reservations and who are treated by Indian Health Services (IHS), said Asetoyer, the founder and director of the Native American Women's Health Education Resource Center in South Dakota. The only large-scale study of AIDS among Native Americans to date has been a seroprevalence study among pregnant women at IHS begun three years ago. While results have still not been compiled, preliminary data indicate that the rate of infection is eight times higher than expected.

CDC Definition

At the close of the conference, participants voted nearly unanimously to send a series of demands to the CDC, including that the agency count the number of AIDS cases among deaf people, other people with disabilities, and lesbians. Conferees also demanded that the CDC revise the definition of AIDS to include the full spectrum of infections occurring in women,

IV drug users, children, and people whose health has been compromised by poverty. That demand has gone virtually unheard by the CDC in recent months, despite the amassing of considerable evidence to support it at a conference sponsored by the National Institute of Allergy and Infectious Diseases last December.

The proposed change would add cervical cancer, chronic and unresponsive vaginal candidiasis, pelvic inflammatory disease, and other diseases, in the presence of HIV infection, to the CDC definition of AIDS. Changing the description would also allow more women to become eligible for Medicaid and Social Security Disability Income.

According to Diane Palladino of the New Jersey Women and AIDS Network, one of the reasons cited by CDC officials for not including chronic vaginal candidiasis in the AIDS definition was that it would send millions of women who suffer from simple yeast infections into a panic. "As if women can't tell the difference between candidiasis that we get during the summer that goes away and a recurrent infection that is unresponsive to treatment," countered Palladino. "And as if having millions of women concerned about whether they could get AIDS would be a bad thing," she added.*

*In 1992, the CDC did revise the official definition of AIDS to include opportunistic infections that affect women as well as men.

JUNE 1994

Safe Sex for Lesbians: What's It All About?

by Judith McDaniel and Judith Mazza

Lesbians are invisible in the battle against HIV/AIDS, we are told, and that invisibility is dangerous to us. In the December 1993 *Sojourner,* we can read that "the CDC [Centers for Disease Control] still has no statistical category by which to survey lesbian AIDS cases" and "there had been no research on lesbian transmission of the virus." Amber Hollibaugh of the Lesbian AIDS Project of the Gay Men's Health Crisis says that "lesbianism is not a condom," meaning that being a lesbian doesn't make a woman immune to HIV. This kind of rhetoric, we would argue, like the call for lesbian CDC categories and research on lesbian transmission of HIV, is not helpful to lesbians and does not describe the HIV problem that faces the lesbian community. Why?

In most discussions about HIV, the rap is that safe sex means barriers. Latex barriers. Lesbians talk with grave familiarity about dental dams, surgical gloves, condoms, and finger cots. Lesbians are getting tested for HIV before they take their clothes off. Spontaneity is possible only in the context of protecting ourselves from any contact with another woman's bodily fluids.

And yet, we have little evidence that supports the rap. Lesbians who are HIV positive, by and large, did not get the virus from sex with another woman. The largest percentage got it from sharing injection drug needles or "works." The next largest group are HIV positive due to having sexual intercourse (anal and/or vaginal) with an HIV-positive man. By far the smallest group of lesbians were infected in the course of "rough sex"[1] with another woman when blood was present or from oral sex when menstrual blood was present. We have no evidence that woman-to-woman transmission is possible in the absence of blood.[2]

To ask why there has been no research on lesbian transmission of HIV misstates the issues; moreover, the assumptions behind this question create panic and paranoia rather than clarity. There has been research on the acts, which some lesbians perform, that allow or promote the transmission of HIV. But none of these acts are performed because we are lesbians—anyone can do the same things, with the same results. These acts include:

- sharing injection drug works, including needles and works that have not been cleaned with bleach;
- having unprotected anal intercourse with an HIV-infected man or penetration with anything (e.g., fingers, dildo) that hasn't been cleaned or washed with bleach since the last, similar use; and
- having unprotected vaginal sex with an HIV-infected man.

That's the short list. Lesbians need to acknowledge that some of us practice behaviors that can be risky rather than asking for research on behaviors that have no known risk factor.[3]

Not all injection drug users get HIV, only those who share unclean needles or works. You can shoot drugs for 50 years, but if you never share, you won't get HIV from shooting drugs. Not all men who have sex with men get HIV, only those who have unprotected sex with an HIV-infected person. The categories of groups—Men Who Have Sex with Men, Heterosexual Contact (Male and Female), Injection Drug Users—are not useful in terms of research because behavior, not labels, spreads HIV. Adding lesbians as a CDC category would accomplish nothing useful that we can see.

Education about safe sex, on the other hand, does need to be targeted, when possible, to those people who are most likely to perform certain acts. Lesbians need education about safe sex that addresses our issues. Blanket statements about dental dams and latex gloves, however, don't fill that need.

The question is, what sexual practices will put a woman in danger? We know that HIV is primarily transmitted by semen or blood. Yes, that includes menstrual blood. And we know that saliva does not transmit the virus because it doesn't carry the virus in quantities that will infect. Saliva, unlike semen, is one of the body's protectors.[4] Saliva tries to kill germs that might be coming in through your mouth, which is why you are alive today, not dead from breathing, eating, and so on. Saliva inhibits HIV, which is why you would need an open cut in your mouth for HIV to get into your bloodstream from contact with blood or semen in your mouth. Getting to your blood through the digestive system is just too difficult.

We've heard lesbians insist that vaginal fluids are just like semen—that is, they carry the virus. That's why, they argue, a latex barrier is necessary any time you have oral sex with a woman. But vaginal fluids act like saliva, not like semen. Vaginal fluids *prohibit* potentially infectious things; vaginal fluids act to protect a delicate area of our anatomy just as saliva does. Very young women—preteens and early teenagers—are at greater risk for HIV infection because the walls of their vaginas, which are lined by the mucous membranes that produce vaginal fluid, are thinner and contain fewer immunity producing cells than those in women of mature childbearing age.[5]

Even if you don't want to take a chance on vaginal fluids, or if you're not sure whether menstrual blood is present (and menstrual blood is a risk just as any blood would be), dental dams are not high on any official safe-sex-practices list. The CDC and the New York State Department of Health, for example, don't take a position on dental dams (or cut-up condoms or plastic household wrap) for use in oral sex on a woman because they haven't been tested and there is no proof that they prevent the spread of anything. Furthermore, dental dams aren't "containers" in the way that condoms are. (After ejaculating, a man can slip off the condom and tie it, containing the dangerous semen. You know where the semen is and which side of the condom is in and which out.) Dental dams are only a barrier until they slip off at a crucial moment or are dropped on the floor in the heat of whatever. ("Oh god," she moaned, "which side was me and which was her?") They give an illusion of safety that may be more dangerous than simply paying attention to things such as the presence of blood or open sores. If dental dams turn you on though, some sex stores do sell panties with open crotches and devices to fasten the dental dam into place.

If you have *significant* open cuts or sores on your hands, and if you are unsure of your HIV status or that of your partner, then latex gloves or finger cots may be a good idea. They protect you from HIV and other nasties like herpes, and they protect the woman to whom you are making love from your blood.

Each lesbian must make her own decision about the level of risk she is comfortable with. We all take risks every day. Getting in the car and driving to work is a risk. Some mornings, we're tired or distracted enough to recognize this; other mornings, we never think about it. We're more likely to die while driving to work than because we've had unprotected sex with another woman.[6] The assertion that we can prevent either of these untimely demises is probably true; but it is also true that most of us don't want to live our lives from such a protected stance. We prefer to take the small risks and accept the consequences. The alternatives are too limiting—would we ever go out of our homes if we were afraid of what might happen to us outside of them? We'd never drive a car or fly in an airplane; but most of us want to do the things that taking those risks allows.

Lesbians need correct information about how HIV is transmitted and exactly what acts could transmit it with what likelihood. Without that information, we could be like women living in a relatively safe neighborhoods who treat the environment outside their homes like bombed-out Sarajevo. As women, we have a long history of being told that we shouldn't enjoy sex, that sex is for men and procreation is for women. As lesbians, we have a long history of being told that the sexual expression of our love is shameful and disgusting. We don't need to tell ourselves and one another that it is never safe to be sexually spontaneous.

Finally, it's important to note that when we say that lesbian sex is really pretty safe compared to other risks we take in our daily lives, we are not abandoning the gay men who are struggling with a much more serious sexual risk factor. The AIDS crisis has affected every homosexual person, and that has occurred because of homophobia, because the world out there does not distinguish between gay men and lesbians. We know lesbians who were not allowed to donate blood because they said yes on the form that asked if they were homosexual. The official in charge couldn't distinguish between a male risk factor and a female risk factor and turned away a potential donor from one of the lowest risk groups (although we don't talk in terms of groups at risk, only risky acts). Not even on Phil Donahue or Oprah Winfrey do straights want to know what queers do in bed (other than sleep), so it's not surprising that America-at-large is afraid of catching something dreadful from all of us, male and female.

But we know the difference. And we need to protect our lesbian community from sex-negative messages that are unwarranted and from paranoia about sex while, at the same time, recognizing that the struggle against homophobia generated by the AIDS crisis is one we share with gay men.

1. *"Possible Female-to-Female Transmission of Human Immunodeficiency Virus," by M. Marmor, L.E. Weiss, M. Lyden, et al. Annals of Internal Medicine 105:969, 1986.*

2. *"AIDS Commentary: Biological Factors in the Transmission of Human Immunodeficiency Virus," by S.D. Holmberg, C.R. Horsburgh, Jr., J.U. Ward, H.W. Jaffe. Journal of Infectious Diseases 160:116, 1989. "It is only during active menstruation that cells capable of hosting HIV are secreted from the cervix."*

3. *"Sexual Orientation versus Sexual Behaviour," by J. Chetwynd, A. Chambers, T. Hughes. New Zealand Medical Journal 937(105):388, 1986. This is one of several studies that indicate women who self-identify as lesbians do have anal and vaginal intercourse with men.*

4. *"Female-to-Female Transmission of HIV," by P. Greenhouse. Lancet, August 15, 1987, 401. "Although HIV can be isolated in low titre from saliva there is no good evidence to show that it could be of sufficient concentration or viability to be transmissible."*

5. *"UN Finds Teen-Age Girls at High Risk of AIDS," New York Times, July 30, 1993. "Author of the study, Dr. Karen Hein of the Albert Einstein College of Medicine in New York...said in an interview that the genital tracts of teen-age girls have not developed characteristics that protect older women from transmission of disease. The vagina in young girls is lined by thin mucous membranes. These thin membranes are a less efficient barrier to the human immunodeficiency virus than the thicker vaginal walls of older women, the report said. In addition, mucus production is thinner than in older women and offers less protection against abrasion and contains fewer immunity producing cells."*

6. *"No Evidence for Female-to-Female HIV Transmission among 960,000 Female Blood Donors," by L.R. Petersen, L. Doll, C. White, S. Chu. Journal of AIDS 5(9):853, 1992.*

Response to Previous Article:

JUNE 1994

TRANSMISSION, TRANSMISSION, WHERE'S THE TRANSMISSION?

by Amber Hollibaugh

The following article was solicited by Sojourner *as a response to Judith McDaniel and Judith Mazza's "Safe Sex for Lesbians: What's It All About?"*

At a Health Forum about HIV-positive lesbian health care needs, sponsored just last week by the Lesbian AIDS Project—GMHC (Gay Men's Health Crisis), of which I am the director, two women in a room of 150 people finally spoke out late into the program. Each unknown to the other until that night, first one stood, then the other, and said, "I am here as an HIV-positive lesbian infected through sex with my HIV-positive female partner. I have been ridiculed and dismissed in talking about this, but I am here to say that I am not a liar or an exception. Before I was infected with HIV, I did not believe that lesbians could get AIDS. And like many of you in this room, I didn't believe that women could pass this virus sexually to other women. But I know differently now. The question for me is, how many more of us will have to stand up and testify about our own lives and our histories of sexual transmission with another woman before we are believed? Two of us know more now. And so should you." Their eloquence silenced us all.

The Lesbian Tip of the HIV Iceberg

I am the director of the only, to date, lesbian-specific AIDS project in the world, but I work with a network of over 100 frontline lesbian and bisexual health care workers who confront, in similar ways, what I see daily. Each of us has been appalled at the growing numbers of lesbians with AIDS or HIV with whom we work, while at the same time the consciousness about this issue in different segments of our communities remains so low. And though we often don't agree among ourselves on the exact or most probable female sexual routes of transmission, we all agree that we are seeing the numbers grow in all categories of risk, including this one.

When the project began, I felt it was vital to reach and serve lesbians with AIDS, regardless of our numbers; today I have met hundreds of lesbians with AIDS. The HIV+ Lesbian Leadership Project of the Lesbian AIDS Project (LAP) has just begun to organize the first conference only for HIV-positive women-who-partner-with-women. We are expecting 100 to 150 HIV-positive lesbians to attend this local one-day conference, and we're already worried that we are undercounting. Those of us doing this work see the crisis broadening, yet, at conference after conference, we recount to one another our local horror stories of who in our own communities still discounts the expanding reality of lesbians and HIV.

Disheartened by denial within our own communities, those of us on the front lines also recognize that we face a government that continues to confuse visibility, identity, and behaviors. This is the same government that brought us the idea that a woman is a lesbian *only* if she has not slept with a man since 1977, and the same government that refuses to recognize or track *our behaviors*, rendering us paralyzed when we try to figure out exactly what is going on and why. Having so little to go on when we struggle to create sound, conservative, clear-eyed descriptions of our risks as women-who-partner-with-women and to quantify our numbers for HIV leaves many of us who are doing the work angry and bitter. We know that listening to the government is always tricky, but as in all else concerning our survival, we have to use every tool at our disposal. However, we fear that what many of us are seeing is just the lesbian tip of the HIV iceberg in our communities...a warning that we can pay attention to or dismiss at our own eventual peril. This is not about scare tactics, it's about survival.

Still, from its beginning two years ago, I have resisted LAP being pulled into the female-to-female sexual transmission debate. It was clear to me that people wanted to define our vulnerability and need for recognition, research, and AIDS services solely through this one question, rather than understanding that *whatever* we eventually learn scientifically about sexual transmission between unprotected female partners, lesbians as a *people* are uninformed about *all the ways* in which we may be vulnerable to HIV. Consequently, our communities lack vital and lifesaving information that would prepare us adequately to access all our risks and vulnerabilities to HIV.

The tragic results of this misguided and entrenched polemic concerning female-to-female sexual transmission, which is still positing that lesbians cannot transmit the virus to each other sexually, has had broad and terrible consequences in our communities. We have been told we are not at risk for HIV sexually and, therefore, are the "lowest" risk group overall for contracting the virus. This has led to many erroneous and tragic conclusions as lesbians try to understand our own personal risk for HIV.

The catastrophe is laid bare when a lesbian says that she doesn't know how she contracted AIDS because she only shared needles with other lesbians and, since lesbians are not at risk for AIDS, she thought she would be safe from the virus; or when another dyke says that she and her HIV-positive female partner called the AIDS hotline for safer-sex information and were told that there was little to no risk in "regular" lesbian sex and now she, too, is positive; or when a woman calls the hotline crying that she is a lesbian, really, has been all her life, though she was raped once, but the CDC, because of the rape, insists on listing her case as heterosexual transmission, even though she has buried two female lovers to AIDS. As a *lesbian body politic*, we remain unreached and untargeted as a people trying to confront the intricate truth of our own histories, memories, conversations, assessments, knowledge, and geography.

In the midst of this tragic confusion, with little official or community recognition regarding all our risks (including that our primary exposure for HIV is still drug use and unprotected sex with infected men), the third and smallest category of women with HIV, those who attribute their infection to HIV-positive female sexual partners, continues to grow. These women have been vilified and belittled in many AIDS and lesbian communities and disbelieved by many health care providers. In addition, most of the research to date was set up explicitly to try to discount their knowledge and clarity about how they became infected. Despite these obstacles, more and more lesbians continue stubbornly to report female-to-female unprotected sex as their only or primary risk for HIV.

Who Are "We"?

Understanding lesbian HIV infection within this framework, when I first received Judith McDaniel's and Judith Mazza's article, it put me in a rage. I found myself muttering arguments to them in my head as I walked down the street or laid in bed at night. I was tired of this fight—tired, sad, angry, and frustrated—and I was especially upset that women whose work I respect had written this piece, essentially suggesting that lesbians have such a minuscule risk of contracting HIV when we have sex with other women (the probability-of-driving-a-car-and-having-an-accident theory of risk) that we really don't have anything to worry about. Worse, their article suggests that those of us who are trying to talk about HIV in our communities, and, as one part of our work, are talking about safer sex, are condemning the women we reach and their communities to rigid, fear-based unspontaneous sex; unnecessary terror of lesbian desire itself; and a sexual paranoia that could result in a dangerous crisis of erotiphobia and sex-negative messages both internally and externally. They argue that we are already deluged with millions of messages that try to undermine our right to our own desires for women and that this bullshit about safer sex, for most of us, is both unnecessary and dangerous.

This fight about the sexual transmission of HIV between women needs to be seen for what it is: a political battle, often between friends, about what we are seeing and hearing and how we interpret that information. Though I disagreed with McDaniel and Mazza both scientifically and theoretically, I was equally disturbed by a set of ideological assumptions that could not be shoveled under the "scientific" or "HIV medical expert" rug. These issues are painful to discuss and hard to bridge. They force us to ask difficult questions. How do we talk class and race in our various women-who-partner-with-women communities? Who are the "we" when we generalize the demographics of our lives and activities vis à vis any risk, and where does that leave us when we try to understand something as complicated as HIV jeopardy or when we grapple with what "we" do in bed?

Bottom line, I don't believe their unspoken construction of "our" lesbian community serves us well when thinking about HIV risk; the underlying presumption in their article is that "we" are a nearly monolithic, mostly middle class, probably mostly white, serially monogamous group of women who sleep with each other and rarely if ever do the things identified with AIDS risk: not much shared needle drug use or unprotected sex with men and certainly not much "rough sex," whatever that means. Do those assumptions really serve us well? Is that really who "we" are or do we need much more rigor when any of us writes or speaks about HIV risk, so that we call forth the range and complexities of the many ways we present ourselves as a group— that ever-changing combination of *ages* and *identities* and *colors* and *behaviors-over-time* and *class stratifications* and *coming-out histories*—which McDaniel and Mazza's article all but disappears?

Their article was poignantly instructive of the much larger problem each of us faces when "we" write about each other. Who is being spoken to or about and who is being included in the construction of community and HIV risk? And who remains invisible or has been dismissed with a sentence or a footnote as unimportant or not significant to this discussion? Do the places where we can most easily document HIV among lesbians, such as prisons, outpatient clinics, shelters, and drug recovery settings, suggest to many lesbians that they can dismiss any significant risk for themselves because they see themselves as different from "those kind of women"? "They," as the article suggests, are much more middle class and/or white and, therefore, don't have to take on the issue of lesbian HIV infection.

These acted-on, but usually unstated, prejudices have led to a kind of lesbian sexual apartheid when we talk about HIV: "It's over there, for *those* kinds of dykes, in *those* bars or *those* outside communities, but it is not about *us* and, therefore, *we* have nothing to learn from *those* others, because *we* have named *ourselves* out of danger. In the meantime, we hide or at least discourage discussion of *our* many similarities, as well as *our* differences. Conversations about this issue have become nearly impossible to translate through the passion because, at the core, we are fighting about the race, class, and sexual differences between us.

This refusal to confront our differences, and the meanings we assign to them, significantly influences the overall understanding of HIV in various lesbian and women-who-partner-with-women communities. Research of any kind is painfully scant, but what we do have indicates the *frontline vulnerability* of various parts of our communities—young lesbians, women who are coming out, poor, working class and/or lesbians of color. This paucity of documentation cries out for a passionate insistence by all of us for more research, more inclusion, more inquiry, and more subtle tracking mechanisms, which can begin to unlock the rich, tangled meanings and the significance of behaviors, activities, orientations, identities, and demographics. When we are asking about ourselves, our identities and behaviors, *whom* are we asking about, *whom* are we imagining in our mind's eye? We have so little information or data about ourselves that when we come up against any of the Big Topics—parenting, breast cancer, chemical dependence and alcoholism, suicide, sex with men, sex with women—we have the skimpiest information upon which to draw. This, sadly, is a literal reflection of our oppression and our need.

A Research Agenda

So we stare out at an uncomfortable reality: we have no power to demand the research we need in order to understand what's happening in our communities. There is no long-range, significant research into the possible transmission activities that might be suggestive when looking at the arena of unprotected sex between women and HIV; no research on the different progressions and intensities of HIV viral load in a woman's bodily fluids over the course of HIV infection through to AIDS; no research to see if a woman's having HIV as well as a yeast infection or other sexually transmitted disease (STD) leads to having a greater concentration of HIV in her vaginal secretions. Where is the research on cervical warts and cancers and their impact on virus distribution in vaginal fluids? What of the human papilloma virus (HPV) and HIV? Where is the research to help us determine the potential for transmission when a lesbian who has just contracted HIV has unprotected sex with an HIV-negative female partner with herpes simplex?

Where can we find the work we need that reflects the reality of how few lesbians access any kind of preventive health care, let alone get Pap smears or pelvic exams? What do we do when a lesbian's own medical provider tells her she doesn't need these procedures "since lesbians don't have sex with men"? What do we do when chlamydia, which often remains hidden without specific testing, is being endlessly passed between female sexual partners without adequate medical interventions? When will we understand that as lesbians, as women, we are not taught how to understand our own bodies or our own sexuality?

It is a perfect circle back to the magical-lesbian-free-of-contagion message reflected in McDaniel's and Mazza's simplistic and dangerous representations of "the healthy vagina." True, both saliva and vaginal secretions are structured to fight infections. But there is an important piece of counterinformation that any woman reading this article can access for herself. Consider your own pelvic history. For most of us, it is a history of cyclical yeast infections, tric, chlamydia, bacterial vaginitis, herpes, endometriosis, pelvic inflammatory disease, interrupted menstrual cycles, and unexpected spot bleeding, to name just a few.

Sometimes I think our memories of our vaginal and pelvic histories are like our phenomenal ability to "forget" when our periods are coming, month after month, year after year. As women, we have vaginal memory loss, something the feminist and lesbian health movement struggles against year after year.

There is also little relevant and useful research about all our "crossover" activities. We need research that reflects accurately the varieties of our sexual activities and our shared drug use, research that would begin to sketch out a more elaborate map of what we are doing sexually and socially and how those activities may contribute to or mask our risks for HIV. Deadened codes like "lesbian sex" or "rough sex" tell us nothing; we must demand serious, multifaceted sexuality and drug-use studies that ask a complicated trajectory of questions in order to capture the web of actions, desires, identities, and ideologies we practice in bed or while putting things in our bodies.

Unfortunately, McDaniel and Mazza omit the bitter history of the "sex wars" and the correspondingly lost or hidden sexual narratives in many lesbian communities. These wars, and their earliest foundation in our female socialization, are the chronicles of our painful legacy as women kept ignorant about our bodies and our sexual options. When we speak of who we are and yet fail to mark out the tremendous effect of this silencing and lack of knowledge on our abilities to talk openly about what we really do in bed with another woman (or with a man), let alone acknowledge something as highly stigmatized as substance use or dependency, we have not substantially addressed "safer sex for lesbians." McDaniel's and Mazza's sweeping dismissiveness only encourages the refusal in different parts of our communities to recognize that we are in a world forever changed by AIDS. We merit more than simplistic "don't worry, we're really safe" messages as we confront the complicated nature of our lives as lesbians and bisexual women in the middle of an epidemic. *The question isn't how we are different from each other and, therefore, not at risk, but how we comprehend the actual distance between the most vulnerable among us and the most sheltered.*

So What About Our Sexual Risks?

So, what do I think about transmission of the virus sexually between women? This is my opinion, based on the best thinking and research I can bring to it, but there is still much we need to know to come to any final answer, as I tried to suggest earlier.

I think this virus is much harder to transmit between women who are having any kind of unprotected sex than in situations involving shooting drugs with shared works or when we are having unprotected sex with men. But I do think the virus can be transmitted through our vaginal secretions in high enough concentrations to be infectious over time, especially if there are existing cofactors. I also think it can be transmitted through going down on each other when there is menstrual or any other blood. I don't think that "rough sex" has much to do with it, since vaginal "trauma" occurs with any penetrative sexual act: fingers, fists, or dildos. I know, from the just-analyzed data in LAP's sex survey, that women are practicing a wider range of sexual activities than we previously thought, from rimming and sex-toy play to vaginal and anal fisting and group sex. The key point, I believe, is *repeated exposure,* and given the ways we partner (even casually with fuck buddies whom we often see more than once), we have many community patterns that support our repeated exposure to HIV with a female partner who might be infected.

I am worried that we have no idea how widespread this crisis is in our communities and that cofactors like HPV, herpes, and yeast infections, when they are combined with the notion that we aren't at risk for HIV, dramatically increase our chance of infection. It also seems to me that lesbians don't often know their antibody status until very late in the progression of the disease and, therefore, don't recognize the need to protect their partners. I would also guess that transmission is more likely at the beginning of HIV infection than later in the disease, though it continues to be possible. I think that as more and more of us are infected, in whatever ways we are, the chances of using, sleeping with, or being lovers with an HIV-positive woman, whether she or her lover is aware of it, is increasing. And finally, I think the incidence of crossover activities, both sex with men (often gay or bisexual) and our sharing of needles, is still very underreported and underrepresented in our communities, *all* our communities, and that too increases the numbers of us who are being infected by HIV.

Is saying this "erotiphobic" (ironically, a term I created in 1981)? Or is it to say that as sexual adults we need to look frankly at what we are grappling with, in bed and in our heads, as women and as lesbians, and factor that in when we are sexually active with anyone? If we are still at the point where we often cannot talk to a woman partner about much of anything sexually, of what delights us or what isn't working when we are making love, if it is still hard to say "lower, darling, and harder," where are we when confronting our risks for HIV? If many of us have been systematically excluded from accessing the medical information we need to help us self-diagnosis yeast infections and other STDs and so can't tell when we have medical problems, this also increases our sexual vulnerability. If talking sex is still hard, then thinking hot and thinking safe is a wide stretch for most of us. It is for me. I am 47 years old, and I am still struggling to bring voice and sexual awareness together with my desires and actions.

To know that HIV is present and growing in our communities and to know that working-class lesbians, most often African-American and Latina dykes, are being hit hardest right now, is not to deny HIV's eventual power to affect and infect any of us. As a very diverse set of communities of women who love and have sex with each other, are we only going to believe numbers when it is too late?

Finally, none of the lesbians I know who are doing this work are suggesting that what is happening to us looks like the devastation now visible in the gay male communities. But I have been surprised and moved that gay men are right there when I say, "We need help precisely because it is still possible for us to reach our communities before the scale is tipped from prevention to brush fires; if we get in quickly enough, we might be able to be one of the few remaining communities who could still turn this around." This battle for recognition of our risk to HIV and the numbers of lesbians now struggling with AIDS is not "virus envy." We are not trying to scare our various women's communities. But in a culture that hates and reviles us, refusing to recognize how and where and in what ways we are being affected by HIV is not acceptable. Pointing out where that will ultimately lead is mandatory. We need to learn from the powerful histories of women and gay men that surround us and name this crisis now.

When I said *lesbianism is not a condom,* I meant exactly to confront what McDaniel and Mazza will not: that we are not immune to this virus, that our communities and behaviors and identities are extraordinarily broad and complex, and that HIV/AIDS is not insignificant in our communities. Our numbers of infected lesbians and women-who-partner-with-women continue to grow, while our access to health care and diagnosis remains minute. We can no longer afford to hide behind the false shelter of our identities while we watch our numbers grow.

Author's note: I would like to thank my lover, Marj Plumb, Beck Young, Laura Ramos, Melissa Murphy, Anita Rosa, Rochelle Burroughs, Alice Terson, and Ana Oliveria and all the HIV-positive lesbians whom I work with. I would also like to thank the s/m lesbian community for its early commitment and safer-sex training to the broader communities of women-who-partner-with-women. Thank you all.

REFERENCES
"Transmission of HIV Presumed to Have Occurred via Female Homosexual Contact," by J.D. Rich et al. *Clinical Infectious Diseases* 17(6), 1993.

HIV Seroprevalence and Risk Behavior among Lesbians and Bisexual Women: The 1993 San Francisco/Berkeley Women's Survey. San Francisco Dept. of Public Health AIDS Office, October 1993.

Health Behaviors among Lesbians and Bisexual Women, A Community-Based Women's Health Survey. San Francisco Dept. of Public Health AIDS Office, October 1993.

"Out of the Question: Obstacles to Research on HIV+ Women Who Engage in Sexual Behaviors with Women," by Nancy Warren, M.P.H. *At Issue with AIDS: About Women,* SIECUS Report 22(1), 1993.

Bibliography of Lesbian Health Literature, by Ryva Rankow, National Center for Lesbian Rights (New York and San Francisco).

DECEMBER 1975

DES, A Double-Edged Sword
by Mimsi Dorwart

In the last five years, literally hundreds of young women have been diagnosed with what had previously been an extremely rare type of vaginal or cervical cancer. The sudden and dramatic emergence of the cancer prompted medical scientists to embark on a campaign of intensive research; it was subsequently discovered that the single thing these women had in common was that they had been born to mothers who had taken DES during the first trimester of pregnancy.

DES is the acronym for a drug named diethyl stilbestrol. It is a synthetic estrogen, developed during the '30s and marketed in the '40s, '50s, and '60s to reduce the incidence of miscarriage in pregnant women. It was linked in 1970 with the development of adenosis in daughters born to those pregnant women; adenosis is a precancerous condition that can develop into a rare and thoroughly dangerous form of vaginal cancer called clear cell adenocarcinoma.

Mounting evidence of the improper research and irresponsible use of DES in the past finally prompted the Food and Drug Administration (FDA) to issue a warning against its use during pregnancy; the *New England Journal of Medicine* stated outright that "there should no longer be doubt that synthetic estrogens are absolutely contraindicated in pregnancy." Retrospectively, medical scientists cannot justify the administration of this drug, which has since proven to be not only ineffective in its purpose, but also potentially harmful to the mother and to any female fetus she is carrying. An estimated three million daughters have been born to women who took DES during their pregnancies: the chances are nine out of ten that these "DES daughters" will develop adenosis and that the potential (or real) threat of cancer will be with them all their lives.

The cancer is one that will strike this generation of young women especially. It is their mothers who were administered DES in the '40s and '50s; it is upon their maturity in the '50s and '60s that the condition became manifest (aggravated by normal estrogen release at puberty). It is of absolute vital importance to every woman born between 1940 and 1965 to find out if she is a DES daughter. She may find out directly from her mother, from her mother's doctor, or from hospital or pharmacy records. If she is a DES daughter, she should seek an examination immediately.

While DES has been disappearing from the counter as an antimiscarriage drug, it has also been developed as another "wonder drug," more potent and more popular than ever before: the "morning-after pill." The morning-after pill, although approved by the FDA in 1973, is nothing less than a massive dose (250 mg) of DES or a related estrogen. Medical scientists warned that such a dosage should be used only in emergencies (e.g., in instances of rape), and then only with full, informed consent and in absence of contraindications; many physicians feel that any estrogen, given at comparably high doses, would be as dangerous as DES. But despite the loudest warnings, the morning-after pill has come into general use.

The morning-after pill contains such a huge amount of estrogen as to cause the uterine lining to slough off, preventing the implantation of a fertilized ovum and thus preventing pregnancy; to be effective, it must be taken within 72 hours of conception and must be taken in its full amount. Most women would think twice before taking the pills if they were fully informed about the drug. Most do not know, for instance, that DES was recently in the news when the FDA banned its use as a growth hormone in cattlefeed, because a small amount of DES was remaining in the beef and was found to be "unfit for human consumption." This amount was three-hundredths of a microgram. Astoundingly, the amount of DES contained in the morning-after pill is 835,000 times that amount. Though the drug has proved highly carcinogenic in animals, it is felt that there is not sufficient data collected to actually say whether this incredible dose of DES is, in itself, dangerous to women—the pills have only been in use three years, and the latency period for DES-induced cancer is ten to twenty years. But testimony before the Senate hearing on DES in cattlefeed described the drug as a "chemical of bizarre and far-reaching properties, chief of which is that it is a spectacularly dangerous carcinogen." (Frank Rauscher, head of the National Cancer Institute, stated that unless DES can be made subject to the strictest controls, it should be taken off the market altogether.)

It is almost incredible that the U.S. government would ban a barely traceable amount of DES in beef and yet would approve the administration of a massive dose to young women. It was suggested that, in 1972, when women of the Advocates for Medical Information charged the FDA with allowing human consumption of this experimental, FDA-unapproved drug, the federal agency was sufficiently embarrassed to *approve* it. Be that as it may, the story of the morning-after pill gives chilling witness to the recalcitrance of the FDA, the drug industries, and the medical profession to learn from tragic experience. Until further evidence is collected and until sufficient concern can spur the government and the pharmaceutical industries to more responsible action, women are on their own; no one is watching out for them.

This article has been edited for length and clarity.

SEPTEMBER 1989

Cancer as a Feminist Issue
by Susan Shapiro

From the time my mother was diagnosed with breast cancer until she died of it eleven years later, it did not occur to me that her illness was a feminist issue. Even my own experience of having cancer did not arouse my sense of politics. Like most people, I had learned that cancer was a personal tragedy, a family tragedy; it was not a community issue, certainly not within the realm of feminist causes. But when I recently read about the sexual abuse of women with cancer by a local holistic psychotherapist, I began to wonder about the silence within the women's community. Why could I not find one feminist cancer support group? Why, despite a wonderfully diverse range of therapy specializations advertised in *Sojourner* (adult children of alcoholics, coming out, incest, stress, depression, self-esteem, single parenting, eating disorders, alcoholism, and work issues—to name a few) was there nothing for women struggling with cancer? (One ad included chronic illness and disability but did not mention cancer.) And where were the other feminists who had cancer? I found it hard to believe that Audre Lorde and I were the only ones out there.

I began an active search for others who had faced this illness and found ten women whose stories, insights, and courage were deeply inspiring. I also began to investigate the politics of cancer—the literature, organizations, legislation, food and drug industries, and more. Information about cancer beyond the most basic facts is not readily accessible, and my list of questions is longer now than when I started. But I did learn two things for sure: that there is a great deal of work to be done, and that there is hope.

The first step toward taking action is in understanding the many reasons why cancer is a women's issue. Feminism has influenced our thinking about almost everything—relationships, economics, the media, religion.... And yet, when it comes to life-threatening illness (with the exception of AIDS, because it is viewed as a political issue), there has been little feminist analysis and consequently no feminist action. Most women with cancer—at a time when we are vulnerable, perhaps terrified—must turn to mainstream resources for both medical treatment and emotional support. ("New Age" and alternative cancer resources are frequently just as sexist as their traditional counterparts.)

Within the patriarchal medical establishment women are subjected not only to blatant sexism but also to male values. We are thrown into a situation where "brave" means not crying, where illnesses are treated instead of human beings. Mary, one of the women I interviewed, described a discussion with her doctor:

We were talking about a bone marrow transplant. It's a painful, high-risk procedure and I was scared. I lost control and a tear slid down my cheek. So he put me on Elavil [an anti-depressant].

For women with cancer, emotional support is crucial not only while facing painful or debilitating treatments but also in dealing with their side effects. Our body images are often affected by scars, hair loss, or weight changes. Women with breast cancer often face body-image problems as a result of full or partial mastectomy. In mainstream support groups, which usually include men, these topics may never come up because women are not comfortable discussing them in male company. Even in all-female groups (generally available only to women with breast cancer), it is important to have a political framework that recognizes the negative influence our culture has had on women's body images.

In addition to generating concerns about the acceptability of our bodies, cancer may mean a silencing of women's voices. We often keep our diagnosis a secret for fear of frightening people away, upsetting family members, or being seen as weak or incompetent (especially in a traditionally male work setting). Also, the role reversal from caregiver to care-needer can be stressful for women. But pretending we are not sick in order to somehow protect our jobs, loved ones, or social roles often means assuming responsibilities we are not up to, and not getting the care we need.

Lorraine, a woman I interviewed, did not tell anyone at work that she had cancer:

Being middle-aged and female in a career filled with young men, it is difficult to convince people of your competence. If I had, in addition, a life-threatening disease, it might be a reason for not promoting me. The game at work is to have as few things against you as possible. So I took on projects that I physically did not have the strength for.

These days, women with cancer may be not only silenced but blamed. Despite evidence that most cancers result from a complex interaction of environmental exposure, genetic predisposition, immune system functioning, lifestyle, and more, New Age "healers" frequently adopt a simplistic blame-the-victim approach. Not surprisingly, many of those blamed are women. Arlene spoke with me about the problems of this New Age approach:

We have the medical profession to create iatrogenic illnesses, we have patriarchal culture which has polluted everything we eat and breathe, and now we have the New Age movement to come along and tell us that it's all our fault. When I was sick, people gave me books that said you got cancer because you're depressed and you've had losses. Fifty percent of the "cancer personality" description probably fits most women. It's similar to what the mental health profession does with "depression" or "masochistic personality disorder." It takes things that define what a woman is in this culture and puts a disease label on it.

The notion that we create our own reality and make ourselves get the disease for some emotional reason or to further our spiritual growth is nonsense. You can find a metaphor for any illness in your life and if you make meaning out of what's happened to you by finding some metaphor for your own spiritual growth that's really an accomplishment. But metaphors don't cause the disease. You can't go back to the beginning with magical thinking and say now that I've made some meaning of this, the meaning is what made me get the disease in the first place.

If there is a grain of truth in the New Age philosophy, it may be that our health is affected by the lifestyles we choose. But the *stressful* and self-sacrificing lives that many women lead are usually dictated and reinforced by society. We are often too busy taking care of others to attend to our own physical and emotional needs. In addition, our stress levels (which affect immune system functioning) may be increasing with the current pressure to be Superwoman, both at home and on the job.

Along with the psychological and emotional reasons for recognizing cancer as a feminist issue, there are many practical matters to be addressed politically. Cows and chickens are routinely given estrogens to increase growth despite the fact that certain cancers (breast, ovarian, and others of the female reproductive tract) are fueled by this hormone. The public is not made aware of this—at the very least there should be warning labels on all products that were exposed to these drugs. In addition, hormone-free meats are expensive and available in few places, making them financially and geographically inaccessible to most people.

Estrogens are also used in treating menopausal symptoms, reducing postpartum breast engorgement, and providing birth control. Most studies and articles that discuss the link between birth control pills and breast cancer are lacking in vital information. Although many different pills have been produced with varying amounts of estrogen, they are lumped into a single category: the Pill. Furthermore, the only age differentiation these reports tend to make is between pre- and post-menopausal women. But young women have significantly different susceptibility to breast cancer. Radiation fall-out during World War II and fluoroscopy treatment for tuberculosis were both factors in the subsequent development of breast cancer—in women below age thirty. Women who become pregnant very young have a significantly lower incidence of breast cancer.

I recently read of a new birth control device, Norplant, approved by the Federal Drug Administration (FDA). It is surgically implanted and releases a progesterone-like hormone. When my mother was pregnant with me, she was given progesterone to prevent miscarriage. Thirty-seven years later, I developed a kind of breast cancer that is highly sensitive to progesterone. While I have no way of knowing whether the drug my mother received contributed to the development of cancer in either one of us, I do know enough to be deeply alarmed by the increasingly widespread exposure to hormones many women are receiving.

Hormones are not the only products that may influence the development of cancer. When it was determined that smoking caused lung cancer (which then affected mostly men), warning labels appeared on cigarette packages, and television advertising was banned. There is now evidence of a link between artificial sweeteners and some forms of cancer. Yet television ads for diet products—which primarily appeal to women—proliferate. It is frightening to think of adolescent girls as the target group for some of these ads, since young people seem to be particularly vulnerable to carcinogens.

While the FDA is contributing to our cancer problem (sanctioning thousands of chemical food additives, irradiated produce, and potentially carcinogenic birth control methods), our legislators are doing little to help. Few current laws protect people with cancer. Informed consent laws requiring physicians to tell women with breast cancer of all their treatment options exist in only fifteen states. I know of no such laws specific to any other kinds of cancer.

Another concern that must be addressed by legislators is the lack of safe and reliable mammography facilities. The American Cancer Society advises women to have a baseline mammogram by age forty, but mammography centers are not legally required to keep the film indefinitely. In some states, such as New York, a woman can find a lump and discover that her baseline mammogram, taken seven years earlier, no longer exists. Many states allow untrained personnel to act as technologists. Furthermore, there is no consistent regulation of radiation dosage or mammography equipment. Radiation dosage for mammography is low and accuracy high under the best of circumstances, but most women are not treated under the best of circumstances. The American College of Radiologists was so alarmed by the results of an FDA study on mammography (with one type of mammogram, the facility using the highest dosage of radiation gave one hundred times the radiation of the lowest) that they set up a voluntary program to evaluate and accredit facilities.

It is no wonder that feminists haven't taken on a cause that on the surface appears apolitical, hopeless, and frightening. Unlike incest, battering, discrimination, and other feminist concerns, cancer does not seem to be an issue of empowerment vs. oppression (although race, socioeconomic status, and gender certainly influence our treatment and, in some cases, survival rates). Decades of research have failed to change the cure rate of most cancers significantly. Furthermore, we live in a culture so phobic about bodily processes that we deny illness and death (as we do aging).

Current statistics show that nearly one-third of all Americans will get some form of cancer. But as women, we are all affected by cancer. For it is females, in our many roles—as relatives, lovers, friends, neighbors, daughters-in-law, and nurses—that most often assume caretaking responsibilities when someone is ill.

The time to address cancer-related issues politically is long overdue. Some of the women I spoke with apologetically expressed resentment about the attention, funding, and political support that people with AIDS have gotten. They feel that people with cancer should be given the same kind of attention. Breast cancer alone has reached epidemic proportions in our country, and the rate is steadily rising. The number of breast cancer deaths in a single year is greater than the total of all AIDS deaths to date. Yet there has been no commemorative effort, no organized demand for education and increased funding, little public attention. One woman with breast cancer who had been involved in AIDS work felt that while the gay community had been incredibly supportive of people with AIDS, there was "no community of women" to offer similar support. Breast cancer activist Rose Kushner noted that funding for breast cancer research has been cut back to $60,894 million this year while $1.6 billion has been appropriated for the fight against AIDS.

Nobody wants to pit one illness against another or to take money away from AIDS. Instead, there is a lot we can learn from the inspiring work and commitment of AIDS activists and the gay community. We can do more than make occasional donations to the American Cancer Society. We must tap into the wealth of human resources at the local level and begin to organize.

Cancer is clearly a feminist issue. We need an organization—of women, for women—that will encompass political action, direct service, and education. We need to question the decisions of the Food and Drug Administration, and call for longer testing periods, warning labels, bans, and consumer action when necessary. We must evaluate and change the laws. We must "feminize" the health care system, making room for our values of connectedness and emotional expression. We must look at cancer research and funding: how much is going toward prevention or alternatives to chemotherapy and how much toward slightly improving the same old drugs that are never going to be very effective? We must pressure political candidates and elected officials to put cancer issues on their agendas. In addition to political action, we must provide widespread education about cancer prevention as well as treatment. Many women, afraid of losing a breast, delay seeking medical treatment because they are unaware of alternatives to mastectomy or of reconstructive surgery. Some of us, afraid of dying, rush into unnecessary procedures or are manipulated into expensive, ineffective, or sexually abusive "treatments."

When it comes to understanding the environmental causes of cancer, we lack a comprehensive picture. One or two chemical additives in a bowl of cereal will not cause cancer. We may be able to tolerate pesticides in the air and on our foods. The radiation from microwave ovens, color TVs, and routine x-rays is probably negligible. But cumulatively, things don't look so benign. We don't have to become fanatics to stay healthy, but we should be able to make educated choices about what risks we are willing to take.

Education about nutrition and environmental issues must begin in the elementary schools. Children today are still taught simply that choices from "The Four Food Groups" constitute a healthy diet—but a Big Mac, a can of peas, a slice of Wonder Bread, and a dish of ice cream can do more harm than good. Children should learn about the additives and preservatives that go into many of our foods. Topics such as the biology of cancer, immune system functioning, and medical advocacy should be presented to older students. Public service announcements should encourage second opinions and inform consumers of various treatment options. The media should give more coverage to cancer research and alternative therapies.

We also need local resource networks—a volunteer program for providing assistance to women with cancer (cooking, driving, child care, etc.); cancer support groups framed with the political awareness of sexism and women's roles in our culture; an annotated directory of professionals (therapists, nutritionists, hairdressers, various healers) indicating wheelchair accessibility and availability to come to the home or hospital; and funding for the services women cannot afford.

We could draw upon the AIDS "buddy" model and set up a system that provides intensive one-to-one support for women with cancer. Or we could organize a network of support groups for individual women. There are many possibilities and ways of involving volunteers with various skills, time, and interest levels. Ideally, we would have a three-pronged approach to cancer activism: direct support, political action, and education. Most of the women I interviewed expressed some feeling of being "left out" or "incredibly alone," even those who had support from friends and family. I think what was missing was the sense of being part of a community that cared.

Author's note: I lovingly dedicate this article to my mother, Tret Shapiro; to Smadar Levin, whose fourteen years of living with cancer were a model of love, courage, and wisdom; and to the women who opened their hearts to me as they told their stories.

FEBRUARY 1990

WOMEN'S COMMUNITY CANCER PROJECT: STATEMENT OF PURPOSE

Following Susan Shapiro's plea, in the September 1989 issue of Sojourner, that women come together to form a feminist organization that would address the politics of cancer, provide support and direct services for women with cancer, and educate the public, a group of women in the Boston area founded the Women's Community Cancer Project. Though Susan died just four months after the publication of her article, she was thrilled to be a part of this project. The cancer project has since become an active voice in the movement to build a health care agenda that addresses women's needs.

The Women's Community Cancer Project is a grassroots organization created to facilitate changes in the current medical, social, and political approaches to cancer, particularly as they affect women. We do not accept the "fact" that thousands of us must die quietly of cancer each year. We are concerned by the insufficient funding for cancer research, treatment, prevention, and education. We recognize the necessity of subsidizing and exploring alternative healing methods in addition to those sanctioned by the traditional medical model. We are appalled by the environmental abuses and unsafe food and drug standards that contribute to our current cancer epidemic. Major changes in our methods of addressing cancer are long overdue—in federal regulating agencies as well as in the medical, pharmaceutical, and insurance industries.

As feminists, we are committed to challenging the various forms of discrimination that exist in many mainstream and alternative cancer establishments—sexism, racism, ableism, homophobia, ageism, and classism. These biases are reflected in the kind of research done and in its interpretation, the attitudes of health care personnel, the accessibility of medical/alternative treatments, and the quality of emotional support services. It is our intention to:

- involve women whose lives are touched by cancer, including women who have and/or had cancer themselves, caregivers, friends, lovers, and families of those with cancer, and women concerned with the political and emotional implications of cancer;
- provide a forum for political activism (investigation and direct action) regarding cancer-related issues;
- create a volunteer system of physical and emotional support for women with cancer;
- produce a directory or referral network of local healers and professionals interested in helping women with cancer;
- compile cancer education resources, both mainstream and alternative.

JULY 1993

The Breast Cancer I Have

by Linda Quint Freeman

VASHON ISLAND, WASHINGTON
JULY 19, 1992
I play like a lazy butter knife in the steaming water of an outdoor hot tub. Mt. Rainier glows behind the red band of sunset, then settles in the cape of darkness, confident and solid, even though unseen. My hand struggles against the urge to touch the lump above the nipple of my left breast. In the last few days, I have felt that spot repeatedly, confirming its reality, summoning healing energy to carry the cancer away, memorizing this part of myself soon to be removed. I circle the edges of the hard bulge, complaining and sore from the doctor's needle and my probing. My lover lays her hand over mine and draws me closer. Beyond the balcony, five soft hoots skitter from a naked limb of a shore pine. A cool whisper of wind, then the answer of five notes. Twilight. It is my time. I am here. My mastectomy is two days away, and I write in my journal and breathe with the life beyond my urban window. I am here, too.

One out of eight women in the United States has heard or is hearing the diagnosis of breast cancer, and it is now the most common cancer in women. Before July 15, 1992, this fact was an unimportant, unexperienced statistic. Now it is me. Now I can visualize these eight women, sisters and friends in a room with eight chairs. I can see their faces—from the 29-year-old expectant mother to the 65-year-old, gray as a weathered fence, newly retired. Their skin is prairie peach to ebony black. One of us will sit down in shock, anger, and grief. One of us will be ill-prepared by our culture to grasp her mortality. And one of us will have the breast cancer she has.

For a month, I repeated the rhythm of taking my insurance card out of my wallet and filling in a succession of forms fixed to a clipboard with a pen that always was just out of ink. Pink forms, blue forms, yellow forms. Name of spouse, person to call in case of an emergency. I practiced self-esteem (as if I always had it) and wrote her name, then "significant other." How do you spell "Gaye"? Gail, Gale, Gabe—the receptionists stumbled to translate for the computer. They spent the most time lovingly copying the insurance card, front side and back—the plastic green card to medical care.

And now I know the meaning of having a disease that she has. We have a disease of women. We are valued with a women's illness in the same way we are valued as women. Many women have no money or insurance to detect the disease early, when the medical community concurs that early diagnosis offers us the best chance of survival. The technologies of detection, from mammograms to stereotactic needle biopsies, glitter from afar for many women. Our medical insurance system creates a privileged class of patients who can go where they will. All women should have this as a right.

"It's nothing. A fibrocystic change," I was told the previous November. In May, after another mammogram and sonogram, it was visible. In June, I visited my internist for a nasty head cold. It was a cyst. She urged me to have it drained. Many, many irregularities in the breast turn out to be normal, but an icy minor scale practiced on my spine. She recommended a competent male colleague. When can you make an appointment? I had pressures at my job. July 1 was a busy date for renewals of our clients. I had a business trip to San Francisco, so I delayed for two weeks.

Western medicine is not the type of exact science where equations promise certainty, no matter how many times or by whom calculated. It is as fallible as the practitioners and patients. As women, our inculcated passivity in the face of authority figures, such as a doctor, leads us to ignore the ultimate responsibility we have for our own life. Too easily reassured, we miss what our bodies are telling us. Besides, with all the pressure of daily life and our focus on other people's needs, who has the time?

"Dr. Wallburger will see you now." I found myself in a cool, yellow metallic room with bad prints, a type of institutional cheerfulness. There were shelves of pamphlets from the American Cancer Society for cancer of the lung, breast, prostate, and colon. All our innocuous organs. I clung to the cyst diagnosis. Hmm, the lump wasn't behaving like a cyst. No fluid drained. He stuck me several times and smeared his findings on a slide. Gaye and I were not really there. Make an appointment with the nurse in two days. We'll have the results by then. The nurse patted my shoulder. I kept asking the same question over and over: am I going to die? The litany of asking fed more anxiety. I was yet to discover the serenity of the present.

Being an American woman is a risk factor for breast cancer. Researchers have noticed that Chinese and Japanese women living in Asia have a much lower inci-

dence—is it the air we breathe, the food we eat, the voluminous list of hard-to-pro-nounce substances (man-made technology we say proudly) at our jobs, homes, and farms, the nuclear tests clouding our deserts and islands during the Cold War? Our approach to health issues mirrors our handling of the environment we live in—com-pensate after the damage has been done, rather than prevent it from happening. But cancer turns on its own terms. In this decade, prevention appears ephemeral. A cure, as every woman with breast cancer knows, awaits lifelong to the next checkup.

The sample had malignant cells. Tears streamed down my face. I had a thousand questions. I could not stop shaking. He offered the pamphlets and asked if I would come back to discuss the next step when I stopped crying. Apparently, women cannot think and cry at the same time. The nurse offered a hug and said that today would be the worst day. After that, everything would start to fall into place.

The breast cancer I have is not like that. There are no smooth transitions; rather, emotions ebb and flow with each successive step, from diagnosis through sur-gery to chemotherapy and follow-up monitoring.

Gaye and I talked and cried on the way home. A finding of breast cancer was hard enough, yet something else felt very wrong. Neither of us was comfortable with Dr. Wallburger's role as expert mechanic, a tourist to my woman's cancer. The nurse was the native face in the office, the caring face. Gaye made some phone calls to doc-tors she worked with, and by some miracle, a woman surgeon in Vancouver, Washington, was willing to see me with four hours notice. I decided to listen to my woman's body and let it tell me what to do and whom to do it with.

It is a curable cancer, but there are 46,000 women who die each year from the disease—how many really died from our insurance-for-profit system, men's priorities and attitudes? We have a disease of women, and to survive, we need to take charge of our own lives. I know I have irrevocably changed what I am willing to leave to others and what I must do for myself.

In my first consultation with the woman who became my surgeon, we talked at great length about the value I placed on survival and my body/breast self-image. I had two basic surgical options: lumpectomy (breast conservation with mandatory postsurgical radiation) or modified mastectomy (removal of the breast). That hour confirmed that survival was most important to me. I did not want the possibility of future operations on the same breast, the "over and done with" school of thought. My choice was not based on the fear that I would lose more than my tumor. I was not any single body part. I was loved, and I could decide for myself freely.

I still struggle to love myself and believe that I am loved. My self-confidence in the world, at my job, and with my body has been tested again and again.

The next few hours were hell. I called the rabbi at the gay synagogue I belonged to in Los Angeles. She told me to get Dr. Bernie Siegel's book *Love, Medicine, and Mir-acles* (Harper and Row, 1986). "Believe in your recovery," she said. My name would be added to the prayer for recovery said at Friday night services. Next I reached out to a lesbian friend in Bakersfield who had had a mastectomy six years ago and was a re-covering alcoholic. She asked me to find the small gold compact she gave me when I moved to Portland with Gaye. Read it every day.

God grant me the serenity to accept the things I cannot change, the courage to change the things I can, and the wisdom to know the difference.

I fished in the black leather bowels of my purse sometimes just to touch those etched words and feel their warmth and serenity. They helped me to call my mother and sister next. My shocked, special sister immediately wanted to be with me. It's difficult and easy to have family around at these moments. The difficult part is they are experiencing their denial and fear out of step with yours. When you are feeling better, they are feeling worse. And a Jewish sister adds an ethnic nuance:

Sister: "Only famous doctors cure people. You aren't serious about this woman shiksa surgeon in Vancouver? Get on the next plane for Johns Hopkins. Are they sure it's cancer?"

Me: "I need to be here. All right, I'll check her diplomas. Why don't you fly here? Gaye could use the support, especially after I get home. Great, you can cook for us. Yes, we like falafel balls. No, I'm not rushing into anything. Gaye and I need a few days away, but I couldn't handle more time than that. The operation is scheduled for Wednesday next week. It's no mistake."

As Audre Lorde has said, first there is hurt and then the tears. Since my diagnosis, tears flow spontaneously at a touch or thought or look.

On Vashon Island, we celebrated my forty-sixth birthday. This one was more than cards and gifts. The lump ached because of repeated needle sticks during the biopsy. Was it my thoughts or the lump that ached? I read Bernie Siegel. I started a journal. I played my new alto recorder. I slowly pulled away from despair and reexamined my life—what was important to me now? I began to repeat positive algorithms to myself: *I believe in my recovery. Wellness and peace are flowing through my body. I believe in Gaye's healing ceremony.*

At night in bed, she would lay her outstretched hand above my breast and pull the cancer into her fingers and shake it away. My shaman, my love.

I am the one in eight women. I am also the one in ten women who is a lesbian woman. And I am in her skin, too, and it is different, offering different insights, problems, and gifts. The articles, pamphlets, books, and newspaper clippings I select to read or are sent to me do not acknowledge my existence as a lesbian woman with breast cancer. Discussions of the relationship issues of breast cancer assume a heterosexual context. The "significant other" is always a husband pictured with his arm around his wife. But even if I were the only one, I exist. I know there are thousands of us with invisible lives. Only our tumors are seen.

VANCOUVER, WASHINGTON
JULY 22, 1992

My sister, Gaye, and I check into the hospital at 8 a.m. The intake clerk has a problem on "religious preference." It takes a while to find J2, Jewish. Then I am ushered to radiology for a chest x-ray. Gaye's daughter examines the plate with the seriousness of an inquisitive, detached medical student. Some people are hopeless, I think. Next there is a blood draw and the shedding of my clothes in the surgical preparation room. I have had enough already of needles and there is an IV to come. Tears punctuate my passage to the next place—the pre-op holding area and a conference with my surgeon and anesthesiologist. I have written down twenty or more questions during our stay on Vashon. Things like, how long will it take before I wake up after surgery? Will you tell Gaye and the family right away? I play classical piano: will I lose feeling in my left hand? I shiver under a thin sheet, but Gaye tells the nurse to get me a blanket. I tell them not to say anything negative while I am under. An injection and I start to count backwards—99, 98, 97, up, up, and away my beautiful balloon.

Is it relevant that this cancer happens to a woman? We are all human beings, aren't we? But it is a cancer of the breast; it is a cancer She has; it is a cancer I have. Start with the basics: what is a breast anyway? Defined in Webster's, *it is the "fore part of the body, between the neck and the belly; the heart; the conscience; the affections." Breasts are just a fatty protuberance of the body, certainly not as weighty or important as a colon or a penis.*

Our breasts nourish human life and move with erotic feelings. To a woman, a breast is much more than fat, ducts, nipple, and skin. Breasts noticeably change with a woman's cycle, sometimes sore, lumpy, and swollen with water. They participate in the joy of a woman's sexual experience and her experience of motherhood, whether the woman is straight or gay.

I awake to blurry faces, a morphine drip, and the verdict of breast cancer. I glance down and see a bra attached in the front with a Velcro strip. On the left side under the cup is a small mound of gauze. My surgeon does not have her patients wake up to a grotesque mass of bandages. She knows about the loss I feel beyond physical pain and the mourning voices I hear inside. She tells me the lymph nodes look normal, but the pathology report will have the definitive answer on whether the cancer has spread to the lymph nodes. I didn't realize there would be two painful drainage tubes. She says she will get them out as quickly as possible. See you tomorrow.

We are the "out couple" at the hospital. Gaye finagles a cot in my room and keeps vigil through my fits of sleep, broken by wakefulness and pain. The breast is gone. What is left?

The emotional dilemma is in other meanings. In our culture, breasts define a woman's desirability, and, in that a woman is desirable, she is valuable. Many women lose their partner after the loss of a breast. With the loss of life at stake, a woman with breast cancer struggles with the value of her living self in her eyes and in the eyes of others.

Cards, flowers, visitors, telephone calls, and a new face. Georgie is a tall, daisy blond Texan with tanned, anorexic legs who announces like a public address announcer at a rodeo that she is "mah nurse for the swing shift. Let's get you out of bed. If you expect to go home, you'll have to do your chores. That's it. Hang on to the stand and sit down on the toilet slowly." Her soft grin. You made it, honey.

Back on the bed, I try several times to lie back without the insistent stab of the drainage tubes. Let me help, Georgie says. Finally, I settle back, and she reattaches the plastic device that squeezes my legs like soft oranges every minute or so to prevent blood clots. "I know about your surgery," she says, "but look here, it's not the end of the world. I want to show you something." The privacy curtain whisks around my bed. I stare at her like a child at a magic show. She unbuttons the front of her neatly pressed uniform and unhooks her bra. There loom two exceptionally symmetrical, softball-sized marvels that are the same color as her face, complete with darkened nipple and areola. I am pleasantly stunned and hope Gaye cannot see my face. Before I can breathe, she asks if I would like to touch them. "Yes, no, yes, no, okay, but only for a second." Hers have a perfect give and bounce. My original breast could never do that. Silicone, girl. You can look this good, too.

We women search for wholeness, each in our own way. Dow knew their silicone envelopes could leak and poison us, profiting from the legitimate desires of women to be whole and comfortable. But the battle scar of our mortality cannot be concealed.

PORTLAND, OREGON
JULY 24, 1992

Home. I cannot sleep in the waterbed; the firmer bed downstairs feels better. It takes quite a while to find a position where nothing hurts beyond tolerance. My arms are propped under and on top of pillows; I am unable to turn on my side, unable to be held. Sleep comes in segments. A relaxation tape sometimes helps, sometimes doesn't. My sister stays three more days and fusses over us. On Sunday, friends arrive and gingerly assist me out the front door to look at the roses and feel the sunshine. I planted three miniature patio tea roses out front last spring—an uproar of purple, yellow, and red. They panic when my drainage box snaps open unexpectedly, and they are unable to press it back into place.

The drainage tubes are removed earlier than anticipated, and my delight grows to cosmic proportions when the surgeon breezes into the examination room, smiling. The lymph nodes are all negative for cancer cells! We discuss the next step, chemotherapy. How much and what kind will be dictated largely by my age and the in-depth pathology report on the tumor. In the meantime, I am instructed to keep up the exercise—a snail-like crawl of the fingers up a wall to straighten the arm. I am making slow progress with Gaye's prodding.

I buy a temporary prosthesis for the next two months, something soft and light. An elderly woman with hair the color of candy corn found me a tear-drop foam shape to insert in my bra. Uncanny how much it matches the shape of the other breast. Wait six months or so before you choose reconstruction, my surgeon advises.

I need to be reconstructed from within. The prosthesis is for my passage through the outer world.

VANCOUVER, WASHINGTON
AUGUST 19, 1992

Given the characteristics of the tumor (and being only in my mid-forties), the oncologist changes her mind and opts for a shorter, intense bout of drugs. I learn what the chemotherapy protocol "CA" means—cytoxan and adriamycin. The oncologist coolly lists the "side effects" that I will learn to live with intimately for the next four months: hair loss within seventeen days after the first treatment, nausea, and fatigue. Other women who have experienced chemotherapy give me the most valuable advice.

I have an uneasy feeling about my doctor's distance, her use of her nurses as a wall, and short explanations, but I stay with her through three difficult treatments. If I had been more self-caring and decisive, I would have changed doctors sooner and not have suffered unnecessarily from nausea and vein damage. The fourth and last treatment is given in much more controlled conditions with my new oncologist. One night I had pushed myself to attend a seminar on breast cancer at a local hospital, and she was one of the speakers. Good karma, I guess.

Chemotherapy challenges the depths of my spiritual and physical resources and strains the fibers of my closest relationships. It begins with my hair coming out in large chunks in the shower, thirteen days after the first treatment. My network of wise women tell me to get a wig fitted before my hair is gone, then shave it off completely rather than grieve as each strand falls. I become depressed, angry, and withdrawn. My hair is woven into my very existence as a woman and as a person. Its loss feels like a loss of self. I am becoming a cancer patient. I stop making love. Again, a woman comes to my rescue. She specializes in wigs for cancer patients, and she patiently creates one that resembles almost exactly my own lost hair. "No, that's not right," I say. "It is a little shorter on the sides."

Chemotherapy is as a cleansing, scouring river, flushing the cancer cells out of my body. I visualize myself sitting in the front of a canoe being paddled across this river by a great medicine woman. The ride is bumpy and scary sometimes, but I see the grassy slopes of the opposite shore. I believe in my recovery and go on.

How inadequate are words like "fatigue" to describe how I feel. Just as the Eskimo have dozens of words to describe the nuances of ice and snow, our culture should develop a lexicon for illness. I have known the stone numbness of mind and body, the gnawing depths of nausea. But it passes. My job provides an anchor and an objective each day—dressing, commuting, functioning—all are small victories.

I have been purposely vague at work as to the nature of my illness. Cancer is perceived as the Industrial Revolution's black plague, a disease with mythical killing powers. An obese man at work had a triple bypass. Everyone assumed he would be around to collect his raise and promotion. Would a woman with breast cancer be treated the same way? I become protective with the knowledge of my illness. However, my sallow face and thimble-sized energy are apparent to many of my coworkers. The office gossip fills in much of the rest. Many compliment me on my hairstyle. They will be quite disappointed when my real hair grows back!

Cry, laugh, let someone in. Yoga classes with my new tribe of one-breasted women, positive messages clipped to the mirror of my bathroom, acupuncture, short walks to see birds are all part of my healing. There are no formulas and no guarantees, but I know my immune system responds to everything inside and outside me.

PORTLAND, OREGON
OCTOBER 26, 1992
And the chemotherapy ends. Like a bare-scrubbed field in winter, my hair sprouts all over the places where it had been last summer. It is a different texture, curlier, but there. Gaye and I visit Israel, and I place a scrap of paper in a chink of the Western Wall, my prayer for health, love, and strength. I begin again as a lover.

I am no longer the woman I was—I am more and I am different. I used to see only the house I lived in and what seemed to be the endless vista around it. Now I see the house and fence that surrounds it. It is not limitless. Today I savor the beauty of this house with clearer and keener senses.

I have already had my two false alarms for the year, so my surgeon remarks. Aches and pains I would have ignored or would have attributed to my treatments and inactivity for almost six months, I magnify and mull in my worried mind. I have lost confidence in my own body. Can I learn to trust it again?

The breast cancer I have is my own, but I am connected to all women survivors. We greet each other with smiles in the waiting room of our oncologists. We value the strength of each other and find our bald heads beautiful. We share our doubts and fears without trying to suppress them or judge them. We talk of our experiences so that women will care for their own bodies and each other's, and we will never accept the disparities in health care that shorten women's lives. We are challenging patients.

MARCH 1982

She Ain't Heavy, She's My Sister...
by Molly Lovelock

The Elizabeth Stone House, a Boston-area program for women in emotional distress, has written a pamphlet, *Mental Health: 13 Myths and Realities*. The realities are that there are basic, straightforward ways women can help each other, and in particular, help women who are labeled "crazy." The Elizabeth Stone House is built on these realities. It provides a unique residential program for twelve to fifteen women. With structure, people to break down the isolation, and the ability to keep her children with her if that makes sense, a woman is given the time to be who she needs to be, to think about what she needs to do.

The Stone House began in 1974, primarily through the efforts of Mary Raffini, a woman who herself had been in psychiatric institutions. Originally, it was a project of the Cambridge Women's Center. It's named after Elizabeth Stone who, in 1840, was committed to the Charlestown McLean Asylum, because her conversion from Methodist to Baptist clearly indicated she was "insane."

Over time, the Elizabeth Stone House has offered a variety of programs, including a long-term residential mental health center, a short-term crisis center, a referral network, services to battered women, education, and outreach. As a feminist program, this has often been done despite incredible constraints of staff and money. The Stone House recently bought and renovated a three-story house in the Jamaica Plain section of Boston, and the staff now concentrates on the long-term therapeutic community, emergency services for battered women referred from other shelters, and education and outreach, including the distribution of their videotape, *The Road I Took to You.*

When I visited the Stone House, I was immediately struck by the warmth and supportiveness even of the building itself. There is brick; there are bright bedrooms, a great kitchen and family room, and an office with a beautiful bow-windowed front wall. And because most of the women are there for five months (the maximum stay), there is a settled-in, home-like atmosphere.

One of the myths the Stone House pamphlet talks about is that "crazy women cannot function effectively, they cannot take on responsibility, participate in meetings, give support, etc." On the contrary, say women of the Stone House, the chance to take responsibility in a supportive setting can be a key thing for a woman in emotional distress. Residents are required to go to twice-a-week house meetings and participate in major decisions of the house. Before a new woman is admitted to the program, she must be interviewed and approved by the other women who are already there. Day-to-day mundane responsibilities—meals, chores—are also shared, and several residents I spoke with emphasized how well this works.

Other myths are that crazy women are "fragile" or "too much for me to deal with." At Stone House there are no psychiatrists on the staff, no nurses in residence. Staff members include women who have been through psychiatric institutions themselves and some who have not. The emphasis on volunteers at the Stone House also helps de-mystify emotional distress. Drawing upon one's own experience, listening, being honest and direct, having fun and doing social things: for volunteers to do this runs counter to what women experience in institutions.

The Stone House is also associated with the traditional mental health system. Many women, particularly those just out of an institution, come to the Stone House already working with a therapist. Or, at a woman's request, the staff can make an appropriate referral: to a neighborhood clinic, a therapist who is a mother, a lesbian. About half the women at the Stone House are seeing therapists.

The Stone House has no specific stand on medications. On this issue, as elsewhere, much is left up to the women themselves. If someone wants to get off medications, the staff will help her do this in the best way.

Setting goals, dealing with practical realities, is one of the key things about the Stone House, and one of the many things that distinguishes this residential program from a traditional halfway house. Women don't necessarily come to the program with goals already set, but they establish goals and work toward them during the five months. For instance, housing is something that is dealt with early on, with the help of a housing advocate.

Of course, what really distinguishes the Elizabeth Stone House is its feminist analysis. The reality is that "craziness is a response to an oppressive environment." Institutionalization, in particular, "is highly correlated to real practical problems like poverty and abuse." Some 95 percent of women at the Stone House have histories of violence whether as victims of child abuse, incest, rape, or wife-beating. Most have some history of institutionalization, and half may be coming directly from hospitals. Another half may be leaving relationships.

From their analysis of the roots of emotional distress comes Stone House's insistence on dealing with practical problems—that working on housing, medical, or children's issues simultaneously creates progress on emotional problems. And the program, at $54 per month, is something women living on AFDC (Aid to Families with Dependent Children) or other limited incomes can pay for.

Finally, one of the key things about the Stone House as a woman-centered program is its emphasis on issues of children. About 75 percent of the women there are mothers, although many are not with their children. For women who have custody, the Stone House is one of the few therapeutic programs where their children can stay with them, and there is support, such as child care, for this. Other women at the Stone House may have lost their children to protective services or have children who are with relatives or in foster care. For these women, too, dealing with issues of children is crucial, and, in fact, having children at the House creates an additional necessity for focusing on these issues.

One of the final myths the Stone House notes is that craziness is either "hopeless and endless" or "an exciting and fulfilling journey." No, craziness is painful and isolating. It increases a woman's powerlessness. But by changing the assumptions, recognizing the causes of emotional distress, and assuming that women can have some control over their lives, the Stone House staff is doing something very powerful. They are creating new realities for all of us.

This article has been edited for length and clarity.

AUGUST 1990

Where I Bin
by R. Judith Vincent

As far back as I can remember I have been beset by a collection of problems that were never severe enough to be obvious, but that, nonetheless, inhibited my life. I was always dizzy or tired, and was horrible at sports (as in the Janice Ian song, I was *never* chosen for basketball). I had a lousy memory, couldn't concentrate, and was constantly having anxiety attacks. I always felt lost, different, ineffectual, in a fog, rudderless, and isolated. I had trouble holding down jobs and seemed to be going nowhere. I never considered these problems symptomatic of anything other than my inability to handle life, having more or less decided I was dumb, without direction or ambition, a dreamer.

But in 1985, I came across a book that listed every one of my problems and named their root cause as dyslexia. The author proposed a list of medications as a cure, including antihistamines and amphetamines. His explanation of how dyslexia could cause these myriad symptoms made sense to me. I knew I had to see this man.

In December 1986, I went to visit this doctor's clinic, spending over $1,000 of my own money on both the airfare and the tests. The final fee was $750, not $600 as the brochure had said, but I was hopeful that someone could guide me out of the haze, the frustration, and the sadness I had always lived in.

The first shock came when I tried to fill the prescriptions in Massachusetts. The pharmacist refused, since the prescriptions were from out of state. I called the clinic in tears. I asked if they could recommend a local psychiatrist to write the prescriptions for me. They knew of no one. They said that if I mailed them the money (about $50 for all three drugs) that they would send me the medications. This I happily agreed to, also requesting a package insert so I would know what I was taking. A week later I received the drugs without an insert. They had sent me Meclezine, Marezine, and Cylert. I went to the library to look up these drugs in the *Physician's Desk Reference*. The first two were for motion sickness; the last was a drug similar to Ritalin, usually given to children with Attention Deficit Disorder (ADD).

Medical scientists believe that ADD is caused by a structural problem in the brain. The disorder is characterized by an inability to focus or maintain one's attention for any period of time. This causes those afflicted to feel frustrated, as they are unable to accomplish the simplest of tasks. ADD is usually diagnosed in children, but more adults are receiving the diagnosis all the time. Both Cylert and Ritalin, used to treat ADD, are amphetamines—speed.

In addition to sending the drugs without the information I requested, the dosage instructions provided by the clinic were illegible. I called the clinic repeatedly to ask questions. Each time I received a different response, some reassuring, some ignorant and impatient, all of them contradictory.

The first time I ordered my drugs ahead of schedule was as early as January 1987, only a month after I began taking them. No one at the clinic questioned this. I was stockpiling the drugs because I was frightened—frightened of changes occurring in my life, frightened that there would be no one with whom to discuss them. The erratic behavior of the clinic staff scared me as well. I knew there was something weird about the whole thing, but they had promised me so much and I felt that I had so little, I could not let go. "We want to give you more good days," one of the medical assistants told me.

I continued to search the Boston area for anyone who knew of this treatment. Although I found many who were expert in dyslexia itself, nobody had ever heard of this treatment. It seemed the only solid thing that I had were the pills. I realized I was becoming dependent and called the clinic again to discuss this. I don't recall their response, but I came away reassured. I also wrote them many letters full of questions. They never answered me. I developed a rash. They told me it was not unusual.

I felt a rush of energy and clarity with my morning dose, but by afternoon I was crashing badly, so I took an extra pill to get through the day. I quickly developed a tolerance. One pill wasn't enough. I had to take increasingly larger doses to function at all. I knew I was getting into trouble, but my intense fear kept me immobilized. I could not bear the thought of lapsing into what (I thought) was my previous level of functioning. I still believed that the clinic specialists held the key to the world I dreamed of—a world where every day was not a constant, unrelenting battle for clarity and balance.

At least three times I stopped taking the pills altogether. Each time I would sleep for several days and eat huge amounts of food. Then I would begin again at the prescribed dose, but the result was always the same. The early morning rush, the crash, the increase in dosage, etc. Throughout all this, I continued to order the drugs at narrowly spaced intervals. I was never questioned. I didn't know that the effects of Cylert were cumulative; that is, it built up in my system (later taking nearly three months to leave it). I began to experience perceptual changes, such as colored rings around objects, and

I had difficulty attending classes. Tearful, confused, and isolated, I called the clinic constantly, describing my plight, asking for help.

In March 1987, I had a psychotic break. I tore the house apart, begging my boyfriend, John, to save me from myself. I hadn't slept in days and was afraid I would die if I didn't. I accused him of poisoning me. I had stopped taking the Cylert weeks before, but my body was already drenched with it. I kept calling the clinic, begging to speak to my doctor. They hung up on me. Finally, John managed to get him on the phone. In response to my predicament, the doctor suggested a prescription for Valium. "It'll calm the inner ear," he said. Finally, John took me to a local hospital where I was given Ativan, an antianxiety drug. It worked; I slept. I also flushed the Cylert and the other drugs down the toilet. I had had enough.

However, believing that the diagnosis was correct but the clinic's mishandling of the situation had prevented proper treatment, I kept trying. I went through at least four different psychiatrists, three hospitals, two diagnoses (ADD with underlying depression), and five different drugs (all various forms of antidepressants). I even tried another trial with Cylert, this time under proper supervision. Nothing worked. It was suggested that I consult experts at a local world-renowned psychiatric teaching hospital, McLean.

I entered McLean's experimental drug program. In January 1988, a year after my first experience with drug therapy, I was put on a new drug called Adinazolam. I had been taking it for about two weeks and my moods seemed to be lightening a bit, my energy stabilizing. Life seemed all right, until the night of January 2, 1988. I still do not totally understand why I took the overdose. I keep coming to the same question: who was responsible for my behavior that night, me or the doctors at McLean? I suppose it was some of both. I do know that my later discoveries, of memories submerged for almost 30 years, had much to do with it. Also, I was tired of the endless parade of drugs and shrinks; I was beginning to believe there was no answer to my troubles.

It was Sunday night when I took the pills. Monday morning I woke up. I wasn't dead. I told John what I had done and he had me, still groggy, transported to the local emergency room (again). They also decided I wasn't dead and insisted I stay overnight for observation. The only alternative, they said, would be to check into McLean for the night. I preferred the latter choice, since after a quick phone call to the hospital, I was assured that my doctor would be available for a consult.

I planned to be home the next day, so I packed just enough clothes for one night. John drove me to the hospital, dropped me off, and then was told to leave. By now it was about 11 p.m. I was strip searched. Frightened, I asked to leave. Guards were called. They grabbed me and threw me down on a stiff plastic mattress rather like a child's sled. I remember its vivid orange color. I was tied face down, in four-point restraint (or "points" as it is called), with thick leather cuffs around my wrists and ankles. My glasses (without which I am severely nearsighted), my boots, and my jewelry were removed. I cried and begged and pleaded, not understanding this vicious treatment.

Having worked as a counselor for a population of recently deinstitutionalized schizophrenics, I was familiar with the hospital milieu. But now I was seeing it from the patient's side, and it would never look the same again—nothing would.

I was carried roughly to another building and dropped in a quiet room, a room totally devoid of any furnishings except a bare mattress. The principle behind this space is that an assaultive and/or hostile patient can have some time out in a safe environment. While in a quiet room the patient is usually under C.O. (constant observation). I was watched by a male guard. Still tied points, I continued to beg and plead with him for an explanation or just to talk to me. He refused. I asked if I could please be released to use the bathroom. I had to urinate very badly. He informed me that I had to wait till the next shift, since only a female staff person could escort me. (He did offer me a bedpan, but I refused.) I thrashed on the mattress, moaning in pain. I had had a laparoscopy two weeks earlier and my abdomen was still very sore. (Later I discovered that this guard wrote in his report that I was hostile and uncooperative, misinterpreting my pain and anguish. The Restraint Order read, "Patient refuses to contract for safety. Is hostile and uncooperative.")

Hours later, after literally promising to "be a good girl," I was released from restraint and allowed to use the toilet while two women watched. Finally, I slept. I was kept in this room for three days, after which I was transferred to a regular room, which I shared with Carolyn, who was diagnosed as manic-depressive. Carolyn was a very gentle and loving woman. She called me "sweet pea" and tucked me in at night. "We all saw you being hauled in," she said. "We felt so sorry for you." A true veteran of the system, Carolyn had spent many years in and out of mental hospitals, on thousands of types of pills. She kept photos of her three children tacked above her bed.

The power structure in a bin is very clear. The staff are on the top and the patients are on the bottom. Those at the top have the power to effect the course of a person's life, and they have the legal system to back them up. A new patient learns very quickly how to exist within this environment—how to play the game. Carolyn and some of the other patients were kind enough to give me instructions. If I wanted to get out, they explained, I had to go along with whatever the staff (nurses, mental health workers, etc.) said, no matter how bizarre, inaccurate, or demeaning. "They like it when you open up," Carolyn told me. "Give them a few morsels. Ask for their help and guidance."

My initial treatment at the hands of the McLean staff had succeeded in filling me with intense fear. I was so terrified of doing anything wrong that I became very docile and agreeable. I followed Carolyn's advice: yes, it was all my fault, I agreed; yes, I was depressed; of course I trusted them—after all, they knew what was best for me. I received no therapy during my incarceration. There were no organized activities. I was visited occasionally by a group of student interns, who would file into the room and ask me questions, answering none of mine. I felt like a small animal in a cage. Twice a day all the patients would line up for "meds," just like in the movie *One Flew Over the Cuckoo's Nest*.

I spent my days reading and staring out the window. It was only the frequent visits from my friends and relatives that saved me from total despair. Still, when I watched them leave, free to walk out, as I was not, a terrible pain would lash across my abdomen. It was the shame. What could I have done to deserve such treatment? I constantly fought off feelings of horror and depression. After nine days, I was released.

I gave up on the psychiatric profession, no longer believing in the veracity of anything psychiatrists had to say. Having spent some time as both a counselor and a patient, the flaws in the system were glaringly obvious. In my nine days at McLean, I had received no treatment other than drugs, and I had been deprived of my constitutional rights without a trial—something only the psychiatric profession has the power to do. Before this experience, I believed that I was an independent woman living in a country that supported my right to free speech and action. But I had learned a brutal lesson in the bin. By attempting suicide, I had broken one of society's laws, and for this, I was harshly punished. I was not free and never had been. I simply had not yet seen the boundaries of my prison.

As it turned out, the psychiatrists were partially correct. I was depressed, and I did qualify for Attention Deficit Disorder, but I didn't need drugs, I didn't need to be tied down, and I didn't need to be abused, humiliated, and brutalized. Treating a woman like shit doesn't make her feel better.

Through the support and guidance of my therapist (a woman I had been seeing off and on since 1981), after being released from McLean, I turned to the holistic healing route and began to take responsibility for my own health. I had recently become interested in natural methods of healing and had read an article in *Cosmopolitan* (of all places) on food allergies as the cause of emotional and physical difficulties. I managed to locate a doctor who was also an allergist. She had me tested.

I had severe food allergies and needed to eliminate wheat, eggs, dairy products, alcohol, and preservatives from my diet. I was also very sensitive to chemicals, dust, and pollen. I was bulimarexic as a teenager and still suffered periods of binging while under stress. On this diet, the bulimic urges nearly vanished. My other symptoms improved as well. I was generally healthier and happier. I was more myself than I had ever been. I also began working with a chiropractor and with a homeopathic physician. Recently, I have begun working with a massage therapist.

A month or so after my bin experience, and after I had been on my new diet for a while, I was in my local women's bookstore when I felt a strong urge to buy *The Courage to Heal* (Ellen Bass and Laura Davis, Harper & Row 1988). I could not understand why I needed to buy it since I did not identify as a survivor of incest, but I simply refused to let myself leave the shop without it. Several weeks later I began to remember childhood sexual abuse experiences. My mother was the first offender. Then there was the father of the principal of the Hebrew school I had attended from grades two to five. There were others. Eight of them so far. I call them The Parade.

When I remembered the abuse, the urge to binge vanished entirely. My energy level went up. Life was infinitely better than it had been. And it keeps getting better. Although the habit still tries to reassert itself occasionally, I can disassemble it if I listen to what it is I really need: i.e., good food, sex, rest, fun, etc. This healing work continues.

As much as I blame the system for abusing me, I recognize my own part in the drama that landed me in McLean Hospital, for there can be no victimizer without a victim. As much as the psychiatric medical profession is trained to dominate, I, as a woman, was trained to serve. We, as women, are raised to believe that someone else knows what is best for us, that only an *expert* can understand who we really are. We believe that our bodies, our sexuality, our minds, even our spirituality are not within our control; that left to our own devices, we would be fat, soulless, shapeless, lonely, pitiful ciphers (either that or rabid, soulless, flesh-eating nymphomaniacs).

Women are trained from childhood to submit and to see this submission as normal and natural. These concepts are part of the traditional medical/psychiatric establishment, which is a firmly entrenched part of the patriarchy. This system is in our blood and bones. I do not blame myself for what happened, but I understand that in that hospital, I was playing the extreme end of a role that I had been groomed for since birth.

What happened to me, this bizarre journey, is neither unusual nor extreme. I am convinced of that. Many multibillion dollar industries feed off women's troubles, troubles just like my own. How many women have gone to how many shrinks, hospitals, diet centers, therapists, encounter groups? How many women have swallowed how many pills; laid themselves at the feet of how many experts; gone through how much humiliation, torture, surgery, and abuse, all in the effort to try and name the unnameable: that black hole that lives inside us, the place where reality is suspended and reason, logic, love, and light cannot reach?

The problems that childhood sexual abuse can cause are infinite. It affects every aspect of our adult lives. It is up to us to learn as much as we can about what troubles us and to question all modes of therapy, all treatments offered. And if the answers we receive make us uneasy, just the slightest bit, it is up to us to keep on going until we get the help we need, and deserve.

Drugs in and of themselves are not evil. Traditional psychiatric treatment can sometimes be helpful. I have seen these things work. But I have also seen them destroy. They very nearly destroyed me.

NOVEMBER 1991

Psychiatry's Crimes
by Kate Millet

The following is an edited version of a talk Kate Millet presented at the 1991 Ohio Legal Rights Conference.

This month at Provincetown I was on vacation. A chance to live by the sea for a few days. A chance to live somewhere without a telephone. And a chance to write. But first off I had one "duty" to perform: before it was too late, I had to write to an aunt of mine I'd been out of touch with for years. I had to write my Aunt Harriet, an aunt on my father's side, a Millet aunt, the side of the family that had disowned me years ago for being a lesbian. But they had never—like the other side of the family—they had never locked me up.

Thirty-five years ago, I had sinned against the Millets by accepting my Aunt Dorothy's money to go to Oxford, while failing to confess that I was going with a lover the family detested and had forbidden me to see. I was discovered when a friend of Harriet's, functioning innocently as a spy stopped in to visit and returned to report that although I hadn't been at home, he had met my roommate. All hell broke loose; I was denounced by all my aunts.

I had grown up adoring, worshipping these wonderful aunts, but you do not lie to a Millet. They are an old tribe of Norman nobles and falsehood dishonors one forever. Dorothy never forgave me and Harriet is Dorothy's sister.

Writing to Harriet this month and trying to explain the years of *The Loony Bin Trip*, the book I had just written about being locked up in a mental hospital and which she had read in a very puzzled way, I had something of an epiphany...

Namely that people like my Aunt Harriet would never have believed in my diagnosis [manic depression] for a moment. Even now Aunt Harriet probably doesn't believe in "mental illness" nor in psychiatry. She never did when I was little; what might make her unique and wonderful in America is that she may still not believe in these things. Of course, people get put away, they get driven mad or life crazes them or they break under pressure, stop making sense, and withdraw; they are troubled or enraged or eccentric; they are outrageous or mad as hatters and irrational, but they do not get mental "diseases" in the sense of some disorder of the brain, some mysterious unproven organic pathology. That's what "disease" means, physiological pathology. And while you can prove the existence of Huntington's chorea or Alzheimer's, brain tumor or paresis, since they are physiological conditions, what we call mental illness—schizophrenia, manic depression, paranoia—are not organic conditions but are diagnosed as types of behavior—unacceptable behavior at that. My Aunt Harriet would regard the allegation of mental illness for unacceptable behavior as a case of low-grade insult rather than science.

Despite the claims of biochemical theory and psychopharmacology, there is no actual medical evidence of pathology that would justify the use of the term "disease" or "illness." In the past, mental illness was merely a metaphor in whose literal truth most people did not yet believe. The unfortunates out at St. Peter's asylum where I worked the summer after my freshman year in college might have had labels like schizophrenia, hebephrenia, mania and so forth attached to them as a way to justify their abandonment by family and their terrible treatment by the state, but they were few in number and obviously victimized; people didn't get "sick" in the head in the clinical sense, only in the literary sense; in fact, speaking again in literary terms, it was the heart that suffered for the mind.

And while people suffered in their minds unquestionably, suffered mental and emotional distress, the reasons for and causes of their suffering were right before us in life itself: in love's betrayal, in death and disease, in heartbreak and bereavement, in the loss of love or employment or honor or joy, in poverty and discouragement, in disappointment with how little life gave, how much of what man and especially woman endured in living was ultimately tedious and meaningless and toilsome and flat. So there was not only, finally, despair, there was also that puzzlement before life I later learned to call existential—but no one—no one would ever be so naive as to imagine that this common sense reaction to human experience was a disease.

This would presume that any response to life that was not contentment, an easy bourgeois adjustment, was not only faulty but pathological. This was a view of life without spiritual or philosophical, tragic or literary, understanding. Also a foolish apprehension of what is disease; it makes the human condition itself a disease. Think about it and it takes your breath away. Think about it and you will begin to remember the larger dimension in which we used to live, when sadness was natural, grief was expected, predictable, healthy.

Eventually, psychiatry, with its medical model of "mental illness," won out. Psychiatry has since taken over popular belief, gained governmental sponsorship and vast social powers.

When I think of my own loony bin trip now, it is not only with gratitude for my escape, it is, increasingly, with anger. And a sense of shame, even intellectual embarrassment: how could I have believed this stuff, pseudo-science, superstition? How could I have thrown away thirteen years of my life on a lie, swallowing toxins like Lithium, and agreeing to the proposition that they were medicines—a proposition that the best and larger part of my mind knew was not true? How did I lose my way? Trying to describe it to my Aunt Harriet, to grind out some excuse before the gaze of reason, humor, and common sense that she and those like her represented, and even now, I hope may still represent, I mumbled that I had "got lost in America."

I expect she smiled when she read that: it's meant to cover a lot of ground. How—if I knew better—if the better part of me was always unconvinced—how could I ever accede to the proposition that my mind was diseased, was no longer sound, was unhealthy, was permanently affected, afflicted, was the helpless victim of a certain biochemical condition I could neither see nor understand?

Ah, but the psychiatrists could convince me—psychiatry, the power that had taken my freedom. Taken it through the agency of the family, not the Millet side, the other side, which didn't just quietly disown me early on but hung in there and panicked later in the face of other, more public offenses, not just lesbianism—or at least not my earlier private, secret lesbianism, but public, printed lesbianism. Not to mention my support for Black causes, which they regarded as extreme and expensive. And so they resorted to putting me away.

I will never be able to convey to you the extent of this betrayal, how it never goes away, how it is painful to mention even these many years later, even after peace is restored. Because, you see, in being betrayed by those I loved and trusted, I also lost my hope. Of course, they were meddlesome and silly and naive. It was my money, my little royalty from writing a book, and if I wanted to spend it helping Black rebels or affirming lesbian experience, that was my business. The point is that our system permitted them to call a doctor and confine me, lift the phone and ruin me. It was possible to do this. State psychiatry had made it so. Like thousands of others, I was deceived, taken on false pretense to a locked facility, led into a trap.

The trap sprung on all of us—the family lived to regret this bitterly. My sister had no power over me once she signed me over; I'm proud to say that she later became an excellent civil liberties attorney. She now defends people persecuted this way. Long afterward everyone was sorry: it was a mistake from every angle. It took years for us to sort it out, eliminate psychiatric intervention, and unite again as a family. But the damage had been done; from my point of view, it is irreparable. Collectively we feel duped, kicked, used. I say again that I cannot convey to you the enormity of that betrayal; in being so betrayed by those I loved I not only lost my freedom, I lost my hope. I very nearly lost my life as well.

Upon my release from imprisonment in hospital, I returned to a freedom that was no longer there, my reputation broken, my self destroyed, both as I understood it and as others did. All were content to believe I had undergone a "nervous breakdown" and was now a marked individual, the victim of a dread disease, a major psychosis: chronic, permanent, lifelong, and degenerative. An invalid, forever unreliable, unstable, in or out of remission, but at bottom, fundamentally, hopelessly ill, released temporarily from custody but sure to return there, soon and over and over again and in time, to die there, more and more grotesque.

A depressing prospect, you will agree. How easy then, to imagine it was also a disease called depression. Logically, you might call this a locked box—if I was depressed then I must have been manic—a trick, a solipsism, intellectual confusion of the worst sort. Why stoop to agreeing with this? Probably to stay alive, to avoid suicide and despair, merely in order to avoid carrying out the verdict, the order to execute one so unworthy to live, so haunted, so condemned already. I was utterly undone, already the victim of overwhelming self-doubt: is it possible to be the only one in the world to deny what is obvious now to all? For everyone believed, no one disbelieved, there were no skeptics about—not then.

I was terrified of myself. For I had lost myself by losing confidence in my own mind: surely that's who I was, who we are—all of us—we are the space between our ears, the voice that talks to us in our inner dialogues, we are the self we are locked in with. That incorporeal voice, which can be our greatest torment or the voice of the soul. And when the soul has been turned against itself, what hell to be locked in with that. I suffered a torment of alienation and despair that I discovered later others have known as well, imagining themselves to be the only ones; I once heard it called the dark night of the soul.

I was alone. I endured until I could bear it no longer. Then I turned myself in. Exhaustion, cowardice, the instinct just to stay alive and cheat the judgment and sentence of suicide, the impulse of a social animal who cannot live in utter isolation from the rest of the race, and finally—what did I know? How dare I assume—maybe they were right. Doctors, scientists, authorities, explanations, a Calvinistic determination in their genetic certainties, I didn't have a chance, my misfortune was prepared from before time itself: fate, karma, kismet. It was ordained I should be what the Nazis called mentally defective, the first group to be liquidated, the experimental group in fact, useless mouths, beings already condemned by nature itself.

For the doubt had entered me like typhus, like cholera, like cancer, a tumor of terrifying uncertainty. This new fear could only be mollified by taking their drug, agreeing with them, doing as they said, submitting, then the great shape of fright in the gut would recede a bit, one would stop shaking, the panic of the morning, the great unreasonable emptiness of the afternoon, the sudden subterranean sense that one was out of control, that the mind raced in a meaningless haste, running away with itself, no good anymore, without brakes, an unknown, its steering gone. The way a car lets you down, suddenly conks out on the highway, your familiar little horse in an instant a stranger, your enemy. With the mind you can't get out and walk.

So you must trust them, you must capitulate to stay alive, to stay in the pack; they control your mind now because they understand it and you don't. This is an alienation greater than slavery. You are a robot. Directed by drugs. There is no longer any need for locks and bars you police yourself, are your own sentry.

How do you explain this to someone to whom this has never happened? How do I explain it to you, if you are a social worker sitting across from someone damaged by a traumatic experience you have not even guessed at, because you imagined they have been in a hospital, whereas they know they have been in hell? How do I explain it to you, if you are a legal representative sitting next to someone about to lose his or her freedom, someone drugged, sitting half unconscious through the travesty of a commitment hearing, before a kangaroo court that is to decide whether this victim loses every human and civil right, even liberty of person? Your client is a prisoner, drugged by his captors, and, ironically, due to the drug, truly incompetent to stand trial. In those dirty, nasty little hearings, the law truckles before medicine and most lawyers sell their victims down the river without a qualm, because the doctor said the guy was crazy and doctors know. So everything the law stands for—in constitutional guarantees, in skepticism, in demanding proof and evidence—is prostituted before the false claims of fraudulent medicine.

Let me make myself clear: there is mental distress and trouble in living, but to pretend that this is disease in the sense of pathology, we are not thinking clearly. Pathology is physical evidence of disease. As in physical medicine, which is full of the evidence of infection and x-ray and blood test and lab culture: real microbes. To speak of disease without such proof is to forget centuries of learning, to fail to remember what we know, to ignore language and definition, to fail to use our heads.

I wasn't using mine; I was falling for this nonsense—haven't we all? But look what it's done to our logic, our law. Our lives. It nearly cost me mine. I could not live with this stigma; I could not endure the loss of my personhood, my hope, my future, my belief in my own mind. This is not merely bad reasoning; this has consequences. This was thirteen years of my life. Two incarcerations behind real locks and bars, two devastations in self-image to live through afterwards, the long hard salvaging of ego and reputation, two ordeals in the bitter processes of rebuilding my life which had lain about me in ruins: lost friends and lovers, lost studios, bankruptcies of every kind. You come out of these joints stripped naked.

Most people are released from these places of shame and dishonor unemployed, unemployable, marked, homeless. You can't put your entire life back together very many times. Busted often enough, you're broken: a ward of the state, a professional patient. Someone who'll probably never work again, crippled, an invalid. They did you in. And inside, how long can the mind hold out against the endless drugs, eating your brain like acid, destroying the cells, bringing on tardive dyskinesia to ravage the central nervous system, drug treatment withering the cortex or shock burning the precious and beautiful living cells of the brain with electricity? Diabolic circumstances, where the mind is assailed and brutalized, where consciousness is sabotaged with toxins, where thought is derailed, cognition undermined, and the sacred light of understanding, reason itself, is knowingly, deliberately poisoned.

These are crimes, infractions of the Hippocratic oath. The damage done to memory, brain function, and intelligence by electroshock and drugs should be grounds for lawsuit. And only the threat of economic reprisal is likely to thwart the juggernaut of drug money. Finally, it is not a question of being gullible or simple-minded or silly; finally, we are not discussing opinion or even error, but criminal culpability.

There are a great many survivors of psychiatric abuse and imprisonment, a great proportion of them are women. We are coming out of the closet, dangerous as it is to do so, because to fail to do so is still more dangerous for everyone. This is a civil rights movement—but it's more than that. It is also a movement for the human spirit and the human mind. A rescue mission. Like ecology. As the planet has been polluted, so have we been toxified and made ill with psychiatric drugs, our culture itself gradually made to distrust and disuse reason and logic, made uneasy and afraid of the mind itself. Imagination and the spirit have been rendered suspect and eclipsed; we have ceased to wonder and admire before the scope and reach of intellect. We have forgotten that nothing is more beautiful and glorious than consciousness and creativity.

Let us stop being intimidated or ashamed of any workings of the human mind. Let there be no more forced hospitalization, drugging, electroshock, no more definitions of insanity as a crime treated with savage methods. No more interventions into grief or ecstasy with state apparatus. Let "sanity" be understood as a spectrum that runs the full course between balancing your checkbook or memorizing vowel changes on the one hand, and fantasy on the other. At one end, the humdrum but exciting work of the mind, at the other, surrealism, imagination, speculation. In the center there is at times a balance between logic and the creative forces that generally tend to fall upon the wilder side: metaphor, simile, parallelism, abstraction. To one side, reasoning, equations, expository prose. To the other, theater, painting, recollection, the visionary. A spectrum, a rainbow. All human. Known places within the great still unexplored country of the mind. None to be forbidden. None to be punished. None to be feared.

Our minds are really all we have, our very selves. Collectively, this is survival as well as freedom. By siding with reason and imagination against force and cruelty and authoritarianism we're not only on the side of light and the Enlightenment, we're sure to have more fun. We're even likely to get high. Euphoria is on our side. And laughter. Who could resist?

CHAPTER SIX

Sex and Sexuality

Within the feminist movement, few issues have been as divisive as sex. Beginning with the "lavender menace"—Betty Friedan's reference to the threatening presence of lesbians in the women's movement—differences over sexual practices have torn feminist communities asunder. Though by the early '70s lesbianism had become an acceptable and even "revolutionary" form of sexuality, prostitution, pornography, and sadomasochism (s/m) have proven to be much more controversial.

Sex was a hot topic in early consciousness raising groups. Sharing the intimate details of their lives, women discovered that the "sexual revolution" had left many of them dissatisfied. The '60s, it seemed, had provided men with access to female bodies, without addressing either the fulfillment of female desire or the continued vulnerability of women to sexual violence. Through consciousness raising, heterosexual women began to demand more of their male partners; they challenged the myth of the vaginal orgasm and the notion that intercourse provided the ultimate sexual experience, and they empowered themselves by learning to say "no." Many women named nonconsensual sexual experiences "rape" for the first time.

Although lesbians feared coming out in early consciousness-raising groups, it wasn't long before anger at male power and violence transformed the social and political climate. When radical feminists applied the phrase "the personal is political" to sexual relations, heterosexuality became suspect. Soon, lesbian feminists were declaring, "feminism is the theory, lesbianism is the practice," suggesting that giving your energy to men, through sex, marriage, or even friendship was antirevolutionary. Lesbianism became the ultimate feminist political statement.

Many women were attracted to lesbianism because it seemed to offer a safe refuge from the harsh world of male sexuality. Lesbian relationships, they thought, would be egalitarian, free from male dominance and the threat of sexual assault. Sex would be gentler, more loving, and more complete, without the need to focus on the "male desire" for penetration.

In a paper presented at the 1984 National Women's Studies Association conference, Darlaine Gardetto argued that this shift to "political lesbianism" in the early '70s had a damaging effect on the sexual dialogue that had begun in consciousness-raising groups (*Sojourner,* October 1984). For one thing, heterosexual women found themselves silenced. Though lesbianism opened some heterosexual women to a wider range of pleasures, focused less on the act of intercourse itself, nonhierarchical, warm and tender, woman-loving-woman sex quickly became the *only* acceptable sexual practice. If penetration was a violation of the female body, as radical lesbians seemed to suggest, how could anyone admit to finding pleasure in intercourse?

Though heterosexual women may have been first to lose their voice, in fact, many lesbians were also feeling shut out by the narrow range of sexual practice now being prescribed as "politically correct." Some of these lesbians—many of whom had come out prior to the women's liberation movement—identified as butch and femme and engaged in sexual practices seen as inherently unequal by the new political lesbians. Some, like their heterosexual counterparts, enjoyed penetration, using dildos and other sex toys to enliven their sexual encounters. Among both lesbians and heterosexuals, there were women who enjoyed pornography, women who had multiple partners (maybe even partners of different genders), and women who practiced sadomasochism. Few of these women revealed themselves during the '70s, when narrow prescriptions around sexuality dominated feminist discourse.

This silence around sexuality is evident in early issues of *Sojourner,* which contained neither the personal revelation around sexual practice that characterized the early years of women's liberation, nor the acrimony that would characterize the "sex wars" of the '80s. In fact, the topic that received the most attention in the late '70s was the decriminalization of prostitution.

Prior to the emergence of the antipornography movement, feminists wholeheartedly supported efforts by prostitutes to improve their working conditions through groups such as COYOTE (Call Off Your Old Tired Ethics) and PUMA (Prostitutes' Union of Massachusetts). Society's vilification of prostitutes was seen as one more manifestation of the sexism that limited all women's lives. What was the difference, feminists asked, between the institution of marriage, in which a woman essentially provided a man with sex in return for his economic support, and prostitution? There seemed to be a clear connection between the condemnation of prostitutes, their harassment and arrest by police, and the system of male privilege. After all, the men who used the services of prostitutes were rarely arrested; yet, without them, the system could not exist.

Throughout the late '70s, *Sojourner* articles continued to present this position on prostitution. Numerous articles covered organizing efforts by prostitutes (see Margo St. James, "Illegal Prostitution Is Society's Crime," 1980), fundraisers, and conventions. Reports of actions by feminists in support of prostitutes were also common. A 1977 news story covered a street trial staged by Boston Wages for Housework and Black Women for Wages for Housework to protest attacks on prostitutes throughout the world. Similar events took place in San Francisco, Los Angeles, New York, and London.

The case: Women vs. Business and Government. The plaintiff: All Women. Among the defendants: Governor Michael Dukakis, Mayor Kevin White...the Department of Health, Education, and Welfare, President Carter, General Motors, and John Does 1-50. The charges: pimping off the work of prostitutes and pimping off the work of all women. The witnesses: women in different situations: prostitutes, secretaries, waitresses, health care workers, women on welfare, mothers, teachers, students. (Sojourner, June 1977)

Using street theater, these demonstrators made the point that prostitutes are no different from other women. Women, economically dependent on men, sell their bodies in numerous contexts, from marriage to pink collar jobs (where they are often expected to sexually arouse bosses and/or clients). Moreover, businesses use sex to sell products, making money off of women's bodies, while women are arrested for selling the real product. Business and government, the demonstrators argued, want to make it appear that sex and housework are "free" commodities: thus, they, too, are pimping off the work of women.

During this period in which *Sojourner* often reported positively on efforts to organize prostitutes, occasional reports of antipornography actions also appeared in the paper. The movement to fight violence against women, which originally focused on rape and battering, was developing a new focus—sexually violent imagery. Women were defacing magazines in adult bookstores, asking local stores not to carry pornographic magazines, and using graffiti to protest demeaning, and often violent, sexual images of women.

The first major antipornography event covered by *Sojourner* took place in New York in September 1979. This conference actually followed a similar event that had taken place almost a year earlier on the West Coast, "Feminist Perspectives on Pornography." The New York conference, organized by New York's Women Against Pornography (WAP), included a speakout in which women spoke of how they had been physically and psychically harmed by pornography; strategy sessions in which they shared actions they had taken against pornography; and a march on Times Square. Women were encouraged to visit Women Against Pornography's Times Square storefront office from which they conducted tours of New York's red light district.

Not surprisingly, the movement against pornography, with its tours of the sexual marketplace, soon came into conflict with the movement for prostitutes' rights. As white, middle-class women entered into the forbidden zones of the cities in which they lived, they were horrified by what they saw—the violence, the degrading images of women, the exploitation. Thus, antipornography activists became increasingly concerned about the role of women in the sex industry. Were these women coerced into having their pictures taken, performing in pornographic films, dancing in strip joints? Did women collaborate in their own exploitation? Was prostitution really a form of "female sexual slavery" as Kathleen Barry described it in her 1979 book? It was easier to believe that sex workers were coerced, either physically or financially, than to think that women might participate freely in a system that, to antiporn activists, seemed so thoroughly degrading and dangerous.

In 1983, Terri Richards of the U.S. Prostitutes Collective wrote a letter to *Sojourner* criticizing the film *Not a Love Story* for this very reason. Richards said of the film, "Because the filmmakers were intent to show pornography as women's degradation and the root of all evil, they showed the workers that way too and little came out about *real lives*—hopes, problems, the laws, etc., which shape them. As women who work as prostitutes, strippers, and in other branches of the sex industry, we cannot allow such a scathing attack on us to go down" (see "Real Life Distorted," 1983). The film, Richards argued, suggests that either sex workers are pathetic victims who allow themselves to be manipulated and abused by men or, even worse, they are responsible for all the violence and degradation of women's lives because sex workers "collaborate in and cater to men's sexual 'perversions.'"

Prostitutes and other sex workers continue to fight for decriminalization, respect, and better working conditions, but their voices are not often heard in the feminist press. As the antipornography movement gained strength in the early '80s, many sex workers felt that the feminist movement no longer represented their interests. Feminists had begun to "judge" sex workers, to see them as victims rather than sisters. Since 1983, sex workers have contributed to the paper only sporadically—and most often, when they have left the industry (see Jayme Ryan, "Legalized Prostitution: For Whose Benefit?," 1989).

Terri Richards's letter, which appeared in *Sojourner* in January 1983, marked a critical turning point in the feminist debate over sexual politics. Though *Sojourner* made no mention of it, Richards' letter followed eight months after the Barnard conference on sexuality (officially titled "The Scholar and the Feminist IX"). Primarily an academic event, the Barnard conference nonetheless made an effort to include participants who identified as butch/femme lesbians, sex workers, and sadomasochists. New York WAP, consequently, decided to picket the conference, firing the first round in the now infamous "sex wars." Over the next five years, attacks on both sides would cause enormous amounts of pain, anger, and disillusionment among feminist activists.

In February 1983, in a rare attempt to heal the wounds on both sides, Karen Lindsey, who identified strongly with the antipornography camp (sometimes called "antisex" by their "prosex" opponents), wrote of her own horror at the tactics being used by antipornography activists:

Finally, a number of the antiporn people...have done something I can only characterize as shameful. They have taken it on themselves to declare that the women they disagree with aren't feminists at all.... The antiporn women are hurt and angry that the work they've done for so long and with such dedication is being so harshly criticized. They should be. They have the right and the responsibility to argue back with equal vehemence—God knows, they've got good enough arguments. But the sleazy notion that they have the patent on feminism does nothing to advance those arguments ("Debate, Don't Excommunicate," *Sojourner*, February 1983).

This from a woman, who a year later, would write, "The glorification of pain and degradation, the willingness to exploit children's vulnerability, the profound abuse of trust in the defiance of monogamous commitment —appearing as they do in some of the best and most principled feminists and radicals—leaves me with a terrified sense that the kind of morality necessary to save the world from its own physical annihilation is ultimately beyond human possibility" (see Karen Lindsey, "Further Thoughts on the Sexual Revolution," 1984). Though unwilling to "excommunicate" others, Lindsey found herself profoundly disillusioned by the "feminist sexual revolution" of the early '80s, which in her mind, promoted sadomasochism, adult-child sexual relations, and promiscuity.

Though painful, the "sex wars" brought sex back into feminist conversation. To counter the antipornography movement and the narrow definitions of acceptable sexual practice that had emerged in the late '70s, "sex radicals" began to talk more openly about a wide range of sexual behavior. They countered the feminist emphasis on sexual violence by talking about sexual pleasure—what they did, who they did it with, and what they liked. It was in this context, in May 1984, that *Sojourner* published its first issue focused on "love and sexuality." Contributors explored a number of topics that had been ignored for almost a decade, including celibacy, casual sex, using pornography to explore sexual fantasies, and playing with power in sexual encounters.

Though by encouraging women to explore their sexual practices in print, *Sojourner* was attempting to create some common ground among feminists on both sides of the fence, hostility raged throughout much of the '80s. When, in 1985, antiporn feminists began to promote legislation making pornography a violation of women's civil rights (see "An Exchange on the Pornography Ordinance," 1985), feminists against the legislation founded an organization called "FACT"—Feminist Anti-Censorship Taskforce. The legislation defined pornography as sex discrimination, allowing women to sue the producers and/or sellers of this material in civil court. Though it did not promote censorship per se, those who opposed the legislation feared that it would be used by the right wing to censor gay, lesbian, and feminist publications. After all, anyone could walk into a feminist or gay bookstore and decide that a publication with sexually explicit words or graphics offended them. The fear of such suits, anticensorship activists argued, would prevent these bookstores and other outlets from carrying any sexually explicit materials.

During the right-wing '80s, such fears were not unfounded. The antifeminist and antigay, "profamily" ideology of the Right was also decidedly anti-sexual liberation. AIDS only added to the moral panic of the '80s. Right-wing ideologues were more than willing to co-opt feminist antipornography rhetoric for their own ends. This was exactly what happened in Suffolk County, New York, where a right-wing legislator introduced the Dworkin-MacKinnon legislation. Republican Michael Andre changed the bill in a number of ways, including amending the "legislative intent" section so that it stated that "pornography causes 'sodomy' and 'destruction of the family unit' as well as rape, child abuse, and other 'conditions inimical to the public good'" (as quoted in Pat Califia, *Public Sex*, Cleis, 1995). This amended language changed a potentially progressive measure to a right-wing attack on gays and lesbians.

Sex radicals did not, however, let the antisex rhetoric of the '80s deter them from their own agenda. Beginning mid-decade, lesbian feminists began publishing their own pornography, much of which was oriented toward explorations of power. Magazines such as *On Our Backs* and *Bad Attitude* and erotic videotapes appeared in feminist bookstores (although some refused to carry this new genre of feminist literature). Writings by Pat Califia, Gayle Rubin, and Dorothy Allison about sadomasochism appeared in the gay press, if not the feminist press. Joan Nestle and others wrote about their identities as butches and femmes, reclaiming an erotic style that had gone underground, but had never disappeared, during the androgynous '70s.

By the late '80s, this trend toward more open discussion of sexual practices among feminists was evident in *Sojourner* as well. Amy Hoffman, cofounder of *Bad Attitude*, first wrote about women publishing their own pornography in 1986; this was followed by a 1988 roundtable discussion among the editors of women's sex magazines. In the early '90s, women wrote more often about their own sexual practices, including butch/femme identities and s/m (see Sabrina Sojourner, "Making Different Choices," 1991, and Carol Sklar, "Bondage Broke the Bonds of Fear," 1992). Each of these pieces resulted in vehement responses from readers, arguing that lesbian pornography, butch/femme roles, and sadomasochism are antifeminist, male-identified sexual practices (see Julia

Penelope, "Different Choices Require a Different Vocabulary," 1991). Clearly, fundamental differences among feminists remain unresolved.

Yet the silence had been broken. The "sex wars" opened up a discussion of sexual fantasy, dominance and submission, and erotic imagery that led many women into new explorations of their own sexuality. The growth of the grassroots women's sex industry is compelling evidence that women want to explore their sexual desires. Yet women cannot deny that we continue to live in a world fraught with sexual danger. It may be that only by returning to the first principle of feminist consciousness raising—listen, do not judge—that feminists can hope to unravel both the complexities of sexual politics and the mysteries of sexual desire.

APRIL 1977

A Crime against Women

DEAR EDITOR,

A crime *against women* is being prosecuted *by women* in Monticello, New York.

If you remember last winter when a travesty of a film called Snuff burst on our consciousness, you will understand what the court proceedings are about. Women across the United States took action when they saw its pernicious advertising, which implied *Snuff* documented the real torture and killing of a woman "in South America...where life is cheap!" for the sexual excitation of the male moviegoer. Few of us who denounced the film actually saw it, but Jane Verlaine, then a resident of Monticello, did...and she took copious notes.

Fortunately, the advertising was false; the depiction of the dismemberment-murder was faked—but the incitement to the male sadist was real enough. Just before the final scene, a pregnant woman is knifed in the belly and an actor says, "That turned me on." This is followed by the *piece de resistance* of sadism in which the dismemberment and disemboweling of a woman brings an actor to sexual climax!

In Monticello, Women Against Violence Against Women (WAVAW) collected over 1,000 signatures on a petition to the district attorney there, requesting that he seize the film. Although he had previously seized a pornographic movie about a nun—under pressure from the Catholic Church—he refused to act against Snuff but told WAVAW they could prosecute.

Jane Verlaine did, with WAVAW's support.

The trial, which was delayed for ten months by the exhibitor, finally was scheduled for December 23, 1976. The night before, the judge *quashed the subpoena for the film,* and then, on the 23rd, dismissed the case for *insufficient evidence:* no film! In a moving plea to the judge, Andrea Moran, our lawyer, said that had the victim in *Snuff* been an animal, the ASPCA would have protested; had the victim been a Jew, B'nai B'rith would have protested; but the victim is a woman and we are not being allowed to protest.

Leaving the courtroom, Jane Verlaine and two other women were slapped with summonses by the "defense." Among the charges was "malicious prosecution." The summonses were an obvious attempt to prevent the case from going to appeal. Richard Dames, the theater owner, is applying for an FCC license to operate a radio station in Monticello and evidently wants to be free of litigation. But in spite of this intimidation—and in spite of outcries from knee-jerk libertarians that incitement to murder women is every man's constitutional right—we are determined to continue court action to protect the civil rights of women. We are not begging any issues. Sadism is recognized by law as obscene and we agree that it *is* obscene. The portrayal of women as subhuman beasts of prey whose very lives are to be sacrificed on the altar of the male orgasm must be stopped!

In sisterhood,
Barbara Deming
Andrea Dworkin
Leah Fritz
Karla Jay
Robin Morgan
Adrienne Rich
Gloria Steinem

FEBRUARY 1980

Illegal Prostitution Is Society's Crime
by Margo St. James

Prostitution is not a victimless crime; rather, the prostitute is the crimeless victim! And usually a young woman. As in rape, incest, and pregnancy, the victim is blamed—only in prostitution, the blame is codified into law. Cops argue that prostitutes commit other crimes, but the prohibition actually promotes larceny, not the sex industry, and there are laws to cover those real crimes.

It is my hope that public officials and community leaders will begin to address this issue intelligently and, through this issue, face the economic issues that affect all women. The women's movement has been reluctant to address prostitution because of the painful connections between women, money, and power, of which women have little. Prostitutes have a high rate of incest and rape in their backgrounds, and no legal recourse; all civil rights are denied. A defense to rape is that the victim is a whore, or in the case of male rape, homosexual. Many turn to prostitution out of economic need and the feeling that there are no alternatives. They get support and sometimes affection from their tricks...but not the support they need—political support for decriminalization. No small wonder wives don't have the right to say "no" either (except in five states).*

There are male prostitutes—not just young boys or transvestites, but rather ordinary-looking young men in their twenties, who are rarely arrested but can be seen standing around the St. Francis Hotel in San Francisco, 53rd Street in New York, and advertising in most papers independently or through escort services. They rarely work in brothels because the gay men's baths fulfill that need.

While women are much less interested in casual sex, a significant number become interested when there is a financial reward that is far higher than the pay for typing. There are at least five million prostitutes working in the United States, with three to five customers for each prostitute on any given day. The laws say they are equally culpable but the arrest statistics tell a very different story.

About 86,000 people were arrested in the United States on soliciting charges last year. Of these, 75 percent were women, about 15 percent were male prostitutes, mostly transvestites and transsexuals. A mere 10 percent were customers. Another 70,000—85 percent of whom were women—were arrested on loitering with the intent to commit prostitution, attesting to the presence of "thought police."

De facto legalized prostitution occurred over the last decade when most of the major cities, to combat visible street prostitution brought on by the recession, licensed third parties in the form of parlors and escort services. This allowed organized crime into the game. A polite fiction is maintained for the public that these places are not brothels, and they are closed when the public gets wise. Women who work these places are licensed by the police in most cases but are denied the right to work if they have a conviction for prostitution; this keeps up the charade. Although 70 to 80 percent of prostitutes work off the streets, 90 percent of the arrests are of the young and poor who are on the street and most visible to the moralists.

Police in every major city complain of the revolving door that allows the hooker back on the street. They fail to see how the official labeling prevents the prostitute from gaining other kinds of employment, while at the same time increasing her earning power as a prostitute. Police also tend to blame the lenient judges, but it is time they understood the reason the (male) judge is lenient is that judges are part of the consumer conspiracy that keeps prostitution illegal and women powerless and stigmatized by their very gender. The public worries about the recruitment of their precious children, yet fails to see how the police are the actual recruiters. The prohibition is enforced minimally in order to maintain an endless supply of branded women for public access.

As in abortion, the government has only been involved for the last century, having gotten a start in Victorian England when the Contagious Disease Acts were instituted in the 1860s, ostensibly to control an epidemic of venereal disease. In reality, it was the sailors who brought the disease to the citizens, but they weren't jailed, only the prostitutes they infected. It was only after years of work by feminist Josephine Butler, founder of the Abolitionist Society, that these laws were repealed.

In 1949, Eleanor Roosevelt read a set of United Nations Convention Papers calling for the universal decriminalization of prostitution. Although 50 other countries have ratified the papers, the United States has not (though the others have merely instituted the punitive and abusive portions of the papers into their codes). Most serious of these problems are pimping and the renting of premises for prostitution, which most countries consider crimes. The intent of the papers was to lessen the abuse and exploitation, but the opposite has occurred. Although the police say they want the pimps, they arrest very few, and many of these arrests are actually of madams who are not abusive.

Due to the illegality of renting a room to a prostitute, there aren't many safe places for women to work, and they may take to tricking in cars, much to the dismay of the community. Also, many landlords up the rent and the hooker has nowhere to go to complain, being outside the law. Only the poorer hotels are slapped with the "Red Light Abatement Act," usually when some speculator or developer wants to upgrade the neighborhood and make room for luxury hotels and condos. The Hiltons and the Hyatts are never charged with prostitution, although more tricks are turned inside them than inside small hotels. Many police work as security guards; they photograph the suspects, pass their pictures around to the other major hotels, and sometimes even charge them with trespassing to keep them out of the hotels.

The women who are willing to go against all gender codes, to risk rape, assault, or worse, in order to pay the rent and take care of their kids, are seldom deterred by the process of being arrested and jailed. Although it is a traumatic experience equal to rape, it is mostly seen as an inconvenience by the prostitutes and very few recognize it as man's way of enforcing the double standard and stigmatizing all women as a class.

It is time for new approaches to the oldest injustice. It is time for Congress (many of whom have been customers) to pass a federal decriminalization bill that will remove the individual prostitute from the criminal code ... not make it a federal offense as the proposed Revised Federal Crime Code is attempting to do. It is time for people who are affected by prostitution to work together to figure out ways for prostitutes to meet the demand with a minimum of abuse and exploitation, while the rights of the community are protected, too.

The National Organization for Women recently proposed a resolution calling for a National Task Force on Prostitution, but it was a long time coming. Only when women can stop pointing their fingers at their whore sisters will they have the unity and strength to stop the intimidation, the rising rape rate, the sexual harassment on the job, and the general exploitation of themselves. Only when the customers stand up and give witness to the benefits of the service they demand and stop being sexist hypocrites, only when the Christians practice what they preach and ordain women, only then will women cease to be at a disadvantage in a man's world. But in the meantime, humane regulation is more desirable than prohibition. Ignorance is no excuse for a law! It's not the freedoms that are the danger, it is the nonacceptance of change and the resulting fascism bred by rigidity within the family that threatens our democracy.

This article has been edited for clarity.
* By 1995, husbands could be prosecuted in 43 states.

JANUARY 1983

Real Life Distorted

TO THE EDITOR:
Some people would have liked the movie *Not a Love Story* (about pornography) because women, in particular a stripper, were the main protagonists. Women, and men too, want to know what it's like to work in the sex industry. The movie showed live sex acts and had interviews with sex workers, both men and women. This gave the impression that the real

people were speaking for themselves, that the facts about their working conditions and lives were coming out. In fact, only distorted facts came out. Because the filmmakers were intent to show pornography as women's degradation and the root of all evil, they showed the workers that way too and little came out about *real lives*—hopes, problems, the laws, etc., which shape them. As women who work as prostitutes, strippers, and in other branches of the sex industry, we cannot allow such a scathing attack on us to go down.

At best, the movie shows us to be pathetic, rather seedy victims who, in our work, allow ourselves to be manipulated and abused by men because we're too stupid to know any better. In the words of Kathleen Barry, an "expert witness," we're "totally enslaved," "assigned to take all the perversion," etc., in the world. The condescending questions asked by the director Bonnie Klein in the interviews ("What do you feel when you're doing this?" "Does it make you feel good?") were designed to get the kind of answers she wanted to fit her stereotyped view of us, that sexual work ruins your sex life and makes you feel debased. It's ironic that Linda Lee Tracy, the stripper, starts off powerful in the movie, talking about her stripping act and criticizing a Women Against Pornography rally for their moralistic attitude towards hookers. Although she tries to defend her stripping as decent all the way through, as another way of making a living, she's made to feel disgusted with herself in the end.

At worst, the movie blames us not only for our exploitation but for the violence and degradation in *all* women's lives, because we collaborate in and cater to men's sexual "perversion" and this "gets translated back" to women. To single out porn and women in porn and prostitution as the *cause* of violence against women is not only downright simplistic, it's dangerous too, and sounds like the Moral Majority.

It ends up reinforcing the differences between us and "normal" women, dividing us into "good" and "bad." It takes sides with the laws against us, which label us as criminals. Yes, many of us are exploited, but "respectable" alternatives are often much worse. No mention was made of Black women in the industry and how we're at the bottom. The woman in the live sex act who was interviewed said she earned more money that way and didn't want a nine-to-five job with a boss on her back. The filmmakers chose not to pick up on this and nothing was said about the degradation women suffer in "respectable" jobs: for example, according to a recent study published in *Ladies Home Journal,* "anywhere from 36 to 70 percent of working women have been subject to sexual harassment, ranging from a dirty joke to an outright 'get laid or get fired' proposition." Did all those men doing the harassing get their attitude from porn movies and porn mags? We doubt it. We think it's a question of power, that men know we are vulnerable because we're dependent on them for our livelihood, whether it's as boss, husband, customer, father, or boyfriend, and they exploit it and are condoned in their behavior by the laws, courts, and the powers that be.

Wherever we work we're all fighting that dependence, and this is what we have in common with each other. Yes, it's difficult for us to organize because we're illegal, but we can and have been getting together all over the world—hookers, strippers, nude dancers, etc.—with other women on the basis of our interests and struggle. The U.S. Prostitutes Collective is an organization of prostitute and nonprostitute women working to abolish all the laws against us. The filmmakers and "feminists" interviewed chose to ignore our organizing and so were unable to see us except as victims and were unable to come up with any answers about what to do beyond the personal kind of struggle. Hence the pessimism.

According to Bonnie Klein, no distinction should be made between "portrayals of nude dancers and sex acts and hard-core torture scenes." We're against the glorification of violence against women as a sexual titillation. When it comes to women being put through meat grinders, we're definitely against it. We want erotica that is sexy. What's wrong with sex and naked bodies? Surely the women's movement is about our fight to increase our sexual possibilities. Our complaint is that porn is geared toward men and straight sex and, as Kate Millet said in the movie, it's just not sexy. We're tired of being told by some "feminists" what kind of sex we should like, and when it doesn't conform to their pure, spiritual ideas, it's disgusting and pornographic.

We'd like to know how far this campaign against pornography is going to go. Are the Canadian filmmakers taking the lead from their sisters in Toronto, who on a demonstration against sex shops helped the chief of police load the women into police cars during a street sweep and were publicly thanked by him for their support? The movie was made with the assistance of the Toronto vice squad. Is the antiporn movement inviting the vice squad, notorious for their antigay behavior, to close gay sex shops, too? Are they joining forces with the "law and morality" groups who are trying to introduce antiporn laws, antigay and repressive legislation in many states? We have already successfully fought attempts by Kathleen Barry and other "feminists" who, at the International Women's Year United Nations Conference held in 1980, tried to get a vicious resolution passed against prostitutes on the pretext of "helping" us. We had to fight to get a clause in the resolution that stated that prostitutes "have the right to legal protection against maltreatment which they may be subject to for the sole reason of their being prostitutes."

It's about time they came clean about who they are helping and whose side they are on—the side of the police and the laws against us, or our side?

Terri Richards
U.S. Prostitutes Collective

JULY 1989

Legalized Prostitution: For Whose Benefit?

by Jayme Ryan

In the following article, Jayme Ryan discusses her experience working as a prostitute in a legal brothel in Nevada. Ryan is a member of WHISPER (Women Hurt in Systems of Prostitution Engaged in Revolt), an organization of ex-prostitutes and advocates working to dismantle systems of prostitution. She spoke at the Spring 1989 Trafficking in Women Conference in New York City.

In the United States, prostitution is illegal everywhere except in twelve counties and cities in Nevada—Storey, Lyon, Churchill, Elko, Winnemucca, Wells, Ely, Esmeralda,

Mineral, Lander, Lovelock, and Nye. Only five of seventeen Nevada counties—Clark County, Douglas County, Las Vegas, Reno, and Carson City—have made prostitution illegal. Prostitution was never actually legalized on a state level; rather, it has been decided county by county. Of the twelve counties that have legalized prostitution, two legalized it by citizens' referendum, five by county commissioners, and five by municipal decree. When Nevada became a state, its constitution did not make specific mention of prostitution. The first time it was addressed by state law was in 1956, to outlaw brothels in Clark County. In 1971, a court decision made the legalization of prostitution a county option. Subsequently, laws have been passed making specific acts such as pandering, living off the earnings of a prostitute, and streetwalking illegal. Additionally, zoning restrictions that prohibit the location of a brothel within a certain radius of a town, church, or school have been enacted.

Proponents of prostitution claim that there are many benefits to legalization. This system has been defended as the most reasonable way to regulate "sex as a commerce." Supporters say that legalization would save money, as law enforcement resources would not be spent on arresting, processing, and jailing prostitutes. Some believe that this system would eliminate corruption and graft. Others claim that illegal activities associated with prostitution, such as using minors in prostitution and drug trafficking, could be eliminated by registering prostitutes with the police and issuing work cards to them. Also, proponents claim that close medical supervision of registered prostitutes would result in fewer sexually transmitted diseases.

Communities would benefit from regulation, supporters say, as prostitutes would be segregated from the larger population and not annoy or bother other citizens. With prostitutes hidden away in brothels, neighborhoods would not be exposed to prostitution-related activities, and nonprostitute women would not be harassed on the streets by men soliciting them for sex. It is also a widely held belief that legalized prostitution lowers the rate of sexual assault against women in the larger community. Brothel prostitution is also said to contribute significantly to the communities in which they are located. (In fact, communities do benefit from legalized prostitution. Taxation brings in added revenues, which are paid to the counties. Additionally, local stores benefit from prostitutes' business.)

Legalized prostitution is said to have many benefits to the women themselves. Some people claim that prostitutes would be spared stigmatization resulting from arrests and criminal records. Others state that there would be less pimping and pandering because women used in prostitution would no longer need the protection of pimps. Finally, there are those who claim that legalization would allow prostitutes to organize unions to demand better working conditions, medical insurance, paid vacation, holiday and sick time, and pension and profit-sharing plans.

As a 28-year-old woman who survived over twelve years of prostitution—many of them spent in the legal brothels of Nevada—I want to tell you what life was like for myself and other women used in prostitution in a legal brothel. I was first introduced to the brothel in Nevada by my ex-pimp. You can't "work" in a legal brothel there unless you have a pimp that the owner knows or a referral from someone who does. These referrals cost you upwards of $200. When you call the brothel, they ask you for your "qualifications": who referred you, your "work" experience, what you look like.... Once they give you the okay, they tell you how to come and what you're allowed to bring.

When I arrived in Nevada, a madam picked me up at the bus stop and drove me to the edge of town where both houses were located. Before I could catch my breath or put my bags in my room she sat me down at the kitchen table and informed me of the house rules and procedures. The first question she asked was who my "man" (pimp) was and whether he had given me instructions on how the money was to be handled and a telephone number where he could be reached safely. Next I was told that I would have to go to the police station to be registered and fingerprinted. She would, however, allow me to begin immediately and instructed me to hide in the back when the police came to check out the women's work cards. This was done on a weekly basis. The madam told me to use a false address (one of theirs) for my work permit if I wasn't a Nevada resident and not to worry if I wasn't of age because it wasn't verified anyway. I was also told that I had to have a medical exam that consisted of a blood test and a pelvic exam—at my own expense—before I could get my work card. The madam immediately started to alienate me from the other women: the women, she said, would tell me to do things wrong so I wouldn't make money and would get me in trouble with my "man." Finally, came the rules and regulations of the house:

Rule #1: Every "girl" is on call twenty-four hours a day, seven days a week. You "worked" six weeks at a time.

Rule #2: You must take eight-hour shifts sitting in the picture window so that there are at least two "girls" in the window twenty-four hours a day to wave to cars that drive by.

Rule #3: You must have your hair done, have makeup on, and be dressed at all times. So, when sleeping, we lay on our backs very carefully so as not to be mussed up in case of "company" (customers).

Rule #4: You are not allowed to leave the premises unless you are being taken to the doctor or have an "out date" (a customer off the premises). For a while we were allowed to suntan until they decided that we wouldn't be ready for "company." So what we did was walk around the building for fresh air.

Rule #5: You are always to keep a fresh supply of porn books and magazines (at your own expense) in your room and have plenty of nude pictures on your walls.

Rule #6: Your room must be immaculate and your bed made at all times. This was another reason that we so carefully laid on our beds. I don't think anyone ever actually crawled under the sheets and slept like a normal person.

Rule #7: You are only allowed one two-minute phone call per week and are not allowed to receive calls. This was especially hard for those of us who had children, and many of us did.

Rule #8: You are not allowed to go out to dinner, to a bar, or to the casino. Everything we "needed" was brought to us by house-approved salesmen. The madam or owner picked out our wardrobe, our hairstyle, and the type of makeup we would wear.

Rule #9: When company comes you must quickly line up and wait for the barmaid to call you out. Once in the parlor, we had to stand up straight in a row, hands at our sides, with no talking or movement of any kind, say our names and wait for the "gentleman" to pick someone. In no way were we to make him feel rushed unless there was a "full house" (a lot of customers) in which case the barmaid said something to speed things up.

Rule #10: Once you are picked you have to sit at the bar with the gentleman. Not only did we have to sell ourselves but we had to sell drinks, food, and jukebox music. We had to sit with this man, smile at all times, make conversation, get him sexually aroused, and above all, "don't make him feel rushed," unless of course, there was a "full house."

Rule #11: The only things you can refuse to do are to have anal sex, have sex with a Black man, or have sex with a man who appears to have something wrong with his penis. When a Black john (customer) arrived, he would be taken around the back way so that other (white) customers wouldn't see him or you with him. If they saw you with a Black man they might not want to see you again, or worse yet—for the brothel owners—they might leave the house altogether. Once you were in your room with a john, if you suspected that he might have "something wrong" with his penis—venereal disease—it had to be double-checked by someone in charge before you could turn him down; even then, they would try to get another woman to "take care" of him.

Once all the rules were laid out I was shown to my room and told I could take a quick shower before I started to "work." I was allowed half an hour to get ready.

About the "work." When you got a customer in your room, you had to perform any sex act that he wanted. Prior to sex, you had to wash each man's penis as you'd been instructed. Unless you were "lucky" enough to get one of the rooms with a private bathroom, you had to carry a pitcher of water into your room for each new customer. For the most part, one bathroom was shared by two to eight "girls." Once alone in your room with a customer, you had no protection from him. There were many different occasions when a woman was brutally beaten or raped by a john, but as long as he paid the house, it was kept quiet.

All of the women were required to provide "special services" to customers upon request. Some of the house "specialties" included parties with two or more women in which any number of sexual acts would be performed: s/m, "water sports" (acts involving urination and defecation), showers or bubble baths (where you must literally bathe the john), all-night parties, "out dates" where the john could take you out of the house (in some cases out of town), the showing of pornographic movies, and photo sessions—Polaroid or video—with just one woman or "multiple girl" sessions. Usually they wanted us to pose or perform something from a pornographic movie or picture. Sometimes the men demanded that we wear costumes; other times we were filmed or photographed chained up, being whipped, or being penetrated with various objects.

We were strictly forbidden to use condoms unless the customer asked for one, as it took maximum pleasure away from the paying customer. We all had towels on our beds so they wouldn't become soiled or stained. For our birthday, we didn't get the day off; instead, we got a cake and matching towel set: a towel for our bed and a wraparound towel for ourselves. There was no excuse for not "working." One time I was extremely ill; I had a fever, a vaginal infection, and rips in my vagina from so much sexual activity. I went to the doctor and he told me to go home and rest so I could heal. Even my ex-pimp told me I could come home, but the madam got on the phone and told him I could still "work" since there was nothing wrong with my mouth and I could handle all of the customers that wanted oral sex.

Legalized prostitution, proponents claim, increases women's earnings and protects them from being economically preyed upon. We were paid once a week. On payday, each woman was called into the office separately, shown a sheet with the house's account of her earnings, and told to call her pimp. Once you got him on the phone the owner would ask him for instructions on handling the money: how or if he wanted it sent to him, how much you were allowed to keep. He would be told how your week went, if you had done anything wrong, how much longer you were scheduled to stay, and what you'd done in your "spare time." There were some women whose pimps lived in Nevada, so they would come to the house on payday to get the money themselves. If the woman was lucky—and not busy—she would be allowed to speak with him for a few minutes before he left.

Payday also meant paying our bills. The house took 40 percent of our earnings off the top. With the remaining 60 percent, we had to pay the maids for cleaning the communal bathroom once a week, giving us clean bedding every other week and a clean towel once a week, and cooking our one meal a day (which we had to sit and eat whether we wanted to or not). The barmaids also received a percentage of our earnings, and then there was the cost of mandatory weekly visits to the doctor and the rent for our room. Other expenses included having our hair done and purchasing various outfits to "work" in. Then there was the pornography, ranging from magazines to videos, which we had to supply at our own expense. Finally, there were the fines, which could range anywhere from $10 to $100. The fines varied greatly because the house rules varied from day to day. You could be fined for anything from going off the grounds, to visiting another girl's room, to not having your bed made perfectly. The brothel owners controlled every aspect of our lives: the color of our hair, the clothes we wore, where we could go, who we could speak to, when we ate, and when we slept.

I left the brothels of Nevada almost two years ago, and when I did, I left the only "job" I ever knew, the only "job" my ex-pimp taught me I was good for. For two years afterward, I lived in what felt like an endless tunnel of regret and remorse for what I believed were bad choices made by a very bad person—me. Then I became involved with WHISPER and came to understand that prostitution wasn't something I did, rather it was something that was done to me—not because I'm bad, not because I'm stupid, not because I'm neurotic; in fact, it had very little to do with me at all. Prostitution exists because men want it to, and under male supremacy, men's desires become women's reality.

The name WHISPER tells you what we stand for: Women Hurt in Systems of Prostitution Engaged in Revolt. We are an organization that is composed of survivors of prostitution and of other women's advocates working for women and children attempting to escape the sex industry. Our purpose is to expose the preconditions that make women and children vulnerable to commercial sexual exploitation and those that keep them trapped in prostitution, to challenge and invalidate cultural myths that misrepresent women and children used in both prostitution and pornography, and ultimately to end the traffic of women and children for sexual use and abuse. We do not attempt to improve prostitution as an institution through legalization, decriminalization, or unionization. The goal of the institution of prostitution is to allow males unconditional sexual access to women and children, limited solely by their ability to pay for it.

Because of our belief that women and children are hurt in systems of prostitution, we recognize that existing remedies for prostitution have not and will not relieve or eliminate the harms done to women and children used in this system: the physical abuse, the emotional abuse, the stigma, and the list goes on.... We reject the lies that claim women freely choose prostitution, that turning tricks is sexually pleasurable for women, that women can and do become wealthy in systems of prostitution, that women control and are empowered in systems of prostitution, that being a call girl is any less degrading or oppressive than being a streetwalker, or that prostitution can be "fixed" to benefit women.

We expect WHISPER to be a tool for change in our lives and in our lifetime. Our main purpose is to make the sexual enslavement of women and children history. I believe that all organizations working on behalf of women and children used in systems of prostitution should be working toward an end to the exploitation of women and children and a change in how society as a whole looks at—and treats—women. I no longer wish to go along with the patriarchy, which perpetuates and tolerates the exploitation, use, and abuse of women and children because of some unwritten law that this is men's ordained right.

Some people claim that decriminalization is the answer; however, under decriminalization, prostitutes would still be isolated and preyed upon by pimps and others who exploit and abuse women. Prostitutes would still have to comply with zoning requirements, report their income—and "profession"—to the IRS and be accountable to regulations drafted by the Department of Health. This system does not lessen the social stigma attached to prostitution and leaves the woman in no better position than she is in today. The only benefit she would receive is that she wouldn't be arrested if she complied with the above regulations. Some benefit! This is one of the myths about prostitution—that the worst part of being a prostitute is going to jail. The truth of the matter is that in spite of the humiliation of being arrested, prostitutes often view jail time as a respite from the abuse they are subjected to by both their pimps and their johns—the lesser of two evils. The bottom line is that whatever form of regulation is enforced, women used in systems of prostitution lose: the only benefits are to the johns and the pimps.

Proponents of legalization and decriminalization claim that prostitution is about money and not sex. They try to keep our focus on the economics of prostitution and our attention away from the fact that women and children are being exploited by this system of so-called economic freedom. They say that the rights of prostitutes are the rights of all women: I think that this is oppression disguised as liberation. They say that there should be laws preventing prostitutes from being treated as criminals so that they may freely work as independent businesswomen. My question to them is: Are we to believe that the exploitation of women and children through systems of prostitution is a precondition to all women's liberation?

As a survivor of prostitution, I say that prostitution is a matter of violence against women—not sexual liberation, not any form of liberation. Prostitution is a matter of dominance and submission facilitated and maintained by men in a male supremacist society to keep all women in the status of second-class citizens. *Lesbian Ethics* (Volume 2, Number 3, Summer 1987) published an article on prostitution by Toby Summer in which she wrote, "When those who dominate you get you to take the initiative in your own human destruction, you have lost more than any oppressed people yet has ever gotten back." For me, those words expressed all of the things in my life that I couldn't vocalize before. So in telling you about a small part of the abuse I was subjected to as a prostitute, I'm not asking for your sympathy. I don't even want you to think of me; instead, I want you to think of the women who are right now, this very minute, sitting in the windows of Nevada's brothels, waving.

MAY 1984

Further Thoughts on the Sexual Revolution

by Karen Lindsey

In the late '60s and early '70s, many feminists (myself included) wrote critical analyses of the sexual revolution, and our writings represented what, with a number of variations, seemed to typify feminist attitudes toward that supposedly liberating phenomenon. Essentially we felt that the sexual revolution, while claiming to liberate all people from the repressive culture that had so fettered our lives, had in fact simply provided left-wing and countercultural men with better opportunities to exploit women. If we wanted a vision of what liberated sexuality might become, we couldn't depend on men to create it for us—we needed to create our own vision. This made sense as far as it went, but it was, unfortunately, very limited.

Having comfortably lumped myself with the other sexual revolution critics of the past, let me move out from here on my own. My ideas on sexuality and liberation at this point are so conflicted, so pained, so tentative that I really can't stick anybody else with them. What I want to do in this article is to discuss some of the thoughts, positive and negative, I've been having on the sexual revolution and on the concept of "sexual liberation." This isn't especially easy, and the thoughts aren't all as thoroughly developed as I'd like them to be. It's still all pretty confusing to me.

Partly this is because my earlier ideas came out of a belief I no longer hold—and the loss of that belief has been as difficult and disorienting as loss of faith usually is. I was never a separatist, and I never believed in the organic superiority of female nature—I'd known too many nasty women and decent men for me to fall into that trap. But I *did* believe, as many radical feminists did, that our conditioning had made us more morally decent—that as oppressive as our roles were, they had at least forced us to understand the value of tenderness and nurturance; if our sexuality had been repressed, it had at least escaped becoming a force of violence, exploitation, and reification. Hence, I shared a fairly common feminist belief that as women were allowed more and more to experience and express their own sexuality, they would almost of necessity create a new, truly liberated, truly integrated sexuality. I was sure that in spite of *Cosmo* and *Playgirl* and all the distorting efforts of the media and big business to co-opt and exploit us, only a handful of women would buy into their efforts. We were *different*. Above all, we *weren't like men*.

No, Virginia, there is no Santa Claus.

Perhaps the most disorienting and disillusioning experience I've ever had has been to see what's happened to large numbers of women, inside and outside of the movement, as they've acquired a small piece of sexual freedom. In the decade or more since the early critiques of the sexual revolution appeared, there has emerged a wide range of feminist visions, many of which are as ugly and degrading as anything Larry Flynt could dream up. There were always nonmovement women anxious to follow the *Cosmo* line and, more disheartening, there were always feminists who, carrying the banner of antimonogamy, cheerfully slept with people they knew were lying to their unsuspecting spouses and lovers. That these were often otherwise decent, ethical women, who nevertheless buried whatever sympathy they had for a betrayed sister, made it all the more appalling. If the sexual revolutionaries had claimed that sex was just an experience like any other, these feminists went a step further. Not only did they refuse to recognize and respect the special pain of sexual betrayal, but they held themselves to far *lower* standards than they did in other areas of their lives—lying to and cheating on an innocent third person were implicitly acceptable in a sexual relationship. If the relationship was "meaningful," it didn't really matter who got hurt. Still, I determinedly held onto my comfortable belief in women's superior sexual ethics.

But the popularity of male strip joints (for heterosexual women), "Tupperware" parties selling kinky underwear, and beefcake ads, which objectify men as women have always been objectified, made it harder for me to keep kidding myself. And the controversy over pornography, sadomasochism, and the sexual use of children by adults that became an increasingly visible part of the movement in recent years (and which I wrote about at length in *Sojourner* last year) has finally forced me to give up my illusions. Given some degree of choice, women will all too often make the kinds of sleazy choices I once believed only men, degraded by their own power, were capable of.

This has affected me in a strange, difficult, and somewhat interesting way. Painful as the whole "sexual liberation" controversy has been for me, it has, paradoxically, liberated me in one way. It's allowed me to confront the one taboo that no radical ever wants to deal with: it's forced me to look at the possibility that some of what the bad guys say may be true. I'm not talking now just about the wimpy liberals—I'm talking about the *real* bad guys. The folks who believe in sexual repression, in women's place, in enforced marriage and the nuclear family. Archie Bunker. Middle America. The Pope. The *conservatives*.

This is dangerous territory to be embarking on these days, when the conservatives have so much power and are exercising it so murderously, and when so many of the fragile gains we've made are being toppled. But we can't live merely in reaction to the reactionaries—if there's any piece of truth in what they say, we've got to be willing to hear it and to put it into a more decent framework. We can't let them keep it for themselves, any more than we can allow ourselves to embrace ugly values because they seem more radical.

And I think one of the areas in which the conservatives have a piece of the truth—a piece they've twisted and tarnished and distorted (and often haven't really practiced or reflected in their private lives)—is the area of sexuality. I think we have to look carefully at the old sexual values and see what makes sense in them, even as we fight against what doesn't. This is the hardest part to admit—the most dangerous thing to say—and yet it needs to be faced.

There is an essential truth that the power structure has taken and interpreted in a hideously crude, exploitative, and destructive manner, using it to attack lesbianism and homosexuality, to deprive women of the right to abortions, to negate the legitimacy of chosen childlessness, to punish unwed mothers. That truth is the ideal of sexuality as something sacred—something so intimate, so deeply connected to the core of life that it should be embarked on only carefully, tenderly, and in the context of a loving, committed relationship.

Feminist fear of looking at the truth because of the horrors the men who run our lives have attached to it has created a climate in which anything they oppose must be good. This has allowed to emerge (among other visions, to be sure) a vision of sexuality no less destructive than theirs: a vision that encompasses the crude commercialism of *Playgirl,* the more sophisticated political/philosophical glorification of "boy love," sadomasochism, sexual betrayal, and transient, uncommitted sexual activity.

We need to face the fact that sex at its biological and psychological core is *about the creation of life:* this is what makes it sacred. We can remove ourselves from the direct biological implication of that fact, and there's no reason why we shouldn't. The absence of a human estrus cycle, linking sexual desire to fertility, suggests that it is part of our nature to build on the essence of sexuality in ways that are removed from procreation itself, and nothing in this process forces it to be linked with heterosexuality or pregnancy.

But we can never really remove ourselves spiritually or psychically from the initial creativity of sex. Any sexual act is always, to some extent, an act of creation. It is always terribly, awesomely close to the core of life itself. We have never been able to reduce the power of sex to the simple pleasure of orgasm, no matter how people try to persuade themselves that they can. (I think that this creative power—so primal and so profound—terrifies those who try to control our lives. Whether Jerry Falwell, trying to force us into "purity," or Hugh Hefner, trying to degrade and reify our sexuality, they're all controlling in us a force they don't want us to control for ourselves, a force so central to the core of life that without being able to control it, they will ultimately be able to control nothing. There have always been in patriarchy the twin needs to stifle and abuse sexuality—needs that dominate and pervert the recognition of the sacredness of sex.)

The closeness to the core of life organic to sex, our ongoing participation through it in the act of creation, makes *what* we create enormously important. We *make love.* And when, in sex, we are not making love, we are always making something else. I think that what many men in patriarchal culture and what many sexual libertarians in the feminist and leftist movements are often making is hate—whether in the form of rape, sadistic fantasy play, indifferent or exploitative sexual encounters, or sexual infidelity in relationships defined as monogamous. And that is, perhaps, our movement's greatest failure.

In spite of all this, I'm not as unambivalently hostile to the sexual revolution as I once was. Paul Goodman, I'm told, when asked whether he thought the Russian Revolution was a good or bad thing, said that the question was irrelevant: given the centuries-old oppression of the Russian people, the revolution was simply an historic inevitability.

I think much the same can be said of the sexual revolution. For so many centuries, sex has been exploited, reviled, denied, and perverted by its entanglement with violence and oppression that a widescale rebellion was unavoidable—and just as unavoidable was the replication of the system's evil in the rebellion against it.

And the sexual revolution, like other revolutions, has achieved some degree of good. On the most mundane level, it made possible the feminist efforts to define and explore women's sexuality and the lesbian and gay movement's demand that same-sex attraction be respected and validated. It created a framework in which people could consider the possibilities of nonpermanent, nonmonogamous relationships that were nonetheless neither degrading nor exploitative. It made birth control far more accessible to women, married and single, allowing them freedom to act on their sexual feelings with less fear of unwanted pregnancy. It created the first large-scale demands for legalized abortion, which feminists would bring to a far deeper level.

Perhaps most profoundly, the sexual revolution exposed the hypocrisy of so many enforcers of traditional sexual mores, even as it ignored the piece of their vision that was true. It made us see, finally, that not only did the emperor have no clothes, he was protecting his own nakedness by punishing ours. There have always been those who have recognized and decried sexual hypocrisy, of course, but the sexual revolution made such recognition almost commonplace—it was no longer the preserve of a handful of brave rebels. We know now that most of the clients of prostitutes are "respectable" married men; we know that large numbers of church-going fathers sexually abuse their daughters; we know that reciprocal monogamy is a polite fiction that allows men to cheat on their wives, who will still be socially penalized for taking the same liberties their husbands take. (Yet we know, too, that there are at least some mainstream men who do respect the values they profess—who love and are faithful to their wives, who do not act out their sexual fantasies with children, for whom sex is something both joyful and sacred.)

It was perhaps too much to hope that we would escape the tragedy of most revolutions—that we would, in attempting to tear down the old, oppressive ways come up with something less ugly and destructive. Nevertheless, I *had* hoped for it—first from the sexual revolution, then from the women's movement, which seemed to be offering hope of a new, redeeming exploration of women's sexuality.

But honest exploration can lead the explorer to some dangerous and ugly places, without the skills to recognize the dangers. Many of us landed in those places, mistaking them for the promised land. We've been ingenuous; in our desire to escape the sexual guilt piled on us all our lives, we've encouraged the notion that we should be able to do anything we feel like doing. And it's turned out that what some of us felt like doing was as ugly and destructive as the things that had been done to us for centuries. The way that sexual liberation has evolved in much of the women's movement has numbed me, horrified me, and affected my political vision in a way that often seems irrational even to my closest friends and to those who agree with my analysis.

In my despairing moments, which are frequent, I think that the sexual revolution and its recent ramifications have proved finally that humankind is doomed to be destroyed by its own evil (a word I think we need to reclaim, along with "morality," and which we have discarded at our peril). The glorification of pain and degradation, the willingness to exploit children's vulnerability, the profound abuse of trust in the defiance of monogamous commitment—appearing as they do in some of the best and most principled feminists and radicals—leaves me with a terrified sense that the kind of morality necessary to save the world from its own physical annihilation is ultimately beyond human possibility. What I think in my rare but possibly more accurate moments of optimism is that the sexual revolution may be functioning like a lance driven into a horribly infected body. What it's spewing out is inevitably hideous but, at least, is finally leaving the body.

Maybe, eventually, the body can begin to heal, and we can begin working toward a sexuality that many people have partially envisioned, and partially created, over the centuries. It's easier to define what it won't be than what it will be. It won't be an assumption that all sexual impulses are good because they're sexual, or that all sexual impulses should be acted upon to prevent repression. It won't be exploitative, pornographic, or sadistic, and it won't be the arena in which self-hatred is played out. It won't be enforced heterosexuality or enforced monogamy (though I have a feeling that, given real choice and a social frame-work that doesn't make deep love terrifying, most people, gay and straight, will eventually opt for monogamy). It won't involve government sanction though some lovers might still celebrate their commitment with public ritual.

What it will be, I hope, is a force fully respected and revered—enough so that both men and women will seriously consider how and when to act on it, with those decisions no longer governed by a need to rebel against a repressive power structure. It will be caring and committed, and not be afraid of or dulled by permanence. It will be passionate and wild and tender; it will be a form of connection between people that enriches and validates the best in both of them. It will be sacred; it will be creative. It will have become, finally, making love.

SEPTEMBER 1985

An Exchange on the Pornography Ordinance

For the Ordinance

AN OPEN LETTER TO READERS:

A group of liberal academic women and lawyers identifying themselves as FACT (Feminist Anti-Censorship Taskforce) have mounted an attack against the feminist antipornography movement and have solicited the support of some prominent feminists. We, as women who are radically op-posed to pornography and who are committed to its eradication, recognize the potential danger to thousands of women if their actions are not understood and challenged.

Many of you know about the antipornography ordinance written by Andrea Dworkin and Catharine MacKinnon. This initiative, launched in Minneapolis, Indianapolis, and now in Los Angeles, makes pornography actionable as sex discrimination. Rather than placing pornography under the legal heading of obscenity or zoning laws, it names it for the first time in the legal arena for what it truly is—a gross violation of women's civil rights. Dworkin and MacKinnon's legal initiative carefully defines pornography as the graphic sexually explicit subordination of women through pictures or words that also includes women presented de-humanized as sexual objects who enjoy pain, humiliation, or rape; women bound, mutilated, dismembered, or tortured; women in postures of servility or submission or display; women being penetrated by objects or animals. (Men or children who are sometimes violated, like women, through and in pornography can sue under this law also.) The Dworkin-MacKin-non civil rights legislation would allow victims of four activities—coercion, force, assault, and trafficking—to sue civilly those who hurt them through pornography.

What some of you may not know about is the immense public initiative that prompted the writing of the legislation to begin with, and the groundswell of public support that has been behind the law in each of these three cities. In Minneapolis, poor and working people living in neighborhoods where pornography had been forcibly zoned, and whose lives were horrendously affected by it, asked Dworkin and MacKinnon to work with them to tell the city how pornography hurts women in particular. Dworkin and MacKinnon responded with legislation that would address grassroots issues and problems. The ordinance in Minneapolis was supported by many progressive groups there. In Indianapolis, similar neighborhood groups, including many Blacks, supported the ordinance.

It is important to understand that this legislation is both a product of the feminist antipornography movement and a catalyst for coalescing thousands of women, working people, gay and lesbian groups, and racially mixed supporters in the cities where it has been proposed. Two women alone have not made this movement. Hundreds of women have testified in public, in support of the bill, to being abused by pornography. Hundreds more have spoken in private to Dworkin and MacKinnon about the abuse to which they were/are subjected by the pornography industry, describing the pictures for which they were positioned to pose, the knots in which they were tied, the expressions that were facially forced, how the abuse was orchestrated—all conforming to the magazine's code of creating pornographic women for male use. As Andrea Dworkin has written: "I have heard women who have been raped in every sort of way, with every sort of device, with animals, filmed during the rapes, the photographs of the rapes now being sold as protected speech; I have heard transgenerational stories of mother-daughter abuse premised on pornography; *Playboy* and *Penthouse* rapes; women of all ages talking about being violated at all ages, used on one end of pornography or the other." The hearings in Minneapolis included testimony of women raped in marriage, prostituted, and gangraped, all finding pornography at the heart of what happened to them. Many courageous women not only testified at these hearings but also went to the press and demanded to be believed.

Dworkin and MacKinnon's work, persistence, and leadership have brought this testimony into concrete political action. Thousands of women have risked public exposure, harassment, assault, and even their lives in testifying for this initiative. Once it is law, many of the women who have been abused by pornography are prepared to bring complaints against the pornographers. These women *know,* not only in their minds but in their bodies, that pornography itself is a form of sexual abuse. Thousands of other women *know* the same: feminists who work with victims of sexual abuse *know* that pornography is central to the abuse; clinicians who work with sex offenders *know* that pornography provides rapists with the ideas and energy that often compose the reality of sexual abuse and mutilation; wives and girlfriends of men who use pornography *know* that what is demanded of them sexually is constructed by the pornography these men read. For example, "deep throat" became a household "word made flesh" after men saw Linda Lovelace (Marchiano) do it in the movie. Linda Marchiano now tells that it took kidnapping, death threats, and hypnosis (to repress the natural gag response) in order for her to do in this film what men think is a lark. But many refuse to believe her testimony.

Among the many who do not believe either Linda Marchiano or the thousands of women who have testified in favor of this legislation is a group called FACT. This group, and its supporters, have filed a legal *amicus curiae* brief against the antipornography ordinance in the U.S. Court of Appeals, Seventh Circuit, in Indianapolis. FACT's central arguments are that "the ordinance suppresses constitutionally protected speech in a manner particularly detrimental to women," and that "the ordinance unconstitutionally discriminates on the basis of sex and reinforces sexist stereotypes." It does this, they say, because the ordinance depicts men as "attacking dogs" and "women as incapable of consent." The FACT brief maintains that statutory rape laws "reinforce the stereotype that in sex the man is the offender and the woman is the victim."

FACT also contends that "the ordinance is unconstitutionally vague because its central terms have no fixed meaning, and the most common meanings of these terms are sexist and damaging to women; sexually explicit speech does not cause or incite violence in a manner sufficiently direct to justify its suppression under the First Amendment; constitutional protection of sexually explicit speech should be enhanced, not diminished; and the ordinance classifies on the basis of sex and perpetuates sexist stereotypes." "Sexually explicit speech" is their euphemism for pornography.

Worse, the FACT brief says that women need pornography to realize ourselves sexually—that freedom for women depends on access to pornography, and that sex is synonymous with pornography. It says, "Even pornography which is problematic for women can be experienced as affirming of women's desires and of women's equality.... The range of feminist imagination and expression in the realm of sexuality has barely begun to find voice. Women need the freedom and the socially recognized space to appropriate for themselves the robustness of what traditionally has been male language." "Male language" is another euphemism for pornography. In this context, they quote Ellen Willis, who has written: "A woman who enjoys pornography (even if that means enjoying a rape fantasy) is in a sense a rebel, insisting on an aspect of her sexuality that has been defined as a male preserve.... [Pornography], in rejecting sexual repression and hypocrisy,...expresses a radical impulse" ("Feminism, Moralism, and Pornography," *Beginning to See the Light*, Alfred A. Knopf, 1981). This is a vision of sexual and women's liberation that would keep us on our knees. Worse, it is a lie.

Unfortunately, FACT is not a fiction. But what they say about the antipornography initiative, and its so-called dangers to "free speech," is a fiction. And they have many supporters—some who have the reputation of being prominent feminists, such as Adrienne Rich and Kate Millet, but mostly male and female academics and lawyers. They parade the abstract flag of First Amendment rights as they trample over the reality of what pornography does to women. They treat the First Amendment as fundamentalists treat the Bible—as absolute, not as subject to any unorthodox interpretation or amendation, and as admitting no legal counterbalance, such as the Fourteenth Amendment, or the right to equal protection under the law. International feminists will recognize their obsession with First Amendment preservation as a specifically American fetish.

FACT and its supporters prefer deceptive abstractions to realities. To define pornography, they prefer the empty abstraction of terminology such as "sexually explicit speech" over the reality of what pornography really is and what it does to women. Abstractly, they pretend to reverse sexism, while ignoring it in the real lives of real women. Their priorities are misplaced, and that is an understatement. They degrade and caricature the word "feminism" by using it to describe their defense of pornography.

FACT and its supporters express no concern about how their position will be used by the pornographers, pimps, and the $8-billion-per-year pornography industry. Their public position would allow Hugh Hefner, Bob Guccione, and the likes of Larry Flynt to use signers' names in their magazines. Picture the next issue of *Playboy* with the headline, "Lesbian feminist poet Adrienne Rich defends women's access to pornography." Instead, FACT raves about the dangers of how the political Right will supposedly use the antipornography legislation for its own purposes. Dworkin, MacKinnon, and all feminists in the antipornography movement have consistently disavowed any connection with the Right.

FACT's position is a "do-nothing" approach to pornography. Nowhere have they proposed any redress, any protection, for women whose lives have been ravaged by "sexually explicit speech," so explicitly that some are dead from that "speech." Witness the death of Dorothy Stratton—Playmate of the year—said to have been raped by Hefner, pimped up to him by a husband who forced her into posing while under the age of eighteen. Stratton was killed at twenty after being tortured and raped, then was raped again after she was dead. Her murderer-pimp-husband was obsessed with pornography and acted it out on her.

Feminism is a reality to us, not an empty abstraction. Feminism is about real women. We are real women who have real voices, and whose "speech" is no more protected by pornography than Black "speech" is protected by segregation. We think it time that our voices be heard in support of the real women and the real work that has been done by Andrea Dworkin and Catharine MacKinnon and the thousands of women who have had the courage to testify for this legislation.

This letter was signed by 139 feminists, all of whose names appeared with the original printing in Sojourner.

Against the Ordinance

AN OPEN LETTER TO READERS:
This summer, people in Cambridge, Massachusetts, were asked to sign a petition to put an antipornography ordinance on the city's November ballot as a binding referendum question.... Enough signatures were gathered so that Cantabrigians will be given an opportunity to place one of the most repressive, insidious pieces of legal hyperbole on the books of one the most liberal cities in the country.

We are a group of long-time feminist activists who have united in response to this organizing by forming a local chapter of the Feminist Anti-Censorship Taskforce (FACT). Most of us have worked in varying capacities against violence directed at women. However, none of us believes that the antipornography/civil rights approach is a cure for the ills of a misogynist society. We think that, if passed, the ordinance will be used against women and sexual minorities by those in power and further circumscribe our writing, art, work, and sexuality.

The version of the ordinance introduced in other cities is extremely broad and vague. The most controversial section is that which defines pornography. Proponents say that the definition will only restrict "hard-core" pornography, which they define as violent, sexist, and sexually explicit. In fact, the definition would include material that lacks one or two of those three elements. It could include books like *Our Bodies, Ourselves* or Andrea Dworkin's *Pornography*. It could be used to shut down feminist bookstores. It can and will be used against lesbian and gay media such as *Gay Community News* and *Bad Attitude*. It allows anybody, including other women and gay people, to become the self-appointed censors of our communities. These are not just spurious speculations: *Our Bodies, Ourselves* and alternative bookstores have been the victims of censorship under the auspices of other laws seeking to protect us. The proposed ordinance gives another tool to an already erotophobic state.

The fact that this proposed law may have been written by women does not allow it to escape the fact that the judiciary will interpret it. Judges are people schooled in the tradition of preserving the status quo, a male version of reality. They rely on legal precedent and laws designed to protect the interests of a white male, propertied class in a system structured by men. One of the interests to be "protected" is the sexual subservience of women. Unless "feminist" laws are given a "feminist" political, legal, and cultural context, they exist only in the abstract. By using this law, we are giving power to the state, not women, to make more decisions about women. In an area where even feminists cannot agree about the meaning of a sexual image, it is a grave mistake to give that control to the legal system. By encouraging courts to restrict expression, we jeopardize our own expression and our ability to create our own sexual culture.

The proposed ordinance does not censor violent misogynist images generally, but only sexually explicit images. It doesn't touch sexism in the media and in advertising. It doesn't address television's ubiquitous dimwitted woman. It doesn't require filmmakers to cut out the violence. It is incomprehensible to give sexually explicit images special treatment, unless feminists believe, as do many people on the Right, that there is something wrong with most sex.

A goal of feminism has always been the elimination of repressive and constricting stereotypes about women. In earlier years of the movement, women eagerly discussed sex in consciousness-raising groups and wrote about the advantages of freeing ourselves from the sexual double-standard. The ordinance, however, codifies the double-standard by its characterization of women as weak and passive victims of sex. The presumption that women need protection from men makes it the legal equivalent of a chastity belt. In both cases, women are infantilized.

Women are vulnerable to sexual abuse and violence. But women can also be enthusiastic sexual actors. As feminists, we want to challenge and eliminate sexual violence without having to deny our capacity for sexual pleasure or give up our own explorations of sex. We don't want to remain mired in an ideology that focuses solely on our victimization. Both heterosexual and lesbian women have rebelled by creating our own sex publications, books, poetry, photographs, and painting. Call them "erotica," call them "pornography," or call them "art"—if they are sexually explicit, they can be eliminated by this law.

It is not surprising that a law like this is being advanced at this particular time. Five years of the Reagan administration have taken their toll and the country is gripped by repressive forces to an extent that is appalling to those of us who came of political age in the '60s. A "profamily" ideology is rampant—not just among the right wing, but among leftists as well. This translates into increasing attacks on women, gay men, and lesbians. Already marginalized, we are being squeezed out of existence by laws that would deny us access to abortion and deny us equal rights in employment and housing. Antipornography laws are a sign of the repressive times and resonate so perfectly with the right-wing political agenda that Phyllis Schlafly has supported them enthusiastically. Although Dworkin and MacKinnon disavow an alliance with the Right, their law has already been usurped by the Moral Majority. In Suffolk County, New York, when a conservative legislator introduced a version of the antipornography legislation, the hearings were packed with members of the Eagle Forum, Citizens for Decency, and other right-wing groups in support of it. Antipornography legislation is the perfect mechanism for the Right to further restrict women, define our sexuality, and control our access to information.

Defining pornography is so difficult that the word becomes an emotional and political Rorschach test—revealing more about the definer than the material. The language of the proposed antipornography laws is so broad, however, that women with a variety of opinions about pornography oppose them. The laws have been condemned by many women, including those who work in the sex industry and women active in the antiviolence movement. When New York's FACT submitted an *amicus* brief opposing the Indianapolis antipornography ordinance, over 80 individuals and groups signed it, including Adrienne Rich, Kate Millet, Betty Friedan, the editors of *Conditions,* Susan Schecter, and Michelle Cliff. The common element among the many signers was their belief that antipornography legislation is a serious political mistake that would hurt more than help women. Since the brief was submitted, however, many of these women have been publicly attacked and discredited by supporters of the ordinance. In a public statement currently being circulated, the politics of FACT are ludicrously distorted and other opponents of the legislation are condemned. These ardent ordinance supporters advance the naive political argument that anyone who does not support their position cannot be a feminist. This continuous credential baiting does not deepen or enhance political dialogue. Instead, it divides our movement even further. Clearly, there is no single feminist "line" about pornography. Clearheaded discussion and debate about the issues will take us further than name-calling and discrediting dedicated feminists.

As members of FACT, we think it would better serve the feminist movement if we returned to some of the original goals that the women's movement advanced to eradicate sexual oppression. Workplace equity, abortion rights, lesbian/gay liberation, welfare rights, and access to child care will free women far more than the elimination of pornographic images.

Janice Irvine and Donna Turley for Boston FACT

This is an edited version of the original rebuttal that appeared in Sojourner.

THE DWORKIN-MACKINNON ORDINANCE*

The legislation proposed in Minneapolis, Indianapolis, and Los Angeles defined "pornography" as follows:

Pornography is the graphic sexually explicit subordination of women through pictures and/or words that also includes one or more of the following: (i) women are presented dehumanized as sexual objects, things, or commodities; or (ii) women are presented as sexual objects who enjoy pain or humiliation; or (iii) women are presented as sexual objects who experience sexual pleasure in being raped; or (iv) women are presented as sexual objects tied up or cut up or mutilated or bruised or physically hurt; or (v) women are presented in postures of sexual submission, servility, or display; or (vi) women's body parts—including but not limited to vaginas, breasts, or buttocks—are exhibited such that women are reduced to those parts; or (vii) women are presented as whores by nature; or (viii) women are presented as being penetrated by objects or animals; or (ix) women are presented in scenarios of degradation, injury, torture, shown as filthy or inferior, bleeding, bruised, or hurt in a context that makes these conditions sexual.

The proposed ordinance also included the following stipulations:

It shall be sex discrimination through pornography to engage in any of the following activities:

a. To coerce, intimidate, or fraudulently induce (hereafter, "coerce") any person into performing for pornography. Complaint(s) may be made against the maker(s), seller(s), exhibitor(s), and/or distributor(s) of said pornography....

b. To produce, sell, exhibit, or distribute pornography, including through private clubs. (i) City, state, and federally funded public libraries or private and public university and college libraries in which pornography is available for study shall not be construed to be trafficking in pornography. (ii) Isolated passages or isolated parts shall not be actionable under this section. (iii) Any woman has a claim hereunder as a woman acting against the subordination of women. Any man, child, or transsexual who alleges injury by pornography in the way women are injured by it also has a claim.

c. To assault, physically attack, or injure any person in a way that is directly caused by specific pornography. Complaint(s) may be made against the perpetrator of the assault or attack and/or against the maker(s), distributor(s), seller(s), and/or exhibitor(s) of the specific pornography.

d. It shall not be a defense to an action filed under a-c that the defendant did not know or intend that the materials were pornography or sex discrimination.

*As it appeared in the September 1985 issue of Sojourner.

SEPTEMBER 1987

Andrea Dworkin: "What Is Intercourse?"

an interview by Katy Abel

The following interview took place just following the publication of Andrea Dworkin's book Intercourse *(Free Press, 1987). A nationally known activist, Dworkin coauthored with Catharine MacKinnon civil rights legislation that defines pornography as legally actionable sex discrimination (see "An Exchange on the Pornography Ordinance").*

Katy Abel: *How would you describe your purpose in writing* Intercourse?

Andrea Dworkin: I wanted to ask, "What is intercourse really? How do we experience it? What is its real meaning? What is its relationship to male power in the system that we live under, the system of male dominance?" The most crucial question to me was, "Does the experience of intercourse—which is often the antithesis of equality for women—have an effect on women's desire or will to be free, to fight for political freedom?"

I want to ask you about your statement, "Violation is a synonym for intercourse."

I say that is true in the context of male society. In other words, I'm not saying that, outside the world men have made, "intercourse" and "violation" are synonyms. I'm saying that in male culture "intercourse" is used virtually as a synonym for "violating the female body." And there are so many thousands of examples of this that it seemed to me bizarre to labor the point.

For example, any number of contemporary male writers—Norman Mailer, Jerzy Kosinski, Michel Foucault—use "intercourse" as a synonym for "violation." But since they're not taking a critical stance, their view goes largely unremarked; it's taken as a point of fact. But what happens when a feminist comes along and says, "Look, in the society we're living in—a socially constructed thing that we can change—'intercourse' is synonymous with 'violation': male power has made it so and men believe that it is so"? Everyone goes, "Oh, my God! She's saying that 'intercourse' is synonymous with 'violation.' What a horrible thing to say."

You must have expected that reaction.

Actually, I expected that, after fifteen years of feminism, people would understand that in a misogynist society "intercourse" is synonymous with "violation," and could move on from that observation. Since 1974, I've written book after book after book explaining why and how that's true.

I think some people have reacted negatively to your focus on the physical act, as opposed to sexist or uncaring behavior by men. This seems to let men off the hook.

My book uniquely focuses on the meaning for women and men of the physical act of intercourse in a male culture, and that hasn't been done before. Nobody has looked at what happens when, in a society where men are considered superior, a man actually physically occupies a woman's body. So it seems to me that what really has people so upset about my book is that it says intercourse is usually a form of sexist behavior, and that you can't separate the rest of a man's or woman's life from the act of intercourse.

In fact, if you don't deal with this basic expression of male dominance, which everyone takes for granted, you're never going to be able to root out male dominance in the rest of life, because you won't even recognize it. If you pull male dominance apart and look at it, it's based on the basic male idea that anatomy is destiny—and the anatomy in question is sexual. So I've tried to parse the act that they say is biological and inevitable and must happen in this and this and this way, and say, "Let's find out what here is male dominance, as opposed to what is just nature."

What's new and radical and startling about the idea that some idiots believe anatomy is destiny?

It's not just some idiots who hold that belief: we still live in a society—however much those of us who don't like it would like to think otherwise—that is deeply based on that belief. And the question is how to change it.

Do you change it just by saying it's wrong? No. You go to the things that consistently reinforce that belief in people's everyday lives, even when they don't know it is being reinforced. In my opinion, intercourse in a male-dominated society is, sadly, one of the most basic experiences that reinforces—for both men and women—the notion of women's inferiority. But when that belief in inferiority is covered by sexual pleasure, people do not see it for what it is. In other words, if women get orgasmic delight in a sex act that is essentially premised on their inferiority and submission (and women do), it is then impossible for women to understand further how they have internalized the notion that they are inferior, should be submissive, and should not fight for political equality.

It sounds as if you're suggesting it's wrong for a woman to find pleasure in intercourse and that, if she does, she doesn't understand her oppression.

I'm not saying it's wrong for her to find pleasure in it. I'm saying that I want to scrutinize what her pleasure means. The fact of the matter is that most women, according to every study that's been done in the last fifteen years—ranging from the most scientific to the most popular—just don't like intercourse very much. For instance, Ann Landers asked women if they liked intercourse, and 80 percent basically said they did not. It wasn't just that they preferred something else: they didn't like intercourse, and they wanted to be close with men in other ways. This is not some deep, dark secret.

Shere Hite found the same thing.

She found that seven out of ten women do not have orgasm from intercourse. So the real question is why intercourse is the central sex act in our society if it's mostly not bringing women pleasure. I think the reason is the fact that intercourse is the most effective sex act of male dominance, and you can ask many questions around this.

For example, why do men only feel they've had sex when they've had intercourse? They can have orgasms many, many, many other ways, many of which are also much more congenial to women. So what is it that intercourse does for men that makes them feel it is the only act that's really and truly sex? My view is that it's the only act that really makes them feel like men—and that means experiencing a sense of power over a woman. So the question is not women's pleasure, although some women get great pleasure from intercourse. The question is one of power.

Another interesting question is why, according to Biblical and most secular law, heterosexual intercourse has been a state-required activity, especially in marriage. In all the years of talk about sexual values and sexual liberation, people have been talking almost exclusively about the things they have been forbidden to do. But it seems to me that people who care about freedom should also be concerned if the state tells them they have to commit certain sex acts. And heterosexual intercourse in marriage is the one sex act that the state and religious law have said must be engaged in. In fact, until recently, for a woman not to engage in heterosexual intercourse was to break the marriage contract. And, until recently, it was not possible for a married woman to claim that she had been raped. The purpose of marriage was to give her body over to the man for the sake of intercourse.

After I read your book I took out my copy of Our Bodies, Ourselves, *by the Boston Women's Health Book Collective, and under "Sexuality," I found the following description of intercourse: "Think of [it] as reciprocal. You open up to enclose him warmly. You surround him powerfully as he penetrates you." That description deliberately shifts the power relationship so that it is very much shared, and I think many feminists wonder why you don't attempt that, too. Why do you, in a sense, surrender to the male notion of what this act is, rather than striking out in a truly radical fashion and finding new ways to feminize it?*

I do. For instance, in my chapter on possession, I show that we don't have to see intercourse as a form of male possession of women. I describe the vagina as a very strong muscle that encircles the very tiny (by comparison) penis, and I write about the power of that muscle in relation to the penis and the fact that men are usually exhausted after sex, while women's endurance is very great. I have a very long and graphic description of intercourse from that point of view. But does women thinking about intercourse differently make intercourse different?

Yes.

I don't agree with that. The fact of the matter is that, when a group of people are out of power, they can think about what happens to them in dozens of ways, but that doesn't change the fact that someone is expressing real power in the world over and against their bodies. Nothing in women's very liberal, very kind, very benign efforts to reinvent sex in our heads has had the effect of changing male aggression against us in the world.

My first feminist book, *Woman Hating* (Dutton, 1974), published in 1974, had a whole section on ecstatic new ways to conceive of various sex acts—I truly believed that was a way to go. But I don't believe it now, and the reason is that I think women had better face reality. Reality is male power, and you can't change it until you face it. Just thinking about it differently doesn't change it.

No, but the process of thinking about it is a form of empowerment.

I think that women are jumping to pleasant thoughts about intercourse and other forms of male dominance in order to skip over the really difficult and painful understanding of how that dominance works. My book is about how male dominance works through intercourse. It's not a pleasant book—I think it's a very tragic book. But I think it's a true book. And if it's a true book, then it's going to make its contribution, which women who feel that there are more utopian ways of dealing with intercourse can use or ignore.

Is there any way for me to go to bed with a man and not feel as if somebody's running a power trip on me?

Under any system of dominance, there are always pockets of personal freedom that people find, whether in sexual relationships or not. Under the most horrifying historical circumstances, people have made relationships that have made a difference for them. But that doesn't mean they make a difference in general, in the world—and this book is about what happens to women in general, in the world. So, yes, you can go to bed with so-and-so, and it may be an experience of reciprocity and sharing for both of you. But when you get up and leave the house, he is a man and you are a woman; he has power and you don't. And you're likely to encounter his power and your relative powerlessness in intercourse somewhere along the line—the next day, the next month. What he brings home with him is what you will encounter in sex.

That is a very fatalistic view of male-female relationships.
No, not if what you're trying to do is change society so that there's equality between the sexes and sex becomes an expression of equality, rather than saying, "We have to have pleasant attitudes towards sex." Most of the time, that is, frankly, an endorsement of male supremacy. It has to be remembered that women have not loved intercourse: if there's been any kind of consistent resistance to male supremacy, it has been women's personal, individual, repeated, legendary, traditional, over-and-over-again refusal to enjoy intercourse.

It sounds like you're indicting feminists for trying to cover up something uncomfortable to look at.
Well, I think that is largely true of feminism now. I think that feminism, in general, is suffering a real softness in the head, a refusal to deal with the realities of male power. I think we went through a period in the women's movement when we were grateful for the new information that gave us some understanding of ourselves. But now the movement is largely saying, "Don't make me think about anything else. I'm tired. I've had it."

I think people are saying, "I'm going to take control here—I'm going to try in the bedroom and elsewhere to reorient this as something meaningful to me. There will be a feminization of the sex act if I'm to be a participant in it." But even though you write, "Male sexual discourse on the meaning of intercourse becomes our language," I don't feel your book challenges that language and helps to create a new one to help individual women.
My area of endeavor is different. I'm trying to destroy the power that men have over women, and I don't think you can do that just by creating a woman's language, any more than, in the old days, you could do that just by having a woman's coffeehouse or one street in a city where women could walk safely. You need to be able to go into any coffeehouse; you need the whole city safe. There are forms of male power, primarily in the area of sex, that have remained absolutely resistant to change; the exploitation of women is worse, not better, and violence against women in our society is worse, not better. I am determined to do everything I can to destroy male power over women, and that means books, demonstrations, and forms of confrontation that try to expose what that power is and the way it works.

Your book represents an "antisex vision," according to feminist writer Karen Lindsey. How do you feel about comments like that?
I'm pretty appalled by the feminist reviewers who have been that simple-minded. I'm also appalled that in the women's movement, "antisex" is in and of itself a totally dismissive pejorative. It reminds me of when people used to have to sign loyal oaths to the Constitution; now, in the women's movement, we have to sign them to the sex act. I don't see why any area of sexual experience or sexual endeavor should not be open to sexual political analysis and questioning and, in a male supremacist society, to sexual political opposition. Intercourse is the quintessential sex act in a male society and, therefore, outright opposition to it is certainly

part of a feminist geography of response. And a book as complex and analytical as mine is certainly part of a reasoned resistance to simply accepting the premises we've been given.

We have to resist what I regard as the insane optimism in this country—and it has been translated into every serious political movement I've seen in my lifetime—that it's all, ultimately, a matter of your attitude. It's not all a matter of your attitude. Power in the world is real, and the most self-respecting thing you can do is work for a social policy that distributes power, money, resources, and influence equally among all people. That's what I would tell people to do—that's where I believe self-respect for women lies.

JULY 1987

A DISTORTED, ANTISEX VISION: A REVIEW OF ANDREA DWORKIN'S INTERCOURSE

by Karen Lindsey

Andrea Dworkin has written a book guaranteed to be attacked—and, unfortunately, her attackers are guaranteed to be at least halfway right. There's an awful lot of problems with this book, not least among them its premise. It's an old favorite of hers, having appeared before in *Woman Hating* (Dutton, 1974) and *Pornography* (Perigee, 1981): sexual intercourse itself, apart from the context in which it takes place or the uses to which it's put, is degrading and oppressive to women.

In the chapter titled "Occupation and Collaboration," Dworkin develops her argument, and, excellent writer that she is, expounds it eloquently: "There is never a real privacy of the body that can coexist with intercourse.... *Violation* is a synonym for intercourse.... Intercourse is both the normal use of a woman, her human potentiality affirmed by it, and a violative abuse, her privacy irredeemably compromised, her selfhood changed in a way that is irrevocable, unrecoverable." Again and again, she repeats this: intercourse demeans a woman by "communicating to her cell by cell her own inferior status, impressing it on her, burning it into her by shoving it into her, over and over, pushing and thrusting until she gives up and gives in...." Intercourse for a woman, she reiterates, can never be other than demeaning, and woe to the woman who enjoys it! To us she offers a scathing condemnation Jerry Falwell might emulate. Rhetorically, she asks, "Would intercourse cause orgasm in women if women were not objects for men before and during intercourse...? Can intercourse exist without the woman herself turning herself into a thing, which she must do because she cannot fuck equals and men must fuck?" By enjoying intercourse, the woman "begins a political collaboration with his dominance"; she engages in "acts of self-mutilation, self-diminishing, self-reconstruction, until there is no self, only the diminished, mutilated reconstruction." Not only that, but having destroyed ourselves, we are incapable of alliance with other women, since they are what we are, degraded and despised. The rhetoric is powerful, as good fundamentalist preaching is; I find myself feeling like a soiled Victorian maiden, with nothing left but to hurl myself, abject and abandoned by all decent women, over the Bridge of Sighs.

I really hate saying all this: those of us in the antiporn, antisadomasochism camp are so often accused of Victorian morality that it's extremely uncomfortable to use that terminology against another radical feminist. Unfortunately, I don't see an honest way to avoid it. Dworkin accuses those of us who enjoy intercourse of being collaborators, but, tragically, it is she who collaborates—with an age-old male notion that sex is dirty and that women who like it are especially dirty. She has always been a brilliant analyst of the ways men have used their sexuality to degrade women, but by removing the social context and clearly stating that the evil is in the nature of intercourse itself, this intense radical feminist implicitly admits women's basic inferiority. Our bodies are, after all, *built* for intercourse. While that doesn't mean we all have to like it, or that we shouldn't go in for other sexual activities, it *does* mean, I'm afraid, that if intercourse is by nature degrading, women are by nature degraded; our bodies are designed to be violated. It's hardly a new notion—most misogynists would readily agree with it—but it's chilling coming from a radical feminist.

Dworkin tries to back her thesis up by ending the book with some of the history of rape and pornography that she has written about so well before. She still writes well about it. But the section does nothing to prove that intercourse is by nature oppressive, only that the men who have power over us have all too often made it oppressive—as they've made almost everything oppressive, from childrearing to letter-typing.

Finally, there is a disturbing omission from this book that, given the power of Dworkin's rhetoric, is irresponsible. Having eliminated intercourse as a legitimate form of sexual expression, she offers us nothing else in its place. What about other forms of sexual activity? Is anal intercourse degrading, since it can be done by a man with other men as well as with women? Is a woman inherently degraded by performing fellatio on her lover? Or cunnilingus? Is oral sex morally different between a woman and a man than between two women or two men? Is manual sex permissible, and if so, if penetration per se is the issue, is it degrading to enjoy one's lover's fingers entering one's vagina? These are not frivolous questions: Dworkin has earlier dismissed with contempt "the simple-minded prosex chauvinism of Right and Left." Is she telling us that sex itself is degraded and degrading? She might well be: it's significant that in this book about sex by a major feminist, lesbianism is never addressed—or even mentioned.

Nor, having proscribed intercourse, does Dworkin begin to suggest alternatives for women who want children. Should they just bop over to the local sperm bank? Or is artificial insemination oppressive—the sperm still inserted into the vagina, still entering the woman's body? And if so, is pregnancy itself degrading? Dworkin demands that we take seriously her questioning of the essence of intercourse, but she does not demand of herself that she examine fully its implications.

I tend to get angry when the feminist supporters of pornography and sadomasochism take their cue from the "prolife" crowd and dub themselves the "prosex" movement, clearly implying that the rest of us are antisex. But Dworkin, I'm afraid, really is antisex, and her vision in this book is as distorted as that of her enemies within and without the women's movement.

Excerpted from the original.

OCTOBER 1988

Susie Bright: On the Line

by Sharon Gonsalves

Susie Bright, editor and founder of On Our Backs, *a lesbian sex magazine published in San Francisco since 1983, spoke with Sharon Gonsalves during a 1988 visit to the Boston area. A mover and shaker of the women's erotica movement, Bright spoke about the "lesbian sexual renaissance," which continues to thrive even in the face of AIDS and the need to practice safe sex.*

Sharon Gonsalves: *What advice do you have for women who want to be able to talk more easily about sex?*

Susie Bright: Well, you give yourself a little rap about how pissed you are that the subject was suppressed around you. There are very old-fashioned sexist reasons why [women] don't talk about sex comfortably. Most women who can't admit that it's hard to talk about sex know that the reason they feel that way is because of how they were raised. And if you can work up a good feminist steam about how mad you are that you were told not to touch yourself, not to talk about it, not to read about it, not to express yourself, not to expect anything—if you can get mad about that—that is the first step.

You gave a lecture recently in Cambridge, Massachusetts, dressed in a low-cut minidress, fishnet stockings, and heels. What statement are you making with your clothes?

A couple of months ago, the *San Francisco Chronicle* had a front-page article that said, "Soviet women driven to lesbianism by ugly clothes." I straightened out my paper and said, "What?" I don't know how it got into UPI, but it was about some obscure report from a Soviet sociologist who was saying that in Soviet prisons women aren't given anything but ugly clothes and vicious regimentation and this is turning them into lesbians and narcotics users. The idea that ugly clothes and lesbianism are somehow directly related kills the idea that we have any style. And we do have style. I enjoyed the way we [lesbians] dressed [flannel shirts and jeans]. It was a statement about dropping out of society and also about being a lesbian. It was liberating to cut your hair off. At a certain point, I had those same liberating feelings about putting on the petticoats again. I started to realize that there was a whole lot to feminine dress and style that was extremely erotic to me. I met drag queens, and I figured if they could wear a dress, I was gonna wear a dress. It took a man to get me into a dress again, but he wasn't straight.

When you come into your own, with your own style, whatever that may be, and you aren't so much worried about what others think and you start dressing for yourself—it's quite an aggressive move. People who come out looking really distinct and very much in their own style radiate that kind of confidence; so for me, it's a closet issue. Are you out of the closet with your erotic style? The thing about femmes is that so often you pass for straight, although I tend to glory in the way that I look different from straight women.... I mean, I notice all the little details in which perhaps my femme persona is different from theirs. It's not a matter for me of, why can't lesbians be more feminine? It's a matter of, why can't you find out who you are and let your sexual preference and that sense of style bloom?

How do you see women's erotica as being different from mainstream pornography?
Women are new to this business. Men have a lot of pornographic traditions now about what the audience is supposed to want. It's not necessarily what I think men want. Men and women, straight and gay, everyone wants more diversity, more authenticity, originality, better production, contemporary characters; they want all this stuff. Is the business giving it to them? No. Women's erotica is different because it's so small and the market is so tiny and because, as lesbians, we are different from straight people. We have different values about sexuality. They could learn something from us about how important sexual identity is. In some ways we're teaching the mainstream business a lot of things. We're small, but we have a big impact on them because they're surprised by how different our values are and because they know there's a women's market out there. They have so much money and resources; if they would bother to get anybody good doing stuff they could wipe us out. Their own homophobia and sexism and guilt about sex stop them. Their attitude is "well, we make these videos, but we wouldn't want our wives to look at them, and we wouldn't want our daughters acting in them." That's very different from grassroots lesbian erotica where we're in our videos. Our pictures are in the magazine. We're very much on the line, and we embrace everyone who would want to be a part of it. We think it's wholesome. We think hot sex is necessary to your physical and mental health. We don't think it's some trifle. We don't think it's something you do after you've taken care of more serious issues. This is a serious issue. Those are ideas that come from women's liberation, gay liberation, and from the last two decades of sexual politics. It's a radical departure from how sex has been regarded in the past.

What do you tell women who are interested in producing erotica?
I really encourage people. This is your chance to get in on the ground floor of women's erotica, 'cause there is no formula yet. There is no girl-next-door; there is no ideal woman. There may never be. I hope actually there isn't. That would kind of bother me if there was. I like our flexibility and our diversity. But it is inevitable; eventually, there will become genres of lesbian erotica, but right now it's wide open. Anyone can walk in with a well-crafted fantasy and say this is lesbian erotica, and no one's gonna pooh-pooh you because we've hardly looked at anything. Our sexual imagination is like Pandora's box, and it's just barely been opened. Things are just starting to come out. And this is not going to hurt your sex life or your political life. It's going to enhance your understanding of people and give you more personal and political power to understand your sexuality.

What impact do you think lesbian sex magazines are having on the lesbian community?
I think there is a lesbian sexual renaissance going on because we now have media like *On Our Backs*. People are talking about everything from lesbians fucking men to butch on butch to exhibitionism, s/m, how our childhood sexual experiences affect us as adults, all kinds of things.

What about lesbians having sex with men ?

A lot of people think that the reason that we're hearing about lesbians fantasizing about men or fucking men is some kind of drawback or some kind of weakness on the part of the lesbian movement. For me, it's a symptom of the fact that now that we have released our sexual energy, everything's coming out. This will just be one of many subjects that finally gets talked about because we are in a position of strength, and, therefore, we can discuss it. I guess the first step in discussing it is just to acknowledge that it's out there and get over it.

Some women who identify as lesbian might call themselves bisexual if there wasn't so much displacement of the bisexual community—the fact that nobody really wants them. The straight people don't want them. The gay people don't want them. People identify themselves by sexual preference according to how they feel and how they fit into their communities. Bisexuals who feel at home in the lesbian community—maybe they had a long-time lesbian relationship—they feel like it makes sense to call themselves lesbians. Then I think you have what I would call lesbians who fuck men, where their sexual contact with men is rare or it's more idiosyncratic compared to their lesbian practice.

A lot of people want to point to the ultimate reason why lesbians fuck men. Some people point to economic privilege or necessity or they talk about the kind of material social advantages that women have in the company of men. But on an individual level, most people will say, "I did it 'cause I felt like it."

We have to be a little bit more accepting of how sex really works. Our sexual desire [should be] more straightforward instead of a subject of such anguish. I understand the anguish. I understand the sense of betrayal. Let's face it, gay people are shat upon by straight society. They are marking us because of what we do in bed, so if one of our own kind is in both beds, well, that poses a dilemma for a lot of people. I know that when I was the only militant bisexual I knew—my first six years of sleeping with women—it was awful to confide that I was bisexual to a lesbian group. It was instant, you know, to the exit sign.

I love being gay because I found so much of myself sexually with women, and I love gay culture, but I cannot work up a steam about a sense of betrayal in regard to bisexuality. I can only work up a steam about women being in the shadows with their sexual desires and not letting others know because they're afraid they won't have any friends or won't have a place to call home. That's what the tragedy is.

This article has been edited for length.

FEBRUARY 1991

Making Different Choices
by Sabrina Sojourner

Pussy, Cunt, Crack, Box, Purse, Slit, Hole are all names for the genital area of the female body. They are often used by men, and some women, as swear words—words to insult one another. Slang words for male genitalia, even the much maligned term *prick,* do not carry the same weight or impact as swear or insult words.

I have been looking at this phenomenon. Looking at the ways we talk and write and speak about sex. This examination has been prompted by: 1) My having spent the past few months providing information about safer sex primarily to gay men. In doing so, I have found myself reading more literature on sex education: safer sex and unsafe sex. 2) Being 37 years old and unsatisfied with most of what I have been told about sex, sexuality, and sexual orientation, including the resurgence of discussions about roles in the lesbian community. And 3) as a survivor of incest, it has been very important for me to recognize I have suffered a second kind of sexual abuse at the hands of therapists, and well-meaning others, who want me to question my sexuality and my joy of sex. While it has been important to examine the impact of the incest on my life, including my sex life, I resent ongoing and relentless implications that I can never be happy, healthy, or whole sexually because I am an incest survivor.

I am a lesbian feminist who writes erotica. For some women, lesbians and nonlesbians alike, that, in and of itself, is a problem. In the development of a feminist critique of patriarchal culture, many women took on the pornography establishment—and rightfully so. However, as theory, jargon, and rhetoric have unfolded, it has become difficult to distinguish between an antipornography movement and an antisex movement. To rephrase Alfred Kinsey's definition of "promiscuous," the argument often seems to come down to: "What turns me on is erotica and what turns you on is pornography." Without falling into the trap of defining these terms, I would argue that this problematic stance requires a true dialogue—not a wrestling match of ideologies—among women with the idea of developing new paradigms for sexuality.

I enjoy writing erotica because I believe in celebrating the goodness and vitality of passion and Eros. Like power, passion and Eros are not evil. How Eros, power, and passion are used determines the positive, negative, or neutral effect they have on our lives.

In looking at how sex gets talked about in our society, I have observed that heterosexual men (as long as race or ethnicity is not discussed) are viewed as being sexually active. Women of color and working-class white women—regardless of sexual orientation—and gay and bisexual men are seen as promiscuous. Middle- and owning-class white women and older women are seen as sexually passive. Any woman walking down the street, refusing to hide the offense she feels toward catcalls, etc., is often called "lesbian" or "frigid." In having these messages stick out in my mind for more than a few angry minutes, I have had to look at my relationship to *pussy, cunt, joybox, slit, clit, labia, dyke, lesbian, butch, femme,* sex in general, and lesbian sex in particular. I have had to look at how lesbians/women relate to their sexuality.

I have discovered that lesbian attitudes toward sex and sexuality are much more informed by heterosexism than we care to acknowledge. Discussions concerning roles are one good example. My biggest objection is the assumptions behind the discussion. The major assumption among lesbian feminists seems to be that roles are a problem whose solution is the creation of identifiable "lesbian clones." The heterosexism informing this opinion assumes that "butch" women seeking "femme" women (and vice versa) are replicating the worst of male/female sex-role stereotyping in their relationships. As one "enlightened" feminist told me, "There's no way these relationships can be mutual [read equal]."

In other words, if I choose to have an outward appearance which identifies me as "femme," which I do, I am expected to be "wifely" and "deferential" to butches the way heterosexual women are assumed to be toward men. If I dress in a manner which identifies me as "butch," the expectation is I will treat a "femme" in the worst ways heterosexual men treat women. Additional assumptions about femmes include: they cook, clean house, cater endlessly to the needs of butches, and are passive in bed—the list is endless. Assumptions about butches include: they are mannish and tough, don't know what it means to be "real" women, are aggressive in bed, don't like to be acted on in bed, and are into sports—again, the list goes on and on. Underlying feelings further assume it is not possible for women and men to ever have mutual/equal relationships.

If it were not for the pain we inflict on one another as a result of these assumptions, they would be laughable. Clearly, lesbian feminists making these assumptions have bought the entire bill of goods regarding sex and sex-role stereotypes.

For me, being femme means many things. In part, it means I am capable of doing a lot of things in a competent manner; however, I choose not to do certain things, unless an unavoidable need for me to do them arises. And, when appropriate, I am willing to pay someone well to provide these services for me. Thus, I do not work on my car, though I possess the technical prowess. I rarely build shelving or participate in other such projects, though I possess the skills. Yet, I will refinish furniture or lay tile, in part because I find them erotically pleasing, and I also enjoy performing simple wiring and plumbing tasks. It is also about paying attention to myself, giving myself permission to feel good, to feel pretty—something which is still begrudgingly given to me as a U.S.-born woman of color. The outward appearance of being a femme is about celebrating the feminine and wanting that celebration to be known. It is also about reclaiming, reidentifying feelings which have ancestral roots for me and about being strong, including having physical strength. "Femme" is a definition of femaleness which goes beyond heterosexist and white Western definitions about the feminine. Let it also be known I cook when I please, clean house as necessary, and I could probably blast a dozen more stereotypes. Some of the "butch" women I know are wonderful cooks, much better housekeepers, know less about cars than I, and have never heard of the San Francisco 49ers!

For many lesbians, being butch or femme is about breaking, bending, exploiting, and changing the rules, as well as about erotic turn-on and putting a face to the world which is comfortable and enjoyable. It is important to include in this discussion room for women who do not want to identify as butch or femme. Historically, these women were called "kiki" (pronounced *keekee,* or *keyekeye*). Bottom line: we are all women trying to define and determine our relationships to other women and ourselves; we are attempting to let go of other people's expectations of our behavior, and we are determined to exert who we are in ways which are intrinsic to our being.

This does not deny the existence of women who follow through on the worst and the best of sex-role stereotypes. The less affirming styles we choose may have more to do with the models with which we were raised; the different models we are willing to find, define, discover, and uncover for ourselves; and whether or not we recognize the need to do something different. It is the models that need to be attacked, overhauled, and raked over the coals—not the people/women choosing to show a particular style as their face to the world.

In recent issues of *Lesbian Ethics,* publishers have posed several forums for discussing butch/femme. I was distressed by the vehemence with which one writer trashed femmes, holding us responsible for butch oppression and "butch-phobia." It is sex-role stereotyping which oppresses all of us. My supposed "privilege" (her word) as a femme is as long as a man's penis. If I am not connected to that, according to societal myths and realities, I am unprotected and fair game for any male seeking to remind me of my place. That hardly connotes privilege. Nor does it put me in a position to "oppress" butch women.

The notion of femmes "trying to pass" colludes with heterosexism to act as a form of oppressing women. This fear of femmes is based on the belief that heterosexuality is preferable and something anyone would choose over being lesbian, that femmes never behave in ways which challenge heterosexism, and that femmes deny their allegiance to lesbianism at every turn.

Butch, femme, or kiki—any woman grappling with identity may follow through on any or all of the above actions. The issue is not other people's behavior but how we allow our assumptions about their motives to oppress us and/or make us feel bad. Butch, femme, kiki, gynogyne, top, bottom, switch-hitter, sexually active, or celibate, we are women who have placed ourselves as unavailable to heterosexual men. That makes us all sexual outlaws.

If being a lesbian is not about accepting a wider range of expression for what it means to be a woman in this world, then I'm ready to find, define, and develop a new term. As I reclaimed *lesbian* in the '70s, I now reclaim the words that our heterosexist and sexist culture have tried to "pervert": *pussy* and *cunt* and *box* and *crack* and *joybox* and *lotus blossom* and *dripping gulch* and *hole* and *split tail* and *purse* and *pudenda*. I use these words in my writing because in the quiet of my bedroom with my sex partner, I do not say, "I want to lick your vagina"; I say, "I want to eat your pussy." I do not say, "I want to put my fingers in your vagina"; I say, "I want your cunt" or "I want inside you" or "I want to fuck you." And since more women respond positively than not, I suspect I am not alone in that use. Like *lesbian, cunt, pussy, crack, joybox, slit, pudenda, dripping gulch* and *hole* have not always been used negatively. Working-class women in nineteenth-century England sometimes talked about having "hungry cats." It was a polite way of talking about sex. *Cunt* referred to the joys of oral sex, particularly cunnilingus. *Fuck* was originally an abbreviation referring to the English statute that defined "Forbidden, Unnatural, Carnal Knowledge."

I seek to reclaim these words—especially the ones for our body parts. I want to put out to the world my celebration of what it means to be a woman who enjoys sharing sensuality and sexuality with other women. I want a female-centered and -defined sexuality that recognizes the power of surrender and capture, that explores what surrender and capture and power and intensity mean to women—regardless of sexual orientation. I want women—lesbians—to explore the meaning of fantasy, spirituality, penetration (a.k.a. fucking). Let us recognize there is nothing wrong with being or wanting to be a sexually active female—regardless of sexual orientation; that sexually active women are not imitating men—gay or otherwise. I want an examination of how sex-role stereotyping has damaged us all. I especially want us to look at the assumptions we use to judge one another as the result of sex-role stereotyping.

I want recognition of a woman's right to share and express her sexuality in whatever fashion is comfortable for her—without recrimination. Yes, I am including what is currently defined as s/m sex in that statement. This statement does not deny that sex has been used to hurt many women. It is to say it is time to differentiate between the

emotional and physical impact of specific acts with specific people and the joy and ecstasy of sharing our sensuality and sexuality in safe settings. Each of us is entitled to
define what our boundaries are and have them respected. Sex in and of itself is not
wrong. What is done with sex can be very wrong.

I want to recognize a woman's right *not* to share or express her sexuality and be able
to do so without fear of reproach from heterosexuals or lesbians. Whether the choice be mo-
mentary or lifelong, it is a choice that needs to be honored and respected. It can be a place of
healing, of intense spiritual growth, of caring and loving oneself sexually—whatever we
need and want this space to be, it can be.

Let us begin a new sexual healing. Let us begin the creation of a female-centered and
-defined sexuality which honors a woman's choices of sexual expression. Let us begin by affirming our right to be healthy, sane, sexually active women. Let us begin to recognize the
wonderful continuum involved in being unabashedly and excitingly and intensely female.
Let us affirm this woman in the world and in ourselves.

Response to Previous Article:

JULY 1991

DIFFERENT CHOICES REQUIRE A DIFFERENT VOCABULARY
by Julia Penelope

Having argued in the past that the word *erotic* and what it means is inappropriate to describe
lesbian sexuality, I have become more, not less, convinced that it is a misleading, erroneous
word in lesbian contexts. Sabrina Sojourner's article, "Making Different Choices" illustrates
why feminists of any stripe should abandon efforts to "reclaim" the "erotic." *Erotic* leads,
inevitably, to *the feminine, femininity,* to *cunt, gash, slit, pussy,* and thence to the metaphor
LOVE IS WAR, as Sojourner's essay demonstrates. We're being asked to accept not one word
but an ideology of sex conceived by men.

Following Audre Lorde *(Uses of the Erotic: The Erotic as Power,* Out and Out Books,
1978), Sojourner links "reclaiming" the word *erotic* with personal and social change. Describing herself as "a lesbian feminist who writes erotica" and as a "femme," Sojourner
explains that description:

> *I enjoy writing erotica because I believe in celebrating the goodness and vitality of passion
> and Eros. Like power, passion and Eros are not evil. How Eros, power, and passion are used deter-
> mines the positive, negative, or neutral effect they have on our lives.* [Her capitalization.]

This is a familiar argument: nothing is inherently anything, it's what *we* make of
it or what *we* do with it. Asserting that words, actions, and behaviors have no inherent
meaning accomplishes two rhetorical aims simultaneously: it pretends that individuals
have more control over meanings and their contexts than we do and encourages us to
ignore the already entrenched, socially approved meanings. No word or behavior or attitude comes to us without its patriarchal meanings. To pretend otherwise is a delusion.

Eros was a male god. As Sarah Lucia Hoagland observed in *Lesbian Ethics* (Institute of Lesbian Studies, 1988):

> *'Eros,' as developed in the homopatriarchal greco-christian tradition, is quite the opposite of life-invoking; it is death or other-world oriented.... 'Eros' is the will to get and possess, it is a force which strives for perfection, for immortality. In religious terms, 'eros' represents an ecstatic loss of self, a love which is directed toward a god and whose climax, in christian mysticism, is self-annihilation.*

The word *erotic* holds no promise for radical personal and social change for us, as the past decade has shown. Poisoned at its roots, *erotic* signals a reactionary cynicism among lesbian feminists.

As we consider whether or not to use the word *erotic* as appropriate to lesbian sex and sexuality, we should consider what it means in the patriarchal universe of discourse (PUD). Class differences are one source (race is another) of the "sexual tensions" necessary to the titillative effects of male erotica and pornography. Moreover, the labels themselves, *pornography* and *erotica* (which Sojourner refused to define), mark a clear class distinction. Glossy magazines, those labeled "erotica," are more expensive than the pulps; they are published and marketed for those who can afford their costly techniques. Their full-color, gauzy photos show partially clad or naked women standing close but not touching. They hint at deviance for the voyeur. The cheap magazines, on newsprint, containing gray, poorly developed crotch shots, are sold to working-class men. What rich men buy is called "erotica." What working-class men buy is "pornography," "porno," or "porn."

This class difference dictates the different treatment given to "erotica" and "porn." The vices of rich men are always perceived as culturally valuable, and so are protected and preserved, whereas the vices of working-class men cannot claim "socially redeeming value," cannot aspire to be protected or preserved. "Erotica" bills itself as "art," as "literature." "Pornography" is cheaply produced, to be thrown away. "Erotica" is preserved in the special sections of libraries; "porn" ends up in garbage cans. Pornography emphasizes exactly what erotica tries to disguise and make palatable. The content is the same, but the packaging is very different.

The *erotic* carries the fragrance of wealth, luxury, time on one's hands, and the "exotic," that which is Other. In PUD, *difference* is erotically appealing. Whatever is not "of the man" is other, is prey, is "sexy." Difference, of whatever brand, introduces the alien, the unknown to be conquered, beaten, degraded. Difference introduces tension, fear, dominance, submission, conquest, feelings of being powerful or powerless, feelings of being in control or out of control. Dichotomies objectify and exaggerate differences like "masculine" and "feminine." The differences among us underlie and justify the violence of pornographic and erotic images. Both trade on misogyny, require racism, promote male rule.

The result of Sojourner's posture is predictable: extolling "the feminine" quickly follows. Claiming that "the outward appearance of being a femme is about celebrating the feminine," she says that "'femme' is a definition of femaleness which goes beyond heterosexist and white Western definitions about the feminine."

Of course, Sabrina Sojourner isn't the only feminist urging us to embrace the virtues of "the feminine." Those who argue for "reclaiming" it point to the implicit associations of the word: nurturing, nonaggressive, tender, caring. But we can't ignore the PUD function of *feminine* and *femininity* because some women want to emphasize their implicit positive values. *Feminine* labels just, and *only,* the behaviors, mannerisms, activities, and ways of being that men allot to women. *Feminine* means "pertaining to a woman or girl: *feminine beauty, feminine dress.* Like a woman; weak; gentle." *Womanly,* its synonym, means "like or befitting a woman; feminine; not masculine or girlish."

What I've said about the possibility of "reclaiming" *erotic* applies to *feminine.* Attempting to salvage words from their patriarchal context, especially when they, and their meanings, are highly valued to PUD, is futile. Women are supposed expected, required, exhorted to be "feminine."

We cannot wrench words out of their patriarchal context and pretend that our usage will purge them of their oppressive meaning. *Femininity* attributes to women certain specific behaviors that limit and restrain us. *Femininity* is a lie that many women succumb to and try to live out, at the same time accomplishing the day-to-day struggle to survive, often in perilous circumstances.

I don't think I misjudge the consequences of Sojourner's proposal when she says she wants us to "begin a new sexual healing...the creation of a female-centered and -defined sexuality which honors a woman's choices of sexual expression."

As I reclaimed lesbian *in the '70s, I now reclaim the words that our heterosexist and sexist culture have tried to "pervert":* pussy *and* cunt *and* box *and* crack *and* joybox *and* lotus blossom *and* dripping gulch *and* hole *and* split tail *and* purse *and* pudenda. *I use these words in my writing because in the quiet of my bedroom with my sex partner, I do not say, "I want to lick your vagina"; I say, "I want to eat your pussy."*

Sojourner believes that "reclaiming" such words will help us create a new and female-defined sexuality, but I think she's wrong. Using such words will not create "a female-centered and -defined sexuality," because we cannot "reclaim" them. They are patriarchal descriptions that reflect men's perceptions of women. Sojourner's proposal is explicit about where using such words will take us. By "a female-centered and -defined sexuality," she means one "that recognizes the power of *surrender* and *capture,* that explores what *surrender* and *capture* and power and intensity mean to women..." [my emphasis]. *Surrender* and *capture* along with *yield, submit,* and their counterparts, *conquer, overpower,* and *dominate* belong to the vocabulary of the LOVE IS WAR metaphor. To think of female (or lesbian) sexuality in those terms is to behave within the limits of male imagination. Men's words mean what men intend them to mean, and we will not change those meanings in our minds by murmuring them among ourselves. Audre Lorde, in *This Bridge Called My Back* (Kitchen Table Press, 1984), said it best: "the master's tools will never dismantle the master's house." Language is one of the most dangerous tools of patriarchy.

We cannot "reclaim" something that has never been ours, and we should be wary about words prized by men. Every word and phrase Sojourner wants to "reclaim," with, perhaps, the exceptions of *cunt* and *lotus blossom,* belongs to the vocabulary of male misogyny. (We still don't know the origin of the word *cunt,* and *lotus blossom* belongs to the vocabulary of Chinese erotica.) Such exceptions aside, those words were coined by teenaged boys of successive generations and taken with them into adulthood. We have to decide very carefully which words we want to use. The end result of trying to incorporate words like *erotic* and *feminine* into a lesbian-feminist context is that they come trailing all the patriarchal garbage some of us are trying to eradicate from our thinking. We can't simply snip them out of their PUD matrix and transplant them into our own without rending the fabric we've created.

Examining the claims of those who, like Sabrina Sojourner, say they're writing "erotica" because they're seeking "new" paradigms or creating female-defined sexuality, I find that they're promoting the heteropatriarchal model unchallenged, unchanged. Sojourner argues that such "reclamations" will lead us to radical personal and social change, but the words she's chosen and the ideas they denote lead us not to radical change but to "settling for a shift of characters in the same weary drama." The word *erotic* is highly valued in patriarchal society, precisely because it dresses up sex, makes sex sound all silky smooth and luscious. Used in reference to lesbian sexuality, *erotic* conjures for us the images of male "erotica": anatomical perfection (no warts or hairs or scars); a misty, vague sensuality that goes beyond the nakedness of bodies to the atmosphere around the act. It suggests candles or other dim lighting, soft music, warmth, coziness, and intimacy—persuasion, not force. *Erotica* leads to *feminine; feminine* leads to *femme; femme* leads to LOVE IS WAR and all the words that describe the behaviors inherent in the metaphor.

"Reclaiming" too easily becomes separated from its roots in the desire for political and personal change and degenerates to a widespread, thoughtless activity of perpetuating the vilest, most derogatory terms in the PUD vocabulary. It's an easy game, because we already know the words. We've heard them all our lives. We don't have to learn anything; we don't have to risk anything; we don't even have to change; we don't have to live in the unknown, wondering how we're going to say to the woman next to us that we want to nibble and lick her clitoris. Most importantly, we don't have to think. Familiarity and its comforts seduce the word-weary and the unwary as well. Contrary to the empowering effects Sojourner promises by legitimizing *erotic* in lesbian discourse, we're back in the '50s, still butch or femme, still slit, hole, or pussy, still thrashing about in the misogyny of PUD's vocabulary.

The impulse that leads us to want to reclaim a word is obvious and noncontroversial: we want labels for ideas, activities, events, and processes that are essential to our vision of who we can be and how we might live in the future. Being able to name, for ourselves and other women, our changes in consciousness, subtle shifts in perception, more sweeping transformations of how we conceive ourselves in the world is, or should be, important to us. We want to communicate the events we've experienced to other women clearly and without ambiguity. But neither *erotic* nor *feminine* is appropriate to describe lesbian sexuality *if* we intend to construct and comprehend our Selves as radically *different* from who we are understood to be within heteropatriarchy. Part of that project is challenging and discrediting male descriptions of *how the world is*. Eventually I hope we will replace them with our own, more accurate descriptions. Until we have fashioned a language that reflects our perceptions and our desires, we must be cautious when we choose words to describe ourselves.

JUNE 1992

Bondage Broke the Bonds of Fear
by Carol Sklar

Mention bondage and domination in a room full of lesbians and you may find the cry of "Foul!" resonating off the walls. It's a hard moment to sit through as your insides scream, "Tell them how it helped you!" and your outside cowers under peer pressure and the fear of rejection or humiliation.

I know that many women, especially those with abuse in their backgrounds, need to protect themselves from these images and practices as a matter of survival. But I have experienced another side to the story. I trust I am not unique and hope, by my telling, that others may have the courage to reveal themselves.

First, a little of my background. From the time I came out, at age nineteen, I was what we used to call an "untouchable." During any sexual encounter, I would be the aggressor. My "job" was to make sure my partner came, several times if necessary. If she reached out to touch me, I would quickly turn the tables and have her again. The reason for this behavior was twofold. First, I had never learned to trust enough to have an orgasm in front of anyone. If my lover tried to bring me to a climax, I would feel self-conscious, then frustrated, then angry at my failure. Not a pleasant experience for either of us.

The second reason for my aggressive behavior was my strong male identification. If my lover touched my genitals, it reminded me that I didn't have a penis. This threw me into an identity crisis—my role, my part, my game was lost. I would panic and usually run away, literally. This frustration and anger often sent me into thoughts of suicide.

At 21, relief came in the form of alcohol. I found that if I was drunk enough I could let my lover touch me. I could even let her penetrate me. I didn't have many orgasms, but when you get that drunk, who notices or remembers?

At 24, I began to see these sexual limitations as unhealthy. I tried to cut back on my drinking before sex, but the old "untouchable" frustrations quickly returned. I hit bottom with my drinking at 25 and began my recovery from what had become alcoholism. I had a few affairs in my first year of sobriety. All were short-lived, and all were hidden behind a hard mask, ensuring no vulnerability on my part.

Then, into my life she walked—beautiful and seductive. I wanted her from the moment I saw her. After a month of flirting and seducing on both our parts, we found ourselves alone and ready. I removed her blouse to reveal a black lace bra that pushed her bosom up to a luscious cleavage. She was inspiring. As I slipped her skirt down to the floor and she lifted her spike-heeled shoes to step out of the garment, I saw the black-lace garter belt that framed her naked pubic mound. She reached back into her top dresser drawer and pulled out a long silk scarf. I first thought, "How exciting. I can handle this." But, when she backed me onto the bed, knelt over me, and tied *my* hands to the headboard, I was shocked. I wasn't afraid she would hurt me—by this time, I knew her well enough to feel safe in that way. But there was no way I could turn the tables; no way to take control if I came too close to feeling vulnerable. I wouldn't say no to her. I wanted her too much. So, I just laid there, my hands above my head tied to the headboard.

She talked to me, she stroked me, she teased me. She was gentle at times. She was rough at times. She took me, all of me. And, after a while, I gave myself gladly, excitedly, anxiously.

As the months went on, we experimented with handcuffs, riding crops, dog collars. We tried water sports (this was before AIDS), but my bladder wouldn't let go. We also traded roles quite often, and I explored my aggressive side with no shame or hidden agenda.

Because the affair had been primarily based on lust, it didn't sustain itself for more than a few months. But, by the time it had ended, I had grown and changed. The games we had played forced me to sit through my feelings, to ride out my fears. I had been vulnerable and not betrayed. I had learned to love myself as a woman exploring passion with another woman. I could let someone watch me have an orgasm.

I didn't take the props and roles into my next affairs and relationships. I did, however, take with me the freedom I had found.

So, the next time the topic of bondage and domination comes up and that secret inside you becomes a knot in your stomach, maybe you can tell your story. But if you can't tell your story, feel free to tell mine. Tell them you read that it once helped a woman find a place in her that had been covered up by fear. Tell them bondage broke the bonds that had made true intimacy impossible. Tell them it saved my life.

Response to previous article

OCTOBER 1992

SEX AND VIOLENCE

DEAR *SOJOURNER*:

I was very distressed by Carol Sklar's article, "Bondage Broke the Bonds of Fear," in the June 1992 issue. The article describes this woman's previous inability to feel vulnerable with a lover, in part because of her strong male identification. She then goes on to tell how her lesbian lover broke through her inhibitions by introducing her to bondage, including her lover being "rough sometimes," and using "handcuffs, riding crops, and dog collars." I am truly sorry for this woman if she really believes that the way to unlock vulnerability is to have someone handcuff her, collar her, and whip her. What if I, a heterosexual woman, was to write an article for *Sojourner*, describing how my husband helped me become more vulnerable by chaining me up, whipping me, and being rough with me? Would feminists out there say, "Hey, she's really liberated, she can be vulnerable now that someone has taught her to sit still with her feelings and behave?" Or would they say, as I wish to say to Sklar, "She is really confused and totally believes the line of bull that patriarchy has sold her."

Just because it is a woman "disciplining" a woman, *that does not make it okay*. One reason those of us with abuse in our pasts avoid such violence masquerading as sex is because so many of us have had to learn the difference between what was taught to us and what really originates *in* us. I think that many of us have experimented with violent "sex," but we have learned that instead of making us vulnerable, it made us exposed. Instead of liberating us, we became more and more confused on the issue of what we really wanted, and what our abusers told us that we, as women, really wanted.

I am dismayed to see so many feminist journals printing articles that are sympathetic to women abusing women "with their consent." There are so many patriarchal messages going into our heads that sometimes we do get confused and believe that just because something arouses us, then we must really want to do it, it is okay, it is liberating. Plenty of men use porn, even beat or rape women because it arouses them. Just because they are *aroused* by the patriarchal linking of sex and violence, that doesn't make it right.

Please, women, we need to get together and start healing our sexuality in a way that includes the gentler aspects of both women and men, instead of just absorbing the attitudes that misogynists have foisted on us for centuries. Just because it is two women experimenting with abusing each other doesn't make it healthy. It is just another way that male supremacism has infected our minds and souls.

Sandra Antoinette Jaska
Watseka, IL

CHAPTER SEVEN

Violence Against Women

In the United States, according to the National Coalition Against Domestic Violence, a woman is beaten by her boyfriend/husband/lover every 15 seconds. The FBI Uniform Crime report shows that one in three women will be raped in her lifetime (approximately 100,000 women per year). And, according to the National Victim Center (1995), one out of every four girls is sexually abused before the age of eighteen. As this chapter shows, feminists have been fighting this epidemic of violence against women for over two decades. By the mid '70s, they had begun to establish rape crisis centers and battered women's shelters, to gather for Take Back the Night marches, and to organize speakouts where women could publicly name the violence they had experienced. Over the last two decades, they have also changed laws, making it more difficult for attorneys to humiliate rape survivors, extending statutes of limitation for women who remember childhood sexual abuse and wish to prosecute, and, in some cities, establishing mandatory sentencing for batterers. Due to the efforts of feminists, violence against women, once a crime that remained hidden behind closed doors, has become a major public policy issue.

During the first decade of the second wave, feminists exposed three systemic forms of violence that are used to reinforce women's subordinate position in society: sexual harassment, rape, and battery. Through consciousness raising, women discovered that these forms of violence were widespread and highly underreported because women felt ashamed when attacked and, usually, blamed themselves. All had internalized the message that women bring sexual and physical assaults on themselves, either by acting provocatively or by not adequately serving the needs of "their man."

Though the U.S. media seems to think that the public was unaware of the problems of sexual harassment prior to October 1991, when Anita Hill accused then-Supreme Court nominee Clarence Thomas of having sexually harassed her, feminists have been addressing this issue for years. Women, of course, have always recognized sexual harassment as a condition of the workplace. In fact, a 1976 survey in *Redbook* magazine indicated that of the 9,000 respondents, 88 percent had received unwanted sexual attention at work. Sexual harassment was no secret.

In the late '70s and early '80s, *Sojourner* often reported on sexual harassment, providing information on how to respond to unwanted attention in the workplace and encouraging women to take action. Although fewer feature articles appeared in the mid '80s, the paper continued to include news reports of sexual harassment, particularly on university campuses and in nontraditional workplaces. Still, it was not until Anita Hill took the stand that the issue made front page news again. Hill's testimony, along with a 1993 American Association of University Women survey of sexual harassment in the public schools (see Lynn Goods, "Sexual Harassment in the School Yard," 1993), made it clear that feminists had been too quick to assume that legal changes (for example, the 1981 Supreme Court ruling that sexual harassment was a form of prohibited sex discrimination) had significantly changed workplace attitudes or behaviors.

Sexual harassment, usually taking the form of jokes, leering, unwanted sexual innuendo, or pressure to engage in sexual relations, is at one end of a continuum of sexual assault, while rape and murder are at the other. Second-wave feminists recognized that rape was different from other forms of physical assault in that men use rape not only to dominate women but to sully the property of other men. Rape laws, they realized, were written to protect the property of men, not to protect women's control over their own bodies. Thus, the movement to stop rape became a two-pronged effort: first, to provide support for women who had been assaulted, and second, to change the laws that provided more protection for the perpetrator than the victim.

The first rape crisis centers and hotlines were established to provide rape survivors with emotional support for healing and assistance with criminal prosecution. Advocates helped those women who wished to press charges through the often demeaning medical procedures and traumatizing court procedures. But the staff and volunteers of rape crisis centers did not stop at the provision of services. They also lobbied for changes in the criminal justice system. For example, prior to 1975, not a single state recognized marital rape as a crime; by 1995, 43 states had revised their laws so that, under certain circumstances, husbands could be prosecuted for sexually assaulting their wives.

Rape crisis workers have played another role as well: challenging the myths that keep women living in fear. Though women often place limits on their own behavior because they fear "stranger" rape—the man in the dark alley—in 75 percent of rape cases, the victim knows the perpetrator. He may be a husband or lover, a father or brother, a family friend or neighbor, but more often than not he will be of the same race and class as his victim.

As antirape activists have come to understand that most rapes are committed by a known assailant, they have focused their education efforts on the problems of date rape, particularly on college campuses. Though neofeminist writers such as Katie Roiphe (*The Morning After,* Little Brown, 1993) insist that young women are being unduly indoctrinated by a kind of new Victorianism that emphasizes caution over sexual freedom, surveys show that many young men still believe that "no" means "yes" and that a "little" force is okay. Roiphe is right, however, that date rape situations are not always as clear as we might like to assume. As Julia Mines points out in "The Trouble with Verdicts" (1993), U.S. culture thrives on mixed messages when it comes to sex. We cannot expect young women to communicate clearly about their desires, and for young men to understand, if, as a society, we insist on making sex into something that forever divides the "good" girls from the "bad."

Though rape is probably the form of assault that women most fear, physical assaults by husbands and boyfriends (and sometimes lesbian partners) are more pervasive. Up until the last two decades, wife-beating was considered a "family" matter, and police, the courts, and counselors, whether psychiatrists or clergymen, were reluctant to step in. Women were encouraged to make peace with their husbands, to work harder at taking care of their needs. But battering is not simply a case of domestic quarreling. An abusive partner uses violence, whether verbal, psychological, or physical, to control his/her spouse (and often the children as well). If such relationships are allowed to continue, the violence usually escalates, sometimes to the point of murder. (The Massachusetts Coalition of Battered

Women's Services reported in 1995, in their state, a woman was killed by her partner every eight days.) That domestic violence is recognized today as a serious crime is a testament to the hard work of second-wave feminists.

The battered women's movement began in the mid '70s with the founding of the first battered women's shelters. In 1975, in Somerville, Massachusetts, two welfare mothers, both the victims of abusive husbands, opened their three-bedroom apartment to battered women and children. Transition House was an immediate success, housing as many as 25 women and children within its first six months of operation. As Lisa Leghorn explains in "Transition House Shelters Battered Women" (1976), battered women needed places to go. Without temporary housing, emotional support, and protection from their abusers, women could not leave abusive situations.

The grassroots activists who founded the first battered women's shelters saw them not as service organizations but as places of female empowerment. Shelters provided safety, but also political consciousness raising. As they talked about what had happened to them, women learned that their experiences were shared by others. Battered women who arrived ready to blame themselves for years of violence left several months later understanding that violence is a tool used by men to maintain their own power and privilege.

Today, the Massachusetts Coalition for Battered Women's Services has 34 member shelters, the criminal justice system is more conscious of domestic violence, and women are more likely to use the courts in search of justice. These are positive changes, but many feminists are concerned that the provision of services has replaced the goal of political empowerment (see Gail Sullivan, "Women's Shelters House Contradictions," 1982). Among mainstream service providers, violence has too often come to be seen as a problem of "dysfunctional families" or individually brutal men rather than the systematic oppression of women. Institutionalized services may be more financially stable and accessible than poorly funded movement organizations, but professional service providers (social workers, psychologists, etc.) exercise control over "clients" rather than seek to provide the political tools necessary for battered women to take control over their own lives. While it is important to provide services to the women and men caught in the maelstrom of violence, feminists wonder how these services will provide the springboard for the social and political change they originally envisioned.

The movement against violence against women initially focused on sexual harassment, rape, and battering but soon grew to include other systemic forms of violence. In the late '70s, some activists became concerned with violence perpetrated through pornography and sexual slavery; as they became focused solely on these issues, the antipornography movement emerged (see Chapter 6: Sex and Sexuality). By the early '80s, feminists had turned their attention to the culture's most taboo form of violence—incest. Although incest was once considered extremely rare, today many researchers confirm that one out of every four girls (and one out of every six boys) reports that she was sexually abused before the age of eighteen—usually by a family member or friend of the family.

Sojourner first published a feature-length article on childhood sexual abuse in January 1981—an interview with Florence Rush, author of *The Best Kept Secret: Sexual Abuse of Children* (Prentice-Hall, 1980). Rush and interviewer Pat Harrison discussed how difficult it was to get the book published (publishers objected to Rush's statement that father-daughter incest was not taboo) and the reluctance of feminists to form a movement around fighting child sexual abuse. By the mid '80s, however, such a movement did exist, as evidenced by frequent articles in *Sojourner,* the emergence of incest survivor groups, and the publication of numerous books and newsletters that allowed survivors to begin the process of coming out. Reprinted here is a 1985 article by Judith Herman, author of the 1981 book *Father-Daughter Incest* (Harvard University Press). In "Sexual Violence and How It Affects Us," Herman, like Florence Rush, argues that sexual assault is "not prohibited, but regulated." She writes, "having sex with one's own daughter falls well within the regulations, for, in practice, only the forms of sexual violence that involve an assault on another man's property are criminalized."

Today, however, some women are suing their fathers, uncles, or other family members for the damage resulting from childhood rape. As a result, alleged perpetrators and their supporters have formed an organization called the False Memory Syndrome Foundation (FMSF) (see Cathy Wasserman, "FMS: The Backlash Against Survivors," 1992). This group claims that feminist therapists plant false memories in the minds of their clients who, prior to therapy, have no recollection of childhood abuse. FMSF is trying to destroy the credibility of survivors who have found new strength in a movement that rightly claims that child sexual abuse is criminal, regardless of the relationship of the perpetrator to the victim. FMSF's ultimate goal is to make us believe, once again, that incest doesn't really happen.

Feminist analyses of violence against women began with the insight that the violence perpetrated against women in this society is not random, but purposeful. That men use violence to control women, to keep women from attaining power, to ensure that women remain submissive. But this analysis was only partial. It failed to take into account the different ways in which women experience violence, particularly women of color and poor women who are subject to not only sexist violence but racist and classist violence, and the difficult problem of women perpetrators.

Sojourner began to address the issue of women perpetrators in the late '80s, with two powerful first-person accounts of mother-daughter incest (see Roberta James, "Contradictions: Mother-Daughter Incest," 1989). Letters from readers confirmed that others had had similar experiences and had often felt isolated and alone, unable to connect to a movement that placed all the blame for violence against women on men. In her 1991 article, "If Not Now, When? Obstacles to Outrage," Ann Russo argues that feminists must integrate their knowledge that women abuse children and each other (lesbian battering) into their analysis of patriarchal violence if they wish to combat violence effectively. Women, like men, will use the power available to them to control others, Russo maintains. Thus, a feminist revolution that simply replaces the male power structure with a female one cannot possibly succeed in creating a violence-free society that supports the self-determination of all individuals.

Just as a theory of violence against women must provide insight into the role of female perpetrators in perpetuating the system, so must it elucidate the way in which sexist violence plays out differently in communities of color and poor communities, where racist and classist violence are so pervasive. Women of color have been addressing the intersection of race, class, gender, and violence since the '70s, though their early efforts were sometimes ignored or misunderstood by white feminists who had little understanding of the dynamics of racism. In Boston, however, the murders of twelve Black women, along with a series of rapes in a primarily white neighborhood, in 1979, brought women together across race and class boundaries in a relatively early successful organizing effort. The Coalition for Women's Safety, which emerged during that year, attracted a multiracial crowd of 5,000 to its August 1979 Take Back the Night March, calling for an end to the violence (see "5,000 Women March to Take Back the Night," 1979). Articles in *Sojourner* during this period of coalition building reflect a heightened awareness of racism, with analyses of the racist media coverage of the murders, an article on the history of racism and rape (see Tracey Rogers, "Myths: Rape and Race," 1981), and an article on the sexual harassment of Black women. Each of these pieces pointed out that myths about the "sexual promiscuity" of Black women increase their vulnerability to sexual violence.

The Coalition for Women's Safety lasted about two years, and for many of the women involved, it represented a high point in the efforts of feminists to organize across differences (see Barbara Smith, "Black Feminism: A Movement of Our Own" in Chapter 1: Claiming Our Identities). By 1982, however, efforts to organize Take Back the Night marches were once again divided by racism. Women of color were angered by white women who planned their march through neighborhoods of color, implying that men of color were more likely than white, middle-class men to be perpetrators of violence. This myth came back to haunt the Boston community in 1990, when Charles Stuart, a white man, killed his pregnant wife while driving through a city neighborhood so that he could blame the murder on a Black man. As Ann Russo pointed out in a February 1990 *Sojourner* article, Stuart's ruse was effective because "we live in a society with a very deep history of racism, particularly with respect to the fear of Black men attacking white womanhood."

Carol Stuart's murder was only the first of several events in the '90s that would highlight the connections between racist, classist, and sexist violence and, thus, lead to greater attention to these issues in the pages of *Sojourner* and among feminists in general. The televised humiliation of Anita Hill during the Clarence Thomas hearings, the rape trials of William Kennedy Smith and Mike Tyson, and O.J. Simpson's arrest and trial for the murder of his ex-wife, Nicole Brown Simpson, all have raised consciousness around issues of violence against women at the same time that they have highlighted the ways in which racism and classism influence media coverage, outcomes, and the experience of the violence itself. In response to these events, *Sojourner* increased its solicitation of articles that specifically addressed issues of violence from the perspectives of women of color (see Sharon Cox, "A Letter to My Son," 1990, and Cheng Imm Tan, "Confronting Domestic Violence in Asian Communities," 1992).

Although efforts to stop violence against women have fallen far short of our dreams, women have empowered themselves through martial arts and other self-defense methods (see Lyri Merrill, "Awakening the Amazon Within," 1988); through safe-neighborhood watches and Take Back the Night marches; by forming underground networks that protect women and children who have defied court orders to return the children to abusive fathers; and through efforts like the Clothesline Project, a takeoff on the AIDS quilt, in which women use shirts to design representations of the violence they have experienced in their lives. *Sojourner* has covered all of these efforts over its twenty-year history, analyzing our successes as well as our failures in changing the patterns of violence that limit women's dreams and lives.

As we approach the year 2000, violence remains a serious problem in women's lives. Domestic violence is still the primary reason that women use hospital emergency rooms. Sexual harassment, incest, rape, and murder are still all too common. But feminists can claim success at least in their efforts to make violence against women a visible reality and a prominent domestic and international public policy issue. The Clinton administration's passage of the Violence against Women Act, which includes a national 24-hour hotline for battered women, along with the United Nations' recent recognition of violence against women as a human rights violation, are two significant victories. Moreover, feminist efforts to establish services, including rape crisis centers and battered women's shelters, have saved lives for over two decades. Feminists must remain mindful, however, that institutionalized services do not build movements. If the goal is to stop violence against women—rather than just patching up the wounds—feminists will need to return to the movement-building strategies of the '70s, empowering women through consciousness raising and preparing them for a life of active resistance.

SEPTEMBER 1975

Rape!

by Monica Edelman

The laws against rape exist to protect rights of the male as possessor of the female body, and not the rights of the female over her own body.
—"Rape: The All-American Crime," by Susan Griffin,
  Ramparts Magazine 10 (September 1971)

Every minute a woman in this country is raped. Rape is an act of violence usually committed by men against women. Although it is generally thought to be a sexual act, it is not; sex is merely the means used by the rapist to gain control of and to dominate another individual. It is the extreme act of "putting women down" and "keeping women in line."

Rape is a crime committed by people from all classes, races, and religions. Forty-eight percent of all rapes occur between people who know each other either as close friends or acquaintances, and approximately one-half of all rapes are committed in the home.

The Boston Area Rape Crisis Center is a volunteer organization made up of women interested in seeing rape stopped. The group operates a 24-hour hotline that serves the needs of women who have been raped or attacked in the Boston area.

If a woman calls the center immediately after being attacked, we first find out whether she is calling from a safe area, and we direct her to one if she isn't. Then we explain the alternatives available to her—e.g., going to a hospital, reporting the crime to the police, going to court. The final decision is left up to the individual, and we support whatever course of action she chooses to take.

If she wants to go to the hospital and/or the police, we will arrange to have someone either meet her there or take her over. Before the doctor examines her, we explain what the examination will entail. If she decides to prosecute, we can also have someone accompany her to court.

There is extensive follow-up of all cases that come to the center. This includes keeping in touch with the women periodically by telephone to see how they are doing; in-person counseling, if this is needed; holding bimonthly discussion groups so that these women can share their fears, frustrations, anger, etc., with other women who have had similar experiences.

OCTOBER 1976

Transition House Shelters Battered Women

by Lisa Leghorn

The movement in defense of battered women in Boston, as elsewhere throughout the country, has been gathering momentum for nearly two and a half years. It was not until last January, however, that Transition House, the first refuge for battered women and their children in Boston, opened in the small five-room apartment of Chris Womendez and Cherie Jimenez. As welfare mothers who had either been battered themselves or seen their children battered by violent husbands, they understood that a woman in crisis has nowhere to turn in seeking help.

A battered woman's greatest obstacle in trying to break out of her situation is that the agencies established supposedly to aid people in crisis are operating according to the patriarchal status quo. Those administering social service agencies and police, courts, and psychiatrists believe in maintaining the sanctity of the home (and male supremacy, institutionalized in the present family structure) at women's and often children's expense. A battered woman is asked by the courts and police, "What did you do to provoke him?" and by the social service agencies and psychiatrists, "Why have you stayed so long if you don't enjoy (or need) it?" By blaming the victim, help is never forthcoming and continued battering is insured. All the existing mechanisms by which a woman could break out are rendered useless by a housewife's economic dependence on her husband, or a working woman's low pay and the prohibitive expense of child care facilities, which leave her equally as dependent on the perpetrator of her misery. She lives in fear and torment until the day she finally dares turn her back on society's condemnation of a "failed marriage," only to be asked by the police, "Who pays the rent here, anyhow?" or by the courts, "How do you plan to support yourself and the children without him?" Thus her predicament is comparable to that of a woman living with her rapist until her case comes to court.

The concept behind the need for shelters for women physically abused by their husbands or lovers is that women need a place where they can go, with their children, in the dead of night if necessary, and stay in peace in a supportive atmosphere until they determine and work out what their next step will be. If they can overcome the immense sense of shame and humiliation—internalized through society's implicit condemnation of their plight—and face the questions and silent implication that they themselves have failed, battered women can turn to friends or family for help. Even when friends and family are sympathetic, a woman is placing their safety as well as her own in great jeopardy. Angry husbands have been known to burn down houses where their wives and children are staying, drive a car through the front end of the house, throw rocks in the windows where their children are sleeping, etc. Consequently, it is imperative that a refuge for battered women have an unpublicized address and that teachers and nursery school workers are warned of the possibility of husbands coming after the children. When husbands do attempt to kidnap their children, it is often not out of love or concern for them. It is only a means of luring back their fleeing wives who would never dare leave the children alone with violent husbands who often subject the children to their beatings as well.

In order to leave their husbands, battered women must have some income; unless they have been able to tuck away dollar bills in safe places over the years, or have some independent income or a job that can viably support them and their children, they must turn to welfare. However, to be eligible for welfare, a woman must have a separate residence from that of her husband, which she often can't pay for until she has some income. So a refuge breaks the vicious circle by providing immediate shelter and an address she can use until she can receive enough money from welfare to pay for an apartment of her own.

When Transition House first opened, Chris and Cherie, with the help of other committed feminists, responded to the need by attempting to staff their apartment 24 hours a day and to feed all the women who came through with their AFDC checks and food stamps, and bake sales, benefits, and private donations. At times, during the six-month period they operated the house, there were as many as 25 women and children staying with them, sleeping on mattresses on living room and kitchen floors as well as in the three bedrooms. The women were of all nationalities, races, and class backgrounds. Some stayed a few days until they could find friends or relatives to go to, others stayed a month or more; one woman stayed four months and is now committed to continuing to work with the house, as are many of the other women.

Chris and Cherie decided to shut down the house for a month or so in the summer in order to restructure its operation because it was clear that the way the house had been organized, most of the burden of work and responsibility fell on their shoulders.

By the end of September, the house will have opened again in a different neighborhood, a larger space, and with an internal structure able to effectively use all the energy of volunteers, which is so badly needed. The house should be able to comfortably shelter 25 women and children, and many more in a pinch. The policy of the house is never to turn a woman away because of space limitations. The reason for the policy is that the violence always escalates. If a woman is ready to leave her husband and her home, it is usually because she fears for her life, and one more night with him could be disastrous. A Kansas Police Department study conducted in 1972 found that in 85 percent of the cases of domestic homicide, the police had been called at least once before the murder took place, and in 50 percent of the cases, they had been called five times or more before the actual murder occurred. This shows not only police ineffectiveness and indifference in dealing with the problem (more police are killed intervening in domestic violence situations than in all other crimes combined), but the truly grim consequences if a woman doesn't leave.

The house itself provides food and shelter in a supportive environment and serves as a resource center with the following services: 1) a 24-hour crisis intervention center; 2) referrals to and advocacy for legal, medical, and social services, as well as housing and employment information; 3) child care and transportation for children to and from their schools; 4) immediate emergency health care (at no charge) by a nurse-practitioner on 24-hour call.

Transition House is designed to help women with limited or no financial resources. Although the incidence of wife abuse is as prevalent in upper-income brackets as in lower-income families, women married to men with greater financial resources sometimes have more options at their disposal, such as enough money to pay for a motel or transportation to sources of help. If they weren't able to glean any money of their own during the time they lived with their husbands, they find themselves with nothing once they leave, since any financial support they received from their husbands was contingent upon their remaining in their subservient status in the home; at this point, they are as much in need of low-cost crisis shelter as working-class women. A minimal daily fee is requested from each family and can be obtained from emergency food and rent vouchers from the welfare department. Because this sum is deducted from a woman's first welfare check, we keep it as small as possible, so that at the end of a month with us, she will have been able to save enough money to make a security deposit on a new apartment.

The house operates with a self-help philosophy. It is our hope that in a nonviolent and supportive environment women will realize they are not alone and will discover and develop together their individual and communal strengths. Every woman, while she is at the house and after she has left, is asked to join in the cooperative effort of maintaining the house and sharing experiences and knowledge with incoming women. A woman is never advised as to what steps she should take but is given the tools and information necessary to make an informed choice and the support that is so vital to making difficult decisions in times of crisis.

The process a woman goes through at the house is a politicizing one—from the time she first enters with most of her self-respect, hope, and energy battered out of her, to the time when she leaves with a sense of herself and of commitment to helping other women in similar crises. By speaking with other women about their experiences, listening to tapes made by women who have previously come through the house about what happened to them and what they did about it, reading literature and speaking with staffers, a woman no longer feels crazy and isolated and is able to place what she thought of as a private nightmare into a social and political perspective. She realizes that the problem is not just that her husband or some men with drinking or employment or insecurity problems batter their wives, but that men have the social, political, and economic power—reinforced through violence or the threat of violence—to do with their wives, girlfriends, and children as they please. If they do not abuse their "privilege," it is only because they *choose* not to. Her husband's behavior can, for the first time be seen in the context of the structure of an entire society, which upholds male prerogative in the family as well as in other social, political, and economic institutions. Once women see the problem in perspective, they are able to act on it. This process is an incredibly energizing one, and many women who have come through the house continue to help other women as much as they are able to.

This new commitment was beautifully visible in the Women Support Women March and Rally held on August 26 in Boston. Five thousand women marched to protest violence against women, with special emphasis on domestic violence, and over half the speakers were women who had stayed at Transition House. The excitement of seeing them speaking out strongly and militantly about their lives, the lives of other women, and the changes they felt had to come, having seen their own personal transformations, was overwhelmingly inspiring.

Marches and rallies are a beginning—strong, public statements made by women that we won't take it anymore. Refuges such as Transition House, also, are only tools that we can wield in our struggle to end male supremacy. Yet they're very powerful tools, enabling women to survive emotionally as well as physically, freeing us to begin to control our own lives and letting women know that this control *is* possible.

This article has been edited for length and clarity.

SEPTEMBER 1979

5,000 Women March to Take Back the Night

Over 5,000 people marched through Boston neighborhoods on the night of August 18, 1979, to Boston's second Take Back the Night Rally held in the South End's Blackstone Park. The march and rally were held to dramatize and protest the increasing problem of violence di-

rected against women. The following statement was presented at the rally by the march organizers, the Take Back the Night Coalition.

We should all be inspired by the fact that we have come together tonight, women from all races, ages, different communities and different classes, and marched to show our power, our strength, our unity, and our determination to end violence against women. We are each other's inspiration.

The statement we are about to read is a collective statement from the entire coalition to Take Back the Night. On the occasion of tonight's Take Back the Night March, it seems appropriate to look back on what we have experienced since last year's march. We should be energized by our gains and victories. However, 1979 has been a year of brutal violence against women in Boston. The losses cannot be forgotten; they should be held in memory to motivate each of us to continue our struggle against violence against women.

The losses of the past year have been painful ones. You do not need to be reminded of the slaying of twelve Black women and two white women in Boston since January or of the series of eight rapes reported in the Allston-Brighton area between December and February. These horrible incidents are all too well known among us. Yet how many of us know that between November 1978 and April 1979 Boston police received 317 reports of sexual assault. And the unreported, unpublicized rapes and murders continue in every city and institution throughout this country.

In the United States, one out of three women will be raped; one-half of all married women are victims of battering; a woman is raped every three seconds; a woman is beaten every eighteen seconds; one out of every four women experiences sexual abuse before she turns eighteen; and nine out of ten women have received unwanted sexual advances and harassment at their jobs. Women of color have been particularly subjected to acts of violence because of their color. Those of us who are lesbians are targets of male violence not only because we are women but because of our sexual choice. There is *no* safe place for a woman!

The legal system, which we have been taught to rely on for our safety and for justice, betrays us constantly. The racist actions by the police force in framing and arresting Black men, as in the case of Willie Sanders, does not insure women's safety.* Safety does *not* mean arresting a Black man on very flimsy charges. That only perpetuates the rampant racism of this society. We will not be appeased with unjust arrests. We will not have our demand for safety pitted against a community that has little power in this society. We want to be safe— and safety means preventing murders and beatings, preventing harassment. It means creating a society in which those actions are not condoned.

Clearly, the state cannot be relied upon to provide women's safety. We must do that ourselves. Our efforts of the past year have shown that by unifying our energy, women can build strength, take power, and accomplish victories across race and class lines.

Since last year's march, community organizing among women has given birth to programs and networks within which we are creating and controlling our *own* safety systems. The Greenlight programs in Dorchester and Jamaica Plain and the Safehouse program in the Cambridgeport/Riverside community provide women a network of safe places to go when in danger. Women in the Fenway have begun meeting, and there is discussion among them of starting a Fenway women's center. Three new groups for battered women have come into existence: the Harbor Area task force in Chelsea, the Jamaica Plain task force, and the Tri-City task force in Malden, Medford, and Everett. The Massachusetts Coalition of Battered Women's Service Groups, which is comprised of grassroots women-controlled shelters, has expanded. It is now a network of seventeen shelters across the state. In direct response to the recent murders and rapes, CRISIS was begun in the South End and a communication network was begun in Allston/Brighton.

Perhaps the strongest victory this past year has been the birth of the coalition for women's safety, comprised of white and Third World women primarily from Cambridge and Somerville. The formation and continuation of these groups shows that women are joining together and recognizing that violence against women affects women of all races, women of all classes, and women in all communities. This year, more than ever in our past, women have been reaching out to each other with new vigor and awareness, across racial, cultural, class, and community lines.

Yet, while it is true that such violence affects us all, it is also true that it does not affect us all equally. The combination of Third World women's efforts over many years to confront their particular oppression in this society and the brutal violence directed this year specifically against Black women has catalyzed an awareness among white women of what Third World women have known all their lives—that women of color are singled out as targets of violence both because of their race and their sex. White women have begun to learn from Third World women and to organize against the violence particularly affecting women of color.

It is not enough for women to resist and organize against violence. Violence against women will not be stopped by women's efforts alone. If that were true we would have stopped it already. It is time for men to take responsibility. They must change their own attitudes, and they must interrupt and challenge acts of violence, threats of violence, and exploitative attitudes of men against women. They must stop the violence!

The beginnings of such a trend exist in this city, in groups such as Emerge, which is a collective of men who counsel men who batter and that actively works against violence against women. We also encourage men to work with mixed community groups that are working on this issue such as CRISIS.

Before we go our separate ways tonight, let's take a look around us. We are a group with much diversity and much in common. We've shared a powerful experience, which should energize us all to make this coming year at least as productive as the last one has been. Yes, women are fighting back, and we are taking back the night but we will win only if we are unified and strong. We must each reach out to our friends, neighbors, and coworkers and draw them into the movement. We must continue opening and expanding communication to bridge the gaps that divide us; we must continue to build on our commonality across race, class, and community lines; and we must continue to learn about and celebrate our diversity as women and as people of many cultures. Individually, we must each become more aware of our own and each other's oppression. And we must take care of ourselves and each other so that we may become stronger.

Let us each take away from this march inspiration, a sense of power and unity, and the reality that for this one night we have experienced what it might be like to live in a society free of violence against women. Let us take that experience and build a movement that will make it a reality.

We will take back the night. We will take back the day. We will take back our lives and live them as free women!

Willie Sanders was arrested February 1, 1979 for the Allston-Brighton rapes. He was never convicted.

AUGUST 1981

Myths: Rape and Race

by Tracey Rogers

Rape is a special concern for all women—we live in fear of its constant possibility, in awe of its scope and in hope of its prevention. Rape is also of particular concern to Blacks—both men and women, because of the long-standing link between rape and racism in this country. By examining and understanding this connection, we also begin to see how it has affected our present attitudes and approaches to rape. It is important that we look at the mutually reinforcing structures of rape and racism, realize the origins of this interface, and begin to dismantle and dispel the myths that now surround us.

Many myths have grown around the crime of rape, explaining who rapes, who is raped, where and why people are raped. Two of the most prevalent myths today concern race: first, that most rapists are Black and most rape victims are white; and second, that Black women cannot be raped because of their peculiar sexual nature. I will examine the context in which those myths first appeared, explore the purposes these myths served, and offer some suggestions as to how this analysis could help our efforts to prevent the rape of all women.

The myth of Black rapist/white victim is soundly contradicted by national statistics that 85 percent of victims are raped by someone of their own race. The myth that Black men rape white women can be traced at least as far back as slavery times, but the myth probably found its full expression at the end of the Civil War. The end of slavery and the beginning of Reconstruction saw the entrance of Blacks into many areas of society that had previously been closed to them, including governmental positions and educational institutions. An entire social structure was being challenged, and this change, slow as it was, posed a great threat to those who had benefited from the old structure. At this time, the Ku Klux Klan was first organized to defeat Reconstruction and destroy through intimidation, violence, and terror, the efforts of Blacks to gain political power. The KKK's efforts were mainly directed against Black state militias, Black persons daring to vote or run for office, the Freedman's Bureau, and anyone connected with the freedman's schools.

In 1871, a Congressional committee was formed to hold hearings to inquire into the Klan's activities. The transcripts of those hearings provide a picture of exactly what tactics were used—rape being one of the KKK's primary weapons. Witness after witness described how a group of eight or ten men would come to her house, try to intimidate her husband into abandoning politics, not voting, or casting his vote in a certain way. After such intimidation they would rape the woman—often in front of her husband and children. Other accounts tell of visits by the KKK when the husband was not at home, and how the women were intimidated and raped because of their husbands' political involvement or inclination. The testimony of these women destroys the myth that it is only Black men who rape.

Not only was white rape of Black women used as a means of political intimidation, but additionally, the myth of the Black rapist was created to justify other actions and policies also aimed at terror and intimidation. Records show that in a 30-year period in the South, more than 10,000 Blacks were killed by lynchings. As a means of justifying these lynchings, Black men were often charged with raping white women.

White men argued that such lynchings were necessary to protect the integrity of their women—their property. They reasoned that the crime of rape was so heinous that it deserved an equally atrocious punishment. Yet, accounts indicate that often a rape had never been committed. Other times, a voluntary relationship had existed between a Black man and a white woman, but it simply was not accepted at the time that any such allegiance could be voluntary, and the presence of the relationship was taken as proof of rape. In numerous instances it was positively known at the time of the lynching, and proven after the victim's death, that the relationship was voluntary.

A few women of the time recognized the political motivations of the lynchings and the abuse of the rape charge, and sought to lay bare the facts about this oppression. Ida B. Wells Barnett was perhaps the most vigilant crusader against lynching. She pamphleted and lectured on the subject and was instrumental in the founding of the British Anti-Lynching Society. Mary Church Terrell also sought to educate people and point out that it was racial hatred and lawlessness that motivated these lynchings. She confronted the myths then being advanced about why Black men raped. For instance, it was said that Black men were morally stunted and, therefore, did not see the act of rape as that heinous a crime. Others said that now that Blacks were free, they began to acquire a taste for the better things in life and, therefore, took liberties with white women as a way of achieving social equality. She argued that these views of Black men were advanced as a way of justifying the violent treatment meted out by southern whites.

The idea of Black men as natural rapists resulted not only in killings outside the law but in the legal execution of hundreds of Black men. Between 1930 and 1967, 455 men were executed in this country as a result of rape convictions. Of these, 405 were Black, 48 were white, and two were of another ethnic origin. This means that 89 percent of all those executed for rape were Black. Furthermore, no white man was ever executed for raping a Black woman.

The second major myth concerning rape and racism is the idea that Black women cannot be raped. The slave codes show that rape against Black women was not a crime.

In Mississippi, for example, rape of a white woman by a Black man was punishable by death. Yet, the law was indifferent to the rape of a Black woman by a Black man, and the rape of a Black woman by a white man was not considered rape—it was the white man's property right. During slavery times, rape was institutionalized. Black women were considered to be both breeders of slaves and sex objects to any white man.

In her book *Black Women in White America* (Random House, 1973), Gerda Lerner describes how this persisted after the abolition of slavery: "I believe nearly all white men take, and expect to take, undue liberties with their colored female servants—not only the fathers, but in many cases the sons also. Those servants who rebel must either leave or expect a mighty hard time if they decide to stay. By comparison, those who tamely submit to those improper relations live in clover."

Another part of the myth that Black women cannot be raped is the belief that Black women have greater sexual appetites than other women, that they always want sex. If Black women always want sex, the myth goes, even if one charges that she was raped, it is unlikely that much force was needed. This myth seems to have originated very soon after slavery was abolished—when free access to Black women was taken away. Sustaining myths were created in an attempt to perpetuate the rape of Black women.

The myth of the "bad" Black woman, loose in morals, *always* eager for sex, justified denying her the "respect" and "consideration" given to white women. By definition she was a "slut" and, therefore, to exploit her sexually was not met with the same horror, was not as reprehensible. Portraying Black women in this way has had very negative consequences. A Black woman becomes a more likely target of rape; she is afforded even less protection by law than her white sisters; and prosecution of rapists is made that much more difficult, especially when the offender is white.

The rape of white women by Black men is frequently tied to the existing state of relationships between Blacks and whites. The notion that women are the property of men—whether it be their father, husband, brother, or son—has permeated our culture for ages. Rape has long been used as a way of violating other men's property—their women. As Eldridge Cleaver points out in *Soul on Ice* (new edition, Dell, 1992), Black men sometimes rape white women as a way of getting back at white men. By destroying their "property," they avenge the systemic racism whites established and perpetuated. The rape of white women is also seen as a way of obtaining the freedom the Black man justifiably feels he should have.

The antirape movement has suffered from the failure to recognize how the charge of rape and the practice of rape have been used to perpetuate racism in our country. At this time, as we are getting increasingly active in rape prevention, it is important to combat *all* myths about rape, including the myths that victimize Black people in particular. Rape has been used as a tool to keep both women and Blacks "in their place." In the words of Alison Edwards, "It is essential that white women in their very real and legitimate concern about the crime of rape, not create a movement that can plug into the hands of these forces that are trying to rekindle fires of racism in our society and divide Black and white people."

APRIL 1982

Women's Shelters House Contradictions
by Gail Sullivan

Shelters for battered women, unheard of ten years ago, have developed into an extensive network of services run by and for women. Begun by feminists, this movement began with a two-pronged focus: first, to provide escape and a supportive environment to battered women and, thus, help individuals to transform their lives and, second, to change the social and political conditions that foster violence against women.

In the past five years, this movement has shown some of the contradictions involved in providing services with a political focus. Battered women's services were seen as being radically different from those of traditional agencies because they viewed violence against women as a result of women's oppression, not a woman's psychological inadequacy—choosing to raise consciousness rather than focus on therapy—and because they operated on a peer basis, the purpose being empowerment rather than dependence.

Yet these radical services depend upon the resources of a system that promotes violence against women, such as the courts, social services, and funding agencies. This creates a constant pressure to become assimilated into the mainstream, to become co-opted. In addition to this external pressure, there are tensions inherent in service delivery that mitigate against meeting political goals. It's therefore necessary to look at the contradictions that obstruct the movement's ability to end violence against women.

Swimming against the Current: External Pressures
SOCIAL SERVICES

Because shelters rely on social service agencies to refer battered women, and often must use their services in return, traditional services pressure battered women's groups to professionalize. This affects who is considered valuable to do such work, how it's done, and how it's viewed. As services professionalize, the emphasis on peer support and on hiring former battered women for advocacy positions loses ground to concerns for counseling experience and academic degrees.

Professionalization of language subtly changes the analysis of a social problem. For instance, a de-politicization process is evident in the transformation of "woman abuse" to "domestic violence" and "spouse abuse," masking the power relations between men and women. It is also evident in feminist groups' acceptance of terms such as "victim," which boxes a woman into a limited and negative identity defined by one experience, and "client," which connotes a static and unequal relationship between helper and helpee.

An additional influence on battered women's shelters is the "therapization" of the problem: a one-to-one counseling/service model begins to replace the feminist model of battered women realizing, by talking to each other, their common experience and oppression and their ability to become strong and independent.

FUNDING AGENCIES

Funding agencies exert influence over battered women's programs in several ways. Funding decisions are made in a context of acceptable reforms—nothing truly earth-shattering will be funded: both analysis and methods of solving a problem must be watered down or twisted around. Second, both private and governmental funding sources are relatively fickle: an issue builds up credibility and importance, becomes fundable, then after a few years loses its place in the limelight to the next fundable issue. This results in groups twisting themselves like pretzels, changing the focus of their work to meet funding possibilities and sometimes losing self-direction. Further, because funding tends to be on a year-by-year basis, the funding system mitigates against a long-term view of the changes we are trying to create.

Second, the interests of funding sources are often contrary to those of grassroots groups. One reason for governmental funding of rape crisis centers and battered women's shelters has been to collect data and provide funds and information to researchers. As a result, many programs begun on a model of informal peer support now have a myriad of forms to fill out, taking away from the real work at hand.

Third, while many battered women's groups began as collective or cooperative organizations, with consensus decision-making, it has been hard to defend the legitimacy of these alternative structures to funding agencies holding strongly to traditional views on hierarchy being the way to get things accomplished. As a result, some groups have changed their structures on paper, causing confusion between reality and what they claim to their funding sources. Others have completely altered their structures, perhaps having long-term effects on the work and experiences of those involved.

Fourth, funding agencies and social services both promote the bigger-is-better, "big bucks" approach to development: services are most respected if they are well-financed with sizable staffs. Grassroots shelters, which felt pressured to go after big grants, are now feeling the destructiveness of this development. Some groups took a long time to regain their equilibrium after the sudden influx of five or ten new staff members and several new programs required by a large grant. Now, just as suddenly, groups that expanded rapidly through dependence on such funds have been forced to cut back or close when the funds have been cut or the funding agencies dismantled.

Fundraisers for battered women's groups bear a lot of external pressure for the group to assimilate into the mainstream. Because they must keep up relations with many outside agencies, must translate the group's work into acceptable language, and must find the money somehow to keep the group chugging along, fundraisers are in a vulnerable position. They often feel responsible for the overall stability and survival of a group and can become overly protective of their organizations, to the extent of being territorial within the movement. This is particularly threatening now, because as money becomes tighter, the attacks against feminism increase, and traditional, even antifeminist, agencies create services for battered women, the potential for infighting increases. Groups need to recognize the external pressures on the movement and the ways that individuals feel them, and to clarify where to draw the line between the movement's goals and its need to relate to establishment agencies.

Murky Waters: Internal Tensions

POLITICAL DIRECTION

There is a lack of clear political direction in the battered women's movement. While there is a broad vision of ending violence against women, there are seldom explicit goals and objectives that move groups in that direction and little emphasis is put on long-range planning. Political views are often implicit rather than explicit. Without clear direction and planning, groups are crisis-oriented, can't tell when they are being co-opted, and get stuck in reformist work without knowing whether or how it furthers their vision. Lack of a strategy isolates the battered women's movement from sister organizations working on other aspects of violence against women and other feminist issues important to battered women and from other progressive groups working on racism and other issues of importance to us. By focusing on a single issue and being without goals that include relations with other progressive movements, battered women's groups lose sight of the inherent connections between various issues and the need for a common solution.

Without explicit political views, battered women's groups can't define what it means to be feminist services and how they differ from mainstream services and cannot recognize real allies, which leads to simplistic conclusions such as that every woman will support our movement.

SERVICES AND MORE SERVICES

Because shelters desire to support battered women as best they can and are often frustrated with the response of existing social services, there's a tendency to create more and more services. Shelters started out as safe places with some advocacy, lots of informal support, and maybe a little child care. Many shelters are now multiservice programs with full counseling, child care, parenting, legal advocacy, and other components. Though important, these services require increasingly enormous amounts of money and put groups in the position of providing *for* women, rather than supporting women in providing for themselves. Further, feminists become inserted in the middle, between women trying to get their needs met and the social structure which doesn't want to respond, relieving the establishment of the burden of providing for women and, at the same time, taking the brunt of pressure from both sides. It might be more politically efficacious to work with battered women to demand of the existing system that it provide for their needs.

SERVICES OR EMPOWERMENT?

Overemphasis on service leads to workers taking power away from battered women, as when a staffperson who knows the ropes at welfare does all the talking on a woman's behalf. This denies a battered woman the chance to fend for herself and build her own ego and creates a view of staff as experts and battered women as incapable of taking control, contradicting a basic premise of the movement.

Moreover, the increasing emphasis on staff-"client" relations rather than peer support cuts away at the most important contribution of shelters—a place for battered women to talk with each other and discover their common experience.

SERVICES OBSTRUCT ORGANIZING

The focus on services conflicts with an organizing strategy to end violence against women. It is in the interests of those in power to keep feminists overwhelmed by providing services for low wages, supporting individual women through their crises and helping them get the most crumbs they can, rather than having battered women's groups organize those same women to take action in their own interests—i.e., by demonstrating at welfare and housing offices or state capitols. In fact, the burnout and exhaustion of movement workers, and the constant turnover of good organizers, is probably a result of trying to meet battered women's every need in the face of increasing opposition. By doing so, we allow ourselves to be exhausted by women's oppression, without the creative, positive relief that comes from women fighting together for what we need.

An important aspect of organizing, within a service context, is consciousness raising. Battered women's groups don't focus on consciousness raising among battered women coming to shelters or among new staff members and often don't involve battered women in political activity in the movement. Whether because of time constraints, emphasis on services, or fear of "pushing politics down the women's throats," this important work gets pushed aside. Yet consciousness raising helps women to understand their experience in a political way: to see that much of what happens to them is a result of their oppression and they, therefore, share much in common with other women. It is this view that distinguishes feminist from traditional services and it should be emphasized, not downplayed. Consciousness-raising groups could provide a bridge between women of different experiences, races, and classes and provide women new to the movement an opportunity to share in the wealth of experience of the women's movement. Without such efforts, battered women and new volunteers are not truly given access to the movement.

Conclusion

Women's services, rooted in a feminist philosophy and promoting women's empowerment, have been an important part of the women's movement in the past ten years. However, though they were initially planned as one aspect of a broader focus, they have become increasingly central to feminist work and the movement, creating numerous problems, some of which I've addressed. Given the contradictions of service work and given the financial and labor difficulties of maintaining all the many service organizations in the face of little or no available funds, it is time to rethink this direction. Services are not enough and are, perhaps, not even the top priority for the '80s. If we are concerned that future women should not be battered or raped, we must do more than patch up the wounds of some of today's victims. We need a long-term organizing strategy to stop the war on women and to ally with those groups that share our vision.

This article has been edited for clarity.

APRIL 1985

Sexual Violence and How It Affects Us
by Judith Herman

The subject of sexual violence carries a taboo that is firmly impressed in both individual and social consciousness. As a result of the women's movement, discussions of sexual violence have been made public in the last decade. Now we are at a stage where we know a lot about sexual violence, but we don't know how deeply it affects us.

Who Are the Victims?

Research in recent years—inspired and influenced by the women's movement—has provided startling data about sexual assault. For example, in a random survey of 930 California women by Diana Russell, 24 percent reported they had experienced at least one completed rape and 44 percent reported at least one attempted rape. (Incidentally, that means almost half of the women who endured a rape attempt got away, and I believe those women are a hidden resource for all of us. We don't know how they did it—but we need to know.) David Finkelhor of the University of New Hampshire did a similar survey of more than 500 women college students in which 24 percent said they had experienced forced sexual experiences. (We don't know how many of these were raped by a stranger and how many were raped by people known and trusted to some extent, but we do know that from the moment women begin to socialize with men the possibility of sexual assault asserts itself.) Finally, Eugene Kanin and Stanley Parcell did a survey of college women in which 83 percent reported that they had suffered some kind of "sexual aggression"—that is, some attempt at forced sexual contact. Thirty-two percent said they had experienced at least one forceful attempt at intercourse in a dating situation.

Surveys of men are equally revealing. Thirty-five percent of the college men Neil Malamuth interviewed said they would be willing to attempt rape if they were sure they could get away with it. He concluded that these male college students felt entitled to use force to coerce sex in a dating situation. This willingness to resort to force as the ultimate instrument of control persists throughout marriage. Another of Diana Russell's findings—the one that led to her book *Rape in Marriage* (new edition, Midland Books, 1990)—is that one in seven of the married women she interviewed had been raped by her husband. (Russell's definition of rape was the strict legal definition: use of force, or a weapon, or threat of force to obtain intercourse.) In other words, being with men we know and trust doesn't necessarily assure safety. We who are unescorted are at risk for street rape, and we who are escorted by men are at risk for date rape and marital rape.

Childhood does not offer us much protection, either, but that reality has been unaddressed for a long time. In fact, one of the ignored findings in the Kinsey report of 30 years ago was that one woman in four reported a sexual contact with an adult male before reaching the age of twelve and that most of the assailants were known to the children. Kinsey also reported that 6 percent of his sample had a sexual relationship with an older male relative and 1 percent had been involved in father-daughter incest. Those figures are probably conservative; recently, Diana Russell, with a more random sample, came up with much higher figures: 38 percent of her sample had a childhood sexual contact with an adult male, 16 percent had a contact with a relative, and 4.6 percent were involved in father-daughter incest.

These are the statistics on major assault, and they represent incidents that victims generally are ashamed to acknowledge. When it comes to minor assaults, however, there emerges a curious discrepancy. When discussing incidents like obscene phone calls, an encounter with an exhibitionist, or suddenly feeling unwanted hands in a crowd, people usually make light of these assaults and don't hold the victims responsible for them. We give the perpetrators humorous names—"flashers," "mashers," "breathers," "peepers"—and as victims we don't feel ashamed to admit having experienced the minor assaults. I am confident that most people reading this have experienced such assaults, and I am confident that not many of you could laugh off the experience at the time it happened. My experience, and that of most people I talk to, is that such incidents are frightening and humiliating.

Further, I submit that these minor assaults in the war between the sexes are ominous warnings of threats that we prefer to repress, the ultimate threat being the rape-murder. Taken together, the research findings and our gut-level feelings point to a conclusion that no girl or woman is currently safe from sexual assault and that to be female is to be subject to the possibility of a sexual assault.

Who Are the Offenders?

I believe that perpetrators of sexual assault are, for the most part, ordinary men. Let's deal first with the proposition that they are men. In cases of rape or sexual abuse of women and girls, this is generally recognized—for example, studies of incest indicate that about 97 percent of the perpetrators are male. It is less generally understood that even in cases where boys or men are victimized, the vast majority of offenders are male. For example, David Finkelhor also surveyed male college students about their childhood sexual experiences. About 10 percent had a sexual encounter with an adult during childhood, and 84 percent of these adults were male.

Now for the proposition that perpetrators are ordinary people. Of course, we don't know a great deal about perpetrators, because they don't volunteer for study. Generally, the only ones who have been studied are those who have been reported, arrested, tried, convicted, and imprisoned. But according to Diana Russell's survey data, only 6 percent of the sexual assaults were ever reported to the police, and only a small fraction of the perpetrators ever saw the inside of a courtroom, let alone a prison. So imprisoned sex offenders constitute an extremely small minority and an extremely skewed sample of the whole.

How, then, can we find out anything about sex offenders? I believe that the best information source, failing direct observation, is reporting by victims. In my own research with incest victims, we interviewed women who, for the most part, had never disclosed the incest, so it had never come to the attention of any law enforcement, criminal justice, or health authorities. The two descriptions that I heard over and over until they were predictable clichés were that the man was a "pillar of the community" and a "good provider." The other comments I heard over and over were, "Nobody would have believed me" and "Nobody would have believed that this man would do such a thing." I believe that if we could identify and study the husbands who rape their wives or the young men who rape the women they are dating, we would find the same thing. In fact, occasionally when such people do come to trial, it is common to see a parade of character witnesses for the perpetrator, affirming what an upstanding, promising young man he is or what a wonderful husband and father he is.

The "pathology" of sex offenders is simply an exaggeration of accepted norms of male dominance. All too frequently we make the mistake of generalizing from the few losers who get caught—persons who often are quite disturbed—a falsely reassuring picture of the sex offender as a beast whom we would be able to recognize easily. We can't do that. I admit that the first incestuous father I saw was someone I was prepared to hate; already I had seen his wife and his two daughters and I had heard horror stories about him. But he came to my office and he was charming. He was mild-mannered, pleasant, ingratiating; he couldn't understand why this matter had been blown so out of proportion. Really, what was all the fuss about?

Social Attitudes Toward Sexual Assault

Although this offender's presentation of his story was, naturally, self-serving, I believe that, in part, his confusion was genuine. For in his world, which also is our world, most sexual violence either is explicitly sanctioned or implicitly condoned. As the legal scholar and feminist theorist Catherine MacKinnon puts it, sexual assault is "not prohibited, but regulated" ("Feminism, Marxism, Method and the State: Toward Feminist Jurisprudence," in *Signs*, Volume 8, 1983). And having sex with one's own daughter falls well within the regulations, for, in practice, only the forms of sexual violence that involve an assault on another man's property are criminalized.

Marital rape is explicitly sanctioned, and, as feminists in the last ten years have found, it is one of the hardest parts of the rape law to change. Until 1975, every state exempted husbands from the rape statutes. The latest tally shows that 22 states have revised their laws explicitly so that husbands may be prosecuted for rape. The legal basis for the "marital rape exemption," as it is called, is the "Hale Doctrine." Matthew Hale was a British chief of justice in the seventeenth century and a famous witch prosecutor. His doctrine read: "But the husband cannot be guilty of a rape committed by himself upon his lawful wife for, by their mutual matrimonial consent, and contract, the wife has given up herself in this kind unto the husband, which she cannot retract." Or, as California State Senator Bob Wilson said when the California rape law was up for revision, "If you can't rape your wife, whom can you rape?"

Most sexual assaults fall into the category of those that are implicitly condoned. The mechanisms of social approval begin with secrecy and shaming of the victim and, if secrecy fails, escalate to explicit rationalizations and justifications, even celebrations, of rape.

Secrecy is rooted in shaming the victim and discrediting her story, and, frankly, we in the psychiatric profession have had a long and dishonorable role in maintaining the denial of such sexual assault. But we are not alone; the legal tradition has been equally culpable.

Denial within the medical and mental health professions goes back to Freud who, in his early work, saw many upper-middle-class Viennese women complaining of hysteria. What they were hysterical about, they revealed, were sexual assaults by men whom they knew and trusted—frequently, their fathers. Freud initially believed his informants, took them seriously, and in an 1896 essay, proposed the seduction theory, which postulated that at the basis of every case of hysteria was a childhood sexual assault. Within a year, he retracted that theory—not because he found new evidence from patients, but because he could not believe that there were so many incest cases. In other words, he would not accept the notion that there were so many incestuous fathers among the well-to-do bourgeoisie of Vienna. Later he not only repudiated his seduction theory, but also falsified his incest cases, identifying the perpetrators as governesses, uncles, other children. He went on to claim that the women's reports of sexual assault were fantasy, and, on that basis, developed the concept of the Oedipus complex, which has been the core of dominant psychological theory for nearly a hundred years.

Shifting focus from the reality of sexual assault to the fantasy life of the victim certainly drew a veil of secrecy over incest and child sexual assault. It sent the whole question of sexual assault undercover within the mental health professions. Even in the '70s, 25 years after the Kinsey report, the *Comprehensive Textbook of Psychiatry* was still stating that the estimated prevalence of all forms of incest is one case in a million. In my own training, there was no mention of sexual assault, and I think that is true in most psychiatric training.

The legal tradition followed the psychiatric doctrine. John Henry Wigmore is to the legal tradition what Freud is to the psychiatric tradition. He is the author of the "Treatise on Evidence," which still forms the basis and standard of a great deal of legal practice. On the question of sexual assault, Wigmore set forth a doctrine that impugned the credibility of any woman who claimed that she had been victimized:

Obviously, there are types of sex offenses, notably incest, which by the very nature of the charge, bear grave danger of completely false accusations by young girls of innocent appearance but unsound mind, susceptible to sexual fantasies and possessed of malicious, vengeful spirit.

To this day, the worry about false complaints dominates the Western legal approach to sexual assault cases.

Shaming and intimidation are also components of denial. In order to keep the denial going, you have to keep the victims quiet. And until the last ten years, when speakouts began, the technique has been effective—so much so that even in Russell's survey, we learn that only 6 percent of the rapes and only 3 percent of the child sexual assaults were ever reported.

We don't know the real figure for the rates of incest, but Diana Russell's data indicated around 5 percent of women have experienced father-daughter sexual contact.

Some people claim that it may be even higher, for we never know all the women who have repressed the memory entirely.

When secrecy fails, the explicit justifications of sexual assault begin. These are found not only in pornography and men's magazines, which one might expect, but also in all forms of literature, including the professional literature. These are the same as the common rationalizations that one hears from the perpetrators who get caught. The first is that the sexual assault did no harm and, in fact, was good for her. Indeed, there is a substantial school of thought that maintains that women need and desire rape. One of the favorite pornographic fantasies is that of the frigid prude who is transformed by rape into a woman who is not just sexually responsive, but a kind of slavering nymphomaniac.

When Kinsey came across his shocking findings about childhood sexual assault, he didn't actually suppress his results, but he did his best to minimize their significance. His theme was, "Let's not make a fuss about any of this: there's no reason why a child should mind having its genitalia touched." He attempted to quell the prudish reactions of parents, teachers, and society by saying that becoming "hysterical" about it would do much more harm to the child than the sexual assault itself. Underlying this idea of harmlessness is a real failure to distinguish between coercive and consensual sex and a belief that sex between men and women requires male dominance. These themes are not just part of the men's magazine culture; they are part of the professional sex manual and medical culture. This is from a standard medical text, *Novak's Textbook of Gynecology*, published in 1981:

The frequency of intercourse depends entirely upon the male sex drive.... The female should be advised to allow her male partner's sex drive to set their pace and she should attempt to gear hers satisfactorily to his.... Lack of consideration for the male partner's inherent physical drive is a common cause of impotence, and reflects an immature attitude of the female who is using her partner for self-gratification.

And here's a quote from David Reuben's syndicated column on sex—advice to millions of readers:

There are some wives who still suffer strong pangs of guilt over sex and only allow themselves to participate if it is supposedly against their will. If everything is all right once you get started, just remind yourself that you are committing rape by request and contributing to your wife's overall sexual satisfaction.

The second group of rationalizations concedes that sexual assault may be harmful, but puts the blame on someone other than the offender—usually the victim. The "Lolita argument," that "the male is not responsible—she provoked it," got wide publicity in 1982 in Wisconsin, when a judge sentenced a 24-year-old man to 90 days in a work-release program for sexually assaulting the 5-year-old daughter of the woman with whom he lived. In explaining the sentence, the judge said, "I am satisfied that we have an unusually sexually promiscuous young lady, and he did not know enough to refuse. No way do I believe the man initiated sexual contact." Equally prevalent is the belief that sex is an entitlement for men. If a woman provokes a man in some way, rape is often considered a permissible response. This is especially true if the male's sexual demand is frustrated. That is, if a woman "leads him on" but doesn't want sex, rape is acceptable. The male sexual drive is not to be denied, and a woman who has the effrontery to refuse or change her mind deserves to be punished.

Social Functions of Sexual Violence

Why is sexual violence condoned? The only satisfactory explanation that I can derive echoes opinions of feminist writers, Susan Brownmiller and others: although it is carried out by individuals or small groups of men, sexual assault is not simply a personal or individual act. It is a socialized behavior and a means by which male supremacy is enforced and perpetuated. It is a form of terrorism by which men as a group keep women as a group frightened and submissive. It serves the same political function as the lynch threat or the pogrom. Perpetrators understand intuitively that the purpose of their behavior is to put women in our place and that their behavior will be condoned by other men as long as the victim is a legitimate target. Most rape trials still focus on establishing the fact that the victim was a legitimate target and, therefore, that the rape was not a crime.

This rationale also explains the rapist's attitude of entitlement, lack of remorse, and failure to respond to pleas of conscience. Linda Gordon, a historian at the University of Massachusetts, has studied the history of domestic and sexual violence, and she has reviewed incest cases that were reported to the child protective services around the turn of the century. She says the distinguishing feature of the incest cases, in contrast to the physical abuse cases, was the lack of contrition and the attitude of entitlement in the perpetrators. The men who beat their wives or children at least felt some regret after the assault, viewing their own behavior as a loss of control. The incestuous fathers, however, rarely showed remorse.

Strategies for Resistance

If sexual violence serves a political purpose benefiting men as a group, then women cannot expect, certainly in the short term, that men will be a meaningful source of protection. The real source of protection against sexual assault must be ourselves and other women. There are even some research data to support this contention. In several studies of childhood sexual assault, it is clear that girls who are alienated from their mothers, or who are physically separated from their mothers for any length of time, are at much higher risk for all forms of sexual assault. In my own surveys of treatment programs for incest and child sexual abuse, one of the main points of consensus was that if the family could be rebuilt at all, the key to recovery for the victim and the restoration of the family was the mother-daughter relationship. Where that could be strengthened and restored, the victims did well; where it could not, the victims had a much harder time.

Pauline Bart has done some fascinating research on strategies for rape resistance. She interviewed women who got away from their attackers and found that they seemed better prepared to act in a crisis and less afraid to fight back than a group of rape victims she also questioned. The resistance strategies of the rape avoiders included screaming, talking to stall their attackers, and running—often all of these in the same encounter. On the other hand, pleading or appealing to the mercy of the attackers seems not to have been a successful strategy for the women in Bart's study. While Bart cautions that her findings are generalizations and cannot be applied to every situation, her general advice is, "Don't be a lady."

The organized efforts of women in the last ten years, also have changed rape laws in every state, created rape crisis centers in every major city, established the National Center for Prevention and Control of Rape, and ended secrecy and raised consciousness about rape. These results, for women by women, illustrate that ultimately we are the sources of safety and protection.

Implications for Our Development

All of this information and theory has profound implications for female psychological development. First of all, I think we all live in fear of sexual assault all of our lives. The fear is pervasive, but it cannot be expressed directly, since explicit discussion of male sexual violence has been taboo for so long. So my own guess is that the fear of sexual assault, like other repressed emotions, returns in symptoms; for example, consider the traditional female symptom of "frigidity."

Helen Singer Kaplan's book, *The New Sex Therapy* (Random House, 1974), does not have the words "rape," "incest," or "violence" in the index. She cites one case history of a woman with vaginismus who said that after a friend of hers was raped she herself became sexually anxious—and describes this response as phobic. The book reflects no consciousness of sexual assault, and the author's assumption seems to be that heterosexual sex always is sensual and caring. The provisions of sex therapy, the rules of sensate focus, and other techniques are offered as protection from performance anxiety and fear of abandonment, which Kaplan thinks are the main things we worry about when we have sex. But the truth is that they are also protections from forced sex. Frankly, I think this approach to sex—de-emphasizing the penis, de-emphasizing the male-superior position, and de-emphasizing the male sexual rhythm and timing and orgasm—offers some possibility for women in heterosexual relationships to develop their own responsiveness.

Finally, I think the fear of sexual violence has a profound effect on mother-daughter relationships. In our current mythology, mother in the role of protector is trivialized. At best, she is ridiculed as an anxious, restrictive prude; at worst, she is jealous of her daughter's sexuality. Because the real problem can't be named, it becomes mystified as a concern over modesty or virginity. The daughter then sees her mother as a stifling jailer trying to rob her of her sexuality; our popular fairy tales present the heroine's task as escaping from the wicked stepmother into the arms of the rescuing prince. Going back to the original Cinderella story, however, we find the story of a girl whose good mother died, leaving her unprotected. The little girl plants a tree on her mother's grave and waters it with her tears, and it is this tree that grows into the magic source of her gifts. Even in the Disney version, the fairy godmother appears outside in a garden as Cinderella cries under a big tree. That big tree is the disguised representation of the protective mother. For, in fact, the development, in women, of the potential for intimacy and for satisfying sexual relationships probably depends on self-esteem and the capacity for self-protection—which is the internalization of a protective mother who will fight for her daughter and for herself.

DECEMBER 1988

Awakening the Amazon Within
by Lyri Merrill

I'm running, panicked—he's right behind me, chasing me. I know he'll catch me, but still I run, twist, turn, lost, frightened. And then I'm cornered, back against a chain link fence or a brick wall. There's no one else around, no one to hear my screams, to see my terror. He grabs me by my wrists, and I freeze in a moment of realization that lasts forever: he has me, I am powerless, there is no escape.

This dream once frequented my nights. Often I'd wake up, the feeling of helplessness tight in my gut. Other times there'd be only a whisper of memory left in the morning. The man in my dream was my ex-lover who raped me, the grubby man who molested me at the subway, the group of construction workers who leered at me when I walked past them on the street. He was the boyfriend who beat me up, the tall thin man who followed me one afternoon, the teenager who yelled, "Hey babe, hey babe," the boys who shouted slurs from a speeding car. Most often the man in my dreams was unrecognizable. He symbolized *man* and the privilege of any man to threaten and diminish me as a woman.

I dream that dream no more. There lives now a warrior within me—an amazon— and *she don't take shit from nobody.* She is there to protect me, to stand tall in her blazing anger, and to say, No!

I remember the first night she came to life. I remember turning and facing him, telling him he had no right to frighten me, threaten me, invade me. I became big, powerful. I pushed him back; I kicked, I yelled, I punched. I let loose all my pent-up fury from all the years of running from him, from all the years of feeling powerless and living in fear. And when I woke up, still savoring my victory, I knew that something was changing within me, deep down inside.

That amazon was born in me through studying karate, specifically through my training with the Sanchin Women's School of Karate and Self-Defense. I came to Sanchin out of frustration. I was tired of scurrying down the street in fear, tired of the images that ran through my mind of rapists climbing through my bedroom window, tired of feeling powerless and small. I found freedom in Sanchin—freedom from my paralyzing fears and freedom from the man of my nightmares.

My fears and nightmares were born of painful experience. Too many of my dealings with men have been tainted by coercion and violence. I have too many memories of men forcing me to have sex with them.

My experiences were confounded by my own confusion and feelings of guilt. I'd been taught that I was the source of a man's desire for me, that I "turned him on." I'd learned that I was to blame for what men did to me, even if I didn't want them to do it. When I found myself in a position I didn't want to be in, I'd go along with it because I didn't realize I had a choice. Sometimes I protested, but I didn't really believe I had a right to say no. I was well trained to attract a man but I had no skills in setting limits with a man.

This belief system broke down for me when an ex-boyfriend raped me. He had come over to my apartment to clean out his stuff. He attacked me in the kitchen: shoved me around, shook me so hard my teeth rattled. He threw me to the floor, pinned me down, and raped me. I was terrified. I struggled to get away; I screamed at him; I pleaded with him. Finally, I just lay still and went numb.

Afterwards I tried to forget it, pretend it hadn't happened. I told myself it "wasn't that bad," that he'd only "forced me." I'd used these words before to deny my feelings, but this time was too painful and violent; this time I'd fought him too hard, this time the excuses didn't work. I continued to be haunted by his violence long after it occurred.

Feminism opened the door to freedom for me by giving me a word for what had happened to me—rape. The first time I named my experience "rape" my whole world shifted. The word "rape" made it more frightening for me, more devastating—more real. Naming it "rape" claimed the deep shame and hurt I felt. And naming it "rape" carried me out of the fog that had blurred my memory, led me through the pain and betrayal, and brought me to my anger. In my anger, I began my healing. In my anger, I swore it would never happen to me again if I could help it.

I continued to have nightmares about the rape and other painful experiences I'd been through, but I no longer felt I was to blame for them. I found in feminism a vocabulary to describe the men of my nightmares, to understand what it was that felt so erasing about their power over me, to know that it was *wrong* for them to pursue me. Through my feminism I learned that my fear was a common experience of all women. I came to understand sexual harassment and abuse of women as systematic in our culture, part of a social structure that deems women second-class citizens, ever-available to the needs of men. The violence, and the constant threat of violence, keep us off-balance and "in our place."

I understood that I was being oppressed as a woman. I saw how I was being oppressed as a woman. Yet I still cringed when I walked down a street alone. My feminism opened my eyes, but it didn't ease my fears. There was still something missing for me. I still felt vulnerable and scared. It was my summoning of the amazon within me through my training at Sanchin that finally took me beyond the haunting of my nightmares.

When I started training at Sanchin it was so awkward! I had never asked my body to do what I asked it to do in karate. I couldn't touch my toes or balance on one leg. My punches were wobbly and ineffective, my kicks came no higher than a couple feet off the floor and never seemed to go where I aimed them. It was a lesson in patience and in accepting the limitations and uniqueness of my own body.

I've been able to watch myself progress in very tangible ways. In learning to *kiai* (yell), I have found my voice and discovered that it can be thunderous, ferocious, *loud.*

My kicks are now waist high and climbing, my punches are fast, elbow strikes power-ful, my sparring has become more fluid and natural. I've even developed some muscles! I love the way I feel in my body now—comfortable, confident, strong. At Sanchin, I'm encouraged to develop my own natural talents, find my own style. I'm challenged to push myself and reach beyond what I think myself capable of. I am learning to trust my own instincts. I am also learning to feel my own power. Every time I go to class, I am surrounded by powerful women and reminded that I am also a powerful woman. It's hard for me to think of myself as a passive doormat or an invisible mouse when I'm beating the beans out of the heavy bag.

I'd heard that studying a martial art helps you gain confidence, self-esteem. Magical words. I've found them to be true. I've become much more self-confident through studying karate. It has happened gradually, like a gentle spring rain that seeps slowly through the earth to eventually come tumbling out as a roaring creek. It has happened without my even trying to make it happen. My training with Sanchin feeds my soul, nourishes me at my roots. It is one of those precious things in my life that "fits"—like a peg in a peghole. I have a place in this world, and karate is giving me the self-confidence to claim that place and fill it.

Historically, the martial arts were developed as a means of self-defense by op-pressed peoples. I believe they can help us, as women, free ourselves from the oppression we experience in this culture—free us from the grip of helpless fear created by the prevalence of physical violence against women and also shatter the more subtle forms of oppression: the countless images and messages surrounding us every day that seek to limit us, make us feel small, ineffective, powerless, and always "less than" men.

I believe that no one has the right to violate another person; no man has the right to invade a woman in any way. In our culture, men are taught to expect women to be open and available to them and their sexual needs, encouraged to take what they want from women. This attitude is unacceptable. Men who attack women need to know when they've crossed the line, when they're trespassing where they have no right to be. It shouldn't have to be our responsibility to teach these men manners, but hell, if a man invades my turf, he's stepped outside the bounds of common courtesy, and I'm not going to be polite about it—I'm gonna teach him his lesson the hard way. If any man crosses my line, I want him to know he's made a mistake; I want to make it so un-comfortable for him that he hightails it away from me just as fast as he can.

I have resisted every attack ever made against me. I have resisted by trying to be invisible, by trying to ignore it and to pretend it wasn't happening, by begging and pleading, by struggling and screaming, by running away. I have resisted by turning off and going dead inside. I have always tried to protect myself the best I knew how. My goal in studying karate is to develop more effective ways to resist.

I don't want to add to the violence that poisons our world; neither do I want to feed resignation and paralyzing fear. We live in a world in which women are constantly subject to the threat and experience of violence. My goal in learning self-defense is to give myself options. When I choose to resist the violence, I want to have some tools, some skills, to help me in that decision. Now if I choose to fight, my attacker's going to know it. I'm going to fight like hell.

NOVEMBER 1989

Contradictions: Mother-Daughter Incest

by Roberta James

Incest. A sinister word, bespeaking confusion, fear, betrayal, guilt, excitement, penetration of boundaries, violation of trust. It immediately conjures up images of victims who are vulnerable, exploited, shamed, doubted, scapegoated, silenced. Alongside are images of the victimizers: selfish, arrogant, emotionally manipulative, sexually perverse. And, presumably, male.

And women? Do women commit incest? No, say caseworkers and activists alike, only in a minute number of cases, so minute as to be virtually nonexistent. It is a pale imitation of male behavior, nothing more. Incest is still a patriarchal phenomenon. Mother-child incest is but a byproduct of the system, a mere reenactment of the oppression visited upon them. It has nothing to do with female sexuality per se, and certainly nothing to do with us.

I remember my mother as a creature of extremes: subservient and domineering, passionate and puritanical, dogmatic and timid, self-righteous and guilt-ridden, given either to violent rages or uncontrollable tears. A large woman, imposing, with harsh features but a body that literally enveloped you in innumerable folds of comfort and warmth. I was both fascinated and fearful of those wild fluctuations of mood and spent most of my childhood trying to gauge them, adapt to them, or manipulate them when not being simply swept up in the chaos. No one could be more imaginative, playful, or outrageous as she spun fantasies and devised games by the hour—a child's delight. No one could be more fragile, as she became increasingly vulnerable, increasingly paranoid, with the passing of years. No one could be more terrifying, bearing down with murderous intensity, outraged at the slightest infraction of a rule or a contradiction.

My mother's tragedy was that she was too much: too loud, too fat, too religious, too masculine, too intense. An embarrassment to an ambitious husband struggling to the top; an embarrassment to a mother renowned—and preferred—for her feminine grace and charm. I was embarrassed too, learning to disappear in a crowd, trying to quiet her in public, to protect her and myself from others' amused contempt. She was a misfit in the middle-class society of the '50s, wanting desperately to belong—and failing that, to escape.

And escape she did: she converted to Pentecostalism, a religion perceived to be as vulgar and extravagant and ridiculed as she was herself. It was a veritable act of madness for a woman in her position. With no warning, she plunged into a world of faith healers, tent meetings, miracles, possession, prophecies, visions, voices, dreams. It provided an outlet for her rage and pain, which appeared to outsiders disproportionate to the circumstances of her life, and salvation from expectations too much to bear. It filled an emotional emptiness while nurturing a desire for revenge. The world she could not succeed in would be destroyed; the women she could not compete with would be damned; and those who mocked her would be punished, not once, but forever.

It happened when she was pregnant with her second child. My father was then on the threshold of success, and my mother was about to be catapulted into a competitive world that terrified her. It was a pregnancy she experienced as an unwanted invasion and a trap, a punishment for cowardly acquiescence to shameful acts that repulsed her. Over the months, she became increasingly obsessed with evil, not just external evil but an evil within, an evil she believed would eventually kill her. It was a nine-month nightmare as she watched her body expand in grotesque disfigurement, carrying death, her death, her final eclipse in a world that had no place for her. It broke her, as what had passed for mental stability gave way under the strain. It also empowered her and, for the first time, this timid and indecisive woman could say no to the intolerable demands upon her life: no to visitors, no to drinking and smoking, no to social obligations, no to sex. Never again would my parents sleep together, though they continued living together another eight years. The overbearing man who had dominated now moved like a stranger in his own home, intimidated by her uncontrollable fanaticism, her paralyzing judgments.

For all her resistance to my birth, she plunged into motherhood as zealously as she had plunged into religion. While she idealized my quiet and passive older sister, I was the one most like herself: aggressive, hot-tempered, intensely religious, an incurable tomboy. She gloried in my achievements even as she felt threatened by my relentless drive. I in turn adored her, as we played together, fantasized together, slept together. I could not conceive of taking a step without her, dreaded the least sign of disapproval, longed for acceptance, and tried my best to shelter her from the world.

Privacy was unknown. There was no small space she did not dominate, nothing that escaped her attention. Every detail of life, however minute, came under her control. In later years, this would become a matter of contention as my adolescence became an endless stream of opened letters, overheard conversations, rummaged drawers, confiscated books, diaries discovered and subsequently burned. Even today I cannot write without an awareness of her presence. My sister and I learned early: whatever is not hidden will be destroyed.

From the beginning, the issue was always sexuality. It was never a natural part of life—not in that household—but a powerful demonic force, so despised that not even marriage could sanctify it. Conflicts over sexuality surfaced again and again over the years, in various forms, now as weapon, now as bond: it was always what drew us together and what ultimately tore us apart.

My mother's aversion to heterosexuality was the driving force of her life. Sex with men was not so much a sin as a degradation. It was pride that kept her aloof and that was the source of her frigidity. Frigidity was to her both badge of honor and source of shame, rebellion and conquest, failure and revenge.

If sex was the war, then masturbation was the battlefield, the one thing I refused to give up, even for her. Like the heroine in Anne Rampling's *Exit to Eden* (Arbor

House, 1985), from earliest childhood, I have felt a criminal in my own body. She had declared war on a sexuality that was too male, too demanding, therefore unnatural and an abomination.

And yet it is her own powerful sexuality that I remember best: what I saw expressed in her moving to the wild beat of Gospel, swept up in the drama of tent meetings. It was whatever in her responded to the ecstatic surrender of altar calls and the surge of excitement under the touch of a faith healer's hand. Her lectures to me were always belied by those inexplicable eruptions of passion that confused and excited: nights of being held, deep absorbing kisses, penetrating fingers, those welcome and frightening intrusions. Not mother, then, but lover, with all the complexity and urgency that word implies.

The erotic bonds between us weren't always gentle. How could they be, with sex so infused with fear and denial? She brought to sex all the refinements of a medieval ascetic: punishing the flesh while indulging it, heightening the senses, bringing the full range of emotions into play. There was the relentless obsession with cleanliness, the enemas, the ritualized purges; the public humiliations; more rarely, the blows. Did I eroticize to endure, or could I endure because it was so incredibly erotic? I became for her the embodiment of self-hatred and fear to redeem her from a guilt I could not understand. If I hated her, I don't remember. There was only the sense of bewilderment, of desire and helpless need. I feared her, but never questioned. I was aware of the discrepancies, but had no words, no language by which to break free of those damning contradictions.

At twelve she discovered porn in my room; her judgment was immediate and complete. No amount of tears, no degree of repentance could win her back. It is the first time I remember being suicidal. I chose life instead. I chose rebellion. It kept me tied to her but made opposition possible, an alternate view by which I could begin to save myself.

My initial infidelities were with books, in a premeditated betrayal of ideas. Philosophy replaced pornography as I devoured the words of Nietzsche, Kierkegaard, Sartre, Hesse. Writers who glorified the individual, writers who spoke of responsibility, of choice. It was a way to separate, to disarm her, to judge in return—a gateway at last to sanity.

In time, books would be replaced by men as the center of our conflict. There was no man I ever fucked but that it was aimed at her; no man fucked but that I brought her proof of it after: bloody underwear, love bites, torn clothing, semen-soaked sheets, a baby. For what? Confrontation? Forgiveness? Recognition? Revenge?

Our arguments shook the neighborhood that summer I left home, blasting away at the last few remnants of what had once meant comfort and love to us both. She had such a sensitivity to language and the power of words, Pentecostalism being a religion of words, alternately seductive and threatening. "Bitch," "cunt," "slut," "whore"; I have often thought back to the extraordinary obscene discourse of that summer, what was revealed, what remained hidden in those violent expletives, all dealing with sexuality, all referring to women.

The last few years have been quieter. Opening myself to the memories has not eased the opening up between us. A loss of energy on our part, a loss of love? My struggle has moved to interior regions in silent private encounters with the past. As memories come back, I write in a journal now rather than engage in direct confrontation, or work things out with other women I love, women so like her. The real issue, after all, was never men, always women. Always that erotic power that neither of us understood, neither knew how to deal with.

One day, my life crashing down around me, I returned to that house, that bed, with a woman, and made love for three days—in delicious desecration and desperate affirmation of sexuality, our sexuality, of life itself. To name it as not my lesbianism, but ours. To know that however much my mother denied it, whether it should ever have been acted upon or not, that impetus, that desire had been good.

What do I hope for now? Recovery? A word that seems to assume a past that was damaging, a future state known as mental health, and usually a specific set of programs as to how to get there. In feminist circles, recovery is a concept often linked with womb imagery, visions of women's healing through one another's nurturance, a moving beyond the past through return to its mythological beginnings.

Yet if I have learned anything, it's that there are no safe spaces, there was no time of maternal nurturance that was ever free of conflict or pain. And to attempt to recreate that fantasy is to ask too much of one another and not enough of ourselves. The reason so many feminists are uncomfortable with mother-child incest is that it introduces too much ambiguity into a situation already too volatile to deal with and threatens precisely all those romantic notions about women's innate capacity for nurturance and care.

Living in the midst of so much denial has given me a passion for truth(s), and looking at the past, I feel far more than regret. If this experience suppressed my sexuality in some ways, it liberated it in others; if it complicated my relationship with women, it was also the primary source of my passion for them. If I say I was deserving of all that happened, it would be a lie; to dismiss her as perverse, equally so. I need an interpretation I can live with, a way to do justice to both our lives.

So how to disentangle the damaging from the good? How to free oneself from the worst of one's past without repudiating it? What alchemy to use, to transform so much bitterness and pain into blessing?

No answers, no simple solutions. What is healing for one may not be for another, what is helpful at one moment may not be the next. For myself, it has been a process of slowly diffusing the fear: fear that I am what she said I was—a whore—or that I am what others would call me, a victim. Fear that I am like her, fear of the connections, fear of difference. It has been a period of grieving the loss, giving myself the time and space to do so, and a process of continual reversal, voicing what was silenced, embracing what was disowned. There has been a growing acceptance of her complexity and my own, which does not justify our relationship but which places it back into the realm of human experience, human fallibility, and makes some kind of understanding possible. It has been a time of stripping away the sensationalism to get at the realities of sexuality and family, complex dynamics that politics alone do not explain. Finally, it is a process of realizing that the past can never fully be resolved but can become less controlling and remembering that, without such a struggle, self-acceptance or any full engagement with life remains impossible.

SEPTEMBER 1990

A Letter to My Son

by Sharon Cox

Although Sojourner *originally chose to run the following story as a feature, the characters are fictional.*

DEAR RICKY,

I just had to write this, a letter you are past reading and surely will not be able to acknowledge getting. Nevertheless, I just have to share these last few days with you. Please excuse me if I don't get all the facts straight; it's been a traumatic time for me.

Tuesday morning, the phone rang, and a woman identified herself, asked me what my name was and if I had a son named Richard Jenkins. I said I did (notice the use of past tense), I did. She told me that I should come to the emergency room of the hospital as soon as possible. I took my time getting dressed, taking careful breaths past the lump in my chest. I somehow knew there was no reason to rush. Ricky, I wasn't fearful or even surprised. Truthfully, I felt relieved that it was finally over.

When I got there a sympathetic nurse told me that you had been shot. She even accompanied me into the trauma room, where they had cleaned you up some, so I wouldn't be grossed out by the gore. They tried to sanitize your death so I could iden- tify your body. I am still grateful for these acts of kindness. The doctors and nurses told me they worked hard to save you. I believed them and thanked them sincerely. I felt neither the urge nor the need to further burden them with my tears or grief.

The police were there, of course, and they kept asking me questions about who your friends were and if I knew who some of your enemies were. I kept repeating like a demented robot, "What friends? What friends? What friends?" I told them you felt I was the enemy. Maybe I killed you, who am I to speak on enemies? I couldn't bring myself to mention your main man, Tyrone, and all the times I tried to tell you he was a scrub nasty and a slime, but you called him a friend. The police left—I could tell they were disgusted with me and felt I was not cooperating with their investigation. Nothing hurts anymore, Ricky. I am suddenly free of pain; their scorn can't touch me.

I left the hospital alone; I had called no one. I walked out into the overcast new day, having just identified an empty husk as my son. How ironic you were born almost exactly at this same time of day and the sky had looked the same way, eighteen years ago. Isn't that funny, Ricky?

When I got home I just sat for a while. I had to get up the nerve to enter your room. The room was as you had left it, all neat and clean. I guess I did teach you some- thing; I just never thought to teach you how to die and not leave a mess.

I got your one and only suit out, the one you wore to court that time (you looked so good that day, all respectable and clean-cut). Remember Ricky, remember how you looked me right in the eyes and told me that you didn't do the despicable act you were being accused of, my baby, asking me to believe your lies; how I looked back into your eyes and pretended to believe you. Well, Ricky, I knew the truth and deep down inside hoped they *would* send you away. My love locking me into a circle of pretense. So there I was, looking for that nice tie I bought you to go with that suit.

I should have called your grandmother right then, but I just didn't know how to say, "Mama, we've outlived your grandson." I did make myself go over to her house; I wanted to be there with her before your name and what happened hit the TV and the papers. She was/is devastated. I tried to soothe her, but she wasn't into hearing about choices, inevitabilities, or about "What goes around comes around." As you know, she sure loved her some Ricky.

You can only imagine what the papers were like the next day: they sifted through our lives with a fine-toothed comb. They said you came from a broken home—until now I'd never thought of us as broken. They said you were a gang member and your death was drug- and gang-related. You were known to the police and a suspect in various acts of violence and drug dealings.

Reporters came to the house to interview me. I guess they thought I would dissolve into tears, make a good picture for the evening news. They thought I'd say how you were a good boy and play the stupid, pitiful mother. Ricky, I couldn't do it; I couldn't even say you were all I had. I had to let the silence of the house make that obvious statement for me—no blaring rap music, no too-loud TV playing, no phone ringing; only the silence louder than thunder. I just sat there mute, staring at the reporters and camera crew, watching their lips move until they finally left. Left without me telling them what you told me: that the gang was your family, how the home-boys really understood you, and I was to stop interfering in your life. I didn't tell them you died for that family and how the honor of this escapes me. I only know that before we were broken, I would have done anything to keep you alive. I guess I don't understand that family even now. I just understand you are dead.

Ricky, I know you would have loved it. All your boys showed for the funeral dressed in their gang uniforms that they think make them look like individuals. Fades cut to the geometric T. Their young faces wet with tears. And sweating to get revenge, to put a cap into the dude that did this shit to you. Yeah, the Yo boys were revved up, they were all ready, if they didn't get to go. I overheard your main man, Tyrone, saying, "It was some cold shit that your mom didn't even cry or anything." After all, he and the other members of the crew were "bugging out," and there I sat just "fucking chillin'," he said. You would have been proud of me, Ricky; I didn't slap his face. I didn't ask him what he knew about tears shed or the quantity or quality of love. No! I just pretended not to hear them judging me. Those impostors, masquerading as your family—blind zombies moving toward their own genocide in lock step, holding on to their young penises, their staffs of life, as if they were security blankets. As if they weren't being stalked by the specter of death. As if they had a tomorrow.

Ricky, your girl was there; she brought your son with her. They looked good, dressed fresh. She screamed and hollered, tried to drag you out of the casket. She was truly into her act. Your son was wailing, too. I watched her from behind my wall of resentment, wondering if, just once, she made your lying with her contingent on your leaving the gang. I know that's unfair, but mothers don't have to be fair. I don't think she ever did. I can see your thick dope rope hanging from her neck. Its golden glitter a symbol of your enslavement and death, hanging from your woman's neck.

I held your son on my lap (I can't let myself think of him as my grandson), wondering if he would be lost into the void of his mother's loneliness and grief, wherever that might take her. I can't bring myself to comfort her, even though she is entrusted with the only living proof that a part of you lives. I'm too blinded by my belief in cycles. Sorry, Ricky, but I'm not sure I can reinvest my love in your son and woman, even if I have anything left to invest.

Ricky, they all watched and waited for me to bend or break down: they don't know I won't. They don't know how many sleepless nights I prayed you'd come home, how I'd wait breathless whenever news came over the air about a killing and the relief I'd feel when some other woman's son's name would be given. How guilty I'd feel not knowing if it was you who killed her child. The guilt almost as terrible as living with my fear. They don't know how many rehearsals I held in my mind, burying you daily, over and over. You've been dying/dead too long for me to pretend fresh grief. I'm out of tears, fresh out of feelings. My grieving has become routine, a voiceless, constant scream.

Since your burial, I sit by the window, looking down at the white statue of the Madonna standing in the ghetto churchyard. The look of resignation on her face is almost serene, as she looks down at the headless baby held in her arms.

DECEMBER 1991

If Not Now, When?
Obstacles to Outrage

by Ann Russo

The following is the second half of a two-part article that focuses on the ways in which women deny and repress their feelings about the pervasiveness of violence in their lives. In this half of the article, Russo focuses specifically on women as perpetrators of violence against other women.

The mind struggling toward integrity will fight for the significance of her own life and will not give up that significance for any reason. Rooted in the reality of her own experience—which includes all that has happened to her faced squarely and all that she has seen, heard, learned, and done—a woman who understands that integrity is the first necessity will find the courage not to defend herself from pain. The colonized mind will use ideology to defend itself from both pain and knowledge.
—Andrea Dworkin, *Letters from a War Zone* (Dutton, 1989)

The strength of grassroots feminist theory and activism, to me, is that women speak out about the painful and sad truths of our lives. What has been most compelling has not been the rhetoric or dogmatism or even the abstract theories, but the movement's rootedness in women's lives. But like many other political movements, the theories start to take precedence over the concrete daily realities of women in all of our diversity. We tend to ignore or deny contrary evidence or to minimize its significance. For instance, despite the central role racism and classism play in violence and the social responses to it, many feminists continue to articulate an analysis that focuses solely on sexism and misogyny. Similarly, in the case of women's violence against women, many feminists have resisted the evidence and held onto theories that assume violence is solely the result of male domination. I believe we have to challenge ourselves again to return to the truths of our lives, no matter how painful or disturbing, and to change our theories and perspectives when they don't fit with our realities. In this spirit, I have challenged myself to address women's violence against women—because of the truths of my own life and the lives of many women I know.

Women's Violence Against Women

The more women speak the truths of our lives, the more we, as feminists, must recognize that women are not only victims of violence—rape, battery, abuse (physical, sexual, emotional, verbal), and harassment—but also perpetrators. Women, like men, use violence in the service of power and control in lesbian relationships, in the physical and sexual abuse of children, and in other relationships characterized by power and hierarchy (doctor/patient, therapist/client, teacher/student, employer/employee). The recognition of women's violence against women and children challenges the attribution of all violence (and therefore power and control) to men and victimization (and therefore powerlessness) to women. Unfortunately, as with women's racism, classism, anti-Semitism, ableism, and homophobia, many feminists either deny or minimize women's use of violence. For the most part, feminists have not integrated this knowledge into our political theory and activism. This lessens our potential for personal and collective outrage because not all of our experiences are being given voice and recognition.

Many feminists place gender inequality and misogyny (usually defined as men's hatred of women, rather than both men and women's hatred of women) at the center of our analysis of, and work against, violence against women. This makes sense given the pervasiveness of men's violence against women and its connection to the larger context of gender inequality and societal misogyny. But the theory and practice are limited, because they don't incorporate race, class, age, social status, or other differentiating factors into the picture. Nor do they address the fact that we live in a society where violence is socially accepted as a method to gain or maintain power and control. It is fundamentally naive and false for us to assume that women are somehow immune from using aggressive emotional, verbal, physical, and sexual violence to gain or maintain power and control in personal and social relationships. And, besides, it is simply not true.

Mother's Abuse of Children

In some ways it feels strange to have to write these words as if they were somehow "controversial." For years I have lived with the knowledge that mothers abuse children—knowledge I gained through my experience with my own mother and the mothers of many of my friends, lovers, coworkers, teachers, students, acquaintances, and fellow activists. And yet, it has taken me years to begin to incorporate this knowledge into my politics. Some of the resistance to recognizing women's violence against their children stems from feminists having had to fight the automatic mother-blaming of psychoanalysis. This and earlier patriarchal theories put all the responsibility for family problems on mothers.

When I became a feminist, I developed an intellectual understanding of, and even an empathy for, abusive and violent mothers (of course, in the forefront of my mind and heart, though rarely publicly stated, was my own mother). I attributed mothers' violence to their victimization at the hands of their husbands and fathers and to their economic, social, legal, political, and, in relevant cases, racial, class, and ethnic oppression under the larger white-male-dominated system. I understood my mother's status and behavior in the family and society through this feminist lens. If anything, I tended to feel sorry for her, despite her verbal and physical violence. I even felt protective of her against the wrath of my other siblings, as well as the putdowns and condescension she faced in the family, first by my father, followed by us kids as we grew to be adults.

In the last few years (particularly since she died), I've had to shift my feminist lens and face the facts of her abusiveness. Despite my political analysis of male violence and my anger at my father and the line of men who came after him, deep down I was, and still am, angry at my mother. I'm angry at her both for having betrayed us kids in deferring to my father and his craziness and for her own violence against us. Facing my mother's abusiveness has been a necessary part of dealing with the various tragedies of my childhood, but it has been a struggle because it has meant breaking a strong tradition of family and ethnic loyalty. I've been able to do this in part because of the courageous voices of the women who have publicly spoken out about their mothers' physical, emotional, verbal, and sexual abuse. I am still working on what this means for me personally as well as politically. In many ways, my mother was a victim, especially of my father and her social surroundings, but I no longer feel the need to excuse her behavior, nor the need to always protect her by repressing my anger and sadness about her treatment of me and my sisters and brothers. Abuse is abuse, no matter who the perpetrator is, and that has to be the bottom line in our work.

The reality is that many adult women, feminist and nonfeminist, have years of repressed or not-so-repressed anger at how we were treated as girl children by our mothers. Many women (feminists included) have felt silenced by feminist politics because neither our experiences nor our anger are given voice or recognition. What does one do with the anger we may feel toward our mothers? What would our strategies for accountability look like? How do we deal with these issues in a society permeated with woman-hating? I don't have the answers, but these are the questions we must address if we want to change the conditions of our lives—individually and socially.

Giving voice and recognition to these realities will help us transform our anger in the service of social change. Minimizing and repressing our mixed feelings or our righteous anger toward our mothers does not change anything or anyone, least of all ourselves. Refusing to acknowledge this abuse in our analyses disempowers both children and adults abused as children. It perpetuates the silence and complicity that ultimately destroy children's possibilities for a hopeful future.

At the same time, our political strategies around mothers' abuse of children must have at their base an understanding of how the social and cultural system in the United States is inundated with sexism, racism, and classism. I grew up middle class and my family's "privacy" was protected from public, community, and state intervention. As a result, the abuse was denied, ignored, or downplayed. In contrast, a family headed by a single mother and dependent on Aid to Families with Dependent Children (AFDC) for survival is not afforded such privacy. In our work to develop social policy and programs addressing abuse, we must take into account that historically white, middle-class social service organizations have scrutinized and disempowered women of color and poor women. Thus, increasing policing and state intervention cannot be the only answers to these problems. Feminists need to challenge the middle-class biases and assumptions by which these organizations often operate, and women using these organizations' services must be the leaders in designing needed changes. In the meantime, since physical and sexual violence continue unabated across the system, we cannot participate in the social denial and ignorance of women's violence against children.

How can we begin to address some of these issues? First, we would all benefit from directly addressing women's violence within our own networks and communities. Discussions among ourselves about our own relationships to women when we were children and our own attitudes and behavior toward children are important. One concrete strategy used within some battered women's shelters is for mothers to work with each other on developing parenting skills and ways of coping that don't include violence. Women who are involved in children's lives could form similar groups to address the concrete ways that adults disempower kids through manipulation, control, and violence and to devise strategies for change.

Being a political feminist, or any kind of activist, does not preclude the use of power and control in relationships. As feminists, we have a tradition of saying that change begins at home and in our intimate relations—we could begin to follow through with this by examining our behavior in our own relationships, within and outside our families. We cannot naively assume feminists are necessarily better at raising children, especially knowing what we know about the use of power and control by women in our intimate relationships as well as in our own organizations.

Feminists can also directly and publicly address women's violence against children in our political actions and in our outreach and educational efforts. We can encourage women to tell our stories of abuse and violence by women, and we can incorporate this knowledge into our work. These changes would be helpful at many different levels: in empowering women who have been silenced and whose realities have been made invisible by feminist analyses that focus solely on men's violence; in making public a reality that children have to suffer in silence and secrecy; and in forcing us as feminists and activists to be accountable to survivors of violence in all of its cruel diversity.

Lesbian Battering

In recent years, more and more lesbians have come forward and spoken out about the realities of lesbian rape, battering, and other forms of sexual harassment and abuse. And yet battered and formerly battered lesbians continue to face the denial and passivity of the battered women's movement and the feminist and lesbian communities. Why? First of all, central to the denial of lesbian rape and battering are two myths common among feminists and many lesbians. One is that women do not use violence to establish power and control in the same ways that men do. The second is that lesbians have relationships based on equality and mutual respect because we aren't involved with men. Recent surveys described in Claire Ronzetti's *Violent Betrayal: Partner Abuse in Lesbian Relationships* (Sage Publications, 1992), show that battering occurs in one-third to one-half of lesbian intimate relationships (and the surveys did not set out to study lesbian battering). But these myths about equality and nonviolence die hard. Their resilience, in part, reflects how central they have been to our work against violence against women. By labeling the problem as male violence, many women (lesbian and heterosexual) thought that lesbians somehow had a better chance at freedom from coercion and control. Many of us believed we'd find safety and equality in women's organizations (or at least the potential for safety). From the beginning, women have found this to be untrue—many women have felt betrayed by the promise of equality—but the hopeful vision and its attendant political analysis of men's power and violence has held out against evidence to the contrary.

My own process of recognizing and accepting the existence of lesbian abuse and battering has been, again, one of rethinking my own life and the lives of other lesbians. It has been hard to analyze the lesbian abuse and violence I have experienced and known about. When I came out, I desperately wanted to believe that women would be different from the men I had known in my life. It didn't take long to figure out that being a lesbian didn't guarantee me freedom from power struggles, sexual manipulation and coercion, or sexual abuse and violence, in my relationships. But to label these experiences "abusive" threatened my hopes for a different life. Consequently, my political work focused mostly on male violence. While several of my relationships were characterized by the use and abuse of power and control over my mind and body, I believed these problems resulted from my own hang-ups. Self-blame, instilled in early childhood, stood strong in the face of the abuse directed at me. I excused this behavior by focusing on the perpetrators' victimization as children and adults (which they, too, were quick to emphasize). But, as in the case of my family, somewhere in my mind and heart, I knew things were not quite right.

In addition, I have always been aware of abuse in the various lesbian communities I have lived in over the years. In a number of instances, I empathized with, and tried personally to support, lesbians who I knew were being harassed, abused, and battered, but I still didn't directly deal with their experiences from a social and political perspective. I remember being at a Take Back the Night march and crying about a lesbian friend who was in a very abusive relationship. I knew that the speakers weren't telling the whole truth when they said that women didn't perpetrate violence, but I didn't have a language with which to speak. As yet, there was no context within the feminist movement through which to incorporate this knowledge into public discourse. It was just a few years ago that I first made a conscious effort to address lesbian battering, and I only did so because of the efforts of battered and formerly battered lesbians who had been working to address these issues for many years. I went to a session on lesbian battering at a regional women's studies conference in Boston. As I listened to the two lesbians talk about their experience—their descriptions of battering and coercion in its multitude of forms and degrees (physical, sexual, verbal, emotional)—I was thrown into a whirlwind of emotion and confusion about some of my own abusive relationships. The truth-telling of this session profoundly changed my life. The changes, personal and political, have not been easy. The biggest change was that it was no longer viable for me to remain in denial.

The more I listen to lesbians in and outside of my networks, the more I hear about rape, battery, and murder of lesbians by other lesbians. For me, this knowledge has broken apart a number of common myths and arguments that are used to cover up violence within the lesbian community. For example, a common response to lesbian battering is to say that it is really "mutual battery." But battering is not mutual by its very definition, and anyone who listens to a battered lesbian—her fears, her stories of verbal, emotional, physical, and sexual violence, her grief at the betrayal of love— would be hard pressed to say it's mutual anything. Even so, I recognize that on the surface it may be difficult to distinguish who is being battered because both may be saying that the other is a batterer. But this difficulty should not stop us from trying to figure out ways to determine who is the batterer and to support battered lesbians in finding safety, support, and validation. Battered and formerly battered lesbians who have been working on these issues, such as the Boston-based Network for Battered Lesbians, have developed ideas and concrete strategies on how to deal with these issues in the context of developing support groups for battered lesbians.

Another common response is to say that we should not interfere in private relationships. This is justified by the assumption that lesbians, unlike heterosexual partners, are social equals. But, as in heterosexual relationships, "privacy" is used to protect abusers from being held accountable for their violence. Similarly, lesbians fear that breaking through the "privacy" barrier, and making lesbian rape and battering a part of public discourse, plays into society's homophobia. This is a realistic fear, but not dealing with the issue allows the violence to continue unchallenged. And by denying or minimizing the violence in lesbian relationships, we are implicitly condoning the use of violence for power and control in intimate relationships, something we would never accept in a heterosexual context. But ultimately, and most importantly, not dealing with lesbian battering leaves battered lesbians alone and isolated, with no support and no community accountability.

We often excuse lesbian batterers with the same reasoning that we excused our mothers—by saying that the abusive lesbian had a difficult childhood or adulthood. This deflects attention away from the fact that she is battering another lesbian, whose chances for survival and for a better life are being actively diminished. Abuse is not mitigated by claims of love or sisterhood or by the abuser's own experience of abuse. Abusers must be held accountable for their behavior, and we cannot use past histories of abuse to rationalize why we cannot actively support battered lesbians.

In many cases, lesbians who are being battered by their lovers (or whomever) have few options in terms of resources and support. Many lesbians are in life or death situations just like heterosexual women, but homophobia further limits their choices. It is very difficult, if not impossible, in many situations, to rely on the police for protection, and only recently have lesbians been welcome in shelters (many shelters still do not accept out lesbians). Battered lesbians continue to face comments from other lesbians and feminists that their experiences don't constitute abuse, that their batterers have hard lives and so can't be expected to be perfect, and that the abuse isn't that bad. With little to no community accountability to battered lesbians, it is the battered lesbian who ends up moving out of town or out of state; it is the battered lesbian who is afraid to go out to a community forum, an event, or gay pride for fear of running into the woman who raped or abused her; it is the battered lesbian who suffers in silence and isolation.

In doing this kind of work, one of the difficulties is facing the fact that we know (or know of) lesbians who are abusive, who are batterers, who are rapists, and who use these strategies to maintain power and control in their relationships. It is hard to figure out what to do with this information, particularly in communities that deny lesbian battering or minimize its effects. There are lesbian batterers who are active participants, leaders, and workers in our communities, and even in the battered women's movement itself. This is appalling, but true. And despite attempts by battered lesbians within the battered women's movement to address this issue, there has not been a concerted effort to look into and remedy this situation. Why? Beth Leventhal from the Boston-area Network for Battered Lesbians suggests, and I agree, that "the issue is power and control. The battered women's movement is a great cover. I have heard stories from women who have been battered by women who work in the movement, whose batterers have said, 'You don't know what abuse is, I work with battered women every day. I'll tell you about abuse, let me show you these pictures, let me tell you this story. What I'm doing is nothing.' It's a perfect coverup. And who would ever believe it if the battered lesbian came forward and said this leader of the movement is a batterer?" Difficult to believe, but true nonetheless.

What does this mean for the battered women's movement? It means there is a lot of work to do. The bottom line in our work, I believe, is that the movement must become accountable to all battered women—lesbian and heterosexual alike. One way of addressing the issue is to make it a public policy that batterers are not welcome in our organizations or at our events. We must also design strategies to deal with situations that arise around battering. Other ways we can make the movement accountable (and some battered women's shelters are implementing these strategies) are to conduct workshops on homophobia and lesbian battering for staff and volunteers, to evaluate programming in terms of accessibility and safety for battered lesbians, and if accessible, to openly accept battered lesbians into shelters, support groups, and programs. We can also encourage battered lesbians to be involved at all levels of our organizations and to provide leadership in dealing with these issues.

What can we do in our lesbian networks and communities? We can break the silence around lesbian battering. We can make lesbian battering a public issue that we discuss and strategize around in our networks and communities—at parties, at political meetings, at support groups, at community events. A major reason for the perpetuation of "intimate" violence is silence and secrecy. Making lesbian battery an acknowledged reality that needs to be stopped should be on all of our agendas. In our groups, we need to start talking about how to handle cases when they arise among us. How can we actively support lesbians who are being battered? What are some strategies for dealing with abusive behavior that we see and/or experience? How can abusive behaviors be interrupted? How can we support each other in confronting abusers/batterers with an awareness that the control of this confrontation should always be up to the battered lesbian herself? Hard questions, but we can't ignore them any longer.

I urge the lesbians reading this article to make a commitment to working against lesbian battering and abuse within our own networks and communities. Our lesbian-feminist politics are hypocritical if we do not address this issue directly and passionately, not because lesbians are worse (or better) than heterosexual men, but because it's about truth-telling and about reclaiming our lives. It's the only way we can even begin to create areas in our lives that are free of violence and abuse.

Hopes for the Future: Moving toward Outrage

Right now in this city, state, country, and world, it is hard to have hope. Violence, already at epidemic proportions, is on the rise, yet violence against women is rarely on anyone's political agenda. In fact, if the Clarence Thomas-Anita Hill hearings are any indication, our legislators haven't even a clue about the pervasiveness of violence in women's lives.

Programs, shelters, crisis lines, and advocacy groups dependent on government funding are being cut in drastic proportions, leaving more and more women needing services and attention to suffer in silence and isolation. And the women working in the trenches of the epidemic are doing so under worse and worse conditions, with little recognition or support.

Despite all of this, I do have hope. I find hope in the fact that many women—individuals and groups—are continuing our work against violence against women. I am hopeful when I see creative programs grounded in experience and daily reality: for example, the Cambridge, Massachusetts, Dating Violence Intervention Project (a collaborative effort of Transition House, a battered women's shelter, and Emerge, a counseling program that works with men who batter), which includes a peer leader program and a theater project on rape and battering in the context of teen lives.

I've had many women say to me that they don't understand why I do this work: they say, it's so depressing, it's so negative, it's so hopeless. What they don't realize is that it is incredibly empowering and hopeful to do this work exactly because it is facing the grim realities of many of our lives. We are fighting back simply by saying our truths that were meant to be borne in silence and secrecy, as our own burden. In telling our truths we are saying violence is not right, it is not fair, and that no one deserves this kind of treatment. And in so doing, we are creating hopeful possibilities for other women who hear us. We hope they will join us, in all the different ways that women can do this work, in reclaiming our lives and collectively organizing against those individuals, groups, and institutions responsible for our collective pain and misery. Many years ago I came across a quote from Barbara Deming that inspired me to commit myself to the personal and collective struggle against violence against women, and so I leave it with you in the hopes of inspiration. She wrote, in *We Cannot Live Without Our Lives* (Grossman Publishers, 1974):

I suggest that if we are willing to confront our own most seemingly personal angers in their raw state and take upon ourselves the task of translating this raw anger into the disciplined anger of the search for change, we will find ourselves in a position to speak much more persuasively to comrades about the need to root out from all anger the spirit of murder.

Author's note: I would like to thank the following people whom I interviewed in part for this article: Delores Aguirre and Stephanie Poggi (Transition House), Carol Sousa (Dating Violence Intervention Project), Barbara Bullette (Community Programs against Sexual Assault), Beth Leventhal and Deb Borkovitz (Network for Battered Lesbians), and Pam Mitchell (local activist and writer on sexual abuse). Many thanks also to Barbara Schulman Lourdes Torres, and Nancy Anderson. I take responsibility for the views expressed in this essay.

MAY 1992

Confronting Domestic Violence in Asian Communities

by Cheng Imm Tan

Cheng Imm Tan is director of the Asian Women's Project and chair of the Asian Task Force Against Domestic Violence. She gave the following speech at a New England Women's Studies Association conference.

I would like to begin by telling you a little about myself and why I do what I do. My family practiced Buddhism, but I went to Catholic school. My goal at the time was to be a saint. Later I realized that sainthood was too difficult—one has to perform miracles and die first before you can get canonized. And so I gave up and settled for being a minister.

Today I am a Buddhist Unitarian Universalist minister. Not a parish minister, but a community minister. I chose to be a community minister—to work in and within the world—to do whatever I could to help build a world community that is rational, a community of people who care about the earth we live on and about each other. I wanted to build a world in which violence, oppression, and exploitation would be obsolete.

Why? Maybe because as a woman I have come to understand how oppression works, how it dehumanizes and disempowers. I understand what it means to be marginalized, deemed unimportant, unintelligent, or to live in fear because I am female. As an Asian immigrant woman, I understand what it is like to feel like an alien, to not quite fit in because of my color and different culture. But primarily I do what I do because I believe in the connectedness of our well-being as humans.

Ten years ago, I started working in the battered women's movement. I listened to the stories of white women, Black women, Hispanic women, Asian women, Native American women, old women, and young women. Each time, as I listened to a woman, in her pain and in her strength, I saw how our pain and our struggles were the same. I have listened to the stories of the young Filipina woman in Manila and the Thai woman in Pattaya, Thailand, who were forced into prostitution. Each time I look into the eyes of one of these women, I see a human face, a reflection of myself. Each time I listen to the stories of refugee and immigrant women who have survived violence and war, I cannot help but be touched by their courage and beauty. I cannot help but be moved.

My ministry is grounded in our intrinsic human connection. Ministry to me is first and foremost not a job, but a way of living, a way of seeing, a way of relating to the world around me.

And so I do what I do. I try to help make connections locally, nationally, internationally. I just returned from a five-week trip to Malaysia and Thailand, visiting refugee camps, doing workshops—making connections. My work in the Boston area is focused primarily on Asian women's empowerment and on addressing domestic violence in Asian communities. I do this because the voices of Asian women who are victims of violence have hardly been heard and attended to. Listen to the story of Sothi, a Cambodian woman who survived the disruption of war as well as violence in the home.

Sothi did not come from a rich or well-known family. But life was good. She was married to a man who treated her well, and they had a son together. They lived near her parents who had a shop in which her husband worked. Then war broke out. Her husband was drafted into the army, and she was moved to another province to work on a communal farm. Before too long, news came that her husband had been killed in action. Life got increasingly hard. There was not enough food to eat, her son became sick, and medical care was not readily available. Separated from her parents and unsure of what the future might bring, Sothi decided to escape to Thailand to get medical care for her son.

Sothi reached a refugee camp in Thailand. One day while she was getting her daily ration of twenty liters of water, she noticed a man staring at her. She had caught his fancy. He pursued her. He came to the house, brought her little gifts, and tried to get her attention. When she refused his advances, he became increasingly violent and threatened to blow the family up with a grenade if she refused to marry him. Feeling she had no alternative, Sothi married him and together they had three more children. But the violence did not stop.

In 1982, Sothi's family resettled in Boston, Massachusetts. Under the pressure of adjusting to a new environment, her husband's drinking and gambling increased and so did the threats and beatings. He would beat her because he could not find a job, because he lost in gambling, because he felt humiliated at the unemployment office. Isolated in a foreign city, Sothi bore the abuse in silence.

What could she do? With no money, where could she get help? Besides, where would she go? She did not know her way around that well, and she spoke almost no English. The extended family to whom she would have looked for support at home in Cambodia was not around. She was too ashamed to tell friends of the abuse and too afraid of her husband's wrath were he to find out that she had told. Several times, she thought of taking her own life to end the pain, but then who would care for her children? So she endured the pain and prayed that he would not kill her.

Sothi's story is not an unusual one. Her story of abuse is shared by the three to four million women abused annually in the United States and by millions more around the world.

Much has been done over the last fifteen years, since the beginning of the battered women's movement, to address domestic violence. Efforts have been made to educate the public in order to change social attitudes that maintain violence against women, to enact legal protection for women, and to create safe shelter and advocacy for battered women. The efforts of the battered women's movement have been crucial in making the world a safer space for all women.

Yet for most Asian women, these gains have not been accessible. The relative isolation of Asian communities, which has sometimes afforded them protection from outside insensitivities, has meant marginalization and invisibility. Violence in the home continues to be seen as a private family matter. Most Asian women are not aware of available resources or of their legal rights. Many also fear reporting abuse because of their fear and distrust of governments and authorities. Like other people of color, they also fear discrimination and unfair treatment.

Emphasis on keeping the family together makes it difficult for Asian women to leave violent husbands or relatives for emotional as well as financial reasons. For refugee and immigrant women, the choice to leave a spouse or partner is particularly difficult; it often means leaving the only really familiar person in this country. In addition, for an Asian woman, leaving her spouse can mean losing the respect of her community and her connection to the support systems within her culture. Turning to resources outside is seen as an act of betrayal. Consequently, most women do not seek outside help, for fear of humiliation and community ostracization.

Asian refugee and immigrant women are particularly isolated. Many do not speak or understand English, or, if they do, they are not confident yet in using the language. Shelters and hotlines do not have staff who speak Asian languages, and, as a result, few shelters successfully serve Asian women. Many battered Asian women have returned to their abusers because of the unfamiliarity of the shelter environment, language difficulties, and cultural differences, all of which make separation from the community unbearable.

To begin addressing this situation, I established the Asian Women's Project, a bilingual direct-service program and, together with other Asian women and allies, organized the Asian Task Force Against Domestic Violence. The task force seeks to have more wide-ranging structural impact on the institutions that affect Asian women's lives by educating the Asian community about domestic violence and the battered women's movement about issues particular to Asian women.

The Asian Women's Project provides bilingual advocacy and outreach services to Cambodian, Vietnamese, and Chinese women. Cambodian, Vietnamese, and Chinese staff are available to provide emotional support and to help with obtaining restraining orders, welfare services, medical care, divorces, shelter, and permanent housing. Because of the language barriers, advocacy has been very time-consuming. Not only do refugee and immigrant women need help with referrals, but staff have to personally accompany them to almost all appointments. Refugee and immigrant women do not know their way around and, as a result of the lack of bilingual staff in all sectors of the human services system, often need help with translation.

To let Asian women know about their rights under the law and about bilingual resources, the Asian Women's Project has developed a home-visit outreach program. This model has been very successful in creating trust within the community. It is personal and respects the community's cultural systems. Outreach and education around issues of domestic violence in Asian communities has also been done through English-as-a-second-language (ESL) classes, community organizations, and community health centers.

In addition, we have developed an empowerment program designed to provide women with necessary survival skills. This program includes support groups, an ESL tutoring program, a match-a-family program to help refugee and immigrant women learn the ropes of the U.S. system, and a food-catering program called Bamboo Shoots. Bamboo Shoots provides Asian women seeking to live independent, violence-free lives with an opportunity to earn some money as well as to learn new skills by running a small business that caters lunches and dinners for nonprofit organizations.

In the past few years, the Asian Task Force Against Domestic Violence has consistently highlighted domestic violence in Asian communities to bring attention to the seriousness of the issue. In Massachusetts, a woman is killed every 15 to 22 days by her boyfriend, husband, or partner. Last year about 10 percent of these women were Asian even though Asians are only 2.4 percent of the population. Nonetheless, Asian communities hold to the myth that domestic violence is not a problem. Thousands of years of male dominance mean that domestic violence is not taken seriously. In addition, because of other pressing survival challenges as well as the fear that acknowledging domestic violence would add fuel to the fire of racism against Asians, we have not attended to violence against women within our communities.

As a coalition of individuals and organizations, the task force has been able to organize effectively, heightening public awareness—in Asian as well as mainstream communities—of domestic violence in Asian homes. We have reached out to community leaders, human service workers, police, and court personnel through conferences, trainings, focused group discussions, poster campaigns, and vigils. But our most effective outreach tool has been personal interaction. Through personal contacts, we have been able to do the essential work of networking and working collaboratively with individuals and groups inside and outside Asian communities.

Breaking the silence around domestic violence and advocating for more adequate and culturally sensitive services in Asian communities have not been easy. Asian communities are growing rapidly. An influx of refugees and immigrants in Massachusetts has led to a 200 percent increase in the Asian population within the past decade. Of Asian Americans nationally, 60 percent are immigrants. These largely immigrant communities are subject to this nation's increasing antagonism toward people who are viewed as "foreigners." Asians are seen as outsiders who are taking American jobs and other resources; thus, it is difficult to get mainstream institutions to support our efforts to curb violence within our own communities.

Yet things are looking hopeful, because the struggle to eliminate domestic violence is first and foremost about women's empowerment. It is about women saying no to violence of any kind, whether physical, sexual, psychic, or economic. It is about each woman reclaiming self, reclaiming power, reclaiming her abilities to care about herself, the world around her, and all people. Although there is still much to be done, including the creation of an Asian women's shelter where women would feel safe and supported, we have made great strides.*

The prevalence of violence against women all over the world is only one example of how men have been hurt and can no longer lead alone, if we are to transform the world. If we want a world where sexism, racism, classism, heterosexism, ageism, environmental abuse, exploitation, and oppression no longer reign, women must take the lead. But the participation of all women is necessary in building a world characterized by right relationship to each other and to the earth, a world where we are not afraid to openly care for one another and to enjoy each other's humanness. The beauty of our differences needs to be understood, our connections reclaimed. The transformation of the world requires all of us to be empowered, rational leaders. To quote the Gospel according to Shug, from Alice Walker's *Temple of My Familiar* (Harcourt, Brace, Jovanovich, 1990):

Helped are those who love the entire cosmos rather than their own tiny country, city, or farm, for to them will be shown the unbroken web of life and the meaning of infinity.

*An Asian women's shelter opened in Boston in July 1994.

NOVEMBER 1992

FMS: *The Backlash Against Survivors*
by Cathy Wasserman

Incest is so much more than the violation of a body by another body.... [It] is a betrayal based on the lie "I love you but I'm going to do this to you anyway."... To admit that you're a survivor...is to admit that you weren't loved.... There are just no words to describe the agony of that. It's not something that one admits lightly.

Lynne Yamaguchi Fletcher's above description of how difficult it was to face the fact that she suffered incest makes it particularly disturbing that an organization has formed to disprove the memories that incest survivors struggle to come to terms with. In February 1992, the False Memory Syndrome Foundation (FMSF) was started by a group of parents who believe that they "have been falsely accused [of incest] as a result of their adult children discovering 'memories' in the course of therapy." Executive Director Pamela Freyd, whose husband has been accused of incest, finds many of these memories so preposterous that she says, "What makes the process of recovering repressed memories of incest any different from the process used [to recover memories of] past lives and extraterrestrials?" Thus, Freyd states that the organization's principal objective is "to inform the mental health community, the legal profession, the media, and the public that a serious health crisis exists [and] to advance the care for our children by pointing to the mistakes of the rush to solve the problem of child abuse...that are destroying our families."

Freyd says that this work has been very successful. With the main office in Philadelphia and satellite groups already starting in Michigan, Utah, Oklahoma, Florida, and Southern California, FMSF frequently conducts meetings to connect "falsely accused" families with each other (500 thus far), puts out a monthly newsletter, has a hotline, and sends out a 26-page survey to all callers in order to gather data on how and why "false memories" develop. Freyd states in their April newsletter, "News of our existence is spreading like a grass fire" and "several sympathetic producers of outstanding television programs" have contacted them. FMSF has also garnered the support of seventeen "scientific and professional advisors," fifteen of whom are current members of either the American Psychological Association or the American Psychiatric Association.

With the backing of these respected professionals, substantial grassroots support, and a driven, organized leadership, FMSF can neither be easily dismissed nor viewed as an isolated phenomenon—it is clearly part of the growing backlash against feminism. As women gain more and more access to political, economic, and social power in this country, they are increasingly being forced to justify their right to do so. When an incest survivor speaks up, she directly challenges these power structures, because most often the person she is accusing belongs to them; i.e., sexual abusers are usually men. If her word is taken over his, then it is being given more value than his. In effect, she gains power and he loses it. Thus, FMSF's attempt to disprove survivors' stories can be viewed, in part, as an effort to preserve the existing power structure.

Elaine Westerlund, a psychologist who has been working with incest survivors since 1980, sees FMSF in exactly this light. She describes it as "another piece of [this] backlash that's alarming." Wendy Stock, assistant professor of psychology at Texas A&M University, echoed her concern: "FMSF is on the warpath." But Stock is also quick to point out that you "don't get this kind of backlash unless [the recovery movement] pose[s] a real threat." Calling on therapists to speak out against FMSF, she thinks we need to educate people about just how prevalent incest is. Ellen Bass, coauthor with Laura Davis of *The Courage to Heal* (Harper & Row, 1988), concurs that neither survivors nor therapists should despair. On the contrary, she has called on survivors to become still more vocal to prevent FMSF from silencing them.

And many survivors *are* speaking out. Lynne Yamaguchi Fletcher recently contributed to an anthology of healing art, *She Who Was Lost Is Remembered: Healing from Incest through Creativity* (Seal Press, 1991). When told about the existence of FMSF, she was angered: "It's not a surprise—though the capacity of perpetrators to deny what they've done never fails to astonish me." She emphasizes that the perpetrators "have to be liars" in order to live with themselves. Fletcher describes abusers' denial of incest as "so across the board [because they] are so far out of touch with reality."

But FMSF insists that it is survivors and therapists, *not* their members, who are out of touch with reality. They claim that incest is much less common than people think. Dr. Ralph Underwager, a member of the FMSF board of directors, thinks that the media's frequent coverage of incest and the recovery movement for survivors has created the false impression that incest is rampant. In particular, he and FMSF target *The Courage to Heal*, a self-help book that is often seen as the "bible" of the recovery movement. FMSF claims the book is "a political statement that preaches anger and revenge." Arguing that the personal stories of abuse included in the book are far too subjective to be meaningful, Underwager says that *The Courage to Heal* "turns the basis of Western civilization [i.e., logic] on its ear" and could cause us "all [to wind up] living in caves [again]." Although Underwager does not deny that incest occurs (he is currently seeing four incest patients), he maintains that it is uncommon. To support his view, he cites the National Center for Child Abuse and Neglect's statistic that only 5 percent of the total population has suffered incest, and he holds that incest may only be correctly diagnosed when someone has a memory from the time the abuse first occurred.

Underwager neglects to mention the explanation that the National Center for Child Abuse and Neglect gives for these low numbers. The 1986 report, from which these figures were taken, states that "many experts believe that sex abuse is the most underreported form of child maltreatment because of the secrecy or 'conspiracy of silence' which so often characterizes these cases."

Many professionals agree and estimate that the real incidence of incest is much higher. Diana Russell, noted expert on incest and author of *The Secret Trauma: Incest in the Lives of Girls and Women* (Basic Books, 1986), puts the figure for girls under eighteen years at 16 percent. In *The Courage to Heal,* Bass and Davis explain that denial "is almost universal where incest is concerned." They write, "If the significant adults in your life told you that your experience didn't really happen or that it happened in ways radically different from the ways you perceived it, you probably became confused and distressed, unsure of what was real." They emphasize that "so far, no one we've talked to thought she might have been abused and then later discovered that she hadn't been."

But FMSF believes that it is misguided and uninformed therapists who create "false memories," needlessly placing the label of incest survivor on their patients. Pamela Freyd says, "We hear over and over again about successful, thoughtful, gentle, loving children who enter therapy and become obsessed, selfish, cruel." Asked why he thinks therapists supposedly create "false memories," Dr. Underwager says only that it gives them a feeling of power and "a sense of virtue."

John Kihlstrom, an FMSF advisor who does memory research, concurs with Underwager: "A large number of clients are being forced to fit a particular set of expectations" and this is "a most profoundly disturbing trend...caused by therapists who have a particular theoretical axe to grind." Although Kihlstrom places blame on therapists, he sees less malice on their part than does FMSF. He believes that therapists diagnose incest too frequently because they know of horrible, true cases, and they think that quickly identifying their patient's problem will speed her recovery.

Elizabeth Loftus is another FMSF advisor who does research on memory. She, too, thinks "therapists are partially responsible for what's going on here," often creating a history of incest in their patients in an attempt to heal them. Loftus firmly believes "therapists should be looking for disconfirming evidence [of incest] as much as affirming evidence." If they do not, she says, they will continue to "[drag] down a lot of innocent families."

Many therapists, however, strongly dispute the idea that they are rushing to diagnose incest and creating "false memories" in their patients. Elaine Westerlund emphasizes that recognition of incest almost always begins with the patient, *not* the therapist: survivors seek out therapy in the first place because they are having trouble dealing with memories of their abuse. "Ultimately, those people who have a feeling find something out."

Elizabeth Matz, the psychotherapist who brought FMSF to *Sojourner*'s attention, says, "The overwhelming phenomenon is that we don't want to know [about incest], don't want it to be true," not that women are eager to admit it happened. Matz emphasizes that some therapists underdiagnose incest. "I am concerned about a therapist influencing a client to believe or disbelieve that she suffered incest at that point in therapy when neither of them knows if it happened or not, and my experience is that denial of the possibility of incest seems more prevalent."

"The reality is that if survivors have trouble knowing what's real, it's because they've been lied to all their lives, and it's the perpetrators who have lied to them. Recovery is a process of uncovering the truth," Fletcher says. And she stresses that when therapists do say something inappropriate, survivors do not necessarily easily accept it. Fletcher says that when, on occasion, a therapist said something that did not seem to fit her experience, she was able to maintain her own sense of reality—to say "that's not my life." Like Dr. Kihlstrom, she points out that therapists who prematurely diagnose incest most likely do so because it is difficult for them to watch their clients suffer from the pain and isolation of not having identified their problem when they at least appear to exhibit the classic patterns of a survivor. Fletcher explains that in her own case it was "not until I presented myself clearly and unequivocally as a survivor and named my perpetrator that any of my therapists [did so].... I was very much the one to tell them what had happened to me and to discover for myself what fit my knowledge of my past." She emphasizes that, ultimately, the survivor alone is responsible for her own well-being: "the therapist can [only] point the way."

But FMSF rejects the idea that the patient plays an active role in realizing she has suffered incest. According to their literature, it is not possible for someone to suddenly begin having memories of an incident that occurred many years before. Dr. Underwager says that "body memories," which many survivors claim are their first recollection of abuse, is "a completely false and erroneous concept." Body memories refer to the physical reexperience of incest caused by some current sensory stimulus. Underwager argues that such delayed memories do not "conform to the laws of human behavior" and that there is "no scientific evidence to support the repression of events that occur repeatedly and across time."

But many professionals in the field of psychology adamantly attest to the strength of repression. Bass and Davis write, "The human mind has tremendous powers of repression" and thus "recovering occluded memories (those blocked from the surface) is not like remembering with the conscious mind; often the memories are vague and dreamlike, as if they're being seen from far away."

Although not a lot of research has been done on how survivors forget and then later remember their incest, in 1987 Elaine Westerlund conducted a study of 43 adult survivors to find out exactly that. In her study, "Memory Retrieval, Management and Validation," she found that dissociation as well as repression were key factors in "forgetting" abuse. She used the DSM-III-R *(Diagnostic and Statistical Manual of Mental Disorders,* third edition, revised) to define the terms. DSM-III-R states that "dissociation allows the child to manage the event(s) of victimization by separating intolerable feeling, physical sensation, and/or experience of self from the event(s)" and "repression allows the child to 'forget' or 'not know' the experience of victimization by blocking the event(s) from consciousness." Westerlund's study clearly stresses the impact of both of these defense mechanisms. Of the participants, 77 percent reported psychically "numbing" themselves, 70 percent reported physically "numbing" themselves, 51 percent reported "leaving their bodies," and 40 percent reported observing themselves from nearby at the time of the event (note: "numbing" refers to dissociating so that you have neither any physical sensations nor emotional perception of the incest and "leaving your body" refers to experiencing yourself as outside of your own body during the incest). In adulthood, 53 percent said that they still used dissociation as a way of coping and 85 percent said that they had repressed all memory of the incest. Of particular note, Westerlund found that "most women were in their late twenties or early thirties before memories began to surface and most experienced a lengthy period of active memory retrieval." Fletcher says that it was not until she was in her late twenties that she began recovering memories; after five years, she is still working to remember fully.

So why do people remember their abuse? Dr. Westerlund explains that while repression and dissociation *can* keep someone from knowing they have been abused for a long time, eventually "memories begin to surface in response to present life circumstances that are somehow reminiscent of the past." Wendy Stock elaborates on this idea, explaining that incest is often remembered when the survivor's body or psyche receives some insult that requires all of her energy, thus taking away from her ability to keep the memory in her unconscious. While dissociation, according to Stock, is used by children instinctually, "allowing [the child] to survive,...a memory [is] generally only held down as long as it needs to be"; i.e., as the child matures, her cognitive and physical means to protect herself from threatening situations improves and, thus, she dissociates less and remembers more.

"The whole process of how [memories] are revealed [forms] a characteristic pattern," according to Dr. Westerlund. She elaborates that these recollections may come in images, but just as often they are body memories, unaccompanied by anything visual. Elizabeth Matz underscores how important both these types of memories are, saying "when body memories come and it's all five senses along with a flash, a mental image—this is what you can trust."

Dr. Bessel Van Der Kolk, the director of the Trauma Center at Massachusetts Mental Health Center, has done extensive research on memory and posttraumatic stress disorder (PTSD). In "The Intrusive Past: The Flexibility of Memory and the Engraving of Trauma" *(American Imago,* Volume 48, Number 4, Winter 1991), he details why these memories can be trusted. Van Der Kolk says that "victims [of posttraumatic stress disorder] tend to dissociate emotionally with a sense of disbelief that the experience is really happening...[because some events] can be so overwhelming that they cannot be integrated into existing mental frameworks," leaving them to be organized as physical sensations (body memories), nightmares, and flashbacks. He says that there is concrete biological data to support this view: "severe or prolonged distress can suppress hippocampal functioning [the hippocampus is the region of the brain that puts memories into context], creating context-free, fearful associations that are hard to locate in space and time. This results in amnesia for the specifics of [trauma] but not the feelings associated with them."

Fletcher says that this amnesia has resulted in "large chunks of my life missing." But she states that "the body remembers what the mind can't deal with.... It never forgets." Thus, according to Fletcher, "Body memories are key to the whole process [and they] leave me without a doubt as to the fact that I was violated."

Not only does FMSF dispute the truth of these psychological processes, Dr. Underwager goes so far as to say that "people persuade themselves that something they fantasized about is true." Thus, FMSF views women as, on some level, desiring abuse.

But if, as FMSF suggests, we cannot trust women's bodies or minds, why should we trust that FMSF is not representing pedophiles? Stating, "We are a good-looking bunch of people: graying hair, well-dressed, healthy, smiling," Pam Freyd indicates her belief that something as superficial as a member's appearance should be proof of her or his good character. She adds that some members have taken lie detector tests in an effort to prove their innocence. Freyd explains, "While we all know in our minds their limitations, polygraph is the best tool that we have to tell the world the truth of our stories."

However, both Dr. Underwager and Dr. Kihlstrom believe that the "burden of proof" lies with the *accuser,* not the accused. Though Kihlstrom acknowledges that the courts are biased against women and thus "make mistakes," Underwager is not unwilling to tip the scales in favor of the accused. He serves as an "expert witness" for the defense in many child abuse cases, testifying that the defendant does not fit the psychological profile of an abuser. However, many experts dispute such a profile exists. Patricia Toth, director of the National Center for the Prosecution of Child Abuse, which serves as a clearinghouse of information for prosecutors, says that there is "no known and acknowledged psychological profile of a sex offender." She adds, "Dr. Underwager is very controversial; many people...question his motivation and expertise." It is believed he receives large sums of money for testifying.

It seems that FMSF wants people to give them the benefit of the doubt that they are unwilling to give to survivors. And perhaps more troubling, FMSF is more than willing to let women fall prey to the "mistakes" of our "justice system." Only too recently, we have seen just how big these "mistakes" can be, with the treatment of Anita Hill in front of the Senate Judiciary Committee. Nothing she said could convince the committee that she had been sexually harassed: no character witness' statement, no statistic on the high prevalence of harassment at the workplace and, most disturbing, no description of Thomas's lewd comments. The bottom line is that Hill's word was simply not given nearly the same weight as that of Thomas. Watching the senators' brutal interrogation of her, it appeared that *she* was the guilty party. Similarly, when a woman attempts to get some recompense by bringing her rapist to court, often it is she, *not he,* who has to provide proof of good character; i.e., that she did not ask for it by wearing "provocative" clothing or smiling "seductively."

This basic distrust is greatly magnified with incest because children's views, sadly, are given even less weight than those of women. The very nature of incest makes it difficult to "prove"; much like sexual harassment or rape, incest rarely occurs with any witnesses (or at least none who are willing to speak up). Furthermore, Fletcher points out, "There is no proof that is convincing enough to the perpetrator" and many of them could even pass a lie detector test because they have convinced themselves of their innocence. Thus, if we were to use the same standards of "proof" that FMSF uses, it would almost always be impossible to convict an abuser. Because this denies the reality of so many women's experiences, we should fight for different "standards" of evidence. Perhaps, if the existence of FMSF leads enough women to this conclusion, then we *can* learn something from them.

We can begin this fight by pressuring the courts to give more credence to the testimonies of character witnesses and, more importantly, survivors. Our judicial system should respect women. For example, the value that is currently placed on the flashbacks of Vietnam veterans should also be given to those of survivors, and questions about what a rape victim was wearing should be inadmissible in court. One way to apply this pressure is by encouraging women to continue to have faith in their convictions and to speak out about what they have endured. It has taken many women a long time to tell their stories at all, let alone about incest. Now that women are beginning to "speak," they should not stop because some people do not like what they are hearing. If women's stories are ugly, it does not mean that they are untrue. Unfortunately, it may take our judicial system a long time to recognize this truth. In the meantime, we should not lose hope. When women recount their stories of incest, whether to the larger world or just to themselves, they engage in a radical social act, disrupting the system by not allowing it to silence them.

JANUARY 1993

The Trouble with Verdicts
by Julia Mines

Our foreman asked us for the last time if we could live with our "not guilty" verdict—we had waffled for half a day. He looked over the lot of us, and in particular, at the juror who mumbled a final "I know he did it" under her breath. When we did not stop him, he signed the verdict and sealed it in its envelope. Then he pressed the buzzer for the court clerk who would summon the judge. Our work was clearly over. The mumbling juror began to cry.

Myself, I was too muddled to cry, and there were other women, too, who looked bewildered. Eight women and four men, we had been impaneled on an acquaintance rape trial. It was a case extraordinary for its ordinary details. No press attended. No expert witnesses took the stand.

Being asked to sit in judgment on a crime that targets slightly more than half the population could have been a feminist's fantasy come true. Could have been, but wasn't. Given a commitment to right causes, who would want to think, then, that having been handed this particular gift of civic duty (the chance to convict a man who raped) that the case could be more gray than black or white? That evidence could be lacking? That high concepts such as *good* and *evil* would never even play a part? Given this rightness of purpose, shouldn't the accused have been required to march his flaws right in? Wouldn't that have been more fair? Who would have thought, given the chance at forging justice, that the man on trial might be a baby-faced boy who put a condom on—who stopped when he was asked to?

It was prom night, Middlesex County, Massachusetts, but it could have been Anywhere, U.S.A. There was the requisite alcohol and a joint, several soirées and a limousine, a small coed slumber party at the home of a teenager whose single parent didn't seem to mind as long as it was all kept downstairs. In the living room, the lights low, the movie *Dirty Dancing* played on the VCR.

A young man and woman, acquaintances from school, were on the couch underneath a blanket, toe to toe. The young woman's boyfriend didn't like proms so was out with other friends that night. Our boy thought she could do better, perhaps with him.

As he tells it, he'd been fondling her leg for quite some time when she lifted her backside up so he could slip off her stretch pants and underwear. When she was naked from the waist down, he put a condom on and entered her.

In her version, she was fast asleep ("dead asleep," was the prosecutor's phrasing) but woke up when she felt pressure on her chest. There he was, on top of and inside her. Her mother testifies that she's slept through fire alarms before, in fact requires, in the morning, one-half-hour prodding just to get her out of bed.

Both sides agree he had only just entered her, that she shoved him and said "get off," that the accused did so after being shoved a second time. Both agree she tried to call her boyfriend but that the young man pushed the phone down, asking her not to tell him what had happened. Both agree she tried again, this time unhampered, but no one answered. The defense asked why she didn't call her parents next. "I'm not gonna call my mother, I called my boyfriend. He's my protector." (In the jury box, some of us were visibly squirming as she applied an old formula to a new era.) Both agree, on the smaller sofa, the young man's brother was fast asleep.

She went upstairs to tell her friend who lived there, cried for hours, and stayed there until morning, when the friend called the young woman's mother to tell her what had happened. By this time both couches were empty, but only recently; the young man had slept the remainder of the night there. The friend took the woman home, where her boyfriend now waited with her mother. Together they drove down to police headquarters.

Sitting on a rape trial requires, among strangers, an instant intimacy. In tones usually reserved for doctor's visits, we talked about sex and body parts and human sexual motivation. This wasn't easy talk. A dignified, older gentleman was first to call a "guilty" verdict; he wouldn't say why, but he wouldn't sway either. What was it that he knew but wouldn't say? Was it cultural? That in his day, sex wasn't talked about, and especially not in mixed company? To my surprise, talking sex with this group at first made me a little squeamish. Did I ascribe to the "mixed company" dictum as well? Was it only that these others were strangers? And then I wondered, have we grown so numb in a pornocentric culture that public, honest discussion of sex is so unfamiliar as to be embarrassing?

Despite our awkwardnesses, we argued. *Was she sleeping?* We used our own lives as reference points, pulled from what we knew—our quiet biases—and by default learned about each other's takes on sexuality. The man reading *The Leadership Style of Attila the Hun* in downtime raised the boys-will-be-boys-they-just-can't-help-it hormone theory. This theory quickly got a counterpunch (and died) on grounds that just because one feels one's hormones raging, one is not exempt from being in control of them. And almost by accident, as if to weight a point of view, there were the individual spillings of personal detail: the woman who in college had had sex in her dorm room while her sleeping roommate tossed and turned but never woke; the man who would "never be allowed" to simply slip his wife's clothing off while she was sleeping...

The men among us shared what they knew on the subject of the budding sexuality of boys. We women listened, fascinated (we'd never heard this before). "I hate to say it," one man said. "You're at the movies and you put your arm around her. Then you see how far you can get. You try for a little and if she doesn't stop you...you always try for a little more." Silence equals consent. The men were all nodding. "But what if it just means she doesn't know she can say no?" "Hate to say it..." another man joined in. And another, "Hate to say..."

But if in those earlier days the goal was to cop a feel, how much more dangerous the same etiquette becomes when paired with today's heightened expectations of sexuality. In our MTV culture, the prosecutor's closing argument came as something of a revelation. He reminded us of the possible slow steps to sexual intimacy, led us through kissing, then fondling, then last stop, intercourse, pointing out that our teen had missed preliminary steps along the way. But did this foreshortened sense of foreplay constitute rape or was it just the stuff of careless, bad first sex? In the defense attorney's closing statement, he hoped we'd think the latter. We argued. *Was she sleeping?*

In deliberation you must push your point of view—be an advocate—or lose it. But just what was the correct point of view? We had begun by presuming his guilt not his innocence (an idea initially more forcefully pushed by the men among us). So why were we unable to sustain the verdict? Had the more passionate among us failed?

We buzzed the clerk so that we might ask the judge to again read us the definition of rape and "reasonable doubt," a turning point. After that, it seems we considered everything but evidence—of which there was precious little: the friend upstairs and the sleeping brother; an agreeably nice detective who retold the story as he saw it; the testimony of the victim's mother; and exhibits A, B, C, and D—a pair of panties and the stretch pants, a pair of socks and a pubic hair. We considered whether our teen would go to prison (though we were expressly told his fate was not to determine our verdict). So unsure of what we had before us, we even looked, at a low point, to TV for inspiration (where were *our* dozens of witnesses as on television?). And then it came to words. Her words and his words. *Was she sleeping?*

Perhaps insidiously, it also came to what seemed to be the accused's "good behavior"—the condom he wore and the seeming lack of violence. Looking back, I see that had there been more violence, the verdict could have gone another way, making it seem as if only through greater drama or physical pain could a guilty verdict have been justified. But I see now what I did not then: that acquaintance rape—particularly in our case—is not like murder, where a dead body is proof of damage done. We found the accused "not guilty" because we chose to err on the side of our "reasonable" doubt. But when the damage is not so visible, when a case boils down to word against word, when would there not be doubt? As the prosecutor later pointed out to me, rapes usually aren't done before an audience; therefore, it often comes to words. If the goal really is justice, how then can these cases be tried using the same rules of evidence that apply to other crimes?

As for the condom, what if the accused was merely proof that education breeds success? Would it be paranoid to think that lurking in the coming century are rapists who will want to spare themselves disease?

Although we found the accused "not guilty," we did not find him "innocent." It's an important distinction, but one for which the law does not allow. When afterward the judge came into our jury chamber to congratulate us on our verdict, it occurred to me that I had learned less about justice than perhaps about group dynamics and the limits of the law. When I asked the judge about some other kind of verdict for a case with shades of gray, he talked about Scotch law's third option, "no verdict." There were those of us who wanted to see him punished but not sent to jail. What about educational programs as punishment, I asked, not unlike those for drunken drivers? Clearly, my line of questioning incensed the fellow who had been reading about leadership styles. He suggested I might move to another country (presumably one more communist in nature. But hadn't he heard? That was now all passé...).

I left the courthouse feeling strangely that I'd witnessed some page out of Darwin. Clearly, there is evolution to be had. I felt nothing if not Neanderthal, and my fellow jurors looked no better to me. If we found the accused "not innocent," we found others in this story not innocent, too. The parents. The young woman herself. The towns they come from. We found ourselves not innocent, too. We could not find the behavior of the participants quite so different from our own. We found we could not make our teen "an example" for our cultural confusion around sexuality.

I wonder what our teens will take from this experience. What interpretations will they have? Sadly, the verdict we chose could not bring with it a guarantee of thoughtful self-reflection on the acquitted's part. Sadly, perhaps no verdict ever could.

I lost sleep as a juror, and when it was over, I felt little comfort, little safety at night again in that bed. Had we twelve conspired to set free, in embryonic form, a rapist? Our verdict was more than just one lost for the prosecuting attorney. It was a loss for our young woman—was she wrong to assume her safety on the couch?—and for the rest of us, a loss symbolic of women's losses everywhere. Of our bodies lost to violent crime and to abuse, of our voices lost to the pain and humiliation that followed.

What will it take to end this crime that targets our gender? Perhaps other questions must first be answered. How, for example, will we enable men and women to court similar social and sexual expectations? Or rally around a common definition of what constitutes violation? Or piece out from sex the list of attributes that get confused with it—love, power, pain, the acting out of previous victimization? How might we instill in our culture a respect for (if not an interest in) a sexual intimacy based on mutual affection, on an equality of desire, evolve a more conscious sexuality?

And can we feel free to challenge the cultural messages that promote the wedding of violence and sexuality, cozy up to that discussion without being written off as puritan or prudish (or *Republican*)—or worse, a First Amendment enemy? The trouble with verdicts is that we must live with them and then with ourselves and the complex questions verdicts raise. The answers to these questions, however, cannot fall only to jurors in times of deliberation. Until our society comes to a thoughtful consensus on how to end sexual violence in all its shades of gray, violence that undermines women's safety and self-esteem and human dignity, then jurors will need some greater courage for the painstaking work ahead.

DECEMBER 1993

Sexual Harassment in the School Yard
by Lynn Goods

Splashed all over the front pages of major newspapers last summer were the results of a study, the first-ever conducted nationwide, on the issue of sexual harassment in U.S. public schools. The researchers of this study, which was conducted by the American Association of University Women's (AAUW) Educational Foundation, found that 4 out of 5 of the 1,632 students surveyed in grades 8 through 11 (both boys and girls) reported having been subjected to some form of sexual harassment in school. Equally disturbing was the finding that over half of the respondents said that they knew of charges of harassment that had gone uninvestigated by their school. The study showed that while many schools had regulations regarding sexual harassment, these policies were rendered moot due to lax or nonexistent enforcement. This study corroborates the findings of an earlier survey conducted by *Seventeen* magazine in which 39 percent of respondents said they experienced some form of harassment every day.

Defined as "unwelcome and unwanted sexual behavior that interferes with your life," the various types of harassment documented were divided evenly between physical and nonphysical forms. Overall, fourteen types of harassment were documented, running the gamut from leering to rape. Such behavior included sexual comments, jokes, gestures, or looks; touching and grabbing; brushing up against someone; spreading rumors; pulling off clothes; cornering or blocking someone in a sexual way; and forced kisses. Over two-thirds of all respondents reported that they had been the object of comments and jokes. At the other extreme, 11 percent reported having been forced to do something sexual other than kissing.

Consistent throughout the study was the finding that in nearly all categories of harassment, girls were harassed much more frequently than boys. For example, 65 percent of girls vs. 42 percent of boys experienced pinching and grabbing. Similarly, 57 percent of girls reported having been brushed up against, while this experience was reported by 36 percent of the boys. Moreover, twice as many girls as boys reported having been blocked or cornered in a sexual way and 13 percent of girls (vs. 9 percent of boys) said they had been forced to do something sexual other than kissing. Out of the fourteen types of harassment documented, only two were more frequently perpetrated on boys than girls: being called gay and being shown or given unwanted sexual notes or pictures.

This gender gap was also reflected in the differing responses of boys and girls to harassment. Overall boys were less likely to be negatively affected. The idea that harassment was just a part of life, "no big deal," was held by 41 percent of boys who admitted to engaging in such behavior as opposed to 31 percent of girls who said they had harassed others. As one fourteen-year-old boy put it, "I don't care. People do this stuff every day. No one feels insulted by it. That's stupid. We just play around. I think sexual harassment is normal." Contrast this statement with the thoughts of one girl who stated that being subject to harassment "made me feel low. Thought that I was dirt. I just wanted to die."

According to the study, 64 percent of girls who said they had been harassed felt embarrassed, while only 36 percent of boys reported feeling that way; nearly three times as many girls as boys described a loss of self-confidence as a result of harassment, and 39 percent of girls vs. 8 percent of boys reported that their experiences had left them feeling afraid. The impact of harassment on educational performance was also more pronounced for girls than boys. Of the 81 percent of students who reported having been the object of harassing behavior, girls were more likely to say that harassment had made them less likely to speak in class and more likely to have difficulty studying and paying attention. This resulted in cutting classes more often and making lower grades.

The results of this study demonstrate how the experience and effects of harassment differ according to gender. This difference is analogous to that which people of color make between racism, which is discrimination exercised by a dominant ethnic group against a less powerful group, and prejudice, which can be practiced by anybody regardless of social or economic status. The former is regarded as more pernicious because it's institutionally sanctioned and perpetuated. Similarly, while discrimination against women is ingrained in our culture and in our institutions, the same cannot be said for discrimination against men. Girls are more profoundly affected by harassment than boys, precisely because men have more power in this society than women. The two types of harassment cannot be equated, although both are equally reprehensible.

Such distinctions went largely ignored in media accounts of the study. Press coverage basically fell into the "oh-isn't-this-terrible-we-must-do-more-to-educate-our-youth" camp, followed by the expected calls for the establishment and enforcement of strict regulations regarding appropriate and inappropriate behavior. At the same time, however, these reports called into question the study's findings by chalking up much of the behavior defined by the researchers as sexual harassment to routine adolescent hijinks. The *Wall Street Journal*, for example, stated that the problem was a general coarsening of society manifesting itself in the behavior of children and adolescents. The author went on to state that "common sense tells us that it is preposterous to label most behavior by children, however inappropriate, as sexual harassment. The menacing title of the AAUW report, 'Hostile Hallways,' sounds like the name of the latest slasher movie in which, no doubt, Freddie would stalk the corridors of P.S. 22 looking for a bra strap to snap." The problem, the author concluded, was not one of sexual harassment but of moral laxity. Even those whose opinions were more in accord with the study's findings took its conclusions lightly. One educator was quoted in the *New York Times* as saying that while harassment was indeed a problem, a distinction had to be made between behavior that was merely insensitive and disrespectful to that which was truly harmful and dangerous.

Much of the confusion over the term "sexual harassment" and its credibility as an issue stems from a lack of agreed-upon standards in a society undergoing great social and cultural change. Although popular convention has it that these changes are an inevitable result of this country's increasing pluralism, diversity is only one side of the coin. The United States has always been a pluralistic society. What's really happening is that as historically oppressed groups challenge accepted norms and attempt to rewrite the rules of behavior more in their favor, they are encountering a lot of resistance.

Not surprisingly, then, we find that the question of what constitutes sexual harassment is undergoing fierce discussion. How much of what is now defined as harassment encompasses actions that used to be called flirting or sexual banter? How much of this behavior is the inevitable by-product of children and adolescents learning both social skills and the boundaries of acceptable and unacceptable behavior? Like men in the workplace who claim that they no longer know how to relate to their female colleagues around the water cooler, school-age boys are now saying they don't know how to act either and stress that the matter becomes particularly confusing when girls respond to their suggestive comments and gestures by smiling or laughing (although a girl's smile can just as likely be attributed to her fear of being reproached by peers if she displays disapproval as to her enjoyment of the attention). Finally, how much of this behavior is actually an expression of adolescent male rage, as many experts contend? Clearly, this is not territory that is easily navigated.

Celebrated neo-/anti-feminist Kate Roiphe (depending on which side you're on) takes this discussion in another direction with her views on sexual harassment, which she states, arises from miscommunication between men and women (*The Morning After*, Little Brown, 1993). In the old days before multiculturalism, "students came from the same social milieu with the same social rules, and it was assumed that everyone knew more or less how they were expected to behave with everyone else. With the introduction of Black kids, Asian kids, Jewish kids from the wrong side of the tracks of nearly every railroad in the country, there was an accompanying anxiety of how people were to behave. When ivory tower meets melting pot, it causes some confusion, some tension, some need for readjustment."

Although her take on the miscommunication argument speaks specifically to campus relations, Roiphe's reasoning is similar to conservative thought on sexual harassment in general in that it largely dismisses harassment as a myth and absolves the perpetrator from responsibility for his or her actions. When Roiphe states that miscommunication arises when "the southern heiress goes out with the plumber's son from the Bronx," she displays an appalling paternalism cum cultural relativism that says, in effect, that people of different classes/ethnicities cannot be held to the same standards of conduct as affluent white protestants, and that the hysterical, privileged white women crying date rape and harassment just don't understand the mores of the poor brown hordes. Yet, the fact is, women of all races and classes are speaking out against harassment within their own cultures and within the culture at large. I've witnessed these struggles both in blue-collar jobs and within the walls of academia.

As various groups assume more power in this society, the folks who have historically been running everyone can no longer make all the rules. Most, but not all.

Miscommunication or not, the question becomes: Whose rules do we follow? Do young girls get to help frame the debate? Roiphe's logic fits in neatly with the anti-p.c. brigades who use the excesses of those who are attempting to create a more equitable society (is "vertically challenged" going too far?) as an excuse for discrediting the whole issue of sexual harassment. Largely composed of conservatives who are pissed off that their heretofore unchecked privilege of being able to say and do whatever they want to whomever they want is being called into question, this group clings to the concept of boys-will-be-boys.

The sexual harassment discussion sheds light on how we as a people take for granted the routine objectification of women. That there is even controversy over whether or not unwanted comments directed at young girls' body parts constitutes harassment is testimony to how ingrained this objectification is. The question of school-age harassment has been approached as if it existed in a societal vacuum. What are the links, for example, between harassment at such a young age and the results of an earlier study that showed how girls of twelve to fourteen undergo a remarkable decrease in self-esteem compared to boys of the same age? The educational impact of harassment on girls detailed earlier, along with their inclination to feel more embarrassed, self-conscious, and ashamed as a result of such unwanted attention undoubtedly contributes to this loss of self-esteem. We might also ask: Is there a correlation between the high level of harassment in schools and the portrayal of women as victims and sex objects in the media, which has become in recent years ever more sexually graphic and violent? What is the relationship between harassment and the very real violence to which women are increasingly subjected? Unfortunately, no connection to these issues was made in the barrage of media accounts that accompanied the release of the AAUW study.

Even more disturbing is the extent to which young girls themselves internalize our society's tacit condoning of harassing behavior. The four girls I recently spoke with—Naimah, Jamila, Angela, and Ramona, all juniors and seniors at Brooklyn College Academy in Brooklyn, New York—spoke with matter-of-fact acceptance about the harassment they are often subjected to, and they shared with me their tactics for dealing with unwanted comments and gestures. Depending on the situation, their strategies ranged from saying hello while quickly walking by to giving a guy a fake phone number. Why not merely walk on by? As any female growing up in New York knows, to ignore such a comment is to invite verbal abuse, at the very least. As Naimah stated, "Sometimes I talk to them just so not to get cussed out." Others have had cigarettes and bottles thrown at them by the boys they ignored. Who usually harasses them? Old men, young boys, and every type in between. In light of these violent realities, I wonder how these young women would respond to this following bit of wisdom from Ms. Roiphe: "Someone I knew in college had an admirable flair for putting offenders in their place. Once, when she was playing pinball in Tommy's Lunch, the coffee shop across from Adams House, a teenage boy came up to her and grabbed her breast. She calmly went to the counter and ordered a glass of milk and then walked over and poured it over his head.... Most of us probably have less creative ways of handling 'sexual harassment,' but we should at least be able to handle petty instances like ogling, leering, and sexual innuendo on the personal level."

Clearly, countering the serious emotional, social, and educational effects of harassment on girls will require much more than facile pronouncements about individual deportment. Until school-age harassment is recognized as the serious form of institutionalized gender discrimination that it is—and one that basically trains girls to assume their eventual second-class status as women—girls will continue to be ogled, pinched, fondled, and assaulted within the confines of what is supposed to be a protective and nurturing learning environment.

© 1983 Marilyn Humphries

© 1995 Ellen Shub

CHAPTER EIGHT

Building an Inclusive Movement

Coalition can kill people; however, it is not by nature fatal. You do not have to die because you are committed to coalition.
    —Bernice Johnson Reagon,
      "Coalition Politics: Turning the Century"*

No doubt, the greatest challenge to second-wave feminism over the last twenty years has been building an inclusive movement. The mainstream and radical feminist movements that emerged during the mid to late '60s were primarily white, middle-class movements, which failed to incorporate the diverse experience of women across race, class, sexual orientation, age, and ability. As we saw in Chapter 1, by the mid '70s, these differences were already beginning to reshape feminist theory and activism, though it was not until the '80s that these differences began to have a significant impact on *Sojourner* itself.

In November 1979, Alison Platt, *Sojourner*'s editor at the time, wrote, "Heterosexual women aren't talking to lesbians (and vice versa), white women aren't talking to women of color (and vice versa), middle-class women aren't talking to working-class women (and vice versa), and worst of all, feminist women aren't talking to nonfeminist women." Though Platt felt that the movement had become fragmented, in hindsight, we can see that this dissension marked the beginning of real challenges for a movement that had assumed that "women" shared some kind of universal experience of oppression. As Andrea Hairston wrote in response to Platt, "Clearly we have to go beyond our own experiences (which does not mean abandon them) and reach across barriers, get up off the convenient, the easy methods, and find ways to bring all women to mutual understanding and solidarity. We need not proceed...without the inclusion of more than white women" (*Sojourner,* December 1979).

The struggle to do so has not been easy. As Bernice Johnson Reagon says, "Coalition *can* kill you." That is because coalition requires self-examination. It involves seeing ourselves as both the oppressor and the oppressed; questioning our privilege and the power inherent in that privilege; giving up power and allowing someone else to take leadership, while, at the same time, using our power to support each other's struggles. If we have not taken leadership in the past, it involves finding a voice, taking power, and refusing to allow others to define our agenda. Sometimes coalitions are built on solid "common ground"; sometimes they are more tenuous, an offer of support across differences, which may yield common ground in the future. The articles in this chapter look at feminist coalition efforts from a number of perspectives: attempts to create a more inclusive feminist agenda, international solidarity and the movement toward global feminism, and efforts to move beyond traditional feminist boundaries to create a broader progressive movement.

The feminist movement, by its very nature, is a coalition effort. As we discovered in the '80s, there is not one movement, but *many* movements. Some of these movements are constructed around issues—reproductive rights, violence against women, health—and some around identities— women of color, low-income women, fat women, old women, lesbian women. All of these movements overlap and intersect, just as the issues and identities overlap and intersect within our lives. Moreover, feminist movements intersect with a large array of other progressive movements—for example, movements for national liberation, civil rights movements, gay liberation movements, labor movements, and antimilitarist movements. The real challenge of the coming century is to build coalitions across all of these movements, in order to create a political force that can challenge right-wing attempts to limit human rights and civil liberties both in the United States and around the world.

Creating an inclusive agenda involves much more than simply "welcoming" the less privileged into the ranks of the privileged. When women of color challenge the racism of white women, they are not asking to be incorporated into an existing movement; they want that movement to change, to build an agenda that meets the needs of women who face constant deprivation and humiliation in a white supremacist society. As Bonnie Thorton Dill said at a 1984 National Women's Studies Association plenary (*Sojourner,* September 1984), the question is not "Is feminism the agenda of women of color?", but rather, "Does feminism, as it's currently defined, fully incorporate the issues, ideas, and concerns of women of color?" The answer, for many women of color, has been a resounding no. The agenda needs to change. As is evident from the preceding chapters, the demand for reproductive rights needs to include public funding for abortions, an end to sterilization abuse, access to prenatal care, addiction recovery programs for poor, pregnant women, and community midwifery services, not just the "right to choose." The health care agenda needs to include free medical care and culturally sensitive, accessible community practitioners, not just self-help groups for women interested in examining their own cervixes. The economic agenda needs to include the right to adequate public assistance, free day care and education and training, and passionate support for affirmative action for people of color as well as white women, not just an end to sex discrimination in the workplace.

The same has been true for lesbians, for Jewish women, working-class and poor women, old women, disabled women, and fat women. Building an inclusive movement has meant building an inclusive agenda. Disabled women want access to the women's movement—through sign-language interpreters, wheelchair accessibility, audiotape and Braille—but they also want an agenda that recognizes able-bodiedism as a temporary condition; that ensures reproductive freedom for disabled women as well as for able-bodied women who do not want to abort disabled fetuses; that guarantees disabled women the right to productive and fulfilling work. Fat women want to be accepted and appreciated just as thin women are, but they also need a feminist movement that draws connections among an epidemic of eating disorders in young women, cultural disdain for women who are fat, and the multibillion dollar diet and cosmetic industries that keep women powerless by keeping them obsessed with body size and appearance (see Judith Stein, "Fat Liberation: No Losers Here," 1981).

An inclusive movement, by attending to the needs of the least privileged, serves the needs of all women. By this, we do not mean that a social movement will provide services for "the poor and the elderly," but that its role is to analyze the forces of oppression as they affect those with the least power and develop its agenda accordingly. As Barbara Macdonald notes in her article, "An Open Letter to the Women's Movement" (1983), a lesbian movement inclusive of old lesbians is not one that creates retirement homes. An inclusive movement would see that the needs of old lesbians intersect with the needs of many other lesbians: lesbians of all ages are poor, though old lesbians are the poorest; lesbians of all ages may be depressed or isolated; lesbians of all ages may be terminally ill. A movement that empowers lesbians must address these issues across age, race, class, and other differences. Or as Angela Davis exhorts in "Lifting as We Climb" (1987), "If we are serious about plotting strategies for the empowerment of all women, we must identify with and associate ourselves with those of our sisters who are the most oppressed. And when they lift themselves, when they climb, we are all lifted in an upward direction."

Problems arise when we continue climbing, without lifting. If feminists insist that we can create a "diverse" movement without each of us examining both the ways in which we are privileged and the ways in which we are oppressed, without the more privileged among us relinquishing some of our power and sharing our resources so that women who have been marginalized can develop leadership skills and organizational strength, we will not lift as we climb. This was essentially the criticism leveled at the feminist movement during a 1990 roundtable organized by *Sojourner* (see "Whatever Happened to Women's Liberation?"). All of the participants expressed sheer dismay at the continued racism of the "white women's movement." African-American activist Barbara Neely insisted that the mainstream women's movement had little to do with her work: "I have considered myself, certainly over the last fifteen years, as trying to work for women's liberation. I do not see the mainstream women's movement as a place where women's liberation is the goal. It appears that the goal is to have equality with white men, and that's just not the same thing."

Though the participants in the roundtable discussion—Barbara Neely, Milagros Padilla, Connie Chan, and Ruthie Poole—looked to the future to a time when white, middle-class women would "begin to understand that...what is good for women of color and for poor women [is good for all women]," in 1990, they saw greater possibilities in coalition building than in a "multicultural" women's movement. As Padilla remarked, "I think that white women and women of color could work together in coalitions or on some common goal. But as a woman of color, I would not be urging women of color to join white women's organizations. I want us to be in our own organizations." In fact, Padilla passionately expressed her distaste for the language of muticulturalism that had emerged during the '80s:

> *But this new terminology of "culturally relevant" or "multicultural-*
> *ism" that is being used—I hate those terms, because they obliterate what*
> *the problem is all about. It's about racism; it's about power. Culturally*
> *relevant or culturally sensitive—I truly am not concerned about that. I*
> *want you to be willing to give up your power; that's it. I could care less if*
> *you know anything about my culture. Just give me the power to be who I*
> *am, and give up your power to oppress me. That's all I want.*

This is a theme that *Sojourner* writers have returned to throughout the '90s (see Joanna Kadi, "Whose Culture Is It Anyway?" 1992, and Delia Aguilar, "What's Wrong with the 'F' Word?" 1994). As our larger society has become more sensitive to cultural difference, we have incorporated those differences into a consumerist model of cross-cultural experience, in which white, middle-class people (feminist or otherwise) eat ethnic food, buy ethnic art, and listen to ethnic music but hold evermore tightly onto the reins of privilege. Outside progressive movements, we see this death grip on privilege in the dismantling of affirmative action; in the passage of Proposition 187 in California, denying public services to "illegal aliens"; in increased violence against people of color and gays and lesbians. Within the feminist movement, we see a similar dynamic when white women engage in Native American rituals but fail to support the struggles of Native American women for health care, reproductive freedom, and treaty rights, or when, as Delia Aguilar notes, white feminists acknowledge the liberation struggles of other peoples but fail to "take into account asymmetries of power." Aguilar's point is that in the "celebration of difference" we eclipse the process by which those differences have come to exist: the way in which women's lives are defined by their unequal access to economic, political, and social resources.

Hollow celebrations of multiculturalism, and the superficial diversity they inspire, create a weak foundation for coalition building. In the '80s, however, we saw numerous honest attempts to examine privilege in a domestic and international context, to find common ground, and to build coalition efforts in the hope of creating a broad-based progressive movement. Particularly important during this period were international solidarity movements, which supported revolutionary struggles in Nicaragua, El Salvador, Guatemala, South Africa, and the Philippines and emerging women's movements around the world (see Charlotte Bunch, "Global Feminism: Going Beyond Boundaries," 1985). Although solidarity work often avoids the more difficult and complex task of confronting racism in our communities at home, it has encouraged U.S. women to examine their privilege within a global context and to broaden the feminist agenda to include U.S. imperialism and militarism, which is rapidly diminishing the prospects of women throughout the world (see Roxanna Pastor, "How the United States Militarized Honduras," 1986). Moreover, by providing material resources to Third World women's struggles and publicizing the impact of U.S. intervention on women's lives around the globe, U.S. women, in the words of Audre Lorde, "use our power and privilege in the service of what we believe" (*Sojourner*, January 1986).

In the mid '80s, Mab Segrest, a lesbian activist in North Carolina, became a paid organizer in the anti-Klan movement. She writes of her transition,

> *I had sat in many rooms and participated in many conversations between lesbians about painful differences of race and class, about anti-Semitism and ageism and able-bodiedism. They had been hard discussions, but they had given me some glimpse of the possibility of spinning a wider lesbian movement, a women's movement that truly incorporates diversity as strength. But in all those discussions, difficult as many of them were, we had never been out to kill each other. In the faces of Klan and Nazi men—and women—in North Carolina, I saw people who would kill us all. I felt I needed to shift from perfecting consciousness to putting consciousness to the continual test of action.* ("Fear to Joy: Fighting the Klan," 1987)

Segrest made the decision to be open about her lesbian identity and she began to build bridges between the predominantly white lesbian and gay community and predominantly heterosexual and African-American communities resisting white supremacy in North Carolina. She opened herself to the lessons of antiracism work that only those with daily experience could teach her while insisting that the anti-Klan movement take the threat of homophobic violence equally seriously. Though the white supremacist movement is virulently racist, anti-Semitic, and homophobic, North Carolinians against Racist and Religious Violence was the first anti-Klan organization in the country to add antigay violence to its agenda.

These are the alliances of the future. Suzanne Pharr writes in "Rural Organizing: Building Communities Across Difference" (1994) about how lesbians and gays can fight homophobia in fundamentalist Christian communities of the South by making connections with people around issues of economic injustice. When lesbians and gay men make themselves a visible presence in community struggles against environmental hazards, for affordable housing, for youth centers and food banks and for better schools, they build alliances that have the power to disrupt sexist, racist, and homophobic policies and rhetoric. The same is true for feminists, who can build alliances with women who reject the "feminist" label by supporting women where they are at any moment in time: by joining in the struggle to unionize factory workers who face hazardous working conditions, tyrannical bosses, and substandard wages; by establishing battered women's shelters in communities outside urban centers; by supporting efforts to create cooperative day care centers.

Today we face the task of pulling together the multiple movements that have emerged from the last 25 years of feminist struggle, not necessarily into a single movement, but into a broad coalition that reaches beyond individual experience to an understanding of the intricate web of domination that affects women's lives at home and abroad. To do so, we must all address the power and privilege that we have acquired by the happenstance of birth—men must deal with their sexism, white people must deal with their racism, heterosexuals must deal with their homophobia, women living in the United States must recognize their privilege as residents of the most powerful country in the world. As feminists and progressives, we can no longer afford the divisiveness of the '80s. We must seek common ground, share resources, and build alliances that have the strength not only to withstand increasingly vicious assaults on the civil rights of women and people of color—attacks on welfare, immigrants, public education, affirmative action, lesbian and gay rights, national health care, and reproductive rights— but to build a common vision of hope. Only in building coalitions and providing an alternative vision for the future can feminists and their allies counter the disillusionment and despair of late twentieth century U. S. society, maintain the gains that women have made since the '60s, and expand those initial victories to include the liberation of *all* women throughout the world.

* Bernice Johnson Reagon, "Coalition Politics: Turning the Century," *Home Girls: A Black Feminist Anthology*, ed. Barbara Smith (Latham, N.Y.: Kitchen Table Women of Color Press: 1981)

MARCH 1979

Racism and White Feminists

DEAR *SOJOURNER*:

I am writing to comment on the issue of racism and white feminists, only partly as a response to the review of the concert "Varied Voices of Black Women" and the correspondence which you subsequently published.

As you say in your January editorial, "Few of us talk about or try to resolve problems stemming from racism and are, therefore, not as sensitized or sensitive to these issues as we ought to be." In an essay which will appear in the next issue of *Chrysalis* ("Disloyal to Civilization: Feminism, Racism, and Gynephobia"), I have tried to unravel some of the reasons why, among white feminists in the '70s, this is so; some of the history behind this fact; and what all this means for women of color and white women who are trying to create a movement whose viability depends on its breadth and depth of reference, its accountability to all women. I hope very much that other feminists will add to, criticize, build upon, go beyond, that essay (meaning, literally, "attempt") of mine.

It seems to me that the first question we who are white feminists must ask ourselves, as individuals and in groups, is *why* we think the issue of racism is important, to ourselves or to this movement. Where does it belong, for us; do we care about it at all? If we care, do we care intellectually, as a "correct political attitude"? or out of unexamined, reflex guilt feelings? or from the same emotional depths that allow us to identify with the raped or beaten woman, the victim of botched illegal abortion, the victim of psycho-surgery, who might be, and sometimes is, ourselves? Does racism make us incapable of *meeting*—i.e., of having honest intellectual or emotional conflict and struggle with Black women or other women of color? What does the word "racism" itself bring to our minds, what images, associations? Do we have a feminist understanding of female racism, and if so, what does this mean?

Racism, it seems to me, is not something any American woman can afford not to think about, whether she's the daughter of Irish immigrants, Jewish anarchists, Wyoming cattle-herders. I grew up out of a Southern background and had to take it seriously out of my childhood experience; but in fact, it is so embedded in American history, like sexual oppression, that its meaning and that of class and sexual oppression are totally related, race and sex above all not to be construed without reference to each other.

In a period when the "personal growth" and "human potential" movements have swiftly moved in to assimilate even some of the most precious, early insights of feminism, when "self-development" has become a banal religion, when much of the women's spirituality movement veers at the edge of light-headed denial of evil, when electoral politics are represented as a "radical" perspective—at this time it is vital to recognize that what we are, as white feminists, can only be understood and acted upon by understanding and acting upon the facts of institutionalized race hatred and violence in America. We may seem to have the choice—as women of color don't—to enter or avoid a realm which is *not* consoling, which is both painful and potentially instructive, ugly and potentially clarifying, the realm sketchily depicted under the term "racism." (By "choice" I mean only that most of us are not forced into a daily consciousness of racism, its pervasiveness, its structures, its destructiveness to our lives.)

I refuse to believe that we, white feminists, really want *not* to know, not to face the full spectrum of female experience in this country, this world. If we don't take this seriously, we don't take ourselves, our history and our movement seriously. To ignore and evade our complex, tortured, historic relationship to racism, which when deeply examined might yield a more healing knowledge than we have as yet—is to choose denial, collaboration, setback, tragedy such as our movement has already seen in the past. Whatever the "options" offered white women now, we all know the whole thing ("personal growth," selective permissiveness) could reverse itself in a matter of months. Maybe there really is no choice for us, either.

In sisterhood,
Adrienne Rich
New York City

FEBRUARY 1981

Fat Liberation: No Losers Here
by Judith Stein

Finally, "fat" has gone public. From the deepest closets of obscenities, denials, and disguise, women are realizing that yes, some of us are fat; and that yes, some of us who are fat are also healthy; and that yes, what we were taught about fat equaling unhealthy is simply not true. Some women are even reclaiming the word "fat" and using it with pride!

The fat liberation movement is a loose coalition of groups and individuals, all of whom believe that fat people are oppressed *because* of being fat; all of whom know that the effects of fat oppression range from psychological devastation to physical death, and all of whom believe that only profound changes in society will end the oppression of fat people. An enormous part of our work consists of undoing the myths and lies all of us, thin and fat, were taught about the causes of fat, the results of being fat, and the "true" nature of fat women.

Because the lies about fatness are so deeply ingrained, disbelief and denial are often the first reactions to fat liberation material. Every piece of medical information in this article has been documented thoroughly, within the most conservative, established medical sources.

What Is Fat Oppression?

Fat oppression is the systematic hatred and ridicule of, and discrimination against, fat people by this society. It is based on the belief that fat people are not as good as thin people, and that fat people remain fat because we are lazy, eat too much, lack willpower, or are stupid. This belief is part of the social order which oppresses people because of their age, race, sex, sexual preference, and physical abilities or disabilities.

Being fat means being the butt of jokes, hostility, and public slurs in every social situation—from movies, TV, friends, and family—and being expected to tolerate or enjoy the experience.

Being fat means getting lower-paying jobs, having less job mobility, and being refused jobs for which you qualify, because you don't fit the company image, or the boss thinks you can't do the work, or they have a "policy" against hiring fat women. Being fat means you have *no legal recourse* if you are refused a job, fired, or harassed on your job because of being fat.

Being fat means living with the constant assumption that you want to be thin; it means living with the public assumption that you are dieting or feel guilty for not dieting; and it means living with the reality that *any* person, from close friend to store clerk to jerk on the street, feels free to comment about your size, your appearance, and your need to diet.

Being fat means being harassed, ridiculed, and discouraged when doing sports or athletic activities, and then being told that your fat is a result of your sloth and inactivity.

Being fat means dieting, maybe losing weight, gaining that weight back (and usually more), and then living with the self-hatred and public hostility this failure produces.

Being fat means literally making yourself sick by dieting and then being told you are sick because of being fat.

Being fat means getting desperate and having your jaws wired shut, your stomach stapled smaller, or a large piece of your intestines cut out (a surgery with a death rate of six women in 100—from the operation alone), and then, when even these drastic methods fail, killing yourself.

These experiences are not fantasies, and they are not uncommon. They are as frequent for women who move within the feminist community as they are for women from all other walks of life. One step in changing this is for feminists, who are accustomed to examining our other socially-dictated beliefs, to begin changing the attitudes and practices within the feminist community that continue to oppress fat women.

The Myths Underlying Fat Oppression

The first and most difficult task of fat liberation is to undo the lies that keep fat women weak from dieting, harassed on the streets, and dying on operating tables. These same lies keep thin women terrorized about becoming fat and keep all of us separated and divided. The fear of getting fat, or getting fatter, keeps all of us preoccupied with our bodies and keeps us from using that energy to fight the real oppression, a sexist society which tells us how we are to look and how we are to live.

Here are the facts:

1. *Fat people are not fat because we eat too much, eat the wrong foods, or have metabolic problems.* Over 100 studies have attempted to prove that fat people eat more than thin people—and every one of them has failed! On the average, fat people eat the same amounts and types of food as thin people. In fact, in one study, a group of adolescent fat women said they ate more than their thin friends even though an actual tally of food consumption showed that they ate far less than their thin friends.

The relationship between food intake and weight is murky at best. Most people seem to have a range of normal body weights, and when repeated dieting does not interfere (e.g., when people lose weight, then gain it back, they often gain more than the original loss), eating patterns seem to create shifts within that "normal" range. Women who have dieted over long periods of time may have a higher "normal" body weight, *as a result of the dieting,* than they would have had had they never dieted. Eating less, even over a long period of time, does not produce permanent weight loss, because the body adapts to the decreased calorie intake.

2. *Fat people cannot change our "problem" of being fat by dieting—even on medically supervised "sensible" diets.* Medical research has consistently shown that diets have a long-term failure rate of 98 to 99 percent. This means that 99 out of 100 fat people who do lose weight will gain all the weight they lost (and usually more) within five years.

In fact, the dieting process itself is unhealthy: it has been shown to increase the risk of heart attacks and strokes, hardening of the arteries, diabetes, gallstone problems, kidney disease, and more. The inevitable yoyo-ing that fat women go through with repeated diets causes repeated exposure to a traumatic body process that is *known* (unlike the fact of being fat) to cause health problems.

3. *Fat people are not less healthy than thin people nor are we unhealthy because of being fat.* Fat people range from very healthy to very ill—just like thin people. Any attempt to actually prove that being fat causes illness has failed in a confusion of third factors (such as presence of other diseases). Not one study has successfully proven that being fat causes any of the diseases attributed to fatness. In addition, the diseases thought to be caused by fat are all stress-related (like high blood pressure) and are more likely caused by the combination of repeated dieting (a high-stress process for the body) and fat hatred in this culture.

"Cures" for being fat—like intestinal bypass surgery and gastric stapling—have high death rates and only make fat people sicker. Diets like the liquid protein diet have led to over 60 known cases of death by starvation. These "cures" are medical malpractice at its height—just as clitoridectomy (removal of the clitoris) was when used as a "cure" for women's independent sexuality. Both are rooted in the same hatred of women in this society and the demand that women conform to men's ideals of female sexuality. It is up to the feminist movement to recognize these "cures" as the barbaric practices they truly are—and to speak out about the false claims of ill health that are the basis for these extremely devastating "treatments."

Despite the ever-accumulating evidence to the contrary, the medical establishment continues to use false information as a basis for medical practices. The diet industry is a billion-dollar, multifaceted industry, which includes medical professionals, therapists, publishers, weight loss clinics, camps, and salons and which has an enormous stake in keeping women terrorized by the spectre of becoming fat or getting fatter.

Women committed to the control of our own lives can begin by taking control over our own bodies—and learning the truth about eating and weight and health. Women can trust our own bodies as a guide to eating. Thin women must learn to believe fat women when we share our lives and experiences and must let go of their illusion of superiority over fat women. All of us together are needed to confront and defeat the medical and diet industries, which abuse us, cheat us, and keep us physically weak.

Women must relearn what we know about fat and health as we have relearned all the other lies we are told about our lives. Fat oppression is no less deadly, and the struggle against it is no less serious. We owe ourselves, all of us, the right to be the size we truly are. And fat women, remember—you have nothing to lose.

JANUARY 1983

Shared Silences/Shared Love

by Demita Frazier

A Memory: Chicago, late summer, 1967
I was visiting my friend Anne; it was the first time I had been invited to her home. The clean-swept streets, manicured lawns, and the semi-formal courtyard gardens were worlds different from the working-/lower-middle class neighborhood I came from. She lived in an imposing brick apartment complex, with a sort of Swiss chalet facade, popular in Chicago in the '30s when it was constructed. Anne's family lived in a large, airy apartment filled with sleek Scandinavian furniture and Persian rugs; built-in bookshelves filled with books lined the walls in their library. Two Alexander Calder mobiles whirled slowly in their respective quiet corners in the living room.

Anne's father was away on business and her brother had already left for Princeton, so that left Anne, her mother, her father's mother and me. Secretly, I was glad we were "just the girls."

After introducing me to her mother, Anne led me down the cool, darkened hallway into the dining room. A voice called from the kitchen, "Anna..." and then a string of words which I guessed were Yiddish. Anne told me her grandmother wanted her to bring her friend into the kitchen so she could meet me. The smell of just-baked cookies wafted toward us, sweet with vanilla and the slightly sharper scent of apricot.

I followed Anne into the kitchen which was warm with the heat of cooking and late summer sun.

"Bubbe, this is my friend, Demita," Anne said in Yiddish, "and Demita, this is my grandmother, Mrs. Rabin."

Anne's words trailed off. Her grandmother was staring down at my proffered hand. She looked up at my face, then at Anne. A torrent of words came, again in Yiddish. The already hot, bright room quickly grew warmer. Anne was deeply flushed and her mother, who had been in the dining room setting the table, came running. The words in Yiddish swirled around me, the cadence rising and falling as Anne pulled me from the kitchen. Silence fell between us. We finished setting the table. I admired the china.

There wasn't any discussion of what happened in the kitchen at dinner. Mrs. Rabin ate her dinner on a tray in her room. For dessert, Anne's mother served the tender apricot-filled butter cookies Mrs. Rabin had made, along with Russian spiced tea. We discussed our college aspirations and the war in Vietnam. I left and took the subway back to the South Side.

A few days later, I asked my friend Alan Isaacs what the word "schvartze" meant. Looking slightly embarrassed, he said, "Sometimes black. Sometimes, though, it means nigger."

My dinner at Anne's was neither my first nor my most intense experience as a Black woman among Jews. It was not the most painful. However, it represents an experience that has been repeated many times since that summer day: Black and Jewish women left silent because of fear of certain realities and seemingly unconquerable differences. This subjective, deeply personal essay/meditation is an attempt to ferret out why and how such shared silences create the barriers between us; how it thwarts meaningful communication and coalition building and, finally, how, left unexamined, it threatens our survival as sisters/lovers/friends and interdependent feminist communities.

A Memory: Boston, late autumn, 1979

Everyone in the news media was oohhing and aaahhing over Andrew Young's "impolitic dalliance" with a representative of the Palestine Liberation Organization. It is as if the dirtiest secret ever suddenly found daybreak. The heads of the major mainstream Black and Jewish organizations rushed to point the accusing finger, each outraged and righteously indignant at the pronouncements of the other. Vehement letters blanketed the op-ed pages of the *New York Times* and the *Boston Globe*; magazine headlines proclaimed that Jews and Afro-Americans were completely disenchanted with each other and that the "era" of the great liberal coalition, while having been recognized as long dormant, was officially dead.

Naturally, all the extant characters in this death/debacle are men: Black *men* and Jewish *men*. No others need apply.

At the time, I lived with a Jewish woman. Naomi and I marveled at the enormous waste of energy and egocentric posturing of the NAACP, the American Jewish Congress, the Urban League, National B'nai B'rith, etc. As two radical lesbian feminists—a Jew and a Colored woman—we knew why they hadn't bothered to ask us what we thought of the condition of the relations between Afro-Americans and Jews. We would have told them a truth they were completely uninterested in hearing. Alive, well, living as friends/sisters/compañeras in Jamaica Plain, in spite of you all.

Private conversations, however, remained simply that. We never took our conversations and analysis any further than our immediate circle of Colored and Jewish womenfolk. The silence on the issues and conflicts between our larger communities of Black and Jewish peoples/Black and Jewish feminists remained unbreached.

My first awareness of anti-Semitism came along with my first social interactions as a high school student with white people. I overheard two students talking at their lockers, and one of them was describing the origin of the hatred of Jews—that Jews were responsible for the death of Jesus. I was dumbstruck. Pontius Pilate was a Jew? Clearly, because I had been brought up as essentially nonreligious, at least nondenominational, my knowledge of religious history was lacking. And wasn't Jesus a Jew? I just didn't get it. Since I had not accepted that Jesus was the one lone Christian savior, I had no investment in his life or death. I was too afraid to ask my friends who were Jews what they thought was at the core of such hatred, and since my only white friends, save one girl, were Jewish, I had to wait a few more years before the political and sociological history would be revealed to me.

I never heard my mother, my only parent, make anti-Jewish statements. Naturally, I was raised with a survival mythology vis-à-vis white people: beware of white men; you can never really trust what a white person says; white people are racist, etc., therefore maintain a safe distance between oneself and them. But my mother claims that her life was saved by a young Jewish doctor and his wife who took her in as a maid when she was seventeen and had run away from her mother's home in St. Louis. And Abe, her long-time boss at the old Rexall drugstore, once came out through a violent Midwestern snowstorm just to bring her medicine when she had pneumonia. She led us to believe that Jews were a step above the average white person. Through Abe we got presents of smoked white fish and chopped liver, pastrami, rye bread, great dill pickles and my absolute favorite, corned beef.

I wrote off anti-Semitism as one more example of regular white folks' aberrant behavior, and once I understood that that pathology was what motivated the annihilation of the Jews of Europe during World War II, I was certain that I shared, in some way, with my Jewish friends, a common role in the larger white world—that of the pariah. Later in life, white skin privilege and other factors would cause me to at least reassess my intellectual set on things (just as I would have to rethink much of what I had learned/thought about the destruction of African cultures by the slave trade upon learning of the complicity of African and Semitic people in that trade). However, the emotional/psychic connection remained and was what made it possible for me to struggle in spite of Jewish racism and classism.

A Memory: February, 1981, The Jewish Women/Women of Color Workshop,
New England Women's Studies Association Conference on Racism
There were 125, perhaps 150 women in the auditorium. The majority of the women were white; from what I could discern, most were Jewish women. The rest of us, Afro-American, Latina, and Asian women, were scattered throughout the room.

The tension all around was palpable. There were far too many women present to make a workshop possible. The workshop facilitators seemed overwhelmed and underprepared. While I was certain they were well-intentioned, it was clear to me that they had not spent a great deal of time preparing nor did it seem that any of them were particularly skilled or experienced as facilitators. Only the Latina woman offered a personal perspective on the possible roots of whatever anti-Jewish feelings she had. The Jewish woman on the panel did not speak at all to whatever feelings of racism she might harbor, having grown up a white woman in the South. I have only a vague memory of the Afro-American woman's remarks and I think that is because she offered little by way of personal sharing. There was no analysis or historical perspective set out. After such an unbalanced and unfocused beginning, the workshop went recklessly out of control. There we were, 100 plus women trying to have a totally formless and undirected discussion about such charged and painful things: attitudes of racial and cultural inferiority/superiority; class and white skin privilege; "passing" and the resentment of those who are able to do so; the anger on the part of those who ostensibly could pass at those who think passing is a real option as opposed to the self-hatred and social death it exemplifies; the attempts to disown our past insensitivities to one another; the careless assumptions of knowledge and ignorance of ourselves and each other; the meaning of the shameless scrambles made for the larger share of righteous pain and anger over who was/is the most oppressed. Here and there, coherent, meaningful statements are made by both Colored and Jewish women, but those bits and pieces are swallowed up by the chaos. Many women are silent; the many unasked questions, unexplored thoughts, and untouched emotions eddy and surge all around us. I am totally furious and frustrated at the facilitators for their lack of readiness and skill. I feel that I and every woman in the room has been merely toyed with. At bottom, I am angry and saddened by our passivity as participants. In the beginning, in the face of our huge numbers, why didn't some of us, any of us who had experience leading workshops approach the facilitators and offer ideas for an alternative structure so that real communication would have been possible? In our collective silence we shortchanged ourselves and our collective desire to learn and share.

Somehow, the workshop lurched to an end; the talking and debate continued long after the workshop had officially ended. Later on, the women of color met to discuss the women of color/Jewish women workshop and the rest of the conference. An Afro-American woman who had made an ignorant and clearly disrespectful comment was gently but firmly confronted by a number of Black lesbian feminists. Somehow, in spite of the fact that she was leery of them (a little homophobia afoot?), the sisters were able to communicate. A small bit of the silence was broken by those Black feminists.

What I Want

I think it is time for feminist women of color and Jewish women who care about future communication and coalition work between us to come together for a weekend of intellectual and cultural sharing. The sheer variety of the cultures within each of the amalgamous groups demands much more time than a single workshop; the historical relationships as they intertwine could easily take a few days to explore. However, I believe that with careful planning by a representative group of women, we could create a weekend's worth of exchange and creative struggle at the end of which we would be richer for it. It would be a time of supportive risk-taking and would be reflective of the planning process. There would be time for

Afro-American, Latina, Asian, Arabic, and Jewish women to meet with just themselves to explore the separate mythologies that we've developed as women of color and as Jews about the other(s). Cross racial/ethnic workshops on class could establish what and how class perspectives develop and delineate the cultural/ethnic differences. Cultural sharing could include an examination of the different ways racial/cultural/sexual oppression has affected our cultural expression as women and also explore those modes of expression which are in some sense simply untainted and outside of the sphere of racial/sexual/ethnic oppression. The poignancy and depth of different songs, dances, dramas, and incantations can teach us in ways which intellectual discourse cannot. Just as our cultural expressions help us to comprehend and illuminate each of our group experiences, I believe those same expressions of joy, pain, life, and sense of destiny can bring new understanding of each other.

I should say here that I realize all the different communities of feminists/women are, at this time, at various stages of evolution and reconstruction, and that it may be felt by many sisters (and rightfully so) that these times are perhaps better spent focusing on intragroup development and struggle. Indeed, it would be politically naive for me not to take those considerations into account. However, my vision is not bounded by a specific timeline, and I believe these issues will be vital when we feel we have the energy to devote to their exploration. I do ultimately believe in the interdependence of our various feminist communities and that because of our feminist principles and our need to see the larger feminist community move forward and become a truly representative and whole movement, we will confront and dispel the silence.

The poet/writer Audre Lorde once commented that in this country we are taught to deal with difference in three ways: to become it, to ignore it, or to annihilate it. I am certain that by refusing to languish in the silences between us, we can, as feminists, overcome those mainstream cultural imperatives, and lead the way, as our peoples so often have, to a fuller more coherent way of being in the world.

MAY 1983

An Open Letter to the Women's Movement
by Barbara Macdonald

I have been reading and writing for Sojourner for years, and it strikes me that nobody (including myself) has sent you a true picture of who old women are and what we really feel like. I hope to do that with this open letter. The fact that I am old, lesbian, and white does not make the letter less pertinent for all women—young, or heterosexual, or of different cultural backgrounds. Despite the many differences in our past experiences, all of us are going to have the common experience of coming up against the ageism in this country.

The following letter was written in response to a questionnaire (of 165 questions) sent to me by a university women's center planning a service for lesbians over 65. It is obvious that the planners had not done the necessary work on their own ageism. I send my response as an open letter because if I and others do not speak out, this is the questionnaire we will all get and this describes a service we will all be expected to use—lesbian or heterosexual—until we begin to talk about our ageism and change it.

I have received your questionnaire for lesbians over 65 with your description of the proposed service, and I am pleased that your university is committed to dealing with ageism in the lesbian community. What follows is not so much a criticism of your individual effort but of the lesbian community and our own years of neglect of the older lesbian and our unwillingness to recognize and work on our own ageism with the same vigor that we have worked to eradicate sexism and racism. Any organization with the courage to make a start must inherit the problems resulting from this neglect—neglect by the women's movement and by the lesbian community. The problems cited here are ours, not yours.

Your service promises to bring older lesbians out of "their often self-imposed isolation so that their needs can be met, their problems solved, and their accomplishments recognized by an appropriate service organization." To fulfill this purpose, you foresee providing services such as "sympathetic visiting," "protective escorts," "bereavement support," and a "congenial meeting site for those lonely and depressed, where they can make new social contacts."

My first gut response is to say that as an old lesbian, I do not want to be addressed as "them," I don't want my problems solved for me, I don't want sympathy, and I don't want my accomplishments recognized by an appropriate service organization.

Your enclosure clearly implies that most lesbians over 65 are "incapacitated" (a word that insults the physically challenged woman of any age) and that the rest of us are lonely, depressed, bereaved, and probably need advice about our wills. Such stereotyping is offensive and segregating. SAGE [Senior Action in a Gay Environment] in New York City (the model for your proposed organization) estimates an active membership of approximately 250 gay men and women who go through their center in a month. Of those receiving services because they are homebound, they estimate fewer than 25 women. Many lesbians 20, 30, and 40 years old are physically challenged or lonely or depressed or bereaved and dying of cancer and need advice about wills. Thus it seems misleading to segregate lesbians over 65 and address "them" from the point of view of "their" neediness. Why just us? Why not set up a service for *all* lesbians, and if those of us over 65 need the services provided for all, we will use them. If you think that lesbians over 65 won't come because we are suffering from self-imposed isolation, just put a few old lesbians in leadership roles, along with lesbians of all ages, and see what happens.

It is not my intent to single out for blame either your agency or SAGE. The description, the language used, is all too familiar, and could be used to describe most of the traditional, patch-up services found in the larger community. Publishing such descriptions of the oppressed group as unable to meet their own needs maintains the hierarchy of the service organization who serves them, whether they do so for salaries, grants, recognition, or out of a gratifying spirit of altruism—and it gives the service organization no incentive to eliminate the sources of the oppression.

Is that the best that the lesbian community can offer? We are a small community, less unwieldy than the larger heterosexual community, less rigid, our institutions newer, more flexible, our prejudices (we can hope) less entrenched. We have both the vision and the will to eradicate prejudice at the source, not cover it up or patch it up. Consciousness raising, our method of getting at the source of prejudice, has been successful in making inroads into our sexism and our racism. We may not yet have been able to effect the changes we would like to see in the larger community, but we are taking care of the first piece of business—the sexism and racism in ourselves. Through consciousness raising we have been encouraged to feel our anger, and this has empowered us to take charge of our own lives and to enter into leadership.

White women were slower to recognize our own racism in the women's movement (and in the lesbian movement), and we made a lot of mistakes. We sat in workshops and large conferences and described ourselves as the women's movement. We talked of doing something about racism. We went so far as to invite a few militant Black women to policymaking meetings as speakers to explain our own racism to us. And when these few women refused to be tokens, we said that we didn't know any other women of color and we couldn't find any.

But there were a lot of mistakes we didn't make in dealing with our sexism and our racism. Even though we recognized that most of us were poor and deprived of opportunity, we didn't follow the methods of the larger community by gathering old clothes. We didn't set up groups to deliver turkeys at Christmas. White women didn't approach the problem of our racism by setting up consciousness-raising groups for Black women. White women didn't set up women's centers for women of color that were separate but equal. We didn't tell them that their oppression was self-imposed or organize bountiful ladies to solve their problems for them.

So why do we now go back to such obsolete methods for solving our own ageism? Those methods breed the same evils they always did—they stereotype, segregate, patronize, and stigmatize. They blame the victim, then having blamed her, they set up services to change her, solve her problems and meet her needs, then they pity her, and finally—I must point out—they exploit her.

Even with the best of intentions, traditional services get caught up in blaming the victim because the success or failure of the service depends upon producing change. The oppressor is very resistant to change and often unaware of being the source of the oppression. But the oppressed are much more vulnerable to intervention, which is soon equated with somehow not doing it right—like "their self-imposed isolation."

I don't believe the oppression of Jews or people of color is self-imposed. And I don't think my oppression as an old lesbian is self-imposed. I have no difficulty in locating the sources of it—in the larger, patriarchal society, in the women's community, and in the lesbian community.

Briefly, let's examine the lesbian movement and ask ourselves some questions. How many lesbians over 65 attend rallies, workshops, readings? How many over 60? Over 50? Where are we? Why don't we come? Before we start blaming the victim maybe we ought to first ask, "What is really there for older women?"

Let's look at our publications. I subscribe to nine—three are lesbian, the others are radical feminist journals and newspapers. I know of only one that has pursued an outrageous, over-65 lesbian to join their editorial staff to raise their consciousness about ageism or to edit out some of their published ageist material.

Your enclosure speaks of first having to locate and get data on lesbians over 65. That reminds me of the reasons the all-white women's movement used to give for not including Black women in our planning and leadership—we couldn't find any, we didn't know any. Only now, as we begin to see able, verbal, creative women of color throughout the lesbian community, are white women forced to recognize that they were always there but we had made them invisible.

The Second Wave recently ran an ad saying that they wished to add women of color to their collective, which they described as "diverse in our class backgrounds and ages." So I called in order to find out about the older women in their collective and learned that they had one woman who was 31 and that they had once had a woman who was 40. That's invisibility.

Nor did the women of *The Second Wave* come by this curious notion of age on their own. Probably one of their earliest impressions of what the women's movement is all about would have come from *Sisterhood Is Powerful*, edited by Robin Morgan in 1970 (Vintage Books), which included 44 articles and 14 poems on all aspects of women's oppression. This very excellent anthology has one article on ageism, "It Hurts To Be Alive and Obsolete: The Aging Woman," written by Zoe Moss. Moss, 43, writes: "I am bitter and frustrated and wasted, but don't you pretend for a minute as you look at me, 43, fat, and looking exactly my age, that I am not as alive as you are and that I do not suffer from the category into which you are forcing me." Should we be surprised that *The Second Wave* felt they had an aging woman in their collective?

A look at some of the most recent issues of lesbian publications shows the need for the active participation of lesbians over 65 on their editorial staffs. By far the most glaring offense of almost all of them is the omission of any articles that address old lesbians. But the editors also need to become more aware of the unconscious ageism in the material they publish. For example, in a dialogue in *Conditions* #8, Barbara Kerr explains: "I went to live with my 70-year-old grandmother. She was not the sweet-little-old-lady type." Such stereotyping is offensive to me; perhaps the offensiveness will become more evident if you substitute Jew or Black—"the aggressive, rich Jew type" or "the happy-go-lucky Black type"—stereotypes this collective would never be guilty of.

In *Sinister Wisdom* #19, "Nadene Pagan's Last Letter Home," by Judith Katz, the assumption that Nadene makes—that her mother exists solely to serve as a witness to her daughter's bravery and heroism—perpetuates attitudes that are destructive to older women, as I tried to show in my reply in issue #21.

A letter published in *Lesbian Lives/Common Lives* #4 I find much more serious, because it is written by one of the editors and published as a model for other lesbians to use. I refer to "Dear Aunt Ethel," by Carol Rising. The attitude of this 40-year-old dyke toward her 80-year-old aunt, who she hopes will send her $50,000, is exploitative and insulting, and renders the older woman invisible. I find it incomprehensible that the editors were so insensitive as to publish it.

Stereotyping and segregation do not end with innocent, unconscious prejudice. (We segregated Blacks in this country and exploited their labor. We segregated Japanese

during World War II, and then took their businesses, their lands, and their other property.) Stereotyping and segregation eventually lead to exploitation. I begin to see the
signs of this in the lesbian community.

Carol Rising's model letter suggests to lesbians that they write old women relatives for money and that old women relatives include them in their wills. But Carol
Rising is not alone in this. Your own proposed organization offers to help old lesbians
write their wills, and your questionnaire asks the old lesbian to list the amount of her
income and the sources. I make no accusation. But when I then find that SAGE sends
out flyers to their membership saying, "You can also support SAGE, Inc., by including
us in your will," along with the suggested wording for such a bequest—it is time for the
entire lesbian community to take a good look at what we are doing.

It is not any of the particulars of your service that I object to. Lesbians of all ages
are homebound, sick, dying, and certainly that is also true of lesbians over 65. Lesbians
of any age can be killed in an automobile accident tomorrow, and there is nothing
wrong with providing legal services to advise all lesbians about their wills and to remind all lesbians of the needs of the lesbian community in making out their wills. My
objection to your service is only in the segregated way you are beginning and the implications about lesbians over 65 that can be drawn from such a beginning.

I can support a strong organization, coordinated out of your university, committed to stamping out ageism in the lesbian community—a community that is
contributing to the "loneliness and depression" of the old lesbians that you speak of. If
your organization is committed to empowering old lesbians, working actively to make
us visible in positions of leadership, you won't need to "locate *them*" and "gather de-
scriptive data about *them*," you will know us.

As a beginning, I would suggest that your university women's center:

1. Organize consciousness-raising groups, a process in which old lesbians should
be visible. The women's movement has given lip service to opposing ageism, but no
real work has ever been done to raise the consciousness of women about ageism
enough for us to even recognize it.

2. Take leadership in insisting that the National Women's Studies Association devote an annual meeting to the issue and commit themselves to long-range plans for
combatting ageism in every field of study.

3. Set up an ongoing group assigned to monitoring feminist and lesbian publications and to addressing the editors, requesting retractions of published ageist material.
Not only would editing staffs become more aware, but the publishing of such letters
would increase the awareness of a much larger population—their readers.

The following are a few suggestions for working on our ageism:

1. Don't expect that older women are there to serve you because you are
younger—and *don't think the only alternative is for you to serve us.*

2. Don't continue to say "the women's movement," as I have in this letter, until all the
invisible women are present—all races and cultures and *all ages* of all races and cultures.

3. Don't believe you are complimenting an old woman by letting her know that
you think she is "different from" (more fun, more gutsy, more interesting than) other
old women. To accept the compliment, she has to join in your rejection of old women.

4. Don't point out to any old woman how strong she is, how she is more capable in certain situations than you are. Not only is this patronizing, but the implication is that you admire the way she does not show her age, and it follows that you do not admire the ways in which she does, or soon will, show her age.

5. If an old woman talks about arthritis or cataracts, don't think old women are constantly complaining. We are just trying to get a word in edgewise while you talk and write endlessly about abortions, contraception, premenstrual syndrome, toxic shock, or turkey basters.

6. Don't feel guilty. You will then avoid us because you are afraid we might become dependent and you know you can't meet our needs. Don't burden us with *your* idea of dependency and *your* idea of obligation.

7. By the year 2000, approximately one out of every four adults will be over 50. The marketplace is ready now to present a new public image of the aging American, just as it developed an image of the young American and the "youth movement" at a time when a larger section of the population was young. Don't trust the glossy images that are about to bombard you in the media. In order to sell products to a burgeoning population of older women, they will tell you that we are all white, comfortably middle class, and able to "pass" if we just use enough creams and hair dyes. Old women are the single poorest minority group in this country. Only ageism makes us feel a need to pass.

8. Don't think that an old woman has always been old. She is in the process of discovering what 70, 80, and 90 mean. As more and more old women talk and write about the reality of this process, in a world that negates us, we will discover how revolutionary that is.

9. Don't assume that every old woman is not ageist. Don't assume that I'm not.

10. If you have insights you can bring to bear from your racial background or ethnic culture—bring them. We need to pool all of our resources to deal with this issue. But don't talk about your grandmother as the bearer of your culture—don't objectify her. Don't make her a museum piece or a woman whose value is that she has sacrificed on your behalf. Tell us who she is now, a woman in process.

I wish you luck in your beginning. We are all beginning.

This article also appeared in Look Me in the Eye: Old Women, Ageing, and Ageism, *expanded edition, by Barbara Macdonald with Cynthia Rich (Spinsters Ink, 1991).*

JUNE 1985

Global Feminism: Going Beyond Boundaries
by Charlotte Bunch

The following article is adapted from a May 1985 speech given by Charlotte Bunch. At the time, she was helping to coordinate explicitly feminist participation at the Non-governmental

Organizations [NGO] Forum to be held in conjunction with the official United Nations Conference on Women in Nairobi, Kenya.

I have just returned from Peru, where I was involved in workshops that were a follow-up to the feminist *encuentro*, or meeting, held in Lima in 1983 with over 600 Latin American and Caribbean women present. At that time I was one of a handful of North Americans invited to offer ideas and developments from the women's movement in this country, but I hardly opened my mouth—I was overwhelmed by the things happening in Latin America. The energy reminded me, as a veteran of the early days of women's liberation in the United States, of the excitement and sense of discovery we felt then. I also realized something that is becoming more and more true: the latest burst of energy and ideas for feminism is coming from the Third World. (By that I mean both feminists in Third World countries and women of color in the United States, who are raising issues that are often similar to developments in Third World feminism.)

As a white U.S. feminist I celebrate this, because it brings insights and imagination that enable us to break some of the boundaries of our thinking—even though (as all of us who have been through various movement conflicts know) it isn't always easy to hear new ideas, or listen to criticisms of feminism in the last two decades. After three or four years of intense activity in one area, one of the best things you can do is listen to feminists emerging from some other place, whether it's Peru, New Zealand, a different part of the United States, or any other cultural context different from your own, even within the same city. Close attention to the perspectives and energy of women outside our own class, race, and culture helps us see more possibilities rather than fewer, to see what feminism can mean as we all grow and evolve a definition that goes beyond any particular cultural boundaries. Of course, no process of taking diversity seriously and listening to different points of view is without challenge, discomfort, and conflict, but I think it's well worth the price.

Understanding this process will be especially crucial at the U.N. conferences in Kenya in July, although I think it will be much more possible to do at the nongovernmental meeting than at the governmental one. The U.N. graciously declared 1975 "International Women's Year," and sponsored an international women's conference in Mexico City that was in many ways the first acknowledgment of women as a global force. A "Decade for Women" was announced after the recognition in Mexico City that the elimination of women's oppression would take more than a year, and a "mid-decade" conference was held in 1980 in Copenhagen. Now we're at the end of the decade, and progress for women seems in many ways to have been minimal; poverty is increasing among women worldwide, there has been very little significant rise in the political power of women—and these are only two of the hard statistical problems we face at this "end of the decade."

But there has been enormous growth in the women's movement during the last ten years: we see women everywhere defining their reality for themselves. To me, the first step in taking any kind of power in any culture is refusing to accept the patriarchal definition of who you are and what your reality is, and this is the stage that I think most women in the world—including this country—are in. But as we each define our own reality, we also must recognize women's diversity. The first step—"We are women, we are distinct, we are oppressed, and there is a women's consciousness"— then must lead almost instantly to, "And yet at the same time there is no one 'women's reality,' except perhaps in the general fact of the subordination of women in every culture—a subordination that takes many varying cultural and individual forms." So the stage of seeing ourselves as similar, seeing ourselves as women, and feeling the excitement of being in a group is followed by the more difficult realization that as a group we are a multitude of groups who are not always united. The struggle for unity requires first recognizing and examining our differences and then asking which of those are strengths and which are simply based on oppression.

It seems clear to me, however, that at the Kenya conferences the worldwide media will use these very differences to say that women are hopelessly divided and that feminism is dead. Our diversity—a source of potential strength—will be manipulated by forces that do not wish to see feminism thrive. But I'm hoping that, in the midst of all the predictable conflicts in Kenya, a number of women will do what we've done over and over in the past decade: build networks around shared concerns, places where we can see our common oppression and work together to solve it. Recently I've worked mostly in the area of sexual violence against women, but coalition building has also happened in many other areas, such as in the women's health movement and among women working in rural development, including U.S. women who face conditions similar to those in some so-called "developing" countries.

By the way, I hope one of the first items on our agenda will be elimination of language like "developed" and "developing": the condescending notion that the Western industrialized world is "developed" is highly questionable outside any but a strictly industrialized interpretation of that word. For lack of a better phrase, I refer to most of the nations of Asia, Latin America, and Africa called "developing countries" as the "Third World," an equally difficult term, but one that at least suggests the possibility of nonalignment with the U.S./U.S.S.R. blocs. This question of terminology raises the related issue of how women, as we define ourselves, can also redefine the ways in which the world is categorized. At the United Nations—created initially to be a place of world unity—you see especially clearly how the various power blocs have developed and solidified. It is very difficult for women there to talk across governmental and bloc lines. The official U.N. conference is a meeting of over 150 patriarchies, not a gathering of the women of those countries or women who see themselves beyond nation-state definitions. The official Kenya conference will be women and men representing patriarchal governments without the freedom to speak what they feel and think—and this is as true of the U.S. delegation as any other. As we saw in Copenhagen, delegates will be pulled in whenever they start to talk beyond bloc lines. Under these circumstances, we cannot expect much more than a reading on how governments view women from the official U.N. conference in Nairobi.

But the NGO Forum can be quite a different matter. I see women there being able to break down barriers, because we will not be under the same obligations to state powers and can examine our positions and the divisions between us. In fact, this conference may be unique because of the emergence of feminism in the Third World in recent years. In 1980, feminism was a term that most women in Third World countries were afraid of, or didn't like, or rejected completely because the media had portrayed feminists with the kinds of stereotypes we know so well in this country. We were described as women who only wanted to get to the top within an oppressive world power system—and why would peasants in Latin America identify with a few women trying to become the head of General Motors? We were also caricatured as crazies, women who hated men, lesbians who couldn't have men, and so on. Feminism has been ridiculed and stereotyped worldwide, and the issues we have raised have usually not been taken seriously by the media.

But remarkably, despite this bad press, feminism has continued to grow. Women's groups all over the world, but especially in the Third World, are taking up issues ranging from housing, nutrition, and poverty to militarism, sexual and reproductive freedom, and violence against women. We face these issues in the United States, too, of course, but their forms vary depending on the culture and where women feel the most intense oppression at any moment. For example, women in shantytowns around Lima, who live on the very edge of survival, are organizing communal kitchens called *comedores populares*, or "popular restaurants." In their traditional role as food providers, they are creating a means to feed their families that is leading them to challenge the whole structure of society and the basis for survival. In shopping together to get better prices, they are starting to ask questions about inflation—why, when food is grown so close to their homes, is it so expensive—and about the worldwide food business in which many countries export certain foods as cash crops while their people starve. And in fixing meals together, they are evolving a sense of community, of being together as women; one group, after talking about violence in the neighborhood, set up a system in which a woman blows a whistle if she is being beaten.

This is only one example of the many ways in which women around the world are saying, "We will no longer be silent about any part of our lives in which we are oppressed." And that statement makes very clear that there is no such thing as a separate "women's issue," although there are women's special concerns and women's perspectives. When we talked about "women's issues" early in the women's movement, we were trying to place on the political agenda things women cared about that had not been considered political: equal rights, reproductive freedom, lesbian rights, child care, violence against women. But we have to say today that all of these are issues of human justice, of human society, not just women's issues.

And, as important, all of the concerns which have been called "larger issues" must be considered women's issues. This became especially clear to me at the Copenhagen conference, where a Western woman said that to talk feminism to a woman who has no home, no food, and no water is to talk nonsense. A group of us, feminists from both Western and Third World countries, wrote a response pointing out that feminism has to do with everything in the world, and so *is* a perspective on food, home, and water. But we also saw the challenge in what she said: if her words become true, then feminism will not fulfill its potential to be a transforming force in the world, although it may do some useful things. I'm hopeful that in Kenya this summer a larger body of women than ever before will develop feminist perspectives on issues like food, shelter, and water.

I also hope that U.S. feminists there will avoid some of the traps that we often fall into, like the tendency to relate to global feminism from one of two extremes. One is to be guilty and overapologetic, to say, in effect, "I have nothing to say because my country is so terrible that nothing I could offer would ever be of use to anybody anywhere else. Please tell me what I should do, and I'll do anything you tell me." Nobody wants that; it's not a partnership, not a real sharing and learning, not the kind of connection that feminism is all about. It may be useful to somebody to have your help, but that approach is patronizing and not the basis of fundamental change. The opposite attitude is "feminist imperialism," which implies, "Feminism started in the United States, after all. We will show you the way. You're in a stage in a process that we've already gone through, and five years from now you'll agree that we were right." I hope we'll be able to say instead, "My experience is valuable and authentic, and I will share it. But I also want to learn about what others are doing, and, without feeling guilty, I want to see where I have been culture-bound and how I can go beyond my particular boundaries." The point isn't to browbeat ourselves or to get defensive if, for example, somebody points out something as racist; the point is to try to understand what that means and begin working to change it. Such a stance—which is not so unnatural, and can actually be quite loving—will be crucial in Kenya.

We will also need to bring home from there what we learn from this approach. We don't want to be "international experts" who no longer relate to our own country, a nation which is, after all, one of the problems in the world. We have to address what the United States does, rather than simply feel apologetic or defensive about it—and we have to look at how our work as feminists affects people's lives worldwide. For example, when U.S. women succeeded ten years ago in getting certain birth control devices outlawed, we didn't understand, because we didn't have a global consciousness, that they would simply be dumped on women in the Third World; I think we know now that if we're going to ban things from the shores of the United States, we also have to make sure they're destroyed. And we will increasingly be concerned about people in other countries not just because "we ought to be," but because we're all so closely connected: secretaries who form a union may lose their jobs when their company responds by sending clerical work via satellite to Barbados, where it can pay starvation wages—thus exploiting two groups of women.

There is a group of women on the Mexico-Texas border working against the manipulation of women's jobs back and forth across that border, and this is the kind of networking we will have to do if feminism is to continue to grow and to realize its global potential. It is also the kind of networking that I hope will happen in Kenya, with roomsful of different women exploring the issues at the heart of our lives—recognizing that all are "women's issues"—and asking, "How can we as women look at these in new ways? What can we learn and offer from our experiences so that there might be some solutions?" We won't resolve all the conflicts created by 2,000 years of patriarchy in a short time. But I do expect to hear the dialogue that must happen in the '80s and

'90s if feminism is to reach toward those solutions and respond to the world's enormous need for new perspectives based on women's experiences.

NOVEMBER 1986

How the United States Militarized Honduras

by Roxanna Pastor

The following speech was given by Roxanna Pastor in July 1986. At that time, Pastor was director of the Honduran Information Center, based in Somerville, Massachusetts.

When the Nicaraguan revolution came to power in 1979, the United States government lost its main ally in Central America. The Sandinistas were not interested in playing Somoza for the United States—and the United States began seeking a replacement, a place from which to influence the countries of the region.

Guatemala was then headed by a military regime that didn't care one bit about the attitude of the U.S. government. They said, "You don't like our human rights situation? You're going to cut out aid? Fine—bye." And, indeed, Guatemala could not really have been seen in the world's eyes as the democratic friend of the United States in Central America. El Salvador's civil war, meanwhile, was becoming a prolonged struggle. The United States knew it would have to play a very important part in maintaining the Salvador army in power, and that during that effort the Salvadoran government would be uninterested in what was happening in other Central American countries. Costa Rica was of interest to the United States because it's seen as a democracy and offers more public services; in the eyes of the international community, Costa Rica is the "Switzerland" of Central America. But, attractive as it is, Costa Rica doesn't have an army, and U.S. policy in the region is totally based on military principles. So the United States kept looking for its new main ally—and began to consider Honduras.

Honduras was then a quiet country, the second poorest in the hemisphere (only Haiti is poorer). It had been known to that point as a banana republic, a "backward place." The only thing people in this country connected to Honduras was the Chiquita banana they bought in the supermarket. When I moved here from Honduras in 1978, people asked me, "Did you have mail there?" and "Are you from Africa?"

Honduras, in other words, was not known—the United States didn't have to worry that the international community would question its role there, as in Guatemala and El Salvador. The United States found out two other important things, as well. First, the Honduran government, at that point a military one, had the best air force in the region. And, second, although Honduras was very, very poor, it was not on the brink of revolution: the U.S. government could expect its Honduran counterpart to forget about its own people and concentrate on the work of the United States in the region. So, in 1979, Honduras changed from a banana republic to a military base.

One of my best friends is a woman from Puerto Rico, and I remember talking with her at a 1980 demonstration at the Vieques base there about how horrible it is to feel your country totally occupied by a foreign military presence. I never dreamed at that point that in less than three years I would be in worse shape than she—that Honduras would become the military base for the United States in Central America. The military infrastructure has so permeated my country now that we can't even point to this or that place as a base, because there are bases all over and they're not being called what they are. We're finding that it's hardest to fight an enemy that is not publicly identified as such.

How did this transformation occur? The United States made a deal with the Honduran government in 1979 that if the army, which had then been in power for seventeen years, allowed free, democratic elections, the United States would pump in a huge amount of military aid and train the army in all possible ways. This has proved a bonanza for the military. They now have far more power and aid than in 1979, but without any responsibility for the problems of country. When they controlled the government, they were questioned by the people about the economic slowdown, unemployment, acts of war. They had to respond then as chiefs of state. But now, as they merely execute orders from the United States, they are in a more comfortable position.

Having struck its bargain with the United States in 1979, in 1980 the Honduran government began helping the Salvadoran state put down the insurrection against it. Honduras's role was initially defensive, consisting in 1980 to 1981 of protecting the border with El Salvador. Salvadorans trying to flee from persecution by their country's army were turned back by a newly created barrier maintained by the Honduran army, and complex international accusations began to be made against the forces of both nations as Salvadoran women and children trying to cross the river at the border found themselves fired upon from both banks.

At this point, the Honduran army could claim not to be at war with anybody, just to be helping their brother soldiers from El Salvador. But as the Salvadoran civil war intensified, El Salvador's forces became more incompetent and the Honduran army took on a more important, less defensive role. It not only patrolled the border but also attacked certain refugees in the camps inside Honduras and supported strategic offenses by the Salvadorans. Little by little, Honduras became better known in the United States largely as the hostess nation for Salvadoran refugees. I began to be asked, "So, have you been in those camps?"

But Honduras's role didn't end there, unfortunately; it changed as U.S. policy in the region altered. As the United States became aware that the Salvadoran army was just not going to be able to sweep the country and win its civil war and that a long struggle was in store, it began developing very specific, concrete strategies against Nicaragua in which Honduras was very important. At first, when the United States was denying its support for the Nicaraguan contras, Honduras was the intermediary between them and the United States. It was Honduras that gave the contras their first chunk of U.S. military aid, $19 million in 1982; it was Honduras that became home for thousands of contras, allowing all kinds of offices, hospitals, and other facilities to be installed in the capital city for the anti-Sandinista forces.

But it was not Honduras that decided to extend support to El Salvador and the contras; it was the United States. In fact, this support contradicts Honduran history, in which the Salvadoran army has been the enemy, never the Nicaraguan army or people. Because of this, some members of the Honduran armed forces even today oppose U.S. policy in the region; they are not pro-Sandinista, but they can't understand why they are helping their traditional main enemy, the Salvadoran army, win a war. They are not convinced that if the Salvadorans again decide that they are powerful enough to become involved in other countries they will not invade Honduras, as they did in 1969. Many people in Honduras share these suspicions about El Salvador—a good example of how U.S. policy in the region doesn't take into account the history, needs, rights, or feelings of the people there.

So, as Honduras became increasingly involved in the contra war, not only providing logistical support but also moving troops, supplying food, and locating people, the Honduran army began to ask, "Okay, but what are we getting in return for all this? How can we play a more important role?" The United States army and government saw that as a wonderful opportunity, and in 1983, began what are called "joint military maneuvers" between the United States and Honduras—although the ratio of North Americans to Hondurans in them is something like four to one. And, interestingly, the U.S. participants are not your average North American blond, blue-eyed citizens. Very often they are Spanish-speaking and can walk through the streets passing for any Central or Latin American—except when they decide to wear T-shirts emblazoned "Big Pine War" or cut their hair too short.

The impact of all of this upon Honduras has been tremendous, as could be expected of any policy ignoring the needs and rights of a people. The Honduran government has slighted its own citizens in supporting U.S. interests, and disillusionment has resulted. At first, most Hondurans thought, "If you're an ally of the United States, you get all kinds of benefits." Well, we're not getting any benefits. In reality, the conditions of daily life in Honduras are deteriorating every day.

I'll give you an example: the Honduran government has been forced to cut its health and education budget every year since 1984 in order to increase defense spending. Even though the costs of the joint military maneuvers are supposed to be borne by the United States, Honduras has to pay the gas bills for them—and has to cut human services to do so. This is tragic in a country where people die of hunger every day, where health and education facilities are practically nonexistent. Honduran education has particularly suffered: an independent economics institute has reported that 6,000 teachers are out of work because, even though thousands of children lack teachers, there are very limited school facilities and no funds for new ones. As Nicaragua has become militarized, its day care centers have been destroyed, but in Honduras, day care has not ever been attempted—and will never be until the present militarization ends.

Typically, women have been particularly hard hit by militarization. As Honduran unemployment has risen sharply, women have been the first to lose their jobs. Prostitution has increased dramatically. The first Sunday that U.S. soldiers were allowed out into the town of Comayagua (near Palmerola, the main U.S. facility in Honduras), the Honduran prostitutes' rates were six times higher than usual. It's now estimated that more than a thousand women come to this very, very small town on weekends to make enough money to survive in their own villages during the week. Some U.S. personnel argue that at least "our doctors" make sure that the prostitutes serving "our boys" don't have any venereal disease, but six women have already been diagnosed with AIDS. Four essentially disappeared after the diagnosis, so rather than being treated, they'll probably continue to spread the disease and, eventually, die themselves.

A few months ago, however, 5,000 Hondurans marched in the streets of Tegucigalpa against the military presence in the country. The protest resulted from the discovery by a teacher in Comayagua that six or so Honduran boys had been sexually abused by North American soldiers in exchange for dollars, which are highly valued because they can be sold in the black market at a high rate. Many of the children's mothers knew what was going on, but also knew that the only way they could buy food was to continue to allow their children to go and see the soldiers. Unfortunately, the Honduran government and many Honduran institutions have focused only on the specific sexual incidents, rather than on the conditions that created the situation. The fact that over a thousand women were used by the same soldiers since 1983 without street protest suggests the value placed on women in Honduran society: the women were expected to become prostitutes, but the U.S. soldiers weren't expected to use Honduran boys. But the demonstration broke the public silence over the presence of the soldiers, although discussion has so far focused more on specific sexual incidents than on what U.S. soldiers are doing in Honduras in the first place and how militarization so greatly affected the economy that the women and children were forced to take the attitudes they did.

The militarization of Honduras has also meant increasing human rights violations. These are often dismissed because they are fewer than those committed in El Salvador or Guatemala. But they are increasing, and they are taking the same form as in the other countries ten years ago, so we can expect things to get worse. As in other places, however, women have organized committees to seek information about "disappeared" relatives, realizing their relative powerlessness as individuals. And, interestingly, many of these women have gone on to found or join other women's organizations, identifying not only as the relatives of men arrested or assassinated but also as activists against U.S. intervention in Honduras and for women's equality. Women now head both established groups, like labor unions, and new organizations of their own that are asking why women are the first to lose their jobs in factory cutbacks and the first hired by U.S. companies in "tax free zones" where wages are especially low. Peasant women, too, are organizing—an important development in a country where 75 percent of the population are peasants. Peasant women's groups are taking over land and are forming cooperatives to sell their products without middlemen.

Militarization has made Honduras into a land where the people have lost our right to make decisions about our short-term future. We are acting as a launching pad against Nicaragua and El Salvador, and we have become totally dependent on U.S. economic and military policies. But these facts are becoming more and more apparent, especially to women, who have begun to organize and even to analyze the situation from a feminist viewpoint (for the first time, there are courses in the national university discussing Honduran problems from a feminist perspective).

Finally, U.S. policy toward Central America and, specifically, toward Honduras is going to fail. It may not fail tomorrow or in six months, but it will fail eventually, because any policy that completely ignores the rights and needs of the people must fail. And the last thing the United States cares about are the interests of the Honduran people, who do not need $80 million in military aid or helicopters or a war against Nicaragua. We need jobs, health facilities, schools, and food—and we are organizing to meet our needs.

NOVEMBER 1987

"Lifting As We Climb"
by Angela Davis

The National Women's Studies Association annual meeting, held at Spelman College in June 1987, featured a plenary session entitled "The Political Empowerment of Afro-American Women." Angela Davis, Byllye Avery, and C. Delores Tucker spoke about the experiences of Black women and the future of the feminist movement. The following is an edited version of Davis's speech.

We are reflecting on the process of empowering this morning, as Afro-American women have been collectively seeking to develop strategies for empowerment for almost a hundred years. The Black women's club movement was born during the last decade of the nineteenth century, after repeated unsuccessful efforts to be accepted on a basis of equality within the mainstream women's rights campaign. In 1895, the first National Conference of Colored Women was convened in Boston. Unlike their white sisters whose organizational policies were seriously tainted by racism, its participants envisioned their movement as one open to all women. They said, "Our women's movement is a women's movement in that it is led and directed by women for the good of women and men, for the benefit of all humanity.... We want, we ask the active participation of our men, and too, we are not drawing the color line. We are women—American women—as intensely interested in all that pertains to us as such as all other American women. We are not alienating or withdrawing, we are only coming to the front, willing to join any others in the same work, and cordially inviting and welcoming any others to join us."

The following year the National Association of Colored Women's Clubs was formed. The association's motto was "Lifting As We Climb." And I think that today when we reflect on the process of empowering Afro-American women, and indeed all women, our most effective strategies will remain those guided by that principle. We must seek to lift as we climb. And we must climb in such a way as to guarantee that all our sisters, and indeed all our brothers, climb with us.

Now this decade has witnessed a resurgence of activity within the women's movement. And Afro-American women, Latina women, Asian women, Native American women, working-class women, particularly women in the organized labor movement, are coming to the forefront. I think that we can say that if the first wave of the women's movement began in the latter 1840s and the second wave in the latter 1960s, then we are about to find ourselves on the crest of a third wave of the women's movement in the latter 1980s. So, we should pose a question to ourselves: When the feminist historians of the twenty-first century attempt to recapitulate this period, will they be allowed to ignore the important participation and accomplishments of the masses of Black women who have historically and consistently dedicated themselves to the struggle for equality, simply by virtue of the fact that the racist tendencies of the women's movement have often forced Afro-American women to conduct our struggle outside the ranks of the established movement? Will this continue to justify our systematic omission from the rosters of women who have constituted and, indeed, led the women's movement? Will there continue to be two distinct continuums of the women's movement—one visible and the other invisible; one publicly acknowledged, and the other ignored except by the conscious progeny of those women who forged their hidden continuum, women of color and white working-class women? If this question is answered in the affirmative, that will mean that the fatal flaws of the first and second waves of the women's movement have become fatal flaws of the third wave.

But how can we guarantee that this historical pattern is broken? As advocates of women's equality in the latter 1980s, we must begin to merge that double legacy into a single continuum which solidly represents the aspirations of all women in our society. We must begin to create a revolutionary, multiracial women's movement, which reflects the central importance of issues affecting working-class and poor women. This will not be a simple process. It will not happen simply through intensified efforts to attract Latina, Afro-American, Asian, or Native American women into the existing organizational forums dominated by white women, often those from the more privileged economic strata. For many decades, white women activists have complained that women of color refuse to respond to their appeals: "We invited them to our meetings, but they just didn't come." Susan B. Anthony wondered why her outreach to working-class women around the ballot was frequently met with disinterest. The fight for suffrage was an indispensible element of the overall quest for equality, but the way in which that struggle was conceptualized, based on the particular condition of white women of relatively privileged classes, made it hardly relevant to the needs of working-class women. So it's not surprising that many of them told Ms. Anthony, "We want bread, not the vote." Eventually, working-class white women, and Afro-American women as well, reconceptualized that struggle, defining the vote not as an end in itself but rather as an important weapon in the continuing class struggle, in the continuing battle for higher wages, for better working conditions, in the continuing battle against racism, for an end to the omnipresent menace of lynching.

Afro-American women bring to the women's movement a strong tradition of struggle around issues that link women to the most progressive political causes. Often we've been accused of having one foot in the women's movement, and the other foot somewhere else, but, as a matter of fact, we have always had both feet in the women's movement and both feet elsewhere as well. This is the meaning of that motto "Lifting As We Climb."

This approach reflects the often unarticulated interests and aspirations of masses of women of all racial backgrounds. Millions of women today are concerned about jobs, working conditions, higher wages, racist violence, plant closures, homelessness, repressive

immigration legislation, homophobia, ageism, discrimination against the physically challenged. We are concerned about Nicaragua, about Winnie Mandela in South Africa. We
share our children's dreams that tomorrow's world will be released from the threat of nuclear omnicide. These are some of the issues which should be integrated into the overall
struggle for women's rights, if there is to be a serious commitment to the empowerment of
women who have been rendered historically invisible.

An issue of very special concern to Afro-American women is unemployment. We cannot talk about empowerment if we do not recognize that its fundamental precondition is the
ability to earn an adequate living. The Reagan government boasts that unemployment has
leveled off to 7.5 million. But Black people are twice as likely to be unemployed as white people, and Black teenagers are six to seven times as likely to be unemployed as white adults. And
we should remember that these figures do not include the millions with part-time jobs, a
greatly disproportionate number of whom are women. They don't reflect those whose unemployment insurance has run out. They don't reflect those who have never had a job.
Women on welfare are not counted among the unemployed. So there are probably at least
eighteen million people of working age in this country without a job.

These critical levels of unemployment contribute in a very basic way to the impoverished status of Afro-American women. The most glaring evidence is the fact that women and
their dependent children constitute the fastest-growing sector of the four million homeless
people in the United States. There can be no serious discussion of empowerment today if we
do not embrace the plight of the homeless as passionately as we embrace issues more immediately related to our own lives. If we are serious about plotting strategies for the
empowerment of all women, we must identify with and associate ourselves with those of our
sisters who are the most oppressed. And when they lift themselves, when they climb, we are
all lifted in an upward direction.

How many of you know that the United Nations declared 1987 as the Year of
Shelter of the Homeless? The developing countries were the focus of this resolution,
but it is becoming very clear that the United States is an undeveloping country. Two-
thirds of the four million homeless in this country are families. Forty percent of them
are Afro-American. There is a trend toward workfare for the homeless. We must militantly challenge that pattern. New York has a "work incentive program" for the
homeless. Homeless women and men are compelled to clean toilets, wash grafitti from
the subway trains, and clean parks for 62 cents an hour—less than one-fifth of the
minimum wage. In other words, the homeless are being called upon to provide slave labor for the cities. Black women scholars and professionals, and indeed, all women
scholars and professionals cannot afford to ignore the condition of our sisters who are
acquainted with the immediacy of oppression in a way that many of us are not.

If we are to lift as we scale the heights of empowerment, we must be willing to
offer militant resistance to the proliferating manifestations of racist violence across the
country. A virtual race-riot took place on the campus of one of the most liberal institutions in the country, the University of Massachusetts at Amherst.

In the aftermath of the 1986 World Series game, white students on that campus,
fans of the Boston Red Sox, vented their wrath on Black students when the Red Sox
lost to the New York Mets. Apparently they perceived the students as a surrogate for

the Mets, which they saw as a Black team. A young woman was attacked; she was called "Black bitch" by white students in the crowd. A Black man attempting to defend her was seriously wounded and rushed unconscious to the hospital.

At Purdue University recently a cross was burned in front of a Black students' cultural center. Last Christmas, in a suburb of New York, Michael Griffith was lynched by a mob of white youths. And, not very far from this city, last January, civil rights marches were attacked by a mob led by the Ku Klux Klan. But perhaps the most outrageous recent example of the condoning of racist violence was the acquittal of Bernhard Goetz, who on his own admission, attempted to kill four Black youths, when he felt threatened by them on a New York subway.

When the Black women's club movement was organized, it was largely a response to an epidemic of lynching. They demanded passage of a federal antilynch law and involved themselves in the women's suffrage movement to secure that legislation. We must become activists today, all of us, in the effort to have racism legally declared a crime.

As extensive as racist violence is today, many racist crimes go unnoticed because law enforcement does not specifically classify them as racist or anti-Semitic. A person, for example, scrawling swastikas or "KKK" on an apartment, if charged at all, may be charged with defacing property or malicious mischief. Just recently, a Ku Klux Klan sympathizer burned a cross in front of a Black family's home and was charged with *burning without a permit*. This is why we need federal and local laws against acts of racist and anti-Semitic violence.

As we organize, lobby, march, and demonstrate against racist violence, we who are women of color must be willing to appeal for multiracial unity again, in the spirit of our sister ancestors. Like them, we must proclaim, "We do not draw the color line." The only line we draw is one based on our political principles. Empowerment for the masses of women in our country will never be achieved, if we do not succeed in pushing back the tide of racism. It is not a coincidence that sexist violence, specifically terrorist attacks on abortion clinics, has reached a peak during the same period which has witnessed a rise in racist violence. Violent attacks on women's reproductive rights are nourished by these explosions of racism. The vicious antilesbian and antigay attacks are part of the same menacing process, and our political activism must increasingly manifest our understanding of these connections. We must always be lifting as we climb.

When we as Afro-American women, as women of color, ascend toward empowerment we lift up with us our brothers of color, our white sisters and brothers in the working class, and all women who suffer under the reign of sexist oppression. Therefore, our agenda must necessarily encompass a wide range of demands—demands for jobs, demands for the unionization of unorganized women workers. Unions must be compelled to deal with such issues as affirmative action, pay equity, sexual harassment on the job, and paid maternity leave for women. Black and Latina women are AIDS victims in disproportionately large numbers: we have a very special interest in demanding emergency funding for AIDS research. And at the same time we must militantly oppose all instances of repressive mandatory AIDS testing and quarantining.

There are forces in our society that gain enormous benefits from the persistent and deepening oppression of women. The Reagan administration speaks for the most racist, the most anti-working-class, the most sexist circles of contemporary monopoly capitalism. The corporations prop up apartheid in South Africa, and they profit from the spiralling arms race while encouraging the most vulgar and irrational form of anti-communism to justify their ventures. Our agenda for women's empowerment must radically challenge the reign of monopoly capitalism. This socio-economic system functions as the main obstacle to achieving equality. If we wish to adopt a revolutionary stance, if we wish to be radical in our quest for power—and, of course, "radical" simply means grasping things at the root—let us learn from the strategies of our sisters in South Africa and Nicaragua. As women of color, as progressive women of all racial backgrounds, let us join our sisters and our brothers across the globe who are attempting to forge a new, world-socialist order. Our problems will not magically disappear in a new socialist society, but that order, I believe, will provide us with the opportunity to continue our struggle with the assurance that eventually we will thrust the ingredients of our oppression into the dust bin of history.

NOVEMBER 1987

Fear to Joy: Fighting the Klan
by Mab Segrest

The following talk was presented by Mab Segrest at the National Women's Studies Association convention held at Spelman College in Atlanta, Georgia, in June 1987. Segrest spoke alongside Esther Chow, Ada Deer, Tandi Goabashe, Beverly Glenn, bell hooks, and Alicia Partnoy at a session entitled "Spinning Threads of Women's Movement."

I am proud to be speaking today as a lesbian on this panel, "Spinning Threads of Women's Movement." We have been asked to address problems identified with our "societies" as well as solutions, strategies, and visions arising from the struggle with those problems.

As a lesbian, of course, my "society" is different from that of others represented here; it is not based on racial, ethnic, or tribal identity, or a heritage passed through each generation by kinship ties. We lesbians are a people who must always reconstitute ourselves, who must find our own identities, and then go in search of our sisters each generation. In the process we are often cast out by our families and by institutions in the home cultures (such as the church) that other peoples rely on for protection and strength and continuity of struggle.

You may have detected that I also speak as a Southerner. Like Angela Davis [who also spoke at NWSA] I was growing up in Alabama when four Black girls, three of them my age, were blown up in a church in Birmingham. And that experience, as well as many others like it in Alabama during those years, informs what I have to say.

Meeting here in Atlanta, lesbians don't have to look far for a problem encountered by our culture. Last summer, in *Hardwick v. Bowers*, the U.S. Supreme Court upheld the constitutionality of sodomy statutes used to oppress homosexuals in half of the states. The case originated with the arrest of Michael Hardwick, a gay man, in his own home here in Atlanta. Mr. Bowers is the attorney general of the State of Georgia. The majority decision of the justices made it clear that the right of lesbians and gay men to physical, passionate expressions of love is not included in the "concept of ordered liberty upon which this country's history and traditions are based." As Chief Justice Burger explained: "Decisions of individuals relating to homosexual conduct have been subject to state intervention throughout the history of Western civilization." Our mere "personal preferences," according to the justices, have little weight against a "millennia of moral teaching" and the "legislative authority of the state." In other words, I speak to you today as a felon in the state of Georgia, and in the state of North Carolina, which is my home. I consider that a problem.

And it is a problem—this antipathy of Western civilization to my "society"—that I share with every other woman on this panel: being on the death list in the United States. It is one of the common threads with which we are spinning movement. The same Constitution that protected slavery (counting Africans as three-fifths human for the purpose of determining propertied white male votes) protects the institution of heterosexual marriage. The same country whose slave codes once prohibited marriage between slaves and broke up and sold down the river the families of Africans, last year upheld the sodomy laws that give lesbians in this room no right to "family relationships, marriage, or procreation." The same Western tradition that arrived on this shore with guns and armor and began decimating native peoples finds lesbians anathema as well. Let me make it clear that I am not saying anything else was like slavery in our history. I am saying that conquerors employ similar tactics on populations they want to control or destroy: they go for the heart.

The Klan/Nazi Movement

In 1983, I saw this repressive climate working itself out in North Carolina in deadly ways. Organizers from the National Anti-Klan Network and Klanwatch reported that North Carolina has the worst Klan/Nazi problem in the United States. Nazi paramilitary troops were marching through Carolina towns to the strains of "Dixie" and Wagner; Klan/Nazi leaders were running for public office, using free television to purvey the rawest bigotries and legitimize deadly ideologies; they were amassing legal and illegal weapons, openly working for an Aryan revolution that would eliminate every non-Aryan person from the face of the globe. All of this was happening within a vacuum of official response. In fact, when concerned citizens presented the governor's representative with evidence of this resurgence and a crisis in racist violence, he looked them in the face and said, "It's not the responsibility of the state to uphold the law." The racism, homophobia, anti-Semitism, antifeminism, and antilabor bigotries of the Klan/Nazi movement found resonances with a North Carolina political culture that elected Jesse Helms and helped create Jerry Falwell. And this Nazi/Klan resurgence is not just happening in North Carolina or in the South. It's happening all over the country. It's not where you are. It's what you see.

The situation presented an opportunity for strong coalition work, because Nazis do not make the subtle distinctions about differences between us that we sometimes make. Their motto, in the words of a song sung by Tom Metzger's White Aryan Resistance in California:

> Gas 'em all, gas 'em all, we're coming to power
> Gas a Jew every hour
> What the hell, gas 'em all.

I had this interchangeability of target groups pointed out to me when I got a phone call from our number one Nazi in North Carolina. I had just gone on TV to say, "Arrest this man."

He said, "Ms. Segrest, I am writing an article on you for my newspaper, and I want to know more about your background. Is your Jewish origin from New York or Miami?"

I hung up on him. Now I was raised Methodist, but I was proud to be mistaken for a Jew—especially in that situation. I mainly thought: "No, you sorry shit, I'm a lesbian. And boy, do you have bad intelligence!"

Beyond Consciousness

When I went to my first anti-Klan meeting in 1983, I was chiefly concerned with being included as a lesbian in the efforts. I did not imagine then that I would end up one of the people leading the charge. In 1985, I became a paid organizer, coordinating an organization we put in place to deal with this resurgence.

I had found myself both inspired by and frustrated with the lesbian-feminist movement within which I had been working. I had heard Barbara Smith say too often, "I don't live in the women's movement. I live on the streets of North America." I had sat in many rooms and participated in many conversations between lesbians about painful differences of race and class, about anti-Semitism and ageism and able-bodiedism. They had been hard discussions, but they had given me some glimpse of the possibility of spinning a wider lesbian movement, a women's movement that truly incorporates diversity as strength. But in all those discussions, difficult as many of them were, we had never been out to kill each other. In the faces of Klan and Nazi men—and women—in North Carolina I saw people who would kill us all. I felt I needed to shift from perfecting consciousness to putting consciousness to the continual test of action. I wanted to answer a question that had resonated through the lesbian writing I had taken most to heart: "What will you undertake?"

At this point, none of my old buttons would do. I had a friend make me new ones. The first said, "Race Traitor." The second, "Pre-Mature Anti-Fascist." I also added another question to "What will you undertake?" and that is, "What will you accomplish?" I have had to learn to think in terms of goals and the strategies to achieve them.

So we wanted to stop the Klan in North Carolina. First we had to prove the extent of the problem through monitoring and research. Then we had to raise public consciousness through the media, and through going anywhere that any group asked us to speak. Then we had to try to focus that public consciousness on public officials—on law enforcement to actively seek convictions where there is clear lawbreaking; on the governor to take a stand as the highest elected official in the state. At the same time, we worked with victims and communities to ensure that those who had been attacked did not remain vulnerable and isolated.

I have been surprised, frankly, how much we have been able to accomplish in four years: today over 25 Klanspeople/Nazis have been convicted or pled guilty to crimes ranging from civil rights violations to paramilitary organizing to perjury. The governor has appointed a task force to deal with racial and ethnic violence. And we have models of how to work to deal with victim/communities "when the Klan comes to town."

The additional problem that I set for myself was: how much of this organizing could I do openly as a lesbian, and one, *stay alive,* and two, not be kicked out by the straight people I worked with. I felt that more models were needed of out lesbians doing work on progressive issues. I also didn't want the larger movement to have it both ways: homophobia is not important, but if you come out it will destroy our work.

In the past three years, I have often resisted my impulse to screech up to the phone booth in front of the Gulf pumps at dusk at the country grocery store full of stale moon-pies and no-telling-who-else, to call Barbara Smith and say: "Well, here I am girl. What do I do next?" But I would generally go inside and buy a moon-pie and a Coca-Cola, and my head would clear immediately so I'd know what to do.

In working with heterosexuals I wasn't sure I would have allies who would understand my vulnerability as a lesbian. It was a leap of faith that was entirely justified. I learned that when the chips were down the best heterosexuals came through. When I was hired by a board of ten straight people, eight of whom were Black, two of those preachers, I explained how I was a homosexual felon with a "profile as an activist" and got hired anyway. My employment came with the organization's commitment to work on homophobic issues, something no other organization that works on Klan/Nazi issues, state or national, has yet done. The real test came when opposition from "my side" finally crystallized, as I pushed an affiliate organization to deal with gay/lesbian issues. Its director (now its former director, a white woman) sat across a kitchen table at the home of a Klan victim and explained how she had dragged her feet about the organization's taking a stand on antigay violence because she didn't want to "encourage homosexuality." And my friend whose home it was, a white woman in her fifties who had bought the house out of weekly savings from her salary as a waitress, stayed in the room when everyone else split. I said, "It's not about heroin, it's about the right of people not to be hurt and killed because of who they love," and my friend—whose life had been threatened because of her love for a Black man, but who often was afraid to speak because she had been beaten by the white men in her family—said, "That's right." I got back to Durham and reported the conversation to a Black woman friend also involved in the work. She said: "This homophobia is like racism. It's got to be opposed." And she helped me to raise the issue within the affiliate organization.

Then, in 1986, the fundamentalist preachers of Durham launched an attack on the gay/lesbian community and on our progressive mayor because he had signed a pro-gay proclamation. The campaign was fronted by two Black fundamentalist churches, although the impetus for it was coming from the Congressional Club and the Right. The Black women with whom I had worked for two years against racist violence came to me urging, "We need to work on this issue now"—not only to oppose homophobia, but because they knew that they couldn't let the Black church become a front for fascism.

And when my lover, Barbara, and I found out she was pregnant through artificial insemination, the successful culmination of both of our longings for a child, I wrote to another friend, a Black minister and long-time freedom fighter, about my happiness and fears. I explained that the culture's concepts of family were as destructive as its concepts of race, as riddled with ownership. "But I feel very fierce, and hopeful, and determined to take our happiness," I wrote him. "Because you are my friend, I wanted you to know." I mailed the letter, a bit apprehensive about whether he would prefer Leviticus and Paul to me. The very next time I saw him, he said immediately: "How's your family?" It took organizing against the Klan and Nazis to show me that lesbian space is, ultimately, the world.*

From Fear to Joy

Finally, I want to talk about fear and joy, since they are the emotions that have moved me most strongly over the past several years. First the fear. I am a person who, for much of my life, has been guided by fear. This philosophy brought me to my fear of Nazis. Since I was a little girl, I have had a fear of men in packs. One of my recurring nightmares is being chased by groups of men with weapons from hiding place to hiding place, none of which was ever safe. With the Greensboro Klan murders in 1979, followed by the Reagan administration, the pack took on a definite identity: storm troopers who busted down doors in the middle of the night to take people away. Within three years, there was a Nazi paramilitary organization within two hours of my home. What else could I do? I went into the task afraid that the work would increase my nightmares. I found it has diminished them. My experience was echoed in the experience of another white woman friend, at whose home a cross was burned because of an interracial relationship. After the first attack, she explained to me, sometimes she and her lover would wake up in the middle of the night, imagining flames at the window. But when a group of interracial couples who had all been attacked came together for support, her life changed. "After that," she said, "I began to believe that there are other people, real people, who felt like me. So the Klan—they might kill me—but they could never scare me like that again."

Organizing against the Klan and Nazis helped to open up a world beyond the fear of death: to turn me from fear to joy. The phrase came back to me like a boomerang I had thrown. "Go toward what you fear," I had told a friend who was still figuring if she could be a writer, in a long walk through the Chapel Hill campus. And a year or so later, in a poem by Jean Swallow in a journal, it came back: Yes, Mab, but what about the joy? So I put on my list: *fear of joy*.

And it was pure joy I felt as I talked with Annie through Barbara's stomach, and she kicked against my hand. Pure joy watching a body I had loved for years grow large with a little one we would love together for years to come. Pure joy—and tremendous relief—watching her head poke out into the immense new space as her birth team (two dykes and two faggots) at Durham County General Hospital wept and cheered; pure joy now as she rides my hip into Woolworths and we pick out a new rattle and diapers and pins.

And it was joy mixed with grief when the three of us returned home for my mother's funeral, at the saddest moment, to carry my lesbian family back into the old kinship circles—friends from the neighborhood, Sunday school teachers, cousins, sister and brother and their children—and find that finally, I had it all as home.

It is this finding our many ways home, this circling back with lesbian selves intact, to family or race or tribe or region, and carrying those selves into an increasingly rich lesbian culture, and an increasingly powerful women's movement and people's justice movement, that is our final answer to the death wish that the Klan and Nazis, and corporate board-rooms, and the Supreme Court, wish on us all.

* After I gave this talk, a Black lesbian shared with me her anger at these remarks. I had not acknowledged the fact that I could get this Black minister's approval as a white lesbian much sooner than she could as a Black lesbian.

SEPTEMBER 1990

Whatever Happened to Women's Liberation?

edited by Karen Kahn, Tracy McDonald, and Eva Young

During the summer of 1990, in honor of its fifteenth anniversary, Sojourner asked four community activists to get together to talk about issues of diversity and inclusion within the women's movement over the last fifteen years. We wondered, had the movement become more diverse (or less so) over the years? How did racism and classism continue to divide the women's movement and prevent diverse organizations or even coalitions from emerging? Barbara Neely, Connie Chan, Milagros Padilla, and Ruthie Poole agreed to participate in the roundtable discussion.

Barbara Neely is the former director of Women for Economic Justice (WEJ), a multicultural women's organization that does projects related to poor women, particularly women of color, emphasizing economic issues. Connie Chan is a professor at the College of Public and Community Service at UMass/Boston. Her work focuses on Asian-American women and gay and lesbian issues. Milagros Padilla is active in the Puerto Rican independence movement and around women's health care, particularly reproductive freedom for women of color. And Ruthie Poole is a community organizer, who in 1990 worked with the Coalition for Basic Human Needs (CBHN), a statewide welfare rights organization.

Sojourner: How do you see the work you do in your communities in relationship to the "feminist movement"? Do you see yourself and the work you do as part of that movement or outside of it?

Barbara Neely: If what we mean by the feminist movement is the mainstream, white, middle-class women's movement, then I would say in my work in WEJ, because it's a multicultural women's organization, there has been a large overlap. We do a great deal of work with other women's organizations that consider themselves feminist and progressive.

But if I had to answer that question in terms of my own work over the last fifteen years, I would have to respond differently. I have considered myself, certainly over the last fifteen years, as trying to work for women's liberation. I do not see the mainstream women's movement as a place where women's liberation is the goal. It appears that the goal is to have equality with white men, and that's just not the same thing.

Milagros Padilla: Throughout my development, politically and as a person, I've worked in pieces of what is called the feminist movement. My thinking about women's liberation has had a lot to do with my work in traditional health care settings. But the work I've done in Puerto Rican groups has intersected very little with that other feminist work.

I remember when I first came to the United States. I was sixteen years old, and I came to Rochester, New York. It was a growing community created by people who came to pick fruit on the farms in that area. There was nothing there, so organizing efforts began in the city. It was the early part of the feminist movement, but many of the things that were going on never touched us. That kind of isolation happens often, and it makes it difficult for women in our communities to cross into feminist movements.

Then, I became part of the movement for a women's health collective. I was there because I was a health care provider who was interested in teaching a very poor community how to take care of themselves. The feminist movement has something to teach, so I was there for that, but no one else from my community was there. When they were talking about health care, they weren't talking about health care for the poor women that came to the health center I worked in. The other members of the collective did not think of race, or class for that matter, ever.

Connie Chan: When I first started being active in what I would consider not feminist issues, but women's issues, was somewhere in 1980. I was involved in the Take Back the Night marches in Boston. The core group of people involved with that— maybe half were lesbians—were trying to get more women of color involved. I thought, well that's a good idea. It seemed to me that of all people who need to take back the night, women of color are the ones who can't walk in their neighborhoods the most. Some of these women were trying to be inclusive of women of color, but the concerns of those organizing and the route of the march were still very white and middle class. It was oriented toward Jamaica Plain as opposed to understanding where women of color really live in this city, and what our issues are.

The two key issues again were class and race. Although the feminist movement is trying to address class in a better way, they don't address it in the context of race. Race as a context of class is a very different interaction than just white women and class. When you lose sight of that interaction, you've really lost women of color.

The feminist movement has failed to address the concerns of women of color who are from different classes, particularly from the working class. And I think what's happened is that when you say "feminism," it's equated with white feminism. In my classes, we spend hours on this issue. Students say, "We've got to redefine feminism; we can't let the whites take it over." I believe we can redefine feminism in a way that can be ours; it doesn't have to be white feminism. The question is how can we make it ours? Women's liberation is, I think, the key, and yet feminism doesn't address that. The true root of the word "feminism" isn't just equality, it's really empowerment, and we've lost the empowerment part. Feminism and women's liberation are worlds apart. That dichotomy in the last ten years, if anything, has gotten worse.

Ruthie Poole: I feel like I'm echoing Barbara, Connie, and Milagros. Most of the women I work with are white, low-income women. It's interesting to hear that women of color have felt really isolated because low-income white women also feel isolated. I went on a retreat with the Coalition for Basic Human Needs board, and we had this wonderful discussion about diversity and inclusion and around accepting differences. But when we got on the topic of feminism, every single woman in that group said, "No, I'm not a feminist; that movement doesn't include me. I'm not a feminist at all." They felt separate from what they defined as feminist. I've never said, "The work I do is with a feminist organization," because the women I work with don't define themselves as feminists. They don't see feminists recognizing mothering as work, and they see the movement as very much focused around choice, without recognizing how your choices are limited by race and class.

Milagros: Connie referred to women's issues vs. feminist issues. Women of color have been involved in working in women's issues for a lot longer time than what the white women's movement refers to. We have been involved in housing issues, which are women's issues; and we have been involved in liberation struggles to end colonialism, which are women's issues. But then, suddenly, somebody determined that feminist issues revolve around getting a better job or abortion rights only and that unless you were involved in those movements you weren't legitimately a feminist. That allows this feminist movement to say, "Women of color are not interested in feminist organizations."

I remember, in 1978, I went to a conference of Latina women, and this Chicana woman was giving a talk. She said that part of the inability of white women to acknowledge how much women of color were really working for their liberation had to do with the fact that many times we women of color find ourselves working on our knees, and that white women thought the only way to work was standing up. They had forgotten what a long way you could travel on your knees. Our aim is to travel on our feet, but we work within the context of a system that wants us lying on our backs. We're on our knees, and we're doing pretty good! White women have to look at that. It has taken a lot of work to get from flat on our backs to our knees. It's very easy to run when you start standing up.

When I get impatient, and wonder why all these Puerto Rican women don't want to join me, I remember the Chicana woman's reasoning. She helped me define a lot of the kind of things I wanted to work on; before I thought, "Oh, God, I'm not going to work on that, that's so traditional."

We have come a long way. We are no longer working on our knees, but as women of color we do deal with a lot of forces that make us look at the problem in a bigger way. For example, we look at housing not as, "Let me get this job so I can get to live in the Back Bay," but can I get housing and can I have an impact on policies, not just for me but for other people? Middle-class women talk about housing in terms of neighborhood safety, but for many women, their whole lives are consumed with whether they are going to have housing or not.

Barbara: One of the reasons why we don't see this work as intersecting is that we have very different agendas. One of the basic reasons for this is racism. There are women, I am sure, who are Ku Klux Klanettes and conservative Republican women that consider themselves feminists.

For me, very early on, and historically, there's been no reason for us to connect with the white women's movement. They've never included us; they have shafted us often—over issues of the vote, for example. The women's movement has not offered us any reasons why we ought to join, because while they may have begun on their feet, once they started running, they started running right down the patriarchal path. Women of color do not blend easily into white women's organizations, because many times those organizations are both classist and patriarchal. White women need to look at the way their organizations are structured, if they truly want to involve women of color.

Individually, some white women are trying to put together a multicultural women's movement, but it's still being done very much from the perspective of either middle-class white women or middle-class women of color. The issues of poor women are not being addressed. Poor women are the majority. None of that is going to change until the whole women's movement can begin to understand that what is good for women is what is good for women of color and for poor women. This needs to be the focus of the women's movement, because if what you're doing is focusing on people who already have $50,000 in the hope that they can get $150,000, this doesn't mean jackshit to poor women.

Milagros: I think that white women and women of color could work together in coalitions or on some common goal. But as a woman of color, I would not be urging women of color to join white women's organizations. I want us to be in our own organizations. I would be willing to work with either individual women or a collective group of women who want to share one specific topic. But to build an organization together, and I mean an activist organization that is setting an agenda for what we are to do at this moment, I would say there is no way to do this together.

Barbara: Well, how could you? We have such very different worldviews; I don't know how to get beyond that. I think that women of color, at least women of color that I work with, recognize that our liberation is both spiritual and material. We need to guard our cultural borders as well as build our collective material base. White women have a very different sort of worldview. The spiritual is not a big piece of it; it is the material piece. It is whether or not you can get a guy's job; it's not whether or not you have the luxury to stay home and teach your kids about their culture. These differences make it very hard to see any sort of serious intersection. So what you end up with is the powerful group using their definition of power and pulling in what they consider to be a less powerful group in order to present some sort of multicolored view of an organization that is still basically, in terms of its policies and practices, a middle-class, white women's organization.

Connie: I don't think you can underestimate the split between cultures. Certainly we have different political agendas, but it's not just politics. We have a country that pretends to be a multicultural country but it's not, it's a monocultural country, and the feminist movement comes from that culture. Even if you have common agendas, items where you can work together—for example, the abortion/choice issue. Certainly that's an issue that affects both women of color and white women. It affects white, middle-class women in different ways than it affects fifteen-year-old white teenagers or women of color who have no access. We have threads of the same cloth here, a common agenda on which we could work together, but that falls apart in terms of cultural sensitivity. The whole way of relating and being is so different, there is little comfort in being in the same room. When you're talking about this kind of movement, you're talking about being close—you have to be close physically and emotionally and really trust the person if you're going to build an organization, do a sit-in, or whatever. The cultural difference is so wide that we don't have that trust. It's very hard to see how we can get that.

White folks don't have to understand any other cultural view; they're comfortable wherever they go. We have to challenge them and educate them, but they don't have to educate because we know their culture. It's too much effort and that's why things fall apart. It's very sad.

Barbara: If you're going to put that kind of energy into bridging a cultural gap, for me, the logical way to do that is to look around at other women of color. I know that, at least on one whole set of issues, we are in the same place. If you are a woman of color in this society, it doesn't matter whether that color is eggplant black or as close to white as you can get, there are certain experiences that you share. And there are certain expectations that you have of this society that make it possible for two women of two very different cultures to be in a room with two white women and have them say something to each other and have two women of color turn and look at each other and know precisely what the other one is thinking. As women of color, in addition to our individual cultures, we share a culture, the kind of culture that grows out of being oppressed people. So, for me, that's the place where I always want to put most of my energy. If I'm going to make that cultural leap, it's going to be with other women of color.

Milagros: I think at this moment we really need to become a unified force, because as people mentioned before, we are going bonkers. Racism seems to be growing. It's no longer correct to want to house people and feed them; that's all passé. It makes more sense for me to be in a group with Southeast Asian women, Chinese women, African-American women, Panamanian women, talking about our differences and really coming to some kind of understanding and some kind of agenda around how we are going to get out of this hole together. I don't want to spend this energy haggling with white women.

Barbara: One of the things that makes it very difficult to make pact with the average white feminist, and the unaverage white feminist who is sensitive on our issues, is that white feminists insist on ignoring the every day indignities we women of color endure.

For many, many white women, racism is an abstraction. For women of color, it is something that we live with every day. Every time I go into Filene's Basement, I expect to be frisked or to have some shop clerk talk to me as though I'm dogshit on the pavement. Every time I go into a restaurant, I expect to have to wait twenty minutes. This is a reality; this is not what white women are talking about when they're talking about racism. We're not even speaking the same language.

What do you mean when you say, "It's gotten worse?"
Connie: I think there are many reasons why it's gotten worse. Certainly because of the political climate, there's less available to everyone and, when there's less available, people focus much more on their own needs and don't make time for anyone else's. Coalition building is much harder when the pieces of the pie are just getting smaller and smaller. The political and economic climate since the Reagan years has contributed to this.

Also there are no joint areas of communication. In the past, people used to think of *Equal Times* and *Sojourner* as being newspapers for more women. Now the perception is that *Sojourner* tends to be, according to the people I work with and my students, focusing on issues that are not relevant to them. It doesn't focus on their worldview. And I think that if we had better lines of communication, while I don't think that would bring our movements together, at least we could keep track of what each other is doing and work together where possible.

Milagros: There seems to be a general climate that it's okay to be a radical and a racist. For a while, if you were a radical you kept your racism quiet. Now they are more willing to speak out and say, "Oh, why should we go out of the way to invite women of color?" It is very difficult to build an organization with diverse women. So, white women behave as if, why go through all that work if there is nobody outside pushing for that anymore? It takes so much energy. Before, I thought there were sincere efforts by white women to do antiracist work. But this new terminology of "culturally relevant" or "multiculturalism" that is being used—I hate those terms, because they obliterate what the problem is all about. It's about racism; it's about power. Culturally relevant or culturally sensitive—I truly am not concerned about that. I want you to be willing to give up your power; that's it. I could care less if you know anything about my culture. Just give me the power to be who I am, and give up your power to oppress me. That's all I want.

Connie: I agree. The terms "multicultural" and "cultural diversity" are very dangerous. It sounds like we're just all different, rather than focusing on racism and the harmful effects of racism.

Barbara: That's all part of this new mindset out there, that we all ought to be grateful for being here because this is the greatest country in the world and it has done something for minorities. Well, what the fuck has America done for us? It has oppressed us and our histories and our languages and our children and our men and our mothers. Still, somehow we're expected to make this huge leap over that into all holding hands and swaying together. It's ridiculous. This country that has always siphoned off the vitality of people of color for whatever it needs. Our music, our language, our idiom, our clothes, all of that. Anything that is needed from us is ripped off. And then we are totally discarded. That hasn't changed; it seems to have accelerated.

Behind all of that is the mindset that all people of color want to be white. That is one of the operating myths in the women's movement: we all want to be white, so therefore we're all prepared to act white, and if we're not prepared to act white then it isn't that we want to hang on to our cultural differences, it's that we're ignorant.

My analysis is that we may not ultimately need the women's movement, but the women's movement needs us. The women's movement will succeed only after women of color's liberation has taken place. Just as the women's movement in its latest form did not get off the ground until it had the civil rights and the Black nationalist movement and the Puerto Rican liberation movement to give it some form and some direction in which to go, the women's movement ultimately will not succeed until we once again show the way.

OCTOBER 1992

Whose Culture Is It Anyway?
by Joanna Kadi

My grandparents brought little with them when they emigrated from Lebanon, an unsurprising fact given their poverty. Three cultural artifacts made it across the ocean: a woven tapestry, a water-pipe for smoking hashish, and a derbeke. The brass drum with nickel finish and elaborate engravings figured prominently in our lives. The der-beck-ee (also known as a dumbek) always appeared at our numerous extended-family functions involving food, music, and dancing; these functions held critical importance as we tried to keep our culture alive in a city where we were the only Arabs. Since we didn't have other musical instruments, we used the drum to accompany Arab music heard through a cheap, tinny phonograph. We'd hold hands and do folk dances around Cousin Millie while she belly-danced. A male cousin played the derbeke, and someone kept an eye on the record player.

Derbekes are made from clay or brass, although recently someone devised a way to make them out of recycled aluminum. They are hourglass shaped with an open bottom and range in size from one to one and a half feet high with a head varying from a few inches to twelve inches across. Arab tradition dictates that you cradle the drum under your left arm, the bottom under your left elbow. The two most common strokes are the *dum* (use the right hand and wrist to strike near the center of the head and gain a resonant tone) and the *tek* (use the tip of one finger on the edge of the head to produce a bell-like tone). Other strokes include slaps, finger rolls, and finger snaps. Producing a pure tone with each hit is as important as producing a good rhythm.

Last year when I decided I wanted to drum, my decision to play a derbeke was not so much a choice as an instinct. Arabs have played derbekes for thousands of years.

And even though I've never set foot in the Arab world, its tones and rhythms are familiar and comfortable; they feel like home.

I began searching for a brass derbeke because of its happy associations from childhood on. My lover and I spent a day combing Arab businesses in Dearborn, Michigan, a city with the largest concentration of Arabs outside the Arab world. I didn't expect any difficulty finding what I wanted. As it turned out, we found plenty of ceramic derbekes but no brass ones. "Import problems," shop owner after shop owner told me.

Not knowing where else to look, I momentarily gave up the search. Two months later, my derbeke appeared. It was January 1991, and I had traveled twelve hours by car to Washington, D.C., for a demonstration opposing the U.S. war against Iraq. Ironically, while there, I chanced upon a store specializing in musical instruments from around the world. Here I found a brass derbeke.

I say "ironically" for a number of reasons. Defined by the Oxford dictionary as the "ill-timed or perverse arrival of event or circumstance in itself desirable," irony is a common feature of the lives of those of us with a foot in two cultures. Here I am, brought to D.C. for yet another futile demonstration, trying unsuccessfully to assuage my grief and rage over the devastation of my people and our homelands. Then I happen upon an object that connects me with these people and homelands. I am elated—but how can I celebrate when my Arab sisters and brothers are being murdered in the Middle East and Arab-bashed on U.S. streets?

Not only did I find my derbeke in a Washington, D.C., store at the moment when the U.S. government was destroying an Arab country. There was a second ironic twist: I had vowed to buy my derbeke from an Arab-owned business, but now, after a long search, I had finally found one here—in a store that appeared to be owned and staffed solely by white people. Yet I felt good about buying the drum. The salesperson seemed to respect me and my culture; he knew the history of the derbeke and the proper way to play it and spent a great deal of time with me.

Ironic twist number three: after going to all that trouble to find a brass derbeke, I found out they're harder to play than ceramic ones. Often, brass derbekes are given as wedding presents and used decoratively. I don't know why my family ended up with the derbeke they did, and there's no one alive to answer the question. That part of the story is lost.

I'm not the only feminist who's taken up drumming. Scan any bulletin board listing women's events and you'll find notices about drumming circles, groups, lessons, rituals. Why is it so popular? On good days, I think it's because drums can be bought cheaply and are thus financially available to many of us, are relatively easy to play, and usually involve playing in groups. On my more cynical days, I think it's a combination of two things. First is the feminist obsession with therapy; one therapeutic concept—that of getting in touch with our inner rhythms—has somehow become attached to drumming. Second is the rip-off of Native spirituality by white people, with a particular emphasis on drumming and chanting. Native drums are a particular favorite among white feminists.

It may be some combination of those two reasons that accounts for feminist popularity of drumming. In my own case, I began looking for a derbeke as I became more connected with my racial/cultural identity. I regularly listened to Arabic music and began wishing I had the drum my grandparents had brought from Lebanon. Finally, it occurred to me that I could buy one and learn to play it.

As I've learned to play the derbeke, I've noticed that along with congas and Native drums, derbekes are becoming popular among white feminists. Unfortunately, most of the white women I've observed ignore the cultural traditions associated with the drums. Usually, they hold the derbeke between their knees and use neither a *dum* nor *tek* stroke. Rather, they apply both palms to the center of the head.

The first few times I saw white women playing derbekes incorrectly, I experienced an exponential increase in blood pressure. After my initial anger subsided enough so that I could think coherently, I realized this was cultural appropriation—white women taking possession of my culture by appropriating an important instrument and the music it produces. Anyone who understands the derbeke's key connection to the distinctive style of Arab music would not be surprised at my rage.

What makes hitting a drum incorrectly cultural appropriation? The derbeke, and its playing style, is an important piece of Arab culture, with thousands of years of history attached to it. To disregard our culture and history and play however one chooses is to whitewash the drum and, by implication, Arab culture. When the drum is stripped of this historical legacy, it is placed outside Arab culture, suggesting that Arab culture and history are not worth taking seriously. Even though Arabs have created something valuable and life-enhancing in our music, that fact is of no consequence. White people can and will choose to perceive the drum as ahistorical and culturally empty—a plaything that can be given whatever meaning the player chooses.

I am not opposed to white women playing the derbeke if it is done with respect, knowledge, and seriousness and if these attitudes are manifested in concrete action. If you wish to play a derbeke, learn its culture and history and the proper way to play it. Whether you're learning to play a piano or a derbeke, you can better appreciate your effort and the instrument if you know its background. And then take this knowledge a step further. Learn about and take action against the imperialism, racism, and genocide Arabs are experiencing today. It is not enough to celebrate cultural difference by learning the language, music, or history, when a people are at risk. Respect and integrity call for action.

Feminist drumming is not an isolated phenomenon. Drumming is part of the dominant culture's latest obsession: "multiculturalism." Strange things are happening under the guise of "honoring diversity."

Not surprisingly, given the brutal racism endemic to our society, much of "multiculturalism" is covert and overt cultural appropriation. It's a form of cultural genocide—as cultural practices are usurped by a dominant white culture that refuses to take our practices seriously, the intrinsic meanings are watered down and their integrity diminished. Today, items from various communities of color are all the rage, but I don't get excited when I see the walls of white people's homes adorned with African masks, Asian paintings, and Native ceremonial objects. Behind all this rhetoric and hype, I perceive the same white attitudes of entitlement and privilege that form part of structural racism. For the most part, these people have not done the homework necessary for any white person interested in becoming an ally of people of color. They know little or nothing about the current global struggles of people of color, as defined and articulated by people of color. They do not engage in acts of solidarity concerning specific issues such as Native self-determination or Palestinian liberation. They do not read the writings of radical authors of color.

Further, these white, middle-class people have not done their homework around a monster related to racism—and that is classism. To be more specific, all of us need to be clear about how and where capitalism fits into the picture. We need to ask critical questions. Is "multiculturalism" the latest capitalist fad? Will our art continue to garner interest or will the release of a new line of Nintendo games signal the end of this phenomenon?

And who is making money, now that it's popular to hang African masks on living room walls? Could it be people of color? Hardly. As more and more people of color are forced to live on the streets, white entrepreneurs are making big bucks selling our art, music, and spirituality. Watching them profit by exploiting and appropriating our cultures, when for years we experienced hostility and scorn for trying to preserve them in a white-dominated society, is truly galling. I grew up with white people belittling and "joking" about my family's choice of music and dancing; now I can watch those same people who made fun of us rush to sign up for "real" Arab belly-dancing lessons. Taught by a white woman, of course.

Moreover, capitalism relies on class stratification, and in this country, many people of color are working class or poor. Consequently, we often can't afford to buy the music, paintings, musical instruments, and books from our cultures that are now available. We often can't afford trips to our countries of origin. Observing white, middle-class women (and men) buying paintings and music we can't afford, and hearing them talk about traveling to our homelands, adds yet another layer of anguish and complexity to these issues.

Capitalism is necessarily an exploitative economic system—it is beyond repair. But in the meantime, we still need to think about where our money goes. It makes a difference. As already mentioned, I bought my derbeke from white people, who were profiting from selling instruments belonging to the cultures of people of color. Yet the white man who helped me cared a great deal about the drums and where they came from. It wasn't a perfect experience, but the respect I felt for my culture and the willingness to spend time with me meant a great deal.

That business was a far cry from two crafts booths at the last women's music festival I attended. Both booths exhibited ceramic derbekes made and sold by white women. They sat with various drums from other cultures, all without names. My fury rose to dizzying heights because the erasure and whitewashing of the drum tapped into my fury about the number of times I have been erased and whitewashed. Even among people who understand the ways in which Native, Latino, African, and Asian cultures have been exploited, there is an appalling ignorance about Arabs. For example, the most recent issue of *Sinister Wisdom*, written and edited by lesbians of color, did not include a single piece written by an Arab lesbian. It was a familiar absence—one I have felt throughout my life.

Drumming continues to be a popular activity at women's gatherings, festivals, rituals, and circles. We need ongoing dialogue, education, and action about drumming and the larger issues to which it connects. Who is drumming, how are they drumming, why are they drumming, and what are they drumming on? Whose culture is involved? Is it treated with respect?

If a non-Arab woman, whether a woman of color or a white woman, is playing a derbeke, is she aware of its history? Does she attend rallies supporting the liberation of Palestine? Does she talk about anti-Arab racism during discussions of racism? Has she read Edward Said and Fadwa Tuqan?

These suggestions are not meant as "nice" actions to take. Genocide is looming on the horizon for many groups of people of color; action must be taken now. The quincentennial celebrations around Columbus's "discovery" of America drive that point home. Literally millions of people in this country are paying homage this month to a person and system representing racism, genocide, and imperialism. However, it's been gratifying to know that feminists, both of color and white, have been celebrating 500 years of Native resistance and mourning the physical and cultural devastation wrought by the arrival of white people on this continent. Let's continue this movement with a renewed commitment to antiracism work and to learning about and appreciating each other's cultures within that context.

JUNE 1993

Out of the Closet and into a Straight Medal Jacket?

by Neta C. Crawford

The debate about gays in the military is disturbing on several levels. On the face of it, the arguments against gays in the military made by those who want to keep the ban are simply wrong, thin disguises for homophobic attitudes. It is saddening to hear stereotypes and misinformation repeated in the Senate hearings about the ban. But the quest for the right for homosexuals to serve openly in the United States military raises even deeper issues about priorities for the human rights and gay liberation movements. Simply put, in the rush to end the ban on gays in the military, some proponents of civil and human rights have perhaps missed the ironies of the situation. Homosexuality and the gay liberation agenda is, first of all, about love and the freedom to love (sex included) whomever one chooses, while the military is, first of all, an institution of violence, quite often used for offensive purposes. The use of violence, except in self-defense, violates human rights.

My argument is simple. First, I agree with those who want to lift the ban on homosexuals in the military and applaud those, especially members of the military, who have taken a courageous stance to end the ban. Second, I argue that though ending discrimination is an important goal, the institution of military service itself is not one that should be viewed uncritically: it's "not just a job." Third, it is troubling that, in the debate about gays in the military among members of the gay and lesbian community, there is a virtual silence on the issues raised by service in an institution dedicated to violence.

No one should suffer discrimination of any kind in the choice of jobs that they wish to pursue. The arguments for the ban on homosexuals in the military rest on stereotypes of gay men and lesbians as both promiscuous and predators of heterosexuals. Some of the arguments put forward by those who want to keep the ban are:

1. *The risk of HIV infection and of AIDS will increase.*

2. *Allowing openly homosexual service members will reduce military readiness and effectiveness. Specifically, lifting the ban would undermine discipline, good order and morale, mutual trust and confidence, unit cohesion, recruitment and retention.*

3. *Homosexual service members are vulnerable to blackmail.*

The only argument of quasi merit made by proponents of the ban, that open homosexuality could jeopardize unit cohesion, is based on a recognition and acceptance of homophobic attitudes. The point about unit cohesion, according to proponents of the ban, is that "bonding in combat promotes heroism and self-sacrifice." The fear is that "with openly gay and heterosexual personnel together, sexual tension would fester 24 hours a day.... Romantic interests, even if unconsummated, would shatter the bonds that add up to unit cohesion. If the bonds that prompt men to risk all and die willingly for each other are lacking, combat performance will decline, with tragic consequences for people and missions" (Bernard E. Trainor and Eric L. Chase, "Keep Gays Out," *New York Times,* 29 March 1993). According to that logic, unit cohesion will be destroyed because gays supposedly care more about sex than their duty and because straight men and gay men don't get along. (Women don't come up too much in this context because they were, until recently, banned from combat.) But if straight men and gays don't get along, it is because of the sort of heterosexual intolerance, fear, and hate that led some naval seamen to beat to death an openly gay sailor, Allen Schindler, in Japan last year.

Most people, including gays and lesbians, don't join the military to kill; they join because they need a job or an education or they want to do something patriotic. But, like the recruitment advertisements say, military service is "not just a job."

Military forces are part of foreign policy. The issue, then, is not the military per se but militarist beliefs embodied and practiced by the military. If the United States and other countries only kept militaries for defensive purposes, then I would not object to military service and I would have no reservations about working to end discrimination of any kind in the military. There is something to be said for defending our country against attack, but no clear and present danger to the territory of the United States exists. There is also something to be said for aiding those who are the victims of aggression—for example, the Bosnian Muslims, who are the victims of Serbian aggression, or the Angolans, who are the victims of UNITA's (Union for the Total Liberation of Angolans) relentless attempt to win power by force (having lost at the ballot box last year). When nonmilitary measures—for instance negotiation, arms embargoes, and economic sanctions—fail, then military force may be appropriate and useful. But military force is too often used for offensive purposes—to change the composition of governments that our government doesn't like. The Dominican Republic, Guatemala, Angola, Grenada, and Panama come to mind.

In other words, even though military service is a job, and the Pentagon one of the world's largest employers, for most members of the military, their jobs involve preparing to kill, killing, and/or assisting in the job of killing. Fundamentally, military force imposes the value of "might makes right" and the use of military force means that another human's rights are denied. There is something quite Orwellian about a discourse that champions human rights so that members of a group that is discriminated against may join an organization that all-too-frequently violates human rights.

And although I hesitate to raise this in mixed (gay-straight) company, the way that much of the gay liberation movement talks about gays in the military brings up troubling issues of militarism within the gay community. Clearly, the homophobic arguments of those who would retain a ban on homosexuals in the military must be met. But, at the same time, we should critically appraise militarist ideas and the whole content of United States foreign policy. This has not happened. Instead, the Campaign for Military Service and the Human Rights Campaign Fund, while doing an excellent job of refuting homophobic arguments, argue in terms of patriotism. It is true that homosexuals can love their country as much as heterosexuals can. But patriotism is not, fundamentally, the point.

To step into even murkier waters, it is also ironic that members of both the gay and straight communities sometimes wear dog tags, combat boots, and camouflage fatigues to demonstrate their support for lifting the ban. Thousands of men and women, gay and straight, wore "Lift the Ban" dog tags at the April 25 March on Washington. One catalogue of gay merchandise advertises "Medals of Honor"—"Support our military brothers and sisters with our exclusive faux medal set. Wear them separately or as a trio. $1 goes to Lambda Legal Defense and Education Fund." There is something disturbing in an image of gay men and lesbians shouting "two, four, six, eight, we can kill as good as straights" at rallies or wearing dog tags as testament to their patriotism and militarism.

When we wear items that imitate military dress, we consciously or unconsciously identify with the institution. The reality of the military, that it is about the use of violence to impose our will on others, is glossed over. We need to come to terms with this reality—that militaries are used to threaten and fight wars and that war means mutilation, separation of families, and death abroad, while at home militarism often coincides with censorship and intolerance—in order to change it.

There is little difference between the attitudes that say it is all right to use force to change another country's government and those that allow and contribute to domestic violence and gay-bashing. There is also little difference between militarism and anti-Semitism, racism, and practices such as "ethnic cleansing." There cannot be a truly "New World Order" as long as violence is used to decide international politics. Violence should be the last resort of those who seek to build a world based on respect for others, even those who are different from us.

In our hearts, we already know these arguments. Among others, Audre Lorde, in "The Master's Tools Will Never Dismantle the Master's House" (*Sister Outsider,* Crossing Press, 1984), and Cynthia Enloe, in *Does Khaki Become You?* (South End Press, 1983), made similar points close to a decade ago. And Ellen Goodman noted some of the ironies of the present debate on women in combat and gays in the military, in a recent column in the *Boston Globe,* "Why the Military Is a Combat Zone in the Fight for Rights."

But, why is there so little open critical discussion within the gay and straight communities today? Have gay men and lesbians who prefer nonviolence or are critical of U.S. foreign and military policy been silenced or self-censored in this debate?

There are some dissenting voices. At the March on Washington, for instance, some signs protested the focus on gays in the military ("The U.S. Military Is *Not* Liberation," "The Enemy Is Militarism, Not Difference") and a contingent of hat-wearing marchers identified themselves as "Gays in the Millinery." One group, the Autonomous Anarchist Action of New York City, chanted "Make Love, Not War, Be All You Can Be, Mutiny, Mutiny" while hundreds of former and active duty members of the military marched in front of the White House.

But, on balance, the March on Washington and much of the debate in both progressive and gay media have ignored the ironies of working to lift the ban. Instead, patriotism and uncritical support of the military have been the order of the day. The quest for inclusion means that many of those who oppose militarism have been silenced and the gay community as a whole co-opted—straightjacketed for military service.

If the gay and lesbian community had a clear political analysis of the world as it is, and a vision of the world as we would like it to be, then opposition to militarism would be part of the present debate on gays in the military. But several problems, practical and philosophical, are raised by this approach.

First, there is the immediate and practical concern about ending discrimination against homosexuals in the military. It is difficult, although I don't believe impossible, to debate issues of militarism while struggling to open up the military institution itself.

The second practical problem is jobs. Despite the fact that the military is downsizing with the end of the Cold War, it is still a huge full-time and part-time (reserves) employer. For some, military service appears to be the only—or best—option for escaping urban unemployment or for getting an affordable education—one reason that African- American women make up nearly 50 percent of all women in the Army. On the other hand, if the priorities of the U.S. government were oriented toward nonmilitary spending, it is likely, according to the Council on Economic Priorities and congressional studies, that after conversion as many or more jobs (and money for education) would be available in nonmilitary sectors of the economy. A gay agenda that included re-examining the role of the military in U.S. foreign policy, while encouraging democracy and the peaceful resolution of disputes abroad, would accelerate the process of shifting from military to nonmilitary spending.

And third, there is a philosophical question. In a community as diverse as the gay and lesbian community, can a humanist lesbian and gay ethics be articulated that responds to the challenges posed by militarism? Is it time for a queer ethics that starts with the premise of respect for differences and a commitment to helping those who need help to overcome violence, danger, or oppression?

Identity politics isn't good enough. Uncritical support of agendas only or primarily because they are said to benefit members of an identity community (women, lesbians and gays, African Americans, disabled persons) may lead to supporting causes that keep in place institutions and practices that themselves ought to be questioned, modified, or eliminated. This is the case with the debate about gays in the military. Identity politics, in the long run, cannot work without issue politics—that is, talking about and changing the beliefs and practices that keep all kinds of people from living safe and fulfilling lives.

The main obstacle to achieving gay liberation may be that straight people don't see gays as fundamentally the same as they are—as human. Ending discrimination in all forms would go a long way toward humanizing others. But militaries are not about humanization: military institutions are specifically designed to dehumanize the other, the enemy, in order to make it possible for soldiers to kill. Homosexuality is about love and the gay liberation movement fundamentally about tolerance and equal rights for both same-sex and opposite-sex relationships. Seeing others who are different as worthy of full human rights is more difficult in a society in which dehumanization of others exists in any form, for any purpose.

So, we should honor those who work, often at great personal risk, to end the ban. There is no doubt that gay men and lesbians make excellent military service personnel and that discrimination must end. But we should also recognize that the particular institution this battle is about is one that perpetuates oppression because it says that the use of force to compel others to do our will is acceptable. We reject this principle when it is associated with child abuse, rape, and gay-bashing; we should also reject the use of force, except in self-defense, among nations. Lesbian, gay and bisexual liberation, at least in this case, doesn't necessarily follow from equal rights.

JUNE 1994

Rural Organizing: Building Community Across Difference
by Suzanne Pharr

In 1993, Wanda and Brenda Henson purchased land to create a women's education center and retreat in Ovett, Mississippi. When the townspeople came upon a newsletter that, among other things, indicated that lesbians were involved, there was a highly emotional reaction to this perceived threat to the local community. After organizing by some preachers and local officials, two town meetings, relentless media coverage, intervention by Janet Reno, and supportive responses from lesbians and gay men nationally, the situation in Ovett today can be described as an emotionally charged, potentially violent standoff.

The complicated conflict that has unfolded between the women of Sister Spirit and the townspeople of Ovett, Mississippi, has been much on my mind for some months now. I have been fearful that someone would be killed: a member of Sister Spirit, a townsperson, or a visitor arriving to observe the situation. With trepidation, I have watched the widespread media coverage help keep emotions intense and people stratified.

The conflict has been depicted as between diametrically opposed groups, with little middle ground: the dykes against the bigots. I've been wishing, however, that I could see more of the middle ground. I know it's there, because I'm standing on a little piece of it. As a lesbian, I have strong identification with the women of Sister Spirit, and as a woman from a low-income rural Southern family, I identify with the working-class people who make up Ovett. They are both my people.

I have a vested interest in these groups learning how to make community together, for if they and others like them cannot, how then can lesbians such as myself live openly with and among our rural families and friends? If we cannot do rural organizing around lesbian and gay issues, then rural lesbians and gay men are left with limited options: leaving our roots to live in cities; living fearful invisible lives in our rural communities; or with visibility, becoming marginalized, isolated, and endangered. Not one of these options holds the promise of wholeness or freedom. We are compelled to do rural organizing because we cannot accept freedoms restricted by geography—or by race or gender or class or any other boundary our society uses for exclusion.

Ovett, then, becomes for us an opening to talk about rural issues, about how to create social change in all of our communities, without exception.

It's difficult for me to talk about rural life without first talking about the antirural attitudes that are prevalent in this country. Urban dwellers, particularly within the lesbian and gay movement, are pretty consistently disrespectful of rural people, especially Southerners. Our first clue is in the language that describes rural places as "hinterlands," "boondocks," "the sticks," "back side of nowhere," and the people as "rednecks," "clods," "bubbas," and "bigots." For a movement that touts "difference" as positive, this level of prejudice and ignorance is appalling. Articles in the lesbian and gay press, as well as the mainstream press, about Sister Spirit have been filled with these antirural attitudes.

It is remarkable to me that someone writing from the chaos and deterioration of our major cities would assume a position of condescension toward rural people. We all have our troubles in this country, no matter where we live. I believe, however, that antirural attitudes are based in class prejudice. The rural United States, outside of resort and retirement communities, is mostly working class and often low income. Because of isolation and an inadequate tax base due to low population density and income, rural areas are often characterized by limited services. We must remember that lack of access and economic standing do not equal ignorance or stupidity or bigotry. Culture simply gets shaped along different lines, with different values. Both urban and rural life offer positive and negative values.

The first rule of rural organizing (as it is for all other groups) is that it needs to be done by the people affected, not others imposing their vision and will. Since resources in rural areas are often limited, this organizing should be supported but not driven by urban people. To achieve this partnership, we all have to get over our bad attitudes: urban disrespect and rural resentment of outsiders.

I believe that the basis of all of our organizing has to be building relationships. This belief runs counter to the notion that we are in a war and a shoot-out is required as we line up along strictly marked and separated sides. In Ovett, community has to be built if Sister Spirit is to stay on their land and thrive; otherwise, there will have to be a shoot-out of one kind or another (guns, lawsuits, increasing harassment), and there will be death or flight or the restricted and tortuous life of two armed camps. It is through building relationships that we achieve transformation.

One day, when I was being particularly angry at the people of Ovett (having very little information about them and forgetting that they were my people), I began thinking about my own rural background. I remembered my first sixteen years of lesbian invisibility, how terrified I was of losing my family and community relationships, and how I lost their authenticity anyway because I cut so much of myself off from them. I thought about how everybody lost: I lost part of my humanity, and they lost a chance to develop theirs through knowing me. The road to coming out publicly was long and slow. Building relationships based on authenticity (our whole and true selves) is slow work. Now, 25 years later, I have deep, loving relationships with my large rural Georgia family, people very much like the townspeople of Ovett. Yet, here I was in 1994, judging the people of Ovett harshly because they couldn't do overnight what it took me, as a lesbian, sixteen years to do: to overcome my fear, my misunderstanding, my lack of information and support, and my homophobia. I had to stop myself and say, "Isn't it a bit much to ask the local people to do immediate change?" Yes, far more information is out there now to help them (and young lesbians and gay men), but who is delivering that information and how?

Relationships are not built on abstractions but on human interactions: they have to have a human face. Part of our work is to figure out how to put a human face on what for most people is the *idea* of homosexuality, to transform it through genuine relationships with lesbians and gay men.

In rural communities (and elsewhere), whether we are just becoming public about being lesbian or gay or are moving in from the outside, we are usually entering the community for the first time. It is, in a sense, someone else's community, because we have not had a presence there as who we are in this part of ourselves. Consequently, we have to be thoughtful about how we enter. We have to ask if immediate confrontation gives the best result; i.e., does it open up the most space for living freely, for creating the most productive dialogue?

In the early '70s, I spent four years on a women's farm in a thinly populated rural farming area in the mountains of northwest Arkansas. Our household ranged from five to twelve women and children, plus dogs, cats, goats, and countless visitors who were part of the great lesbian migration back and forth across the country at that time. Our farm was both isolated and exposed, and we could not survive there without strong relationships with our neighbors.

We built those relationships slowly in numerous ways. The first was by introducing ourselves to our neighbors and to those who lived in the small town and by constantly asking for advice. We hung out where the local people did—at stores, the lumber mill, restaurants—and had long conversations about ourselves and about the area. We purchased goods and services from people who lived around us. When people drove by and stopped on the dirt road by our house to chat, we stopped whatever we were doing and talked. We went to community events such as basketball games and estate sales and church fundraisers. People became interested in our successes and disasters and our stubborn hard work. They thought we were strange but good hearted and often amusing.

Our sexual orientation was not directly announced to the community at large but lived openly and talked about to some privately. While trying to live as openly as possible, we also tried to respect the community's customs. For example, almost every urban lesbian who arrived at our door to visit wanted to 1) take off her shirt and "be free" and 2) let her dog off its leash to "be free." We did not permit either. This was not a simple nor an easy decision. We understood that bare breasts had become symbolic of women's freedom (if men can bare theirs...) and that urban women had dreams and fantasies of some isolated place where they and their dogs could run free. We lived among farming people, however, and the dogs, untrained in farm behavior, threatened both our animals and the animals of our neighbors. As for the bare breasts, we decided that this was not the issue that we would choose as the focus for our struggle for freedom. There were many more compelling issues, and besides, we wanted to choose them for ourselves as long-term residents rather than having them pressed upon us by someone who was merely passing through.

This work was not always easy or successful. One of the local teachers at Kingston (town of 300, now notorious because of Whitewater) was fired for being a lesbian because she was seen hanging out with us. Generally, though, the community came to terms with us as we did with them. The greatest dissension and conflict came not from our being lesbians or part of the perceived back-to-the-land hippie lifestyle but from our political work that threatened their economic lives. The major chemical companies were bringing back defoliants from Vietnam and selling them to local farmers to clear their mountain land of trees and brush. These defoliants (now called Agent Orange) contained dioxin and were already causing concern about their effect on the community's health. We were documenting stillbirths, deformities, cancer, and other ill effects and vigorously and publicly opposing the use of 24-D and 245-T, the chemicals used. It was this work that brought rage from farmers because they felt hurt economically when they could not use this new technology to clear previously impossible-to-reach pastureland.

The lessons we learned then remain true now in this time when lesbians and gay men are under massive attack from the Right. All of the polls show that when people personally know lesbians and gay men, they often overcome their homophobia. It is the lack of knowledge that creates the climate for prejudice and bigotry.

I am struck by the fact that those who made trouble for my friends and me in northwest Arkansas for being a lesbian teacher or for fighting Dow Chemical and the policies of the Vietnam era are the same ones making trouble in Ovett. They are rural people entrenched in the literal interpretation of the Bible, unfamiliar with lesbians and gay men, and, most importantly, struggling for economic survival in an economy that is discarding them. The difference is that they are now bolstered by national organizations that provide support and money and who pump out strategic misinformation so fast that people live in a state of heightened confusion. Another major difference is that twenty years ago we had time to deal with our differences and to do it on the community level. Today, a fast, ever-circling media shapes public opinion so rapidly that we are impeded in doing the slow, face-to-face work that must take place in community.

Putting a human face on homosexuality addresses one part of the issue. The Right's primary success, however, comes from being able to scapegoat effectively lesbians and gay men as contributing to economic ills, just as they have scapegoated African Americans and Jews. Their major success has come from linking civil rights to "minority status," which supposedly provides "special rights" such as affirmative action and quotas. In the historic rhetoric of anti-Semitism, the Right argues falsely that lesbians and gay men, though small in numbers, are wealthier than "average" citizens and control institutions such as the media secretly, from behind the scenes. Then, with a leap into the rhetoric of racism, they argue that if lesbians and gay men achieve civil rights enforcement, through "affirmative action and quotas," we will indeed take away jobs from deserving heterosexuals and destroy the small piece of the pie now allotted to low-income people. Clearly, building community will take more than getting people to recognize our humanity as lesbians and gay men; it is also necessary for all of us to learn how to make connections with people around issues of economic injustice. Those were the conversations we failed to hold in northwest Arkansas while we were busy breaking new ground around lesbian and gay issues.

The places where those economic justice connections can be made in rural areas are most obvious in the arena where direct services and community organizing meet: food banks, housing construction (such as Habitat for Humanity), battered women's organizations, youth organizing (especially through community sports), senior centers and meals-on-wheels, and environmental cleanup. These are some of the places where lesbians and gay men belong, a visible presence working for economic and social justice and talking about our lives.

What I have learned from rural organizing is virtually the same as what I've learned from urban organizing: we must build lasting authentic relationships across many boundaries—race, gender, class, sexual identity, physical disability, and so on—but of all of these, the most difficult for U.S. citizens as a whole is class. It is here that we do not make full connections, that we have not built alliances and coalitions. And it is this refusal to deal with economic injustice that will trip us up over and over again and prevent our dream of creating a multiracial, multi-issue movement for justice. We cannot separate ourselves from rural communities or communities of color or working-class communities or any other where economic injustice has had an extraordinary impact. To do so takes the heart out of our work for social justice, and without that center, it will not hold; we will always be working on the fringe of true and lasting social change.

SEPTEMBER 1994

What's Wrong With the "F" Word?

by Delia D. Aguilar

The following talk was presented at a conference entitled "The Feminist Moment/um," held at Sarah Lawrence College in April 1994. Initiated by two white women who were disturbed by what they saw as the continuing exclusiveness of feminism in the United States, it was sponsored by organizations of students of color.

I understand that one of the questions the organizing committee for this symposium wants to see addressed is why young women today are not overly eager to identify themselves as feminists. As I'm sure you're aware, a resident fellow of the American Enterprise Institute has stated that while three-fourths of U.S. women claim they "support efforts to strengthen women's rights," only one-third accept the label "feminist."

I want to tell you that it took me a long time before I could call myself a feminist. Let me narrate my coming to feminism and, in the process, point to some of the areas that I believed were trouble spots during the early phases of the second wave, and what those trouble spots might be today.

My political development began in work here in this country against the Marcos dictatorship in the Philippines. This was mostly support for the national liberation struggle taking place in my homeland. What that meant in practice was that our campaign here was to educate the U.S. public to the fact that it was U.S. people's tax dollars that sustained the Marcos regime. What support work also meant was that we toed the political line drawn by the resistance movement in the Philippines. With respect to what were then referred to as "women's issues," the belief was that participation in the movement in itself represented a break from traditional sanctions placed on women and that national liberation would, therefore, ultimately liberate them.

It wasn't long before I saw the bankruptcy of this position. For several years I went back and forth in dialogue with friends in the Philippines, arguing for specific attention to women's issues. But as you might well imagine, the stubbornness with which my suggestions were received was extremely frustrating, doctrinaire as these folks were. On the other hand, I did not find feminism in the United States terribly appealing either, despite the fact that I had begun participating in women's discussion groups and was teaching women's studies. I was relieved when Black women and other outspoken women of color began to voice their objections to what is now understood as universalizing tendencies in feminism, since they were expressing my reservations. If the nuclear family was regarded as the primary site of oppression for white, middle-class women, what about the ways in which families have formed cultures of resistance in "Third World" struggles? When white feminists fiercely denounced the male chauvinism and homophobia of liberation struggles but condemned U.S. support of repressive dictatorships only when prompted, what could we make of such equivocation? For those of us in-volved in support work for resistance movements, the atomized focus on male/female relations was both distracting and alienating, since as a collective we faced gender, class, racial, and national oppression. I think we know now that the problem was that the women who were most active and visible in the women's movement failed to take into account matters of class (since they assumed their class privilege) and race (since they took for granted entitlements accruing to being white in a racist society).

I remember bringing up just those issues to a feminist study group to which I be-longed. A group of us "Third World" women decided to give a presentation on how feminism as put forth really only embodied the experience of white, middle-class women. We initially observed that even our vocabularies were different, the white women's consisting largely of "patriarchy" and patriarchy-linked terms, while ours re-volved around words like "capitalism," "imperialism," and "revolution." We discussed our own concerns, which at that time had to do with the struggles in Iran, the Philip-pines, Puerto Rico, El Salvador, and other countries fighting for national liberation. Even so, a white member of the group heaved a challenge that in one fell swoop ac-knowledged our presence and then dismissed us: "Should we support national liberation struggles that are patriarchal?" Because this was a Marxist/feminist study group, the response to our prodding, in the end, was a positive one, which resulted in broadening the scope of the topics addressed to include working-class families, families in communities of color, issues in the workplace, workplace organizing, and health care, among others.

I also remember giving a talk along similar lines to the women's studies faculty at my university. The title was a catchy one, "Why Third World Women Reject Bourgeois Feminism." Somehow, at this meeting, my complaint (the universalization of white women's experience) was a little more difficult for my audience to comprehend. I made an argument for class and nation, citing the case of the Philippines, a former U.S. col-ony whose political economy could hardly be labeled sovereign. I explained that a sizable portion of the population, 70 percent, fell below the government-defined pov-erty line and that any reckoning of women's condition would have to take this fact fully into account. Then I described the dilemmas confronting women as workers on the assembly line, or as migrant workers, "hospitality girls," and mail-order brides. As the responses indicated, the information I was presenting seemed to fall outside the purview of the kind of feminism existing at the time, for although there was sympathy for the plight of the poor, my colleagues wondered, "Are class and nation feminist issues?"

In the meantime, changes were taking place rapidly in the Philippines. The assas-sination of former Senator Benigno Aquino drew an impassioned antidictatorship outcry that cut across classes. (This movement eventually led to the ouster of Marcos.) This became fertile ground for the development of feminism in the Philippines because, while the National Democratic Front remained the largest and most disciplined organi-zation, it no longer monopolized the anti-Marcos movement. The emergence of a wide variety of "cause-oriented" groups allowed women who were already active in the re-sistance movement, who had experienced incarceration and torture, to articulate their specific needs not only as revolutionaries but as women, and to appropriate for themselves the term "feminism." This was the change that made it possible for me to call myself a feminist.

Today, political thinking has been greatly altered. The collapse of the Soviet Union has led progressives to question, on the practical level, the viability of a humanely instituted socialist project. These doubts are reflected on the philosophical level as well, where intellectuals now disdain the use of explanatory frameworks (Marxism, for one) that have a wide compass, for fear that this might invoke totalizing thinking, which in turn is believed to lead to totalitarian regimes. These revisions in progressive thinking must be situated in the context of changes that have been taking place since the beginning of the Reagan era. Reaganism and the conservative tide it brought about has left its mark on people's outlook. With the demise of the Soviet Union, even those who held a progressive worldview had their visions of an alternative society profoundly shaken.

Ironically enough, the "New World Order" formally launched by George Bush is new only in that old alignments have been unscrambled, with the United States now jockeying for superpower status with Japan and Western European countries. Outside of this repositioning, however, the picture for the rest of the world does not look too different. Wretched poverty for the majority and the problem of distribution of resources in developing countries have intensified, if anything. In the United States, widespread wanton violence, crime, drugs, homelessness—a result of the flight of industry to more profitable climes—are predicaments that can no longer be ignored in spite of declarations that capitalism has triumphed.

So what are the implications of this new thinking—particularly this disdain for overarching theory—and how has it affected feminist circles? Those of us on the margins should welcome the move away from universalization. Many feminists are now aware that they cannot simply substitute "woman" for "man," proceed to talk as white, middle-class women, and presume to be speaking for womankind. We should be pleased that many feminists now refrain from the use of the totalizing plural "we," and instead take care to give attention to other social relations like class, race, nationality, ethnicity, and so on.

The problem that I see, however, is that the approach of the "politics of difference," as this is called, at its very best fails to take into account asymmetries of power. That is, in its zeal to acknowledge the existence of a plurality of differences—presumably to celebrate these in the age of multiculturalism—the relations of power that have produced those differences are obscured or ignored. So, for example, class—which is the result of power relations and often irresolvable conflicts between the haves and the have-nots—becomes interpreted as a matter of lifestyle and is frequently interchanged with "classism," presumably meaning class bias. So, while on the surface, there is a celebration of difference (and the list of differences can be very lengthy), we never really get to understand how the differences came to exist. This fragmentary thinking is an immediate consequence of not having a larger context, an overarching frame, that would try to make sense of component parts. Viewed from this angle, attempts to resolve racial, class, and other divisions within feminism by specifying and clarifying differences, are closely linked to neoconservative trends that impel the move away from analytical instruments attempting to describe and explain larger social systems.

To crudely sum up for the moment: while early second-wave feminism was blemished by race and class prejudice in white women's fervor to achieve gender unity, the movement existed at a time (the late '60s and '70s) of social ferment and activism. This ferment was characterized by a willingness to call social systems by their names—e.g., capitalism or socialism—and to use analyses of macrostructures to explain social phenomena. To give an example, when we discussed the oppression of women in the domestic realm, we looked at the gendered division of labor and tried to show how this mirrored the inequities in the labor market of capitalism, a profit-based society. We envisioned how those disparities might be eliminated or minimized in a society with the goal of fulfilling people's needs. Many of these explanations, one must admit, were economistic and simplistic. Nonetheless, the temper of the times encouraged the creation of visions of alternate societies that entailed, if not outright revolution, at least some sort of thoroughgoing social transformation. In contrast, in the current period, there seems to be great pleasure in recognizing differences among women and in posing each woman's identity as heterogeneous, fluctuating, and shifting. But all this, given a conservative political climate, is conducted with no notion of an encompassing totality. The differences are flattened out and, in the ultimate analysis, the conditions giving rise to such differences, effectively conserved.

I would like to end with two examples that I think are symptomatic of current trends in feminism. The first is a performance that two friends and I recently saw. Billed as a satirical play that looked at "the history, shortcomings, and progress of the U.S. women's movement," through a pastiche of vignettes, The "F" Word was wildly entertaining and very funny. It was cleverly and imaginatively executed with a minimum of props and, addressed to the "converted," poked fun at the deficiencies of feminism, particularly its race and class leanings. Now, on the surface, it had all the required elements of "diversity"—of color, class, sexual orientation, etc. The audience laughed and applauded vigorously at various junctures, for it was outrageously humorous indeed. One song took a direct jab at the ethnocentrism of U.S. feminism by chanting, "Why, oh why, is the women's movement so white?" In spite of this, I felt as strangely alienated as I did in the '70s when white feminists unabashedly presented their class- and race-bound views as universal. Why did I feel this way? During the open forum afterward, Susan Porter Benson, a white historian, was the only one who put her finger on the problem. Everyone else thought the presentation was terrific. Using the example of the abolition of slavery and the movement for women's suffrage, Benson pointed out the play failed to make the necessary connections. The latter was an offshoot of the former, but the play simply located them side by side. And that was exactly how the play laid out its multicultural ingredients—side by side, as though each operated in isolation, a perfect illustration of the politics of difference that holds currency at this historical moment.

The second example is a review by Leslie Hazleton of Naomi Wolf's widely publicized book, Fire with Fire (Random House, 1993), and Hazleton's response to a reader's comments. The review was overwhelmingly positive and completely uncritical of the notion of "power feminism" (Wolf's antidote to what she sees as the prevailing conceptualization of women as victims) and its preponderantly white, middle-class foundation. That it was printed on the front page of *The Women's Review of Books*, a respected feminist publication, is probably not an insignificant matter. The subsequent issue carried a reader's "left-wing" critique, arguing that ending gender discrimination within capitalism would still condemn the vast majority of women; in other words, this reader emphasized the class-boundedness of Wolf's point of view. In response, Hazleton queries the reader: is she or isn't she for women? For Hazleton, "as women gain more power...they do so thanks to a determination and a sense of possibility created by feminism." Maybe so, but which "women"? She writes about "a feminist high," which she gets from attending a U.S. car company meeting where twelve women employees meet with twelve journalists to discuss women and cars. Organized by men, the meeting was taken over by women who turned the focus to "aiding and abetting each other's careers and women's issues in general." For her the "camaraderie...felt very similar to that of consciousness-raising groups in the '60s."

From what she says, one cannot doubt the sameness of the camaraderie she felt, then as now. In the absence of a critical analysis of societal structures and societal goals, how easily the plurality of "difference" in the first instance can slide into the univocality of "women" in the second!

What is wrong with the "F" word is that so far it hasn't carried its promise far enough. In articulating gender, it originally disregarded women for whom other factors like race, class, and ethnicity were more salient. In articulating a decontextualized politics of difference, race, class, ethnicity, sexuality, and other forms of "difference" now receive a great deal of emphasis. But expressions of the specificity of difference that are deployed without a comprehensive view of society, in the final analysis, merely become another useful camouflage for the preservation of exploitative social arrangements.